14

THE CERTIFIED MANAGER OF QUALITY/ ORGANIZATIONAL EXCELLENCE HANDBOOK

Also available from ASQ Quality Press:

Principles of Quality Costs: Financial Measures for Strategic Implementation of Quality Management, Fourth Edition
Douglas C. Wood, editor

ASQ Pocket Guide to Root Cause Analysis
Bjørn Andersen and Tom Natland Fagerhaug

The ASQ Quality Improvement Pocket Guide: Basic History, Concepts, Tools, and Relationships
Grace L. Duffy, editor

Root Cause Analysis: The Core of Problem Solving and Corrective Action
Duke Okes

The Lean Handbook: A Guide to the Bronze Certification Body of Knowledge
Anthony Manos and Chad Vincent, editors

The Quality Toolbox, Second Edition
Nancy R. Tague

The Quality Improvement Handbook, Second Edition
ASQ Quality Management Division and John E. Bauer, Grace L. Duffy, Russell T. Westcott, editors

Performance Metrics: The Levers for Process Management
Duke Okes

Process Improvement Using Six Sigma: A DMAIC Guide
Rama Shankar

Mapping Work Processes, Second Edition
Bjørn Andersen, Tom Fagerhaug, Bjørnar Henriksen, and Lars E. Onsøyen

The Internal Auditing Pocket Guide: Preparing, Performing, Reporting, and Follow-Up, Second Edition
J.P. Russell

The Certified Six Sigma Black Belt Handbook, Second Edition
T. M. Kubiak and Donald W. Benbow

The Certified Six Sigma Green Belt Handbook
Roderick A. Munro, Matthew J. Maio, Mohamed B. Nawaz, Govindarajan Ramu, and Daniel J. Zrymiak

To request a complimentary catalog of ASQ Quality Press publications, call 800-248-1946, or visit our website at http://qualitypress.asq.org.

THE CERTIFIED MANAGER OF QUALITY/ ORGANIZATIONAL EXCELLENCE HANDBOOK

Fourth Edition

Russell T. Westcott, Editor

Contributors
*Milt Krivokuca, Jd Marhevko, Heather McCain,
Ken Sadler, Jan Tucker, Doug Wood*

*Quality Management Division,
American Society for Quality*

Quality Management
Division
ASQ The Global Voice of Quality™

ASQ Quality Press
Milwaukee, Wisconsin

American Society for Quality, Quality Press, Milwaukee 53203
© 2014 by ASQ
All rights reserved. Published 2013
Printed in the United States of America
19 18 17 16 15   5 4 3

Library of Congress Cataloging-in-Publication Data

The certified manager of quality/organizational excellence handbook / Russell T. Westcott,
    editor ; contributors, Milt Krivokuca [and five others].—Fourth edition.
      pages cm
    Includes bibliographical references and index.
    ISBN 978-0-87389-861-4 (hardcover : alk. paper)
    1. Total quality management—Handbooks, manuals, etc. I. Westcott, Russ, 1927–

    HD62.15.C42 2013
    658.4'013—dc23   2013033022

ISBN: 978-0-87389-861-4

Acquisitions Editor: Matt T. Meinholz
Managing Editor: Paul Daniel O'Mara
Production Administrator: Randall Benson

ASQ Mission: The American Society for Quality advances individual, organizational, and
community excellence worldwide through learning, quality improvement, and knowledge
exchange.

Attention Bookstores, Wholesalers, Schools, and Corporations: ASQ Quality Press books,
video, audio, and software are available at quantity discounts with bulk purchases for
business, educational, or instructional use. For information, please contact ASQ Quality Press
at 800-248-1946, or write to ASQ Quality Press, P.O. Box 3005, Milwaukee, WI 53201-3005.

To place orders or to request ASQ membership information, call 800-248-1946. Visit our website
at http://www.asq.org/quality-press.

 Printed on acid-free paper

Quality Press
600 N. Plankinton Ave.
Milwaukee, WI 53203-2914
E-mail: authors@asq.org
The Global Voice of Quality™

Table of Contents

List of Figures and Tables

Preface to the Fourth Edition

QUALITY MANAGEMENT—AN EVOLVING REQUISITE OF SOCIETY

Quality management has and continues to evolve from a rigid, structured function founded exclusively to monitor manufacturing processes to a more well-rounded function of total organizational performance. The traditional view of quality as a manufacturing-specific organizational cost center is rapidly becoming obsolete and being replaced by a more holistic approach to the functional definition of quality. The ASQ Futures of Quality study, conducted every three years, continues to reflect these perspectives of quality in our global society. The need for a holistic approach to quality is necessary to address the social responsibility, environmental, and sustainability concerns of society. This holistic approach extends an organization's place in society, going beyond providing products and services that are safe and reliable, to also being a respected member of the local community and global society. Organizations must recognize the expanded role of quality and how the principles of quality management have transitioned to those of organizational excellence. Any and every organization, from the sole proprietor entrepreneur to the largest multinational corporation, can benefit from the Certified Manager of Quality/Organizational Excellence (CMQ/OE) body of knowledge.

This increased complexity of societal expectations of organizations necessitates professionals who can demonstrate superior knowledge of the traditional functional areas of business while maintaining objectivity in assuring that organizations accomplish their mission and vision. The manager of organizational excellence understands how a delicate balance is necessary to meet customer satisfaction, global stakeholder concerns, and internal process efficiencies.

Since the inception of this certification, the title has been changed to reflect the current responsibilities of this profession. In this the fourth edition, significant changes have been made, and the body of knowledge has been revised, with additional emphasis placed in several sections.

CONTINUOUS LEARNING—PERSONAL EXCELLENCE AS A BASIS FOR ORGANIZATIONAL EXCELLENCE

The personal accomplishment of becoming a CMQ/OE provides professionals with the distinction of being formally recognized not only for superior knowledge, but also for exceptional comprehension of the complex issues affecting organizations and their performance. Additional opportunities are afforded those who possess formal recognition for their accomplishments, knowledge, and professionalism. These key CMQ/OE attributes are indicative of role models who thoroughly understand and are able to apply the principles of organizational excellence necessary to achieve world-class performance.

The body of knowledge is reviewed every five years through a very robust process. Extensive research related to the content of the body of knowledge and its applications is conducted utilizing a variety of quality methodologies. Conducting this analysis on a regular basis assures that the content of this handbook and the body of knowledge reflects the current responsibilities of mangers of organizational excellence.

The CMQ/OE body of knowledge remains in constant transition as global economic conditions, societal concerns, and technology continue to change. The transient nature of elements that impact organizational excellence requires that the CMQ/OE recertify every three years. Recertification assures that the CMQ/OE continues to have the most current knowledge of the issues and concerns of the global community.

Managers of organizational excellence will be tasked with applying critical, out-of-the-box thinking to solve complex issues facing organizations. The personal accomplishment of attaining the CMQ/OE recognizes that the fundamental skills and knowledge are in place to meet these challenges.

USE AND DEVELOPMENT OF THE FOURTH EDITION OF THIS HANDBOOK

This handbook is a comprehensive reference source designed to help professionals address organizational issues from the application of the basic principles of management to the development of strategies needed to deal with the technological and societal concerns of the new millennium. The content of the fourth edition is very similar to the previous edition, but theories and applications have been revised to reflect a more current global perspective. The residual value of this handbook is immeasurable. Although this handbook thoroughly prepares individuals for the ASQ CMQ/OE exam, the real value resides in post-exam usage as a day-to-day reference source for assessing quality applications and methodologies in daily processes. Along with the display of the CMQ/OE certificate, this reference source should be visible and readily accessible. The content is written from the perspective of practitioners, and its relevance extends beyond traditional product quality applications.

The contributing authors are all subject matter experts (SMEs) from the leadership team of ASQ's largest division, the Quality Management Division (QMD). This team consists of volunteers who are advocates for improving organizational performance. The royalties arising from the sale of this book are applied to the QMD operations budget and are used for funding additional activities designed to enhance QMD membership value.

For the fourth time, thanks to Russ Westcott and his six new contributors.

Milton Krivokuca, DBA
Chair—Quality Management Division
American Society for Quality

Acknowledgments

To colleagues Milt Krivokuca, Jd Marhevko, Heather McCain, Jan Tucker, Ken Sadler, and Doug Wood, who have contributed to this revised edition.

To Jerry Rice for his painstaking analysis of the impact of the changed body of knowledge.

To the staff at ASQ Quality Press as well as the hardworking copy and production editors who have ably corrected grammatical goofs and made valuable suggestions for improvement.

To the contributors to the first, second, and third editions, who laid the foundation for this edition.

Russ Westcott
Editor, Fourth Edition

Introduction

HISTORICAL PERSPECTIVE

In early agricultural situations, quality resulted largely from screening and culling inferior product, and grading the acceptable product. Careful selection of seed and breeding stock, attention to site, and good husbandry lowered the incidence of poor product, but did not eliminate the need to cull and grade. Farmers did their best, but their output was the result of natural processes mostly beyond their control. The "make it, then sort it" approach to quality is still prevalent in this industry.

Craft workers had somewhat more control over their inputs and processes. For example, potters recognized that their outputs varied depending on the type of clay, glaze, and firing method used. Inherent (undetectable or uncontrollable) variations in materials and methods still limited their ability to make a uniformly high-quality product. Their best work was excellent, but consistency varied. This craft-like method existed in the preindustrial era where sales, design, manufacturing, finance, and quality were integrated, and one worker performed all these functions, perhaps with the help of an apprentice or family members.

This tradition persisted until the development of the factory system, in which supervisors were placed to oversee workers. All employees were involved with production, but only the supervisor judged quality. A distinction between making product and checking it had been introduced. Factories developed into highly organized enterprises, with much specialization of labor. Quality was still tested in, and the testers and inspectors became a separate, specialized group. Usually, this group was part of manufacturing, close to the point of production and familiar with the needs of other workers.

These assumptions are still made by many: we can only make so much, it will come out in various grades, and better product is rare, so high quality is opposed to high productivity. If quality and productivity are opposed, then it is a conflict of interest for quality control workers and production workers to report to the same managers. To get independent judgment, the quality organizations became autonomous, reporting to their own managers rather than to managers of manufacturing. This was also institutionalized in government contracts.

The foundations of modern quality control were developed by Walter Shewhart, who published *Economic Control of Quality of Manufactured Product* in 1931 based on his years of experience at Western Electric. This book advocated techniques better than "make a lot and sort out the good ones." The concepts of measuring and controlling the process, reducing the variation in the system, and distinguishing between special causes and common causes contributed to a new approach for achieving quality.

During World War II (1940–1945), the military needed large quantities of highly uniform product. A three-second fuse needed to take exactly that long; the consequences of variation were quite unsatisfactory. The propellant charges for artillery shells had to be uniform to control trajectory. Tanks, airplanes, and other equipment had to have closely matched parts to function reliably. Thousands of personnel in the American war industries were trained in the practice of *statistical process control* (SPC).

For the most part, some engineers (not operators or statisticians) applied quality principles and technologies (especially SPC) and came to be called *quality engineers*. Because it was recognized that many of the problems experienced in production and service were due to design practices and decisions, a specialized group, reliability engineers, emerged. The experiences of the best-performing organizations made it clear that high levels of quality demand careful planning, analysis, and communication between functions, and close cooperation among all functions.

Present enlightened understanding recognizes that increased quality and productivity go hand in hand, so the need for independence and autonomy of the quality function is lessened. The enterprise is more integrated with the adoption of this new view. Each worker is responsible for work quality. Each worker must have the necessary training, tools, and power to perform work correctly. The production cycle is becoming similar to the days when each worker was master in the shop, often dealing with customers, making the product, and controlling its quality. Management of the total process or subprocess calls for many skills, requiring educated, motivated, and extremely competent workers.

OBSERVATIONS ABOUT THE QUALITY FUNCTION

In a manufacturing environment, the quality function and manufacturing are often organized in parallel, whether by product or by process. How this is done depends on the size and complexity of the operation, the nature of the customers or markets served, the variety and quantity of products involved, and the variety of processes used. If A employs several dozen people at one site to produce one or two products that are distributed locally, and B employs 10,000 people on four continents to make and support dozens of product lines, clearly, their quality functions will have to be very different.

If various parts of the organization are very different, then it may be beneficial to have quality functions at each location. The intent is to have what is needed where it is needed.

The larger the organization, the easier it is to justify the costs of specialized groups located in one central place to serve other dispersed groups. Some common examples are laboratories, calibration facilities, auditors, and trainers. It is often more cost-effective to divide the expense of central shared services among many users than to physically divide the function.

The notion of critical mass says that a certain threshold in size and amount of activity is required for some functions to work well. For example, if equipment used in the quality function requires calibrating only a few times per year, then it makes little sense to own all the necessary equipment and to have an underutilized expert in calibration. It might be better to make arrangements to outsource the activity. In some circumstances, the quality function might be spread over many other internal functions.

When *total quality management* (TQM) is successfully implemented, the distinctions between staff and line activities can become blurred as empowered teams become responsible for both plans and action as the layers of management decrease.

The role of the quality function may include:

- *Quality control (QC).* Providing techniques and performing activities that focus on controlling or regulating processes and materials to fulfill requirements for quality. The focus is on preventing defective products or services from being passed on.

- *Quality assurance (QA).* Planning systematic activities necessary to provide adequate confidence that the product or service will meet the given requirements.

- *Quality management system (QMS).* Defining the structure, responsibilities, procedures, processes, and resources for implementing and coordinating the QMS.

- *Metrology.* Ensuring that the measurements used in controlling quality are meaningful and accurate. Ensuring that measurement equipment is calibrated and traceable to the National Institute of Standards and Technology (NIST).

- *Inspection.* Managing or overseeing the inspection activities.

- *Training.* Providing training and/or training subject matter that supports employee skills training and education in quality-related topics. May also include training for suppliers and for customers.

- *Auditing.* Managing or overseeing the activities involved with auditing products, processes, suppliers, and the QMS to ensure that the organization's strategies, principles, goals, objectives, policies, and procedures relative to quality are followed.

- *Reliability engineering.* Working with design and production functions, determining the probability of a product performing adequately for a specified length of time under stated conditions with an aim of lowering total cost of ownership of the product, and satisfying customers.

- *Initiating and/or participating on problem-solving teams.* Working where needed to apply expertise, such as the tools of quality control and root cause analysis.

- *Supplier quality.* Managing or overseeing the activities that ensure that high-quality suppliers are selected and that incoming purchased parts and materials are acceptable in grade, timeliness, and other characteristics.

- *Product/service design.* Working with sales, design, and other functions to ensure quality in products under development.

The priority (importance and authority) attributed to the quality function is not based on the size of the quality department (budget, head count, floor space, or location in the organization chart), but on consideration of a number of factors, including:

- An organization's vision, mission, strategic goals and objectives, and the emphasis placed on quality principles and practices

- Total costs of quality and the allocation to the types of costs, that is, prevention, appraisal, and failure costs

- Resources allocated and the time spent on quality by management at all levels, especially the higher levels

- Senior leadership's visible and personal involvement in and support of quality efforts

The quality function is not:

- A prevention squad. When the quality department is viewed as the owner of quality, the rest of the organization tends to abdicate its role and responsibility.

- A policing function oriented primarily toward defect detection.

- A screen or barrier to protect the customer from problems and defects. Advertisements may emphasize that the customer can be confident of satisfaction "because we have X number of inspectors and testers checking the product." This could be viewed as an admission that an organization may not have dependable processes for making a good product.

- Just one more task among many. This occurs when managers and workers approach quality as another task on top of or after all the other tasks.

Quality is an extremely important function in an organization, but it is not the only important function. The quality function needs to practice humility and respect in dealing with other functions within the organization. Quality is not alone in bringing about success for the organization and is not exempt from blunders, mistakes, poor judgment, or human error. There are good and bad ways to work for quality. Thus, the quality function should be scrutinized just as any other function is evaluated, and continually improved.

BIG Q AND little q

Dr. Joseph M. Juran illustrated the difference between managing to achieve quality across the board, in all functions of the organization, and for all products and services (Big Q) and managing for quality on a limited basis (little q). Quality control activities are little q. Quality assurance may be little q or Big Q depending on how it functions within an organization.

LEVELS OF ORGANIZATIONAL MATURITY

To gain an overall perspective of the implications of applying quality principles and practices, scan Table I.1.

THINKING LIKE A QUALITY MANAGER/ DIRECTOR

The roles and responsibilities of the quality manager/director—and approaches to quality management—vary depending on the type of industry or the size of the business entity. The Certified Manager of Quality/Organizational Excellence (CMQ/OE) Body of Knowledge (BoK) (see Chapter 20) is a product of inputs from many sources and reflects areas of common interest and importance. The intention in the development of examination questions is to measure the level of knowledge and skill that a person possesses relative to each area of the BoK, and how to apply the BoK as an integrated system, regardless of each person's job, organization culture, or industry practice.

For individuals planning to take the ASQ CMQ/OE examination, getting into the mind-set of the role for which the certification was designed is a major key to a successful outcome. Some recommendations for establishing a successful mind-set in using this study guide and preparing for the examination include:

- Visualize or think of yourself as a corporate director of quality for a multi-facility organization, perhaps with locations globally. In reality, in businesses in which products and services are not highly regulated by government legislation, and in smaller business enterprises, the quality manager may not have a support staff to perform quality engineering–related tasks and make day-to-day quality decisions. As a result, you might spend the majority of time acting in the capacity of an engineer, and assume that mind-set in studying for and taking the exam. *That might not work well for you.* A wider and higher-level mind-set needs to be assumed for exam purposes.

Individuals taking the CMQ/OE examination need to place themselves in the context of having to think strategically. For instance, after placing yourself in the role of a corporate director of quality for a multi-facility business, envision addressing such questions as "What can the quality function do to help the company identify or implement initiatives that will enable it to break into new markets, or gain a greater share of the present markets served?"

- Think of yourself as having to integrate the needs of the quality function with the needs of the management team and all other business processes. In addition to managing the quality department, the quality manager's role includes facilitating deployment of quality approaches, principles, and practices in other functional areas, such as supplier quality in purchasing and customer satisfaction in marketing/sales.

Table I.1 Levels of organizational maturity. What is your organization's level?

Level 1 Dysfunctional system	Level 2 Awakening system	Level 3 Developing system	Level 4 Maturing system	Level 5 World-class system
Economy of scale focus with long runs preferred. Time-consuming changeovers are the norm. The customers' voice is rarely heard, and then only at the top.	Quality steering committee has been formed; quality systems are assessed; quality initiatives are planned. A customer focus is a goal.	Tested practices are deployed to all major areas of the factory. Customer involvement is sought.	Seeks out and learns about best practices. Adapts improved practices for all areas. Customers, suppliers, and employees are integrated into the systems.	Retaining satisfied customers is key. Plant uses single-piece flow with cellular techniques. Improved throughput achieved through reduction of bottlenecks.
Rigid plant layout, nonintegrated systems, erratic workflow prevalent. Buffer stock everywhere. All jobs are rush. Firefighting is the norm.	Applicable lean management practices have been identified. Training is being conducted.	Flexible production layouts and cells are introduced. Cleanliness and neatness of individual work areas is stressed.	Production system allows short runs, greater product mix, speedy introduction of new products, and shorter cycle times.	Plant layout is agile and clean. Workers are self-inspecting their work. Lean manufacturing tools and techniques are liberally applied.
Machinery runs at maximum speed without regard for its life or performance quality. Workplace is unorganized and unclean.	A small project is under way to implement and test improved quality management practices.	Pull-type production system under test in one area. Employee qualification system is in place.	Operating information is provided immediately with computerized displays. Errors are prevented with mistake-proofing devices.	Preventive maintenance ensures availability and optimizes quality, efficiency, and lifecycle cost.

Continued

Table I.1   *Continued.*

Level 1 Dysfunctional system	Level 2 Awakening system	Level 3 Developing system	Level 4 Maturing system	Level 5 World-class system
No teamwork. Fiefdoms fiercely guarded from encroachment by other functions. No linkage between any overall strategy and production scheduling.	Bottlenecks and non-value-added functions in process flow are being examined. An equipment maintenance program is under development.	Cross-functional teams promote adherence to standards and ensure continuous improvement.	Teams, some self-managed, aid adherence to high standards, the focus on customers, and continual improvement.	Management is personally and visibly involved in continual improvement. Quality of information and decision making at all levels is exemplary.
Management by command. Poor workforce commitment and involvement.	A cross-functional team is being initiated to work on cycle time reduction.	Systems are implemented to provide data for performance measurement, improvement.	An effective strategic planning process is instituted.	All employees are highly motivated, involved, and empowered.
Communication is one way (downward) with few or no feedback loops.	Weekly production review meetings are held, chaired by the VP manufacturing.	A supplier certification program is in place.	Overall strategy is linked to production planning and process improvement.	Supplier relations are based on collaborative communication and partnerships.
Adversarial supplier relationships focus on price.	A supplier qualification approach is under study.	Overall performance is about equal to industry norms.	Plant benchmarked by others in industry.	Plant benchmarked by others outside industry.
Customers frequently get poor quality and delivery.	Overall performance remains below industry norm.		Performance is above industry norm.	Performance is world-class.

• Think in the context of the *plan–do–check–act* (PDCA) model. Constructed response questions are purposely designed to assess the ability of the test taker to integrate and apply the BoK from a broader perspective. Therefore, using PDCA to structure responses will often help ensure more complete answers to many of the described situations.

Keep uppermost in your mind that your role as test taker in answering constructed response questions is not to solve the problem, but to define a process, based on the principles of quality management, that would enable the issues presented to be effectively addressed. The planning step of the PDCA cycle often also involves first assessing the current situation, as well as past efforts, before moving forward.

• Develop an understanding of how all the elements of the BoK are interrelated. A good way to practice the use of critical-thinking skills that will further aid in answering constructed response questions is to select two or more elements or sub-elements of the BoK and consider how they are related, such as the linkages between leadership and strategy development/deployment, or how quality control methodologies can lead to customer satisfaction.

A link in one direction is that leadership of the organization is ultimately responsible for both defining and carrying out the strategic management process. Viewed from the reverse direction, when defining strategy, the characteristics and processes of leadership that currently exist in the organization should be considered in light of how they will support or block implementation.

STRUCTURE OF THIS HANDBOOK

The handbook follows the body of knowledge scheme as set forth in Chapter 20. Throughout each section of this handbook, the categorical BoK requirements associated with good quality management practices for that section are shown in a box preceding the pertinent text. These BoK requirements represent the range of content and the cognitive level at which multiple-choice questions can be presented. Also, there is a separate BoK pertaining to constructed response questions in Chapter 20.

There is some overlap of topics within the BoK. An attempt has been made to cover a given topic in depth in one section and where necessary provide cross-references to that one explanation.

Additional references to material for each chapter are presented in Appendix A. When a topic is new to a test preparer, or knowledge has faded, the test preparer is urged to seek more information from one or more of the resources listed. There is no way this single handbook can provide the depth and breadth of knowledge you should have on any given topic in the BoK. A few years back, one test preparer referred to the BoK as "a mile wide and an inch deep." The new 2013 BoK is updated where needed, and wider and deeper than before. On the subject of reference material, do not forget the wealth of information available via the internet—most of it free! That includes a sample test and the extensive, wide range of information on the ASQ website and available from the ASQ Knowledge Center, www.asq.org or (800) 248-1946.

In order to provide a broad perspective of quality management, this book has specifically been written to address:

- Historical perspectives relating to the evolution of particular aspects of quality management, including recognized experts and their contributions

- Key principles, concepts, and terminology relevant in providing quality leadership, and communicating quality needs and results

- Benefits associated with the application of key concepts and quality management principles

- Best practices describing recognized approaches for good quality management

- Barriers to success, including common problems that the quality manager might experience when designing and implementing quality management, and insights as to why some quality initiatives fail

- Guidance for preparation to take the Certified Manager of Quality/ Organizational Excellence examination.

Not every quality manager will equally possess expertise in each BoK section and topic. The handbook's primary purpose is to help readers properly focus their study efforts in preparation for the examination. However, this handbook should prove useful as a reference guide back on the job.

TERMINOLOGY

The ISO definition of *product* as "the result of a process" includes categories of hardware, software, services, and processed materials. The word *product* is used throughout the handbook, with and without the accompanying clarification that it also applies to services. It is expected that the reader will have the flexibility to interpret the words in the context in which they are used and to substitute terms that are more apropos for their own industry or experiences to help them clarify the material.

DISCLAIMER

The body of knowledge for the Certified Manager of Quality/Organizational Excellence is largely based on conceptual ideas and models rather than on exact mathematical formulas or tangible items that can be held up as correct. For some of the areas of the BoK, there could be multiple correct views because of differences in industry, organizational maturity, geographic location, competitors' strategies, and so on. Even the gurus of quality differ in their philosophies, priorities, and approaches to quality. For example, multiple-choice questions often may appear to have at least two right answers. It will be your task to choose the one answer that best applies to the content and context of the question. (No one ever said that making decisions as a manager/director is simple.)

Furthermore, you should know that ASQ policy maintains a strict separation between the people who prepare the examination, those who score the completed examination papers, and those who present material (in whatever medium available) for people preparing to take the examination. As a result of this separation, the content presented in this handbook may differ from the intent of the creators of the BoK and/or the writers of the examination questions. Therefore, any questions you may have regarding BoK intent or details about answer scoring can not be answered by the editor of this handbook nor by course instructors.

Success as a quality manager requires experience and a mature understanding of the various principles, concepts, and practices, as well as the specific knowledge obtained from this or any other reliable source. The best to you in your quest to become a Certified Manager of Quality/Organizational Excellence. *Good luck!*

Russ Westcott, Editor

Part I
Leadership

1. *The only definition of a leader is someone who has followers.*

2. *An effective leader is not someone who is loved or admired. Popularity is not leadership.*

3. *Leaders are highly visible. They . . . set examples.*

4. *Leadership is not rank, privileges, titles, or money. It is responsibility.*

—**Peter F. Drucker**

Leadership is not so much the exercise of power itself as the empowerment of others.

—**Warren Bennis and Burt Nanus**

If you want one year of prosperity, grow grain.

If you want ten years of prosperity, grow trees.

If you want one hundred years of prosperity, grow people.

—**Chinese Proverb**

Chapter 1

A. Organizational Structures

It's appropriate that a book on the management of quality begin with the subject of leadership. Perhaps no other factor has a greater impact on an organization than how well it is led on both a strategic and an operational basis. Additionally, leadership is not solely the responsibility of those who reside at the higher levels of the hierarchy, but is instead an activity in which anyone involved in the success of an organization can take part.

Strategic leadership includes defining the structures to achieve the overall vision and mission of an organization and its strategies and systems.

Define and describe organizational designs (i.e., matrix, flat, and parallel) and the effect that a hierarchical management structure can have on an organization. (Apply)

Body of Knowledge I.A

ORGANIZATIONAL DESIGN

A major role of leadership is to ensure that an organization is designed to carry out its mission, goals, and strategies. Understanding leadership requires a fundamental understanding of organizations and the design factors that must be considered.

The design of an organization is the formal framework for communication and authority, and is determined by three major factors:

- *Complexity.* The number of different entities (for example, job titles, reporting levels, functional departments, and physical work locations) that will exist in the organization.

- *Formalization.* How much the organization will rely on standard guidelines and procedures to instruct and direct employee activities.

- *Centralization.*[1] Whether decision-making authority is located primarily at upper management levels or is delegated to lower levels.

These three aspects can be combined to create many different organizational designs. Purposes of organizational design are to:

- Divide the total work required into logical functional groupings (for example, departments, work units) and the jobs within the functions.

- Assign specific tasks and responsibilities to each individual job.

- Allow better coordination of diverse organizational tasks.

- Establish relationships among individuals, work units, and functions.

- Establish formal lines of authority and decision making.

- Allocate and deploy organizational resources.

To create an appropriate design, a decision must be made as to how work activities will be organized both vertically and horizontally. The vertical structure typically categorizes positions as top managers, middle managers, first-line managers, and operations personnel. Creating the vertical structure includes determining these categories and defining the interaction between the levels by deciding who reports to whom, and who has the authority to make what types of decisions.

VERTICAL ORGANIZATIONAL DESIGN

One concept used in creating the vertical structure is *unity of command,* or the idea that a subordinate should be directly responsible to only one superior.[2] Although structures such as a matrix organization do not follow this rule, the basic intent of vertical design is to avoid conflicts, misunderstandings, or misuse of resources. Organizational designers also must determine the types and amount of authority and responsibility that organizational members will have. Authority refers to the rights inherent in a managerial position to expect orders to be followed, and are related to the position, not the person. Traditionally, authority is delegated downward to subordinate managers, giving them certain rights while specifying limits within which to operate.

There are also different forms of authority: line and staff. *Line authority* is the superior–subordinate relationship extending from the top of the organization to its lowest levels (along a chain of command). A manager with line authority has the right to direct the work of subordinates and to make certain decisions without consulting others. As organizations become larger and more complex, however, line managers may lack the time, expertise, or resources to do their jobs effectively. In response, staff functions are established, such as human resources (see Chapter 8, Section 4) that have the authority to support and advise.

Organizations now recognize that one does not have to be a manager to have influence, nor is influence always correlated to organizational level. Authority is an important concept in organizations, but focusing exclusively on authority produces a narrow, unrealistic view of sources of influence in organizations. Today, authority is recognized as one aspect of the larger concept of power.[3] For example, some individuals in an organization may have considerable informal authority due to their knowledge or personality.

Span of control is another design factor and refers to how many subordinates a manager can effectively and efficiently supervise. Although no consensus exists on an ideal number, many managers favor small spans—typically no more than six—in order to maintain close control.[4] The level at which this decision is targeted affects this number. As managers rise in the organizational hierarchy, they deal with a greater variety of complex and diverse problems. Typically, top executives have a smaller span of control than do middle managers, and middle managers require a smaller span than do supervisors. Therefore, to a large degree the span of control determines the number of levels and managers in an organization. Other things being equal, the wider or larger the span of control, the more efficient the organizational design.

Today, many organizations have reduced the number of managerial positions through restructuring while increasing the spans of control. The optimum span of control is increasingly determined by issues such as:

- Amount of employees' training and experience

- Similarity of subordinate tasks

- Complexity of the tasks

- Physical proximity of subordinates

- Degree to which standardized procedures are in place

- Sophistication of the organization's management information and internal communication systems

- Strength of the organization's culture

- Preferred style of the manager[5]

- Employee turnover

- Available resources

- Financial and competitive pressures

- Organizational beliefs and values

HORIZONTAL ORGANIZATIONAL DESIGN

In addition to a vertical dimension, an organization's design also has a horizontal dimension that determines how work activities are organized at each level of the organization. This involves answering questions such as "How will work activities be allocated?" or "What form of departmentalization will work best?"

Division of labor means that rather than an entire job being performed by one individual, it is broken down into a number of steps, with separate individuals completing each step. In essence, individuals specialize in doing part of an activity rather than the entire activity. Assembly-line production, in which each worker repeatedly does a standardized task, is an example of division of labor. Fast-food companies use the concept of division of labor to standardize the process of taking a customer's order and filling it quickly and properly. Because some tasks require highly developed skills, while unskilled workers can perform others, division of labor makes efficient use of the diverse skills and capabilities of employees. If all workers in an organization were engaged in each step of the production process, every worker would need the skills to perform both the most demanding and the least demanding jobs. The result would be that except when performing the most highly skilled or highly sophisticated tasks, employees would be working below their skill levels. Because skilled workers are paid more than unskilled workers and their wages tend to reflect their highest level of skills, paying highly skilled workers to do easy tasks would be an inefficient use of resources.

Historically, management has viewed the division of labor as an unending source of increased productivity. Eventually, certain drawbacks of division of labor exceed the economic advantages, including problems such as boredom, job stress, low productivity, poor quality, increased absenteeism, and high turnover. Organizations have discovered that by giving employees a variety of activities to do, allowing them to do a whole and complete piece of work, and putting them together into teams, jobs are more interesting, and higher quality often results.

CENTRALIZATION/DECENTRALIZATION

Centralization/decentralization refers to how much decision-making authority has been delegated to lower management levels. Few organizations could function effectively if all decisions were made by a select group of top managers, nor could they do so if all decisions were delegated to the lowest levels of the organization. Fayol lists centralization as one of his 14 principles of management and notes that the proper amount of centralization or decentralization depends on the situation.[6]

Organizations have traditionally been structured as pyramids, with authority and power concentrated at the top and with relatively centralized decision making. As organizational environments became more complex and dynamic, many organizations began to decentralize decision making. Many executives now believe that decisions should be made by those people with the best information to make the decisions, regardless of their level in the organization.

More decentralization might be needed under one or more of the following conditions:

- The environment is complex or uncertain.

- Lower-level managers are capable and experienced at making decisions.

- Lower-level managers want a voice in decisions.

- Decisions are relatively minor.

- Corporate culture is more open to allowing managers to have a say in what happens.

- The organization is geographically dispersed.

- Effective implementation of the organization's strategies depends on managers having more involvement and flexibility to make decisions.

Organizational designers should select the amount of centralization/decentralization that best allows management to implement goals and strategies. What works in one situation might not be best for another.

TYPES OF ORGANIZATIONAL STRUCTURES

In resolving issues such as distribution of authority, reporting relationships, span of control, and centralization/decentralization, the structure of the organization will result. It is worth noting that the current tendency is to move to flatter organizations having fewer hierarchical levels and more flexible reporting arrangements. Although a flatter organizational structure implies a wider span of control, information technologies have greatly simplified the processes of communication and decision making, allowing authority to be more widely dispersed.

Organizations are becoming managed more as horizontal processes (for example, as a part of the supply chain or value chain), rather than vertical hierarchies. A *matrix structure* is one way of formalizing a structure that provides both effective horizontal, operational decision making as well as allowing development of functional specialties. Another structure often used when an organization desires to implement a significant change is to create a temporary *parallel* or *collateral organization*, which consists of a group of employees (often a diagonal slice of the organization) who meet on a regular basis in order to guide the change process. Once the organization has made the transition, the parallel structure is dissolved.

Earlier, some of the aspects that affect organizational design—such as division of labor, distribution of authority, span of control, and employee knowledge and experience—were discussed. Many different structures can result from these decisions, and which one an organization selects is also impacted by larger factors, both internal and external.

Each organization has its own way of grouping work activities (departmentalization). Groupings may be according to the:

- Work functions performed

- Product or service provided

- Customers served

- Geographic area or territory covered

- Product–customer process flow

The method(s) used should reflect the grouping that would best contribute to the attainment of the organization's strategic goals and objectives as well as the objectives of individual units. Following is a discussion of each of these structures, plus additional forms in which boundaries are more fluid.

- *Functional*. One of the most common ways to group activities is by the function performed. A manufacturing plant might be organized by separating engineering, accounting, manufacturing, human resources, and purchasing specialists into departments as shown in Figure 1.1. Functional departmentalization can be used in all types of organizations, with the name of the functions changed based

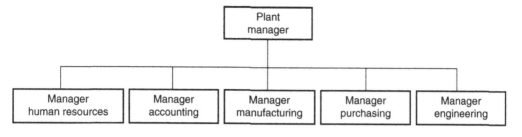

Figure 1.1   Functional departmentalization.

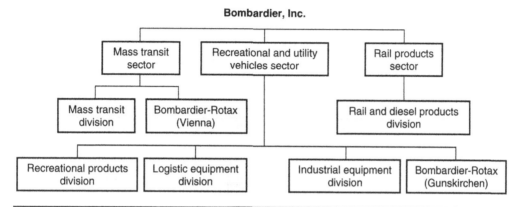

Figure 1.2   Product departmentalization.

on the types of skills required to achieve organizational objectives. For example, a university hospital might have departments devoted to health research, patient care, facilities management, and finance.

• *Product.* Figure 1.2 illustrates the product departmentalization structure. Each major product group is placed under the authority of an executive who specializes in and is responsible for all aspects of that product line. A clothing retailer also uses product departmentalization, basing its structure on its varied product lines, such as women's and men's footwear and apparel and accessories. This type of structure allows portions of the organization to focus on particular categories of product, allowing greater expertise to be gained of the market and product technology.

• *Customer.* The particular type of customer an organization seeks to serve can also be used to define structure. The sales activities shown in Figure 1.3 for an office supply firm can be broken down into three departments: those serving retail, wholesale, and government customers. Textbook publishers often organize by customer, such as those serving primary schools, high schools, and college or university levels. The assumption underlying customer-stratified organizations is that customers in each grouping have a common set of problems and needs that will best be met by specialists who can focus on their needs.

Part I.A

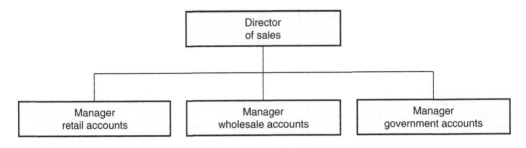

Figure 1.3   Customer departmentalization.

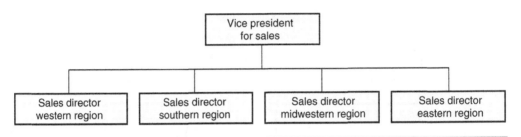

Figure 1.4   Geographic departmentalization.

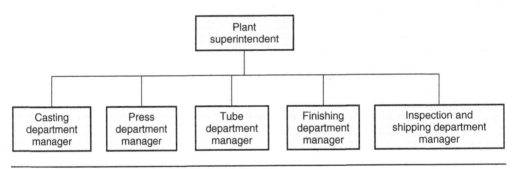

Figure 1.5   Process departmentalization.

• *Geographic.* Another way to organize is by geography or territory. An organization's sales function might have western, southern, midwestern, and eastern regions, as shown in Figure 1.4. A large school district might have six high schools to serve each of the geographical areas within its district. Geographic organization is valuable when an organization's customers are scattered over a large area, allowing the specific needs of the location to be addressed, as well as reducing business costs such as logistics.

• *Process.* A flow form of departmentalization is shown in Figure 1.5, which illustrates the various production departments in an aluminum extrusion processing plant. Each department specializes in one specific phase (or subprocess) in the production of aluminum tubing. The metal is cast in huge furnaces and sent to the press department, where it is extruded into aluminum pipe. It is then transferred to the tube mill, where it is stretched into various sizes and shapes of tubing. It then moves to finishing, where it is cut and cleaned, and finally arrives in the inspect, pack, and ship department.

• *Team.* The competitive drive for improvement has made organizing by teams more common. This structure often overlays or replaces the rigid boundaries of departmentalization, bringing together individuals with needed competencies for a particular mission. In a team-based structure, the entire organization consists of work groups or teams that perform the organization's work. Employee empowerment is crucial because no rigid line of managerial authority flows from top to bottom. Team members are free to design work processes in the way they think best, and are held responsible for all work activity and performance results in their areas. For example, an insurance company reorganized its customer representatives into eight-person teams trained to expedite all customer requests. Rather than switching customers from one specialist to another, a team now takes care of every aspect of a customer request.

• *Matrix.* A matrix structure assigns specialists from different functional departments to work on one or more projects led by a project manager. This arrangement was developed in the 1960s by the U.S. aerospace industry to cope with the demands of managing a number of concurrent projects. Figure 1.6 shows a sample matrix organizational structure. In a typical matrix organization, specialists report to a line or project manager to integrate their expertise with those of other specialists. They also report to a functional manager responsible for departmental human resource issues such as hiring, skill enhancement, assignments to line or project units, and performance reviews.

• *Cells.* Parts of an organization may be structured in work cells. A *cell* is a self-contained unit dedicated to performing all the operations to complete a product or process or major portion of a product (see Figure 14.12).

• *Boundaryless.* A different view of organizational structure is called the boundaryless organization (also referred to as a *network organization, modular corporation,* or *virtual corporation*). It is not defined by, or limited to, the boundaries imposed by a predefined structure. The *boundaryless* organization breaks down the artificial boundaries created by a design such as departmentalization and hierarchies, and the external boundaries separating the organization from its suppliers, customers, and other stakeholders (see *virtual teams* in Chapter 3).

Many factors have contributed to the rise of the boundaryless organization. One is the need to respond to rapidly changing, highly competitive global markets. Another factor is new technology that permits organizations to work more effectively. For example, a world leader in credit card authorization systems has no corporate headquarters, secretaries, or paper mail. The chief executive officer calls his organizational structure the "blueberry pancake model, very flat, with all blueberries equal."[7] Employees have a vast amount of information at their fingertips through the company's e-mail network.

The authors of *The Boundaryless Organization: Breaking the Chains of Organizational Structure* discuss the means for structuring a boundaryless organization attuned to the needs for integrating resources to serve the customer, strengthening the value chain, and crossing geographic boundaries.[8] Authors of *The Virtual*

Part I.A

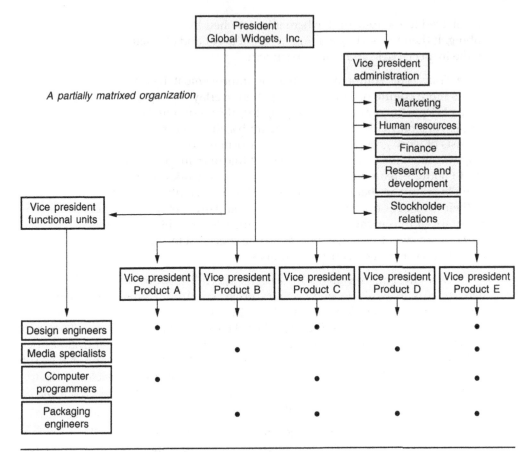

Figure 1.6   Matrix organization example.

Corporation focus on the powers of information, new technologies, and a new kind of worker.[9]

Beyond the ways an organization groups its work activities, there are other factors to consider. They are:

• *Strategy.* Since organizational structure will impact the ability to achieve strategic objectives, structure should be based on the organization's strategy (see Chapter 5). This means that if the strategy significantly changes, structure will likely need to be modified to support the change. A low-cost provider strategy may utilize a functional structure sharing the same support resources with many facilities (for example, centralized purchasing, human resources, and engineering), while a strategy to develop close, long-term customer relationships would call for a more decentralized structure (for example, sales offices for each major customer or geographic location).

• *Size.* The size of the organization affects structure due to the fact that a larger organization will tend to have more specialized and diverse activities to be managed. This increased differentiation can easily lead to narrowly focused or transactional management, although this may be mediated by where the company's product is in its life cycle. For example, a company that has grown large as a result of gaining a significant market share in a new product line may find a need for transformational management as the product enters the mature, low-growth stage.

 • *Technology.* Another factor affecting structure is the range of technologies used by the organization. Every organization uses various forms of technology to convert inputs into outputs, and the type of technology will impact organizational structure. For example, a chemical firm using continuous-flow processes will be organized differently than a hospital or a law firm. The management styles are also likely to differ, since professionals in a hospital or law firm are knowledge workers who would expect a freer reign than employees whose job is to load and unload railcars of raw material and finished goods.

 • *Core competencies.* Organizations can be structured to focus on the core competencies that differentiate the organization from its competitors. Core competencies may consist of unique capabilities of its workforce, specialized technologies, the knowledge and experience of its management, track record for innovation, world-class service policies and practices, a unique niche the organization's products and services fulfill, and so on.

 • *Regulatory, legal, and other requirements.* Constraints and mandates due to regulations, laws, and standards may influence organizational structure. For example, ISO 9001 registrar organizations must clearly separate their registration auditing organization and services from their consulting services organization. Certain customers may specify that the products they purchase be produced in facilities and by workers separate from products their supplier produces for other customers to protect proprietary designs and processes. Because of potential contamination, laws may prohibit the commingling of production of certain products, for example, food products and chemicals. The types and levels of security mandated for certain industries, for example, products and services for the U.S. military, will influence organizational structure. Regulations governing occupational health and safety affect organizational structure, and laws governing allowable emissions are critical to certain industries.

 • *Union.* Employees represented by a union are a kind of parallel organization within an organization. In an ideal situation, the union leader participates with top management of the organization in strategy development as well as decisions affecting the ongoing business of the organization. In the more traditional situation, and, sadly, still the more prevalent situation, the union and organization management may coexist in an adversarial relationship.

Union leadership may influence organization structure and reporting relationships, job design, work standards and practices, compensation and benefits, purchasing decisions, supplier selection, employee disciplinary actions, facility expansion or closure, process improvement initiatives, and so on. Disagreement over the terms of the labor–management contract can result in a production slowdown or strike.

• *Competition.* The competitive environment in which the organization operates will also affect organizational structure, as a higher pace of change requires a more flexible organizational design that can quickly adapt to new market opportunities. In this environment a team structure and participative style (see Chapter 8) are more likely to succeed than a functional structure with autocratic management.

• *Workforce issues.* Availability of sufficient workers and/or of skilled workers is a factor affecting organizational design. All of the considerations necessary to attract and retain the workforce are factors, for example, availability of housing, transportation, schools, religious entities, shopping, entertainment, and adequate community infrastructure.

• *Facilities.* The present and future availability of land, buildings, utilities, rail service, roadways, airport, and so on, are important considerations.

• *Other environmental factors.* The prevailing weather patterns, the political climate, and the presence or absence of crime all are factors.

• *Combinations.* Most large organizations will utilize a combination of methods of organization and management. At the local facility level they might be organized in teams or in functional or process groups, and at the division level organized by product. At higher levels there may be a geographic structure that allows focusing on a particular part of the world (for example, United States, Europe, and Asia).

MANAGEMENT HIERARCHY AND INFLUENCE ON THE ORGANIZATION

To ensure that an organization achieves its desired outcomes, someone must plan, allocate resources, and monitor results. These are major activities for which management personnel have responsibility. *Top management* (also called *senior management* or *executive management*) is responsible for providing direction in defining the vision, mission, strategies, goals, structures, policies, systems, and objectives. These managers are also responsible for managing the boundaries between the organization and its major stakeholders, such as investors, business partners, and the communities in which the organization is located.

Middle managers are responsible for carrying out the policies and procedures necessary for achieving the mission, goals, and strategic objectives. Their emphasis is more operationally than strategically oriented, playing a key role in day-to-day communication and decision making. Middle management's role also parallels that of top management in the sense of being responsible for leadership of a particular part of the organization.

First-level supervision (line management) is responsible for overseeing the workforce assigned to produce the products and/or services for which the organization is designed. Supervisors, while usually considered to be part of management, have the difficult role of thinking and behaving like a manager and at the same time dealing empathetically with the concerns and problems of the workers. In this role, supervisors must communicate downward the vision, mission, principles, and strategic objectives of the organization, take the actions necessary for their work unit to respond appropriately to those objectives, monitor and maintain the processes and people under their supervision, and be accountable for the quality and quantity of product and service required. How effectively supervision establishes a motivational environment has a direct effect on the stability of the workforce and the outcomes achieved by the organization.

In some structures, a quasi-supervisory role exists: the lead operator. Not an official member of management, the lead operator is often charged with the responsibility for some scheduling, instructing, and inter–work unit liaison activities in addition to performing production work.

The role of supervisor, and to some extent the middle manager, may not be needed in some types of organizational structures, for example, where teams are the predominant structural element in a virtual organization, or when information technology has adequately bridged the gap between the workers and management.

Organization culture has an overarching influence on organization structure (see Chapter 8, Section 2 for discussion of culture).

ENDNOTES

1. S. P. Robbins and M. Coulter, *Management*, 5th ed. (Upper Saddle River, NJ: Prentice- Hall, 1996).
2. H. Fayol, *Industrial and General Administration* (Paris: Dunned, 1916).
3. D. Kipnis, *The Power Holders* (Chicago: University of Chicago Press, 1976).
4. L. Urwick, *The Elements of Administration* (New York: Harper & Row, 1944), 52–53.
5. D. Van Fleet, "Span of Management Research and Issues," *Academy of Management Journal* 26, no. 9 (1983): 546 –52.
6. Fayol, *General Administration*, 19–42.
7. T. Peters, "Successful Electronic Changeovers Depend on Daring," *Springfield Business Journal* (August 8, 1994): 15.
8. R. Ashkenas, D. Ulrich, T. Jick, and S. Kerr, *The Boundaryless Organization: Breaking the Chains of Organizational Structure* (San Francisco: Jossey-Bass, 1995).
9. W. H. Davidow and M. S. Malone, *The Virtual Corporation* (New York: Edward Burlingame/Harper Business, 1992).

See Appendix A for additional references for this chapter.

Chapter 2

B. Leadership Challenges

I believe leadership lies more in character than in technical competence,
but these two are interwoven. As people grow in competence, they gain
awareness of a new dimension of their character. Then, as they begin
to develop that aspect of their character, they find that their competence
also increases.[1]

—**Stephen R. Covey**

When is a manager not a leader? When is a leader not a manager? The answer to these questions begs for a precise definition of *leader* and *manager*. Yet, try as we often do to differentiate between the two roles, ambiguity creeps in to blur the line of demarcation. The fuzziness is exacerbated by common usage (or "misuse," depending on your point of view). One observation is that the title "leader" is rarely found on organizations' lists of position titles, although occasionally "team leader" may appear. Does this mean that a leader is some ethereal entity that doesn't truly exist in the real world? Not so.

A *leader* is an individual recognized by others as the person to lead an effort. One can not be a leader without one or more followers. A leader might or might not hold an officially designated management-type position or officially have people reporting to her or him. A leader leads people. An organization can also be referred to as a leader, in the sense that it is on the leading edge (in technology, innovation, products, services, market share) compared with its contemporaries.

A *manager* is an individual who manages and is responsible for resources (people, material, money, time). This is a person officially designated with a management-type position title. A manager is granted authority from above, whereas a leader's role is earned by having followers. Managers manage organizations, processes, systems, projects, and themselves.

According to Deming, "The job of management is not supervision, but leadership."[2] The roles of leader and manager can be fulfilled by the same individual. It's really what the individual does, how he or she does it, and from where the individual derives the power to act that relate to which term is most applicable in a given situation.

Leadership focuses on doing the right things; management focuses on doing
things right.[3]

—**Stephen R. Covey**

This chapter discusses techniques and tools available to leaders/managers that include those used to overcome organizational roadblocks (change management). Also discussed are techniques and tools used in applying, evaluating, and creatively using interpersonal skills (motivating, influencing, negotiating, resolving conflict, and empowering). These are leadership challenges.

Strategic leadership involves creating both technical and social systems that are effectively integrated and that address the needs of both customers and employees. Operational leadership requires ensuring that organizational processes are effectively carried out on a day-to-day basis, monitoring performance, and addressing constraints. It involves ensuring that employees understand what is to be done and that they are provided with the appropriate authority, responsibility, requisite skills, tools, and work environment with which to do it.

The levels of employee motivation and empowerment and how conflict is resolved shape as well as serve to measure the organizational culture. Leadership must effectively attend to these softer issues that also affect organizational performance.

1. ROLES AND RESPONSIBILITIES OF LEADERS

> Describe typical roles, responsibilities, and competencies of people in leadership positions and how those attributes influence an organization's direction and purpose. (Analyze)
>
> **Body of Knowledge I.B.1**

Debate continues as to whether leaders are born or made. A consensus, but with no conclusive evidence, indicates both are possible.

Much effort and countless pages of print have been expended in attempting to develop a universal profile for a leader. It appears to be an endless and (perhaps) pointless task, each effort adding but another viewpoint on what constitutes a leader. It has already been stated that the line between the roles of a leader and those of a manager tend to be blurry and often overlap. Let's explore some of the attributes that tend to identify an individual as a leader, under several different situations:

- *Organization leader.* Most often holding a position with managerial or supervisory responsibilities, this individual exhibits leadership qualities that enable her or him to accomplish more than the position calls for. This individual may be perceived as a leader by his or her subordinates, peers, and bosses for exhibiting one or more of these attributes:

  - Knowledge

- Skills

- Experience

- Charisma

- Action

- Convincing speech

- Empathy

- Ethics

- Empowerment

- Collaboration

- Support

- Trust

- Multidimensional personality

- *Cause leader.* May work either behind the scenes or be highly visible to followers. Through personal motivation and power of persuasion, this leader gathers followers to a common goal, sometimes inciting the followers to take physical action against a targeted group. This type of leader has the ability to communicate in the language of the followers to stimulate their emotions, the stamina to build and sustain a high level of personal energy, and the ability to be seen as a fellow group member with issues the same as or similar to those of the group. This person is usually from the worker ranks of an organization or, sometimes, a "hired gun" who looks and talks like the followers.

- *Transactional leadership.* A transactional style is one in which the manager views the relationship as one of getting the work done through clear definition of tasks and responsibilities, and providing whatever resources are needed. This view might be likened to a contractual relationship, with rewards (positive or negative) being associated with achieving the desired goal.

- *Transformational leadership.* Transformational leadership is a style whereby a leader articulates the vision and values that are necessary in order for the organization to succeed. It is sometimes equated to charismatic leadership, but is aimed more at elevating the goals of subordinates and enhancing their self-confidence to achieve those goals. Bob Galvin accomplished this transformational leadership at Motorola with the Six Sigma program, an approach that positioned Motorola to become a high-quality, reliable competitor in its market.

- *Other kinds of leaders.* Bass identifies several additional leadership types, namely:[4]

- Educational leaders

- Public leaders

- Opinion leaders

- Legislative leaders

To be a leader, one has to believe in oneself, but with reasonable doubt and humility. One has to have a zeal for the role and genuinely care for people (the latter does not apply to ruthless dictators who lead through fear). "Leaders of the future can no longer afford to maintain insularity. It is simply not an option in increasingly boundaryless organizations driven by customer power . . . now they must destroy those walls and replace them with bridges."[5] Key roles of a leader include being a:

• Facilitator

• Appraiser

• Forecaster

• Adviser[6]

• Enabler[7]

• Follower[8]

Requirements for good leadership are similar, regardless of the functional department a manager oversees. Some specific requirements for quality managers in leadership roles include the following:

• Personal commitment to process, product, and organizational quality

• Strong sense of value for others' work and leadership

• Skilled application of a broad base of knowledge of the quality field and an understanding of how to apply this knowledge in functional areas

• Wisdom about both people and things, and an understanding of how to integrate them to get work accomplished (see Section 3)

• Absence (or control) of temperamental or emotional characteristics that might interfere with the ability to work with others

Some critical personal attributes that leaders in the quality management area should exhibit include creativity, patience, flexibility, and self-discipline. Good listening skills, excellent coaching and training skills, sensitivity to customer and employee issues, and a personal commitment to excellence are all essential. Finally, a leader must be a mentor, capable of leading change, and willing to empower followers.

Kouzes and Posner describe a three-phase model of leadership strategy called *VIP—vision–involvement–persistence*.[9] The leader has visions of an exciting, highly favorable future for the organization. The leader involves many others in the organization in making the vision a reality. This takes hard work and the persistence to stay the course.

Just as organizational structures, processes, and priorities have changed in recent decades, so too have the defined roles and characteristics of an effective leader. Some writers have defined the difference between management and leadership as being the amount of control exercised over people. Kouzes and Posner define leadership as a shared responsibility, and state the difference as "managers . . . get other people to do, but leaders get other people to want to do."[10] Warren Bennis defines the differences between the two as doing the right thing (leadership = effectiveness) versus doing things right (management = efficiency). Others have recognized that the type of leader needed often depends on the particular situation, such as the organization, its mission, strategies, and competitive environment, and the makeup of the individuals being led.[11]

Some issues that make leadership difficult to define include:

- Leadership of an organization may be an appointed role (for example, president or department manager).

- Leadership may be taken on at various times by different people who are working together on a particular project. That is, the role of leadership is based on who has the competence necessary during a particular phase of a project.

- Increasingly, in a knowledge-based environment the person being led has more knowledge of the tasks to be accomplished than the individual who is regarded as the leader.

- The increase in virtual teams, in which a group of individuals is jointly responsible for a particular outcome, but where team members do not have face-to-face contact (for example, where technologies are used to communicate).[12]

- Schein described paradoxes of leadership when stating that leaders of the future will be persons "who can lead and follow, be central and marginal, be hierarchically above and below, be individualistic and a team player, and, above all, be a perpetual learner."[13]

- Deming described the primary responsibility of leaders as "transformation of the organization."[14]

- Another leadership role is to ensure that the organization works effectively with respect to the interactions between individuals, groups, and business units both within and outside the organization, and that behaviors meet accepted standards for business ethics.

The traits and actions of leaders will, or should, vary based on the contingencies they face. Hersey and Blanchard's situational leadership model focuses on three factors:

1. Task behavior

    - The level of work-related detail and guidance a leader must provide to a performer

- The extent to which direct action must be taken with the performer

2. Relationship behavior

   - The extent of the communication required with the performer

   - The amount of interpersonal support given a performer

3. Employee maturity or readiness

   - The ability a performer has to assume a task

   - The willingness of the performer to assume the task

Considering the maturity factor, the task and relationship behaviors comprise four situational leadership styles:

1. *High task, low relationship.* Specific instructions and close supervision of performance are indicated (a telling mode). For example, a new or transferred employee is assigned a task for which he has no prior training and needs continual supervision until skill is developed.

2. *High task, high relationship.* Decisions are explained and there is opportunity to clarify and ask questions (a selling mode). For example, a newly trained operator is trying to apply the training to the task at hand, but doesn't understand the need to follow the prescribed sequence of steps and requires supervisory support.

3. *High relationship, low task.* Ideas are shared, encouragement is provided, and the leader acts as a coach (a participating mode). For example, a trained operator is hesitant to assume full responsibility for the entire task assigned and needs help to build confidence.

4. *Low relationship, low task.* Responsibility for decisions and implementation are turned over to the employee (a delegating mode). For example, an experienced operator knows what to do and how to do it, as well as how to troubleshoot a problem should one occur, and assumes full responsibility for the task assigned without requiring direct supervision.

The keys to effective situational leadership are:

- Being able to determine, situation to situation, the leadership style most appropriate to apply in working with performers

- Realizing that one style does not fit all situations

- Realizing that the style used last with a performer may not be the best next time

- Realizing that there are other factors that can influence performance, such as:

  - The performer's physical and/or mental health

  - Events in the performer's personal life

- Influence of coworkers

- Lack of material, tools, equipment, and so on

- Inadequate working conditions

Another aspect to leadership is the emotional competence of the incumbent leader. Daniel Goleman identifies five dimensions, three personal and two social, and related competencies:[15]

1. Self-awareness

    • Emotional awareness

    • Accurate self-assessment

    • Self-confidence

2. Self-regulation

    • Self-control

    • Trustworthiness

    • Conscientiousness

    • Adaptability

    • Innovation

3. Motivation

    • Achievement drive

    • Commitment

    • Initiative

    • Optimism

4. Empathy

    • Understanding others

    • Developing others

    • Service orientation

    • Leveraging diversity

    • Political awareness

5. Social skills

    • Influence

    • Communication

    • Conflict management

    • Leadership

    • Change catalyst

- Building bonds
- Collaboration and cooperation
- Team capabilities

Good leaders challenge the status quo. They inspire and enlist others. They encourage collaboration and enable others to take action. Effective leaders share their power and information to strengthen others. They look for and recognize people who are doing things right. Respected leaders set an example, recognize others' contributions, and celebrate successes. Exemplary leaders continually strive to improve both their intellectual intelligence (cognitive capacity) and their emotional intelligence. Leadership is a daily balancing act: juggling responsibilities and withstanding pressures.

2. ROLES AND RESPONSIBILITIES OF MANAGERS

The inherent preferences of organizations are clarity, certainty, and perfection. The inherent nature of human relationships involves ambiguity, uncertainty, and imperfection. How one honors, balances, and integrates the need of both is the real trick of management.[16]

—Richard Pascale and Anthony Athos

> Describe typical roles, responsibilities, and competencies of people in management positions and how those attributes contribute to an organization's success. (Analyze)
>
> **Body of Knowledge I.B.2**

What Managers Do

Managers attend to the work and resources of the organization—a stewardship role. This may include obtaining, allocating, distributing, using, disposing, and accounting for the resources that fall within the purview of the position to which they are assigned. Primary categories of resources include:

- Money
- Time
- People
- Material
- Physical assets: equipment, facilities, land, and water
- Information
- Intellectual property

Managers may be assigned a variety of different position titles, some of which are:

- Chief executive officer, chief operating officer, chief finance officer, chief information officer

- Vice president of _____

- Director of _____

- General manager of _____

- Manager of _____

- Superintendent of _____

- Supervisor of _____

- Staff supervisor of _____

- Designer of _____

- _____ engineer

- Purchasing agent/buyer for _____

Labor laws differentiate between exempt employees (employees free from certain laws pertaining to hours and compensation) and nonexempt (employees covered by laws relating to hours worked and compensation). Generally, management employees are exempt (however, the nature of one's work and compensation received are key determinants of exempt versus nonexempt status; for example, some management employees receive overtime pay as nonexempt employees do).

As stated earlier, there is often overlap between the roles and responsibilities of a leader and a manager. A significant difference is that the manager's role is mandated by some higher authority and is in effect as long as the higher authority so states. The role of leader is less permanent and, in fact, may either be shared through rotation or acquired through acceptance by followers. Being recognized as a leader often has no relationship to an organizational position title. Thus, a manager may or may not be recognized as a leader. A worker may be recognized as a leader without having any managerial-type title or responsibility. Organizations often interchange the two terms, for example, calling someone a project leader when the intention is really project manager. A chairperson may be a leader and/or a manager, depending much on the influence he or she may have on an organization and the decision authority granted.

Managers' roles may include:

- *Strategist.* Establishes direction for the enterprise through strategic planning and deployment of the plan's goals and objectives

- *Architect.* Builds an enterprise structure that supports the strategic goals and objectives

- *Organizer.* Organizes, people, ideas, and things to achieve the enterprise's objectives

- *Business generator.* Grows and sustains a viable business by creating and retaining satisfied customers

- *Value creator.* Adds value to the enterprise's processes, products, and services

- *Innovator.* Continually seeks ways to introduce, improve, or replace processes, products, and services to further the strategic goals of the enterprise

- *Administrator.* Optimizes the use of and results obtained from resources available

- *Entrepreneur.* Redeploys resources from activities producing poor results to activities where improved results may be obtained

- *Supporter.* Provides visible support, personal involvement, and reinforcement in furthering the efforts of the workers in fulfilling the enterprise's objectives

- *Ethicist.* Embraces the principles, standards, morals, and norms of the society in which the enterprise operates

- *Environmentalist.* Operates the business with high regard for sustaining and improving the physical environment in which the enterprise exists, with responsible use of land, air, and water, and safeguarding of wildlife

- *Mentor.* Provides a personal role model and guidance for the development of future managers

- *Motivator.* Creates and sustains a work environment that stimulates motivation in others

- *Coach.* Sets an example and guides others in achieving excellence

- *Trainer.* Imparts knowledge and teaches skills to others

- *Communicator.* Keeps others informed

- *Integrator.* Brings previously disassociated people and processes together

- *Harmonizer.* Balances and harmonizes major functions of the enterprise

- *Controller.* Oversees the financial affairs of an enterprise

- *Evaluator.* Tracks, measures, analyzes, and evaluates the performance, outputs, and outcomes produced by the enterprise, and the contribution toward achieving the strategic goals of the enterprise and addressing the needs of society

Sometimes a person may be titled a manager even though she or he is an individual contributor (makes a personal professional contribution to benefit the enterprise) and is not responsible for managing people.

Management functions may be grouped as follows (see Chapter 8, Section 2 for more):

- *Planning*
  - Mapping the work unit's processes and interfaces with other work unit's processes
  - Defining the work unit's performance objectives and linkage with the organization's mission, strategic goals, and objectives
  - Identifying the actions and activities needed to achieve the unit's objectives

- *Organizing*
  - Acquiring or assembling the resources needed to meet the unit's objectives
  - Establishing the structural framework (systems and procedures) for managing the unit's processes and resources

- *Staffing*
  - Selecting, hiring, assimilating, and training personnel needed to achieve the unit's objectives
  - Developing the unit's individual and collective competence level to meet or exceed the planned objectives
  - Retaining the unit's competent personnel by creating a motivational environment

- *Directing*
  - Directing the actions and activities of the unit's personnel in achieving the planned objectives
  - Providing the support needed by the unit's performers in realizing the product or service produced by the unit

- *Controlling*
  - Monitoring unit performance and comparing actual results to plans
  - Taking appropriate corrective actions as needed
  - Identifying areas for continual improvement

Competencies needed by managers cover a wide range.[17] (See Chapter 8 for a discussion of management skills and abilities.) Typical managerial competencies may include:

- *Technical competence,* for example:
  - Value streams
  - Techniques and tools

- – Enterprise resource planning
- – Process and quality auditing
- – Process benchmarking (see Chapter 12, Section 3)
- – Information technology (see Chapter 8, Section 3)
- – Knowledge management (see Chapter 8, Section 7)
- *Business competence*, for example:
  - – Strategic planning (see Chapters 5, 6, and 7)
  - – Customer relationship management (see Chapter 17)
  - – Finance (see Chapter 8, Section 5)
  - – Metrics (see Chapter 15)
  - – Risk analysis and management (see Chapter 8, Section 6)
  - – Project management (see Chapter 10)
  - – Performance management
  - – Organization structures (see Chapter 1)
  - – Marketing (see Chapter 8, Section 3)
  - – Processes (see Chapter 14)
  - – Legal requirements
  - – Ethics issues (see Chapter 4)
  - – Stockholders/ownership issues
  - – Supply chain management (see Chapter 18)
- *People competence*, for example:
  - – Personality types (see Chapter 8, Section 2)
  - – Managing styles (see Chapter 8, Section 2)
  - – Diversity issues
  - – Behavior management
  - – Interacting
  - – Communicating (see Chapter 9)
- *Human resource competence*, for example:
  - – Hiring
  - – Training
  - – Affirmative action
  - – Benefits

   – Recognition and rewards

   – Compensation

   – Safety and well-being

   – Professional development

 • *Environmental competence*, for example:

   – Factors affecting the world

   – Politics and power issues

   – Earth sciences

   – Competition

Drucker identifies four tasks of management:[18]

 • *The task of economic performance.* Business enterprises exist for the purpose of economic performance—profitability. Other societal needs can not be fulfilled without a surplus of economic resources.

 • *The task to make work productive and the worker achieving.* Performance is accomplished through work. Achieving implies consideration of the human resource as human beings and not as things.

 • *The task of managing the social impacts and the social responsibilities of the enterprise.* No institution can exist outside of community and society.

 • *The task of managing within the dimension of time.* Management always has to consider both the present and the future, both the short run and the long run.

See Chapter 8 for a discussion of management principles, skills, and abilities.

Persons holding management positions lower in the organizational structure usually are responsible for designated short-term outputs, for example, parts produced, engines serviced, reports generated, and so on. Managerial personnel at the high end of the organizational hierarchy are more likely to be responsible for longer-term strategic outcomes affecting the profitability, growth, and overall success of the enterprise.

3. CHANGE MANAGEMENT

Use various change management strategies to overcome organizational roadblocks and achieve desired change levels, and review outcomes for effectiveness. Define and describe factors that contribute to an organization's culture. (Evaluate)

Body of Knowledge I.B.3

Techniques for Facilitating or Managing Organizational Change

External change is inevitable; internal change is probable. Organizations that continually improve their processes will have a greater probability of success than those who only react to problems. As an organization evolves, there are not only incremental changes, but also increasingly major shifts in strategy, technology, and work organization. Change can occur as a result of outside forces or inside forces.

Fear of change is also a real and valid concern. People are afraid of change because of its potential impact on them. Corporate downsizing and outsourcing cause major disruptions of people's work and personal lives, and continual improvement efforts are sometimes blamed for job losses.

Change management is a process for ensuring that the people affected by change understand the nature of the change and the reasons for it, with the expectation that the new methods of operating will be internalized without creating undue resistance, conflict, and fear. To reduce fear, it's important that the vision of the future be well communicated and that jobs be protected when feasible. Ongoing and open communication during any change process is paramount. Although these precautions will not totally remove fear, they can remove some of the uncertainty of not knowing the direction in which the organization is headed.

Change Agents

Change agents are individuals who play a specific role in the planning and implementation of the change management process.[19] They may be members of the organization or may be outsiders. Collaboration of an internal change agent with an external change agent who has extensive experience in the type of change to be implemented can be a useful strategy.

An internal change agent is a person within the organization designated, usually by management, to facilitate a particular change effort. Internal change agents possess an understanding of the organization's culture, infrastructure, and the business, and also have a vested interest in seeing change efforts succeed. However, they can be hindered by political pressures that can influence objective feedback when problems arise. They might also lack perspective of the big picture or have a vested interest in preserving certain traditions that keep them from seeing specific opportunities for improvement. The role of the internal change agent may be filled by a staff or line person depending on the type and magnitude of the change being implemented.

An external change agent is a person from outside the organization who has been retained to advise and help facilitate the change process. An external change agent often has a greater degree of freedom and should be better able to objectively assess activities and provide honest feedback to senior management without fear of repercussion. Also, organizational members are less likely to have previous experiences with the change agent that might impact effectiveness, and the agent does not have a vested interest in preserving long-held organizational traditions. The danger, of course, is that organizations can become so dependent on an external change agent that the change process is adversely affected when the agent leaves. Another disadvantage of external change agents can be their lack of familiarity with the specific corporate culture.

External change agents must work diligently to build a relationship with the client organization. This includes becoming familiar with company norms, shared beliefs, and behaviors, as well as understanding both formal and informal leadership structures. In most organizations, the change agent needs to become acquainted with persons who serve as informal leaders and to whom others turn for new ideas. Building a relationship between informal leaders can be beneficial because other members of the organization will check with them for affirmation that it is beneficial or safe to support the change process.

Deming emphasized the role of change agents in his view of organizational transformation by stating, "A system can not understand itself. The transormation requires a view from outside."[20]

Guidelines for Implementing Change

The following steps are key to implementing change:

1. Create an awareness of the need for change.

2. Organize a project with sufficient authority to guide the process.

3. Define the vision and strategies for achieving it.

4. Communicate the vision and demonstrate personal commitment to it.

5. Remove obstacles that prevent others from acting on the vision.

6. Go for early and visible successes.

7. Build on success by rewarding supporters and involving more people.

8. Institutionalize the new methods by aligning other systems with them.[21]

The following are common errors made in managing change:

- Not sufficiently emphasizing the urgency and allowing people to be complacent.

- Those guiding the process do not have sufficient power.

- Lacking a clear and compelling vision or not communicating it strongly and/or frequently enough.

- Failing to manage the forces that resist change.

- Not ensuring some early successes that encourage others.

- Celebrating victory prematurely.

- Not changing other organizational systems and cultural elements that are required for long-term continuation of the change.[22]

In Peter Senge's *The Fifth Discipline,* he refers to the parable of the boiling frog to emphasize how threats to corporate and personal survival are perceived when transformational change is taking place: A frog suddenly placed in boiling water— the turbulence of organizational change—will scramble out. Placing a frog in water that is room temperature will not upset the frog. In fact, the frog might even be calmed. Now the water can be gradually heated until it is boiling. As the heat increases, the frog will become groggier until it can no longer climb out. When the water is boiling, the transformation is now complete. The frog's internal apparatus senses the change as a threat to survival and instinctively seeks to avoid the situation. For effective organizational change, use a slow and gradual process change, while paying attention to the subtle reactions from employees.

At the same time, a significant lesson that psychologists will emphasize is that the change process, from an individual perspective, is a progressive one that usually occurs over a considerable length of time. For major changes in culture, this is also true at the organizational level. Trying to shortcut the process may create an illusion of speed, but will not produce the desired results.

Techniques and Roles of Change Agents

Change agents may assume several roles and use a variety of techniques, such as:

- Coaching top management to:

  - Create an environment in which change can take place with minimum resistance.

  - Develop and support an improvement plan.

  - Provide the resources to implement the plan.

- Supporting and advising management colleagues on how to:

  - Deal with technical issues.

  - Cope with intellectual and emotional resistance.

  - Measure, monitor, and report progress.

  - Handle behavioral issues.

  - Provide performance feedback, including reinforcement of top management for the decision it made and reinforcing the work of those implementing the change.

  - Use the change agent as a facilitator when needed.

- Managing a specific project or segment of a large project to:

  - Fill in where no other suitable resource person is available.

  - Serve as a role model for other project management efforts.

- Guiding the development of a network to:

  - Support the implementation of the change.

  - Deploy the principles and practices for managing change throughout the organization.

- Guiding the assessment of the results and closure of the change, including:

– Reviewing lessons learned.

– Evaluating the economic case for the change.

– Documenting the change.

Organizational Roadblocks

Organizational change is difficult, partially due to the inherent nature of how organizations are designed and operated. That is, by constructing an organization in one way (for example, defining the specific roles and processes to be used), other options are excluded by default. Although the boundaries of organizational structure, policies and procedures, and norms are actually quite permeable, the fact that they are defined, documented, and reinforced makes them appear permanent in the minds of many employees. This may be especially true in an organization with a history of success, where that success is linked mentally to the way things have been done in the past.

The division of labor in an organization, both horizontally and vertically, creates several roadblocks. Following are some examples along with methods for reducing the effect on the organization's ability to change:

- *Lack of cross-functional collaboration.* Functional or other forms of work units are created in order to help clarify the mission and focus of each particular group in the organization. An organization, however, is a system with interdependencies in many different directions. When the interdependencies (for example, internal customer–supplier relationships) are not clearly defined and fostered, each work unit may view a request for change only as it relates to their own processes, rather than the entire organization.

A possible solution is to ensure that improvement initiatives, performance measures, and rewards are designed such that collaboration (teamwork across boundaries) will be necessary in order to achieve objectives. Develop internal customer–supplier agreements and performance measures, along with ongoing joint reviews of progress.

- *Lack of authority.* The reason for dividing up work processes and tasks is because time and/or skills constraints prevent any one person from carrying out all the necessary activities. This means that responsibility and authority are divided among many. When a change in work activity is required, however, new roles, responsibilities, and processes may not fit into the predefined boundaries.

A possible solution is to ensure that someone (for example, a champion/sponsor) is identified who has authority over the entire area to be impacted by the change, and that they have a direct link to higher levels of the organization in the event they need additional support outside their area of authority.

- *Inward focus.* Similar to the lack of cross-functional collaboration is the problem of the boundaries between the organization and its environment. By definition, each organization consists of only certain processes and people, and outside these boundaries are suppliers, customers, regulators, and other stakeholders. The day-to-day attention of many members of the organization, however, is on internal

Part I.B.3

processes, resources, and knowledge. Being willing to look externally for ideas, support, and feedback may not come naturally.

A possible solution is to have employees go outside the organizational walls, for example, visiting customer sites, locations where the final product/service is in the hands of the final user, or where other sources of information on new ideas might exist (such as trade shows, conferences, workshops).

• *Internal competition for resources or rewards.* All organizations have limited resources and opportunities, and must allocate them so as to best accomplish the mission with high efficiency. Limited funds, people, or promotions can cause employees to compete against each other—not wanting to suboptimize their area—instead of seeing their efforts as needing to be focused on maximization of the enterprise.

A possible solution is to ensure that strategic and operational plans clearly indicate the priorities and strategies of the organization, and where and how resources are to be allocated. Involve employees in creating these plans through a catchball-type process (see Chapter 7).

• *Lack of understanding.* In a typical organization there are so many different strategies, initiatives, projects, and day-to-day activities always going on that it is often difficult to keep everyone fully informed. People therefore put their focus where it seems best placed, but this may not agree with what is actually expected or desired.

A possible solution is to communicate, communicate, communicate! The biggest problem noted in many employee surveys is lack of adequate communication. When people have gaps in their understanding, they often fill them in as best they can, even though what they hear or think may be incorrect. Management must ensure that information relative to organizational direction (for example, vision, mission, values, strategy, objectives, projects, and performance) is continuously communicated, with the amount and type of communication being adapted to the message and audience (see Chapter 9 for more on communications).

• *Slow decision making.* Although an organization may have clearly communicated plans and have good cross-functional relationships, levels of the hierarchy slow down and frustrate some people who are actively working on improvement initiatives. Vertical communication is meant to ensure ongoing alignment of goals and activities, but is often slower than optimal due to the number of channels through which it may travel and differing time perspectives at each level.

A possible solution is to ensure that authority levels are clearly spelled out for typical situations and use an exception basis where a few key people have the authority to act if the decision involves crossing a particularly difficult organizational boundary. Specify decision-making channels that do not require everyone in the hierarchy to be involved in all decisions, especially those related to improvement opportunities.

Those who study human development discover a tension within many individuals who on the one hand want to improve their lives, but at the same time want a life that is stable and without chaos. Similar paradoxical issues impact an organization's ability to change. Following are some examples:

- *Lack of willingness to invest for the long term.* Managers are often measured according to the end-of-quarter financial results. Yet, a significant commitment of funds and other resources is usually required in the early part of organizational transformation, with the more strategic payoffs occurring perhaps three or more years later.

- *Wanting results fast.* Many of the cause-and-effect relationships dealt with on a day-to-day basis in organizations are quickly resolved. This gets translated into people's expectations for many other issues, although there is often a significant time lag between cause and effect. People become impatient and want to stop taking action if they aren't seeing results.

- *Be selective in what to work on first.* Take the classic low-hanging fruit approach. Make sure that initial efforts are focused on areas where success and payoff are highly probable.

- *Poor history of change.* Some organizations have a long record of unsuccessful change efforts, which causes people to become cynical and to want to avoid future attempts.

- *Learn from errors.* Study and admit past mistakes, and ensure that future efforts don't repeat them.

- *Fear of the unknown.* By definition, change means that things will be different than in the past. People are often uncertain of what their new roles will be and whether they will be able to adapt to the changes, or want to.

- *Provide support for change.* Allow employees to talk with others who have been through similar changes. Provide reassurance that necessary support will be available throughout the change.

- Ensure that there is a common vision of change; communicate the purpose and importance. Figure 2.1 depicts the change process and causes for resistance to change.

Current state	Change process	Future state
• Like the current condition	• Don't like change	• Future status unknown
• Indicates time is wrong	• Poorly communicated	• Fear of failure
• Poor history of change	• Wrong people, method, timing	• Additional workload

Figure 2.1   Causes for resistance to change.
Source: Reprinted with permission of APLOMET.

- Understand the emotional impact of change.

- Understand the systems view—that is, be aware of how changing one process or part of the organization will affect other processes or parts.

- Communicate what will and what will not change.

- Model the behaviors that are desired.

- Provide effective feedback, rewards, and consequences.

- Be consistent in responding to resistance.

- Be flexible, patient, and supportive.[23]

Constraint Management

Managing change is particularly complex due to the fact that much of what must be changed often consists of intangibles such as beliefs, behaviors, and policies. These types of constraints are more difficult to identify and manage than issues such as the capacity limitation of a piece of equipment. Conceptual models or diagrams are useful for representing situations, however, making them more visible and aiding understanding of intangible constraints that may need to be addressed. Following are some examples of how these diagrams can be used. (Chapter 14 contains additional information based on Goldratt's theory of constraints.)

Identifying Constraints with an Interrelationship Digraph. Creating the interrelationship digraph is a method for representing several elements involved in a process and their cause-and-effect relationship. The digraph involves first developing an affinity diagram, then analyzing and organizing the components into their respective relationships (see Chapter 13 for more about constructing an affinity diagram and an interrelationship digraph).

Figure 2.2 is an example of a diagram developed by an organization that was considering developing a suggestion system. Some people had reservations about whether it would be worthwhile, so the management team developed the diagram to represent its thinking about the issues involved. Team members included whether the relationships between components were positive or negative (for example, would or would not be beneficial) as some members of management had reservations about the costs, both resource and financial, of administering the program. They subsequently discovered that they could design the system to fit their particular needs rather than basing it solely on the systems they'd seen and read about. The diagram helped them understand the true cause-and-effect relationships involved and that the design they selected would be the major driver for both costs and resources. An organization unhappy with an existing suggestion system might also learn from a similar analysis.

This type of analysis allows a group to develop a common view of how something is working or should work. The model can also be used as a diagnostic tool to guide collection of data to determine which components of the system are not working as desired. Managing constraints requires understanding the issues involved in the situation, how they are interrelated, which have the most leverage, and which will or may block the desired outcome.

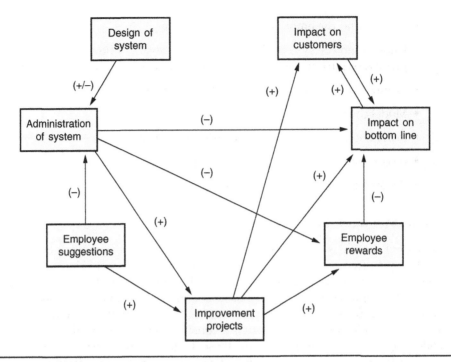

Figure 2.2   Analysis of an employee suggestion system.

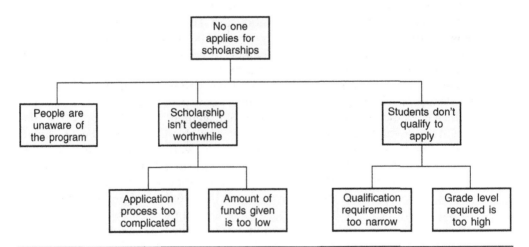

Figure 2.3   Logic tree analysis.

Identifying Constraints Using a Tree Diagram. Another approach to finding constraints is to break the situation down into component parts using a logic tree diagram. Figure 2.3 demonstrates the use of the process by an organization that has offered a scholarship program for three years, but had no applicants. The organization had widely publicized the program, so elected to not look at that branch of the tree. By breaking down the other two branches, however, it found some likely sources of the problem. It may again ignore some of the branches (for example, keeping the required grade level at what is deemed necessary for true scholarship purposes) and either investigate or alter other aspects of the program in order to affect the next application period.

The logic tree diagram uses a top-down approach to analyzing the situation. As with many improvement tools, the process can also be enhanced by involving key stakeholders in developing the model and in gathering information to identify the constraint(s) for which action will be taken.

4. LEADERSHIP TECHNIQUES

> Develop and implement techniques that motivate employees and sustain their enthusiasm. Use negotiation techniques to enable parties with different or opposing outlooks to recognize common goals and work together to achieve them. Determine when and how to use influence to resolve a problem or move a project forward. (Create)
>
> **Body of Knowledge I.B.4**

It is impossible for one person to motivate another person. Motivation is derived from within a person—a person needs to feel motivated. Therefore, motivating a person can only be done by creating an environment in which the person feels motivated. When one person (for example, a supervisor) says she is going to motivate a subordinate, she means (or should mean) she is going to do something that will cause the subordinate to become motivated. The idea that a "kick in the butt" will motivate a subordinate is incorrect; it may just move the subordinate, and usually will make the subordinate angry and/or afraid. That kind of movement is erroneously perceived as motivation.

Theories of Motivation and Influence

Two types of motivation have been identified:[24]

- *Extrinsic motivation.* The satisfaction of either material or psychological needs that is applied by others or the organization through pre-action incentive or post-action reward.

- *Intrinsic motivation.* The qualities of work itself or of relationships, events, or situations that satisfy basic psychological needs (such as achievement, power, affiliation, autonomy, responsibility, creativity, and self-actualization) in a self-rewarding process.

Abraham Maslow developed a model demonstrating a *hierarchy of needs* through which he believed people progressed.[25] Maslow's pyramid (see Figure 2.4) assumes that once humans satisfy the basic, physiologically driven needs, they will then be

Part I.B.4

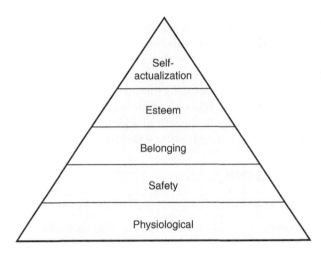

Stage	Process	Needs
1st	Physiological	To eat, sleep, have shelter
2nd	Safety	To have economic and physical security
3rd	Belonging	To be accepted by family and friends
4th	Esteem	To be held in high regard; status
5th	Self-actualization	To achieve one's best

Figure 2.4   Maslow's hierarchy of needs.

motivated by higher-level needs, and this process will continue until achieving self-actualization. The workplace is obviously a key aspect in allowing an individual to satisfy physiological and safety needs, but someone who has satisfied these levels and is working to satisfy higher levels can quickly return to the bottom of the hierarchy in the event of a job loss. The workplace can also allow them to reach higher levels, assuming there are job opportunities that enable their personal desire for recognition and achievement to be satisfied. It is important to note that since Maslow's theory is based very much on values, it would not necessarily apply to people from all cultures or socioeconomic strata.

Frederick Herzberg identified two categories into which work motivation factors could be classified—*satisfiers* and *dissatisfiers*.[26] Dissatisfiers included factors such as work conditions, salary, company policies, and relationship with one's supervisor. He also called them *hygiene factors*, since although they create dissatisfaction if not adequately addressed, correcting the deficiencies would not create satisfaction. Satisfiers included items such as responsibility, achievement, advancement, and recognition.

There are also three motivational theories specifically related to recognition and rewards:

- *Equity theory.* Job motivation depends on how equitable the person believes the rewards (or punishment) to be.

- *Expectancy theory.* What people do is based on what they expect to gain from the activity (Victor Vroom).

- *Reinforcement theory.* What people do depends on what triggers a behavior initially (the antecedent) and the consequences that have in the past resulted from such behavior, or the consequences the performer believes will happen as a result of a behavior (B. F. Skinner).

What motivates one person may not motivate another. McClelland and others have posited that:

- An individual who enjoys working closely with other people is motivated by affiliation.

- Someone who works in order to accomplish personal goals is motivated by achievement.

- A person who works in order to contribute to the well-being of others is motivated by altruism.

- Someone who wants to have control over their work is motivated by power.

These motivations are not mutually exclusive, nor is any one person driven only by a single factor. In fact, in order to satisfy their many different needs, people are often involved in several different activities at work, in their local community, and in other organizations.

A paradoxical view of motivation is the division between intrinsic motivation and extrinsic motivation. Some people are driven more by their own internal needs or desires, while others are motivated primarily by external factors. This is partially a function of whether the person has an internal or external locus of control—whether you believe your future is impacted more by your own actions or by actions/decisions of others.

Caution is advised in assuming that what stimulates motivation for an individual in one situation or time frame will continue to motivate the next time. Also, what provides motivation for one person may not do so for another.

Consider this example: Work is backing up, and the manager tells her work unit personnel that the unit will have to work overtime each day for the next 10 days. Rose, a young woman who is saving money to buy a dirt bike, is delighted about the prospect of extra compensation. Ray, a single father whose baby is cared for during the day by a babysitter, is distraught because he has to be home by 6 p.m. to relieve the babysitter and realizes that any other option would cost more than he will earn on overtime. Rose is motivated, Ray is not. Six months later, the same need for overtime occurs. Rose resents the mandate (she has purchased her dirt bike and wants to ride it in the early evening before the sun sets). Ray's aunt has moved in with him and now cares for the baby. Ray needs the additional compensation to help with his expanded family. Ray is motivated, Rose is not.

Negotiation

In order for multiple parties, whether individuals or groups, to work together to achieve common goals, there must be agreement on the goals, the methods for achieving them, and what will occur when difficulties arise. Each party will typically have different values and priorities that need to be addressed, and that calls for negotiations resulting in an agreement acceptable to all parties. Management–union negotiations are perhaps the most widely discussed example, but negotiation also occurs as part of many other normal business processes, such as:

- Establishing specifications for purchased components for a new product

- Setting performance measures for a process or department

- Defining the desired outcomes for an improvement project

- Identifying personal development goals

Parties involved in such negotiations might include customers and suppliers, senior management and middle management, sponsor and team leader, or manager and employee.

A difficulty in the negotiation process is that the two parties often approach the task as though there were only two sides to the situation, when, in fact, there are multiple views that could be taken. This is exacerbated when a win–lose attitude is taken, as the process will become divisive and usually result in outcomes that are not seen as beneficial by either party. There are four orientations to negotiation: win–win, win–lose, lose–win, and lose–lose. When both parties approach negotiation with an anticipation of achieving mutual benefit, both parties tend to win. The other three orientations leave the parties striving not to lose at any cost.

Principled negotiation based on a win–win orientation includes:

- Separating the people from the problem

- Focusing on interests, not position

- Understanding what both sides want to achieve

- Inventing options for mutual gain

- Insisting on objective criteria

Timing also affects negotiations, both long-term and short-term. For negotiations that recur on a long-term periodic basis (such as labor agreements), the years between sessions allow the parties to store up their frustrations and release them just as they come together to forge a new contract. At the same time, allowing a break between negotiation sessions allows the parties to back off from what may be an emotional discussion and reflect on their primary purposes.

Negotiations should take place in an environment that is conducive to open discussion and allows all involved to see each other face to face. Rather than making presentations to each other, both parties should focus on a conversation with each other, which means that listening in order to understand the other person's viewpoint is a key requirement. A set of ground rules or a third-party mediator may be useful if the negotiations involve a highly controversial or emotional subject.

Some techniques that have been found to improve the negotiation process include:

- Focusing on common objectives before discussing areas of difference.

- Avoiding power strategies such as lying about one's priorities in order to get the other party to submit to lowered expectations.

- Doing something for the other party, even if symbolic, to create positive energy.

- Separating out discussion issues that are not interconnected so that they can be discussed based on their own merit.

- Bringing in other parties that may have additional or different information about the situation.[27]

Additional techniques include:

- Identifying, up front, a range of acceptable outcomes—and why you want what you want.

- Determining the real intentions of the other party: the goals, objectives, and priorities.

- Being prepared with supporting information.

- Not rushing the process.

- Keeping the most difficult to resolve issues for last.

- Being sensitive to face-saving needs of the other party.

- Being firm, fair, and factual.

- Always controlling your emotions.

- Evaluating each move against your objectives and assessing how it relates to all other moves.

- Being adept at formulating a win–win compromise.

- Being aware of the effect of the outcomes of the present negotiation on future negotiations.

- Actively listening and seeking clarity of expectations.

- Being flexible with your position and being able to step back and look critically at your position—there may be multiple ways the same overall objective can be achieved. This view involves going up the vertical hierarchy of one's cognitive view of the situation, rather than only going horizontally across perceived options.[28]

Figure 2.5 is a portion of a decision option hierarchy for reducing deficit spending by a city government. Negotiations between city officials and the school board often focus only on option C, while negotiations with the citizenry focus only on options A and B. By limiting the focus to the *hows*, the larger picture of the higher *why* is often ignored, which means that option D is often not even understood as a possibility.

Negotiating is a skill very much needed in the project management arena. Often, the project manager/leader has less authority than ongoing operations

Part I.B.4

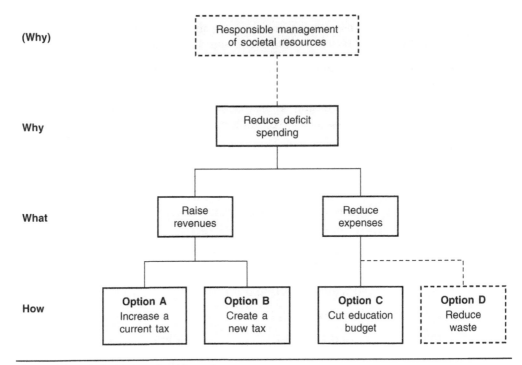

Figure 2.5   A decision option hierarchy.

managers, and that necessitates negotiating for needed resources. This is especially problematic when the project team is not dedicated solely to the project. Then, one of the largest problems is ensuring that the project team members get the release time needed to work on the project.

Negotiating in a different culture can be a challenge, but is essential in the growing global marketplace. Communicating in a global economy is discussed in Chapter 9, Section 3.

Change management usually involves negotiation in eliminating organizational roadblocks and managing constraints. (Change management will also involve conflict resolution.)

Some common uses for negotiation are:

• Customer–supplier purchasing contracts

• Negotiation of compensation terms between a potential new hire and the organization

• Labor–management contracts

• Facilites/equipment rental contracts

• Negotiating for approval of the annual budget for a work unit

Having effectively completed negotiations usually means that the relationship between the parties will continue and that the agreement should be documented. The agreement should include the standards against which compliance of each party will be compared, a frequency or process for reviewing performance, and what is to take place if a violation should occur.

Conflict

Sources and Views of Conflict. Because organizations consist of individuals and groups with different backgrounds and responsibilities, some conflict is inevitable. A conflict might occur between two individuals (for example, between a manager and an employee, or between peers), between groups (for example, departments or teams), or between organizations (for example, customer and supplier). Although conflict will often be created by disagreements over goals or resource allocation, beneath the surface are differences in values, priorities, roles, and personal styles that cause the conflict to become emotional and/or personal.

Conflict occurs when two or more options appear to be mutually exclusive, and a viable alternative is felt to be absent. Conflict can not be resolved when the parties involved firmly believe that what each wants is incompatible with what the other wants.

Conflict may be due to personal issues or may be caused by underlying organizational issues (for example, incongruent policies or unclear boundaries). The effect is that energy that should be focused on the organization's mission instead gets transferred to activities that are unproductive. Regardless of whether the activities are unseen or visible, it is in the best interests of the organization to identify and address the conflict. Quality managers, because of their expanded role in facilitating cross-functional cooperation for strategic alignment and continual improvement, should be aware of and develop their conflict management abilities.

On the plus side, conflict can also be viewed as an energizing force. Management and resolution of differences between individuals and groups can unlock creativity. "Contrary to conventional wisdom, the most important single thing about conflict is that it is good for you. While this is not a scientific statement of fact, it reflects a basic and unprecedented shift in emphasis—a move away from the old human relations point of view where all conflict was basically seen as bad. In brief, in our new frontier environment, conflict is the order of the day."[29]

One model for understanding conflict resolution is based on the dimensions of assertiveness (extent to which a party attempts to satisfy his/her own concerns) versus cooperativeness (extent to which the party attempts to satisfy the other's concerns).[30] The resulting matrix (see Figure 2.6) has been incorporated in an assessment instrument that can be used to evaluate conflict-handling style. Interpretation of the instrument emphasizes that each conflict mode might be appropriate for a particular situation. The following list further expands on these options:

- Approach it as a problem to be solved. Utilize facts and information that can be useful for looking at and evaluating different options.

- Smooth over the conflict by emphasizing the positives and trying to avoid the negatives. This is obviously only a temporary solution if the conflict is substantial.

- Transfer the problem to a higher level of authority.

- Resolve any scarcity of resources that is creating the conflict.

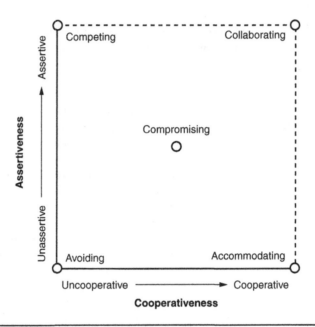

Figure 2.6   Conflict-handling modes.

- Avoid the conflict if it is not in the organization's best interests to continue to pursue it.

- See if compromise will resolve it to the satisfaction of both parties.

- Change the minds of the people involved.[31]

Since the latter option involves trying to change a person's mind, it is not a very viable one. Research indicates that people's basic personality does not change substantially over their lifetime, so changing a mind is obviously difficult. Additionally, organizations do not have the right to change a person's thought processes per se. The option is viable if interpreted differently—people may be transferred or otherwise removed from the conflict situation as a final option. In a quality organization, however, it is more likely that additional methods for resolving the situation would be attempted.

Techniques for Conflict Resolution. The best method for resolving a particular conflict depends on the situation. If there is clearly a solution that simply needs to be identified and agreed to, and the parties involved are not adamantly opposed to each other, then simple discussions utilizing brainstorming, multivoting, and consensus may be sufficient. The brainstorming process can be used to identify several possible solutions, followed by a multivoting process (see Chapter 13) that narrows the list to a smaller, more viable list. Looking at the positive and negative attributes of each option may then result in agreement of all parties on what action(s) will be taken. This discussion can be aided by looking at each of the activities that would be required by each party in the conflict, the effort it would require, and the impact it would have both on resolving the issues and on the relationship between the parties.

A more difficult situation arises when, although there may be several viable solutions, the involved parties do not appear to be prepared to work cooperatively in order to reach a joint decision. A process such as *interest-based bargaining* (also called *principled negotiation*) might then be used to attempt to satisfy as many interests as possible using the following steps:

1. Define the problem in a way that distinguishes it from the people involved.

2. Clarify the interests of the parties (as opposed to their positions on the issue).

3. Identify new and creative options beneficial to all parties.

4. Determine objective criteria to be used to evaluate fairness of the outcomes for all parties.

Conflict resolution may also involve intervention by a third party. For example, a person trained in human process interventions might help parties involved in a conflict by engaging them in dialogue. Strategies that might be used include:

• Helping the parties avoid the factors that trigger conflict

• Setting guidelines for interaction of the parties

• Helping the parties find ways to cope with the conflict

• Identifying and eliminating the underlying issues[32]

Real dialogue involves not only listening to what the other party says, but also taking care to truly comprehend his or her perspective and why it is important to him or her. It also requires that one understand the values and assumptions underlying one's own position and be willing to share them.

Core Issues in Conflict Management. Conflict management is difficult when people take a "What's in it for me?" viewpoint. A win–win approach provides the following benefits:

• A unified direction—a platform for achieving the organization's goals and objectives

• Higher employee satisfaction, especially when active listening is used and the search for alternatives is expanded

• Improved health and safety of employees due to encountering less stress in their lives

Following are components of an approach to resolving conflict to the mutual benefit of all involved parties:

• Define the conflict as a mutual problem.

• Identify goals common to all parties.

• Find creative alternatives that satisfy all parties.

• Ensure that all parties understand their own needs and communicate them clearly.

- Emphasize mutual interdependence (as opposed to independence or dependence).

- Be certain that contacts are made on a basis of equal power.

- Communicate needs, goals, positions, and proposals openly, honestly, and accurately.

- State needs, goals, and positions in the opening offer.

- Empathize with and understand others' positions, feelings, and frames of reference.

- Reduce defensiveness by avoiding threats, harassment, or inconveniencing other parties.

A conflict is not likely to be resolved successfully when either party does the following:

- Defines the conflict as a win–lose strategy.

- Pursues his or her own goals or hidden agenda.

- Forces the other party into submission.

- Increases power by emphasizing independence from the other party and the other party's dependence on them.

- Tries to arrange contacts based on power relationships.

- Uses inaccurate or misleading communications.

- Overemphasizes needs, goals, and position in the opening offer.

- Avoids empathy and understanding of others' positions, feelings, and frames of reference.

- Would rather both parties lose (lose–lose) than have the other party get his or her way.

5. EMPOWERMENT

> Apply various techniques to empower individuals and teams. Identify typical obstacles to empowerment and appropriate strategies for overcoming them. Describe and distinguish between job enrichment and job enlargement, job design and job tasks. (Apply)
>
> **Body of Knowledge I.B.5**

One of the core components of quality leadership is having everyone in the organization involved in managing and improving quality of the processes for which they are responsible. This might be done as part of day-to-day operations as a member of a natural work team or a self-directed team, or in becoming part of a group that is going to take on a special process design or improvement project. Regardless of the way it occurs, it involves giving employees greater responsibility and authority, and is commonly labeled *empowerment*.

Empowerment is based on the belief that employees have the ability to take on more responsibility and authority than has traditionally been given them, and that heightened productivity and a better quality of work life will result. Different words and phrases are used to define empowerment, but most are variations on a theme: to provide employees with the means for making influential decisions. Juran defined empowerment as "conferring the right to make decisions and take action."[33]

Empowerment means different things in different organizations, depending on culture and work design; however, empowerment is based on the concepts of job enlargement and job enrichment. *Job enlargement* means changing the scope of the job to include a greater portion of the horizontal process. An example would be a bank teller who not only handles deposits and disbursements, but now distributes traveler's checks and sells certificates of deposit. *Job enrichment* means increasing the depth of the job to include responsibilities that have been traditionally carried out at higher levels of the organization. An example would be if a bank teller also had the authority to help a client fill out a loan application and complete initial screening to determine whether or not to refer the customer to the loan officer.

As these examples show, empowerment of employees will require:

- A work environment and managing style that supports empowerment

- Training in the skills necessary in order to carry out the additional responsibilities

- Access to information on which decisions can be made

- Willingness and confidence on the part of the employee to take on greater responsibility

Empowerment also means management giving up some of the power traditionally held by it, which means management must take on new roles and responsibilities and gain new knowledge. It does not mean that management relinquishes all authority, totally delegates decision making, and allows operating without accountability. It requires a significant investment of time and effort to develop mutual trust, assess, and add to individuals' competencies, as well as develop clear agreements about roles, responsibilities, risk taking, and boundaries.

Empowerment is difficult to implement because it is often a major culture change from past ways of working. It involves behavioral changes in all members of the organization: management, operations personnel, and support staff. Therefore, it is critical that the organization lay the appropriate groundwork. To start, an organization should develop an operational definition of empowerment and communicate a strong commitment to it, starting with top management. It should develop a time-phased implementation plan and build or modify the necessary organizational systems to support empowerment.

Empowerment requires the transfer of authority with a clear agreement about expectations, responsibilities, and boundaries. This process takes place over a period of time as both managers and workers become comfortable with the concepts and implications of empowerment. Four principles that foster this transition are:

1. Give people important work to do on critical issues.

2. Give people discretion and autonomy over their tasks and resources.

3. Give visibility to others and provide recognition for their efforts.

4. Build relationships by finding them sponsors and mentors.[34]

Empowerment often also calls for restructuring the organization to reduce levels of hierarchy or to provide a more customer- and process-focused organization. Empowerment is often viewed as an inverted triangle of organizational power. In the traditional view, management is at the top while customers are on the bottom, whereas in an empowered environment, customers are at the top while management is in a support role at the bottom (see Figure 2.7).

For empowerment to be successfully implemented, the leader's role must shift from that of a traditional manager to that of an enabler. Leaders must balance their need for personal control with the ability to provide freedom for others to act on their own authority. This is a mind-set as well as a negotiated agreement between leaders and their subordinates. Leaders who empower others create an environment in which this balance can take place. They involve their subordinates in planning, delegate responsibility, clarify the scope of authority, delineate boundaries, encourage, provide a motivational environment, and reward accomplishments.

The process also needs to occur from top to bottom. Frontline managers need to understand how to implement the process and how to transition from a traditional role to that of an empowering leader. Middle management needs to work to remove barriers to empowerment and to help coach frontline managers in their

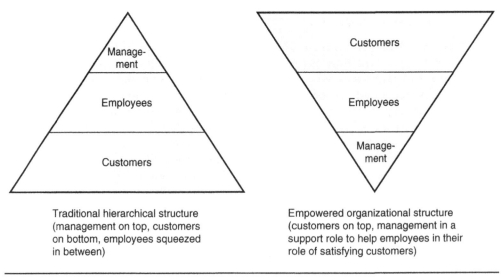

Traditional hierarchical structure (management on top, customers on bottom, employees squeezed in between)

Empowered organizational structure (customers on top, management in a support role to help employees in their role of satisfying customers)

Figure 2.7   Traditional versus empowered organization.

new roles. Changes in performance review and compensation systems are usually required to align these systems with the new responsibilities.

People who are well matched with the jobs they hold don't require force, coercion, bribery, or trickery to work hard and produce quality work. They are internally motivated.

An example of a mismatch is assigning a usually gregarious extrovert to spray-painting parts in an isolated room, wearing a protective mask all day. This would certainly be totally dissatisfying and lead to poor work. Another example would be reassigning an operator who formerly worked on a help desk solving customers' problems to a role as a telemarketer where he or she has to cold-call prospective customers. Initiating customer contact may be a totally distasteful job for the individual. Type of personality, personal beliefs and interests, fear of danger, and so on, are all factors to consider when matching people to jobs—assuming a motivated workforce is desired.

For a person to be internally motivated from the job itself, the person must:

- Receive sufficient skills training and knowledge to succeed in the job assigned

- Know what level of performance and result is expected of him or her

- Be provided with appropriate tools, equipment, and a workplace conducive to producing a quality product or service, within a safe, secure, and healthful (physical and mental) environment

- Experience responsibility for the results of the work

- Experience a challenge, but not be overwhelmed

- Have the authority to make decisions commensurate with the job responsibilities and personal competence, and within preestablished boundaries

- Experience the work as contributing value

- Know how the results from personal work contribute to the organization

- Know how work is measured and evaluated

- Have the opportunity to improve the processes used in the work

- Know that management is aware of, supports, and appreciates the work

Although work design is the most visible change in empowerment, the relationships of managers and employees is perhaps the most significant and difficult aspect of that change. Table 2.1 summarizes these changes, emphasizing the inherent difficulty in trying to change from a traditional to an empowered organization.

Common mistakes and barriers to empowerment include:

- A lack of a clear commitment. To succeed, top management must clearly communicate its support. Without this commitment, empowerment will be impossible to implement.

Part I.B.5

Table 2.1   Relationship changes in an empowered organization.

Issue for comparison	Traditional organization	Empowered organization
Employees' primary focus is on:	Management	Customers
Management's role is:	Monitoring and controlling	Facilitating and coaching
Management–employee relationship is:	Boss-to-subordinate	Peer-to-peer

- Failure to define empowerment. Failing to develop an operational definition of empowerment results in confusion and inconsistent implementation. Many managers do not understand the term and can unwittingly block its effective implementation by sending conflicting messages.

- Failure to establish the boundaries within which employees can be empowered.

- Failure to provide appropriate training to management and the performers.

- Failure to implement appropriate incentives. People who have been rewarded for behavior that serves a traditional hierarchical system will resist transitioning to a new role unless incentives to encourage change are in place.

- Lack of an implementation plan. Empowerment consumes time, resources, and up-front costs for training and organizational support systems. An implementation plan is essential to prepare this groundwork. An organization that does not think through all the implications sets up serious barriers to success.

- Inability to modify organizational culture. Many traditional organizations will hinder empowerment by virtue of their hierarchical structures, reward processes, and cultural values. Unless appropriate changes are made, empowerment will fail.

- Some people will resent a shift to empowerment. They often don't want to assume the responsibility involved. Others may feel management is trying to pass down their responsibility in order to save money or whatever.

- Not everyone will buy in at first. Some will wait and see if this is just another "here today, gone tomorrow" scheme of management. Some are terrified at the new freedom, fearful they might make a dreadful mistake and be punished for it.

- Middle and first-level management resent giving up their authority (and perhaps the curtain they've been hiding behind). Learning and practicing new behavior is tough on those who grew up in the "old school" ways.

- If top management is not visibly and continually seen using empowerment techniques, the effort will likely not succeed.

- Changing the culture from a traditional hierarchical mode to one where empowerment is practiced takes a long time and costs money. A high level of sustained commitment is needed for years.

- The organization structure and reporting relationships will need to be changed.

- Major systems and processes will require modification or replacement, for example, strategic planning process, compensation system, employee recognition and reward process, customer service processes, expense reimbursement procedure, and so on.

Benefits from Empowerment

Aubrey and Felkins reported a survey administered in several companies to evaluate the perceived benefits of employee involvement. It indicated significant improvements in attitudes and behavior. For example, results showed an increase in individual self-respect, increased respect for employees by supervisors, increased employee understanding of management, reduced conflict, and increased employees awareness of why many problems are not solved quickly. A similar survey administered to management indicated that employee involvement seemed to increase productivity.[35]

Customer satisfaction also typically improves when personnel are given the authority to make decisions directly related to customer problems or needs. For example, a major credit card service organization reported that through its employee empowerment program, customer delight helped to propel the organization to the number two spot in the bank credit card industry and helped it win the Baldrige Award. Other Baldrige Award winners report similar results.

The very highest leader is barely known by men.

Then comes the leader they know and love.

Then the leader they fear.

Then the leader they despise.

The leader who does not trust enough will not be trusted.

When actions are performed without unnecessary speech

The people say, "We did it ourselves."

—Lao-tzu

This chapter has discussed a number of leadership challenges and issues. While the expression " _____ is a born leader" may be true in some cases, for the rest of us, being a good, effective leader is a learned skill. In transforming ourselves to become a good leader we may have to change our behavior—

sometimes drastically. We may have to disregard traditional teachings and practices from our early years. We're in a rapidly evolving world that calls for innovative, adaptive, and ethical leaders. Relationships with people are critical, especially as technology tends to lead us toward dehumanizing internal and external organizational interactions.

ENDNOTES

1. Frances Hesselbein, "The Habits of Effective Organizations," in *Leader to Leader: Enduring Insights on Leadership from the Drucker Foundation's Award-Winning Journal,* ed. F. Hesselbein and P. M. Cohen (San Francisco: Jossey-Bass, 1999).
2. W. E. Deming, *Out of the Crisis* (Cambridge, MA: MIT Center for Advanced Engineering Study, 1986).
3. S. R. Covey, "Three Roles of the Leader in the New Paradigm," in *The Leader of the Future: New Visions, Strategies, and Practices for the Next Era*, ed. F. Hesselbein, M. Goldsmith, and R. Beckhard (San Francisco: Jossey-Bass, 1996).
4. B. M. Bass, *Stogdill's Handbook of Leadership*. New York: The Free Press, 1990.
5. R. M. Kanter, "World-Class Leaders: The Power of Partnering," in *The Leader of the Future: New Visions, Strategies, and Practices for the Next Era*, ed. F. M. Hesselbein, M. Goldsmith, and R. Beckhard (San Francisco: Jossey-Bass, 1996).
6. D. H. Maister, C. H. Green, and R. M. Galford, *The Trusted Advisor* (New York: The Free Press, 2000).
7. C. Farren and B. L. Kaye, "New Skills for New Leadership Roles," in *The Leader of the Future: New Visions, Strategies, and Practices for the Next Era*, ed. F. M. Hesselbein, M. Goldsmith, and R. Beckhard (San Francisco: Jossey-Bass, 1996).
8. D. K. Smith, "The Following Part of Leading," in *The Leader of the Future: New Visions, Strategies, and Practices for the Next Era*, ed. F. M. Hesselbein, M. Goldsmith, and R. Beckhard (San Francisco: Jossey-Bass, 1996).
9. J. M. Kouzes and B. Z. Posner, *The Leadership Challenge: How to Get Extraordinary Things Done in Organizations* (San Francisco: Jossey-Bass, 1987).
10. Ibid., 27, 135.
11. W. Bridges, "Leading the De-Jobbed Organization," and E. H. Schein, "Leadership and Organizational Culture," in *The Leader of the Future: New Visions, Strategies, and Practices for the Next Era*, ed. F. M. Hesselbein, M. Goldsmith, and R. Beckhard (San Francisco: Jossey-Bass, 1996).
12. C. Handy, "The New Language of Organizing and Its Implications for Leaders," in *The Leader of the Future: New Visions, Strategies, and Practices for the Next Era*, ed. F. M. Hesselbein, M. Goldsmith, and R. Beckhard (San Francisco: Jossey-Bass, 1996).
13. E. H. Schein, "Leadership and Organizational Culture," in *The Leader of the Future: New Visions, Strategies, and Practices for the Next Era*, ed. F. M. Hesselbein, M. Goldsmith, and R. Beckhard (San Francisco: Jossey-Bass, 1996).
14. W. E. Deming, *The New Economics* (Cambridge: Massachusetts Institute of Technology, 1994), 116.
15. D. Goleman, *Working with Emotional Intelligence* (New York: Bantam, 1998).
16. R. T. Pascale and A. G. Athos, *The Art of Japanese Management* (London: Penguin Books, 1986).
17. R. T. Westcott defines "competency = knowledge, experience, skills, aptitude, and attitude—KESAA Factors," and discusses examples of competence requisites in "The Metamorphosis of the Quality Professional," *Quality Progress* (October 2004): 22–32.

18. P. F. Drucker, *Management: Tasks, Responsibilities, Practices* (New York: Harper & Row, 1974).

19. D. W. Hutton, *The Change Agents' Handbook: A Survival Guide for Quality Improvement Champions* (Milwaukee: ASQC Quality Press, 1994).

20. Deming, *New Economics.*

21. J. P. Kotter, *Leading Change* (Boston: Harvard Business School Press, 1996).

22. Ibid., 16.

23. D. W. Okes, "Developing Effective Change Agent Skills," 32nd Annual Quality Clinic, Knoxville, TN, March 1991.

24. J. M. Brion, *Organizational Leadership of Human Resources: The Knowledge and the Skills, Part I, The Individual* (Greenwich, CT: JAI Press, 1989).

25. A. H. Maslow, "Self-Actualization and Beyond," in *Challenges of Humanistic Psychology,* ed. J. F. T. Bugental (New York: McGraw-Hill, 1967).

26. F. Herzberg, "One More Time: How Do You Motivate Employees?" *Harvard Business Review* (January–February 1968).

27. K. W. Thomas, "Conflict and Conflict Management," in *Handbook of Industrial and Organizational Psychology,* Vol. II, ed. M. D. Dunnette. (Chicago: Rand McNally, 1976).

28. J. F. Brett, G. B. Northcraft, and R. L. Pinkley, "Stairways to Heaven: An Interlocking Self-Regulation Model of Negotiation," *Academy of Management Review* (July 1999): 435–51.

29. J. Kelly, "Making Conflict Work for You," *Harvard Business Review* 48, no. 6 (July–August 1970).

30. K. W. Thomas and R. H. Kilman, *Thomas-Kilman Conflict Mode Instrument* (Tuxedo, NY: XICOM, 1974).

31. M. A. Bittel, ed., *Handbook for Professional Managers* (New York: McGraw-Hill, 1985).

32. T. G. Cummings and E. F. Huse, *Organizational Development and Change,* 4th ed. (St. Paul, MN: West Publishing, 1989), 171.

33. J. M. Juran, *The Last Word: Lessons of a Lifetime in Managing for Quality* (Wilton, CT: Juran Institute, 1993), 332.

34. Kouzes and Posner, *The Leadership Challenge.*

35. C. A. Aubrey and P. K. Felkins, *Teamwork: Involving People in Quality and Productivity Improvement* (Milwaukee: ASQC Quality Press, 1988).

See Appendix A for additional references for this chapter.

Chapter 3

C. Teams and Team Processes

A team is a group of people who perform interdependent tasks to work toward a common mission. Some teams have a limited life, for example, a design team developing a new product or a process improvement team organized to solve a particular problem. Other teams are ongoing, for example, a departmental team that meets regularly to review goals, objectives, activities, and performance. Understanding the many interrelationships that exist between organizational units and processes, and the impact of these relationships on quality, productivity, and cost, makes the value of teams apparent.

Many of today's team concepts were initiated in the United States during the 1970s through the use of quality circles or employee involvement initiatives. The initiatives were often seen as separate from normal work activities rather than being integrated with other organizational systems and processes. Team designs have since evolved into a broader concept that includes many types of teams formed for different purposes.

Difficulty with teams in the United States is often blamed on a cultural emphasis on individual accomplishments versus shared responsibility and success. The problems are also due to inadequate organizational support structures. For example, since reward systems often reinforce individual performance, it is logical that people would be less interested in sharing responsibilities. Formal gainsharing programs that reward individuals financially based on performance of the company, division, facility, product line, and/or project of which they are part are more likely to reinforce the need for working together toward common goals.

Just as individuals develop over their life-span, groups tend to change over time. Being aware of this normal progression and ways to overcome difficulties that arise can help the team process be a very positive experience. As Senge pointed out in *The Fifth Discipline*, if a team really jells, the resulting experience can be a highlight of one's career.

The team process also helps an organization change and begin working in different ways. If decisions are made in a multidisciplinary way, the team will consider a broader perspective and will be likely to better address problems. Other members of the organization will often more readily accept the decisions. Some work design changes mean that people from formerly separate functional areas now work together in a newly designed process. These types of changes require more significant attention to organizational change issues to help the group focus on its new mission.

Team processes offer the following benefits to the organization:

- Synergistic process design or problem solving
- Objective analysis of problems or opportunities
- Promotion of cross-functional understanding
- Improved quality and productivity
- Greater innovation
- Reduced operating costs
- Increased commitment to organizational mission
- More flexible response to change
- Increased ownership and stewardship
- Reduced turnover and absenteeism

Individuals can gain the following benefits from teams:

- Enhanced problem-solving skills
- Increased knowledge of interpersonal dynamics
- Broader knowledge of business processes
- New skills for future leadership roles
- Increased quality of work life
- Feelings of satisfaction and commitment
- Sense of being part of something greater than one could accomplish alone

Numerous reasons have been noted for why teams often fail to reach their full potential. Common reasons are:

- Failing to integrate cooperative work methods into the organizational culture
- Lack of organizational systems necessary to support the team process
- Minimal up-front planning of how the organization plans to utilize teams
- Failure to prepare managers for their changing roles
- Failure to prepare team members for their new roles
- Inappropriate recognition and compensation systems
- Inadequate training
- Impatience of top management with the time needed for maturation
- Incomplete understanding of group dynamics

1. TYPES OF TEAMS

> Identify different types of teams and their
> purpose, including process improvement,
> self-managed, temporary or ad hoc (special
> project), and work groups or workcells.
> (Understand)
>
> **Body of Knowledge I.C.1**

Team Configurations

Consider the differences between a baseball team, a jazz quartet, and a bomb squad. They differ according to the number of members, the range and complexity of skills required, the forms of leadership used, the frequency of working together, and the total time spent working together. As Louis Sullivan, a mentor of Frank Lloyd Wright, stated, "form follows function," and this also applies to teams. Although they may take different names in different industries or organizations, this section presents eight types of teams:

- Process improvement teams

- Self-managed teams

- Temporary/ad hoc teams

- Work groups

- Cellular teams

- Special project teams

- Virtual teams

- Combinations of two or more of the above types

Process Improvement Teams. A process improvement team is a project team that focuses on improving or developing a specific business process and is more likely to be trying to accomplish breakthrough-level improvement. The team comes together to achieve a specific goal, is guided by a well-defined project plan, and has a negotiated beginning and end. Such teams are typically cross-disciplinary, bringing together people from different functions and with different skills related to the process to be improved. The team may have a management sponsor who charters the team and ensures that the team has the appropriate resources and organizational support.

The leader of a process improvement team is usually selected by the project sponsor, and the team meets on a regular basis (for example, weekly) to plan activities that will be carried out outside the meeting, review information gathered since the previous meeting, and make decisions regarding implementation of process changes. An independent facilitator who has no involvement in the process to be improved may also work with the team if team members do not have sufficient skills or experience with team facilitation.

In today's fast-paced environment, many organizations also do process improvement through an accelerated team process sometimes called a *kaizen event* or *kaizen blitz*. These teams spend three to five consecutive full days focusing on a very narrow project scope and implement many of their recommended changes during that period. Gains on the order of 70 percent (for example, increase in productivity or reduction in changeover time) are not uncommon. In order to accelerate the pace of progress, the facilitator typically has more authority than with most teams.

Self-Managed Teams. Self-managed teams are groups of employees involved in directly managing the day-to-day operation of their particular process or department. They are authorized to make decisions on a wide range of issues (for example, safety, quality, maintenance, scheduling, and some personnel decisions). Their responsibilities also include processes traditionally performed by managers, such as setting objectives, allocation of assignments, and conflict resolution. These teams are also called *self-directed teams* or *high-performance work teams*. They give employees much broader responsibility and ownership of a work process.

The leader of a self-managed team is usually selected by the team members, and in many cases the role is rotated among the members over time. Also often rotated is the responsibility for providing within-team coordination of particular technical aspects of the team's processes, such as safety or scheduling.

All the elements that apply to work groups also apply to self-managed teams. Self-managed work teams, however, require more up-front planning, support structures, and nurturing. The transition will usually take a significant time period, and needs consistent support from management.

The following key lessons related to self-managed teams were identified during a study of a financial organization:

- Implement a well-thought-out structure to design and guide the implementation process, such as a steering committee, a design team, and a pilot effort.

- Provide special training to managers and supervisors to help them make the transition from their current role to the new support role.

- Develop a careful plan to manage people throughout the transition. The new team structure will cause changes that will appear threatening to many involved, as they interpret the changes as a loss.

- Set realistic expectations that consider the long and energy-consuming time required for the process to become integrated into the business.[1]

Comprehensive training is also critical in order to move from a traditional to a self-managed work environment. For example, one Fortune 500 company provides training in the following subjects:

- How to maintain a focus on the customer

- How to develop a vision and mission that are integrated with the larger organization's mission

- Understanding of roles and operating guidelines

- Skills required for working together to make decisions, plan work, resolve differences, and conduct meetings

- The concepts and strategy for empowerment

- Setting goals (objectives) and solving problems for continuous improvement[2]

Self-managed teams are more likely to be successful when they are created as part of starting up a new facility (a greenfield site) since the cultural change required if an existing facility (a brownfield site) attempts to transition from a traditional work design is so dramatic. In order to smooth the transition to self-managed teams, an existing organization may begin by first implementing cross-functional process improvement teams and/or work teams as a means for learning.

Temporary/Ad Hoc Teams. In a flexible organization, a need for a temporary team may be identified due to a specific problem or situation. Although such ad hoc teams may not use the same formal structures (for example, agenda, regular meeting frequency), the same general principles and processes are still necessary. An empowered organization often sanctions the use of such teams when deemed useful to carry out a short-term mission. For example, many organizations regularly use temporary teams to conduct internal audits of compliance of their quality management system with the ISO 9001 standard.

A problem or situation may arise that requires immediate and dedicated attention, for example:

- A flood or fire has occurred, and decisions have to be made regarding temporary relocation of the process. What emergency plans need upgrading to deal with a similar future emergency?

- A major customer is sending in an auditing team to assess the adequacy of your quality management system. What needs to be done to prepare for the audit?

- Your information management computer system has been compromised by an outside virus. What processes have been affected, and what emergency steps must be taken to recover from the infected data and programs? What safeguards need upgrading or replacement to prevent a similar future disaster?

Usually, management designates the person to form the team to address the situation. Typically, and depending on the nature of the situation, the team will be small and cross-functional, and will call on other technical expertise as needed.

Situations less critical than those listed may also be addressed by a temporary team, for example, the disposition of an unusually large return or recall of unacceptable product.

Work Groups. Work groups, sometimes called *natural teams*, are teams of employees who have responsibility for a particular process (for example, a department, a product line, or a stage of a business process) and who work together in a participative environment. The degree of authority and autonomy of the team can range from relatively limited to full self-management depending on the organizational culture. The participative approach is based on the belief that employees will be more productive if they have a higher level of responsibility for their work (see Chapter 2, Section 5). Since the team understands the work processes, the members should monitor and improve the processes on an ongoing basis. The team leader is usually the individual responsible for the work area, such as a department supervisor.

Work groups function similarly to quality circles, in which department personnel meet weekly or monthly to review performance of their process. They monitor feedback from their customers and track internal performance measures of processes and suppliers. These teams focus on continual, incremental improvements in their work processes. They are similar to process improvement teams, with the key differences being that they are neither cross-functional nor temporary. Again, a facilitator is usually available for teams if needed. Other outside personnel may be brought in as resources on a temporary basis.

More effective use of the work group team design involves applying it at all levels of an organization, with each level linked to the one above and below it (see Figure 3.1). The top management team monitors performance of processes for which it is responsible (for example, overall business performance), teams at the next level monitor and improve their processes (for example, logistics and delivery performance), and teams at the next level track and improve their performance. Since performance of a work area can be impacted by issues outside the team's control, one work group might request that another (for example, the supplier work group) improve a particular process. Alternatively, a process improvement team may be organized that involves both departments working together.

Since work groups are an ongoing organizational structure, it is critical that the organizational systems and values support the effort. Certain basic elements should be considered when an organization is attempting to initiate work groups:

- Top management support
- Clear communication
- Improvement objectives and expectations
- Team training
- Appropriate competencies
- Supportive compensation and performance appraisal systems

Other issues to consider include:

- Team's scope of responsibility and authority
- Degree of autonomy
- Information needed by team and where obtained
- Decision-making process
- Performance measures and success factors
- Recognition and rewards for performance
- Competencies that must be developed

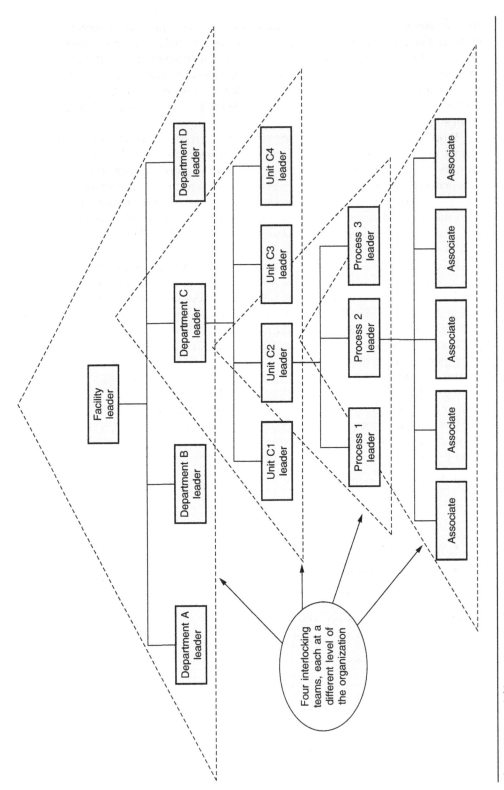

Figure 3.1   Linking team structure.

- Selection process for leaders and facilitators

- Risk management process

An implementation plan including the necessary support systems should be defined before initiating such groups. If work groups are being introduced into an existing organization where a participative management style has not been used before, a pilot program in a department where it is likely to succeed is highly recommended.

Cellular Teams. When processes are organized into cells, the layout of workstations and/or machines used in a given part of the process typically is arranged in a U-shape (see Figure 14.12) configuration. This allows operators to proceed with a part from machine to machine, performing a series of sequential steps to produce a whole product or a major subassembly.

The team that operates the cell is usually totally cross-trained in every step in the series. Team effectiveness depends on coordination, timing, and cooperation. Team members' competencies must be as closely matched as possible to maintain a reasonable and consistent work pace and quality.

Cell team members usually assume ownership and responsibility for establishing and improving the work processes. Leadership of the cell team may be by a person designated as lead operator, or a similar title. In some cases, the role of lead operator may be rotated among the members. The lead operator is usually responsible for training new team members, reporting team output, and balancing the flow of work through the process. A cellular team is a specialized form of a self-directed work group.

Special Project Teams. Often, a need develops to form a long-duration, totally dedicated project team to implement a major new product, system, or process. Some examples are:

- Reengineering an entire process

- Relocating a major segment of the operation

- Mergers, acquisitions, or divestitures

- Replacing a major information system

- Entering a new market with a new product

- Preparing to apply for the Baldrige Award

Such special project teams may operate as a parallel organization during their existence. They may be located away from the main organization, and even be exempt from some of the policy and work-rules constraints of the main organization. The core team members are usually drafted for the duration of the project. Persons with additional expertise may be called into the team on a temporary, as-needed basis. Usually, the project is headed by an experienced project manager. Depending on the nature of the team's objectives, external specialists or consultants may be retained to augment the core competencies of the team members.

Virtual Teams. In today's global and electronic business environment, it may be expedient to have team members who do not work in the same geographic location. These virtual teams also require many of the same roles and processes, but the substitution of electronic communications (for example, e-mail, video-conferencing) for face-to-face meetings provides an additional challenge to team leadership. A key competency of team members is the ability and motivation to self-manage their time and priorities.

Virtual teams have special needs, some of which are:

- Telephones, local area networks, satellites, videoconferencing

- Computers, high-speed and wireless connections, internet technology, e-mail, web-based chat rooms/forums, and so on

- Software for communications, meeting facilitation, time management, project management, groupware, accessing online databases

- Combinations of the above may facilitate communication and performance

The benefits of virtual teams are:

- Team members may work from any location and at any time of day.

- Team members are selected for their competence, not for their geographic location.

- Expenses may be reduced or eliminated, such as travel, lodging, parking, and renting/leasing or owning a building, office equipment, and furniture.

Team Selection

Management selects the team leader. Team members may be selected by either management or the team leader. When the choice of the team members is left to the team leader, however, some methods and tools may be used. To begin, the team leader should identify the competence needed. Five factors (KESAA) comprise competence:

- *Knowledge.* Formal education, degrees, educational certifications, professional certifications, and self-study achievements

- *Experience.* Years spent applying knowledge and skills in pertinent types of organizations and industries, and in jobs/positions held

- *Skills.* Skill certifications, training received, and demonstrated proficiency in use of pertinent tools and equipment

- *Aptitude.* Natural talent, capability, capacity, innate qualities, deftness, knack, adaptability to change, natural ability to do things requiring hand-eye coordination, and fine motor skills

- *Attitude.* Manner of showing one's feelings or thoughts; one's disposition, opinion, mood, ideas, beliefs, demeanor, state of feeling, reaction, bias, inclination, emotion, temperament, mental state, frame of mind, ease in accepting and adopting new or changed plans and practices

By analyzing the tasks facing the team, the team leader can complete a *KESAA requisites analysis* for each individual role, major task, or task cluster.[3] A sample from staffing a project team is shown in Figure 3.2.

In addition, the *Myers-Briggs Personality Type Indicator* may be used to determine how each potential team member is best suited to the team tasks and team

---

Project Staffing—KESAA Requisites Analysis

[Define KESAA factors for each key project participant planned on the resource requirements matrix—personnel]

Task/work package name: Train project managers in using new Microsoft Project software
Task/WP number: 3.10.01.01
Job/position category/title: Application software specialist

Knowledge	• Knows proven techniques for designing and delivering software training to people with diverse knowledge, experience, and skills • Extensive knowledge of project planning and management techniques, tools, and practices • Received Microsoft certificate for completing the advanced MS Project five-day training program within last four years • Earned college degree (software major)
Experience	• Has instructed project teams in use of MS Project at a previous employer, two or more times • Used MS Project on two or more previous large-scale projects • Has demonstrated proficiency in providing software technical support for MS Project users working on large-scale projects • Has demonstrated proficiency in using thorough, rapid, and user-friendly techniques for training new software users
Skills	• Possesses excellent communication skills (reading comprehension, instructing, technical writing, and listening) • Proficient in using all Microsoft Office software • Trained in using proven instructional technology in training design, delivery, and evaluation
Aptitude	• Has capability to adapt the MS Project training to the special needs of each participant • Has worked well in a team environment that is subject to frequent changes. Fast learner.
Attitude	• Enjoys imparting his/her knowledge and skills to new software users • Measures his/her success on the improved performance of those trained by him/her • Believes that MS Project is the best selection of project management software, at this time and place • Exhibits "What can we do to make this happen?" demeanor

Additional comments:

_____

_____

_____

_____

Prepared by: Anna Lyst   Date: June 30, 2013

Figure 3.2   Project staffing–KESAA requisites analysis.
Source: Reprinted with permission of R. T. Westcott & Associates.

dynamics anticipated. The *DiSC* model and instrument may also be used (see Chapter 8). Team leaders should also consider any problems obtaining cooperation from a selected person's boss relative to time constraints and conflicts, prior commitments (unfinished work on regular assignment), priorities (which work is most important?), and reporting relationships (to whom does selected person report?).

A selected individual's reluctance to join a team may be because of the potential for losing interaction with colleagues from the same discipline and the potential for losing an opportunity for further education and training in the individual's chosen field, and potential impact on pay raises and promotion.

2. STAGES OF TEAM DEVELOPMENT

Define and describe the classic stages of team development: forming, storming, norming, performing. (Apply)

Body of Knowledge I.C.2

Teams will progress through stages of growth and maturity as the members work together over time. Understanding these development stages is valuable for the effective management of the team process. The stages can vary in intensity and duration depending on the type of team, the environment in which it works, and the individuals who constitute it. A generic model for the phases of team development, described by Tuckman,[4] is shown in Figure 3.3:

- *Stage 1: Forming.* When team members first come together, they bring with them individual identities and the values and the priorities of their usual environment. Each team is a new experience, even for those who have previously been members of teams. Individuals enter this situation cautiously, feeling uncertain of what their role and performance will be in this new environment. During the forming stage, the team usually clarifies its purpose, identifies roles for each member, and defines rules of acceptable behavior (often called *norms*).

- *Stage 2: Storming.* During this phase, the reality of the team's task sinks in. Team members still think primarily as individuals, and might attempt to form decisions on the basis of their individual experiences rather than pooling information with other members. Collaboration has not yet become the norm as team members fluctuate in their attitude about the team's chances for success. The behaviors exhibited during this time may involve argument, testing the leader's authority, attempts to redefine goals, and competitive or defensive acts.

- *Stage 3: Norming.* In this phase, the individuals coalesce into a team by shifting their focus from personal concerns to that of meeting the

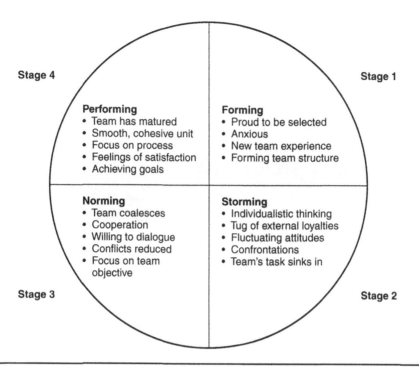

Stage 4

Performing
- Team has matured
- Smooth, cohesive unit
- Focus on process
- Feelings of satisfaction
- Achieving goals

Stage 1

Forming
- Proud to be selected
- Anxious
- New team experience
- Forming team structure

Norming
- Team coalesces
- Cooperation
- Willing to dialogue
- Conflicts reduced
- Focus on team objective

Storming
- Individualistic thinking
- Tug of external loyalties
- Fluctuating attitudes
- Confrontations
- Team's task sinks in

Stage 3

Stage 2

Figure 3.3   Team development phases.

team-related challenges. Interpersonal conflicts and the tug of external loyalties are reduced. Team members are willing to discuss differences for the sake of the team, resulting in more cooperation and dialogue.

- *Stage 4: Performing.* At this stage, the team has matured to the point where it is working as a smooth, cohesive unit. Team members have a good understanding of each other's strengths and weaknesses and how they support the mission, and are now able to work through group problems. There is a better appreciation of the team's processes and a general satisfaction with team membership. During this phase, the team is making significant progress toward achieving its goals.

Although the four stages of development indicate a logical sequence that occurs over time, the actual progress made by each team will vary. For example, a team that has progressed to stage 3 or 4 may fall back to stage 1 or 2. This may occur if they learn that previous assumptions about one another are not true, information they have been using for decision making is found to be inaccurate, or team membership changes.

Some teams might never progress beyond an earlier stage because of limited project duration or poor resolution of group dynamics issues.

Some authors have added a stage to Tuckman's original model: *adjourning.* It is the process of closure that occurs when the team has accomplished its mission. The team should take time to review the lessons learned and what was accomplished, complete documentation, celebrate, and formally disband. Frequently, this stage is either skipped over or incompletely performed, or in some cases, project teams just continue to meet without "closing" the project and without a continuing business purpose.

Team development can be enhanced by making sure that team members have a basic understanding of how to (1) interact in positive ways, (2) deal with difficult people or situations, (3) contribute to accomplishing the team's goals, and (4) give or receive constructive feedback.

3. TEAM-BUILDING TECHNIQUES

> Apply basic team-building steps such as using ice-breaker activities to enhance team introductions and membership, developing a common vision and agreement on team objectives, identifying and assigning specific roles on the team. (Apply)
>
> **Body of Knowledge I.C.3**

Team Processes

There are two major groups of components in team processes—task-type and maintenance-type. Task-type processes keep a team focused and moving toward its goal, while maintenance processes help build and preserve the effectiveness of relationships between team members. Key task components include:

- Reviewing and documenting the team's objective(s).

- Preparing an agenda for every team meeting and staying focused on the agenda. If other issues come up that need to be addressed, the agenda can either be intentionally modified, or new issues can be placed on a list for the next meeting agenda.

- Defining or selecting, and following a technical process that fits the particular project mission (for example, a seven-step problem-solving model if the team is trying to solve a problem; see Chapter 13).

- Using decision-making techniques (for example, consensus, consultative) appropriate to the situation.

- Defining action items, responsibilities, and timing, and holding team members accountable.

Maintenance tasks are somewhat less easily defined, but can also dramatically impact team performance. An outsider might see only the tasks involved with meeting objectives as important, but for team members, the dynamics of interactions between team members can be just as critical. Theories and practices of team dynamics have come from fields as diverse as sociology, psychology, anthropology, organizational development, and political science, where group behavior has been studied in working, living, academic, and therapeutic environments.

Team maintenance tasks are meant to help alleviate the problems created by the fact that each individual on the team has his/her own perspectives and priorities. These are shaped by individual personality, current issues in the person's personal life, and the attitudes of both the formal and informal groups within the organization to which the individual belongs. This means that although the team may have a specific objective and agenda, each individual perceives things differently.

Preventing Problems with Team Process. Two common ways of preventing team dynamics problems are to use *norms* and *roles*. A list of behavioral expectations (norms) is defined by the team during the first meeting, or a predetermined set of norms used by all teams within the organization might be adopted. Following are a few examples of norms and the purpose of each:

- "Be on time for meetings." Emphasizes that meeting time needs to be used effectively, and to wait for someone to arrive is a waste of others' time.

- "At least four (of five) team members must be able to attend." Recognizes that vacation, business travel, and other events may prevent some team members from attending a particular meeting, while ensuring that meetings are not held and decisions made by only a small proportion of the members.

- "No side conversations." Ensures that members are fully present and listening to what is being said, making sure that each person's ideas are heard and considered.

- "Staying on the agenda." Although somewhat task oriented, this emphasizes that team meetings are not the place for personal gripes, and that the team has an important mission.

- "Participation by everyone." Clarifies that all are expected to play an active role, even though the particular skills and activities may differ.

- "Use the *parking lot*." For issues not on the agenda that are set aside to be dealt with at a later time.

- "No phones or other electronic devices" are to be used in a team meeting unless specifically required to accomplish the task at hand.

- "The management of team members must be apprised that the need for absolute dedication to the team objectives by team members is not to be interrupted, except for extreme personal or business emergencies."

Having team members take on particular roles helps get them involved and reduces the likelihood of their feeling that their time is being wasted. Two common roles often rotated among team members are scribe and timekeeper. A *scribe* is responsible for capturing information from the team meeting in a record of meeting minutes and distributing them appropriately following the meeting. A *timekeeper* monitors how well the team is progressing against the timeline spelled out in the agenda, and will notify the team if they are straying off the scheduled times.

Another method for getting team members more involved and working together is to have them work in even smaller groups on narrow activities. For example, if the team needs to acquire some data that are readily available, having two team members work together to get and present the data will provide an opportunity for them to develop a closer working relationship that can carry over into the overall team process.

The first team meeting can set the tone for the entire team effort, and it is therefore important that it be well planned. Following are some actions that can enhance the first meeting:

- Have the sponsor or other stakeholders attend the meeting to emphasize the importance of the project, and the support that will be provided.

- Ensure that all team members have a full understanding of the team's mission and scope.

- Allow team members to get acquainted.

- Clarify team members' roles.

- Work out decision-making issues.

- Establish meeting ground rules (norms).

- Define or select the technical process improvement methodology/ model to be used.

- Define/review the project plan and schedule.

- Draft the team's objectives (may be modified in second meeting).

- Define the structure for future meetings.

Special exercises (often called *icebreakers*) can also be conducted during the first meeting to help team members feel more comfortable in the new environment. (Training material providers offer a plethora of such exercises.) Aside from structured exercises, team members can be asked to state what they hope to personally gain from the project experience. The team can come up with a name for the group. Team members can discuss previous experiences with working in teams and what they learned from them. Activities such as these allow the personalities and values of individual team members to become more visible, and bring team members closer together.

Setting the Team's Objectives. Setting objectives not only gives the team some work to do, it begins the team's development and helps to begin to clarify the task ahead. It is likely that the first draft will require modification at a subsequent meeting. As a template, consider the *S.M.A.R.T. W.A.Y.* (Table 5.1).

Decision-Making Method. Consensus decision making is the process recommended for major project issues. The approach is more time-consuming and demanding, but provides the most thorough and cohesive results. It allows the team to work out different points of view on an issue and come to a conclusion that is acceptable. Consensus means that the decision is acceptable enough that all team members will support it. To achieve consensus, all team members must be allowed to express their views and must also objectively listen to the views of others. The decision and alternatives should be discussed until consensus is reached.

4. TEAM ROLES AND RESPONSIBILITIES

Define and describe typical roles related to team support and effectiveness such as facilitator, leader, process owner, champion, project manager, and contributor. Describe member and leader responsibilities with regard to group dynamics, including keeping the team on task, recognizing hidden agendas, handling disruptive behavior, and resolving conflict. (Analyze)

Body of Knowledge I.C.4

Of the seven roles described in Table 3.1, the roles of timekeeper and scribe are the only ones that are optional depending on the ability of a team member to effectively fulfill a dual role of participating member and either scribe or timekeeper. While the remaining five roles are essential, they may be combined in a variety of ways. Crucial roles for the success of the team, once it is formed, are the team leader and facilitator roles. The *team leader* is responsible for the content, the work done by the team. The *facilitator* is responsible for ensuring that the process used by the team and team dynamics are the best for the stage and situation the team is in.[5]

There is a need for a trained facilitator when:

- No team member is trained for, capable of, or willing to assume this role in addition to functioning as a participating member.

- The team has been meeting for some time and is incapable of resolving conflicting issues.

- A new member has been added, thus upsetting established relationships.

- A key contributor has left the team.

- There are other factors, such as running short on resources, project cancellation, or major change in requirements, that may disturb the smooth functioning of the team.

Supplementing the team with on-call experts can often compensate for a shortfall in either the number of members or members' competencies. Such temporary members must willingly share their expertise, listen attentively, abide by team norms, and support team decisions.

The selection of a team member to serve as a timekeeper may be helpful, at least until the team has become more adept at self-monitoring time usage. When a timekeeper is needed, the role is often rotated, giving consideration to whether the selected member has a vital role to play in the deliberations at a particular meeting.

For some team missions where very formal documentation is required, a scribe or notetaker may be needed. This role can be distracting for a member whose full attention may be needed on the topics under discussion. For this reason, an assistant, not a regular member of the team, is sometimes assigned to take the minutes and publish them. Care should be taken to not select a member to serve as a scribe solely based on the person's gender or position in the organization.

All team members must adhere to expected standards of quality, fiduciary responsibility, ethics, and confidentiality (see Chapter 4). It is imperative that the most competent individuals available are selected for each role. See Table 3.1 for attributes of good role performance.

Frequently, a team must function in parallel with day-to-day assigned work and with the members not being relieved of responsibility for the regularly assigned work. This, of course, places a burden and stress on the team members. The day-to-day work and the work of the team must both be conducted effectively. Not being able to be in two places at one time calls for innovative time management, conflict resolution, and negotiation skills.

Steering Committee

Top management is ultimately responsible for organizational performance improvement. One of top management's key roles, then, is to identify and prioritize opportunities, and initiate teams to address those of greatest value to the organization. Projects might be selected on the basis of new strategic initiatives (for example, developing a new service for a new market niche), customer satisfaction data, cost-of-quality reports, or other strategic or operational performance measures or initiatives (for example, capacity, throughput, and lean projects such as waste reduction).

In order to carry out this process and to simultaneously provide opportunities for learning, a special group called the *steering committee* is often set up for guiding and tracking of team efforts. The group usually includes key leaders in the organization (for example, president, operations manager, quality manager) as well as others who represent particular interests. In an organization working under a union contract, the union representative is also likely to be a member of the steering committee. The steering committee is often a diagonal slice representing all levels of the organization.

One role of the steering committee is to initiate desired organizational improvement efforts. It is vital that each team have a clear understanding of its purpose and how that purpose is linked to and supports the organization's strategic plans. This is done through a written charter that defines the mission and objectives of each project, as well as key personnel (for example, team leader, members, facilitator) and project timing. The charter is a formal document agreed to by both the

Table 3.1 Roles, responsibilities, and performance attributes.

Role name	Responsibility	Definition	Attributes of good role performance
Champion	Advocate	The person initiating a concept or idea for change/improvement	• Is dedicated to seeing it implemented • Holds absolute belief it is the right thing to do • Has perseverance and stamina
Sponsor	Backer, risk taker	The person who supports a team's plans, activities, and outcomes.	• Believes in the concept/idea • Has sound business acumen • Is willing to take risk and responsibility for outcomes • Has authority to approve needed resources • Will be listened to by upper management
Team leader	Change agent, chair, head	A person who: • Staffs the team or provides input for staffing requirements • Strives to bring about change/improvement through the team's outcomes • Is entrusted by followers to lead them • Has the authority for, and directs the efforts of, the team • Participates as a team member • Coaches team members in developing or enhancing necessary competencies • Communicates with management about the team's progress and needs • Handles the logistics of team meetings • Takes responsibility for team records	• Is committed to the team's mission and objectives • Has experience in planning, organizing, staffing, controlling, and directing • Is capable of creating and maintaining channels that enable members to do their work • Is capable of gaining the respect of team members; serves as a role model • Is firm, fair, and factual in dealing with a team of diverse individuals • Facilitates discussion without dominating • Actively listens • Empowers team members to the extent possible within the organization's culture • Supports all team members equally • Respects each team member's individuality

Continued

Part I.C.4

Table 3.1   *Continued.*

Role name	Responsibility	Definition	Attributes of good role performance
Facilitator	Helper, trainer, adviser, coach	A person who: • Observes the team's processes and team members' interactions and suggests process changes to facilitate positive movement toward the team's goals and objectives • Intervenes if discussion develops into multiple conversations • Intervenes to skillfully prevent an individual from dominating the discussion or to engage an overlooked individual in the discussion • Assists the team leader in bringing discussions to a close • May provide training in team building, conflict management, and so forth	• Is trained in facilitating skills • Is respected by team members • Is tactful • Knows when and when not to intervene • Deals with the team's process, not content • Respects the team leader and does not override his or her responsibility • Respects confidential information shared by individuals or the team as a whole • Will not accept facilitator role if expected to report to management information that is proprietary to the team • Will abide by the ASQ Code of Ethics
Timekeeper	Gatekeeper, monitor	A person designated by the team to watch the use of allocated time and remind the team members when their time objective may be in jeopardy.	• Is capable of assisting the team leader in keeping the team meeting within the predetermined time limitations • Is sufficiently assertive to intervene in discussions when the time allocation is in jeopardy • Is capable of participating as a member while still serving as a timekeeper

Continued

Table 3.1   *Continued.*

Role name	Responsibility	Definition	Attributes of good role performance
Scribe	Recorder, note taker	A person designated by the team to record critical data from team meetings. Formal "minutes" of the meetings may be published and distributed to interested parties.	• Is capable of capturing on paper, or electronically, the main points and decisions made in a team meeting and providing a complete, accurate, and legible document (or formal minutes) for the team's records • Is sufficiently assertive to intervene in discussions to clarify a point or decision in order to record it accurately • Is capable of participating as a member while still serving as a scribe
Team members	Participants, subject matter experts	The persons selected to work together to bring about a change/improvement, achieving this in a created environment of mutual respect, sharing of expertise, cooperation, and support.	• Are willing to commit to the purpose of the team • Are able to express ideas, opinions, and suggestions in a nonthreatening manner • Are capable of listening attentively to other team members • Are receptive to new ideas and suggestions • Are even-tempered and able to handle stress and cope with problems openly • Are competent in one or more fields of expertise needed by the team • Have favorable performance records • Are willing to function as team members and forfeit "star" status

team and by management. It legitimizes the team's effort and documents a tacit agreement from management to provide whatever support is necessary to sustain the team. The charter should also include boundaries of the scope of work, authority and responsibility and related limitations, relationship of the team to other teams or projects, the team's reporting relationships within the organization, and the expected deliverables. (See Chapter 10 for more on project management.)

If a process improvement team is chartered without a clear mission or objective, the team will either do nothing or will go in the direction it believes best. One way to test understanding is to ask, "What will you measure to determine whether the objective has been accomplished?"

The steering committee may also have the responsibility for approving the team's recommendations, and certainly has the authority to enable implementation. This helps ensure that teams' recommendations are acted on. Inaction will result in the belief of team members that management is not serious about the process, and employees will be reluctant to get involved in future efforts.

Another role of the steering committee is to ensure that managers and team members are trained in all aspects of the team concept. This should include team dynamics, project management, process design and improvement methodologies, empowerment, managing organizational change, attributes of leadership and the transformation process, and how to motivate and reward efforts.

Team Structure

How a team is structured will depend on the scope of the process on which it will work. A cross-functional team is most widely used for process improvement, as it may be necessary to cover the full range of job functions that the process involves. The dynamics of individual personalities will affect the team's development and performance, and should be taken into account when selecting team members. Every team needs a leader, appropriate team members, and, in some cases, a facilitator.

Team Leader. The team leader is responsible for coordinating meetings, which includes scheduling of meeting rooms, creating agendas, guiding the team through the agenda (including reviews of homework assignments), and reporting progress to the steering committee. The team leader may also coordinate implementation of the team's approved recommendations. The team leader should have a vested interest in the process, and may be a process owner responsible for the results of the process. The team leader must have strong organizational and interpersonal skills, and should be sensitive when dealing with diverse opinions.

Team Members. Other team members are those involved with the process to be improved and may also include internal or external customers and suppliers. Technical experts and outsiders with no vested interest in the process are sometimes added to help provide additional knowledge, objectivity, or creativity. The team members will generally have action items to accomplish outside the team meetings, and will often take on special roles during a meeting (such as scribe or timekeeper).

Team Facilitator. The team facilitator has the responsibility of helping the team to work effectively. The facilitator can play a critical role by asking questions, thereby encouraging the group members to look at the technical process on which they're working from different points of view. It is important that the team facilitator understand quality management theory. In particular, he or she should recognize the impact of individual and social psychology in groups. The facilitator may also provide or arrange for training to assist the team with the technical tools of improvement, such as process mapping, selecting data collection strategies, using relevant analysis tools, and ultimately, guiding the development of a project plan to carry out improvement recommendations.

Dealing with Team Process Problems

Team members are most productive in an environment in which others are responsive and friendly, encourage contributions, and promote a sense of worth. Peter Scholtes spelled out 10 problems that frequently occur within teams and are typical of the types of situations for which team leaders and facilitators must be prepared. Following is the list along with recommended actions:[6]

Problem 1. Floundering or difficulty in starting or ending an activity. *Solution:* Redirect team to the project plan and written objectives.

Problem 2. Team members attempt to influence the team process based on their position of authority in the organization. *Solution:* Talk to the members off-line; clarify the impact of their organizational role and the need for consensus, and ask for cooperation and patience.

Problem 3. Participants who talk too much. *Solution:* Structure meeting so that everyone is encouraged to participate (for example, have members write down their opinions, then discuss them in the meeting one person at a time).

Problem 4. Participants who rarely speak. *Solution:* Practice gatekeeping by using phrases such as, "John, what's your view on this?" or divide tasks into individual assignments and have all members report.

Problem 5. Unquestioned acceptance of opinions as facts, or participants making opinions sound like facts. *Solution:* Do not be afraid to ask whether something is an opinion or a fact. Ask for supporting data.

Problem 6. Rushing to get to a solution before the problem-solving process is worked through. *Solution:* Remind the group of the cost of jumping to conclusions.

Problem 7. Attempting to explain other members' motives. *Solution:* Ask the other person to clarify.

Problem 8. Ignoring or ridiculing another's values or statements made. *Solution:* Emphasize the need for listening and understanding. Support the discounted person.

Problem 9. Digression/tangents creating unfocused conversations. *Solution:* Remind members of the written agenda and time estimates. Continually direct the conversation back on track. Remind team of its mission, objectives, and the norms established.

Problem 10. Conflict involving personal matters. *Solution:* Request that these types of conflict be taken off-line. Reinforce ground rules.

Solutions to conflicts should be in the best interest of the team. Team members should be nonjudgmental, listening to team discussions and new ideas. Group feelings should be verbalized by periodically surfacing any undercurrents or by giving feedback.

One important skill needed in working with teams is the ability to provide constructive feedback during and/or at the end of a meeting. Feedback is an important vehicle to help the team mature. This feedback can be provided by the facilitator or by team members.

There are two types of appropriate feedback: motivational and coaching. *Motivational feedback* must be constructive, that is, specific, sincere, clear, timely, and descriptive of what actually occurred in the meeting. *Coaching,* or *corrective feedback,* specifically states the improvements that need to be made. Scholtes provides the following guidelines for providing constructive feedback (obviously, destructive or degrading feedback is not acceptable behavior):[7]

- Be specific.

- Make observations, not conclusions.

- Share ideas or information, not advice.

- Speak for yourself.

- Restrict feedback to known things.

- Avoid using labels.

- Do not exaggerate.

- Phrase the issue as a statement, not a question.

Having a team do a self-evaluation at the end of each meeting can be useful in helping the team to further develop their team skills and to take more responsibility for team progress. Team members can be asked to write down how well the team is doing on each of the norms (for example, on a scale of 1–5) and to list any additional norms they believe need to be added. A group discussion of the information can then result in revised norms and specific actions the team will take to improve in the future.

Team Facilitation Techniques

A *facilitator* is a person who helps a team manage the team dynamics and relationship processes. A facilitator does not normally get involved in the content— the technical aspects of what the team is working on. The role of the facilitator is instead to act as:

- A guide to circumvent the pitfalls of a stoppage or detour in difficult situations

- A catalyst to assist in developing a plan that provides follow-up to all management levels, thus maintaining continuity of support

- An objective evaluator and auditor of team progress, identifying any roadblocks to success and opportunities to improve performance[8]

Some specific responsibilities of the facilitator include:

- Cultivating an unbiased and impartial environment

- Ensuring that a full examination and discussion of issues takes place

- Providing an objective framework

- Reinforcing focus on mission and objectives

- Helping organize multiple and diverse viewpoints

- Regulating interruptions

- Ensuring that everyone on the team has the opportunity to participate in discussions and decision making

- Defusing destructive behaviors

- Encouraging visual or verbal tracking of ideas

In order to carry out these responsibilities, the facilitator typically does the following:

- Encourages reluctant participants to speak

- Helps to resolve conflict between team members

- Provides feedback to the leader and/or team

- Ensures that ground rules (agreed-to group norms) are followed

- Ensures that members are listening to and understanding others

- Legitimizes everyone's perceptions and feelings

- Verbalizes what is going on

- Checks for agreement

- Maintains or regains focus on the meeting agenda or topic of discussion

- Provides ideas on approaches for gathering or analyzing data

- Ensures consensus

- Periodically summarizes results

A well-trained facilitator is a valuable asset in any team situation. A combination of formal training and considerable experience will produce the best results. Facilitators should be trained in meeting process facilitation, conflict resolution, training and coaching skills, interpersonal skills in a group environment, basic behavior management skills, quality management principles and practices, and appropriate use of quality tools.

Facilitators are less necessary as the team becomes more experienced and capable. Initially, the facilitator is more of a coach and referee in the team process, and therefore requires good communications skills as well as some technical knowledge of the subject, meeting facilitation skills, and the ability to resolve conflict when it occurs. If performance of the team remains dependent on the facilitator, however, then the facilitator has not done an effective job of helping the team to develop. A highly developed team should have the knowledge and ability to deal with problems that might arise, such as a deviation from the agenda, interpersonal conflict, or ineffective decision making—in effect, to become self-facilitating.

Sponsor. Each team usually has a sponsor responsible for ensuring success. The *sponsor* is an individual who has a significant stake in the outcome of a particular team project. He or she is often the process owner. Such a person must be at a level high enough in the organization to be able to address any difficulties encountered by the team. In the early part of a continuous improvement effort, the sponsor may also be a member of the steering committee. A sponsor's responsibilities include the following:

- Helping to initiate the team effort by authorizing the activity
- Defining the purpose and scope of the team
- Coordinating the front-end planning
- Helping to select the team leader, facilitator, and members
- Negotiating additional resources needed

During the team effort, the sponsor maintains an awareness of team progress, monitors team performance problems, acts as a liaison to the steering committee, top management, or other departments or teams, helps obtain any additional information and resources that are outside the team's authority boundaries, and acts as a coach to the team leader.

Team Leader. The *team leader* is responsible for the team's ongoing success. Responsibilities include:

- Organizing and managing team meetings
- Working with the sponsor to develop and monitor the project plan
- Keeping the team effort on track
- Providing status updates to the sponsor and steering committee
- Addressing group dynamics issues
- Serving as a liaison between the team and other parts of the organization
- Helping to resolve problems
- Handling administrative duties and keeping team records

A team leader is also responsible for contributing to the team's content, although he or she must be careful that those contributions do not receive greater status

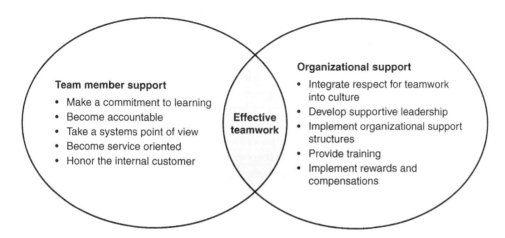

Figure 3.4   Supporting factors for effective teamwork.

than those of other team members. When a facilitator is not involved, the leader also has the same responsibilities as a facilitator relative to team dynamics and relationships.

A team's growth is the responsibility both of individual team members and of the organization. As shown in Figure 3.4, both must create the cultural synergy that makes teams productive.

A new type of organizational leadership is necessary to provide teams with the authority they need to be successful. This requires a transformation from the old type of autocratic leadership to the new facilitating, coaching, participative approach.

5. TEAM PERFORMANCE AND EVALUATION

> Evaluate team performance in relation
> to established metrics to meet goals and
> objectives. Determine when and how to
> reward teams and celebrate their success.
> (Evaluate)
>
> Body of Knowledge I.C.5

Team members and top management will quickly become frustrated if teams are not making progress. The organization should be tracking progress to identify problems, such as poor meeting attendance, failure of other departments to provide the necessary support, or lack of specialized technical knowledge. Long-term projects also require more-complex project management skills and processes (see Chapter 10). Measuring and communicating the effectiveness of a team can help promote necessary changes and stimulate improvement. The feedback is important to management to indicate the degree to which a team is meeting its objectives.

Objective measures directed toward the project goal could include data such as changes in process performance (for example, increase in first-time yield, reduction of customer waiting time), resource utilization (for example, number of person-hours invested in the project, funds spent), and timing against the project plan. The team may also use internally oriented measures such as overall percentage of team member attendance at meetings and the team's evaluation of meeting effectiveness. A team should take responsibility for self-evaluation, with appropriate measures reported to the sponsor and steering committee.

One way a team can evaluate itself is to select criteria based on team effectiveness guidelines included in team training materials or based on the team's list of behavioral norms. A list of questions and a rating scale can then be used at the end of each meeting to monitor how well the team performed. The evaluation criteria can also evolve over time as the team develops. Standard instruments available from providers of training and organization development materials can also be used.

Questionnaires or interviews can be administered to outside-the-team personnel—such as internal and external customers, other teams, or management—and used to capture metrics related to perceived progress on attributes such as relationship building, effectiveness of the team's progress, and efficiency of the team's process. Maintaining a list of lessons learned can also help the team to see what additional benefits are being gained, and these lists can be shared with others to accelerate organization-wide learning.

Teams, like individuals, deserve recognition for their efforts. This recognition can also provide encouragement for future progress and success. In an organization that is just beginning to use the team process, this might be the single most important factor for sustaining momentum. The following suggestions for recognition and rewards are described by Aubrey and Felkins:[9]

- Supportive comments and helpful suggestions provided by management during team presentations

- Public recognition through professional societies or through publication of results in such journals as *Quality Progress* or industry publications, as well as company newsletters and bulletins

- Performance appraisals that reflect employees' personal growth and contribution as team members

- Material rewards such as certificates, pins, coffee mugs, and lunches

- Gainsharing, or distributing some of the cost savings or revenue enhancements to team members

- Bonuses or other monetary rewards

What is measured (and recognized/rewarded) and how it is measured and administered requires careful thought and team members' input. Applying recognition and rewards fairly implies the creation of standard performance definitions and values. Ignoring some achievements, recognizing or rewarding under-standard achievements, and giving the wrong weighting to an achievement are reasons why care and good judgment are critical, and each are causes of disappointment, disillusionment, and discontent among team members.

Nonmonetary forms of recognition are used to acknowledge a team's efforts in a majority of cases. Examples are public recognition in articles published in the organization's newsletter and/or community newspapers, verbal mention at group meetings, plaques and certificates, T-shirts, pins, and other visible, but low-cost items. Recognizing an entire team with one standard reward can be less effective than when team members choose their own rewards, within a value range. Catalog programs have evolved to service this approach. Sustained performance excellence may be rewarded by promotions and preferred assignments for team members.

Rather than focusing on rewarding performance, some organizations create a pay-for-skills plan. As employees progress through a ladder-style development program, their pay is increased at predefined increments. This is especially relevant in a self-directed team environment.

In addition to external recognition, it is important that team members and leaders provide internal recognition for team progress when important milestones have been accomplished. Recognition might also be given to individuals whose contributions are exceptional or above expectations, or to people outside the team who have provided valuable support.

Formal recognition for team-based efforts often involves ceremonies at which top management recognizes teams that have made significant contributions (for example, excellent project outcomes and/or significantly enhanced organizational learning). The recognition might also involve a symbolic award (usually not financially based). Formal efforts to reward team performance are likely to include a modification of performance evaluation criteria to include the new behaviors desired, with an increase in financial compensation or greater job opportunities being a possible outcome for good performers.[10]

Groupthink

In the team selection process, as well as when the team is functioning day-to-day, care must be taken to avoid groupthink.[11] *Groupthink* occurs when most or all of the team members coalesce in supporting an idea or a decision that hasn't been fully explored, or when some members may secretly disagree. The members are more concerned with maintaining friendly relations and avoiding conflict than in becoming engrossed in a controversial discussion. Actions to forestall groupthink may include:

- Brainstorming alternatives before selecting an approach

- Encouraging members to express their concerns

- Ensuring that ample time is given to surface, examine, and comprehend all ideas and suggestions

- Developing rules for examining each alternative

- Appointing an "objector" to challenge proposed actions

Final Thought

An effective team leader can provide an environment in which team members feel motivated. This can be achieved by applying the *six R's*:

1. *Reinforce.* Identify and positively reinforce work done well.

2. *Request information.* Discuss team members' views. Is anything preventing expected performance?

3. *Resources.* Identify needed resources, the lack of which could impede quality performance.

4. *Responsibility.* Customers make paydays possible; all employees have a responsibility to the customers, internal and external.

5. *Role.* Be a role model. Don't just tell; demonstrate how to do it. Observe learners' performance. Together, critique the approach and work out an improved method.

6. *Repeat.* Apply the above principles regularly and repetitively.[12]

ENDNOTES

1. C. C. Manz and H. P. Sims Jr., *Business without Bosses: How Self-Managed Teams Are Building High-Performance Companies* (New York: John Wiley & Sons, 1993).
2. Ibid.
3. R. T. Westcott, *Simplified Project Management for the Quality Professional* (Milwaukee: ASQ Quality Press, 2005), Chapter 5.
4. B. W. Tuckman, "Developmental Sequence in Small Groups," *Psychological Bulletin* 63, no. 6 (1965): 384–99.
5. J. E. Bauer, G. L. Duffy, and R. T. Westcott, eds. *The Quality Improvement Handbook* (Milwaukee: ASQ Quality Press, 2002), Chapter 3.
6. P. R. Scholtes, *The Team Handbook* (Madison, WI: Joiner Associates Consulting Group, 1988): 6–37.
7. Ibid., 6–24.
8. J. L. Hradesky, *Total Quality Management Handbook* (New York: McGraw-Hill, 1995), 57.
9. C. A. Aubrey and P. K. Felkins, *Teamwork: Involving People in Quality and Productivity Improvement* (Milwaukee: ASQC Quality Press, 1988).
10. J. M. Juran and F. M. Gryna, eds., *Juran's Quality Control Handbook* (New York: McGraw-Hill, 1988), 8.6–8.7.
11. J. E. Bauer, G. L. Duffy, and R. T. Westcott, eds., *The Quality Improvement Handbook* (Milwaukee: ASQ Quality Press, 2002), Chapter 3.
12. Ibid.

See Appendix A for additional references for this chapter.

Chapter 4

D. ASQ Code of Ethics

> Identify and apply behaviors and actions that
> comply with this code. (Apply)
>
> Body of Knowledge I.D

It is important that people in an organization know and understand the behaviors that are considered acceptable. Therefore, another critical role of leadership is to ensure that the organization has defined those behaviors and the principles behind them as clearly as possible. Documenting and communicating the values and principles that should be used as a guide for day-to-day decision making is one way employees learn what is acceptable. Another way is through observation of the actions of persons in leadership roles and others in influential or powerful positions. Therefore, it is important that a leader's actions be congruent with the stated principles and values.

For some fields of professional practice, codes of conduct are defined by professional organizations. Following is the code of ethics for quality professionals established by the American Society for Quality (ASQ). It provides both general principles and specific actions designed to ensure that ASQ members demonstrate ethical behaviors in their relationships with the public, employers, customers and clients, and peers. The code is critical to quality decisions and behavior, and valuable when designing systems as well as in day-to-day communications.

It is important for leaders in organizations to take action on the basis of how well employees meet ethical guidelines. Employees who demonstrate ethical practices, especially during difficult situations, must be commended for their actions, whereas those who do not must be dealt with appropriately.

Use the ASQ Code of Ethics as a model to assist your organization in developing its own code as well as using it to develop your personal code of ethics. Refer often to your organization's code and your own code. Ensure that you are behaving at or above the ethical level embodied in the code.

One thing to consider, though, is that unethical behavior in one country may be an acceptable behavior in another locale.

Although the term *supplier* is not specifically mentioned, the intent of an ethical relationship between a customer and a supplier may be implied from the intent

ASQ CODE OF ETHICS

Fundamental Principles

ASQ requires its members and certification holders to conduct themselves ethically by:

I. Being honest and impartial in serving the public, their employers, customers, and clients.

II. Striving to increase the competence and prestige of the quality profession.

III. Using their knowledge and skill for the enhancement of human welfare.

Members and certification holders are required to observe the tenets set forth below:

Relations with the Public

Article 1—Hold paramount the safety, health, and welfare of the public in the performance of their professional duties.

Relations with Employers, Customers, and Clients

Article 2—Perform services only in their areas of competence.

Article 3—Continue their professional development throughout their careers and provide opportunities for the professional and ethical development of others.

Article 4—Act in a professional manner in dealings with ASQ staff and each employer, customer, or client.

Article 5—Act as faithful agents or trustees and avoid conflict of interest and the appearance of conflicts of interest.

Relations with Peers

Article 6—Build their professional reputation on the merit of their services and not compete unfairly with others.

Article 7—Assure that credit for the work of others is given to those to whom it is due.

of the ASQ code. A code developed for use by a different type of organization would, no doubt, include specific principles applying to supplier ethics.

There is an increasing concern that the *social responsibilities* of an organization, its management, employees, and subcontractors be addressed in any code of ethics. Although this concern is not specifically mentioned in the ASQ Code of Ethics, it can be assumed the intent exists. The ISO 26000 standard provides guidance.[1]

This is a short chapter, but the importance of embracing and sustaining ethical behavior permeates every aspect of organizations' operations. Laws and regulations have been enacted to control certain industries and types of organizations and punish wrongdoers. Behaving ethically, however, has to derive from personal values and integrity. Controls are useful reminders, but individuals must believe in and feel the need to conduct themselves ethically.

ENDNOTE

1. American Society for Quality, ASQ/ANSI/ISO 26000:2010 *Guidance on social responsibility* (Milwaukee: ASQ Quality Press, 2010).

See Appendix A for additional references for this chapter.

Part II

Strategic Plan Development and Deployment

Part II

The transformation to world-class quality is not possible without committed, visionary, hands-on leadership.

—Steven George

Although strategic planning is billed as a way of becoming more future oriented, most managers, when pressed, will admit that their strategic plans reveal more about today's problems than tomorrow's opportunities.

—Gary Hamel and C. K. Prahalad

An environment which calls for perfection is not likely to be easy. But aiming for it is always a goad to progress.

—Thomas Watson Jr. (IBM)

The purpose of a business is to gain and keep customers.

—Fred Smith (Federal Express)

Chapter 5

A. Strategic Planning Models

If you always do what you've always done, you'll always get what you've always gotten.

—Origin unknown

An organization's strategy defines what it strives to become and the means by which it will achieve it. Tregoe and Zimmerman define strategy as "the framework which guides those choices that determine the nature and direction of an organization."[1] Mintzberg further describes strategy as a plan or a course of action into the future, as a pattern providing consistency in behavior over time, as a position, namely, the determination of particular products in particular markets, and as a perspective, namely, an organization's way of doing things.[2]

Strategic planning is the continuous process of making present entrepreneurial decisions systematically and with the greatest knowledge of their futurity, organizing systematically the efforts needed to carry out these decisions, and measuring the results of these decisions against the expectations through organized, systematic feedback.[3] Planning is a continual process because the competitive environment is dynamic. Effective, continual planning guides an organization toward achievement of goals and prepares it for changes in internal and external factors that can affect its future.[4]

The origin of the term *strategic plan* has been traced to H. Igor Ansoff's *Corporate Strategy*, published in 1965. For the following two decades, Ansoff continued to write about this concept of planning and managing with a strategic intent. By the mid-1990s, Henry Mintzberg had contributed a vast amount of writing on strategic planning. A critical factor in strategic planning is the subject of quality.

Long-range planning, a term often confused with *strategic planning*, consists of extrapolating future plans based on what is known of current operations. In this sense, long-range planning and *forecasting* are synonymous. Strategic planning develops a view of the future, then delineates plans for the near term that will, when achieved, address the future needs as envisioned.

The Baldrige Performance Excellence Program criteria describe strategic planning as the process that addresses strategic and business planning and deployment of plans, with strong customer and operational performance requirements. The award's strategic planning category emphasizes that customer-driven quality and operational performance excellence are key strategic business issues integral to an organization's planning.

The span of a strategic plan may be as short as two or three months (for fast-moving organizations in a rapidly changing marketplace) to 30 years or more for a public utility (planning electric generation capacity for the future with an average of 30 years to find and acquire land, design, certify, and put a new plant into operation). For most organizations, the planning span is three to five years.

Strategic Planning Concepts

Strategic plans communicate the organization's priorities throughout the enterprise. A strategic plan provides a road map of how to get to specific targets and directs everyone in the organization to work to reach those same targets. Strategic planning should not be the work of a few select managers. It should involve people from all levels of the organization in the planning and execution of actions needed to help the organization focus on customer needs, remain flexible and responsive, retain employees, satisfy the needs of other stakeholders, and achieve excellence.

The development of an overall strategic plan is affected by various internal and external forces. Internal forces such as corporate culture, finances, worker skills, and other resources have an effect on the strategic plan. External forces such as changes in technology, customers' requirements, accrediting and regulatory agencies' rules, and competitors' actions relative to products/services have an effect on the strategic plan. In addition, various functions within the organization need to develop their own strategies that are closely aligned and integrated with the overall strategic plan. Examples of these are service strategies, marketing strategies, quality strategies, and operational strategies.

The strategic planning process is a continual process. As part of the planning process, there is opportunity to determine whether previous strategic plans have been met. If the plans have not been met, the organization needs to determine why. Answers might range from a flawed planning process that needs improvement, to unrealistic objectives, to organizational weaknesses.[5]

Controversy has arisen over the viability of strategic planning. Because strategic planning spans several years, it does seem somewhat less useful for organizations that face extremely rapid change, such as organizations in a volatile marketplace, organizations facing exploding technological advances, or the production of products with short-term appeal (for example, toy action figures and computer games). Nevertheless, organizations operating within such rapidly changing contexts also require an established strategic planning process to avoid falling prey to knee-jerk reactions. Yet, in order to be responsive, the strategic planning cycle in such cases must be sufficiently rapid to remain meaningful.

> Define, describe, and use basic elements of strategic planning models, including how mission, vision, and values as guiding principles relate to the plan. (Apply)
>
> **Body of Knowledge II.A**

Traditional Strategic Planning

Numerous strategic planning models have been developed to assist in the planning process. A generic overview of traditional strategic planning is shown in Figure 5.1. Planning is typically divided into three levels: strategic, tactical, and operational. *Strategic plans* articulate what an organization strives to become and the means to achieve it.

Tactical plans identify how the organization will implement the strategic plan. Tactical plans are those that occupy most of the attention of quality engineers, especially when a new product/service is being planned. The quality engineer works with suppliers, testers, designers, and market and financial analysts to specify what tasks need to be completed to ensure that a product meets its goals.

Operational plans, or *action plans*, are the day-to-day action-oriented plans concerned with the details of who performs what tasks and within what time frame. Operational planning includes scheduling inspections, tests, calibrations, process capability studies, training courses, and other essential day-to-day activities.

Another way to view these levels of planning is that strategic planning is composed of two phases. The first phase is *formulation*, in which strategies and objectives are formulated or defined. The second phase, *implementation*, encompasses the tactical and operational plans.

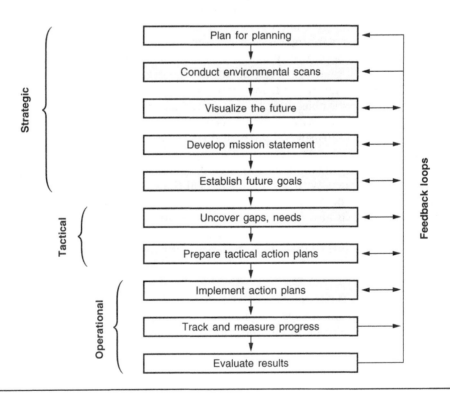

Figure 5.1   Overview of strategic planning process.

Involvement of people during the strategic planning process also changes as the process is deployed throughout the organization. Typically, the organization's leadership drives the strategic planning with input from all functional areas. Next, functional areas formulate their own objectives and strategies (tactical plans) to support the strategic plan in achieving its vision. Farther into the process, individual employees or teams become involved in developing action plans, budgets, and measures to monitor performance against the plans. A strategic planning process continues, with budget information being funneled back up the organization to develop the functional budgets, division budgets, and overall corporate budget.

Measurements complete the process by providing feedback to the various levels. Individuals receive information on how well they are meeting their operational/action plans, functions and divisions receive information on how performance relates to their tactical plans, and the organization gets valuable feedback on how well it is achieving its vision. Measurements close the plan–do–check–act (PDCA) loop by providing the information needed to make course adjustments over time, thus ensuring that the strategic plan is met.

A potential shortfall of traditional strategic planning is that the resulting plan may, because of a lack of committed deployment (for example, ownership), end up on someone's shelf unfulfilled. For this reason, hoshin planning is presented as a model that completes the cycle from planning to deployment to planning again (plan–do–check–act). The Japanese term *hoshin kanri* loosely translates as *hoshin* meaning *policy* or *target* and *kanri* meaning *deployment* or *management*.

Hoshin Planning

The first stage of hoshin planning (Figure 5.2) is to develop, or revise as needed, the vision (for example, future state of the organization, its purpose) and mission of the organization, using information from the environmental analysis (see Chapter 6). There is controversy over whether vision should precede mission or vice versa. The answer appears simple: do whatever makes the most sense for a given organization.

Let's say a healthcare organization has a long-standing mission to deliver exemplary healthcare (for example, efficient and effective care) to its community. That's a given, no need to change the mission. The environmental analysis, however, indicates that rapid and extraordinary changes must be made in the role healthcare will need to take in the future, or the continuance of the organization will be in jeopardy. A vision, or a revised vision, is in order. In this case, mission first, vision second.

Across town, an accounting firm is starting its first strategic planning process. It has neither a vision nor a mission on paper. It has, however, been functioning for years with the founding partners' unwritten concept of what to do, for whom they do it, and how well they do it. This concept needs to be captured in print and examined for currency as well as future implications. A vision emerges from the planning team. The mission statement is then formulated to reflect the products and services it delivers now and will deliver in the foreseeable future. The firm views the mission statement as more likely to change to reflect changing client needs and as it expands into different service markets. In this case, vision first, mission second.

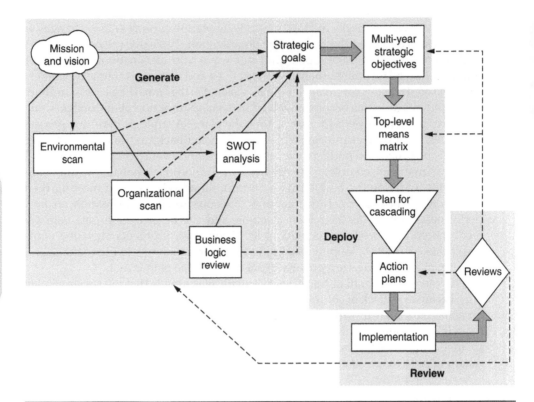

Figure 5.2   A typical view of the hoshin planning process.

Creating a Vision Statement. The purpose of the *vision statement* is to express what the organization would like to accomplish and/or where it would like to be in the future. A vision statement should be brief, inspire and challenge, describe an ideal condition, appeal to all stakeholders, and provide direction for the future state of the organization. The following are examples of vision statements:

- To become a $125 billion company by the year 2000. (Wal-Mart, 1990)

- To knock off R. J. Reynolds as the number one tobacco company in the world. (Philip Morris, 1950s)

- To become number one or two in every market we serve and revolutionize this company to have the strengths of a big company combined with the leanness and agility of a small company. (General Electric Company, 1980s)

Why create a vision statement? To articulate a vision, an organization should visualize the future and define its role in it. Once the vision becomes clear, the organization can work toward achieving it by developing the strategic plan. Although the terms are often used interchangeably, mission statements and vision statements are distinctly different. "A mission is for today's goals and the vision is for tomorrow's goals."[6] Vince Lombardi, Super Bowl–winning coach of the Green Bay

Packers, is credited with saying, "The best coaches know what the end result looks like, whether it's an offensive play, a defensive play, a defensive coverage, or just some area of the organization. If you don't know what the end result is supposed to look like, you can't get there. All teams basically do the same thing. We all have drafts, we all have training camps, we all have practices. But the bad coaches don't know what they want. The good coaches do."[7]

Likewise, all organizations do basically the same thing. They all sell products and services to customers, and they all utilize the same resources (for example, people, equipment, and money). Successful organizations know where they are headed and have plans to get there.

Guiding Principles or Values. Some planners choose to develop guiding principles or values to specify how business is to be conducted (for example, the protocol for completing transactions). Guiding principles or values help establish and define the organization culture and form the basis for decision making. Guiding principles or values may be customer focused, innovative, ethical, and risk taking. These principles or values are the fundamental beliefs that guide actions.

Defining the Mission. To effectively develop a strategic plan with all its ancillary objectives, means, and action plans, the organization must state its mission. The mission defines the purpose of the organization. "Mission defines the core purpose of being, in terms of the accomplishments needed that will result in realization of the vision."[8] The mission statement is infrequently revised. The following are examples of mission statements:

- The mission of Levi Strauss & Co. is to sustain profitable and responsible commercial success by marketing jeans and selected apparel under the Levi's brand name. We must balance goals of superior profitability and return on investment, leadership market positions, and superior products and service. We will conduct our business ethically and demonstrate leadership in satisfying our responsibilities to our communities and to society. Our work environment will be safe and productive and characterized by fair treatment, teamwork, open communications, personal accountability, and opportunities for growth and development.[9]

- Our mission is to continuously provide unprecedented customer satisfaction.

- We administer Prudential Assurance life business. Our purpose is to delight our customers by delivering a quality service, in a cost-effective manner, through the contribution of everyone.[10]

- We are Bread Loaf, a family of building professionals dedicated to and empowered by the strength of our people. We seek challenges to create innovative solutions that make statements demonstrating our commitment to excellence. As we grow into the twenty-first century, we shall continually focus upon employee wellness, community responsibility, and a sensitive balance between personal and professional fulfillment.[11]

Establishing Strategic Goals. Keeping the vision and mission before them, planners integrate information derived from the environmental analysis to formulate strategic goals (strive for no more than three or four goals).

Setting Multiyear Strategic Objectives. From the goals, planners then expand into multiyear strategic objectives (for example, what the objectives will be for the first year of the planning cycle, the second year, and so on). As with all objectives, they must be measurable. Each goal may have one or many objectives. Table 5.1 is a template for the S.M.A.R.T. W.A.Y. to establish objectives.

Creating the Means Matrix. Using the goals and the objectives, a top-level means matrix is prepared. The means succinctly answer the *how* question. Additional data are added to the matrix, for example, estimate of resources required, persons responsible for each objective, and the basis for measurement. Each objective may have several means.

A typical means matrix format (Figure 5.3) displays the multiyear objectives (derived from the strategic goals) as columns, and the means for accomplishing those objectives as rows. The relationship of a means to an objective may be coded; for example, a filled circle means has a direct relationship, an open circle means has an impact on the objective. Primary and secondary responsibilities for each mean may be indicated as persons or functions. A macro-level statement of resources required is entered for each means, as well as the most appropriate measure. A Gantt charting of the timeline for each means completes the matrix. If the time span of the strategic plan is five years, the timeline would encompass the five years. As the planning team develops the matrix, it may well be a chart four to five feet long and 10 or more feet wide. Figure 5.4 shows a tree chart of the relationships between the goals and the objectives, and the objectives and the means.

Deploying the Plan. When the matrix has been reviewed and adjustments made (for example, for conflicting times and resources), the overall plans are deployed horizontally and downward throughout the organization (see Chapter 7). At this stage, the strategic goals, objectives, and means are cascaded across

Table 5.1	Setting objectives the S.M.A.R.T. W.A.Y.
S	Focus on *specific* needs and opportunities.
M	Establish a *measurement* for each objective.
A	Be sure objectives are *achievable* as well as challenging.
R	Set stretch objectives that are also *realistic.*
T	Indicate a *time* frame for each objective.
W	Ensure that every objective is *worth* doing.
A	*Assign* responsibility for each objective.
Y	Ensure that all objectives stated will *yield* desired return.

Source: Reprinted with permission of R. T. Westcott & Associates.

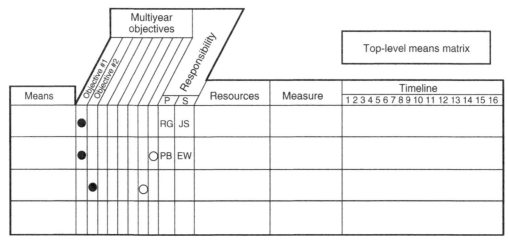

Figure 5.3   Top-level means matrix format.

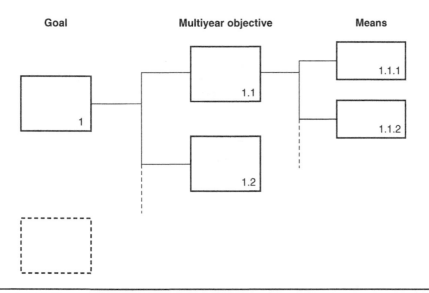

Figure 5.4   Linking goals, objectives, and means.

the organization. The plans move in an iterative way, for example, up and down (vertically) and across organizational functions until consensus is reached, a process the Japanese call *catchball.*

Preparing Action Plans. Action plans are developed for each means by the individuals or teams responsible for executing the plans. There may be several action plans for each means. The action plans are implemented, continuously monitored, and reviewed (see Chapter 7).

Transitioning to the Next Year's Planning. By the end of the third quarter in the planning and implementation process, hoshin planning begins anew for the upcoming year. Results of the first year's implementation become additional information, part of the environmental assessment, for the following year. All goals, objectives, and means are carefully reviewed and adjustments proposed as needed. Typically, some action plans will not have worked out as planned, perhaps leaving work to be carried over to the next year. Some objectives and some of the means supporting those objectives may either be no longer valid, require additional resources to complete, or be postponed to make room for a new or higher-priority activity.

Advantages and Disadvantages of Hoshin Planning. The hoshin planning process should not be confused with management by objectives, which it superficially resembles. Hoshin planning is a tightly knit planning and implementation system that can involve every member of the organization. Hoshin planning is a vehicle for communicating, through every organizational level, the direction of the organization, and for controlling the outcomes. Every person in the organization knows where his or her efforts and ideas fit in the overall scheme. Documented evidence exists at every stage in the process to enable all planners to learn from the process, improve the process, and achieve the planned goals of the organization. Hoshin planning engenders and reinforces team-based problem solving and decision making. It literally forces management to "walk the talk" and to integrate the implementation of strategic plans with daily operations. It surfaces resource conflicts and forces trade-off analysis and resolution. Hoshin planning is a fact-based system for stimulating and managing the growth and development of the organization and its people.

Hoshin planning, through its catchball approach to resolving barriers and its insistence on constant tracking, measuring, and reviewing, succeeds where other less-stringent strategic planning efforts have faltered or failed. For the many years strategic planning has been around, it has always been implied that the plans must be cascaded down through the organization for the plans to be viable. The problem was that no effective and enforced process had been devised for making this happen.

Perhaps the single most troublesome area of hoshin planning for the typical American organization is the emphasis on involvement of the entire organization, with consensus at every level, before implementing the action plans. In hoshin planning, the ideal planning group often comprises the key top management of the organization, who coalesce into a smoothly functioning team, both to make the process work as well as to create a role model for lower levels. Also, the time required to fully implement hoshin planning can be daunting for smaller organizations. An answer, in many cases, is to take on fewer goals.

Hoshin planning is not an easy journey. It requires solid top management support and personal involvement. For organizations that are not accustomed to soliciting feedback from below, or that have never done formal planning before, it involves a significant cultural change. An effectively functioning hoshin planning process might take three years, or even longer, to work out the smooth flow of information and to build realism into the planning.

Scenario Planning

Scenario planning is a disciplined method for imagining possible futures that companies have applied to a great range of issues.[12] By identifying basic trends and uncertainties leading to the future, a series of narratives or scenarios can be constructed. These stories challenge existing assumptions, a kind of looking glass for organizations to see themselves as never before. Scenario planning helps compensate for the usual errors in decision making: overconfidence and tunnel vision. In its simplest form, scenario planning uses three macro (or all-embracing) scenarios: good future, bad future, and wild card. Once scenarios are visualized, alternate strategic (contingency) plans can be developed.

Barriers to Successful Strategic Planning

Undefined and ambiguous terms can be one of the biggest roadblocks to the strategic planning process. Terms can be easily misunderstood because they are often used interchangeably. The term *goal* is often substituted for *objective*. Likewise, *action plan* and *program* are sometimes used interchangeably. Organizations need to clearly define the terms they will be using in their strategic planning process, and communicate them to ensure that they are understood by all people involved in the planning process. When priorities and strategies are unclear, people do not know what to aim for or what to do.

Strategic planning sometimes fails because reward and recognition systems do not support the results of the planning process or promote a sense of urgency. People are motivated to act quickly when they receive rewards and recognition, but in most organizations people are not rewarded for a sense of urgency.

At times, individual departments have their own set of plans, goals, and strategies that might or might not fit with those of other departments. When fragmented responsibilities and functional systems do not support the planning process, the organization can not work together toward a common goal.

Additionally, when management does not "walk the talk" of strategic planning, people become confused by the mixed signals they receive. Excessive procedures, paperwork, and meetings choke out a sense of urgency by miring employees in mundane tasks (an example of lack of focus on the "vital few" of Juran).

These problems are supported by the list of the 10 most important pitfalls of planning as compiled by Steiner:[13]

1. Top management's assumption that it can delegate the planning function to a planner.

2. Top management becomes so engrossed in current problems that it spends insufficient time on long-range planning, and the process becomes discredited among other managers and staff.

3. Failure to develop company goals suitable as a basis for formulating long-range plans.

4. Failure to assume the necessary involvement in the planning process of major line personnel.

5. Failure to use plans as standards for measuring managerial performance.

6. Failure to create a climate in the company that is congenial and not resistant to planning.

7. Assuming that corporate comprehensive planning is something separate from the entire management process.

8. Injecting so much formality into the system that it lacks flexibility, looseness, and simplicity, and restrains creativity.

9. Failure of top management to review with departmental and divisional heads the long-range plan that they have developed.

10. Top management consistently rejecting the formal planning mechanism by making intuitive decisions that conflict with the formal plans.

When the appropriate model and structure for the strategic planning has been determined, the next step in the process is to conduct an environmental analysis.

ENDNOTES

1. B. B. Tregoe and J. W. Zimmerman, *Top Management Strategy: What It Is and How to Make It Work* (New York: Simon & Schuster, Touchstone Books, 1980).
2. H. Mintzberg, *The Rise and Fall of Strategic Planning* (New York: Free Press, 1994).
3. P. Drucker, "The Information Executives Truly Need," *Harvard Business Review* 73 (January–February 1995): 125.
4. T. J. Cartin and D. J. Jacoby, *A Review for Managing for Quality and a Primer for the Certified Quality Manager Exam* (Milwaukee: ASQ Quality Press, 1997), 79.
5. Ibid., 81.
6. J. R. Latham, "Visioning: The Concept, Trilogy, and Process," *Quality Progress* (July 1995): 89.
7. J. Madden and D. Anderson, *Hey, Wait a Minute, I Wrote a Book* (New York: Ballantine, 1985).
8. P. Mears and F. Voehl, *The Guide to Implementing Quality Systems* (Delray Beach, FL: St. Lucie Press, 1995), 32.
9. C. Lee, "The Vision Thing," *Training* (February 1993): 29.
10. J. Cook, "Teams Need a Vision to Work," *Journal of Quality and Participation* 12 (December 1994): 59.
11. T. Lammers, "The Effective and Indispensable Mission Statement," *Inc.* (August 1992): 75–77.
12. P. Schoemaker, "Scenario Planning: A Tool for Strategic Thinking," *Sloan Management Review* 37 (Winter 1995): 82.
13. G. A. Steiner, *Strategic Planning: What Every Manager Must Know* (New York: Free Press, 1979).

See Appendix A for additional references for this chapter.

Chapter 6

B. Business Environment Analysis

Many factors both inside and outside an organization can have a significant impact on short-term performance and long-term viability. For example, current strategy may be invalidated by a new entrant to the market or a change in product liability law, or new product or service opportunities may suddenly become possible due to new technological breakthroughs. A critical role of senior management, then, is to create and implement strategies to keep an organization viable over the long term, taking into consideration customers, employees, suppliers, owners, competitors, and society at large.

Development of strategy requires that an organization understand the external environment in which it operates, its own internal strengths and weaknesses, and how the internal and external factors can best be combined to create a competitive advantage. An organization might choose to be the leader in product or service design, or the low-cost provider in the general market, or may carve out a unique niche in the market that is not currently served by others.

Environment scanning and analysis, both external and internal, should not occur only once a year, just before strategy and budgets are set. In a fast-changing world, an organization must be continually monitoring factors known to be important to performance, as well as be on the lookout for changes that may bring new factors into consideration. Business *environment analysis* is a process that is done as a key input to the strategic planning process.

Figure 6.1 highlights some of the major components considered during an environment analysis. While much of the information gained during the analysis is on the same or similar issues, it is received from several different sources. The process of comparing the information to find agreement or differences can then help validate the information and identify significant opportunities or gaps to be addressed by strategy.

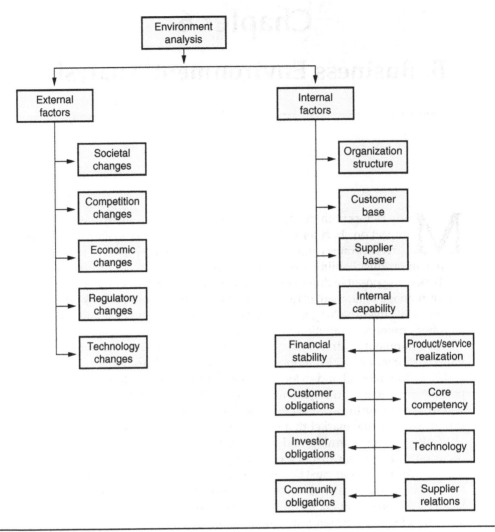

Figure 6.1   Components of an environment analysis.

1. SWOT ANALYSIS

> Analyze an organization's strengths, weaknesses, opportunities, and threats, and develop and prioritize actions to take in response to that analysis. Identify and analyze risk factors that can influence strategic plans. (Analyze)
>
> **Body of Knowledge II.B.1**

A common component of the strategic planning process involves looking at both current internal strengths and weaknesses of the organization's operations, as well as future opportunities and threats in the external marketplace. A SWOT analysis is a systematic assessment of an organization's internal and external environment, and identifies attributes that affect its ability to achieve its vision and to improve and protect its competitive position. A SWOT analysis looks at how the organization fits to the current reality. Following are some of the factors that are looked at in a SWOT analysis.

Strengths and *weaknesses* (focused on internal environment) may include:

- How strong is the organization's image and/or name/brand in the marketplace?

- How strong (stable, effective, flexible) is the organization's leadership?

- How effective is the organization structure?

- How stable is the current and future financial strength of the organization?

- How do features and costs of products/services compare to competitors, and where are products/services in their probable life cycle?

- Is the organization well focused on a clearly defined vital few issues, or are efforts widely dispersed?

- How innovative is the organization? What is the track record of new products/services? Is there a strong research and development effort ongoing?

- How effective are the organization's efforts toward continual improvement?

- What is the condition (for example, age, flexibility, capacity) of major assets (for example, key employees, technology, facilities), and how does that impact the organization's capacity and capability to sustain the organization?

- What additional resources does the organization have available (for example, employees, stakeholders, capital) to enable change?

Depending on the answers to questions like these, the action might be to build on the strengths and address the weaknesses. In addressing the deficiencies, there are several options:

- Remove the deficiency by changing the goal or objective to make fulfillment achievable.

- Invest more in the people, technology, physical assets, improvement efforts, and so on, to be able to turn the deficiency into a strength.

- Outsource parts or all of the process to another organization that can fulfill the process requirements more effectively.

- Sell the part of the business that causes the present deficiency.

Opportunities and *threats* (focused on external environment) may include:

- What new competitors or products may enter the marketplace?

- What viable markets are not currently being served?

- How saturated is the marketplace?

- How are demographics or values changing in the marketplace?

- What new accreditation, legal, or regulatory issues might arise?

- Are customer/supplier partnerships or alliances effective for the organization?

- Does the likely future economic situation pose risks or potential rewards?

Figure 6.2 is an example of a SWOT analysis. Connie is the owner of the two stores that comprise the Brides on a Budget Boutique. She met with her two store managers to commence their first strategic planning process. After an intense three-hour meeting, the items in Figure 6.2 were identified. Other issues were discussed, but the document represents the major items. Following the SWOT effort, Connie and her managers met again to begin to formulate a strategic vision. They prepared for this meeting by discussing answers to, "What will this business be like five years from now?"

SWOT analysis should be based on objective data that review critical events from the past, the present, and the probable future in making comparisons with the marketplace, competitors, products and services, and company performance. Analysis of the information will typically be reviewed for items that provide significant advantages or risks that should be addressed by strategy, as well as the relative ratio of advantages to risks, which may impact the aggressiveness of the strategy. Items affecting the firm's critical success factors must be reviewed in detail.

A SWOT analysis can be done at any time, but it is essential in developing the data needed for strategic planning. Also, there is no reason to prevent a critical

Strengths	Opportunities

• We are trend leaders in both cities in which the stores are located.
• Both locations are ideal for their market niche (high-traffic, multi-store malls).
• Customer retention indicates extreme loyalty and a high referral rate.
• Both stores show a 10% to 12% increase in business in last three years.
• Store A does a higher volume of cash business than store B.
• Layout, displays, and inventory carried is identical for both stores.
• Customer surveys and media coverage acknowledge the superb personalized customer service provided by personnel of both stores.
	• Find ways to improve profitability of store B.
	• Rethink inventory management practices and improve.
	• Assess the products (costs, quantity, style life, and pricing) carried to determine which products are most profitable and which should be dropped.
	• Assess the effectiveness of present advertising efforts and look for more lucrative media and approaches.
	• Examine the potential of new approaches to marketing:
	  – Offer home service (selection, fitting, delivery)?
	  – Explore alliance opportunities with other mall-store owners?
	  – Explore alliance opportunities with caterers, wedding planners, and so on?
	  – Consider presenting a fashion show?
	  – Consider opening an outlet store for previously owned bridal wear?

Weaknesses	**Threats**
• Connie is the only person who understands the billing system. • Because of taking advantage of a manufacturer's close-out, the business currently shows a negative cash flow. • Connie is stretched thin by her heavy work schedule and the growing pains of her business (hiring and retaining competent help, rising benefits costs, slowing economy, other stores closing in the malls, and so on) • Inventory obsolescence tends to be higher than for others in the industry. • An increasing number of crimes committed in the malls is affecting the attraction of potential buyers. • Store B is a cash drain (sales dollars low due to clientele tending to purchase lowest-price items, and number of bad debts increasing).	• Malls have both been bought from original owners, and a rent increase is rumored. • Connie could get sick. • Refurbishing of downtown areas is attracting customers away from the malls. • Malls are becoming hangouts for unruly teenagers, and could be a distraction for brides-to-be. • Mall owners' extension of the mall's business hours impacts personnel costs (often, we staff a store at hours when no potential customers appear, yet must comply with mall rules to be open).

Figure 6.2   SWOT analysis example.

Source: Reprinted with permission of R. T. Westcott & Associates.

discovery from the analysis immediately being turned into an action plan—even before the strategic planning process is complete.

It is vitally important that future initiatives be aligned with findings of the SWOT analysis. Success of previous strategic initiatives should be assessed to determine whether the desired outcomes were achieved. Success or failure may be a function of the method of deployment (for example, process reengineering) or may indicate an issue that will only be resolved through long-term and consistent action (for example, organization culture change).

2. MARKET FORCES

> Define and describe various forces that drive strategic plans, including existing competition, the entry of new competitors, rivalry among competitors, the threat of substitutes, bargaining power of buyers and suppliers, current economic conditions, and how well the organization is positioned for growth and changing customer expectations. (Apply)
>
> **Body of Knowledge II.B.2**

For any product or service to be successful, it must be an effective fit to the economic environment. When shaping strategy, an organization should look for general trends in the marketplace, trends within the industry of which it is a part, and competitor strategies. The competitive landscape is impacted by the strategies of customers and suppliers.

Information on these issues may often be gathered from government sources, newspapers, television, the internet, direct marketing ads, industry groups or publications, trade shows, customers and suppliers, and the annual financial reports of public companies. Some competitive intelligence gathering may be subcontracted to firms who specialize in this area, but management (and in the best organizations, all employees) should continually be on the lookout for changes that can provide opportunities or create threats to present and future strategy.

Some general marketplace issues for which information should be gathered include:

- Government subsidies that can help offset internal or raw material costs, or make competitor products less expensive

- Trade restrictions or tariffs that limit (either by fiat or through economic incentives or disincentives) what can be sold to or purchased from particular markets

- Changes to international monetary exchange rates that have the effect of raising or lowering prices of raw materials used by the organization, or the selling price for goods sold in global markets

- Social concerns, demographic or political changes, or other societal issues that may create opportunities or threats for the organization and/or its products

- Inflation, deflation, or changes in lending rates that impact the costs of borrowing money and of raw materials and labor

- Economic cycles that affect demand for various products (for example, luxury goods)

- Market expansion, stability, or contraction that impacts demand for products (for example, in other countries, the opening up of new markets as a result of changes in political and economic philosophies)

- Social or economic differences (for example, values, relative purchasing power) between regions or countries

Some general issues to watch for relative to specific industries are:

- Amount of capacity currently in existence in the industry relative to total market demand, and the rate at which demand and capacity are changing. For example, in industries where capacity is added in large blocks, if many organizations chase the same existing opportunity, an overcapacity situation may result, creating overstocking and pricing pressures.

- Mergers and acquisitions that consolidate the number of players and may provide greater economic leverage for some.

- Place in the life cycle of a particular product (for example, is it a brand-new or mature product?) and how that impacts profitability and growth potential.

- Potential for an entirely new product or service, or a less expensive version of the existing product or service, coming to market.

- Speed of change in the industry, and how it might call for breakthrough versus incremental change.

- Trends toward or away from regulation of the industry.

- Whether the product/service requires a local or globally focused design orientation.

- Whether the cost of entry for new players in the industry is high or low, and how this affects product, capacity, and pricing issues.

- How much specialized knowledge and/or technology is required for the product/service, and how much of a barrier that may create for new entrants.

- How does/will the bargaining power of customers affect strategy? For example:

  - Just-in-time buyers offering long-term contracts, but expecting price reductions

  - Large-volume customers demanding price and delivery advantages

- Customers pulling back presently outsourced services

- Customers changing to more standard products, making it easier for them to switch suppliers

- Customers in a financial crisis expecting concessions from their suppliers

• Expiring patents.

Competitive Analysis

Comparisons may be made of competitors' strategies and results in relation to one's own assumptions. For example, if a competitor formulates its strategies based on its assumption that birth rates in the marketplace served will increase over the next five years, and the opposite is occurring, there is a strategic gap that can be exploited. If a competitor's strategies are significantly different than what the organization's management assumes, it could lead management to believe there may be an error in strategy that would seriously impact the organization's potential.

Porter provides a framework for comparing the organization with competitors that, among other factors, examines a competitor's "core capabilities, its ability to grow, its quick response capability, its ability to adapt to change, and its staying power."[1]

Comparisons at a product/service level can yield valuable information for strategy consideration: For example, commercial bank A compares itself with its competitors' products and services feature by feature. On the surface, all the banks studied appear to be offering similar services. Closer examination of time to process, contacts available, fees, and linkage to other services reveals that competitors have an edge in supplying direct loans to customers who export. Bank A, in servicing its exporter customers, provides faster service in furnishing letters of credit, at lower fees, and has a wider range of overseas contacts. This detailed type of comparison yields important insights for use in determining whether strategy needs to be changed.

Both quantitative data and qualitative data can be examined in comparing against competitors. Scanning of pertinent news media (newspapers, magazines, radio, TV, and the internet) for qualitative data is productive in finding both factual and speculative indications of competitors' recent and potential next moves.

Types of questions to ask when analyzing an industry include:

• Who are the competitors? How many are there? Where are they located? How do they range in size (number of employees, number of locations, dollar sales, number of customers, and so on)? Which competitor dominates the industry?

• Are the competitors forming consortiums or other types of alliances?

• How aggressively are the major competitors pursuing new product or service opportunities?

- To what extent are the methodologies used by major competitors influencing attraction of new customers?

- What are the primary weaknesses and vulnerabilities of the major competitors?

- Is doing business globally a plus or a minus for the major competitors? What risks are they facing?

- What image and reputation do each of the major competitors have regarding ethical and fair practices, legal practices, leadership strength, type of employer, environmental conscientiousness, and so on?

Organizations in extremely competitive markets establish units of specially trained people to search out meaningful comparative data about their competitors as well as about the environment in which both operate, for example, the pharmaceutical industry and the computer industry.

The results of competitive comparisons not only shape top management's day-to-day decision making but are input to the business environment analysis, impacting the formulation of longer-range strategic plans.

Benchmarking

Competitive comparison differs from benchmarking. Competitive comparisons are done to assess the organization's strategic strengths and weaknesses as compared to the competition. Benchmarking targets performance of specific processes for input to the strategic planning process. It identifies other organizations known for their best practices in those processes and conducts a benchmarking study with other organizations to help define how the practices observed can lead to improvement in one's own organization's performance. Remember, copying a better practice of a competitor makes an organization, at best, only as good as the competitor—not better!

From the process of conducting benchmarking studies (see Chapter 12) data critical to strategic decisions and plans may be available. These data should be integrated with business environment analysis. Examples of potential benchmarking study results include:

- Revelation that a whole new technological approach may be needed to maintain or improve the organization's position in the marketplace.

- Identification of the potential for upgrading the organization's value chain, from supplier through delivery to customers, thus reducing cycle time, improving quality and production, reducing costs, increasing customer satisfaction, and improving profits.

- An indication of how lean manufacturing techniques can reduce inventories, improve process flow and quality, and eliminate the need for additional facilities.

Part II.B.2

- Insights as to how activity-based management can aid in pinpointing products that are unprofitable to continue to produce/provide.

- New knowledge of how to identify and deal with constraints in a major process.

When such data are collected and analyzed, the potential exists for initiating a process reengineering effort or other breakthrough initiative that could have a significant impact on the organization, for example, making a heavy improvement investment at the front end resulting in a significant return on the investment later.

Knowledge of one's competitors is vital, and will typically include looking at:

- Who is producing a new product that can be substituted for an existing product

- How competitors market their products or company (for example, how they try to differentiate their products or company from others) in ads or press releases

- Timing of announcements of new products

- Alliances or mergers between competitors that may impact market coverage or financial leverage

- Other companies who are not already in the market but who may have the expertise, resources, and inclination to enter it

- Pricing strategies that might indicate inherent cost structures or new market initiatives

- Synergies within a competitor's value/supply chain, or within their own organization's product mix, that might give them leverage

- Strength of an organization/product as a brand, and at which market niches the brand is targeted

- Core competencies of competitors

- Position of the company relative to competitor firms (size, image, capital access, niche served)

- Age of competitor organizations and their management, and how this might impact the probability of significant change

As the strategies of customers change, there will usually be a ripple effect calling for adaptive change by those who supply them. Some issues a company might watch for include:

- How good is the relationship between the company and various key customers (for example, regarding field failures, customer complaints)?

- How high or low a cost would customers incur if they decide to switch to a different source?

- How might the customer decide to vertically integrate, producing internally some of the products/services currently purchased externally?

- What large purchasing groups might exist or be formed that could pool their purchasing power, with increased economic power being one result?

- How much does the product/service need to be customized, and for which market segments, applications, or other demographic factors?

- How easy is it for customers to compare prices/sources (for example, ability to shop around using the internet or other means)?

- How are final user priorities and values changing, and how will that impact desired product/service features or methods of delivery?

Supplier strategies can also impact a company. Examples are:

- Is the supplier the only one available for the product/service, and how might that impact its pricing strategy or willingness to adapt to different needs?

- What is the total dollar amount of what is being purchased relative to the total sales of the product for the supplier, and how might that impact its flexibility?

- Might the supplier find other applications or buyers for the product that would cause the supplier to discontinue selling the product according to the existing agreement?

This information allows an organization to begin to more fully understand the environment in which it is working. It must first, however, be combined with additional factors before strategy can be finalized.

3. STAKEHOLDER ANALYSIS

> Identify and differentiate various internal and external stakeholders, as well as their perspectives, needs, and objectives to ensure that the organization's strategic objectives are aligned with those of the stakeholders.
> (Analyze)
>
> **Body of Knowledge II.B.3**

Stakeholders are individuals, groups, or organizations who will be directly or indirectly affected by an organization carrying out its mission. Although employees, suppliers, customers, community, and shareholders are the stakeholders having the most directly at stake, others such as accrediting organizations, unions, regulatory organizations, and special interest groups can also affect outcomes and should therefore not be ignored.

All stakeholders have particular issues, priorities, and concerns, and it is important that an organization understand each of the stakeholder groups and the issues most important to them. For example, one company may draw a large proportion of its workforce from college students who primarily desire part-time work to help cover tuition until graduation, while another company may consist primarily of middle-aged parents who are concerned about health benefits for their families.

The organization should take steps not only to identify each stakeholder group, but also their interests relative to the organization. An assessment should be done to identify gaps between the objectives and plans of the organization and the needs and interests of stakeholders, and action taken to close the gaps where feasible (see Figure 6.3). The impact of gaps should be considered especially as it relates to legal risks, employee and community health, and viability of the product/service in the marketplace. Efforts should then be focused on the vital few issues.

Stakeholder needs and interests can be gained directly by involving them in the planning process or by gathering input that will be considered during planning. When stakeholders will not be directly involved, it is often advisable to communicate advance information about organizational plans in order to reduce the likelihood of inaccurate conjecture being the only information available to these groups.

Social responsibility is an especially challenging facet of stakeholder analysis. Consider the impacts on stakeholders of each of the following organizational strategies and behaviors:

- Organizational restructuring/reengineering resulting in layoffs

- Diversity issues relative to race, ethnicity, gender, sexual orientation, age, and so on

- Privacy concerns relative to personal test results, chemical dependencies, personal finances

- Sexual harassment

Stakeholder group	Key needs/interests of stakeholders	Goal (G), objective (O), plan (P) that addresses stakeholders' needs/interests	Gap to be addressed
Customers			
Suppliers			
Shareholders			
Employees			
Community			
Special interest groups			

Figure 6.3   Template for evaluating organizational alignment to stakeholder needs and interests.

- Environmental concerns relative to quality of air and water, pollution, flora and fauna, and so on

- Conducting business in locations where the local practices challenge the organization's ethics and beliefs, particularly in such areas as human rights, bribery, gift giving

- Initiating and defending actions that offend or damage relations with the public, for example, insider trading, misrepresenting the organization's financial status, predatory pricing, and so on

To help ensure that stakeholder needs and interests are met, they can be converted to a strategic goal supported by strategic objectives, with measures used to track performance. Stakeholder concerns can also be embedded in values or principles statements used to guide management action. A common mistake is to think of stakeholder interests as incongruent with the organization's interests; in most cases this is not the case if one takes a systems view of society. An organization truly interested in long-term value to society will find that a balanced interface with all stakeholders can be managed.

4. TECHNOLOGY

> Describe how changes in technology can have long- and short-term influences on strategic planning. (Understand)
>
> **Body of Knowledge II.B.4**

In today's rapidly changing world, a new technological development can have a dramatic impact on the life and sustainability of an organization. Organizations must have a means for detecting technology developments, assessing the potential for use in their industry and organization, and effectively implementing those technologies that will likely provide an advantage. Technology may include:

- Electronic-based technologies used for communicating

- Product or service technology

- Production or service process technology

- Support systems technology (for example, designed to serve marketing, engineering, production, customer service, finance, human resources, suppliers, knowledge management, and so on)

- Hardware, software, storage media

Technological developments can enable the creation of entirely new products (for example, handheld devices, distance learning) or may be incorporated into a product or a service process to enhance functionality or reduce costs (for example, online flight reservations, e-tickets, and self-printed boarding passes, even bio-logically implanted monitoring devices). The fact that technological changes often occur outside an organization's industry means that organizations must be continually scanning the environment to identify potential threats and opportunities. A change in one technology can also quickly obsolete another technology (for example, the demise of typewriters, floppy disks, auto carburetors, and a myriad of other now obsolete technologies) or dramatically shorten an expected product life cycle.

Just because a technology is available, however, doesn't mean the organization should immediately adopt it. Some issues that should be considered include:

- Is the technology one in which design standards are necessary or will evolve? If so, can the organization help lead the way toward standardization, or might another source (for example, regulators, stronger competitors, the marketplace) take precedence? What are the risks of adopting the technology before standards have been developed? Will the standards be applicable in all markets or might different countries have their own version (for example, electrical power standards throughout the world)?

- How quickly is the technology likely to diffuse within the industry or marketplace? Will it be widely accepted almost immediately, or will there be a process of conversion over time? How much of the company's R&D resources should be allocated to exploring this technology versus maintaining and improving existing products?

- Does the organization have the technical and financial capabilities to effectively adopt the technology? Should it be a leader and innovator, or a follower who shortens the learning curve by learning from others' successes?

As these questions show, technology is not a panacea and should be implemented with forethought and planning. Understanding the fit between the technology and the organization can be especially important when it involves changing business processes. In using technology to improve service, Berry suggests six basic guidelines:

1. A technology strategy must also address behavioral changes that will be required.

2. Don't apply automation to bad processes.

3. Make sure that the new technology solves a real problem.

4. Technology should allow users to gain more control over the process, rather than to become robots.

5. Choose the lowest technology that will do the job, rather than just going for the latest and greatest.

6. Technology should increase flexibility, customer service, and performance.

The internal capability of the organization becomes important. If there is insufficient knowledge to support the technology, then it can either be acquired or the depth to which the technology is adopted can be scaled appropriately to internal capabilities. The knowledge required may include how to effectively integrate it into the organization's products or business processes, and how to maintain/support the technology itself.

The ability to patent technological developments may also be considered. If a firm can not obtain a patent on a new product, competitors may quickly duplicate the offering and quickly erode profit margins. The ability to provide a unique design for which a patent might be obtained may depend on the creativity of design personnel as well as an understanding of the legal aspects of the patent process.

A match of a new technology to core competencies and other technologies currently used by the firm may also impact whether a new development in technology can be converted to a viable competitive strength. The technology may be one for which not only are new skills necessary, but perhaps an entirely new mind-set.

The time needed to change organizational culture may mean that the organization simply will not be able to take advantage of what initially seems like an opportunity.

Technology is a never-ending challenge in that it affects both the internal capability of the organization and an organization's ability to stay ahead of or at least keep up with competitors' new developments. For example, in some industries, the introduction of web-based selling has totally restructured the marketing, advertising, sales, order processing, product and service delivery, customer billing, and other processes of organizations. The competitor's internal capability, however, is stressed in the attempt to meet the new needs. The strategy question is "Can your organization afford to join in the race, or can it afford not to?" Technology can be a competitive advantage today and a constraint tomorrow.

5. INTERNAL CAPABILITY ANALYSIS

> Identify and describe the effects that influence an organization's internal capabilities: human resources, facilities capacity, and operational capabilities. Analyze these factors in relation to strategy formation. (Analyze)
>
> **Body of Knowledge II.B.5**

Organizational Core Competencies

It is essential to have a clear understanding of the primary competencies that distinguish the organization and its products and services from the competition. Ask:

- What capabilities of the employees enable the organization to successfully compete in the marketplace?
  - What are the unique skills and experience level of the workforce?
  - What creative and innovative talents are embodied in our workforce?
  - What organizational climate, work environment, and management style supports a highly motivated workforce?
- What process capabilities enable the organization to successfully compete in the marketplace?
  - What research and development is unique to this organization?
  - What state-of-the-art organizational structure, facilities, processes, equipment, and tools are unique to this organization?
  - To what degree is the organization integrated with its supply chain?
- What unique difference does our geographic location make?
  - Proximity to major customer segments?
  - Proximity to major transportation hubs, highways, terminals, and so on?
- What unique certifications and other recognition has the organization received?
- How does the organization's financial stability distinguish it from competitors?

Factors that should be considered in developing the organization's strategy are:

- Availability of human resources
  - Is the available labor pool stable, expanding, or contracting?
  - Is the infrastructure supporting the labor force capable of accommodating the organization's expanded or changed strategies in the future? What about transportation issues and housing issues like utilities, taxes, and emergency services? What about schools and other institutions to support families?
  - Is the current labor force and available labor pool capable of acquiring the competencies required to support future organizational strategies?
  - Are there currently, or planned, educational opportunities capable of assisting in the development of the organization's human competencies?
- Are there currently, or available in the future, the facilities, equipment and operational capacity to expand and/or reconfigure to accommodate future strategies?

- Are there funds available or accessible to support growth plans?

- Are there adequate materials, supplies, and suppliers to meet the needs of planned growth?

- Will the quality of leadership, the organization structure, and the predominant managing style support the planned growth?

Much of the information desired from the environment assessment can be gained directly from customers and/or employees. For example, customer feedback can help an organization understand opportunities for modifying product or service features to make them more value-added for the customers. Employee feedback can help to understand how management systems support or hinder implementation of strategy.

A portion of the customer and employee information to be fed into the strategic planning process may come from common sources of information such as customer complaint data and employee exit interviews. Since this type of information is limited to problem areas, however, a special data-gathering process should be developed and implemented as part of the environmental assessment process in order to gain more strategically focused information.

Following are some of the questions that such assessments should be designed to answer. From customers:

- How well are current needs and wants being satisfied, and how could that satisfaction be enhanced?

- What new products/services/features would be value-added?

- How does the organization and its products/services compare to direct competitors or other suppliers with whom the customer does business?

- Does the customer intend to use the organization as a supplier in the future? Why or why not?

- What are some future plans of the customer for which the organization should be aligning internal capabilities and resources?

- Does operation of the organization show alignment with the publicly expressed vision, mission, and values?

From employees:

- How well does the organization's culture fit with its strategy?

- Are skills and rewards appropriate for the industry and strategic direction?

- Are management systems properly aligned to the espoused vision, mission, and values?

- Do employees have the authority needed to make decisions for which they are held responsible (are they empowered)?

- Do employees understand the organization's strategy, and would they be committed to the changes necessary (ownership)?

- Is there sufficient trust and communication to enable the organization to work effectively?

- Was past strategy implementation seen as appropriately deployed?

Significant opportunities or gaps in findings must be translated into action. This might involve:

- Modification of the vision, mission, or values to more clearly spell out what the organization stands for in its design or redesign of a product or service

- Partnering with customers to develop a more long-term, integrated working relationship

- Changes in organizational structure, management systems, technologies, and communications practices to better produce, support, and reward behaviors in line with customer and organization needs

- Enhancement of strategy deployment and employee development processes

These changes would be accomplished through being identified as specific objectives of the strategy, with appropriate projects and resources provided to carry them out, and progress monitored to evaluate their effectiveness (see Chapter 7).

6. LEGAL AND REGULATORY FACTORS

> Define and describe how these factors can influence strategic plans. (Understand)
>
> **Body of Knowledge II.B.6**

Legal Factors

Legal factors relate to laws, the lawmaking process, and rules for litigation. Laws are established by city, county, province, state, or federal governments—and enforceable by threat of punishment.

Understanding the legal requirements of the following is suggested:

- Employment-related laws and litigation

- Product/service liability

- Environment liability

- Protection of intellectual property (patents, copyrights, trademarks)

- Contract-related liability pertaining to customer orders

- Ramifications of the Sarbanes-Oxley Act

- Antitrust laws

- Trade protectionism

Regulatory Factors

Regulations are established by agencies within governments as well as outside organizations, for example, industry associations, self-regulating bodies, and professional societies. Regulations are enforced through self-regulation under the threat of disenfranchisement. Regulations are principles or rules designed to control or govern behavior. In theory, they are voluntary, but often have the force of law. Regulations may span a whole industry, or segments within industries may each have their own specific regulations. Identifying and understanding the pertinent rules and regulations is critical.

ENDNOTE

1. L. L. Berry, *On Great Service* (New York: The Free Press, 1995), 8–16.

See Appendix A for additional references for this chapter.

Part II.B.6

Chapter 7

C. Strategic Plan Deployment

Anyone can make pretty planning documents; transforming those plans into meaningful actions is the hard part.

—(Executive who prefers to remain anonymous)

This chapter completes the strategic planning cycle. Chapter 5 introduced several process models for strategic planning. Chapter 6 discussed various types of information gleaned from the business environment analyses. This chapter covers getting the plans deployed, acted on, and measured.

The individuals who own the action plans, having participated in the formulation of the plans, deploy the plans to where the action fits in achieving an organizational objective. The next step in the process is monitoring and measuring progress and achievement against each strategic objective. The last step, for the current plan, is to assess performance, the outcomes, and the effectiveness of the planning process itself, and to pinpoint areas for improvement—then start over again from lessons learned.

A simple concept, but it does require discipline and solid top management support. Following are the key steps for successful deployment of the strategic plan.

1. TACTICAL PLANS

Identify basic characteristics of tactics: specific, measurable, attainable, relevant, time-specific, and linked to strategic objectives. Evaluate proposed plans to determine whether they meet these criteria. (Evaluate)

Body of Knowledge II.C.1

Action Planning

To transform the organization's strategic objectives into action, an action plan is needed. In actuality, the planning detail that comprises an action plan is a mini project plan. There may be several action plans generated from one strategic objective. It is the systematic approach to initiating actions and the follow-up of those actions that closes the loop toward achieving the organization's strategy. An action plan should include:

- Project identification and description.

- Date project completion is needed.

- Link to the strategic objective and any pertinent mandates.

- Project objectives.

- Scope of the project—Where and for whom will the solution/ implementation be applied? What limitations or constraints will be encountered?

- Deliverables—including both outputs pertaining to the project objectives and outputs for managing the project, and ultimate outcomes.

- Criteria by which the project will be measured.

- Assumptions affecting the project.

- Description of the overall approach.

- Start date to begin the project.

- Estimate of the resources required—time, personnel, facilities, equipment, tools, materials, money.

- Verification that there is sufficient organizational capacity and resources to accomplish the objectives.

- Estimate of benefits versus costs.

- Timeline and person responsible for steps to complete the project (mini Gantt chart).[1]

Figures 7.1a and 7.1b show an action plan example for one of several projects linked to a strategic cycle time reduction objective. Note that the action plan form can also be used for other small projects, for example, corrective or preventive action, process changes resulting from regulatory changes, a kaizen blitz, or an internal audit.

   Action plans, sometimes referred to as *operational* or *tactical* plans, are typically short term (accomplishable within a year). When an action plan is not sufficient because of the scope, size, and duration of a project, refer to Chapter 10 for information on planning for larger projects.

Action Plan		Plan no:	*Q-5*
		Date initiated:	*032913*
		Date needed:	*091013*

Project title: Replace existing laser cutting machine.

Description: Determine, select, purchase, and install an appropriate laser cutting machine that will meet our need through 2009.

Plan no: *Q-5*
Date initiated: *032913*
Date needed: *091013*
Approval by: *T.B.B.*
Team leader: *R.T.W.*
Team member: *T.R.E.*
Team member: *F.P.M.*
Quality team member:

Linked to what (strategic objective, contract, policy, procedure, process, corrective or preventive action, customer mandate, or regulatory requirement)?: PAR # 04-21—Resulting from 2/24/04 process audit and quality council decision of 3/19/04.

Project objectives: To replace existing cutting machine with the most cost-effective laser cutting machine that meets engineering specifications, capital equipment purchase policy, and production criteria, by August 31, 2004. Must meet SMED-type setup requirements and accommodate manufacturing cell configuration changes as needed when lean thinking is applied in the plant.

Scope (Where and for whom will the solution/implementation be applied? What limitations and constraints?): Up to 10 equipment vendors will be contacted with our Request for Proposal. Up to five vendor proposals will be evaluated in detail. Up to three vendors' machines will be subjected to a live demonstration using our materials and specifications. Preference will be given to U.S. vendors, if all other factors are equal.

Deliverables (include outputs re content, outputs re project management, and outcomes):
- Evaluation criteria
- Engineering specifications
- Request for Proposal
- Review of project status at weekly management meeting (time and costs expended)

By what criteria/measures will completion and success of project be measured?:
- Deadline met
- Equipment meeting all specifications and production requirements selected, purchased, installed, tested, and turned over to production
- Purchase within capital project policy parameters

Assumptions made that might affect project (resources, circumstances outside this project):
Machine selected will not require predelivery design modifications.

Describe the overall approach to be taken, data needed, processes to apply:
A three-person team will be formed (leader from quality, members from engineering and production). Within an extended work week (48 hours), the team will:
- Research appropriate vendors and their equipment.
- Prepare Requests for Proposal from selected vendors.
- Evaluate proposals and select machines to subject to demonstration testing.
- Select and place purchase order for equipment.
- Arrange for appropriate operator and supervisor training.
- Provide necessary changes to procedures and work instructions.
- Install, test, accept, and turn over machine to production.

When should the project be started to meet the date needed/wanted?: March 29, 2004.

Estimate the resources required (time, personnel, facilities, equipment, tools, materials, money):
- Quality engineer for 16 hours per week for 22 weeks
- Production engineer for 16 hours per week for 10 weeks
- Production planner for 16 hours per week for 18 weeks
- T & L expenses for trips to machine demonstrations $5000
- T & L expenses for training first operator and supervisor $3000
- Machine replacement (transportation, rigging, etc.) $4000
- Machine cost $850,000
- Other expenses $2000

Is there sufficient organizational capacity and are resources sufficient to meet the objectives?:
Yes.

Estimate the benefits versus costs value: Annualized decrease in setup costs = $75,000. Annualized decrease in cycle time = $200,000. Salvage value of obsolete machine = $5,000. Project costs = $14,000. Annual amortized machine cost = $170,000. Total costs = $184,000. First-year payoff ($280,000–$184,000) = $96,000. Second-year payoff = $110,000.

Outline the major steps and dates on page 2.

Figure 7.1a   Action plan (front).

Source: Reprinted with permission of R. T. Westcott & Associates.

Action Plan—Steps				Plan no: *Q-5*

Outline the *major steps* to be taken, a projected *start and finish date* for each step, and the *person to be responsible* for each step. Attach any backup data.

Step number	Activity/event description	Depends on step	Start date	Finish date	Person responsible
1	Form project team and launch project		032913	040113	RTW
2	Prepare machine specifications and Request for Proposal	1	040113	041213	TRE
3	Research vendors	1	040113	050313	RTW
4	Select vendor and order machine	2, 3	050313	051013	TRE
5	Train initial operator	4	052413	052813	FPM
6	Install machine	4	062113	062513	FPM
7	Conduct trial runs	5, 6	062813	071213	FPM
8	Revise documented procedures and operator training materials	7	072613	080213	RTW
9	Train supervisor	8	080213	083113	FPM
10	Place machine in production schedule	9	082313	083113	FPM
11	Document project and disband team	10	083113	091013	RTW

Figure 7.1b   Action plan (back).

Source: Reprinted with permission of R. T. Westcott & Associates.

2. RESOURCE ALLOCATION AND DEPLOYMENT

> Evaluate current resources to ensure they are available and deployed in support of strategic initiatives. Identify and eliminate administrative barriers to new initiatives. Ensure that all internal stakeholders understand the strategic plan and have the competencies and resources to carry out their responsibilities. (Evaluate)
>
> **Body of Knowledge II.C.2**

Leadership and Management

Strong leadership, diligent management support, and personal involvement are necessary to develop and deploy strategic plans into action. Instituting strategic planning, whatever model is adapted to the organization, takes sustained commitment and a *can-do attitude*. The hard part of the process is deployment and management of the actions (projects) that will, collectively, accomplish the organization's strategic goals and objectives.

For most organizations, initiating strategic planning is a major cultural change. Communication to everyone in the organization is critical at every stage in the process. Encouragement and sustained support is critical to the people who will be transforming the plans into action and achieving the results. The trade-off decisions about resources will require negotiating skills and conflict management. Leadership roles for each stage in the strategic planning process must be chosen wisely.

Resource Availability

One of the principal concerns is how to superimpose and/or integrate action plans resulting from the strategic planning process with everyday business activities. Picture this: The strategic planning team, in its zeal to produce a great plan, goes beyond the capability of its organization to implement the strategic actions as well as continue to "make the donuts." Guess what falls out? Right, one or more of the strategic actions. Guess who gets blamed? Right, the people who compiled the action plans often catch the blame. So, the strategic planning process must be suspect? Wrong, the process is fine—if it is followed properly.

This situation demonstrates another key to successful deployment and integration. Also, there needs to be an organizational culture that permits lower-level persons to challenge the actions they are being asked to implement. These front-line persons must be heard and receive respectful answers to their challenges—without fear of retribution.

One of the several advantages of hoshin planning, discussed in Chapter 5, is that care is taken to ensure that the plans are deemed acceptable and doable by all involved. This includes a consensus on resources needed.

A key question is: Can time be made in the day-to-day activity schedule to integrate the work involved in carrying out the action plans? Or, is it just assumed that the time will somehow be found for these new actions, and nothing will suffer? In this age, relatively few organizations have the slack time to assimilate a lot of new activities without sacrificing something. A strategic planning team needs to understand how far the organization can be stretched before something breaks.

Aside from daily activities, which are crucial, work on other potentially conflicting activities and programs may be under way, such as:

- A process reengineering initiative is planned or under way.

- A new quality management system is being implemented (for example, ISO 9001).

- A new information processing system is being implemented.

- An outsourcing initiative will result in downsizing.

- A merger, acquisition, or divestiture of part of the business is planned.

- A new product/service line of business is introduced.

- Major upgrades to machines and processes are introduced.

- Turnover of personnel due to new, large employers entering the same labor pool area.

- A Six Sigma initiative is being introduced.

- New products/services threaten obsolescence.

- Restrictive regulations mandating mass retraining, new procedures, and controls are in effect.

If any of these conflicting activities or programs are under way, or soon will be, this must be considered in the business environment analysis. For example, assume that one of last year's multiyear objectives was to replace the present information system (IS) within the next three years. System design, programming, testing, and implementation tasks are still going on, and severely draining existing resources. Strategic planning must assess this impact—before making commitments that will conflict. And, if the persons responsible for the means do not challenge the shortage of resources, then those at the action level who will most feel the lack of resources must challenge the feasibility of completing the actions affected.

Allocation of Resources

Before action plans are fully developed (for example, including resource estimates), a spreadsheet (matrix) should be prepared showing the various types of resources required against each of the objectives. This matrix can be at any level of detail needed for decision making regarding resources, for example, including the commitment of resources for day-to-day work. Not only is the type of resource vital to know, but also when and for how long that resource will be required. Many project planning software programs have the capability to provide such a document, as well as the ability to play out what-if scenarios to determine the best mix with the least conflict.

When adjustments have been made, the action plans are developed, and a revised master resource allocation plan is prepared. This becomes the resource allocation baseline against which actual use of resources is measured. Constant monitoring and in-course correction is necessary. Not only will the estimates by which the resource allocations have been made be tested in practice, but the resources available will be subject to changes as time goes on. People leave, training replacements takes time, equipment breaks down, funds are jeopardized by external aberrations, and so on. As initial plans often can not be static, neither can resource allocations be held constant. This doesn't mean planning is useless, but it does mean that without plans there is limited ability to see the potential constraints and what must be done to achieve the objectives.

Deployment of Tactical-Level Means

Steps are taken to ensure horizontal and vertical alignment of plans, as well as integration at mid-level and with functional management. One of the tools for surfacing potential priority and resource conflicts early in the process is a group review of the master means matrix prior to deploying to the action planning level. One organization calls this meeting a *walkabout*. Each person responsible for a means posts a flip-chart paper on the wall showing, by name or job title, the anticipated people, machines, materials, and funds required and when needed. Each attendee, using colored sticky notes, walks about the room examining the postings. When a potential conflict is noted, a sticky note is attached where the conflict is seen. Following this, negotiation and trade-offs take place to resolve the conflicts. Any unresolved conflicts are listed as issues to be resolved before plans are deployed downward. Inasmuch as many of the means are cross-functional in nature, the walkabout begins the integration and consensus process for the second layer (those below the initial planners). This iterative up, down, and sideways integration and conflict resolution process continues, both at the means level and the action levels, until agreement is reached and the plans can be deployed.

Deployment of Action Plans

In some of the traditional strategic planning processes the planners move directly from the objectives to action plans (often failing to convey a clear understanding of the linkage between objectives and action plans). Usually, a gap analysis is employed to surface the steps that may be needed to move from the current status toward the future goals.

In traditional strategic planning it is implied that action planning is a natural extension of the deployment process. Unfortunately, this is where the traditional approach has sometimes faltered for lack of commitment to support and execute the plans. The hoshin planning process described in Chapter 5 is designed to remedy this potential shortfall. The hoshin approach literally involves everyone in the organization with the action planning that pertains to their function. The action plans must be prepared and sent back up the planning hierarchy for acceptance and integration before the implementation of the plan can take place. This *catchball* technique assures not only involvement of those persons responsible for implementing the action plans, but also achieves better buy-in of the plans.

The summation of all the action planning details (that is, time and resources required, including dollars) is reviewed by successive organizational levels back up to the strategic planning team. At this point the plans are given final approval or adjusted and sent back down the organization for replanning and return. This iterative process aids in communicating the entire strategic plan to all employees and allows each employee to clearly understand his or her contribution to the overall plan. Figure 7.2 displays the concept of cascading from top-level (enterprise) objectives down throughout the organization to individual action plans.

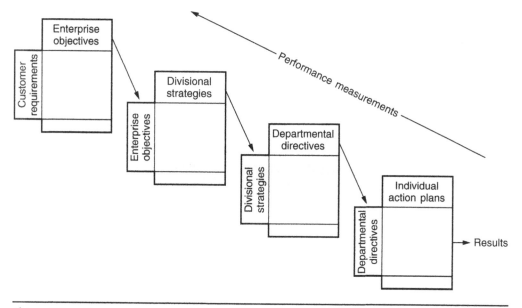

Figure 7.2   The cascading concept (from QFD) used as a strategic plan deployment tool.

3. ORGANIZATIONAL PERFORMANCE MEASUREMENT

> Develop these measures and ensure
> that they are aligned with strategic goals,
> and use the measures to evaluate the
> organization against the strategic plan.
> (Evaluate)
>
> **Body of Knowledge II.C.3**

Designing Performance Measures

Measurements for processes are used to indicate the effectiveness of the processes in delivering products and services, such as product/service quality relative to customer satisfaction. Internal operational measures may include inventory turns, efficiency of the quality management system, cost savings from Six Sigma projects, and so on.

Feedback Loops. Consider the experience of folding and flying paper airplanes, hoping that they would fly straight and true to their targets. Once launched, those planes went where they wanted to. Consider flying a model radio-controlled plane. When the wind blows the plane off course, the radio operator adjusts the rudder and ailerons, and the plane is back in control.

Part II.C.3

This difference contrasts open-loop versus closed-loop performance measurement. In closed-loop measurement, monitoring is continual so that immediate adjustment to the action can be made.

The better the design and construction of the paper plane, and the more experienced the operator, the more likely the plane will fly close to its desired target. This is basic to open-loop operations. Good planning, anticipation of the potential causes of disruption, tightening the process so that it is not easily deflected from the target—all these are useful practices that are effective in the hands of skilled managers. However, closed-loop processes are more likely to succeed in reaching their objectives because they can better handle disruption from unforeseen causes.

Every process should have two outputs: (1) a valuable product or service to satisfy the customer and (2) the information to manage, control, and improve the process. A closed-loop process has many advantages over the open-loop operation. Unfortunately, many processes are open loop, and managers resort to intuition, emotions, and other ineffectual methods in an attempt to eliminate common causes of variation. Management by fact—that is, using closed-loop processes and trend data to monitor continuous improvement—is the preferred approach.

The contrast between open-loop and closed-loop operations shows up early in deployment planning stages. Typically, in open-loop operations, planning focuses on how to detect or measure problems in the inputs and how to plan for contingencies. "What if the Barlow shipment is late?" "How late is too late?" or "What if the weather is too cold?" and "How cold is too cold?" In contrast, closed-loop planning focuses on how to measure the outputs and how to determine the control points where adjustments can be made.

Balanced Measurements. A technique for measuring organizational performance is the balanced scorecard approach (see Chapter 11, Section 3).

Consider the balancing of financial and nonfinancial measures supporting a strategic objective of increasing customer satisfaction, for example:

- Reduce customer order processing cycle time (order entry to order delivery)

- Number of certified suppliers for critical raw material

- Accuracy and completeness of customer billing

- Number of field service technicians qualified to service all of the company's products

- Overall product failure costs reduced

Critical Success Factors. Many organizations designate indicators called *critical success factors* (CSFs) by which to measure the outcomes of the strategic plans. These must be custom fitted to the specific organization. These CSFs, when considered together, provide the focus for steering the organization toward fulfillment of its vision, mission, and strategic goals and objectives. Typically, these CSFs may number eight to 12 indicators and target the life-span of the strategic plans, for example, five years. Partial examples from two different industries are shown in Figure 7.3.

A not-for-profit organization		Company A	
CSF	**Target**	**CSF**	**Target**
Number of subscribers	28% of area population	Sales expansion	$2,800,000 in five years
Fund growth	32% increase in corporate contributors	Pretax income	8.5% of sales

Figure 7.3   Examples of critical success factors for two organizations.

Table 7.1   Annual closed-loop assessment.

Annual closed-loop assessment	Use of metrics
1. Define "business excellence" for your business	Establish strategic measures of success
2. Assess your progress	Compare your progress to world-class competitors and to strategic objectives; identify gaps
3. Identify improvement opportunities	Set annual priorities and improvement goals
4. Deploy action plan	Align key metrics and deploy to all levels of the organization

Metrics and Organizational Alignment

It has been said that *whatever gets measured, gets done*. This is true in many applications and organizations. Unfortunately, the organization that has too many measures dilutes its ability to achieve breakthrough results in any of them. When metrics are considered an integrated element of organizational strategy, they are a powerful means of plan deployment throughout the organization.

An annual closed-loop assessment process, such as the one shown in Table 7.1, can be based on the Baldrige Award criteria, state-sponsored award criteria, or independent criteria. In any case, the overall organizational goal should be to assess progress toward excellence and initiate a new plan to close the gap. Relatively few (four to 10) strategic metrics can focus an organization's efforts and achieve breakthrough performance. A variety of different tactical measures would be important to individual departments or sites that support the strategic plan. Metrics should be limited to the actual process drivers because too many metrics can lead to ineffectiveness. A metric should directly relate to an action to attain an objective, and be attainable.

Some measurements verify that the action item is under way, and other measurements verify that the objective is reached. Usually, both types of measurements are required.

Measurement costs money. There is the time involved in measuring, often equipment and space for collecting and/or displaying the measures, and training of employees in how to measure. Measuring can be seen as a diversion of resources from the main task of producing useful output.

Six factors influence how frequently measurements should be taken:

1. *Purpose.* Does the metric indicate a trend or control output?

2. *Cost.* How much time/money is spent measuring?

3. *Rate of change.* What is the maximum time between measurements?

4. *Degree of control.* Can an unfavorable change be corrected? How soon?

5. *Consequences.* What is the risk?

6. *Baseline.* Are there existing data on how the metric performs over time?

Process maps for closed-loop operations should indicate the points where measurements are taken in a process and the analysis of those measurements.

Monitoring, Measuring, and Reporting Performance

Continual monitoring and review of each action plan/project takes place. This may necessitate various types of project adjustments as the plans unfold into action. Reviews of progress and problems take place at all levels, including assessing the effectiveness of the planning process itself. Formal review reports are presented on a scheduled basis at each level (usually quarterly). The results and lessons learned feed into the subsequent year's strategic planning process.

The hoshin approach—while it often takes several years to achieve a smooth transition from traditional or no strategic planning—does engender greater organizational awareness of the organization's vision, mission, goals, and objectives. Hoshin planning does involve absolute top management support as well as a high degree of participation and personal commitment in carrying out the plans. Usually, by the third year of implementation the process becomes the way of doing business.

In addition to the metrics already implied or discussed, that is, measuring progress against action plan timelines and measuring resources used against resources planned, there are other measures and tools used for performance measures. Key questions to ask:

- Why measure? To take action to ensure success in reaching goals.

- What to measure? Key process elements to help monitor the process.

- Where to measure? As close as possible to where variation could occur.

- When to measure? As often as necessary, but no more often.

- Who should measure? The person closest to the action.

- How many metrics? Only as many as are truly useful in meeting the strategic objective.

- How to measure? As consistently but unobtrusively as possible.

4. QUALITY IN STRATEGIC DEPLOYMENT

> Support strategic plan deployment by applying continuous improvement and other quality initiatives to drive performance outcomes throughout the organization. (Create)
>
> **Body of Knowledge II.C.4**

Formulating Quality Policies

The quality function or department can take several types of support actions relative to the strategic plan's deployment, as well as ensure that the voice of the customer is addressed throughout the organization's processes.

Quality should be integrated with the organization's strategic plans. In a very small organization, most personnel are familiar with all the organization's knowledge, goals, policies, and procedures, much of which may not be documented. As organizations grow in size and complexity, personnel are added, many of whom make significant decisions. To ensure consistency and understanding throughout the organization, quality policies need to be defined, documented, and communicated.

A *policy* is a high-level, overall plan embracing the general goals, objectives, and acceptable practices of an organization. Policies state how goals will be achieved, and are intended to guide decisions. They are future oriented, sometimes for the indefinite future and sometimes conditioned on the presence or absence of some constraining factor. As visions, strategic goals, and objectives are unique to each organization, policies are also (in general) unique to an organization.

A quality policy is a formalized document created to communicate the overall intentions and directions of the organization relative to quality. The quality policy is a guide indicating the principles to be followed or what is to be done, but does not stipulate how. The quality policy should summarize the organization's view on the definition of quality, the importance of quality, quality competitiveness, customer relations, internal customers, workforce involvement, quality improvement, planning and organization, and additional subject matter as required. Examples of quality policy statements are:

- Our products shall be free from all unacceptable substances that may cause property damage or impact the personal health of employees, customers, or suppliers, and shall meet all applicable standards and regulations.

- We will deliver products and services that meet or exceed customers' requirements, on time, and at competitive prices.

- Our policy is to build long-term relationships with customers and suppliers that commit to high quality and continual improvement, as we do.

- Our commitment to quality without compromise will be sustained through state-of-the-art technology, cost-effective solutions, customization, customer support and training, and investment in research and development of ever better products and services.

Establishing a quality policy is a focal point for development of an organization's formal quality system. A clear and brief statement can help people in the organization develop a common understanding about the aims of the organization in dealing with management processes and work activities that affect all aspects of quality performance. The policies should be viewed as adaptable.

In general, senior management formulates top-level policies. The process of formulating an effective quality policy and objectives should be based on inputs from many stakeholders: line organizations, such as manufacturing and distribution; staff functions, such as product design, budget/finance, human resources, and legal; customers; suppliers; regulators; shareholders; communities in which business is conducted; senior management; and enterprise planners. The quality function should contribute input to and support the organization's overall policies.

Quality policies developed by the quality function/department should be clear and provide guides for conduct. Make a quality policy actionable through example. When the culture does not permit or fit, do not attempt to force one quality policy on multiple markets or divisions. Remember—a policy imposed is a policy opposed.

The ripple effect from policy changes, if perceived as negative by any stakeholder, can produce unfathomable damage. Organizations have suffered major losses, and some have been ruined, by the results of saying one thing and appearing to do another. On the positive side, upgrading the quality policy would have favorable effects.

Policies differ from guiding principles. Organizational policies (directives, procedures, guidelines, and rules) are more specific and directive. Usually, the most important are communicated to the workforce through employee handbooks, to suppliers through supplier guidelines, and to customers through product or service guides and warranty and disclosure information (see Chapter 17).

Defining Quality Management Principles

Business principles are the fundamental beliefs or values that are intended to guide organizational behavior. These principles may be integrated and documented as a part of the strategic planning process. Examples are:

- We believe it is better and easier for the organization to retain customers than to replace them.

- We value each customer and grow as they grow.

- We believe in honesty and mutual respect for our customers and employees. This forms the basis for our shared prosperity.

Quality management principles are the guiding beliefs that, when used for organizational decision making, will ensure long-term success from the perspective of customers, employees, and other stakeholders. The quality management principles are the basis for objectives at all levels and demonstrate the depth of the organization's commitment to quality.

Well-formulated principles should be timeless, not dependent on temporary circumstances. The ISO 9000 series of standards includes eight such principles (see Chapter 12, Section 2). Examples of specific quality principles are:

- Problems have special causes and common causes.

- Management must take responsibility for common causes.

- It is better to prevent defects from getting in than to sort them out.

The quality function should recommend wording for the quality principles and support the deployment of the principles throughout the organization. Policies and principles that are nicely framed and hung in the front lobby, but not deployed, are just window dressing.

Quality Objectives

To deploy organizational goals and objectives relative to quality, quality objectives are set to specify what specific actions will be taken, within a given time period, to achieve a measurable quality outcome (Table 5.1). Examples are:

- Errors in processing insurance claims will be reduced from 150 per week to 15 or less per week by the end of the fourth quarter of this year.

- Eighty percent of all platform personnel will be cross-trained and qualified to perform a minimum of five banking functions by the beginning of next year.

- Waste of floor-covering materials will be reduced from 15.6 percent to 0.5 percent, or less, by the beginning of the first quarter of next year.

- Cycle time for family product line 4 will be reduced from 20 seconds per item produced to no more than 1.7 seconds per item produced by August 1 of this year.

The quality function should position itself to review all quality objectives, provide recommendations, and support the deployment of the objectives. The quality function should promote the establishment of responsibility for quality objectives as an inclusion in creating job descriptions, and individual objectives as an agenda item for discussion in all performance appraisals. Inasmuch as individual compensation typically depends on receiving a favorable performance appraisal, the inclusion of quality objectives as measurable performance appraisal factors helps close the loop—pay for performance and support for meeting objectives. Inclusion of quality measurements in the appraisal process supports the adage *what gets measured gets done.*

The quality function should participate in identifying the voice of the customer (VOC) and deploying the VOC throughout the organization. Expertise in using quality function deployment (QFD) (see Chapter 17, Section 1]) should enable the quality professional in facilitating the development and deployment of the QFD output.

Part II.C.4

Summary

A quality function should support the strategic plan deployment by:

- Participating in the strategic planning process

- Helping in promoting the communication (deployment) of the strategic goals, vision, mission, values, and objectives

- Formulating quality policy

- Defining quality management principles

- Setting quality objectives

- Ensuring that quality objectives are included in job descriptions and that performance relative to those objectives is a performance appraisal measure

- Ensuring that the voice of the customer is addressed throughout the strategy development and deployment

- Periodically auditing to ensure that the organization's quality practices meet the intent of published quality policies

- Continually providing performance and environment feedback to the organization's strategic planners, information that is pertinent to the attainment of the organization's strategic goals and objectives

- Identifying opportunities and/or initiating continual improvement efforts to improve the strategic planning process and the deployment of the plans

ENDNOTE

1. R. T. Westcott, *Simplified Project Management for the Quality Professional* (Milwaukee: ASQ Quality Press, 2005).

See Appendix A for additional references for this chapter.

Part III
Management Elements and Methods

Part III

He who runs his company on visible figures alone will soon have neither company nor visible figures to work with.

—W. Edwards Deming

Management's job is not to promote satisfaction with the way things are, but to create dissatisfaction with the way things are and could be.

—Edward M. Baker

Most Japanese companies don't even have a reasonable organization chart. Nobody knows how Honda is organized, except that it uses lots of project teams and is quite flexible.

—Kenichi Ohmae

Chapter 8

A. Management Skills and Abilities

Organizations, regardless of their size, are complex entities. They consist of and require the effective coordination and integration of goals, objectives, systems, processes, employees, information, technology, and equipment, including interfaces with customers, suppliers, and other stakeholders. This is the role of management—to plan, carry out, monitor, and initiate action to maintain the appropriate focus and results, and to ensure viability of the organization in the future.

The complexity of organizations is reflected in the metaphors used to describe them. In the more stable environments of past decades, organizations were thought of in mechanistic terms. That is, they were considered as a predictable amalgamation of tightly linked components that could be relatively easily adjusted in order to achieve desired results. In today's chaotic environment, organizations are often thought of as living organisms that evolve in order to adapt to change. The components of today's organizations operate in more fluid relationships, inasmuch as unpredictability of the future and a need for more rapid change call for a more agile and adaptable way of working.

This also changes the role of management. While mechanistic organizations could operate effectively with a hierarchical structure, organic organizations typically have fewer levels. In many ways, however, the basic functions required for managing are still the same. What has changed is the style of management and how much more widely the responsibilities for management are deployed.

Total quality management (TQM) has contributed significantly to these changes. An emphasis on customer satisfaction means that people now look across the organization rather than up the hierarchy in order to find out how well they are doing. Involvement of everyone in process management and continual improvement means that employees must be more knowledgeable and committed to the organization's mission. Management personnel must now know more about how to acquire competent employees and organize them in ways that allow them to function effectively.

Also, the distinction between a manager and a leader is ever blurrier. While in the past managers were said to manage resources and leaders to lead people, today there is less of a demarcation—the two roles often blend (see discussion of leadership in Chapter 2).

There are three levels of management. *Top management* (also called *senior management* or *executive management*) is responsible for providing direction through defining the vision, mission, policies, goals and objectives, strategies, systems, and structures. Top management is also responsible for managing the boundaries between the organization and its major stakeholders, such as customers, suppliers, employees, investors, and business partners.

An organization that is committed to quality requires that top managers demonstrate their commitment through defining the values and principles by which the organization will operate, and by leading the effort. Some of the core principles of a quality orientation include a passion for excellence, a focus on customer satisfaction, involvement of all employees, and a systemic view of the internal and external relationships of all organizational processes.

Middle management is responsible for carrying out the policies and procedures necessary for achieving the organization's mission, goals, and objectives. The middle manager's role is more operationally than strategically oriented, playing a key role in day-to-day communication and decision making. Middle management's role is often being responsible for managing a particular part of the organization.

First-level supervision (often called *line supervision*) is responsible for managing the work of a functional unit, such as customer service, production scheduling, a sales territory, quality assurance, and so on. First-level supervisors have a daily balancing act to perform, for example:

- They have to follow upper management's strategies, goals, objectives, and directives—and enlist the support of their subordinates in meeting the organization's mission, goals, and objectives.

- They have to be empathetic to, and often defend, the needs and concerns of their subordinates, whose beliefs and attitudes may be opposed to or not completely in accord with upper management.

1. PRINCIPLES OF MANAGEMENT

> Define and apply basic management principles such as planning, leading, delegating, controlling, organizing, and allocating resources. (Apply)
>
> **Body of Knowledge III.A.1**

Planning, Organizing, Staffing, Directing, and Controlling (POSDC)

What business are we in? What resources do we need in order to succeed? How should those resources be organized? What skills and information do employees need in order to do their jobs? How do we know how well we're doing? What should we do if things aren't going well, or if we want to improve?

These are just some of the questions asked by management as part of attending to the processes for which it is responsible. The processes of management (POSDC) are often described in the following categories:

- *Planning* is the setting of goals and objectives and the methods for achieving them.

- *Organizing* involves structuring the organization and the work to be done, obtaining and allocating resources in order to carry out the plans.

- *Staffing* includes acquiring and placing the right people for the right job as well as further developing their competencies.

- *Directing* is guiding members of the organization (see Chapter 1) to achieve the mission, plans, and objectives of the organizational work unit.

- *Controlling* involves monitoring activities and results to ensure that desired outputs and outcomes are obtained.

On a macro or long-term level, *planning* involves defining the vision and mission of the organization as well as the values and principles by which the company will operate. It involves defining the business's goals and objectives, strategies to be used for each product, service, and/or customer segment, and ensuring that appropriate systems and structures are created to carry out strategy. Planning must occur for the overall organization as well as subunits within it (for example, divisions, departments, and work units). The strategic processes are further defined in Chapters 5, 6, and 7.

Operational planning has a shorter-term perspective, and involves activities such as:

- Setting short-term objectives (for example, which university courses will be offered during the upcoming semester)

- Analysis, planning, and allocation of capacity and material (for example, how many flu shots are expected to be needed by a local community health clinic, and how many nurses will be needed where and on what days)

- Planning needed resources (for example, assuring sufficient inventory of winter road salt for a highway department depot)

- Setting out timelines (for example, when user training and operational conversion to a new customer relationship management software package will occur)

Organizing at the strategic level includes determining the organizational structure and design (see Chapter 2) and how work will be divided and authority allocated. It is at this level that basic policies and decisions are made relative to the systems to be used to manage aspects of the business such as finance, human resources, order fulfillment, and research, and the types and locations of facilities to be used in carrying out the processes. At the operational level, organization involves making the appropriate resources available, both human and otherwise (for example, equipment, material, information, and funds), to implement and sustain the processes.

Staffing at the strategic level is identifying the human resources needed and the levels of competency necessary to achieve the organization's mission, goals, and objectives, the acquisition of these resources, the building of a competent workforce that meets or exceeds customers' expectations, and the care and development of the individuals that comprise the organization.

Directing at the strategic level is the communication of vision, mission, values, and strategy in such a way that every business unit understands its role in the success of the organization (see Chapters 5, 6, and 7 on strategic planning and deployment). *Directing* at the operational level is the day-to-day delegation, empowerment, and coaching that enables all employees to effectively apply their knowledge and skills to satisfy the customer (see Chapter 2 on leadership).

Controlling at a strategic level is the monitoring of strategy implementation and results, using macro-level performance measures (for example, sales, profitability, market share growth, new product development, and customer and employee satisfaction). *Controlling* at the operational level is the monitoring of shorter-term measures such as performance against budget, on-time delivery, and customer complaint resolution. Controlling includes initiating corrective and preventive actions when necessary. It also involves recognition and rewards for work done well. Controlling also includes the organization's continual learning and continual improvement.

Management is about the management of processes, whether it's a business process (for example, strategy development or order fulfillment) or a single step within a business process. Regardless of the type and scope of the process, there must be a plan that is organized, carried out, and monitored—the PDCA/PDSA cycle. All employees should be involved in process management at some level, with the primary differences being the scope and time horizon.

Core Values and Concepts

The Baldrige Performance Excellence Program (BPEP) embodies interrelated core values and concepts:

- Visionary leadership

- Creating a sustainable organization

- Communication and organizational performance

- Strategy development and deployment

- Customer-driven engagement and excellence

- Performance measurement, analysis, review, and improvement (management by fact)

- Management of information, knowledge, and information technology

- Building a competent, effective, supportive, and valued workforce

- Organizational and personal learning

Part III.A.1

- Designing, managing, and improving work processes with a systems perspective and emphasis on creating value

- Achieving measurable and effective process, product, customer-focused, workforce-focused, leadership- and governance-focused, financial- and market-focused performance outcomes

- Managing for innovation

- Social responsibility

These values and concepts are the foundation for integrating key business requirements within a results-oriented framework that creates a basis for action and feedback. (See Chapter 12, Section 1 for more about the Baldrige Performance Excellence Program.)

2. MANAGEMENT THEORIES AND STYLES

> Define and describe management theories such as scientific, organizational, behavioral, learning, systems thinking, and situational complexity. Define and describe management styles such as autocratic, participative, transactional, transformational, management by fact, coaching, and contingency approach. Describe how management styles are influenced by an organization's size, industry sector, culture, and competitors. (Apply)
>
> **Body of Knowledge III.A.2**

Overview of Management Theories and Styles

The personal style one uses in working with others depends on many factors. One is the background and perspective of the individual manager, especially the assumptions made about what influences people's behavior. The characteristics exhibited by employees, individually and as a group, may also impact how a manager will approach an issue. A final factor is the particular situation. For example, the manager may act quite differently when carrying out the following two tasks: (1) a one-on-one discussion with an employee about a performance problem and (2) communicating to the entire organization the opportunities for learning that will be embedded in a new company initiative.

Several theories of management have been proposed over time that can help to explain different management styles. Following are some of the more widely known theories.

Scientific Management. Frederick Taylor was one of the first contributors to the scientific theory of management, which focused on finding the one best way to perform a task so as to increase productivity. Taylor emphasized the efficiency, not the satisfaction, of workers. He did this by breaking a job down into small-task components that could be studied to find the most efficient way of doing the task. Essentially, he separated thinking tasks from physical tasks, repositioning thinking tasks as the province of engineers, not the shop floor. Happening at a time when the workforce comprised poorly educated people with few skills, Taylor's approach significantly increased production. Ultimately, though, as more workers became skilled and better educated, the boredom and dissatisfaction of doing repetitive, unchallenging work began to decrease production.

Frank and Lillian Gilbreth also focused on increasing productivity. They developed the motion and time study method in order to analyze work processes. Henry Gantt (developer of the Gantt chart) proposed the concept of providing incentives to employees based on output.

Classical Organizational Theory. As organizations became larger and more complex, the study of management began to look at the management not only of individual tasks, but also the larger enterprise. Henri Fayol developed 14 principles of management that included issues such as how power and authority needed to be subdivided into reporting relationships, and the subordination of individual interests to the common good. Max Weber believed bureaucracy to be the ideal organizational structure since everyone would clearly understand their responsibilities, and lines of authority would provide more predictable and efficient output. Mary Parker Follett added the factor of relationships, both within the organization and between the organization and its environment, as a consideration for management.

Human Relations Theory. In the 1930s researchers performed a series of studies at the Hawthorne Works plant of Western Electric Company to determine the best level of lighting, length of workday, and length of rest periods to maximize worker productivity. As the lighting in the plant was increased, production levels rose. Surprisingly, production levels also rose as light levels were decreased. Researchers eventually determined that the increase in productivity was correlated not to lighting levels, but to the fact that the workers were involved in the study. This change in behavior due to being singled out for attention, now commonly called the *Hawthorne effect*, clearly shows the importance of human factors in motivating employees. Human relations theory then brought a focus on workers—both individually and as a social system.

Behavioral Theories. Behavioral theory is the background on which many motivational theories are based. Two landmark theories related to motivation are discussed in Chapter 2, Section 4. They are Abraham Maslow's hierarchy of needs and Frederick Herzberg's two-factor theory (satisfiers and dissatisfiers).

Douglas McGregor formulated the *theory X versus theory Y* model. Theory X is a negative view of human nature, assuming that most employees do not want to work and will require continual prodding. Theory Y is a positive view, believing that employees want to work and will seek responsibilities that can offer solutions to organizational problems and their own personal growth. Consistently treating workers under either of the assumptions tends to be a self-fulfilling prophecy.

Learning Theories. There are several theories of how people learn. David Kolb formulated the experiential learning model whereby a person (1) has an experience,

(2) reflects on the experience, (3) develops abstract theories based on the experience, and (4) applies what he or she has learned.[1] When the knowledge is applied, it then creates another experience, and the cycle continues (see Figure 8.1). The model is useful not only for designing training programs, but also for understanding how people react to certain types of training since most people tend to prefer particular phases of the learning cycle. For example, some prefer hands-on learning (phases 1 and 4), while others prefer abstract thinking (phases 2 and 3).

Knowledge of one's style can be assessed by a learning style instrument such as the *Learning Styles Questionnaire* by Honey and Mumford. The knowledge can be used to help one identify learning opportunities that one would find more comfortable or desirable, or can help people to know in which areas they might want to expand their learning repertoire.

Howard Gardner proposed that there are multiple types of intelligence, and that people will learn better if the learning experience enables them to apply their own strengths. The intelligences include:

- *Linguistic.* Skilled in the use of words

- *Logical/mathematical.* Skilled in the analysis of concepts

- *Visual/spatial.* Skilled with manipulating symbolic relationships

- *Musical.* Skilled with sound

- *Kinesthetic.* Skilled in physical touch or movement

- *Interpersonal.* Skilled in relationships with others

- *Intrapersonal.* Skilled in self-analysis and development

Differences in skill levels in each of the seven intelligences impact how well one will learn various subjects and in different environments. Most training has traditionally focused on the first two intelligences, while accelerated learning techniques often integrate others in order to take advantage of different learning styles and how each fits with a particular aspect of the topic.

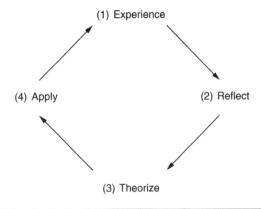

Figure 8.1   Kolb's experiential learning model.

Another view of cognitive learning style focuses on preferences of the learner from two different angles: (1) Do you prefer to receive information in a verbal format or in visual images? and (2) Do you prefer a holistic view or to analyze the details? These two perspectives then create four different combinations of learning styles. Instructors need to ensure that material is not presented in a way that puts one particular style at a significant disadvantage.

Behavior Management. Behavior management is an adaptation of B. F. Skinner's behavior modification/operant conditioning studies. Performance management is a technique involving an analysis of the antecedents of a behavior and the consequences of that behavior for the purpose of reinforcing desirable behavior to obtain or maintain positive consequences. The phrase "positive reinforcement for work done well" has become embedded in many of the processes for training and managing people in organizations.

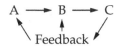

Upon completion of an analysis, a manager can deduce whether the antecedent is appropriate and whether the consequences are positively reinforcing the behavior to the extent that the behavior is likely to be repeated. A–B–C means:

- A—*The antecedent, the trigger that initiates a behavior.* Examples include:
  - A work order received by a machine operator
  - A sign directing pedestrian traffic around an obstacle
  - A customer 's inquiry about her stock market account
  - A nurse frowning when a patient flinches during an injection
- B—*The behavior initiated by the antecedent.* Examples include:
  - The operator starts the job.
  - Pedestrians follow the directions on the sign.
  - The customer service representative (CSR) looks up the account and answers the inquiry.
  - The patient complains about the pain inflicted by the nurse.
- C—*The consequences, to the observed person or group, from the behavior.* Examples include:
  - The worker is satisfied that the job started without a problem.
  - The pedestrians go about their business, without harm and mostly without noticing what they just did.
  - The customer is satisfied with the response of the CSR, but dissatisfied with the outcome of her investment.

- The nurse is defensive, stating that she couldn't help it and it was only a slight "pinch." The patient grumbles and suggests the nurse learn how to do her job correctly.

An antecedent initiates a behavior, but the consequences of that behavior influence the performer's behavior in the next similar situation. In these situations:

- The machine operator may anticipate a trouble-free startup of the next job.

- The pedestrians follow posted directions the next time they encounter a posting.

- The investor seeks out the same CSR when she has another question. The CSR thinks of ways to draw a positive inference from the negative performance of customers' accounts.

- The nurse gripes to other nurses about her experience. The patient tells everyone he encounters about the incompetent nurse. The nurse is nervous when making another injection, tending to make a poor and hurtful insertion of the needle.

Consider the following scenario: John, a new employee, has just undergone training as a bank teller. He is assigned a window and told to begin to serve customers as they step up. He is also told that his performance will be observed and that a discussion will be held, after John has been on duty for two hours, between John and the observer to mutually discuss ways John's performance can be improved.

One of the key points made in the training is to frequently use the customer's name during a transaction. It is this basic behavior that the observer will be targeting in the first improvement discussion. The observer prepares an A–B–C behavior collection form (see Figure 8.2) and stations herself as another teller (with a closed window) next to John.

The observer collects data from the customer interactions. She analyzes the data and prepares to discuss the findings with John.

In the improvement discussion, John is made aware of his behavior and asked what he feels he can do to improve. The observer intervenes with suggestions to

Antecedent	Behavior	A/U	Consequences	P/N	I/D	Impact

A = Acceptable   U = Unacceptable   P = Positive   N = Negative   I = Immediate   D = Delayed

Figure 8.2   Analysis of behavior template.

Source: Reprinted with permission of R. T. Westcott & Associates.

consider, as appropriate. The two mutually agree on a plan of action. John returns to his window to try out the agreed-on changes while the observer collects a new set of data. John is recognized for his use of the desired behavior, if used once or used every time appropriately.

The approach is repeated until John has mastered the desired behavior and has been recognized for work done well.

Possible unintended outcomes from consequences are (1) feedback to the performer is unrelated to desired behavior (inadequate, incorrect for circumstances, not constructive, nonexistent) and (2) consequences tend to reinforce the wrong or inappropriate behavior (extinguishes good behavior rather than stimulating and sustaining desired behavior).

Performance/behavior management has been misused in some organizations and has received some bad press because it is perceived to manipulate people against their will. On the plus side, however, behavior management has achieved mutually beneficial positive outcomes for the individual and the organization when properly used with good intent.

Daniels states, "If you work with other human beings, you are subject to the laws of behavior. And if you don't understand them, more than likely you're impeding, possibly depressing, the performance of your employees, your peers, even yourself."[2]

Situational Leadership/Management. Paul Hersey and Ken Blanchard's *situational leadership* model and instrument (see Chapter 2, Section 1) is useful for the leader-manager in appropriately applying the right amount of direction and supporting behavior to followers as they progress through the four maturity levels.[3] It is also helpful in understanding why performance problems may arise when new procedures are introduced, reorganizations occur, and new members are added (or removed) from a work group or team. It is important for the leader-manager to realize that the process of progressing through the stages will need to differ from person to person, work group to work group, and situation to situation.

Systems Thinking. Peter M. Senge, in *The Fifth Discipline*, discusses the five disciplines of the learning organization: systems thinking, personal mastery, mental models, building shared vision, and team learning. He points out that these disciplines should develop as an ensemble. Systems thinking is the fifth discipline; it blends the disciplines into a coherent body of theory and practice. Systems thinking shifts our mental focus from perceiving ourselves as separate from the rest of the world to being connected to the world.

Through a series of diagrams, Senge maps what he calls *systems archetypes.* Each archetype is described and a principle is stated as well as one or more examples. These diagrams feature feedback loops. Upon mastering this systemic language, the subconscious becomes trained to think in terms of circles rather than straight lines.

Senge states, "While traditional organizations require management systems that control people's behavior, learning organizations invest in improving the quality of thinking, the capacity for reflection and team learning, and the ability to develop shared visions and shared understandings of complex business issues. It is these capabilities that will allow learning organizations to be both more locally controlled and more well-coordinated than their hierarchical predecessors."[4]

Part III.A.2

Complexity Theory. The growing body of knowledge on complexity theory and complex adaptive systems signals the emergence of a meaningful management concept. As a generalization, complexity theory is concerned with the interaction between the parts of a system, as well as the interaction between the system and its environment. A whole complex system can not be fully understood by analyzing its elements. The interactions tend to change and shift. Consider that "The capacity for self-organization is a property of complex systems which enables them to develop or change internal structure spontaneously and adaptively in order to cope with, or manipulate, their environment."[5]

Okes discusses five ways complexity theory can be used to manage and improve organizational performance:

1. Ensure that the mission, values, goals, and priorities of the system are clear.

2. Provide only as much control as necessary for each system.

3. Ensure there is sufficient feedback from the environment so the system can detect and act on signals indicating a need for change.

4. Monitor a wide range of system performance metrics to understand more fully how well the organization is performing.

5. Make many small changes rather than major disruptions to improve system performance.[6]

As these examples indicate, many existing quality management practices support the view of organizations as complex adaptive systems. When and how each should be applied depends on the type of organization and its current situation. Complexity theory provides a lens through which such decisions can be made more easily.

Managerial Grid. Blake and Mouton proposed the managerial grid, a two-axis perspective of managerial attention. The *x*-axis indicates the amount of focus on accomplishing a task, and the *y*-axis a measure of concern for people. A manager who has little of either, of course, is considered to be not carrying out his or her duties. Someone high on task but low on people is focused on authority, while someone high on people but low on task is viewed as a "country club" manager. The ideal in this normative model is a high priority for both task and for people, asking for commitment by all to accomplishing common organizational goals.

Seven Habits. Stephen R. Covey's model and instruments amplify his *Seven Habits of Highly Effective People*. Progressing from *dependence* through *independence* to *interdependence*, the basic model addresses:

- Being proactive

- Beginning with the end in mind

- Putting first things first

- Thinking win–win

- Seeking first to understand, then to be understood

- Synergizing

- Sharpening the saw (exercising the four dimensions of renewal)

  - Physical (exercise, nutrition, stress management)

  - Social/emotional (service, empathy, synergy, intrinsic security)

  - Spiritual (value clarification and commitment, study and meditation)

  - Mental (reading, visualizing, planning, writing)

Covey postulates that organizations function according to principles, whether or not leaders are aware of them. He emphasizes the importance of understanding these principles and how they interact with organizational functions to enable effective changes in quality. His term *principle-centered leadership* applies the seven habits to organizational change.[7] Covey and Gulledge assert that by applying the seven habits at four levels (personal, interpersonal, managing, and the organization's strategy, systems, and structures) an effective environment of trustworthiness can be attained to enable change to be perceived as positive.[8]

Tools

Dominance, Influence, Steadiness, Conscientiousness Instrument. The DiSC profiling instrument is based on William Marston's theories. It measures characteristic ways of behaving in a particular environment. The DiSC dimensions are:

- *Dominance.* This dimension emphasizes shaping the environment, overcoming opposition, and accomplishing results.

- *Influence.* This dimension emphasizes influencing (or persuading) others in shaping the environment.

- *Steadiness.* The emphasis in this dimension is on cooperating with others within the existing circumstances in order to perform a task.

- *Conscientiousness.* The focus of this dimension is performing conscientiously to ensure quality and accuracy within existing conditions.

Within each dimension, the respondent's tendencies and desires are surfaced. An action plan is suggested, including the characteristics of other persons needed and the steps to be taken in order for the respondent to be more effective. DiSC increases self-awareness and points to ways the information can be used in relations with others.

Myers-Briggs Type Indicator. Isabel Myers and Katharine Cook Briggs devised a method of assessing personality type based on Carl Jung's theory of personality preferences. The Myers-Briggs Type Indicator (MBTI) looks at how one approaches life based on the following four bipolar scales:

(E)—Extraverted	or	(I)—Introverted
(S)—Sensing	or	(N)—Intuitive
(T)—Thinking	or	(F)—Feeling
(J)—Judging	or	(P)—Perceiving

Following is a brief summary of the pairs:

- An E gets energy by interacting with other people, while an I prefers to be alone to think things through.

- An S wants lots of detailed information in order to make a decision and is here-and-now oriented, while an N will go with a general hunch and is future oriented.

- Someone who is a T makes decisions based on logic and facts, while an F places more consideration on the emotional impact.

- J people are concerned about getting things organized and completed, while P folks want to keep exploring alternatives.

Personal style is determined by the MBTI instrument scores, defined in sixteen possible styles (for example, ENFP, INTJ, ISFP) with each having a relatively unique (but overlapping) way of looking at the world. The model is useful for helping individuals understand their own behaviors as well as those of others.

The MBTI instrument can therefore be used as a team-building tool whereby members of a team assess and discuss their respective styles, and how it has (or will) impact their way of working together. It can also be used in forming groups, for example, making sure that membership is not too highly skewed in a particular direction (for example, making quick, intuitive decisions, or wanting to collect more and more information to ensure that all possible viewpoints have been considered). The MBTI is in active use after many years of successful application.

A–B–C Analysis. The A–B–C analysis template is used in the systematic analysis of the behavior observed of an individual or a work group. The purpose of the analysis is to collect data that, when analyzed, may indicate what is causing or inhibiting specific behaviors. (See *behavior management* earlier in this chapter.)

Interaction of Management Theories and Management Styles

The theories presented so far offer many different views of management. The personal style that an individual manager takes will be impacted by the theories he or she believes to be more useful, as well as education, past experiences, and view of work and the world. Following are some of the resulting management styles:

- *Autocratic management.* Autocratic managers are concerned with developing an efficient workplace and have little concern for people. They typically make decisions without input from subordinates, relying on their positional power.

- *Participative management.* Participative managers are primarily concerned with people, but might also attempt to balance this concern with the business concerns of the organization. Participative managers allow and encourage others to be active in the decision-making process.

Another approach to participative management is *management by walking around* (MBWA). It encourages managers to periodically roam throughout the organization and talk to employees, listen, and look for improvement opportunities. This technique motivates managers to stay in touch with the people who actually perform the work—those who experience problems firsthand.

- *Transactional leadership.* A transactional style is one in which the manager views the relationship as one of getting the work done through clear definition of tasks and responsibilities, and providing whatever resources are needed.

- *Transformational leadership.* Transformational leadership is a style whereby a leader articulates the vision and values that are necessary in order for the organization to succeed. It is sometimes equated to charismatic leadership, but is aimed more at elevating the goals of subordinates and enhancing their self-confidence to achieve those goals. Bob Galvin accomplished this transformational leadership at Motorola with the Six Sigma program, an approach that, at the time, positioned Motorola to become a high-quality, reliable competitor in its market.

- *Management by fact.* A key emphasis of quality management is that decisions should be based on data such as performance measures and process improvement facts. This style is reinforced by the Baldrige Performance Excellence Program and the ISO 9000 series requirements.

- *Coaching.* A key differentiation in organizational performance is the ability to develop and effectively empower employees. Providing guidance and constructive feedback to employees to help them better apply their natural talents and to move beyond previous limitations has become a style of management. In this role, managers ask questions that will help others reach a conclusion rather than the manager making the decision for them.

- *Contingency approach.* Although many factors have the potential to positively affect performance, substantial obstacles often exist for managers who try to use a formula or single theory. For example, Locke and Schweiger, in their research into the subject of whether participation enhances productivity, did not find clear support for this premise.[9] One reason could be the difficulty of effectively implementing a participative management system.

Other management styles might be more productive in certain environments and conditions. For example, in some cases, the costs of employee participation (ergo, training and support) might be greater than the potential cost benefits and intangible benefits that can be achieved. In some situations, an autocratic management style might achieve superior performance over a participative style, such as when decisions must be made rapidly with information only available to the manager. For example, it is difficult to imagine that the captain of a sinking ship would have better results if he or she approached the crew using a participative style.

The contingency approach is a good place to end this section. It emphasizes that there is not one right way to manage, to learn, or to look at the world, as highlighted by Deming's system of profound knowledge. Managers need to have a good understanding of organizational theory, what drives people, and how learning occurs if they are to effectively utilize the human resources that make up their organizations. Matching people to the job, matching training design to the learners, and matching one's management style to the specific person and/or situation are fundamental to management.

Organizational Culture

The culture that results from the manner in which work is carried out, as well as outsiders' views (customers, suppliers, shareholders, community, and competitors), shape the way members of an organization relate to each other and to the world outside.

An organization is the integration of two major systems:

- The technical system, which defines how products and services are to be realized (and includes the equipment, work processes and procedures, and human resources to carry out the processes).

- The social system, consisting of how people communicate, interrelate, and make decisions. A manifestation of the social system is called *culture*, which is evidenced by employee behaviors.

Culture is a function of the artifacts, values, and underlying assumptions shared by members of the organization.[10] It can be shaped by communicating what standards of behavior are expected and ensuring that policies, procedures, promotions, and day-to-day decisions are appropriately aligned. Culture is manifested in such ways as:

- How power is used or shared

- The organization's orientation toward risk or safety

- Whether mistakes are punished, hidden, or used to guide learning and improvement

- How outsiders are perceived and treated

- Vision, mission, principles, policies, protocols, procedures, and practices

- Artifacts, layout, and amenities (for example, furnishings, artwork, open versus closed work spaces, employee time-out spaces, signage, and so on)

Members new to an organization are soon acclimated to the culture through training and both formal reinforcement and peer influence.

The design of the organization has an impact on culture. If a hierarchical structure restricts cross-functional communications, then close relationships between interrelated functions will be more difficult. Similarly, in a unionized organization the relationship between organization management and union management will set the stage for how cooperatively people are able to work together toward common goals.

Culture will have a significant impact on quality when it is shaped by the words and actions of leadership, how work systems are designed, and what gets recognized and rewarded. If the culture is not proactive, is not focused on customers, and does not use data to guide decision making, the organization is not likely to be highly successful in the continual improvement of quality.

Visible artifacts and the metaphors used to describe an organization are often superficial indicators of culture. For example, a company that talks of "killing the competition" and creates a graphic display showing competitors being "wiped out" would convey a focus on competitors rather than on customers.

Examining the beliefs and values espoused by members of the organization requires deeper probing than just observing obvious things. For example, in a family-owned business, the predominant values are often those of the founder(s). Those values may persist long after the death of the founding individual(s).

At an even deeper level are the shared tacit assumptions of which the organization's members may not be consciously aware. Failure to surface and consider these assumptions can result in serious blunders, for example, a failure to understand the mutual level of demonstrated trust needed for management to introduce major change in a unionized organization where an adversarial relationship persists.

Juran lists five steps for changing to a quality culture:

1. Create and maintain an awareness of quality.

2. Provide evidence of management leadership on quality.

3. Provide for self-development and empowerment.

4. Provide participation as a means of inspiring action.

5. Provide recognition and rewards.[11]

Changing an organization's culture is difficult and requires time. Fear of change must be removed, poor labor–management relations must be resolved, and the company's focus must move away from the status quo. Employees should be convinced of the benefits that a quality management approach will provide, and should buy in to the changes. This often means that employees at all levels will need to change behaviors or perform tasks in a different manner. If strong leadership, motivation, and enthusiasm are lacking, frustration and stress will result.

3. INTERDEPENDENCE OF FUNCTIONAL AREAS

> Describe the interdependence of an organization's areas (human resources, engineering, sales, marketing, finance, research and development, purchasing, information technology, logistics, production, and service) and how those dependencies and relationships influence processes and outputs.
> (Understand)
>
> **Body of Knowledge III.A.3**

The concept of an organization consisting of a system of interacting processes is widely accepted. The quality management system standard ISO 9001 stresses this concept, up to a point. (ISO 9001 doesn't specifically include *all* the functions of an organization.) The Baldrige Performance Excellence Program is more inclusive, covering all the functional components of the business. Yet, in spite of the emphasis placed on systems thinking, many organizations still consist of functional silos or fiefdoms. Such internal silos tend to foster dysfunctional attitudes and behaviors, such as (partial list):

- Optimizing the operation of the subunit to the detriment of the overall organization. (Referred to as *suboptimization.*)

- Having a "that's not my job" attitude—throw it over the wall for the next unit to worry about.

- Inhibiting interunit communication and keeping knowledge in the unit.

- Hiding mistakes. Don't tell, it could make us look bad.

- Competing—attempting to get all the resources we can get, regardless of other units' needs.

- Protecting the boss's reputation at all costs, so he or she will protect us.

- Being wary of the units who provide product or services to us, and the units to which we provide product or services.

- Ignoring the external customer—unless we are in sales or customer service, we have nothing to do with them.

- Making sure we spend all the budget money allocated to us. If we don't, next year's allotment may be reduced.

- Resisting efforts to enlist our unit's people in cross-functional teams.

And the list goes on.

The structuring of an organization into semiautonomous work units or departments developed with the hierarchical, autocratically run organization. The emphasis in this type of organization is centralization of decision making (power and control), the specialization (education and experience) of the incumbents, and a focus on maintaining the status quo.

The modern perspective is a business organization as a system—a group of interrelated processes designed to accomplish a mission. Many of these processes call for specialized skills or functions. At the same time, the organization is not a stand-alone entity—it is part of a larger system that includes other organizations, society, and the world. An organization must ensure that its role in the larger system is carried out appropriately. This requires (1) an awareness of outside issues that affect the organization and (2) knowledge of how to manage the process of interfacing with those external functions.

Business functions can be classified as external or internal. *External* business functions are those that have dealings with the outside world, such as safety, legal, regulatory, product liability, and environmental, and maintaining knowledge of laws, regulations, and standards mandated by authorities at the local, state, federal, and/or international levels. Other external business functions that must be managed include technological and process-oriented activities that might be driven by the competitive or industry environment within which an organization operates.

Internal business functions are those that operate within the boundaries of the organization, including sales, marketing, engineering, purchasing, production, human resources, finance, research and development, information technology, logistics, and other services. Collectively, these types of business functions affect the ability of the organization to meet and adapt to changes in customer and market requirements.

The distinction between external and internal functions exists in traditional, for-profit businesses as well as in not-for-profit educational or government organizations. Regardless of whether the organization is departmentalized according to function, product, customer, geography, process, or a matrix form, both internal and external business functions will exist.

The size and priority of a firm's various functions will also depend on the particular product or service being provided. For example, a firm that deals with dangerous chemicals or drugs will have larger legal, environmental, and safety functions. Companies in fast-changing fields, such as the telecommunications and computer industries, will have a larger research and product development function. In a labor-intensive business, human resources and training might be classified as separate functions; in a capital-intensive business, these functions might be combined, with training being a subset of the human resources function.

Internal Functions

Internal functions are those activities that create and operate the processes that enable the organization to accomplish its mission. Such functions would differ between a manufacturing organization, a healthcare organization, and an educational institution. The following list examines internal business functions found in a manufacturing setting. Although the names may change in a healthcare, banking, or government organization, the same basic processes typically occur.

- *Information technology* is a core enabler for an enterprise. The information technology function is responsible for providing technology that will allow the organization to effectively acquire, process, store, and access information that is of value for achieving results. Information technology strategy should be driven by business strategy rather than simply by adopting the latest technology. Because of the pace of change in information technology, all or parts of the function may be outsourced, and that requires an effective process for managing the subcontractor.

- *Finance* is responsible for planning, controlling, and reporting the flow of monetary funds into and out of the enterprise. It oversees the acquisition of both operating and capital funds. The finance function provides a structure used by the business for budgeting and accounting for operating receipts and expenditures, and ensures that any excess funds are invested until needed. This group reports on the organization's financial status both internally (for example, for monthly operating reviews) and externally (for example, to the Securities and Exchange

Commission [SEC] and to shareholders in the form of cash flow statements and balance sheets). (See Section 5 of this chapter.)

- *Human resources* is responsible for recruiting, training, and, as needed, terminating employment of the organization's personnel. It also oversees compensation systems, development of people for future needs (for example, career and succession planning), and resolution of people problem issues in accordance with the organization's policies and any existing labor–management contract. The human resources function also is usually responsible for ensuring that company policies do not violate laws, such as the Americans with Disabilities Act (ADA) and discrimination laws regulated by the Equal Employment Opportunity Commission (EEOC). In unionized companies the function also coordinates, or is involved with, negotiating labor contracts, and with ongoing labor relations.

- *Marketing* has the responsibility for ensuring that potential customers are aware of who the organization is and what it does, as well as to help translate potential customer needs into product or service opportunities for the organization. It develops communication channels, for example, advertising and timely news releases, using appropriate and available media, to keep the organization visible. Marketing is usually driven by and aligned to the strategic direction of the business to support growth, diversification, and broadening market penetration.

- *Product development* works closely with marketing and sales to develop the products that fulfill changing customer needs. This often drives technological breakthroughs.

- *Sales and customer service* functions work closely with present and potential customers to match their specific needs to current product offerings, resulting in a customer order. Customer service supports sales by ensuring that order requirements are clearly and accurately defined and are communicated to the scheduling function. It also monitors orders to ensure that they are fulfilled as contracted. Customer service also handles customer complaints and product returns.

- *Materials management* (or *logistics*) is often broken into three different functions: purchasing, production control, and inventory management. The *purchasing* process is responsible for identifying suppliers who can deliver needed materials for production—as well as maintenance, repair, and operations items—on time and at an appropriate quality level and price. The supplier management process also includes placing orders and monitoring supplier performance, often helping to improve suppliers, or replacing them if necessary improvements are not made.

  The *inventory management* function includes receiving purchased materials and issuing materials to production. This function also provides warehousing for raw materials as well as finished product. Disposition of scrapped material/ product is also included.

  Production control schedules production of customer orders and arranges for transportation of finished products to the customer. This process is often a key business measurable as customer order fulfillment is determined by both available quantity to meet requirements and on-time delivery.

- *Engineering* can take many forms depending on the particular industry, product line, or organization philosophy. The types of engineering functions include:

- *Product engineering.* Converting the concepts from the marketing or research and development functions into viable products and specifications

- *Process engineering.* Designing product realization work processes, procedures/instructions; developing, acquiring, and installing equipment (for example, machinery, tooling, gaging) that can consistently and effectively produce the organization's products

- *Industrial engineering.* Optimizing workplace layout and material work flow, consideration of ergonomics in process design, and setting and monitoring production standards

- *Facilities engineering.* Maintaining the building, land, central services (HVAC and water), and machinery

• *Research and development* is the process of exploring potential developments and new ideas in order to identify possible new products, services, or processes that can fulfill previously untapped opportunities, and/or replace those that are in the later stages of the product life cycle.

• *Operations* (production) is the key element of any manufacturing organization. In fact, many plants have no responsibility but production, as all other functions are performed off-site. The production function manages the flow of material and its conversion from a raw state to a finished state. All resources—energy, materials, supplies, equipment, and human labor—are combined to make this conversion.

• *Quality* supports the other functions of the organization by defining and ensuring the use of operational systems that meet customer requirements. The quality function supports internal functions by providing special skills necessary for day-to-day operations, for example, supporting human resources in developing a quality-related training curriculum for new employees, and assisting other functions in their continual improvement efforts. The quality function also provides quality control services, for example, product inspection, instrument and equipment calibration, and quality-related training.

Integrated Business Processes

A higher-level view of an organization is shown in Figure 8.3, demonstrating how the various functions must work together in order to become an integrated business system. Strategy development and deployment (see Chapters 5, 6, and 7) is the primary responsibility of senior management. Customer relationship management includes the processes primarily carried out by marketing, sales, and customer service. Product/process technology management includes R&D and various engineering functions that design new products and processes. Order fulfillment includes the functions that acquire and transform raw materials, and deliver the final product to customers. Support processes are the staff functions that provide specialized expertise, for example, information, employees, performance reporting, and enabling the other business processes to work effectively.

Part III.A.3

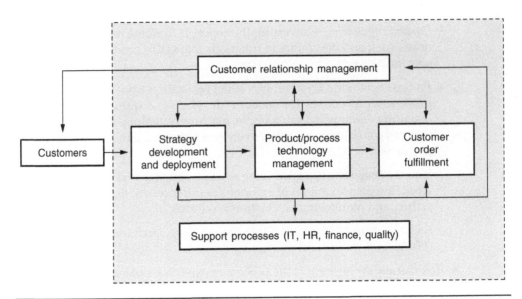

Figure 8.3   Major business processes.

This view of a business emphasizes the interrelationships of the many activities that take place. On a day-to-day basis, work occurs across organizational boundaries, requiring that employees have an understanding of the bigger picture. For example, to the patient who goes to an outpatient clinic at a hospital for an arm injury, it is a single organization. To those within the hospital, at least four different functions are involved—admissions, radiology, subacute care, and billing. Although a different individual oversees each function, and each may have its own mission statement, they must understand how their processes are interconnected in order to serve the overall organizational mission—and the patient.

One problem that often occurs is that each function or department within an organization tries to optimize its own performance without considering the impact on performance (suboptimization) of the overall enterprise. To continue with the arm injury example, consider what can occur if the admissions clerk tries to perform the activity as quickly as possible, attempting to reduce the queue of patients. Some of the effects on radiology, billing, the entire hospital, or the patient might be:

- The patient gets lost due to poor directions to the radiology lab.
- The wrong type of X-ray is taken, and the patient is misdiagnosed and has complications and/or must have additional X-rays taken.
- The bill is sent to the wrong address.
- The treatment is incorrectly coded, and insurance refuses to pay.

It is therefore vitally important that people and functions within an organization understand the system in which they have a role, and how their activities contribute to or detract from overall organizational performance. Optimization of one area often can conflict with efforts to optimize the overall system. Employees must collaborate across functional boundaries, a process for which team structures are vitally important (see Chapter 3).

A classical example of cross-functional collaboration is the process of *concurrent engineering* (also called *simultaneous engineering*), often used by manufacturing companies to expedite the development and launch of new products. The design and launch process has traditionally been done sequentially (see Figure 8.4a) whereby sales talks to the customer, then tells product engineering what to develop. Product engineering creates specifications and drawings for the new product, and hands them over to manufacturing engineering to figure out how it can be made. Manufacturing engineering designs and purchases equipment and tooling, then hands it over to production to operate. This process is frequently called "over the wall" product development, where each department believes that it has completed its task when the next department becomes involved.

In order to overcome the inherent problems with this process, concurrent engineering applies the team concept to get all key players involved simultaneously (see Figure 8.4b). It is a multidisciplinary approach that typically involves product design and manufacturing engineers; sales, purchasing, quality, and financial personnel; and also key suppliers of raw materials and production equipment. By having all work together throughout the product and process development and launch cycle, many errors that would typically be found only after beginning

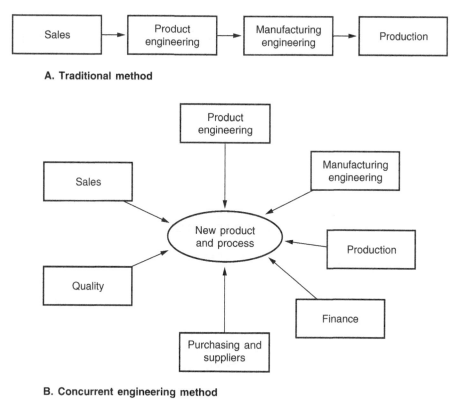

A. Traditional method

B. Concurrent engineering method

Figure 8.4   New product design and launch process.

production are prevented. Concurrent engineering invests the time in design changes before launch of the product, while the traditional method relies on continual engineering changes during production to address the problems. Cross-functional collaboration is a critical component of concurrent engineering and performance of any business process.

Systems Thinking

In thinking of an organization as a system, some caveats are:

- Be clear and objective as to what is to be changed or improved.

- Be specific as to what the desired outcomes from a change are.

- Be prepared to be flexible and adaptable as to the receptivity of feedback received.

- Accept that systems changes need effort and alignment from the outside in, not from the inside out.

- The whole system is more important than its parts; relationships and processes are paramount.

- Every system is linked to other larger or smaller systems in a hierarchy of systems.

- The quest for achieving a steady-state balance, although desired, can be perilous in the rapidly changing world.

- Entropy must be reversed or the system will perish.

- There are multiple ways to achieve the same preferred outcomes.

- Employees support what they participate in creating.

- Root causes and their effects typically do not occur within the same time frame and space.

- Systems consisting of many levels are too complex to fully comprehend and manage from a central control point.

- Solving problems at the level at which they were created is often not possible nor feasible.

Some of the advantages to systems thinking are:

- The organization is freer to commit to more than one approach or best practice relevant to achieving their strategy; for example, Six Sigma methodology is only one option of several available.

- Organizations can integrate multiple approaches, allowing:

  - Choice of the best management method or tool for the situation

  - Time to comprehend the principles and practices involved with each approach chosen, adapting each approach as needed

– More effective integration of each individual technique or tool with other approaches

• With the advent of new, more easily adaptable approaches and methodology, the organization is better equipped to subsume the new approach into its system without the trauma traditionally encountered.

• Systems thinking makes understanding relationships, system to system, easier. This is especially important in understanding and managing supply chain relationships.

• Systems thinking, when it permeates the entire organization, causes all employees to think of the interrelationships within their organization, as well as beyond the physical boundaries to the external stakeholders (that is, customers, suppliers, investors, regulatory agencies, community, and so on).

4. HUMAN RESOURCES (HR) MANAGEMENT

Apply HR elements in support of ongoing professional development: setting goals and objectives, conducting performance evaluations, developing recognition programs, ensuring that succession plans are in place where appropriate. Develop quality-supportive responsibilities to include in job descriptions for positions throughout the organization. (Apply)

Body of Knowledge III.A.4

Part III.A.4

Human Resources Functions

Depending on the size and purpose of the organization, the performance of the various functions relating to human resources may range from being wholly assumed by a person holding multifunctional responsibilities (as in a small organization) to a large HR department with several work units. Subfunctions of HR may include:

• Human resource planning, including succession planning

• Staffing

– Recruiting, interviewing, selecting, testing, hiring, assimilating

– Relocation administration

– Promotion, transfer administration

– Job fairs

- Training
  - Employee orientation
  - Management/supervisory education and training
  - Nonmanagement skills training and education
- Compensation
  - Wage/salary administration
  - Executive compensation administration
  - Job analysis
  - Job descriptions
  - Competency analysis
- Management performance appraisal
- Nonmanagement performance evaluation
- Payroll processing
- Benefits management
  - Insurance administration
  - Health and medical services
  - Vacation/leave processing
  - Pension/profit sharing plan administration
  - Tuition aid/scholarship administration
  - Thrift/savings plan administration
  - Suggestion system administration
  - Employee assistance program administration
  - Recreation/social recognition program administration
  - Career planning and support
  - Stock plan administration
  - Retirement plan administration
- Labor relations
  - Complaint/disciplinary procedures
  - EEOC compliance, affirmative action administration
  - Union/management relations
  - Contract negotiation
- Safety, security, and employee welfare

  - Safety program administration

  - OSHA compliance assessments

  - Security force management

  - Provide or arrange for counseling as needed (for example, substance abuse, family matters, health conditions, gambling, anger management, and so on)

- Employee termination, layoff, medical leave

  - Separation processing

  - Outplacement administration

  - Unemployment compensation administration

  - Worker's compensation administration

- Organization development

  - Employee satisfaction surveys

  - Organizational diagnoses

  - Organizational interventions

- Public relations

  - Community relations, fund drives

- Personnel records

  - Personnel records, reports, and database management

- Other

  - Employee communications, publications

  - Personnel research, for example, surveys

  - Food services

  - Library management

  - Travel arrangements administration

  - Administrative services (mail, phone, messengers, and so on)

  - Facility maintenance services

As you can see, HR is sometimes the home for diverse functions. However structured, there must be a strong collaborative relationship between the HR function, operations, and other staff functions.

Human Resources Responsibilities Shared by HR and Other Functional Managers. The responsibilities of managers of other functions, relative to HR, are to:

- Set functional human resources–related objectives aligned to the overall organization's strategic goals and objectives.

- Clearly communicate personnel resource requirements and specifications to the HR function.

- Learn and apply skills in interviewing job candidates.

- Follow the policies, procedures, and guidelines promulgated by the HR function.

- Learn and abide by the laws and regulations governing personnel behavior as they pertain to the function.

- Seek the counsel and guidance of the HR function on personnel legal issues, labor relations issues, safety, security, and employee welfare issues.

- Ensure that quality responsibilities are addressed in job descriptions and the evaluations/appraisals of employees' performance for all organizational levels within the function.

- Learn and apply a coaching style of managing, including effective performance feedback, and recognition of employees for work done well.

- Support the continual development of the function's personnel (career planning support, promotions, lateral movement to gain additional competence, training and education, and other opportunities for personal development).

- Create and maintain a succession plan for key positions within the function.

- Ensure that all employees in the function are treated fairly and justly.

Identifying Job Positions. Finding employees who will be positive contributors to an organization's mission is an inherently difficult process. Ideally, each employee should be a good fit to the company's values, have an interest in the specific product or service being provided to customers, and have the skills required for a specific position. At the same time, when an organization wants to be flexible, there is also a need to ensure that not everyone thinks alike. Different ideas are the core of innovation; however, this section will focus on finding, hiring, and retaining employees who have the skills for a specific position.

To know what staff is necessary, an organization must first understand the tasks to be performed and the skills necessary. On the basis of the organization's product and process technology, management philosophy, and organizational structure, the work activities are organized into specific job functions/titles, each of which will typically have a description of the primary responsibilities.

The manager who oversees the position should develop the job description, with a review by HR. Having an employee currently in that position also review the description is useful. Job descriptions typically state any educational and/or experience requirements, as well as the level of accountability and authority allocated to the position. The document also includes the following:

- Position title

- Basic job functions

- To whom the individual reports

- Titles of positions reporting to the individual

- Knowledge and skill requirements (including educational and experience qualifications when applicable)

- Limits of authority (for example, maximum dollar limits with respect to decision making)

- Specific job functions

- Performance standards

Any special physical requirements for the job (for example, ability to lift 100 pounds) may also be included in order to reduce the likelihood of legal action regarding discrimination under the Americans with Disabilities Act (ADA).

Some key quality-related processes and activities likely to be spelled out in job descriptions for management personnel who are not in the quality department include responsibility for:

- Supplier quality management—purchasing or materials manager

- Product reliability, design for manufacture, design change control—engineering manager

- Quality of manufactured product—production or manufacturing manager

- Quality of training and organization development—function manager

- Clarity of product application and quality needs—sales manager

- Quality of information and the processes to support it—information technology director

These and other quality responsibilities can be further detailed and included in job descriptions of other personnel within these departments. Job descriptions must also be regularly reviewed and revised in support of organizational changes and continual improvement.

Personnel Selection. Personnel needed for job openings can be obtained by internal promotion or through external recruitment. Internally promoted employees provide the advantage of being a known entity, have a familiarity with the company's products and processes, and may become fully productive more quickly. A disadvantage of promoting from within the company is the possibility that past relationships or performance might affect others' views of the individual and influence the individual's ability to perform. Hiring from outside has the potential of introducing new concepts and ideas.

When a position is to be filled, a list of potential candidates is developed. This can be done by advertising the position both internally and externally, by contacting an external recruiter, or by working with placement personnel from educational, professional, or other institutions. Applicants are then screened through a review of résumés; those applicants whose résumés generate the most interest will be invited to interview for the position. Although special skills and experience could be necessary for some positions (for example, accounting or welding), organizations sometimes consider candidates who they believe to have the aptitude, attitude, and flexibility for change and ability to learn, since specific skills are often developed once the person is hired.

Human resources personnel specially trained in interviewing techniques and protocols, as well as the department manager, typically perform the interviews. Depending on the position to be filled and the work design of the organization, peers and customers of the position to be filled could also participate in the interview process.

Employers are increasingly turning to various forms of preplacement testing. Tests might check for cognitive ability, intelligence, physical ability, personality, and interests. Any test administered must be proven valid and reliable and appropriate for the position for which the testing is done to avoid possible liability or discrimination claims. Checking candidate references is also a valuable step in the hiring process, but legal constraints must be carefully observed.

Once the best candidate has been identified, an offer is made regarding pay and benefits. If it is declined, the next suitable candidate may be offered the position. When the offer has been accepted, the individual must be oriented as to company facilities, people, and practices. The quality manager should ensure that the company's quality policies and procedures are included in such orientations.

Organizational expectations must be made clear to new employees. This includes the specific goals, objectives, actions, and behaviors. Such information should be documented to support the communication process and to allow tracking of performance.

One mistake often made by managers is treating staffing considerations in a reactive mode, responding only as positions become vacant. A more proactive view is that of establishing a succession plan that looks at key positions and individuals in the organization over time. Developing people who will be able to move into other positions makes the organization more responsive to change. Quality managers should ensure that positions critical to quality, especially their own, are considered in the succession planning.

Personnel Selection, Hiring, and Assimilation

Key managers often may participate in recruiting at colleges and job fairs. To perform this role, the manager should develop competence in the following:

- Reviewing of candidates' résumés and choosing potential interviewees

- Interview scheduling at the college or event

- Managing time (interviews often may last only 25 minutes, with five minutes between each interview to record information gathered during the interview)

- Asking questions within the parameters of pertinent laws, organizational policies, procedures, and guidelines

- Acquiring the key information needed to determine if there is a match between the organization's needs and the candidate's competencies, interests, and attitude

- Deciding which, if any, of the candidates interviewed should be selected for further interviewing back at the organization's site

- Compiling interview notes and preparing a report of the recruiting effort

Except for very small organizations, recruiting at the organization's site is usually performed by the HR function. HR, working from personnel requisitions or other specifications, will seek candidates to fill open positions. HR may use a variety of sources, for example, job postings, ads (TV, radio, website, internet searches, newspaper), employee referrals, walk-ins, and so on. HR will screen and contact candidates for the hiring manager to interview.

Managers who conduct selection interviews will need competency in:

- Predetermining the questions they will ask a candidate, and the criteria they will apply in recommending selection

- Managing time to ensure that the manager and the interviewee each obtain the information they require in making their decisions (for example, to consider working at the organization, to consider the candidate an acceptable fit for the organization)

- Asking questions within the parameters of pertinent laws, organizational policies, procedures, and guidelines

- Describing the organization's purpose, the requirements of the job/position under consideration, benefits, compensation range, and so on

- Deciding which candidate(s) are to be offered a job

Candidate interviews may be structured in several ways, such as:

- *One-to-one interview.* Hiring manager alone with candidate.

- *Panel interview.* Candidate faces more than one interviewer simultaneously.

- *Hierarchical interviews.* Candidate who passes interview with a lower-level manager is interviewed by the next higher-level manager with the possibility of being rejected at a succeeding level.

- *Peer interview.* Candidate is interviewed by his or her potential work peers. A variation is interviewing by persons who would be interacting with the candidate after hiring (for example, internal customers, suppliers, external officials, and so on).

- *Group interview.* Candidate is placed in a group with other candidates (often subjected to a series of scenarios) and required to respond to questions from several interviewers and interact with other candidates. In this competitive environment, candidates are evaluated against various criteria (for example, interpersonal skills, assertiveness, stress level, use of prior knowledge, adaptability, and so on).

The manager's responsibility is to collaborate with HR during the hiring process on the following matters:

- Determining the terms of the employment offer

- Obtaining necessary approvals for making the employment offer

- Negotiating terms with the candidate, if necessary

- Preparing for the new hire to enter the organization

  - Preparing coworkers

  - Preparing the workplace

  - Preparing an agenda for assimilation and training

  - Preparing informational materials the new employee will need

New Employee Assimilation. A person is usually highly motivated upon reporting for a new job. It's what is done to him or her after hiring that increases or diminishes the motivation. It is up to the manager to:

- Tell the new employee what performance is expected, and how and when the employee's performance will be evaluated

- Provide any needed skills training and/or education the new employee will need to succeed

- Coach the employee as he or she develops the competency to perform the work assigned

- Provide effective performance feedback to enable the employee to correct and/or improve performance

- Support and recognize work done well

- Support the employee's self-development

Employee Development. The objective of employee development is to improve employees' performance in their current positions as well as to prepare them for future roles or positions. Successful companies recognize the importance of the continuous professional development of employees, as evidenced by the number of companies who operate corporate universities.

The need for professional development is closely linked to the organization's goals and objectives, the individual employee's goals and objectives, and the organization's current performance. Employee development should include the active involvement of both the employee and the manager, with a focus on individual and business performance. Opportunities for development are often identified during the performance evaluation process.

In order to keep professional development aligned with business needs, it is important that everyone know where the business is headed (for example, mission and strategy) and what skills will be needed in the future. The personal interests of each employee should be taken into account as well. Management must be cognizant of employees' skills and abilities and be able to ascertain whether these skills and abilities are sufficient for meeting the organization's current or future needs. Timely plans can then be created to define skills to be developed, explain how this will be done, and ensure the provision of adequate resources.

The quality manager has two primary responsibilities regarding professional development. The first is to ensure that the skills being developed throughout the organization include those that will allow other functions to perform their duties well. Another is to develop the personnel within the quality department, including himself or herself. The American Society for Quality's certification programs and professional development courses are valuable resources for developing quality-related skills.

In earlier times, development of individuals was considered to be a responsibility of employers. During those times, managers led employees in formulating career development plans. Organizations published career ladders and steps individuals should take to broaden their knowledge and skills for growth and development. This effort was not universally successful. It became more apparent that the real responsibility for development rested with individuals, not their bosses. Now, and especially with a more mobile, transient workforce, personal development is the individual's responsibility, sometimes with some resources and support from their employer.

Figure 8.5 is a model showing the mutual investment made by the organization and the individual leading to the individual's growth and personal development. The inner circle suggests what the newly hired individual brings to the workplace, for example, work and life experience, education, capabilities, and aspirations (each individual is different, as characterized by the unique symbol). Some combination of the options, shown in the center ring, affect growth and development of the individual over time, for example, assignments, feedback, exposure to experts, training and education, and so on. As time passes, and the individual continues to grow and develop, certain career enhancements occur, for example, advancement, more money, enriched self-esteem, and so on. The organization's investment is suggested by the factors outside the concentric circles, which fuel the development.

In summary, *development* is an all-encompassing term embracing much more than education and training. Inasmuch as managers can not actually motivate an individual, but can provide an environment in which an individual feels motivated, so too, a manager can not actually develop an individual, but can provide opportunities and resources by which the individual, assuming a desire to do so, can grow and develop.

Performance Evaluation. Accurately evaluating staff performance is part of the continual improvement of an organization. Performance evaluation involves reviewing performance against expectations, identifying strengths and weaknesses, and creating an improvement plan. Performance evaluations are also considered for promotion and salary decisions, and as input into disciplinary actions.

To be fair, performance evaluations must be continual, fact based, and founded on clear, established, and communicated expectations. They must result in the

Part III.A.4

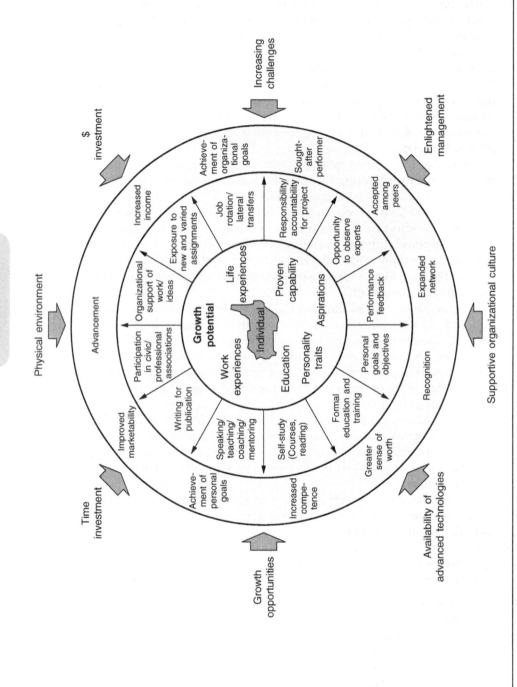

Figure 8.5   Mutual investment in individual development.

Source: Reprinted with permission of R. T. Westcott & Associates.

identification of areas where work is done well, and areas for improvement and/or corrective action. Performance evaluations should evaluate only areas deemed to be important, since they will lose credibility if they focus on trivial matters.

Performance evaluations usually involve scoring the individual's performance against predefined criteria (for example, goals and objectives) and often include narrative comments. Common problems with performance evaluations are that ratings are either forced into a normal distribution or everyone is rated about the same. An additional source of information for evaluation is a record of critical incidents maintained by the manager. This involves reviewing a log of behaviors (good or bad) that the employee used when facing a significant or difficult situation. Critical incidents that will be logged should also be communicated on a more immediate basis in order to provide the employee with feedback for continual improvement or corrective action.

A more recent development in performance evaluation is the involvement of more than the manager and the employee. Known as *360° feedback*, this method solicits feedback from peers, subordinates, and internal and external customers.

A fair performance appraisal system exists when it allows for interaction between manager and employee, and the following criteria are met:

- Expectations are clear and guidelines are established.

- The format (structure, time, place, and protocol) for the evaluation is consistent, with periodic meetings.

- Notes of performance, both good and bad, are discussed and recorded.

- Just-in-time training and/or coaching are used when work performance or behaviors are not appropriate.

- Disciplinary action rarely occurs as a result of the appraisal; however, if it does, an appeals process should be readily available.

- Assessments should consider consistency of output, presence of favorable or unfavorable environmental conditions, the ability to do a better job, the use of discretion (within limits), and the ability to work as part of a team.

- The evaluation should express whether the person grasps the quality aspects of the job and to what degree expectations were met.

Following are some problems that occur when a performance evaluation process is poorly managed:

- When appraisal is not done on a continuous or frequent basis, the performance review will result in some employees receiving unfair evaluation because of inaccuracies. Infrequent appraisals also fail to allow employees to rectify deficient performance in a timely manner.

- Annual reviews might be conducted late and done as a routine action to satisfy the higher-ups in the organization.

- Managers are not trained to give or receive feedback.

Experienced persons have expressed concerns about the use of performance appraisal systems. Deming stated that because the individual is part of a system, it is impossible to differentiate between the contribution of the individual versus the contribution of the system to the resulting performance.

An important role of the quality manager in the performance evaluation process is to ensure that the criteria used for evaluating personnel include measures that are related to product and organizational quality. Thoughtful and continual appraisal can help keep employees aligned with the mission of the organization.

Competency Analysis. Unlike job analysis, which is focused on the tasks contained within a job and the knowledge and skills required, a competency analysis focuses on the competencies of individuals performing the job. The five factors of competence—*knowledge, experience, skills, aptitude,* and *attitude* (KESAA)—are discussed in Chapter 3, Section 1. Figure 3.2 shows a KESAA requisites analysis form for collecting data.

Some of the reasons for conducting a competency analysis include gathering input to:

- Establish a job's level within a hierarchy of job levels and, as such, contribute to a determination of the compensation level of a job.

- Determine the exemplary performer in a work unit performing similar tasks for the purpose of setting or modifying performance standards.

- Help in selecting the members of a team.

- Augment the job description with competency criteria.

- Assess feasibility of job enlargement, job enrichment, and empowerment.

- Help to establish the specifications for a new hire.

- Conduct a competency gap analysis (desired versus present)

- Set objectives for improving competency.

- Determine and articulate the organization's core competency.

Staffing the Quality Function. Depending on the size of the organization, division- or corporate-level quality directors/managers could be involved in defining new strategic initiatives, integrating and standardizing quality methods across the organization, and transferring new technologies. They will often provide policy input to the operation-level quality function, but might not actually have a staff reporting to them.

The range of quality activities within an organization is large and is somewhat dependent on the industry; however, following is a list of typical job titles and activities within the quality function:

- *Vice president of quality.* Establishes the direction for the development and administration of the organization's quality initiatives. Consults with peers on the attitudes toward and practices of quality throughout the organization to develop an environment of continual improvement in every aspect of the organization's products and services. Acts as a champion for quality.

- *Director of quality.* Coordinates all aspects of the organization's quality program, such as developing and administering the program, training, coaching employees, and facilitating change throughout the organization. Responsible for participating in the establishment of strategic plans and policies, as well as procedures at all levels to ensure that the quality program will meet or exceed internal and external customers' needs and expectations.

- *Quality manager.* Ensures the administration of the organization's quality program within a defined segment of the organization.

- *Quality engineer.* Designs, installs, and evaluates quality process sampling systems, procedures, and statistical techniques. Designs or specifies inspection and testing mechanisms and equipment, analyzes production and service limitations and standards, and recommends revision of specifications when indicated. Formulates or helps formulate quality procedures and plans, conducts training on quality concepts and tools, and interfaces with all other engineering components within the company and with customers and suppliers on quality-related issues.

- *Quality specialist.* As their primary assignment, performs a specific quality-related function within the company's quality program (for example, quality training, auditing, or reliability testing). Has either received direct training or has been performing the activity for a number of years. Shows a high degree of skill performing the activity.

- *Quality supervisor.* Administers the company's quality program within a defined function of the organization. Has direct reports that implement some aspect of the policies, procedures, and processes of the quality program.

- *Quality analyst.* Initiates and/or coordinates quality-related data collection from production and service activities, and interprets and reports these data using statistical techniques.

- *Quality coordinator.* Collects, organizes, monitors, and distributes any information related to the functions of the quality department. Might also communicate information on the latest standards, procedures, and requirements related to the company's products or services. Typically generates reports using computer skills and distributes these reports to various users in the organization, customers, or suppliers.

- *Quality technician.* Performs basic quality techniques to track, analyze, and report on materials, processes, and products to ensure that they meet the organization's quality standards. Might calibrate tools and equipment.

Part III.A.4

- *Quality inspector.* Inspects and reports on materials, processes, and products using variable or attribute measuring instruments and techniques to ensure conformance with the organization's and customers' quality specifications.

- *Quality auditor.* Conducts system, process, product and/or supplier audits of conformance to the organization's quality standards, customers' standards, and/or standards of a third party.

- *Quality trainer.* Designs and conducts quality training programs and/or instructs quality modules of wider-scope training programs. Consults with the organization's training function on the inclusion of quality content in other pertinent training programs. Designs and instructs a quality-related train-the-trainer program for personnel who will be instructing in quality programs.

5. FINANCIAL MANAGEMENT

Read, interpret, and use various finance tools including income statements, balance sheets, and product/service cost structures. Manage budgets and use the language of cost and profitability to communicate with senior management. Use potential return on investment (ROI), estimated return on assets (ROA), net present value (NPV), internal rate of return (IRR), and portfolio analysis to analyze project risk, feasibility, and priority. (Analyze)

Body of Knowledge III.A.5

Speak the Language of Management

Increasingly, today's quality professional realizes there is a need to speak the language of management—finance. Whether it's participation in the strategic planning process, seeking approval for a process improvement project, justifying a quality management system implementation and certification, or preparation for a Baldrige-type award—approval and support is mainly based on financial outcomes.

ASQ has mounted an effort to assist quality practitioners in developing an "economic case for quality." Many trade journals, representing a wide variety of industries, are urging their industry members to create an economic case for their activities.

Even past attempts to justify expenditures solely through a simple return-on-investment (ROI) have often failed because the proposal does not relate the request to the organization's bigger picture. For example, a quality manager seeking approval for a major process improvement effort may, considered alone, estimate a reasonable ROI. The proposed initiative, however, may be more than the organization can currently fund based on its financial health, or there are other strategic matters that require the organization's more immediate attention and resources.

Learn some of the terms and tools of finance from guidance offered here and from suggested readings. Invest some time to get acquainted with the financial status of your own organization and the issues management considers important from a financial perspective. Importantly, determine where *quality* fits into the big picture and what it will take to link the measures of quality with the financial measures. Learn what "sells" to upper management and how to approach them.

Financial Reporting

Basic Statements. There are three basic financial statements. They are (1) the *balance sheet*, (2) the *profit and loss* or *income statement*, and (3) the *statement of cash flow.*

These three are considered the required statements under the *generally accepted accounting principles* (GAAP) guidelines. The Securities and Exchange Commission (SEC) requires a statement of shareholder 's equity in addition to the basic three.

Depending on the industry, size, and complexity of the organizational structure, and special requirements dictated by government entities, industry norms, and accounting practices, there may be a number of related reports prepared. For example, one public utility company prepares:

- Consolidated reports and reports for each subsidiary

- Variance reports comparing figures from several past periods with the current period

- Cash flow comparisons

- Capital requirements, past and projected

- Sales and deliveries by business segment and by type of product/ service

- Statement of shareholder's equity

- Statement of changes in net assets

- Statement of expenses by function

- Long-term debt comparisons

- Operating statistics—year-to-year comparison over five years

Bookkeeping Methods. There are two basic methods for bookkeeping: the cash basis and the accrual basis. The *cash basis* is simplistic: income is considered earned only when payment is actually received. Expenses are booked only when actually paid for. The cash basis is used by small organizations (small in physical size and small in the magnitude of transaction dollar amounts). The cash basis is simple, but from a control perspective, the revenues and expenses can mislead the decision maker because of the time gap between an action taken and when money is disbursed or collected.

Using the *accrual basis*, income is considered earned when goods or services have been sold or performed, although payment may not have been received. Expenses are booked as soon as they have been incurred, although they may not have been paid for.

The intent of the accrual basis is to be able to measure the results of operations by allocating to each period the income associated with operations of that period and all expenses and losses associated with the income of that period. This approach more accurately relates costs with income. The majority of organizations use the accrual method.

Many organizations prepare two types of financial statements: internal statements and external statements. *Internal statements* are produced at a macro level for management oversight and decision making. These statements present information about the whole organization. Micro-level reports are used at department level or below, and are oriented to operations, production, use of resources, and so on. *External statements* are prepared for disclosure to the SEC, lending institutions, investor-owners, the public, and other interested entities (depending on the organization's status as for-profit or not-for-profit). External documents are used by third-party auditors and accountants.

The Sarbanes-Oxley Act of 2002 (SOX), enacted after a series of financial scandals, mandates strict requirements for financial accounting and for top management's responsibility and accountability in disclosing the financial status of their organization.

The Balance Sheet. A *balance sheet* shows the assets, liabilities, and owner's equity. See Figure 8.6. It is so named because it conforms to the formula:

$$\text{Assets} = \text{Liabilities} + \text{Owner's equity}$$

The balance sheet components typically are:

- *Current assets.* Included are cash, short-term investments, accounts receivable (reduced by an amount for potential uncollectible accounts), inventory, and prepaid expenses. These assets are convertible to cash within a year. Adding the amounts for cash, short-term investments, and accounts receivable constitutes *quick assets.* Inventory may be valued by two common accounting methods: last in, first out (LIFO) or first in, first out (FIFO). LIFO would be used for materials that are usually stored loosely in piles (for example, sand and gravel). FIFO reflects the way inventory is typically used.

- *Property, plant, and equipment.* Such items are valued at *book value* (cost of acquisition) less applicable accumulated depreciation for the life of the asset.

- *Goodwill and other intangible assets.* This figure may represent the variance resulting from one company buying another for more money than the acquired company's net worth. Goodwill is usually amortized (decreased, written off) over some time period.

Total assets is one key determinant of an organization's size. Another is sales (reported in the income statement).

- *Current liabilities.* This figure represents liabilities that must be paid within a year. Included are accounts payable, dividends payable, accrued wages, and

Company LMN
Consolidated Balance Sheet
December 31, 2013
(In thousands of dollars)

Assets
Current assets

Cash	$ 20,178
Short-term investments	5,160
Accounts receivable (less allowance)	9,912
Inventories	33,428
Prepaid insurance expenses	966
Total current assets	69,644
Property and plant	55,113
Equipment, furniture, fixtures	99,875
Total property, plant, equipment	154,988
Less reserve for depreciation	53,288
Net property, plant, equipment	101,700
Goodwill	2,546
Total assets	173,890

Liabilities and owners' equity
Current liabilities

Accounts payable	$ 14,521
Dividends payable	1,085
Accrued wages and taxes	11,745
Federal, state taxes	5,639
Total current liabilities	32,990
Deferred income taxes	13,112
Long-term debt	31,524

Owners' equity

Preferred stock ($50 par value, 500,000 shares authorized)	
Common stock ($2 par value, 40,000,000 shares)	20,400
Retained earnings	75,864
Total owners' equity	96,264
Total liabilities and owners' equity	$173,890

Figure 8.6   Sample balance sheet.

taxes. Current assets minus current liabilities = working capital (funds for current operating purposes).

• *Deferred income taxes and long-term debt.* These figures comprise amortization of investment tax credits over the life of the asset and debts that will be payable after twelve months, mortgages beyond the next year, long-term promissory notes, and bonds.

- *Owner's equity.* This amount consists of what the owners (stockholders) have invested plus any profits returned to the organization in lieu of paying dividends. Owners'/stockholders' equity may be called *net worth* or *book value.* Therefore, what the business owns (assets) equals the amounts owed creditors plus the claim (equity) owners have on the business.

The Profit and Loss (or Income Statement). The *income statement* shows sales, costs, expenses, and profits for a given period of time, for example, a quarter or a year. See Figure 8.7. The components of an income statement are:

- *Net sales.* This figure represents the organization's *gross* income from the sales of products and services (revenue in not-for-profit organizations). When all costs and expenses are deducted from net sales, a profit or loss results.

- *Cost of goods sold.* This figure shows the cost of all the products that were sold during the accounting period represented by the statement.

- *Selling and administrative expenses.* Often itemized, these figures show what the organization spent to sell the products and operate the organization.

Company LMN Consolidated Income Statement December 31, 2013 (In thousands of dollars, excepting per-share amount)	
Net sales	$289,321
Costs and expenses	
Cost of goods sold	178,428
Selling and administrative expenses	55,743
Reserve for depreciation	7,725
Interest income	(1,335)
Total costs and expenses	240,561
Income before income taxes	48,760
Provision for income taxes	
Federal	12,856
State	2,865
Deferred	3,200
Total income taxes	18,921
Net income	$ 29,839
Net income per share	$ 1.46

Figure 8.7   Sample income statement.

- *Reserve for depreciation.* This figure represents an amount set aside to amortize the cost of assets over the lifetime of the assets. This reserve is depleted as depreciation is written off.

- *Interest income.* This amount is the net interest earned on investments for the statement period. This other income is a deduction from expenses.

- *Total costs and expenses.* This amount is deducted from net sales to show *income* before income taxes. Income taxes are then deducted to arrive at either a *net profit* or a *net loss.*

- *Net income per share.* Net income divided by the dollar value of shares (taken from the balance sheet) results in net income per share.

Cash Flow Statement. The *cash flow statement* shows the incoming flow of cash and the outgoing flow of cash for the reporting period. The purpose of the statement is to make a determination as to whether the organization requires external financing or if the cash flow is sufficient to meet debt obligations and dividend payments. The statement often breaks down the organization's cash flow into three categories, for example:

- Cash related to operations
    - Net income
    - Depreciation and amortization
    - Deferred taxes and wages
    - Net change in accounts payable
    - Net change in accounts receivable
    - Net change in inventory
- Cash related to investing activity
    - Capital expenditures
    - Proceeds from sale of property
- Cash related to financing activity
    - Increase in notes payable
    - Repayment of debt
    - Increase in common stock
    - Payment of dividends
- Net increase in cash and cash equivalents
- Cash and cash equivalents at beginning of year
- Cash and cash equivalents at end of reporting period

Part III.A.5

The benefits of using a cash flow statement are:

- It records the actual cash generated at a given point in time.

- It offers more detail than the balance sheet.

- It indicates the quality of the organization's earnings, the cash backing up the earnings, and the organization's capability to pay interest and dividends.

Caution: The organization's cash flow statement should not be confused with cash flow reports for projects. Project cash flows typically spread the outlay of cash across the time period of the project, for example, expenditures made in each month by category of expenditure. Such statements for projects usually do not involve incoming cash (see Chapter 10).

Notes on Financial Statements. Most financial statements will show notes clarifying statement entries or describing important events or transactions. Notes should always be read. Examples of contents of notes are:

- Detailed costs of major capital expenditures, acquisitions, or initiatives

- Structural changes in the organization or operations

- Pending litigation

- Obligations for pensions

- Special contracts or transactions

Measures—Ratios

Ratios are used for several purposes. Investors and lenders use this tool to evaluate the viability of an organization before investing. Buyers and sellers use ratios as a means for establishing a fair price. Management uses ratios as a metric for assessing organizational performance and as a basis for determining incentive compensation amounts.

There can be four categories of ratios:

- Ratios that view an organization's liquidity and overall financial condition—derived from the balance sheet.

- Ratios that provide insight as to the organization's operations—derived from the income statement.

- Ratios that interrelate information from the balance sheet, the income statement, and other reports (for example, source and usage of funds to show how effectively the organization is using its resources).

- Other ratios that are compiled from reports other than those just mentioned. These ratios are derived from internal operating reports. They may help to analyze workforce utilization, cycle time, and industry-specific comparisons.

Ratios Derived from the Balance Sheet. These ratios are used to analyze the liquidity and financial health of the organization.

- *Current ratio*

$$\text{Current ratio} = \frac{\text{Current assets}}{\text{Current liabilities}}$$

Commonly, the current ratio should be 2.0 or greater to indicate that liquidity is not a problem.

- *Acid test ratio* or *quick ratio*

$$\text{Quick ratio} = \frac{\text{Cash} + \text{Accounts receivable}}{\text{Current liabilities}}$$

Ignoring other current assets, the ratio uses only easily liquidated assets. A ratio equal to or greater than 1.0 indicates that an organization should have no problem in meeting current obligations.

- *Debt/equity ratio*

$$\text{Percentage debt} = \frac{\text{Total long-term debt}}{\text{Total long-term debt} + \text{Total owner's equity}}$$

$$\text{Percentage equity} = \frac{\text{Total owner's equity}}{\text{Total long-term debt} + \text{Total owner's equity}}$$

A capability to borrow additional long-term funds is critical to the organization's financial health. The larger the percentage of total capital that is reflected in existing borrowings, the more difficult it is to borrow more. The debt/equity ratio differs by industry; however, lenders universally feel that the greater the amount of owners' money that is invested in the organization, the lower the credit risk.

Ratios Derived from the Income Statement. These ratios are used to analyze the operations of the organization. *Gross profit* is the profit less the cost of goods sold (by a merchandising or manufacturing organization).

$$\text{Gross profit margin} = \frac{\text{Gross profit}}{\text{Net sales}}$$

A period-to-period trend analysis examines the movement of this ratio over time. Care must be taken when comparing this ratio with other organizations that what is included in the totals is comparable between the two organizations.

    Cost of goods sold is another useful figure. The following example demonstrates how to determine it.

Part III.A.5

(thousands of dollars)	Inventory, January 1, 2013	29,566
	Purchases	181,928
	Incoming freight	747
		212,241
	Less returns and allowance	385
		211,856
	Less inventory, December 31, 2013	33,428
	Cost of goods sold	178,428

Interstatement Ratios. *Inventory turnover* represents the rate at which the organization sells its inventory.

$$\text{Inventory turnover} = \frac{\text{Cost of goods sold}}{\text{Average inventory}}$$

The higher the number of inventory turns, the lower the amount of cash required on hand. This means less borrowing for working capital and more available to invest to earn interest. Also, faster inventory turnover means less of a problem with nonsalable product. Many industries have recorded typical inventory turns for the industry.

The sooner an organization collects receivables due, the lower the amount invested in accounts receivable and the lesser chance of bad debts.

$$\text{Days receivables outstanding} = \frac{\text{Average accounts receivable}}{\text{Net sales}} \times 365$$

$$\text{Average receivables} = \frac{\text{Opening plus closing balances}}{2}$$

The longer the period, the more of a creditor's money is being used, and less of the organization's funds.

$$\text{Days payables outstanding} = \frac{\text{Average accounts payable}}{\text{Cost of sales}} \times 365$$

To support increased sales, total accounts receivable outstanding and inventory tend to increase. Additional working capital is needed to increase sales.

$$\text{Working capital/dollar of sales} = \frac{\text{Average working capital}}{\text{Net sales}}$$

Average working capital = Average current assets – Average current liabilities

If the organization plans to increase sales volume (by an advertising campaign, hiring additional salespersons, and so on), the amount of additional working capital required by that sales growth must be determined.

Return on investment (ROI) is the dollar benefit generated by an investment divided by the amount of the investment. This ratio is frequently used to justify a proposed project or quality initiative, or in demonstrating the financial outcome of a project or initiative.

$$ROI = \frac{\text{Net dollar benefit}}{\text{Investment (Net costs)}} = \frac{\$675,000}{\$109,700} = \$6.15$$

$6.15 is returned for every $1 invested.

For example, net dollar benefit may consist of cycle time reductions, process improvements, productivity improvement, cost reductions, and so on.

There are some things to remember with ROI:

1. ROI and *benefits to cost analysis* may, depending on the figures used, produce the same ratio. (See Chapter 10 on project management.)

2. The computation does not consider the time value of money (money available now is worth more than the same amount in the future because of the potential earnings from using the money).

3. Net dollar benefit may be difficult to identify accurately for a specific project because of other influencing factors or ongoing initiatives.

Return on assets (ROA) is a measure of the return generated by the earning power of the organization's investment in assets. ROA is calculated by dividing net income by dollar value of tangible total assets. This ratio is used when there is a substantial capital investment to be made in physical assets. Things to remember with ROA include:

1. Net income may be difficult to isolate for a particular asset.

2. Payment for the asset usually spans several years and impacts cash flow.

3. During the time in which the asset is being paid for, the interest rates may fluctuate.

4. The computation does not consider the time value of money (money available now is worth more than the same amount in the future because of the potential earnings from using the money).

See Chapter 10 for more detail on ROI, ROA, NPV, IRR, and portfolio analysis.

Other Ratios. A wide range of ratios have been developed for specific industry sectors and purposes. Examples of a few of these ratios are:

• Number of units accepted/Number of units inspected

• Customer-accepted lots/Lots shipped

• Warranty repair costs/Sales

• Cost of quality/Cost of sales

• Profit before income tax/Number of employees

• Number of defectives/Number of units inspected

• Cost to prepare drawings/Number of drawings produced

• Number of engineering change orders/Number of drawings

• Project overrun cost/Total project cost

- Total operations personnel/Customer service personnel
- Satisfied employees/Total employees
- IT hardware uptime/Total IT hardware operating time available
- Jobs completed/Jobs scheduled
- Prevention costs/Total cost of quality
- Nonproductive time/Total time available

Product/Service Cost Structures

The traditional standard cost model is:

Product cost = Direct material costs + Direct labor costs + Overhead costs

Different organizations use different methods for booking costs, for example:

- *Undifferentiated costs*—those costs known or assumed to be associated with producing the product or rendering the service. There is no categorization by cause or type of product or service.
- Costs allocated by a percentage of direct labor dollars or some other arbitrary factor such as amount of space occupied, number of personnel in work unit, and so on.
- *Categorized costs*—costs attributable to appraisal, prevention, or failure (see Chapter 13, Section 5).
- Costs of materials and services allocated by the activity or process (cost drivers) by which they are consumed (see Chapter 13, Section 5).

Traditional cost accounting practice involves computing the sum of all costs from the work unit accounts that have been identified as a part of the direct cost of goods, then adding to this sum the indirect expenses (utilities, space allocation dollars, cleaning and maintenance, and so on). In contrast, *activity-based costing* (ABC) uses a unique assembly of all the components of cost pertinent to each product or service. The ABC approach provides a much more accurate depiction of what it really costs to produce each type of product or service. Some organizations that use ABC have curtailed or discontinued production of some of their products once the more realistic cost to manufacture became known.

Activity-based management (ABM) incorporates ABC as its data source. ABC is historical whereas ABM is more proactive—what are the causes of the cost?

Budgets

Budgeting in larger organizations is an iterative process. As a result of the strategic planning process, a macro-level estimated budget is prepared. Typically, this budget will identify a total of all projected income and expenses for operating the organization for the budgeted period. Operating units then prepare a tentative budget based on their estimated operating needs to meet the strategic plans. The operating budget numbers for all operating units are summed and compared with the top-level target budget. Depending on the organization's culture and practices, either negotiation or mandates occur to reconcile the operating budgets to the overall target budget. This usually involves several passes up and down the organization until agreement is reached. Sometimes, the top-level budget may be modified, but usually it is the operating units' budgets that will undergo change.

Once a budget is approved, the operating units manage their operations to attempt to stay in line with the approved budget. This balancing act requires continual monitoring and analysis of interim results, trade-off actions, and occasionally a request to approve an overrun due to a special occurrence. Measures to link budgets with strategic goals and objectives cascade throughout the organization.

The spreadsheet is the basic tool of the manager in managing his or her budget. The budget for most operating units will include an itemization of all planned expenses spread over the time periods in which the expenditures are anticipated. An income budget is not usually the concern of most operating units.

Managers' concerns include fears that:

- Not spending up to the allowed budget will result in a lower budget being approved for a subsequent period.

- Overspending the allowed budget will result in a poor performance rating and future curtailments to make up for the overrun.

- Concern for making budget may negatively impact customer satisfaction, employee satisfaction, and process and performance improvement initiatives.

- Concerns for financial performance will overshadow pertinent nonfinancial measures that are critical for decision making.

Balanced Scorecard

The basic financial accounting model and reports are based on past events. The balanced scorecard was developed from a need to develop a measurement tool that includes both leading and lagging indicators.[12] The basic model contains four high-level groups of measures, from a financial perspective, customer perspective, internal business process perspective, and learning and growth perspective. The concept of the balanced scorecard can be adapted to any organization and to functions within an organization. By carefully selecting the key measures in each segment of the scorecard, management can more intelligently and confidently make critical decisions affecting the outcomes of the organization. (Chapter 11, Section 3 contains more on this topic.)

Communicating with Senior Management

While the quality professional may be driven by her or his needs to improve quality, customer satisfaction, and processes, senior managers react to an overarching need to show profitability during their time in office. Profitability not only pertains to satisfying the owners of the organization, but also sustains the organization's growth and competitive position in the marketplace. Profitability is also the basis for senior managers' performance ratings, and often their compensation. Senior managers will tell those lower in the organization that "if we don't make money, we will all be out of a job."

An ASQ-sponsored survey revealed that a vast majority of American executives believe that quality impacts the bottom line.

"Selling" quality initiatives and projects to management means:

- Calculating the risks and benefits involved.

- Collecting and analyzing all the pertinent data derived from financial analysis, competitive analysis, benchmarking, and so on.

- Crafting a salable picture of the benefits to the organization and to the executives who must approve the initiative.

- Do the homework before presenting the final proposal:

  - Solicit critique and advice from key people in the organization who have or will have a stake in the outcome of the proposed quality initiative.

  - Present a draft of the proposal to the people who furnished advice, with evidence that the proposal reflects their suggestions.

  - Win support from as many members of top management as feasible.

- Present the proposal for approval, with the support of the people who participated in its preview.

When seeking executive approval for a project or capital expenditure, think and talk the language of finance. It is imperative that quality professionals learn how to convert their requests and needs to financial performance language to achieve buy-in.

ASQ has embraced the concept of developing an "economic case for quality." ASQ provides tools and guidelines for quality professionals to use to sell the case for quality within their organizations. This trend is evidenced by the growing number of articles in a wide range of industry publications espousing the need to develop an "economic case for [insert industry name or function]."

6. RISK MANAGEMENT

> Identify the kinds of risk that can occur throughout the organization, from such diverse processes as scheduling, shipping/receiving, financials, production and operations, employee and user safety, regulatory compliance and changes. Describe and use risk control and mitigation methods: avoidance, reduction, prevention, segregation, and transfer. (Apply)
>
> Body of Knowledge III.A.6

Types of Risks

Most everyone realizes that risk is present in our personal life as well as in the organizations in which we work. Risks organizations face are:

- Events ranging from those causing minor disruption to those catastrophic events that affect the organization regardless of its location, financial stability, and so on.

- Events that can affect each organization differently; a minor disruption to one organization but a major disaster for another.

A risk that becomes a negative event can seriously disrupt your organization's processes and make it unable to meet customer requirements. Identifying and planning for potential risks is critical in the pursuit of customer satisfaction, organizational stability, and profitability, especially under potentially adverse conditions.

Table 8.1 lists risks that could affect an organization. This is not an exhaustive list. The proactive organization, regardless of size, makes an assessment of the potential risks to which it is exposed and establishes feasible means to prevent or lessen loss.

The Risk Management Process

The PDCA steps to take to establish an effective risk management process are:

1. *Plan* the means by which your organization will:

   - Identify and define its potential exposures to loss

   - Quantify the potential financial and nonfinancial risks

   - Examine the feasibility of alternate risk management techniques

   - Select the best risk management technique(s)

2. *Do*. Implement a test of the chosen risk management technique(s).

3. *Check*. Assess the effectiveness of the technique and make necessary adjustments or select a new alternative.

4. *Act*. Implement the full process.

   - Roll out the full implementation of the tested technique(s).

   - Monitor the implemented techniques for adequacy of protection.

5. *Improve* the implemented techniques (return to the plan step).

These PDCA steps are focused on continual improvement to lessen an organization's exposure to loss. Consider the following questions in identifying exposure to loss:

1. What is exposed to a potential loss? Items to consider include:

   - Property (real estate, facilities, equipment, product, material, intellectual property)

Table 8.1   Potential types and forms of risk that could affect an organization.

Legal action	Noncompliance with regulatory requirements
Environmental violations (perceived as unacceptable)	Customer errors
Customer payment delinquencies and nonpayment	Supplier errors
Raw material defects	Subcontractor nonconformances
Errors and omissions	Financial investments (unexpected or unacceptable yield)
Failed projects or inadequate ROI from projects	Product liability
Employee wrongdoing (failure to comply with safety and other rules, theft, physical harm to coworkers, giving incorrect answers, falsifying records, and so on)	Sabotage
Accidents	Catastrophic loss (fire, hurricane, tornado, flood, earthquake, blizzard, and so on)
Civil unrest or terrorist attack	Damage from military action or political upheaval
Vandalism	Product obsolescence
Inadequate or omitted controls (over processes, finances, employees, suppliers, subcontractors, and so on)	Inattention to danger signals from controls
Illegal or unethical behavior on part of management	Disqualification for certifications, licenses, permits
Unwanted buyout/takeover of organization	Unexpected death, disability, or departure of key persons
Other business interruption situations	

Source: Reprinted with permission of R. T. Westcott & Associates.

- Net income (short- and long-term)
- Liability (short- and long-term)
- People (employees, customers, suppliers, community members, investors, others)

2. What situation, event, or peril could cause a loss for each exposure?

3. What are the financial and other business consequences of such a loss?

4. What entity(ies) may potentially suffer the loss?

Table 8.2 provides a detailed look at exposures relating to these four factors.

Part III.A.6

Table 8.2   A detailed look at potential exposures to loss.

Loss exposure	Causes	Financial consequences	Potential entity suffering loss

Property
• Tangible
  – Real estate (land, facilities, things that grow on it)
  – Products
  – Material
• Intangible
  – Licenses
  – Leaseholding
  – Intellectual property (trade secrets, proprietary processes)
	Natural
	Fire
	Wind
	Flood
	Earthquake
	Store (rain, hail, snow)
	
	Human
	Theft
	Vandalism
	Misuse
		• Replacement cost
		• Functional replacement cost
		• Actual cash value
		• Economic or use value
			• Ownership interests
			• Secured creditors
			• Sellers and buyers
			• Tenant interests
			• Employees
			• Community

Net income (Revenues—Expenses) • Near-term • Long-term	**Decrease in revenues** Business interruption Loss of anticipated profits Reduced rental income Decreased collection of accounts receivable **Increase in expenses** Increased operating expenses Increased rental expenses and expediting costs	• Decreased profits • Decreased market share • Decreased stock price • Less capital • Reduction in improvements	• Business itself • Stockholders • Customers • Employees • Contractual interests

Freedom from legal liability
(arises from an entity: being sued for having breached a legal duty or allegedly harming another; becoming obligated under contract to pay for a loss that another entity has suffered)
• Near-term
• Long-term
	Classified by the entity to whom the duty is owed
	Criminal
	Civil
	• Contract
	• Tort
	
	Classified by the source of legal duty
	Common law
	Statutory law
		• Legal costs including:
		  – Judgments against the entity
		  – Attorney fees
		  – Punitive damages
		• Time value cost
		• Loss of reputation
			• Business itself
			• Stockholders
			• Customers
			• Employees
			• Contractual interests

Personnel loss • Key persons • Employees • Customers • Suppliers • Community members	Death Disability Retirement Resignation Employee benefits • Contractual liability • Criminal or civil liability	• Temporary versus permanent losses • Normal versus above normal losses • Fringe benefits	• Stockholders • Customers • Employees • Contractual interests

Source: Adapted from provided by the U.S. Small Business Administration.

Part III.A.6

Risk Exposure Techniques and Tools

Following are 10 suggested techniques and tools for identifying and analyzing loss exposures. Note that the list is not intended to be all-inclusive.

1. *Analyze reported incidents involving potential or actual losses.* The first place to look is within the organization. Search records to uncover information about:

- Payouts for losses for the previous two or three years, including any fines and out-of-court settlements

- Indications and severity of bad debts and delinquent customer payments

- Indications of any losses due to fraudulent actions by suppliers or employees

- Indications of losses due to any revocation of licenses, registrations, certifications, and so on

- Potential loss when a patent period expires

Look next at data from insurance carriers regarding the types and amounts of claims paid on behalf of your organization (for example, liability, health, and accident/disability claims). Also obtain data from any pertinent industry association.

Next, check community records for the past few years regarding local incidents. Such incidents might be repeated because they are commonplace in the community. Such incidents could also trigger copycats to file a claim against your organization. Community records include:

- City/town hall records and historical archives

- Local newspaper archives

- Local library sources

- Local police blotters and fire department records

2. *Data from internal sources.* Conduct diagonal-slice brainstorming sessions with employees from all functions and organizational levels, and use surveys to identify areas of potential risks.

3. *Audit financial statements and supporting documents.* Financial risk exposure is probably the most frequent source of risk for most organizations, yet this risk is often the most cost-effective to fix or prevent. All organizations are required to report financial information to various entities, yet management tends to rely only on external accountants to verify this information. A closer examination of these financial statements, and the data supporting the figures therein, could ensure that the numbers make sense. An audit by executive management could raise red flags where appropriate, keep the accountants on their toes—and keep the organization's executives out of jail.[13]

4. *Complete and analyze process maps.* From process map(s) of key processes, brainstorm where points of risk may be embedded in the process.

5. *Conduct a what-if brainstorming session.* With a group of key persons, using a cause-and-effect diagram, explore as many possible risk situations as time and feasibility allow.

6. *Perform periodic inspections and process audits.* Health and safety inspections not only look for lapses in compliance with regulations, but also surface opportunities to decrease risk. Vigilance and preparedness are maintained with surprise drills. Potential risk–type questions can be incorporated in the internal auditing of the quality management system, as well as in product audits. Continually question whether the organization's product, in the end user's hands, will be safe to use over the product's life cycle, including disposal.

7. *Use failure mode and effects analysis (FMEA).* This technique can help in determining what could go wrong and what impact it could have on the organization's processes and product. The intent is to prevent such failures and their effects. The process of constructing an FMEA is discussed in Chapter 13, Section 3.

8. *Assess the robustness of management systems and processes.* The objective is to determine if there are any gaps in your management system(s) and processes that could expose the organization to loss. Following are examples of systems and processes where risk exposure may lurk:

- Quality management system

- Financial management systems, which include supplier payments, revenues, payroll, investments, asset management, and contingency reserves

- Intellectual property management systems (especially proprietary and patent information)

- Supply chain alliances and partnerships

- Safety and security systems

- Environmental management systems

- Ship-to-stock, kanban processes

- Communications (website, e-mail, electronic data interchange)

- Material handling systems

- Inventory and warehousing

- Other systems

9. *Contract out surveillance services.* Consider outsourcing examination of the organization's exposure to property and personnel security risks, and risks inherent in noncompliance to regulatory and nonregulatory requirements.

10. *Access exposure statistics from insurance carriers, trade associations, and regulatory agencies.* These sources often provide statistics about potential exposures that are common to the organization's sector. Such statistics can point to where to look for potential exposures based on industry history—as history often repeats itself—and what the costs of such exposures could be.

Responding to Risk Exposures

The organization must determine how to respond, and there is no guarantee that responses to all exposures will be possible or feasible. After the organization has identified risk exposures and computed the potential for financial loss, one or more of five actions may be initiated:

1. Find a way to avoid the exposure.

2. Find ways to reduce the potential loss.

3. Find ways to prevent the occasion for the loss to ever occur.

4. Segregate the loss exposures to concentrate efforts on those exposures most probable to occur and/or cause the greatest loss (for example, exposure triage—minimum, medium, maximum).

5. Transfer the risk (for example, through insurance or other contractual arrangement).

In addition to obtaining insurance to cover all or a portion of the potential risk, the organization may initiate contingency plans, including setting up loss reserves, a form of self-insurance. The single most effective prevention approach, however, may be to train employees to recognize hazards and potential areas for loss, and to facilitate communicating the information to appropriate management.

A short story illustrates this well. At one session in a series of employee briefings on potential hazards and risks, one employee mentioned a story his late father, a long-time employee, had told him. The story was about the time when the adjacent river crested 15 feet above normal after an unusually snowy winter upstream. The plant's buildings were badly damaged.

The organization's present management, who had all joined the company within the last five years, was unaware of this potential for loss. This was an especially relevant heads-up notice because the organization had recently planned a new facility—full of expensive new equipment—to be built along the riverbank.

In another company, an employee looked into product liability payouts after a training program. She isolated the reported causes and suggested that engineering explore ways to engineer the products to prevent customers from misusing the product—the cause for the greatest number of occurrences. A resulting engineering design change substantially reduced the number of occurrences as well as the average payout for the few misuse claims submitted. The insurance premium was also lowered.

Assessing the potential risks for a new product at the design and development stage and taking preventive actions is extremely cost-effective. The tool to use in this assessment activity is the FMEA. The U.S. automotive sector has standardized an industry-specific approach in the Big Three's *Failure Mode and Effects Analysis* reference manual, but there are several ways to conduct an FMEA. (See Chapter 13, Section 3 for more on FMEAs.)

Computing Potential for Loss and Taking Action

To generate a credible estimate of the organization's potential for loss, consider the following steps:

1. Prioritize the identified risks. A Pareto chart is helpful.

2. For each of the top eight to 10 risks, envision a worst-case scenario. List all the consequences that could happen. Brainstorming, mind mapping, and cause-and-effect diagrams are effective techniques and tools.

3. Categorize the consequences into clusters of similar happenings. An affinity diagram is a useful tool.

4. Assign dollar estimates of losses to each cluster. Some of the line items you might consider assigning a value for include:

   • Legal defense costs, claim settlements

   • Claim settlements for loss of human life

   • Temporary business loss or business closing

   • Product recall costs

   • Erosion of confidence in your organization and/or its products

   • Increase in insurance premiums

   • Increase in surveillance costs

   • Replacement costs: people, facilities, tools, and so on

   • Product obsolescence

   • Shortages of raw material, energy sources, transportation, staffing, and so on

   • Deterioration or spoilage of raw materials, work in progress, or completed product

5. Determine what it would take (cost of additional resources) to mitigate or eliminate the accumulated potential dollar loss for each cluster/ scenario. Factors to consider include:

   • Insurance or other ways of spreading the potential loss

   • Improved environmental scanning and forecasting methodology

Part III.A.6

- Improved response and preparatory procedures (contingency plans)

- Decentralization of risk-associated functions and facilities

- Relocation of facilities to less risky geographic area

- Discontinuing production of product with high potential risk.

- Lean techniques to reduce or eliminate inventory

- Outsourcing part or all of a process

6. Compute the risk ratio for each cluster (cost of additional resources relative to total value).

7. Decide what action(s) would be in the balanced best interest of all the organization's stakeholders.

8. Decide how and when to take action or not.

9. Periodically reassess the decisions made and make necessary adjustments.

Summary

This review of some of the elements of risk management is intended to build awareness of the need for assessing and managing the risks that can impact the organization. Recall that not every organization that has won the coveted Baldrige Award or other quality awards has survived. Failure has had little to do with their success in meeting the Baldrige criteria and more to do with how these organizations managed their businesses so as to withstand the risks encountered.

Many of the massive business failures of recent times have had little to do with product or service quality problems and everything to do with failures to identify, assess, and manage potential risks. It really doesn't matter if the organization has the world's best ISO 9001–registered QMS when a mudslide from that never-noticed hill behind the plant wipes out the business. All because of the failure to identify the risk and devise a contingency plan! A similar fate awaits an organization if its CEO absconds with the employee pension funds, or its capital equipment replacement project failed to produce the intended payoff and the organization defaults on its loan payments.

Furthermore, in this litigious society, organizations must carefully assess their potential liability from legal actions: actions arising from alleged product failures, end users' misuse of products, inappropriate actions of employees or alleged health, safety, and security violations, or negligence. Legal actions often result in huge payouts to the litigant if the company is found guilty or is forced to reach a huge out-of-court settlement regardless of alleged responsibility. Not being able to sustain a viable organization that fulfills customer requirements and supports your workforce is a quality failure—that is, a *quality of management* failure.[14]

(ISO 31000:2009 provides a standard on risk management implementation.)

7. KNOWLEDGE MANAGEMENT

Use KM techniques in identifying core competencies that create a culture and system for collecting and sharing implicit and explicit knowledge among workers, customers, competitors, and suppliers. Capture lessons learned and apply them across the organization to promote best practices. Identify typical knowledge-sharing barriers and how to overcome them. (Apply)

Body of Knowledge III.A.7

What Is Knowledge?

One view is that knowledge is part of a hierarchy (see Figure 8.8). In this view, data are meaningless until something is done to them. Data can be stored in their raw form or they can be manipulated (sorted, categorized, analyzed, calculated, summarized, and subjected to tests). When the manipulations are completed, the data may be synthesized into information. Information has meaning, but the meaning is based on the interpretation of the user of the information. The value of the information is determined by the uses for which the information is employed. Information can be stored for future use, disseminated to others for their use, or ignored (purposely or not). Typically, information is correlated/integrated with previously known information, as well as rules, policies, procedures, regulations, and so on, to build knowledge.

Part III.A.7

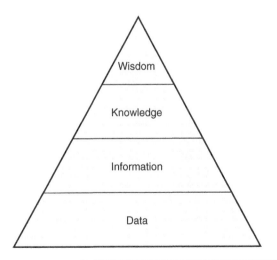

Figure 8.8   Transformation of data.

This new knowledge now has substance in the sense that it is framed by previous knowledge. This enhanced knowledge may be used as developed, then stored (for example, in the human brain, the brains of a closely associated group of people, a computer, or documents in a file cabinet), or ignored and lost. Knowledge may be used in making decisions without the benefit of the next step in the continuum.

Wisdom is derived from the collective database of knowledge built from experience, values, and expert insights. Wisdom provides the capability to exploit the use of the knowledge for informed decision making. Wisdom invokes unique capabilities, such as being able to:

- Visualize the connectivity among seemingly disparate knowledge sets (for example, the concept of a business organization as analogous to a biological system, the potential for adapting a space-age technological development for use in increasing agricultural output, the five-year strategic goals of an organization derived from an environmental analysis and synthesis of voluminous inputs)

- Know or sense the rightness or wrongness of an assumption, conclusion, or decision where objective data may not be available

- Solve problems of a nonlinear nature by attribution of nonquantitative characteristics and values to the pertinent knowledge sets to enable deduction of a solution

Tacit knowledge consists of all the difficult-to-articulate know-how and techniques and processes that are part of an individual's and/or organization's expertise. It typically is not recorded and, while it is part of the corporate knowledge pool, there is no guarantee it will be passed on to the next generation. When an employee leaves an organization, usually the tacit knowledge retained by the employee also leaves.

Explicit knowledge is the captured and recorded knowledge that is codified and can be transmitted between individuals, that is, procedures, processes, standards, and other documents. Much of the current organizational *knowledge management* (KM) effort focuses on attempting to convert tacit knowledge into explicit knowledge without the loss of value.

In recent years, many organizations realized that their collective knowledge was disappearing. This may have happened because no effort was made to transform the mountains of data into knowledge for future generations to reuse. It also occurred when the human repositories of tacit knowledge left the organization. For example, Chrysler created Books of Knowledge to stop the loss of internal automaking know-how and prevent future reinvention of the wheel. The armed forces videotaped and archived many of its war games and other activities as a source for learning. The purpose of these efforts was to enable sharing of knowledge, given the high turnover of personnel.

Not long ago, many people in organizations tended to protect and hoard their knowledge. Knowledge was perceived as power, and to share with another function was to give up this power. With the change from functional (silo) thinking to enterprise/systems thinking, organizations have realized the collective value of their knowledge bases, their intellectual capital. Knowledge, for those who use it wisely, is a key competitive advantage in the marketplace and must be leveraged with other core competencies.

How to Capture, Share, and Access Information

Knowledge management involves transforming data into information, and the acquisition or creation of knowledge. The creation of knowledge from information requires human intervention, and applying wisdom is strictly a human function. Many of the mechanistic functions of manipulating data to generate information, and the storing and accessing of information for use in creating knowledge, can be done speedily and accurately by computers (for example, data mining, neural nets), whereby the software may find patterns of things not readily evident to the human eye. But interpretations from information to knowledge and wisdom typically involve a human capability.

Issues to consider for capturing, sharing, and accessing data include:

- Identifying the types of data to be captured and the media on/in which it is received

- Preparing the procedures for capturing the data and how it will be organized/categorized, for example, scanning documents into a computer database, filing the actual documents received, extracting key data for direct entry to computer storage, or point-of-sale transfer of data from a checkout register directly to computer storage

- Determining how the data may be used to create information (influences accessibility and design of storage medium), and whether certain data will be retained as *data* or in its upgraded form as *information* (for example, detailed machine or data recorder data, or the summarized information version)

- For security purposes, identifying the customers who will use the data and protocols for access

- Designing methods for searching and accessing the data

- Establishing the policies and rules governing data use, maintenance of data (storage, handling, preservation, updating, and so on), retention duration, and disposal

- Determining the protocols for sharing, including whether the data will be made available on request (reactive mode) or will be disseminated to select individuals/departments based on an on-file profile of interests or needs (proactive)

- Establishing methods for continually evaluating the effectiveness of the knowledge management system and the means for improving it

Recognize that data sources may be proprietary, information is vulnerable if not properly cared for, and both data and information can disappear along with knowledge when people leave an organization. Information can be purchased,

Part III.A.7

leased, rented, acquired as part of a merger or business acquisition, or generated within the organization.

No matter the source, there is a cost and a value associated with data, information, and knowledge. With some, the value may depreciate over time, for example, cash flow statements from five years ago or an economic analysis of the Pennsylvania Railroad from two years before its acquisition by Amtrak. Other data, information, and knowledge may appreciate in value over time, for example, lab notes from experiments in mapping DNA (data), the report summarizing the results of the experiments (information), and the board of directors' concerns and conclusions about the use of the information (knowledge). Other knowledge sets, for example, design documents for concept auto #CD0699, or the public communication program used during the construction of the Baldwin Bridge, may have instructional value as well as historical value.

Initiating Knowledge Management

An organization-wide study may be conducted to determine what information and knowledge exists, where it exists, in what form it exists, and who does or will use it. The study team should include a variety of talents and backgrounds. It should probably not be directed and led by the information technology (IT) function in order to avoid emphasis on technology rather than content. Costs (acquisition, processing, storing, accessing, and maintenance costs) and values (worth to users) can be assigned and the knowledge sets displayed on a Pareto chart to aid prioritization. From the knowledge derived, decisions can be made about the knowledge management process (what to retain, how to retain it, who is responsible, who has access, how the activity will be funded, and so on).

The technology approaches used to support knowledge management are exploding in quantity and functionality. The advent of larger computer storage (in data warehouses or in a "cloud") and processing capability enables even smaller organizations to establish a knowledge management system. A very small organization can still reap the benefit of knowledge management concepts without the previous constraints of system complexity.

Consider the example of a small firm specializing in writing and publishing articles on business topics. The firm has established a 400-item topic list. Supporting the list is an internal library of over 1000 books, approximately 10,000 documents (clipped articles, papers, conference proceedings, and so on), and over 400 audio- and videotapes pertinent to the listed topics. The files are continually augmented by internet downloads, clipped articles from over 50 publications, and media purchases. This library of data is stored in easily accessible file drawers and on bookshelves. The topic list aids categorization of input, and speeds access to data needed for a given topic.

The system is old-fashioned in that it is not computer-based; however, it meets the needs of the small number of persons sharing the information, and it is cost- and time-effective. Its shortcoming is on those rare occasions when a cross-topical search is needed to locate data not specifically listed, when a computer "find" function would be useful. The cost and time involved to enter sufficient data into a computer database to support such a search, however, is not warranted for the few times it would be used. The system does meet present needs and far exceeds the functionality and focus of collections at nearby town libraries. Internet search capability supplements the physical collection.

Larger organizations are taking advantage of the innovative uses of intranets (dedicated internet-like internal systems) for sharing information and knowledge, and data mining techniques. Data mining is exploring, via computer, gigantic databases of millions of records to extract valuable data that can be transformed into useful information and knowledge. As an example, visualize the potential uses for information derived from exploring the correlation and permutations of data collected by a supermarket chain. It is the rare shopper who does not dutifully present her or his shopping card to be swiped (bar code read) at the checkout counter. Bargains available only to the cardholder have successfully modified the behavior of the buying public to submit their card, and hence allow the recording of their purchases for the company to analyze.

Other examples of applications of KM include:

- Organizations that carefully preserve the research and design work that went into creating a new product, whether or not the product was ever launched or was successful. All R&D persons assigned a new project must first access the database for pertinent information and knowledge. In these cases it is truly a policy to not reinvent the wheel.

- Legal firms that augment the existent case law (from publishers) with case details from their own experience with clients. It enables attorneys with the firm to access particulars of a case for applicability to a new case. This information also enables newer attorneys to learn how their peers have applied the law, as well as the firm's policies and practices in previous cases.

- Retail store chains that formulate patterns of buyers' habits from huge databases of captured customer data. These data facilitate how they provide the products people want when they want them, which products, from which distributors, in what quantity, when the product is needed, how retail space is allocated to each product, which products should be dropped, and how to schedule human resources for shelf restocking, checkout, and store maintenance. Also, the system is set to enable the issuance of pertinent coupons and notices to customers. Periodic searches of the customer database enable marketing to issue targeted advertisements to customers.

- Many companies archive data, documents, and other physical objects that represent the company's history. These data and items are not only of historical interest to newcomers, but are accessed in support of future planning, as background for publicity and advertising purposes, and objective evidence in legal matters.

- Corporate libraries have expanded from their normal reactive services (acquiring, shelving, and loaning books and publications, data and information searches) to developing profiles of key users of the library and proactively feeding new information to users based on their profile and documented needs.

- A large organization collects, catalogs, and makes available online to field salespeople a range of information. The information includes technical product information (their own and competitors'), sales presentations, sales and marketing practices and strategies, sales promotion materials, customer account information, analyses of buying patterns, and industry trend data.

- A company annually measures the value of its intellectual capital and publishes it to their stockholders.

- Organizations who periodically mine their database for patterns and connections that remain virtually hidden to humans. The resulting information is used in determining the potential for new products and services, establishing new markets, segmenting the customer database, restructuring processes and the organization, and guiding the strategic direction of the organization.

The Learning Organization

As individuals must continue to learn, so must organizations. Essential principles for any learning organization are:

- Recognition that the database is not the KM solution; it is the people effectively using the database who are the real solution.

- Build and reinforce an organizational culture that supports and promotes knowledge sharing, networking, and reusing knowledge rather than hoarding or reinventing knowledge.

- Ensure that organizational management considers knowledge management a key strategy for growth and prosperity of the enterprise.

- Institute a system of policies and procedures to identify what information and knowledge is essential, and specify how the information and knowledge are to be captured, processed, stored, maintained, accessed, and used.

- Nurture an open communication work climate that encourages the identification of new information and knowledge that can be exploited for individual and organizational learning and development.

- Foster the valuing of knowledge management as one of the organization's core competencies in remaining competitive.

As portrayed by Senge, organizational learning goes beyond the mere capture of knowledge to include gaining a deeper and complete understanding of how things work, and involves five learning disciplines:

1. *Personal mastery.* A continual drive for personal and organizational development

2. *Mental models.* Understanding how our cognitive schema affect our view of the world, and continually improving the accuracy of the models

3. *Shared vision.* Working jointly toward a common view to which all aspire

4. *Team learning.* The use of dialogue to move beyond mere conversation to true joint understanding

5. *Systems thinking.* Understanding the multiple cause-and-effect relationships and how they are interconnected in organizations, society, and other systems[15]

Core Competencies

A key to long-term success of any organization is the ability to differentiate itself from competitors. One way of doing so is to possess a unique capability, a core competency, that can be continually leveraged. For example, Honda has the ability to continually refine the technology of small gasoline engines, which has been applied to products such as lawn equipment, power generators, motorcycles, consumer automobiles, and racing engines.

Core competencies are a result of both specific knowledge as well as the ability to integrate various skills and other components of the organization to effectively apply that knowledge. In order for it to remain a core competency, the organization must continually increase the depth of knowledge and ability of employees to utilize it in new ways.

An organization's core competency should then be a driver for company strategy and be maintained and improved through development of employee skills (Chapter 19) and internal capabilities, as well as continual research and development in relevant knowledge areas. An effective knowledge management process supports the capturing, processing, and storage of information so as to make it available to those who need it, while also maintaining the necessary security of that information.

Measuring the Outcomes of KM

- Focus the KM system on the organization's strategic objectives and measuring tangible outcomes.

- Define and clearly communicate the KM measures and how they will be used.

- Create interdependent KM measures tied to the organization's measures of its outcomes.

- To strive for continual improvement, measure only what matters— with a primary focus on the customers of the KM system.

- Encourage the telling of success (and failure) stories of users of the KM system to reinforce the lessons learned aspect of measurements.

Part III.A.7

Organizational Hurdles to Overcome

To effectively implement KM techniques, a number of hurdles or barriers may have to be overcome, such as:

- Lack of top management's interest in, support for, and commitment to KM

  - A knowledge vision may be lacking.

  - The economic case for KM is not developed.

- Failure to consider KM a top-level strategy

  - KM as a competitive edge is not developed.

  - KM is not perceived as integral to doing business.

- Inter- and intraorganizational barriers

  - Organizational structures may either enable or hinder knowledge sharing.

  - Turf conflicts and tendencies to hoard knowledge are power issues.

  - Organizations not structured on a project basis may be less likely to understand and appreciate the value of KM in performing their assignments.

  - There's conflict over funding for the KM system and services.

- Overcoming process barriers

  - Perceiving the IT function as the logical process owner of KM may be ill advised. With IT heading the KM effort, the emphasis may be more on processing data, not on the strategic use and value of the knowledge captured and retained.

  - In examining the process, questions include:

    - What data are to be captured?

    - Why are they needed?

    - Who will use the data and for what purpose?

    - What are the procedures and protocols for data capture?

    - What are the procedures and protocols for transforming data into information and knowledge?

    - How is information/knowledge access and retrieval to be accomplished?

    - Is there a competent person responsible for establishing quality criteria and maintaining the level of quality in selecting data for entry, correctly and completely capturing the data selected, maintaining database integrity and security, and providing accurate and timely access and retrieval of information/knowledge?

- In the case of a large database with a high volume of usage, have the users (internal customers) been segmented so as to optimize service (and costs) to the different segments?

- Infrastructure issues

  - Who ensures that the electronic systems are adequate to serve the growing needs of the organization, that is, the expanding database, the ever faster pace of business decisions, the increasingly innovative workforce, and the organization's commitment to continually improve?

  - Who ensures that all persons interfacing with the KM system are properly trained?

- Cultural concerns

  - Do the organization's strategy, the recognition and reward systems, the organizational structures, the predominant managing style, and other cultural concerns help or hinder the realization of an effective KM system?

  - Have cultural concerns, such as language usage and communication protocols, been updated to mesh with the KM system?

  - Has the voice of the customer (external customer) been integrated with the design of the KM system?

- Individual barriers

  - How resistant to change are the organization's employees?

  - How reluctant will key employees be when required to submit their knowledge to a KM system—and perceive they have lost their power?

  - How much individual fear has to be overcome—fear of failure, fear of exposing errors and mistakes in judgment, fear of giving up personal papers and notes?

Far from an exhaustive list of hurdles, barriers, and issues, this list provides an overview of concerns facing organizations implementing major new systems.

Product Development

Developing a product or service is often performed as a team consisting of representatives from marketing/sales, engineering, production/operations, quality, and finance. The physical location of the function varies from organization to organization, and it may even be outsourced. Numerous disciplines are usually involved, requiring the expertise of people with a wide range of knowledge and skills.

The development may include plans for:

- Funding

- Project planning and management

- Market research

- Customer needs/wants analysis

- Engineering design for manufacturability and for customer use (see below)

- Quality planning and management (design, processes, reliability, and so on)

- Consumer testing

- Marketing the product or service (promotion, selling, distribution, demand forecasting, assessing customer satisfaction, and so on)

- Product safety and liability

A process that has gained recognition is *human factors engineering* (HFE), an interdisciplinary approach to evaluating and improving the safety, efficiency, and robustness of work systems, such as healthcare delivery. HFE is the practice of designing products so that the user can perform required use, operation, service, and supportive tasks with a minimum of stress and a maximum of efficiency. HFE is about designing for the user, instead of forcing the user to accommodate the design. HFE scientists and engineers study the intersection of people, technology, policy, and work across multiple domains, using an interdisciplinary approach that draws from cognitive psychology, organizational psychology, human performance, industrial engineering, systems engineering, and economic theory. HFE addresses multiple aspects of work, including:

- Task analysis and design

- Device evaluation and usability

- Communication, collaboration, and teamwork

- Training

- Systems resilience, adaptation, and failure

HFE engages employees by getting them involved in the design process. It focuses on systems and environments designed by the employees leading to the well-being and function of humans. Systems and environments designed through the HFE process are safer, more efficient, and cost less, and system downtime, maintenance, and injuries are reduced. (See www.medicalhumanfactors.net for more details.)

ENDNOTES

1. J. Giles, "Learning How We Learn," in *Gower Handbook of Training and Development,* 2nd ed., ed. J. Prior (Brookfield, VT: Bower, 1994).

2. A. C. Daniels, *Bringing Out the Best in People: How to Apply the Astonishing Power of Positive Reinforcement* (New York: McGraw-Hill, 1994).

3. P. Hersey and K. Blanchard, *Management of Organizational Behavior* (Englewood Cliffs, NJ: Prentice-Hall, 1977).

4. P. M. Senge, *The Fifth Discipline: The Art and Practice of the Learning Organization* (New York: Currency Doubleday, 1990).

5. P. Cilliers, *Complexity and Postmodernism: Understanding Complex Systems* (London: Routledge, 1998).

6. D. Okes, "Complexity Theory Simplifies Choices," *Quality Progress* (July 2003): 35–37.

7. S. R. Covey, *The 7 Habits of Highly Effective People* (New York: Simon and Schuster, 1989).

8. S. R. Covey and K. A. Gulledge, "Principle-Centered Leadership and Change," *Journal of Quality and Participation* (March 1994): 12–21.

9. E. A. Locke and D. M. Schweiger, "Participation in Decision Making: One More Look," in *Research in Organizational Behavior*, ed. B. M. Staw and L. L. Cummings (Greenwich, CT: JAI Press, 1979).

10. E. H. Schein, *The Corporate Culture Survival Guide* (San Francisco: Jossey-Bass, 1999).

11. J. M. Juran and A. B. Godfrey, eds., *Juran's Quality Handbook*, 5th ed. (New York: McGraw-Hill, 1999), 22.65.

12. R. S. Kaplan and D. P. Norton, *The Balanced Scorecard: Translating Strategy into Action* (Boston: Harvard Business School Press, 1996).

13. See the *Sarbanes-Oxley Act of 2002*, a law that, among other stipulations, requires the principal executive officer or officers and the principal financial officer or officers of public companies to attest to the accuracy of financial reports and the effectiveness of internal controls.

14. R. T. Westcott, *Stepping Up to ISO 9004:2000: A Practical Guide for Creating a World-Class Organization* (Chico, CA: Paton Press, 2003).

15. P. Senge, C. Roberts, R. B. Ross, B. J. Smith, and A. Kleiner, *The Fifth Discipline Fieldbook* (New York: Doubleday, 1994).

See Appendix A for additional references for this chapter.

Part III.A.7

Chapter 9

B. Communication Skills and Abilities

In today's world, the quantity and diversity of available data, information, and knowledge is overwhelming for many people. Access to data from virtually any part of the world, even including outer space, is nearly instantaneous. The quality of such data and information, as well as its usefulness, is often suspect, however. Not only is the capability to communicate quickly, succinctly, and accurately more important than ever, but so is the capability of knowing what information to choose for a given purpose.

This chapter will review what communication is and how communication takes place, and present techniques and strategies for enhancing communication. In addition, the chapter will discuss how to effectively communicate in the global economy, as well as tips on how to use data produced by information systems technology to monitor and manage an organization.

1. COMMUNICATION TECHNIQUES

> Define and apply various modes of communication used within organizations, such as verbal, non-verbal, written, and visual. Identify factors that can inhibit clear communication and describe ways of overcoming them. (Apply)
>
> **Body of Knowledge III.B.1**

What Is Communication?

People working toward a common purpose can not function without communication. Communication is a transmitting and receiving process that depends for effectiveness on both the transmitter's and the receiver's perceptions. This statement appears applicable to both human as well as technological communication. Important to each is the realization that there are filters affecting both what is transmitted and what is received. In the human communication process, these filters may represent cultural beliefs, the consequences of previous communications, conditions at the time of transmission, language disparities, education, experience, and so on. In technological communication, filters are intended to reduce or eliminate noise (interference) along the communications path. Figure 9.1 depicts the communication path from sender to receiver.

Filters intended to help clarify the meaning of the message can, and too often do, muddle the message instead. Note: Some authors refer to *coder* and *decoder* rather than filters. An aid to effective human communication is for the receiver to transmit back to the sender a paraphrased understanding of what the receiver heard or saw. Depending on the complexity of the message and its intent, this exchange may require repeating, in different words, until the intended understanding is reached. In technical transmission this clarification may be accomplished by various types of built-in checks for the technical accuracy of the transmission and then, for clarity of understanding, a return message confirming (repeating) the pertinent data. Keep in mind that unless there is direct machine-to-machine interface (no human intervention between sending of data and reaction to the data), even technological transmission may be subject to human filtering on both ends.

As far back as Socrates it was pointed out that one has to communicate with another on the other person's terms. This applies not only to language differences, but also cultural, educational, and experiential differences. Before communicating, the first consideration is, given the receiver's background, is this communication within the receiver's range of perception and understanding? In the technological realm, this potential for incompatibility is annoyingly prevalent in transmitting data from computer to computer. In this case the unknowing transmitter discovers that the recipient's computer and programs do not have the compatibility for receiving the data as sent, for example, the data appears garbled when received.

Hayakawa stresses that in communicating, the words or symbols are not the actual thing being discussed.[1] This concept emphasizes that for clarity of understanding on the part of the receiver, the sender must work at conveying what was meant by the message and strive to ensure that the receiver *got the message intended.*

Expectation is a critical factor in communication. Humans tend to see and hear mostly what they expect to see and hear. The unexpected message may not be received (ignored, blocked out). This suggests that some knowledge of the

Part III.B.1

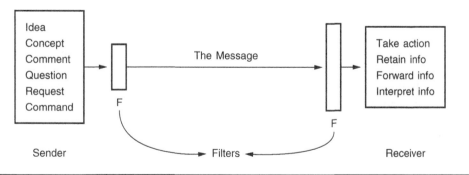

Figure 9.1   Communication path.

receiver's expectations should be known for communication to be effective. (Note: *recognize*, or *re-cognize*, means we see what we expect to see or have seen, ignoring what doesn't fit our mental model.)

Communication has occurred when action is taken. Action can range from immediately perceiving the message as an order and obeying it to deciding that the message contains information that may or will potentially be useful (or entertaining) at some later date, and then storing the message for subsequent retrieval.

A significant problem in human communications is the difference between what the sender says and what the receiver often hears. Because the sender is translating thoughts into words, and the receiver is then translating words into thoughts, many opportunities occur for differences in meaning. Misinterpretation can be caused by background, cultural biases, group norms, and emotional and health factors.

Direction of Communication

Organizational structure plays an important role in communication. Top-to-bottom vertical communication flows from managers to subordinates. The organization's vision and values, strategic goals, objectives and measures, and policies and procedures are typically communicated in this manner. Vertical communication also occurs when a manager assigns tasks to direct reports. Vertical communication also flows upward in the organization, in the context of feedback, problems encountered, and so on. In both downward and upward directions, the content of the communication is subject to filtering as the message passes from one person to another in the hierarchy.

For example, think of the telephone game. It goes like this: A group of people, say 16, are each separated by perhaps six feet. The first person softly reads a short story (up to a third of an 8-1/2 × 11″ sheet of paper) to person number two. Person number two repeats the story, from memory, to person number three, and so on, until person number 16 has heard the story. Person number 16 then repeats the story to the entire group. After a great laugh, the group discusses the changes that took place as the story passed from person to person. Often, the last person tells a version of the story that bears little or even no resemblance to the original.

Bottom-to-top vertical communication occurs when information flows from subordinates to management. Status updates on assigned tasks, employee suggestion systems, and various types of reports are examples of this form of communication. Upward communication may also include notification of deficiencies in materials, supplies, and work orders, as well as employee complaints.

Sometimes, management finds it more efficient to communicate some types of messages to all employees at monthly group meetings. These communications are often announcements of presumed general interest to all (for example, new product/service, new large customer, facility upgrade) and may be used in situations in which the speaker desires an audience reaction.

In addition to vertical communication, information is also transferred horizontally. Information flow among peers or within a team or group is horizontal communication. Examples of situations in which horizontal communication occurs are (1) a cross-functional design team developing a new product, (2) a quality improvement team working on cycle time reduction, and (3) a field sales-person notifying the production scheduler of a pending large order.

In Chapter 7 the deployment of organizational goals and objectives was discussed. A critical feature of hoshin planning, used in strategic planning, is the *catchball* concept. This is using both vertical and horizontal means of communicating (down, up, and sideways). The aim is to ensure that everyone in the organization understands the organizational goals and objectives, and identifies the part they are to play in achieving those goals and objectives. The communications, if carried out well, result in a tightly knit plan with clear linkages (and understanding) throughout every organizational level. Another type of vertical and horizontal communication is the 360° feedback process (see Chapter 8, Section 4).

Methods of Communication

Communications can be written or oral (both are verbal communication), or non-verbal. Examples of written communications include policy and procedure manuals, performance reports, proposals, memoranda, meeting minutes, newsletters, e-mail, and online documents (for example, via company intranets). Examples of oral communications include giving orders, giving performance feedback, speeches, meetings (group or one on one), informal discussions, and voice mail.

Body language—the expression of thoughts, emotions, and so on, through movement or positioning of the body—is yet another form of communication. Detailed studies have been done to analyze the meaning of various facial expressions, positions of arms and legs, posture, and so on, for both females and males, and within different cultures. Body language, especially if it is perceived to be negative (particularly if viewed as insulting, disrespectful, or threatening) from the receiver's perspective can negate a positive oral message.

Picture one spouse giving an emotionally laden oral message to the other spouse, who is intently watching a televised sporting event. The "yes, dear" replies do not reflect whether any of the spouse's messages were received. Also, body language may suggest that the messages, if received, failed to be interpreted as intended.

The negative nonverbal message that body language may communicate is a serious training topic for persons embarking on an assignment to a part of the world where the culture is different. Morrison et al. discuss some of the perils associated with inappropriate body language.[2]

Communication is also either formal or informal. *Formal* communication is planned and delivered as part of standard operating policies and procedures (SOPs) of the organization. A letter offering employment, a product test report, an environmental impact statement, the company's annual report, and performance appraisals are examples of formal communication. Signs, posters, and official posted notices are also formal communications.

Informal communication is not mandated or otherwise required, but occurs as part of helping people function collaboratively. Examples include a discussion between a test engineer and a production supervisor to clarify a specification, or an e-mail message from one employee to another reminding him or her of the need for the two of them to prepare for an upcoming presentation. Classroom

Part III.B.1

training is typically a mix of formal (for example, lecture) and informal (for example, discussion) communication.

The "grapevine" is informal communication. It is often of unknown origin and transmitted orally and/or by other fast, unauthorized media (unsigned posted notes on a bulletin board or e-mail, online postings, and so on). It may include rumor, opinions, gossip, false or true data, or valid information that has not yet been officially made known. Efforts to squelch or abolish the grapevine usually fail and often drive the communication further underground. Interestingly, management has been known to plant information for the grapevine to pick up for the purpose of testing the water to get employees' reactions or to communicate something that might be too embarrassing to document or say officially and publicly. To keep the grapevine from spreading misinformation, the frequency, accuracy, and honesty of management's communications to employees is crucial.

Other forms of informal communication include the pictures, cartoons, and quotations individuals post at their workplace, and traditional greetings and rituals, for example, "Good morning, how are you today?"

Selecting Appropriate Media

Factors to consider in making the choice of media include:

- *Urgency of message.* If the building is burning, a loudspeaker evacuation notice from a top official would be appropriate, whereas the death notification and funeral arrangements for an employee over a loudspeaker could be perceived as using poor taste.

- *Number and makeup (for example, culture, education, experience) of the receivers.* The bulletin board notification of critical safety rules may be inappropriate as the sole communication to workers with poor reading ability.

- *How dispersed are the receivers.* Will priority mail suffice for sending design changes to suppliers in different parts of the world? Or would another medium be more cost- and time-effective?

- *Culture and work climate into which the message will be received.* Would it be prudent for management to deliver its latest dictum on the "we must improve our quality and work harder to keep our customers" theme at an all-hands employee meeting when the workforce is embroiled in a labor contract dispute?

- *Best individual (for example, organizational level, functional responsibility, level of respect) to whom to send message.* Not only is the content a consideration, but also the authority level of the person sending the message will be a significant aspect of the message.

- *Physical and technical constraints (for example, facility size, transmission equipment capability/availability, time zones).* Will the conference room hold all the people needed to hear the message? Does the equipment have the needed capability? Will a phone call and ignorance of time zones awaken an irate customer?

- *Security/privacy/sensitivity issues (for example, of data and/or people).* Where will a manager and worker/associate discuss the performance review? Who might tap into a transmission and pick up proprietary organizational information (vulnerability to hackers)?

- *Safety, health, and environmental issues (for example, adequacy of facility, emotional state of receiver, impact of message on receivers' values).* Is e-mail too impersonal for communicating with certain receivers? In the interest of economy of time and space, will some of the niceties that typically are part of written communication be left out, for example, use of titles, salutation, less direct language, and so on. Will the combination of message and medium convey a conflict of personal values to the receiver(s)?

- *Whether the communication (data or information) should be retained— the methods for storing, maintaining (updating, preservation), accessing (including security requirements), and duration of retention.*

Questioning Techniques

Asking the right questions in the right way of the right people at the right time and for the right reasons is a skill that can be learned. Inasmuch as the quality professional relies heavily on data, information, and knowledge to fulfill responsibilities, this skill is important. The skill of questioning is critical to learning. Examples of a few of the situations in which good questioning skill is essential are:

- Identifying the process used by a bank loan processor in preparing a loan for approval or rejection

- Determining the root cause of a problem

- Getting facts about a customer complaint from a field service technician

- Confirming whether a direct-report employee understands what good performance is

- Confirming that trainees understand the skill and knowledge from their training

- Verifying the spikes on a control chart and obtaining the rationale for each

- Determining the facts behind a supplier's deteriorating quality

- Understanding new requirements, specifications, and other mandates

To obtain data or information from another person or group usually involves asking questions. What is asked and the manner in which it is asked influence the quality of the response received (that is, accuracy, completeness, timeliness, and relevance to other pertinent data). Skilled interviewers such as employment interviewers, consultants, complaint adjusters, systems designers, salespeople, talk show hosts, detectives, trial attorneys, and many others develop the skill of extracting the data they need to meet their purposes. Three basic methods are employed:

1. Plan beforehand what is to be learned.

2. Ask mostly open-ended questions.

3. Actively listen and capture the responses.

Additionally, and depending on the situation, these questioners create a setting conducive to the types of answers they are seeking. For example, they use a professional setting for questions about quality issues, individual performance, and so on, a threatening setting for questions about misbehavior, crimes, and so on, and a warm and comfortable setting for questions soliciting opinions and suggestions, and the like.

Often, a questioner will start with a few short, closed-ended questions to obtain demographic facts or identification, for example, "What is your employee number? What shift do you work? What accounts are you assigned to? To whom do you report?"

Then, to probe the subject of the interaction, the questioner shifts to open-ended questions, such as "Can you tell me exactly the chain of events that led up to Mrs. Smith filing a complaint about the service she received? From your perspective, what could have caused the missing pages in Tuesday's batch of policies mailed?"

The respondent's answers frequently open the opportunity for the inquirer to probe further by asking another open-ended question. Also, some responses may not be clearly understood by the questioner, so the questioner repeats what was heard in the form of a question. For example, "Did I understand you correctly when you said . . . ?" This closed-ended question will usually produce a *yes* or *no* answer, sometimes followed by further explanation, or followed up by the questioner, for example, "Can you tell me about that?"

The technique of *active listening* in two-way communication involves paraphrasing the message received back to the sender. Here's an example:

(Sender) "I need you to get the report you're working on out to Mr. Blank by noon today."

(Receiver) "I understand you want me to get the analysis of perpendicular appendages for our Purple People Eater toy line to Mr. Blank no later than noon today, no exceptions."

(Sender) "You've got it," or "No, that's not the one I mean, it's . . . "

In this scenario the sender knew what was needed, but the receiver could have been working on more than one report. Fortunately, the receiver listened actively by sending back the understanding of the order.

The speed of speech is said to be four to five times slower than the speed of assimilating the spoken word. What is done about the gap is the difference between an effective listener and a mind-wanderer. The effective listener, instead of drifting off to other unrelated thoughts, focuses on the topic at hand, using the gap to begin to formulate questions to ask to learn more (cognitive multitasking). Examples of questions to oneself using this technique are:

- "What is being said, what does it really mean?"

- "How does that relate to what was said earlier?"

- "Where is this going, what point is the speaker attempting to make?"

- "How is what I'm hearing useful to me?"

- "Am I getting the whole story, what's being left out?"

- "What evidence is being given to back up the points made?"

- "Do I really understand what's being said, should I ask for clarification?"

2. INTERPERSONAL SKILLS

> Develop skills in empathy, tact, friendliness, and objectivity. Use open-minded and non-judgmental communication methods. Develop and use a clear writing style, active listening, and questioning and dialog techniques that support effective communication. (Apply)
>
> **Body of Knowledge III.B.2**

Using Interpersonal Skills and Techniques

Interpersonal skills and techniques the effective communicator may use include:

- *Showing empathy.* The communicator identifies with and understands the needs and interests of the receiver. The communicator fosters a harmonious relationship with the receiver.

- *Tactfulness.* The communicator is polite and respectful, and avoids using insensitive, vulgar, or profane language.

- *Open-mindedness.* The communicator conveys her or his openness to consider other viewpoints and opinions. Without being hostile, the communicator provides constructive criticism when help is wanted.

- *Showing a friendly attitude.* The communicator evokes a feeling of warmth and helpfulness to receiver.

- *Sensitivity.* The communicator is kind and caring, attuned to receiver's feelings and concerns.

- *Trustworthiness.* The communicator is perceived to be and/or is known to be worthy of the receiver's trust.

- *Ethics.* The communicator embraces common codes of honor and integrity.

- *Fair-mindedness.* The communicator treats others as equals and is fair in communicating with all constituencies.

- *Authenticity.* The communicator is perceived as being congruent with reality. What you see and/or hear is what you get.

Benefits of Effective Communication Techniques

- Employees understand organizational strategies, goals, and objectives, and their role in meeting them.

- Costs are reduced as the organization accomplishes tasks effectively, eliminating the costs and time delays associated with miscommunication.

- Open communication channels make it easier for management to perceive the real issues and problems.

- Employees are more receptive to change and prone to offer creative solutions for problems.

Organizational communication is most effective when the following are present:

- Open channels of communication are maintained. This enables employees to provide the correct information. Trust between the manager and the employee is enhanced.

- Employees are highly motivated.

- An appropriate recognition and reward system is in place.

- Communication is timely. When communication is timely, employees feel that they can trust management and that management will act on the information provided. This applies to both top-to-bottom and bottom-to-top communications.

- The organization is flat. Reduction in the number of management layers helps reduce communication distortion.

- Employees are empowered. When teams or individuals are empowered, their participation and motivation increases, resulting in improved efficiency. Because they are closer to the problems, they are better positioned to make decisions rather than having to work through several management layers.

- Employee training in effective communication is provided.

Written Communications

The probability of distortion in formulating and conveying a message in writing versus orally depends on the competence of the sender in composing clear, concise, consistent, and comprehensive content. It also depends on the competence of the receiver in comprehending the intent, context, and content of the message. There is a tendency sometimes for the receiver to misunderstand written communication, especially when the message is shortened and the speed of transmission is increased. For example:

• A cryptic message delivered via a handheld device may be easily understood if communicated between two teenage friends, but could appear unintelligible to a mature adult.

• A handwritten note attached to a document may rely heavily on the knowledge and experience of the receiver. Consider this situation: A vice president, noted for his stern demeanor and attention to perfection, habitually handwrote short notes on his personalized blue paper, attaching the notes to pertinent documents. The notes were written using blue or black or red ink. His assistant hand-delivered the noted documents to the addressees.

The receivers usually stopped their work to read the notes, making the following judgments: if the blue bullet, as the notes were called, was written in either blue or black ink, the action taken and the response to the message could be delayed (slightly). If the message was written in red ink, all work was stopped until the indicated action was taken or an answer to the question was determined, and a response was made to the VP.

All but one of the VP's direct reports reacted in this way. This person had made it a point to observe the VP writing the blue bullets and learned that the VP had a desk drawer full of blue, black, and red pens. When the VP wished to write a note to attach to a document indicating the action he wanted or the question he had, he reached in his drawer and grabbed a pen—any pen. The color had no significance! The employee also realized that some blue bullets were of much lower priority and could be "aged" to see if the message became self-evident, or meaningless, over time. If not, those remaining blue bullets were dealt with eventually.

• E-mail messages often lack attention to the feelings and beliefs of recipients. Messages sent via e-mail are usually short, blunt, and lack the typical politeness of letters. Such messages can lack the completeness a receiver may need to understand and react to the message. Also, because the message is not delivered face-to-face, the sender may deliver a more aggressive and/or offensive message. And e-mails are usually composed quickly and sent without much, if any, proofreading or fact checks. Haste sometimes does make waste. As a habit, all e-mails should be checked for spelling, grammar usage, and clarity of meaning—before sending.

• The writer of the message does not have the advantage of observing the body language of the receiver, hence the writer is unable to judge how the message is being received. For example, does the receiver understand the message intent and content? Is the receiver disturbed (stressed, offended, confused) by the message and how it is worded? Is the relative importance or level of urgency the sender intended being correctly perceived by the receiver? Is the receiver perfectly clear about what action the sender intends the receiver to take, and when and how? Is the receiver clear about any confidentiality precautions the sender wants taken (whether the wishes are explicitly stated or implied)?

- Signage can be both the object of humorists and the curse of the confused. Two or more meanings attributed to a sign or a printed notice can produce unforeseen, even tragic results. On the humorous side, until recently, a sign on a major highway leading into San Diego read, "Cruise ships take next exit." A sign outside a university cafeteria said, "Shoes are required to eat in this cafeteria."

More seriously, a yellow notice attached to a new regulation for handling a dangerous chemical demanded, "Destroy this message after reading." A help wanted ad requested, "Person to handle dynamite. Must be prepared to travel unexpectedly."

Listening

I know that you believe that you understand what you think I said, but I am not sure you realize that what you heard is not what I meant.

—Unknown

Hearing and listening are distinctly different. People hear with their ears. They listen through their head, eyes, heart, and gut. Listening is often an afterthought in everyday communication. How often have you had a flashback to what you thought you heard and realized you had not listened carefully? Good listening should involve:

- Preparing yourself to listen.

- Paraphrasing to clarify understanding.

- Paying close attention to all that is being said. Showing genuine interest.

- Listenening without judging—keeping an open mind.

- Focusing on receiving data and information, not on the speaker's appearance, tone of voice, accent, beliefs, and so on.

- Asking relevant and meaningful questions.

- As the communication turns in a new direction, intervening with a summary statement of what you think you heard up to that point. It's better than waiting until the end to find you've been off track for much of the communication.

- Clarifying objections. For example, what part of what was said prompted the objection?

- Responding with statements echoing similar situations to clarify your assimilation and application of what is being said.

- As appropriate and comfortable, jotting down key words or ideas from the speaker.

- Taking mental note of what you are learning, how it will benefit you, and what you can tell others.

- Being aware of your talking to listening ratio. It's a truism that we should talk less and listen more.

What to avoid includes:

- Interrupting the person speaking.

- Changing the subject in the middle of the communication.

- Getting comfortable and drifting away to daydream.

- Completing the sender's statements.

- Solidifying your opinion or judgment of what is being said before you hear it all.

- Attempting to document every word the speaker says.

- Working on shaping your response while the other person is speaking.

- Doing something entirely different during the communication, such as computer work, answering your cell phone, reading papers, and so on. Avoid multitasking while communication is occurring.

Feedback

Feedback may be informative, constructive, or a combination of both. *Informative communication* is passing information from one person or group to another person or group. Its intent is to inform, not to instruct, direct, or control.

Constructive communication (also called *corrective feedback*) is intended to provide information that will cause action by the receiver. For example, in providing performance feedback, the management person must:

- Refer to a standard, specifications, objective, or other basis by which the performer is being measured (the baseline).

- Give specific data related to performance in relation to the baseline.

- Enlist the performer in jointly planning the action that will improve their performance.

- Provide positive reinforcement for any performance improvement, including actions taken to attempt to improve performance.

- Set a specific time for achieving the planned improvement, and obtain mutual agreement.

- Discuss the consequences for not achieving the desired performance level within the time frame planned.

* Provide interim encouragement to the performer until the objective is reached.

Roadblocks to Effective Communication

The disturbance or barrier distorting or blocking an intended message is often called *noise*, a term common to both human communication and technological communication. Examples of this noise include:

* The means for communicating is faulty or ineffective, for example, access to e-mail is blocked by a surge in usage due to a natural catastrophe occurring, the location of the sender or the receiver is too loud for the person to be heard completely or accurately, or the cell phone connection keeps breaking up as the phone moves from location to location.

* The cultural difference between sender and receiver presents obstacles due to language (including dialects), beliefs, habits, and practices.

* Communicators tend to selectively listen, not allowing themselves to hear the message as intended because of their own bias and beliefs.

* Sender and receiver place a different value on the message and from whom it is received, preventing reception of the entire message and/or understanding the intent and content of the message.

* The level of trust may cause either party to pay undue attention to the search for an underlying agenda and perceived manipulation or falsification rather than the face value of the message itself.

* Detection of, or perception that, the information conveyed in the message has been manipulated or altered to portray a more positive spin than the data warrant. For example, the subordinate tells the boss what the subordinate thinks the boss wants to hear—rather than the true facts.

3. COMMUNICATIONS IN A GLOBAL ECONOMY

> Identify key challenges of communicating across different time zones, cultures, languages, terminology, and business practices, and identify ways of overcoming them. (Understand)
>
> **Body of Knowledge III.B.3**

The obstacles shown in Table 9.1, and more, complicate and hinder effective communication within a global enterprise. Overcoming each obstacle requires:

Table 9.1   Some of the communication obstacles facing organizations operating globally, and possible remedies.

Obstacle encountered	Possible remedies
• Differences in cultures (politics, religion, social practices, business practices, and so on) Example: The business practices are alien to employees of the organization's new plant opened in a former Soviet Union country.	• Set the learning about the differences as a strategic objective for offshore facility management and headquarters management (immersion training). • Establish and distribute a newsletter to all employees, with side-by-side articles published in each of the languages used in the organization's locations. • Create a position at each organization's location that will be responsible for answering employees' questions regarding the organization's policies and practices. • Periodically convene a diagonal slice of the organization's employees, at each location, to assess the effectiveness of internal communications and uncover areas for improvement. • Carefully monitor complaints or any hints of displeasure with the handling of cultural issues, and take corrective and preventive action as needed.
• Language differences (multiple languages and dialects, even in the same country) Example: The workforce hired by the new plant will be drawn from a multiethnic population comprising persons from three different tribes (each with their language variations) as well as two large groups originally from India and from China (each with different language variations).	• Cross-train key personnel from both offshore locations and headquarters in everyday common business languages of the offshore locations and headquarters. • Provide glossaries/dictionaries to personnel in the offshore locations as well as headquarters containing the common business terms and idioms in use. • Provide orientation training for new hires in offshore locations stressing critical oral and written expressions and warnings that could affect their safety and security.
• Time differentials (time zones as well as differing perceptions of time) Example: Most of the local population do not own clocks or calendars and have no experience in adhering to schedules.	• Establish and publish the business hours and protocols for communications to and from offshore locations. • Through orientation and daily communication, address the importance of the day and time issue with offshore employees where the local culture tends to regard the day and time as more flexible than do headquarters personnel.

Continued

Part III.B.3

Table 9.1   *Continued.*

Obstacle encountered	Possible remedies
• Additional risks (disaster- and political unrest–prone geographic areas, financial instability of regions and/or industries, predominant ethical and moral attitudes and customs of a geographic area) Example: Operating in a country where extreme poverty exists, crime and corruption are rampant, and the local leaders expect the incoming organization to "contribute" to the community in exchange for protection and ease in transacting business.	• Assess and continually update the assessments of additional risks that are likely when operating in specific offshore locations. • Establish the responsible persons, in both the offshore locations and headquarters, who will continually administer the programs and actions necessary to minimize or eliminate the risks. • Establish a system of listening posts (key people who will watch for local events and actions that could affect the risk exposure of the organization) and the means for reporting and acting on the information gathered.
• Incompatibility of organizational structures and managing styles Example: Working with local tribal leadership.	• Recognize and address local perceptions of how the location/facility should be organized and managed. • Accommodate local preferences as long as such preferences can be integrated into the business practices without negative impact to the organization.
• Incompatibility of managerial and workforce competencies • Incompatibility of organizational structures and managing styles Example: Newly hired managers have no experience in coaching and participative management techniques. The newly hired workforce expects to be told what to do and does not expect to offer improvement suggestions.	• Assess and address the differential in managerial and workforce competencies between what the organization normally expects and what exists at the offshore location. • Establish training and education to address the gaps in knowledge, experience, skills, aptitude, and attitude. • Establish temporary coaches and advisors to facilitate operations until trained local personnel are fully capable. • Establish appropriate incentives for individuals' improving their competencies.

Continued

Table 9.1   *Continued.*

Obstacle encountered	Possible remedies
• Incompatibility of financial matters (currency, rates of exchange, accounting methods, pricing issues, inventory valuation, invoicing practices, payment collection practices, and so on) Example: Local payment collection practices vary based on from whom the payment is due. Some payments from certain constituencies may be waived in exchange for favors.	• Assess and address differences in handling financial matters. • Establish training and education programs to clarify the organization's objectives and to ensure that pertinent policies, procedures, and regulations are understood and followed. • Establish auditing programs to surface deviations from accepted practices and identify areas for improvement.
• Incompatibility of electronic interfaces Example: Customer order data are garbled in transmission from the United States to the plant in Malaysia.	• Assess and address incompatibilities due to equipment design and operation, and/or incompatible programs. • Set up a corrective action team, including users and supplier, to work out solutions to the problems. (May be a virtual team.) • Create temporary communication processes to mitigate the condition and enable communication to continue. • Establish help desks and remedial programs to quickly correct problems. • Form preventive action teams to continually improve electronic interface systems.

- A commitment to find a way to overcome the obstacle.

- The willingness to adopt and adapt to new ways of communicating, and to integrate those ways with the practices of the organization.

- The ability to accept that there may always be differences, but the best approach that can be expected has been subjected to discussion with and consensus of the parties involved, and agreement as to the practice or protocol has been reached.

- Top management's commitment to continual improvement for the mutual best interest of all stakeholders is paramount.

Succeed in the Global Workplace

The following list is not intended to be a complete list of competencies in the global workplace, but merely suggestive:

- Study and understand the philosophies, beliefs, regulations/laws and strategies of the global markets in which the organization does or will operate.

- Understand pertinent global business protocols, procedures, and practices.

- Develop global networks, both personal and organizational.

- Learn the business language of the pertinent global location.

- Gather information about, study, and understand the pertinent global cultures, especially as they relate to doing business.

- Modify the communication media, protocols, and styles to address the needs to be faced in the targeted global location, with care taken to sustain the organization's ethics and social responsibilities.

- Build or modify negotiation and decision-making skills to effectively deal with persons from the pertinent global location.

4. COMMUNICATIONS AND TECHNOLOGY

> Identify how technology has affected communications, including improved information availability, its negative influence on interpersonal communications, and the new etiquette for e-communications. Use appropriate communication methods to deliver different kinds of messages in a variety of situations. (Apply)
>
> **Body of Knowledge III.B.4**

Uses of Information Systems

Information technology (IT) plays a fundamental role in organizational communications. Following are examples of just a few changes that have occurred in organizations since computer technology became a core part of business systems:

- A bank teller checks his or her employee benefits information by looking on the corporate intranet instead of reading a printed brochure formerly mailed home.

- A professor sends students an e-mail message asking why they've missed class, rather than calling them by phone.

- A technician monitors performance of a machine by looking at a graphical display in a control room instead of reading an analog dial located at the machine.

- A sales agent checks availability of a product by using a laptop computer (accessing the inventory database through a wireless link) or handheld e-device such as a tablet or cell phone with wireless applications, instead of looking at a two-week-old, three-inch-thick printed inventory report.

- A construction firm checks the status of a shipment using the shipping company's web-based tracking system.

- A vice president or sales director shares sales trends using a webinar application and sharing computer screens

Information systems are used by organizations for three primary types of tasks: operations support, day-to-day decision making, and strategic analysis. Operations support includes processing transactions, for example, a bank ATM, a point-of-sale connection in a retail store, or online registration for a conference or course. Operations support also includes process monitoring and control. Monitoring and control applications might be a robotic assembly operation or the automatic pilot on an aircraft. Day-to-day decision making is the analysis of process and business performance measures. Examples would include tracking of sales, on-time delivery, cycle time, and quality indicators, as well as financial and customer satisfaction metrics. Strategic analysis of longer-term indicators provides data for supporting decisions made from examining market sector and product line trends in order to project future business performance requirements.

Following are a few examples of how an effective information system enables analysis, control, and/or projection of performance:

- A regional salesperson can compare sales with objectives, verify that the product mix is appropriate, see if the plant or warehouse is experiencing difficulty meeting requested delivery dates, and check on commissions earned in the period to date.

- The regional sales manager is able to have information for managing development of specific customer types, managing the sales force, and providing performance feedback to salespersons.

- The vice president of sales can access data for deciding how to allocate sales territories, manage the regional sales managers (support, coaching, performance feedback), and look at actual-versus-budget comparisons.

- The marketing vice president can use cumulative information for forecasting buying trends, look at geographical differences in product preference, and evaluate the impact of regional advertising.

- The operations plant manager can have early indications of product mix changes that will affect production schedules, inventories, purchases of raw materials, and the need for additional resources.

- The finance vice president can get a heads-up on any significant potential upward or downward trends in sales revenue that could impact the financial position of the organization.

Part III.B.4

- The human resources vice president and staff can utilize early indications of potential needs for staffing and training.

- The product development group can see how recently introduced products are selling, where traditional product sales are slumping, and where new needs may be developing.

Information systems are used to manage data about customers, suppliers, employees, finances, products, and processes. A well-designed system will allow the information generated at one level to be used at other levels. Figure 9.2 shows an example of some of the processes a bookstore might integrate into an information system.

Some of the more important information needed by an organization for long-term success is not generated internally. Information system design should consider the need for input of external information about competitors, markets, noncustomers, and societal trends. Sources for acquiring such information should be identified, as well as how it will be analyzed and integrated with, or compared to, company-specific information. Additionally, information systems increasingly need to be able to communicate information externally, such as for supply chain optimization.

The importance of information systems can be clearly seen by looking at their impact on various aspects of quality management. For example, both process management (see Chapter 14) and problem solving (see Chapter 13) require accurate and timely information. A well-designed information system can simplify decision making through the use of graphic displays of statistical and trend

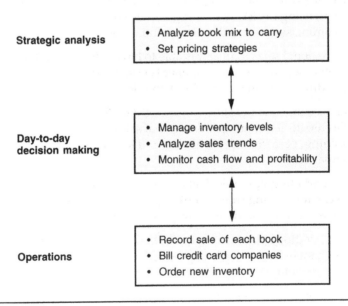

Figure 9.2   Levels of information systems.

analysis (see Chapter 15). Information systems are also key to successful employee empowerment (see Chapter 2) and cross-functional collaboration (see Chapter 8) since distributed information access is required in order for groups and employees to make quicker and better decisions.

The Technology in Information Systems

Depending on the types and volume of information, as well as differences in distribution needs, many information systems, like organizational structures, combine aspects of both centralization and decentralization. Mainframes may be used to manage organization-wide information pertaining to products and customers, while personal computers (decentralized) handle functional or process-specific information (for example, a computer-aided design [CAD] system for engineering, a workstation computer showing machine operations status). Local networks and the internet allow the information on these separate systems to be shared with or accessed by others. Wireless technology also expands the availability of information to and from any location.

Technology decisions are also important to having a reliable information management system. Redundancy of portions of the hardware or software and databases may be necessary to enable some processes to operate if a system fault occurs. Staying abreast of changes in technology while also maintaining a common core (for example, customer databases) is vital to competitiveness. Control of both applications software and databases is increasingly seen as proprietary to the business and, therefore, requires confidentiality and security. With the increasing trend toward external (cloud) data storage systems, this security issue becomes a business risk.

Design of the information system, although enabled by new technologies, should be based on the organization's strategy, structure, and business systems. That is, information system strategy should be driven by business strategy, rather than vice versa. Organizations frequently have a chief information officer whose role it is to facilitate this integration. In an organization where the information system is well integrated with strategy, the system becomes a business model of the organization, showing what is measured, what is considered important, and how widely information is dispersed. This means that as strategy, structure, and/or business processes change, the information system will also need to be modified. The particular measures tracked and reported, at least at the decision-making and strategy levels, will also shift. The effect of rapid technological change and the increasingly competitive environment means that information technology investment has become a growing proportion of the capital investment of most organizations.

Employee competency must be adequate for effective use of the information technology applications provided, meaning that proper training and ongoing technical support of hardware and software are critical to the successful use of technology. The design of any information system should consider these fundamental questions:

- What specific information is needed, and by whom?

- What precision is needed, and how often should data be collected and analyzed?

- What standard reports should be available, and how should they be delivered?

- How long should the information be maintained (for example, archived)?

Not only is information itself vital to quality performance, but also the quality of the data themselves is critical. This requires that the process for collecting the data, whether manual or automatic, be validated. It is also important to ensure that the process for subsequent (and often automatically generated) computer analysis of the data be confirmed. For example, ensuring that auto accidents are correctly recorded (location, time, people and property involved, and cause) is important for each insurance claim. Accident information may then be automatically compiled for a state highway department, which relies on correct accident categorization and geographic grouping by the computer's software.

Distribution of Information

In formatting data and reports, consider that some situations for which the information will be used are structured and predictable, while others are unstructured and unpredictable. In many cases users need the ability to look at the information in different ways. For example, sales data are useful when organized by segment (see Chapter 16). Allowing data to be viewed as text, numeric summaries, or graphics allows users to look for different types of patterns. Multidimensional graphics—for example, using 3-D and color, as in geographic information systems (GISs) (see Chapter 15, Section 5)—and computer data mining can surface very complex relationships that would otherwise not be discernable.

Of course, not all information will be viewed or analyzed on a computer screen. Processes must be defined for distribution of appropriate information, usually in summary form, to other sources for communication such as bulletin boards, management reports, meetings, newsletters, or the company website. Reports should take into consideration different personal decision-making styles (see Chapter 8) and how information may need to be presented in a variety of formats.

Information must be available at the point of use. It should enable each user access to something on which they are to act or that provides them with a broader picture to allow them to make more system-based decisions. As much as possible, the information should be integrated into the process being carried out rather than having it captured at a different location and then reported to the user. The purpose of process information is to:

- Allow action to be taken to impact current performance

- Verify that past actions were appropriate

- Predict actions that need to be taken (or not taken) in the future

Not all information captured by an organization is of the same level of importance. In some cases analysis and reporting can be done on an exception basis, although the rules for what is to be considered an exception must be carefully defined. Computer models, expert systems, neural networks, and other techniques can be useful when the decisions to be made involve many variables or a complex and dynamic process, or when it is vital that many people take similar actions based on the same information.

Using Information for Managing Organizational Performance

Alignment and integration of business processes and performance measures is necessary in order for the information captured to support the organization's strategic goals and objectives. Alignment includes both vertical and horizontal aspects.[3] *Vertical* alignment makes sure that performance measures used at lower-level processes in the organization support the measures used in higher-level processes, while *horizontal* alignment means measures at one process will support effective performance of upstream and downstream processes, including those of suppliers, customers, and other stakeholders. *Integration* calls for making sure that the various systems, and their performance measures, work together rather than against each other, and that the measures effectively implement the organization's stated values and strategies.

Analysis of performance measures should be defined according to who is responsible for the analysis (and subsequent action) and the frequency of the review. Reviews might be done by individuals or groups, and the frequency vary from continual to perhaps monthly or quarterly. In general, lower-level measures (for example, operational) are monitored much more frequently than higher-level (for example, strategic), although modern information technology is allowing this to change (for example, an organization that is able to perform a traditional type of financial closing at any time, within an hour). The information needed to support the deployment of strategic goals, objectives, and action plans, and the monitoring, measuring, and reporting of actual versus planned performance, is critical to sustaining a viable strategic planning process (see Chapters 5, 6, and 7).

Some related issues and concerns are:

- Care must be exercised to alleviate personal information overload to the extent possible.

- Security of data and information, and potential for misuse, requires increasing vigilance.

- The high risks of upgrading to the newest technology must be carefully assessed.

- Care must be taken to not emphasize technology to the detriment of stakeholder relations and needs.

- Service excellence is measured from a different perspective when looking from the inside out, rather than as perceived by the service receiver.

Part III.B.4

- Information systems can be either a competitive advantage or a disadvantage, depending on how used, for example, in the impact of these systems on an organization's customers, in their ability to be responsive to the marketplace, and in their capability to support a high level of performance (quality and quantity).

- An information system is only as effective as the quality of the planning that created it, the quality of the people who manage it, and the quality of the uses to which it is put. A highly sophisticated system, poorly designed, poorly operated, inappropriately used, or inadequate to meet the needs for which it was intended, is a drain on the resources of an organization.

Obsolescence in the Blink of an Eye

Companies that produce electronic gadgetry are stumbling over each other, pushing new products that obsolete yesterday's technology—even intentionally obsolescing their own products. Examples of technology changes and changes in users' habits are:

- *Cell phone.* Cell phones have rapidly evolved into smartphones, which provide instantaneous business and personal communication worldwide. This ability to review, prepare, send, and receive documents as well as follow world news and events has transformed any location where we might be into an effective business office. With these technological advances, problems have developed. Many professionals find it difficult to distinguish when business concludes, and how to separate personal activities from professional activities.

- *Internet.* The World Wide Web (www) offers a myriad of means and methods for communicating, reactively as well as proactively. Even the most obscure business can now portray themselves as a major player through the magic of animated and interactive websites. Bona fide sharers of information can post their articles, newsletters, and viewpoints, and join chat groups to discuss issues. Sellers can directly accept customers' orders and payments through their website. Buyers can track the progress and shipping status of their order. Researchers can access a seemingly infinitesimal number of resources through powerful search engines. Weblogs (blogs) created by individuals or organizations provide another outlet for recording and disseminating news and views. Short seminars (webinars) are offered, often in 15–20 minute chunks, for learners with a myriad of interests and needs. Many educational institutions provide degree programs that can be completed without ever attending the brick-and-mortar site.

It's mostly true that if you want information and know how to search for it, you will find more than you ever expected, needed, or wanted. Also, larger organizations have implemented *intranets* that operate within the organization and its physical locations.

On the negative side is the horrendous quantity of data and information considered to be objectionable by many internet users (for example, pornography, solicitations for participation in unprintable acts, criminal advice, hate messages, and so on). Such material is so easily accessed, organizations have had to issue policies and disciplinary guidelines to attempt to quell the curiosity of their employees.

• *E-mail.* The expansion of electronic mail is rapidly replacing a large percentage of regular mail (or "snail mail"). An e-mail message takes seconds to transmit and be received. Even with lengthy attached electronic documents, the elapsed time is negligible. Documents with electronic signatures are now widely accepted. Basic e-mail etiquette is continually being updated. Lists and suggestions range from discussions of brevity to grammar and punctuation usage, layout, font type and size, and things not to do.[4]

Access one of the many websites by searching "e-mail etiquette." The speed with which e-mail is usually composed and the informality of its use has caused concern. Oft forgotten by e-mail users is the fact that the received e-mail is a direct reflection of the organization issuing it. Sloppy grammar, misspellings, incomplete information, incorrect information, and lack of good manners can, without careful checking by the sender, convey the sending organization's image, bad or good.

Finally, depending on the receiver's e-mail service, the user may be inundated with spam (unwished-for messages), with the organization's legitimate messages buried amongst the junk. Remember the junk mail that used to fill the organization's postal mailbox each day? Multiply that by a huge number and that's the amount of spam many users get. At least the U.S. Postal Service has laws governing the types of messages being mailed! And the organization that sets up a spam sorter and automatically dumps the spam may miss an important message buried in the spam!

• *Multifunction electronic devices.* The wireless laptop computer has evolved to notepad technology. These miniature electronic devices are replacing desktop and laptop computers. Their ease of use and small size makes them very convenient for professionals required to travel or who work from different locations. And, with voice-over-internet capability, the laptop competes with the smartphone for visual, as well as verbal, contact with the other parties involved in the call or meeting.

These technological advances have transformed your automobile into a mobile communications center. Voice-interaction including access to cell phone messages, internet, and emergency service is provided by most vehicle manufacturers.

Assess the Risks

Highly integrated systems are, like any multipurpose machine, subject to breakdown if any one component fails to function properly (the weakest link). Before considering and buying the latest and greatest information-age system, care must be taken to think through the multitude of possible scenarios that a malfunction could cause, and assess the impact and risks of each. Can a disabled information system be survived? For how long, and at what cost? If the organization chooses to buy it, what data safety and backup provisions will be needed?

ENDNOTES

1. S. I. Hayakawa, *Language in Thought and Action* (New York: Harcourt Brace Jovanvich, 1972).
2. T. Morrison, W. A. Conaway, and G. A. Borden, *Kiss, Bow, or Shake Hands: How to Do Business in Sixty Countries* (Holbrook, MA: Adams Media Corporation, 1994).
3. L. L. Silverman with A. L. Probst, *Critical Shift: The Future of Quality in Organizational Performance* (Milwaukee: ASQ Quality Press, 1999), 96 –97.
4. One website is http://www.emailreplies.com/.

See Appendix A for additional references for this chapter.

Chapter 10

C. Project Management

roject management is a collection of proven techniques for proposing, planning, implementing, managing, and evaluating projects, combined with the art of managing people.[1] Projects are actions performed by people, usually with limited resources. Projects have a beginning and an end, whereas most everyday operations are ongoing. Projects may be needed at any organizational level. They can range from a massive effort (for example, a satellite global warming monitoring system) to a small, short-term project involving a few people from a single organizational entity (for example, a weekend relocation of a 10-person function to an office on another floor).

Projects are initiated for a variety of reasons, such as to:

- Develop or modify a product or service

- Start up a new business

- Implement a new process or system, introduce new equipment, tools, or techniques

- Reengineer a process to reduce customer complaints, decrease cycle time, eliminate errors

- Relocate or close a facility

- Reduce environmental impact

- Comply with regulatory mandates

- Address a community issue

Activities and/or events that can trigger the initiation of a project may include the need to:

- Implement strategic goals and objectives by deploying strategic plans downward in the organization to where action plans (projects) are initiated

- Respond to an audit finding

- Take action resulting from a deficiency uncovered in a management review of existing processes

- Resolve an existing or potential process, product, or service deficiency identified through trend analysis
- Prepare to address identified threats to market share, customer retention, and profitability
- Address identified opportunities to expand and/or change focus in how products/services are marketed, produced, and delivered
- Take advantage of unrealized core competencies, strengths, or resources by initiating an innovative service development

Short-term projects are generally those that can be completed within one year. The short-term objectives that trigger these projects are called *tactical objectives*. Typical characteristics of short-term projects are:

- They require less rigorous or no risk analysis.
- They require few resources.
- They are not cross-functional.
- They produce immediate cost savings.
- They require only a limited set of project management tools and at a lower level of sophistication.
- They are easier to obtain approval, funding, and organizational support for.

Examples of short-term projects include:

- Improving the quality of residential electric service installations by 25 percent
- Reducing defects on production line 2 from five percent to one percent
- Reducing the cost of claim processing data entry errors by 10 percent within the calendar year
- Assisting the hospital's pharmacy in reducing cycle time in fulfilling drug orders

Long-term objectives are strategic and lead to projects typically taking longer than one year to implement. Typical characteristics of long-term projects are:

- They require risk and feasibility analyses.
- They are most often cross-functional.
- They have a major impact, over a long period, on internal and external organizations.
- They typically require a large commitment of resources.
- They are often a breakthrough initiative.

Examples of long-term projects include:

- Establishing or buying a new business

- Designing and implementing a customer–supplier strategic alliance between a custom packager and a distributor

- Implementing a quality management system in a contract metal products fabricating company and certifying it to the ISO 9001 standard

- An educational institution preparing for and applying for the Baldrige Award

- Designing and implementing a municipal waste treatment program and facility

All but very small projects tend to be cross-functional, meaning they require direction, cooperation, and resources from multiple contributors. For example, in a manufacturing environment, changing a component's outer case from aluminum to plastic would affect engineering, purchasing, production, shipping, sales, and possibly other functions (including suppliers). Because there may be a number of initiatives competing for the same resources, project leaders should take into account the needs of all the affected organizational entities.

1. PROJECT MANAGEMENT BASICS

Use project management methodology and ensure that each project is aligned with strategic objectives. Define the different phases of a project: initiation, planning, execution, monitoring and controlling, and closure. Recognize the importance of keeping the project on-time and within budget. (Apply)

Body of Knowledge III.C.1

Project Life Cycle

The life cycle of a project may be defined in five stages:

1. Visualizing, selling, and initiating the project

2. Planning the project

3. Designing the processes and outputs (deliverables)

4. Implementing and tracking the project

5. Evaluating and closing out the project

Part III.C.1

Understanding a project's life cycle leads to better estimation of what resources need to be applied and when. Identifying the stages also provides for intermediate decision points (go/no-go) as a stage nears completion. The advantage of planning by stages is that fewer contingencies need be built into the estimates of the total project, as funding and resource allocations are made stage by stage, with greater knowledge of actual requirements just prior to each new stage.

Methodologies for Visualizing, Selling, and Initiating the Project

Risk Assessment—Determining If the Project Is Feasible. All projects that consume organizational resources involve risk. Risk assessment is important inasmuch as the project might not achieve a level of results acceptable to stakeholders, might not be accomplished on time, or might require more financial capital than initially anticipated.

Potential risks can be identified through brainstorming by a team, input from stakeholders, or reviews of other projects. Quantifying risks involves looking at the probability of a particular event's occurrence and its resulting impact by using a tool such as failure mode and effects analysis (discussed in Chapter 13, Section 3).

Project managers should carefully consider the risk orientation of the particular organization and stakeholders for which the project is being undertaken and not allow their own perspective to overly influence subsequent decisions.

Benchmarking (described in Chapter 12, Section 3) may be an initially useful tool to help determine what levels of performance other organizations have achieved, how the results have been accomplished, and what benefits were derived from the project.

As businesses respond to changes in markets, technology, and strategic emphasis, they allocate or reallocate financial resources for many purposes. The careful selection and successful implementation of business projects plays a large role in organizational change. An organization's future economic success and long-term survival are dependent on the financial benefits of projects outweighing the associated costs.

Benefit–Cost Analysis. Top management must approve funding for projects that require significant financial resources. Therefore, before a proposed project is initiated, a benefit–cost analysis using projected revenues, costs, and net cash flows is performed to determine the project's financial feasibility. This analysis is based on estimates of the project's benefits and costs and the timing thereof. The results of the analysis are a key factor in deciding which projects will be funded. Upon project completion, accounting data are analyzed to verify the project's financial impact on the organization. In other words, management must confirm whether the project added to or detracted from the company's financial well-being.

In today's competitive global environment, resource allocation is complicated by the fact that business needs and opportunities are greater and more diverse, and that improvements are often more difficult to achieve. Many of the easier projects have already been done. Therefore, top management requires that project benefits and costs be evaluated so that projects can be correlated to overall revenues, costs, customer satisfaction, market share, and other criteria. These factors are analyzed to maximize business returns and to limit risks and costs. Therefore, quality improvement projects are considered to be business investments—as are all cash or capital investments—in which benefits must exceed costs. Quality managers are additionally challenged in that many of these benefits and costs are not easily quantifiable, as is normally expected by executives, accountants, and financial officers.

Benefit–cost analysis strives to evaluate the benefits and costs associated with a project or initiative. Two types of benefits can be evaluated: direct or indirect. *Direct benefits* are easily measured and include issues such as increased production, higher quality, increased sales, reduced delivery costs, higher reliability, decreased deficiencies, and lower warranty costs. *Indirect benefits* are more difficult to measure, and include such items as improved quality of work life, increased internal customer satisfaction, and better-trained employees. Similarly, two types of costs can be evaluated. *Direct costs* include equipment, labor, training, machinery, and salaries. *Indirect costs* include downtime, opportunity costs, pollution, and displaced workers.

$$\frac{\text{Sum (\$) of all benefits anticipated (say, \$855,000)}}{\text{Sum (\$) of all costs anticipated (say, \$90,000)}} = 9.5$$

This means $9.50 in benefits for every dollar expended.

Typically, a benefit–cost analysis is conducted on the basis of direct costs and direct benefits to:

- Assist in the performance of a what-if analysis

- Compare the benefits, costs, and risks of competing projects

- Allocate resources among multiple projects

- Justify expenditures for equipment, products, or people

Because many indirect benefits and costs are difficult to quantify, and time is needed to identify such costs, some worthy quality projects or initiatives could fail to obtain the necessary funding.

Quality professionals are expected to help their organizations profit from quality investments, so no project should receive automatic approval and resource allocation. To be competitive, companies must find ways to increase profitability while providing customers with high levels of satisfaction. The challenge, then, is to find the link between critical business performance measurements, such as profitability, and quality investments for improvement projects, programs, and initiatives. Although some quality benefits and costs are difficult to measure or are unknowable, the quality manager still must help determine and measure quality's effect on the organization's finances. One way is by measuring the cost of quality (discussed in Chapter 13, Section 5).

Project Selection Decision Analysis. Understanding the relationship between quality and profitability requires knowledge of:

- How meeting customer quality requirements affects customer satisfaction

- How quality initiatives are linked to satisfying customer requirements and expectations

- The relationship between quality investments and gross profits

- How to ensure that quality improvement focuses on the greatest returns

- How to track elements of the cost of quality

- How customer returns and customer satisfaction affect revenues

- How to quantify customer satisfaction

Projects approved and funded by top management affect an organization's growth and development as well as its ability to remain competitive and to survive. Success depends on a constant flow of new investment ideas that are activated through these projects. Accordingly, well-managed organizations go to great lengths to develop an effective process for submitting project proposals.

Project screening procedures must be established so that projects with the most merit are approved. Screening quality capital expenditure proposals can be a complex activity. Benefits can be gained from a careful analysis, but such an investigation has its own costs. Projects should be selected not only on the basis of their potential financial payback, but also on the basis of their fit to overall business needs (for example, new product development, improvements in support systems, or improvement of the order fulfillment process).

Ranking and Prioritizing Projects. Several methods are commonly used to rank and select projects for inclusion in the organization's cash/capital budget. Projects may be accepted or rejected based on the limitations of capital or other resources. Five analysis methods are discussed:

1. Payback period

2. Net present value (NPV)

3. Internal rate of return (IRR)

4. Potential return on investment (ROI)

5. Estimated return on assets (ROA)

- *Payback period.* The payback period is the number of years it will take the results of the project to recover the investment from net cash flows. The first formal method developed to evaluate capital budgeting projects, the payback period is easily determined by accumulating the project's net cash flows to locate the point where they reach zero.

The payback period method provides a measure of project liquidity, or the speed with which cash invested in the project will be returned. Organizations short of cash may place greater value on projects with a high degree of liquidity. The payback period is often considered to be an indicator of the relative risk of projects inasmuch as managers generally can forecast near-term events better than those more distant. Overall, projects with relatively rapid returns are generally less risky than longer-term projects.

• *Net present value (NPV)*. To improve the accuracy of cash/capital project evaluations, discounted cash flow techniques were developed to take into account the time value of money. One such method, NPV, consists of finding the present value of each cash flow, discounted at an appropriate percentage rate, which is determined by the cost of capital to the organization and the projected risk of the flow. The higher the risk, the higher the discount rate required. Compute the project's NPV by adding the discounted net cash flows. When the NPV is positive, determine if the project is a prospect for acceptance. If two projects are positive, the one with a higher NPV is a more likely choice.

• *Internal rate of return (IRR)*. This is a discount rate that causes NPV to equal zero. If the IRR is greater than the minimum required by the organization (for example, cost of capital or alternative investment options), the project is likely to be accepted.

• *Return on investment (ROI)*. This analysis method is used both as an estimating tool to determine the potential return on an investment contemplated, as well as a measure of actual payoff upon project completion. ROI tends to be more useful for evaluating the payoff potential of shorter-term projects inasmuch as it ignores the time value of money.

The four methods just discussed may be applied either to projects involving a one-time investment, for example, purchase of a major facility or equipment, or to a project involving cash outlays over several time periods. Figure 10.1 is an example of the latter.

Here's a scenario: Assume an organization is considering implementing a quality management system and seeking certification to the ISO 9001 standard. The time frame from start through registration is estimated to be 18 months. Following certification, the registrar will conduct semiannual surveillance audits.

Rate	9%							
			D	E	F	G	H	
A	B	C	Net cash	Cumulative	Cumulative	ROI	Cum. net	
Year	Cost	Benefit	flow	investment	benefits	ratio	cash flow	
1	$(15,000.00)	$800.00	$(14,200.00)	$15,000.00	$800.00	0.05	$(14,200.00)	
2	$(12,200.00)	$5,600.00	$(6,600.00)	$27,200.00	$6,400.00	0.24	$(20,800.00)	
3	$(4,000.00)	$45,000.00	$41,000.00	$31,200.00	$51,400.00	1.65	$20,200.00	
4	$(4,000.00)	$61,000.00	$57,000.00	$35,200.00	$112,400.00	3.19	$77,200.00	
Totals	$(35,200.00)	$112,400.00	$77,200.00					
NPV	$(29,952.40)	$83,409.55	$53,457.15	(Excel NPV calculation)				
IRR			99%	(Excel IRR calculation)				
Payback			In year 3	(See column H)				
ROI ratio			3.19	(Column G = Columns F/E)				

Figure 10.1   ISO 9001 quality system implementation and registration.

The contract with the registrar will be for three years. One driving force for considering the project is the potential for acquiring a major new customer's business upon certification. Management's policy is to approve only major projects that can begin to produce a payback within three years from implementation and a return-on-investment ratio of at least three to one.

Using a spreadsheet and the *insert function* capability, the quality manager constructs a table. The manager employs the *finance* functions of the spreadsheet to compute the NPV, using a 9% discount rate, and IRR. Estimates of benefits are gleaned from internal sources, for example, marketing, for the value of additional business. The computations and analysis indicate a payback in the third year (1½ years following registration), an NPV of $53,457, an IRR of 99% (obviously positive), and a 3.19 to 1 ROI ratio. The manager presents his proposal to management, and the project is approved for inclusion in the annual budget. (Note: The IRR computation was not really useful for this particular decision, but was included to show how the spreadsheet function is used.)

In practice, all of the capital decision rules described previously are used; however, these methods can lead to different conclusions. Obviously, the best method is the one that selects the set of cash/capital projects that will maximize value to an organization.

Three properties must be exhibited by a project selection method if it is to lead consistently to making favorable capital budgeting decisions. The method must consider all cash flows throughout the entire life of the project and the time value of money, such that dollars acquired sooner are valued more than later dollars. In addition, when a method is being used to select from a set of mutually exclusive projects, it must choose the project that will maximize the organization's value.

In the example, the payback method fails the first two considerations by not addressing all cash flows and ignoring the time value of money. Both the NPV and the IRR provide appropriate financial accept/reject decisions for independent projects, but only the NPV method indicates maximization under all conditions. ROI ignores cash flow and the time value of money, thereby rendering the method useful for only rudimentary analysis, or smaller, short-term projects.

Return on Assets or Return on Net Assets. Projects that involve primarily the acquisition of assets are often proposed on the basis that the asset will earn more than the asset cost. Capital invested in an asset is recovered through the money derived from the use of the asset over the useful life of the asset.

Here's an abbreviated example: Assume an asset has an initial cost of $5000 and an estimated useful life of five years, with an estimated salvage value of $1000. The interest rate is estimated at 6%. Total estimated benefit derived from use of the asset over its useful life is $475,700.

The simplified return on assets (ROA) ratio calculation is:

$5000/5 years = $1000 + ($1000 x 6%) = $1060 [Asset cost per year]

$1060(5 years) = $5300 [Gross estimate of asset's cost for useful life]

$5300 – $1000 = $4300 [Asset cost less estimated salvage sale value]

$475,700 ÷ $4300 = $110.63 [Estimated net ROA—$111 return for every $1 spent]

Factors complicating the computation of ROA could be adjusting for the time value of money (not included in the previous calculation), the varying rates at which benefits are realized during the life of the asset, and an asset being paid for incrementally over several years impacting the cash flow, possibly meaning a time-delayed investment and different interest costs. As a tool for selection and prioritization, ROA may be computed using only direct costs and primary benefits to develop a ballpark estimate.

Portfolio Analysis. Usually, the comparative value of the proposed projects to the organization is a major consideration in the acceptance of projects. This comparative value pertains to the financial impacts of ongoing projects relative to the potential impact on resources of the proposed projects. A common fallacy is to accept new projects solely on the basis of their projected positive ratios, ignoring the fact that the organization may not be able to absorb further depletion of its resources within the time frames projected. For these reasons, it is prudent to create a comparative table or chart (for example, a decision tree, discussed in Chapter 13, Section 2) showing the relative financial impacts of ongoing projects versus proposed projects. The results of each of the five computations may be displayed in a table or spreadsheet for analysis of the projects (present and proposed). Thus, analyzed as a portfolio, decision-making tools (see Chapter 13) may be applied to aid in the selection, postponement, or elimination of proposed projects.

The Boston Consulting Group developed a framework for analyzing portfolios (BCG matrix) that focuses on three aspects of each alternative considered: sales, growth of market, and whether it absorbs or produces cash. The goal of the analysis is to develop a balance between the alternatives that use up cash and those that supply cash. Porter discusses the use of this analysis technique.[2]

Prioritization Matrix. A two-dimensional, L-shaped matrix compares project alternatives against weighted criteria.

Strategic Fit Analysis. The basic question is "Does the project fit within the organization's near-term and long-term strategy and available resources?" A potential project may suggest unsurpassed benefits to the organization but not be feasible given the organization's debts and volatility of the market. Essentially, this is a form of risk analysis.

With the strategic decision that a project should be planned, the planning and estimating stage begins.

2. PROJECT PLANNING AND ESTIMATION TOOLS

> Use tools such as risk assessment, benefit–cost analysis, critical path method (CPM), Gantt chart, PERT, and work breakdown structure (WBS) to plan projects and estimate related costs. (Apply)
>
> **Body of Knowledge III.C.2**

Part III.C.2

Risk Assessment

A basic rule of thumb is that all projects should be frequently assessed from the earliest stage through completion and implementation. See Chapter 13, Section 3, for failure mode and effects analysis, and Chapter 13, Section 2, for prioritization matrix, in support of risk assessment.

Methodologies for Planning the Project

Table 10.1 shows a typical project planning sequence. The sequence of steps will vary depending on the organization's needs. Following are a few examples of the variations:

- Project would not need to be justified if it has already been mandated by management or a regulatory requirement. Jump to sequence number 3.

- Project is small, involves only one work unit, should be completed in six weeks, and will cost less than $20,000, including a capital expenditure to replace one machine. Follow sequences 1, 2 (benefits to cost ratio only), 3 (project scope and objectives), 5 (pick two members of unit familiar with the situation), 6 (probably can skip unless revision is needed), 7 (list all deliverables), 9 (do, and add persons responsible as notes to the timelines), 10 (probably can skip, if Gantt chart clearly shows dependencies at a glance), 11 (combine with budget), 13 (combine budget and resource requirements), 14 (define metrics and reports), 15 (detail depends on policy of organization— a simple memo approval may be all that is needed).

- Project involves a major reengineering of a whole product line, including product redesign, new facilities, and new processes. Use the full range of the project planning sequence, including PERT charting and interim stages/gates.[3]

- Project plan is not approved on the first pass, necessitating a return to any pertinent place in the sequence to recast the plans and work back up to the approval stage.

Project Concept/Scope Statement. To initiate the planning sequence, a clear, concise statement is needed. This statement describes the situation and gives an overall concept of what the project is to accomplish, including long-term outcomes as applicable.

Stakeholder Requirements Matrix. Identify stakeholders and their needs. Stakeholders are those persons or groups who will be directly or indirectly affected by the project and its outcomes. A process map can be used as an aid to ensure that all stakeholders are identified. In addition to helping to identify areas from which team members should be selected, a process map provides the project team with an understanding of the current process. The stakeholder analysis for a customer response project is shown in Figure 10.2.

Table 10.1   A typical project planning sequence.

Seq.	Tool/technique	Comment
1	Statement	The kernel of an idea, basic concept, problem, deficiency, or opportunity to be realized is carefully defined to help later in clarifying project scope.
2	Project justification • Payback period • Net present value (NPV) • Internal rate of return (IRR) • Return on investment (ROI) • Return on assets (ROA) • Benefits to cost ratio	Risk analysis and feasibility assessment leading to a go/no-go decision.
3	Drafts: • Mission statement • Project scope • Project objectives	Documents to clarify the overall direction of the project, what it is to accomplish, breadth and depth of project, and the measurable objectives by which progress and completion are to be measured.
4	Stakeholder requirements • Matrix • Process map (to identify areas from which potential team members should be selected)	Listing of stakeholders and their requirements: (1) those with a direct commitment to the project team, and (2) those without involvement but who can influence project results.
5	Project team formation • Matrix (from sequence 4) • Myers-Briggs Type Indicator* • DiSC profile* • KESAA assessment*	Team members selected from stakeholder groups to be represented and/or based on specific skill sets needed. *Discussed in Chapter 8, Section 2 (See Chapter 3 about teams and team processes.)
6	• Mission statement (updated) • Project scope (updated) • Project objectives (updated) • Project charter • Request for project planning funds	Team members refine the original drafts, prepare charter and request for funds to plan the project. (A benchmarking study could be appropriate to better define target outcomes. See Chapter 12, Section 3.)
7	Deliverables • Project outputs (objectives of project) • Outputs used to plan and manage the project	Team members compile a list of all contractually required or agreed-on outputs (identify, define, and document). Internal outputs used in managing the project are also listed.
8	Work breakdown structure (WBS)	Project work is further defined by breaking the work into a hierarchy of work categories (clusters/families of like work, down to individual task level). Boxes in the WBS diagram may be annotated with "person/work unit responsible," "resources required," "cost estimate," and various other cross-references.

Part III.C.2

Continued

Table 10.1   *Continued.*

Seq.	Tool/technique	Comment
9	Gantt chart (matrix)	Major project steps or task clusters are listed vertically on a timeline chart, with each such item's estimated start to finish time shown as a horizontal bar across the chosen time intervals (days, weeks, months, quarters). As the project progresses, the same chart may be used to show actual time expended adjacent to the estimated timeline. Major milestones (check points, action dates) may be shown as points along the time bar for each listed item.
10	Time-dependent task diagram: • Activity network diagram (AND) • Critical path method (CPM) diagram • Program/project evaluation and review technique (PERT) diagram	Depending on the size, complexity, and duration of the project, the Gantt chart may not be sufficient for plotting the time dependencies of each task in relation to other tasks. AND shows the interrelationships of each task, or task cluster, in the project. CPM adds the dimension of normal time estimated to complete tasks and allows for computing the critical path (longest time line through the project steps). PERT adds two additional time estimates for each task (optimistic and pessimistic) allowing computation of what-if estimates of timing. Typically AND is used for short-term, simple projects. CPM is used where there are data or knowledge available to make reasonably accurate estimates of times. PERT is most often used for projects when there are no prior estimates known.
11	Resource requirements matrix (RRM)	An RRM is used to identify and describe the various types of resources needed, when they are needed, quantity, and cost (for example, personnel, facilities, equipment, materials, consultants, funding).
12	Linear responsibility matrix (LRM)	Used in larger projects, the LRM defines who has responsibility for what tasks, and to what degree (e.g., primary, secondary, resource only, need to know).
13	Project budget • Summary project budget • Cash flow budget	An itemized budget, prepared by the team, based on the project time and cost estimated.
14	Measurements and reports • Milestones/stage gates • Project monitoring • Data analysis methodology • Reporting protocols	The quantifiable measurements, defined by the team, whereby the project progress and project completion will be determined.
15	Completed project plan • Executive summary • Backup documents supporting plan • Funds request • Plan approval sign-off	Final approval to proceed with project is obtained.

Source: Reprinted with permission of R. T. Westcott & Associates.

Stakeholder	Requirements	Impacts
Project team	• Project plans • Project management	Approval Successful implementation
Customer	• Timely initial response • Courteous response • Timely call-back response, if needed • Satisfaction with action taken or reasonable explanation as to why no action will be taken	Satisfaction with complaint response and resolution process
Customer service rep (CSR)	• Effective procedures, tools, and techniques for handling customer complaints • Positive reinforcement for work done well • Organizational objective to achieve a balance between serving volumes of customers quickly and serving customers satisfactorily • Well-trained and available support/supervision	Productivity loss due to overload of inadequately handled customer complaints. Customers' mood and satisfaction with responses. CSRs' demeanor and satisfaction in serving customers. CSRs' morale and motivation.
Complaint investigators (experienced CSRs removed from customer contact duties)	• Reduction in number of complaints to investigate • Reassignment of CSRs to customer contact duties	Elimination of complaints escalated to CEO's office. (Average = 2000/month with investigation cost of 20 CSRs/month)
Customer service management	• Senior management commitment to customer satisfaction as top priority • Revised measurements that reflect more appropriate balance between achieving customer satisfaction and productivity	More satisfied customers Lower operating costs Less employee turnover, fewer grievances and disciplinary actions Time better spent on preventive actions
Operations management	• Senior management commitment to preventive action to reduce occasions causing customer complaints	Reduction in customer complaints
CEO	• No poorly handled customer complaints to deal with	Time better spent on future planning, attracting and retaining investors
Stockholders	ROI	Investor confidence in company

Figure 10.2   Customer response project–stakeholders.
Source: Reprinted with permission of R. T. Westcott & Associates.

Part III.C.2

All stakeholders have their own interests, priorities, and concerns regarding a project's outputs and outcomes, as well as the processes used. Any stakeholder groups that will not be represented on the project team should have an opportunity to provide input. Their information is important for identifying processes to be used, boundaries (for example, of authority) to be observed, and performance measures to be tracked.

Project Team Formation. The team should consist of representatives of as many stakeholder groups as is feasible. It is especially important that those responsible for implementing any project recommendations are represented on the project team. Team membership must also take into account any particular technical skills that may be required. When the need for a member with specialized skills will vary over the life of the project, such a person may be called in on an as-needed basis.

When an opportunity exists to be selective in project team membership, the level of sincere interest shown by potential project team members is a primary consideration. Some organizations take into account the personal styles of potential members (as identified through a personality profile, such as the Myers-Briggs Type Indicator) to ensure team diversity.

The process for selection of team members can vary. Team members may be selected by the project sponsors (for example, a management group) or may be representatives appointed by the various stakeholder groups affected. The project team leader may be appointed and given the authority to select or solicit other team members. The approach used to select members may depend on the scope and importance of the project, likelihood of success or the potential impact of failure, the culture and values of the organization, or the dominant style of management within the organization. See Chapter 3 for more on team member selection and team formation.

Deliverables. The project team collects, categorizes, and documents all contractual requirements and all planned deliverables expected from the project. Also, where applicable, use of required documents and/or actions required by regulatory agencies may also be documented. In addition, the outputs needed to manage the project are also listed. An example of project deliverables is shown in Figure 10.3.

Work Breakdown Structure. Except, perhaps, for extremely small, short-duration projects, a *work breakdown structure* (WBS) is created by the project team. If any pertinent organizational groups are not represented on the project team, such groups should be consulted before committing them to work responsibilities on the WBS.

Typical terms for the descending levels of a WBS are *project level, subproject level, work unit/component level* (optional), *work package level,* and *task level* (may be optional). Usually, cost accumulation reaches down to the work package level. Figure 10.4 shows a three-level WBS under development (project level, subproject level, and work package level only). The task level has not yet been added, nor have the identification numbers for each box (usually a decimal hierarchy to aid accounting in building costs from the lowest to the highest level), the name of the person or function responsible, nor time and cost estimates.

The WBS is the focal point for planning. It provides the structure of the project and the basis for estimating time and costs. The WBS also enables the project team

Name of deliverable	Description/purpose of deliverable
Project management outputs	
Time and cost tracking system	Procedure, software to collect project data
Progress reports	Weekly "exception" reports of variables
Evaluation report	End-of-project evaluation of results
Project documentation	Critical documents for knowledge base
Team effectiveness evaluation	Members' performance evaluated
Team celebration	Members recognized for contribution
Project work outputs	
Engineering specifications for machine	For use in selecting and purchasing machine
Vendor selection criteria	For use in selecting vendor
Purchase order	For purchase–lease of machine
Floor plan	Layout for new machine workspace
Installation plan	For replacement of old machine with new
Operator training plans	For off-site and on-site operator training
Trial run plans	To test new machine, acclimate operators
Revised work instructions	For changed process
Revised plant scheduling system	For changes in production scheduling
Turnover plans	Turning over responsibility to production
Post-installation process audit	To determine if planned outcomes were achieved

Figure 10.3   Deliverables (hypothetical).

Source: Reprinted with permission of R. T. Westcott & Associates.

Part III.C.2

to visually see the relationships of all parts to the whole: the deployment of tasks and responsibilities, and the accounting structure by which costs will be accumulated and measured against budget.

Note: A WBS may be created in outline format, the line indentations indicating the levels of the structure. Advantages of the outline format are that the outline is easy to compile (word processing) and easy to modify. A disadvantage is the difficulty in clearly seeing the overall view of the project and its interfaces. The input to some project management computer programs that compile the WBS and other documents is similar to the outline format. A sample WBS in outline format is shown in Figure 10.5.

Gantt Chart. After the WBS has been created, the tasks or steps are time-phased on a *Gantt chart*. Gantt charts may be created at any level of detail needed for managing the project, although not generally at the work unit level. Figure 10.6 shows a partial Gantt chart at a work package level. As project planning progresses, the chart can be amended to display milestones (critical points for measurement), and as work progresses bars added representing actual times elapsed, and other symbols to indicate project status.

Part III.C.2

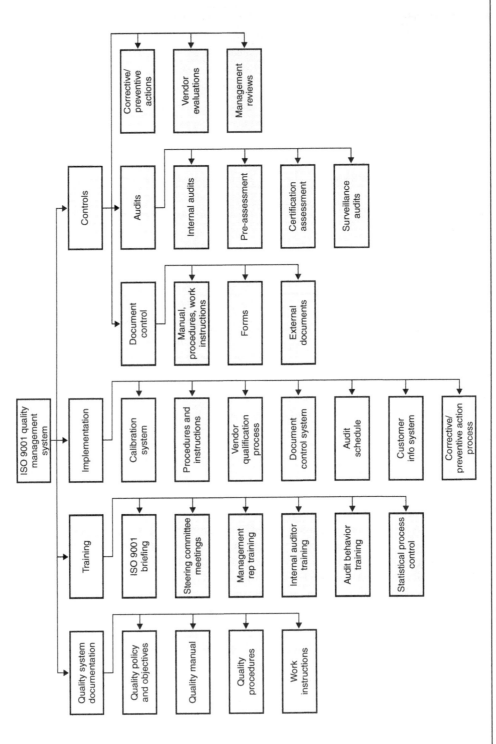

Figure 10.4 Work breakdown structure (work package level).

ID #	Activities	Resp. person	Start date	Finish date	Time est.	Cost est.	Depends on
02	New garage project	Russ	040113	092213	102	42,125	0
02.01	Purchase drawings	Russ	040113	040113	1	25	02
02.02	Select builder	Russ	040113	041213	2	0	02.01
02.03	Obtain permits	Russ	041413	043013	1	150	02.02
02.04	Order building materials	Bud	050513	052713	2	3,000	02.03
02.05	Construct garage	Bud	050513	091313	88	36,150	02.04
02.05.01	Lay foundation	Bud	051713	052713	5	3,500	02.05
02.05.01.01	Prepare lot	Ron	051713	052013	3	1,500	02.05.01
02.05.01.02	Set forms and pour concrete	Bud	052413	052713	2	2,000	02.05.01.01
02.05.02	Erect structure	Bud	060713	081113	45	19,350	02.05.01.02
02.05.02.01	Framing	Pete	060713	063013	15	6,750	02.05.02
02.05.02.02	Roof	Bill	062113	071913	12	5,400	02.05.02.01
02.05.02.03	Windows and doors	George	072113	073013	3	450	02.05.02.02
02.05.02.04	Siding	Al	072213	081113	15	6,750	02.05.02.03
02.05.03	Finishing structure	Bud	072613	091313	38	13,300	02.05.02.03
02.05.03.01	Electrical work	Oscar	072613	081813	15	5,250	02.05.03
02.05.03.02	Plumbing work	Tony	072813	082013	10	3,500	02.05.03
02.05.03.03	Interior finish, painting	Stan	082313	083113	7	2,450	02.02.03.02
02.05.03.04	Exterior finish, painting	Stan	083113	091313	6	2,100	02.05.03.03
02.06	Property reconstruction	Bud	081613	092213	8	2,800	02.05.03.02
02.06.00.01	Driveway	Rashid	081613	083113	4	1,400	02.06
02.06.00.02	Landscaping	Rashid	083113	092213	4	1,400	02.06.01

Figure 10.5   Work breakdown structure (WBS)–building garage (outline format).
Source: Reprinted with permission of R. T. Westcott & Associates.

Advantages of a Gantt chart include:

- It is easy to understand and modify.

- It is a simple way to depict progress status.

- It is easy to expand to identify tasks that are critical to monitor.

Disadvantages of a Gantt chart are:

- It does not as clearly show interdependencies among project activities as does a network diagram.

Part III.C.2

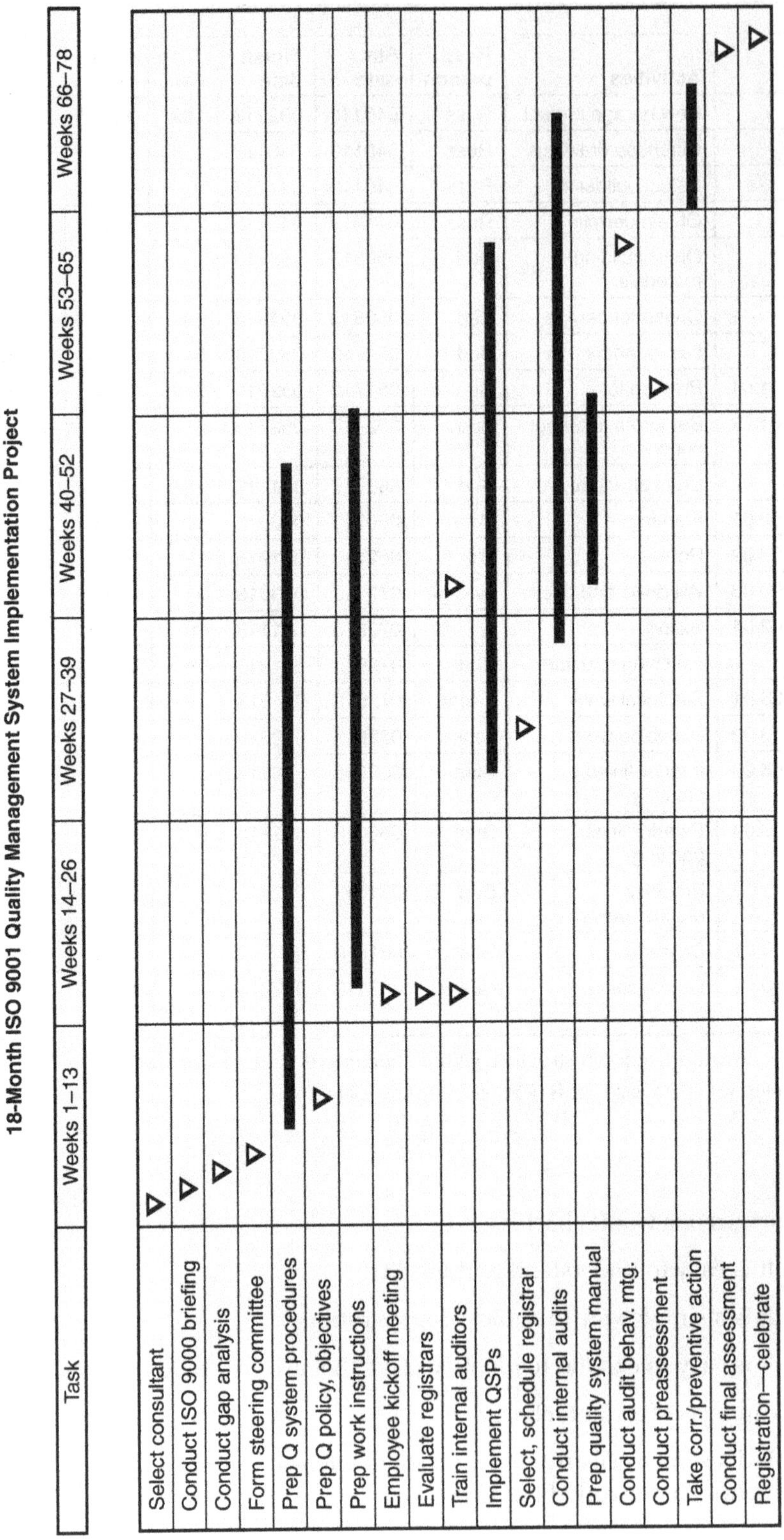

Part III.C.2

18-Month ISO 9001 Quality Management System Implementation Project

Task	Weeks 1–13	Weeks 14–26	Weeks 27–39	Weeks 40–52	Weeks 53–65	Weeks 66–78
Select consultant	▷					
Conduct ISO 9000 briefing	▷					
Conduct gap analysis	▷					
Form steering committee	▷					
Prep Q system procedures	▬					
Prep Q policy, objectives	▷					
Prep work instructions		▬				
Employee kickoff meeting		▷				
Evaluate registrars		▷				
Train internal auditors		▷	▷			
Implement QSPs			▬			
Select, schedule registrar			▷			
Conduct internal audits				▬		
Prep quality system manual				▬		
Conduct audit behav. mtg.					▷	
Conduct preassessment					▷	
Take corr./preventive action						▬
Conduct final assessment						▷
Registration—celebrate						▷

Figure 10.6   Gantt chart.

- It can not show the results or consequences of either an early or late start of project activities, thereby giving little or no clue as to the impact of slippage on the project completion date.

- It is unable to show uncertainty, that is, the effect of the longest, shortest, or most likely time estimates.

While a WBS depicts a project hierarchy and delineates the work to be done, the Gantt chart graphically indicates the timeline for each significant piece of work or event, and the current status of each. For smaller projects, the task dependencies may be sufficiently visible to obviate the need for time-dependency charting.

Activity Network Diagram. An *activity network diagram* (AND) is a simple chart showing the dependencies of each task on other tasks in the project (what has to precede a given task and what has to follow). This chart is used in understanding and communicating task relationships within the project.

Critical Path Method. A *critical path method* (CPM) chart is an expanded AND showing a time estimate for each activity. The sequence of interrelated activities that takes the longest is the *critical path*. CPM charts are commonly used for projects where there are prior data or experience in documenting reasonably accurate time estimates. Computer software is usually employed for more complex projects.

Figures 10.7a and 10.7b follow the ISO 9001 Quality Management System Implementation Project, showing the development of a CPM chart. The critical path is the series of steps taking the longest time. No slack time exists on the critical path.

Program/Project Evaluation and Reporting Technique. A *program evaluation and reporting technique* (PERT) chart expands the CPM concept by including three time estimates (optimistic, most likely, pessimistic) for each activity. From these data, comparative paths can be generated. Also, slack time may be computed for activities not on the critical path, thus providing decision information for reallocating resources and schedules. PERT is usually used where there is a paucity of estimate data and little to no prior experience with a similar project. Computer software is needed for complex projects. A significant feature of both the CPM and PERT methods is the ability to test the feasibility of different scenarios to find an optimum path.

Note that project management software often integrates the AND, CPM, and PERT concepts and computations into one tool—*network diagramming.* Examples of questions that can be answered with network diagramming are:

- What are the task dependencies?

- Where is slack or float apparent? Tasks with slack can be delayed without delaying the entire project. Tasks on the critical path have no slack. Float may be used to do certain tasks simultaneously, or delay noncritical tasks and divert resources where needed so as not to affect the total critical path time.

- What task sequences can be overlapped and performed simultaneously?

ISO 9001 Quality Management System Project

#	Tasks	Start in	After task #	Before task #	Weeks to complete
1	Select consultant	Wk 01		2	3
2	Conduct ISO 9000 briefing	Wk 04	1	3	1
3	Conduct gap analysis	Wk 05	2	4	1
4	Form steering committee	Wk 06	3	5	1
5	Prepare QSPs	Wk 07	4	16	57
6	Prepare quality policy and objectives	Wk 09	4	8	1
7	Prepare work instructions	Wk 14	4	16	39
8	Employee kickoff meeting	Wk 15	6	11	1
9	Evaluate registrars	Wk 26	4	12	1
10	Train internal auditors	Wk 26	6	13	2
11	Implement QSPs	Wk 29	5	16	35
12	Select and schedule registrar	Wk 33	9	16	1
13	Conduct internal audits	Wk 39	10	18	37
14	Prepare quality system manual	Wk 42	6	16	13
15	Conduct audit behavior meeting	Wk 64	11	16	1
16	Conduct pre-assessment	Wk 65	5	17	1
17	Take corrective/preventive action	Wk 66	16	18	12
18	Conduct final assessment	Wk 78	17	19	1
19	Registration notice—celebrate	Wk 79	18		1

Figure 10.7a   CPM data table.

78–Week Quality Management System Project

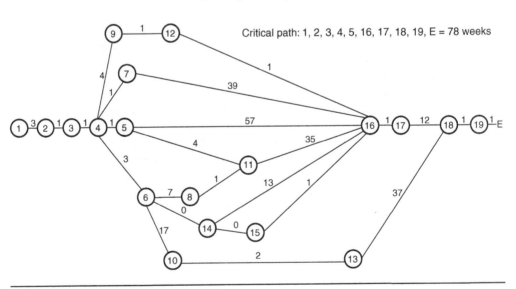

Critical path: 1, 2, 3, 4, 5, 16, 17, 18, 19, E = 78 weeks

Figure 10.7b   CPM chart.

- What tasks have to be *crashed*, meaning applying more resources to complete the task in a shorter time or on time?

- What is the cost effect of a late start or an early finish?

- What is the probability of completing the project on time and within budget?

- What is the cost effect of a project cancellation, an imposed temporary suspension of the project, or a mandated early completion of a re-scoped project?

- What other alternatives are feasible? Subject the plans to *what-if* scenarios.

Resource Requirements Matrix. Requirements matrices are helpful for documenting resources required. A typical *resource requirements matrix* (RRM) may be prepared for each major resource, at any level of detail essential for managing the procurement and deployment of resources.

For example, an RRM spreadsheet for personnel could have left-column labels for the major categories of personnel needed, and the columns to the right showing time periods (for example, weeks, months, quarters). The quantity posted in each applicable cell represents the number from each resource category needed in each time period. Column totals show the total number of personnel needed for each time period; the horizontal totals show the number of each category of personnel needed for the project. Similar RRMs can be compiled for facilities, equipment, materials, and contract/consulting personnel.

A sample RRM for personnel is shown in Figure 10.8.

How resources are to be acquired, including special needs that might not have been considered in advance, should be determined as part of the project plan (for example, who has the authority to make such decisions?) and communicated to personnel responsible for allocating resources.

Some resource questions to ask are:

- *What resources will be furnished, and by whom?* For example, if one resource is a work area within existing space, have arrangements been made and affected departments informed that they must provide such space? If the resources are people, what qualifications must they have?

- *When must these resources be available?* A piece of equipment might need to be available immediately or only during a particular phase of the project. Holidays and vacations might conflict with the project schedule.

- *How will the resource be delivered?* This factor can affect both cost and timing (for example, consider the arrival difference between shipboard freight, rail freight, truck freight, and airfreight).

- *How much will it cost, and when will payment be made?* The detailed costs and timing must be known in order to manage cash flow.

- *Who will pay?* This must be known in order for each direct stakeholder to budget and make decisions about the project's timing.

Part III.C.2

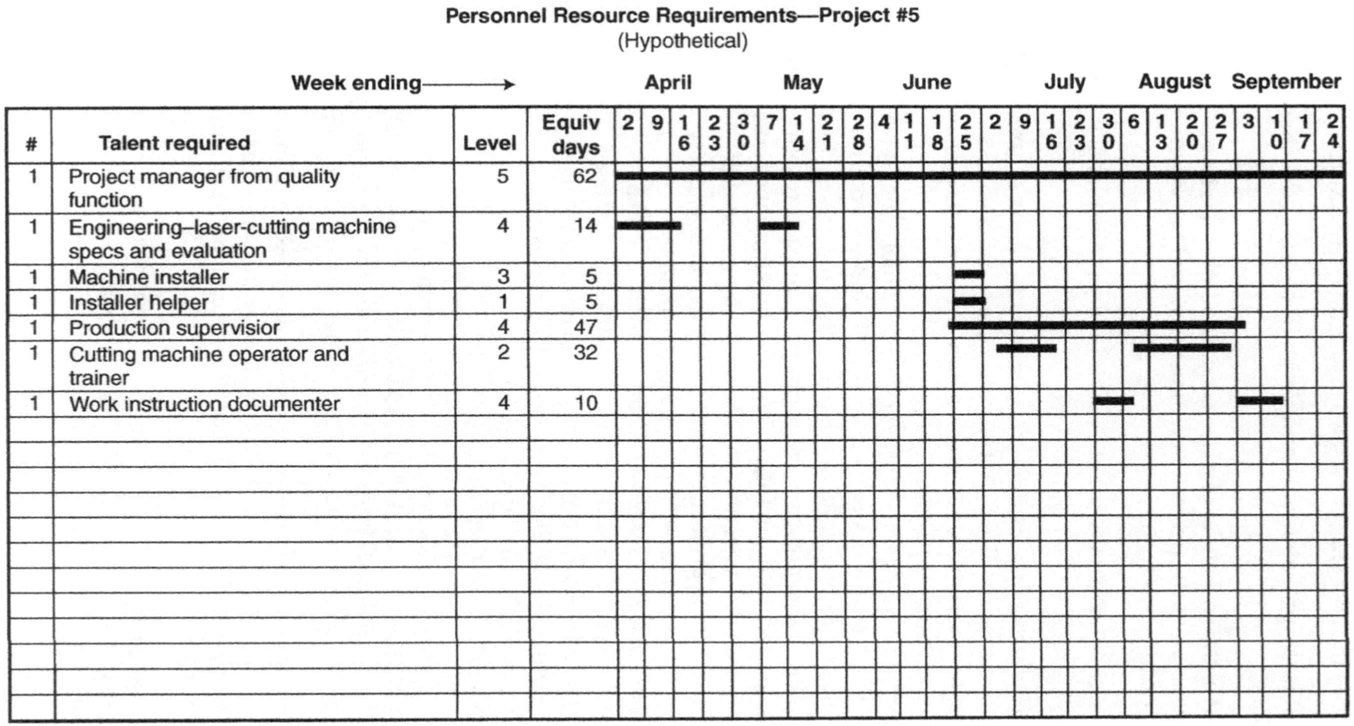
Personnel Resource Requirements—Project #5
(Hypothetical)
Week ending
April
May
June
July
August
September
#
Talent required
Level
Equiv days
2 9 16 23 30 7 14 21 28 4 11 18 25 2 9 16 23 30 6 13 20 27 3 10 17 24
1 Project manager from quality function 5 62
1 Engineering–laser-cutting machine specs and evaluation 4 14
1 Machine installer 3 5
1 Installer helper 1 5
1 Production supervisior 4 47
1 Cutting machine operator and trainer 2 32
1 Work instruction documenter 4 10

Figure 10.8 Personnel resource requirements matrix.

Linear Responsibility Matrix. For large projects with multiple responsibilities, a *linear responsibility matrix* (LRM) is helpful for documenting a three-dimensional view of the project responsibilities. One way to construct an LRM follows: List tasks in the left column as row labels; identify the persons or functions responsible as labels for additional columns to the right. At the junction (cell) where a task relates to a person/function, a symbol is placed (the third dimension). Several types of symbols or codes may be used. Typical symbols denote the level of relationship, for example, primary, secondary, resource only, or need to know. Looking at a column, it is readily apparent for what tasks a person or function is responsible/involved, and to what extent.

Project Budget. A project budget sets financial expectations for project implementation. The budget plan details the magnitude and timing of projected financial resource inflows and outflows over the project's duration. Typically, management is concerned with the cash flow requirements and when the payback will be available.

A budgeted quality project is expected to be completed (1) within the time schedule approved, (2) within the approved costs and capital expenditures, and (3) within the approved scope and specifications. Typically, budgeting involves:

- Identifying the resource requirements for each of the defined project activities

- Estimating costs to complete the activities

- Communicating the requirements to top management for funding approval

Typical budget revenue estimating factors include:

- Increased sales

- Improved process capability

- Increased profits

- Increased equipment uptime

- Reduced defects

- Reduced spare parts inventory

- Reduced scrap

- Reduced customer cancellations

- Lowered warranty claims

- Fewer returned products

Quantifiable budget cost factors may include:

- Cost of money

- Energy costs

- Personnel costs

Part III.C.2

- Subcontracted work costs

- Overhead allocations

- Cost of materials

- Equipment costs—purchase, rentals, leases

- Fees—permits, licenses, and applications

- Consulting charges

- Reserve or contingency for unanticipated events

In general, a project budget should be:

- The mechanism for planning, authorizing, allocating, and controlling resources

- A basis for comparison of multiple projects (portfolio analysis)

- A baseline from which to measure the difference between the actual and planned uses of resources

A sample budget is shown in Figure 10.9.

Measurements and Reports. Developed and set in place early in the planning stage, a feedback system is designed to monitor the project to detect and report deviations from the plan so that corrections can be made as needed. Feedback is necessary to surmount communication barriers, which can include physical distances, priority conflicts within the company, language difficulties (for example, foreign, technical, and perceptual), work shift differences, interpretation of drawings and requirements, and rumors concerning the project status. Feedback is also useful for identifying learning opportunities for the current or future team.

The design of a tracking/monitoring system should consider:

- The objective for each type of feedback

- Providing data that can be used to initiate any corrective action needed

- How the data provided tie in with the planning documents, that is, Gantt charts, network diagrams, and resource matrices

- The frequency and timing of data (for example, hourly, daily, weekly, or monthly)

Key measures should be selected by persons at each responsible level in the project team who can reliably see the status of both the whole project and their own part of the project. Factors to consider in planning these measures are:

- Time status (relative to plans/critical path, percentage completed)

- Resources expended status (relative to budgets, percentage expended)

- How future outcomes/impacts on the organization will be measured, when, and by whom

Project: Improve Filler Cap Quality

Expected outcome: 50% reduction in returned products

Labor budget

Team	$/hr.	Planned hours per stage					Dollars of labor per stage				
		1	2	3	4	Total hrs	1	2	3	4	Total $
Beth Esda	20	10	15	15	25	65	200	300	300	500	$ 1,300
Anna Lyst	15	8	8	6	12	34	120	120	90	180	510
Ed Ifye	18	0	15	25	20	60	0	270	450	360	1,080
Jule Ly	9	0	20	20	25	65	0	180	180	225	585
Ali Ghator	10	10	5	10	15	40	100	50	100	150	400
Total		28	63	76	97	264	420	920	1,120	1,415	$ 3,875

Non-labor dollars budgeted per stage

Category	1	2	3	4	Total $
Facility rental	4,500	4,500	4,500	4,500	$ 18,000
Equipment rental	1,950	1,950	1,950	600	6,450
Materials	675	0	1,250	7,800	9,725
Consulting fees	20,000	0	5,000	18,000	43,000
Process changeover	0	0	0	235,000	235,000
Total	27,125	6,450	12,700	265,900	$ 312,175

Total budget per stage

Category	1	2	3	4	Total $
Labor	420	920	1,120	1,415	$ 3,875
Non-labor	27,125	6,450	12,700	265,900	312,175
Total	27,545	7,370	13,820	267,315	$ 316,050

Projected reduction in returned product—year one	$1,498,000
Estimated project costs	316,050
Projected net benefit from implementing project	$1,181,950

Figure 10.9   Sample project budget.

Care must be taken to ensure that project status reports are useful to those requiring them for decision-making purposes. Project planning must consider:

- What reports are needed by whom

- The frequency and timing of reports, for example, daily, weekly, or monthly

- Media by which data are reported

- How and from whom the project team is to request help when necessary

- How and by whom project plans and timetables will be updated

Project Funding Approval Request. For larger projects when the funding has not been approved or allocated up front, a funding approval request is often required. The project planning documents just described serve as backup for the funds requested. In some organizations this document may be called an *appropria-tion request*.

Project Plan Approval. Depending on the organization's policies and procedures, the scope of the project, the planned cost, the planned outputs and outcomes, and the requirements of stakeholders, the approval may take many forms, such as:

- A signature affixed to a project plan document (for example, funding request, project budget)

- A memo from an authorized person

- A sign-off sheet signed by key management

- Verbal approval from an authorized person for very small, short-duration projects

For larger projects, the documented project plan, represented by these documents, is packaged with an executive summary and presented to senior management for approval. If the team's work has been done well, the plan may be approved on first pass. Senior management, however, often has knowledge of pending sit-uations that may impact the timing or the potential effectiveness of the project's outcome. A project may be delayed, the plans sent back for revision, or the project canceled entirely. An example is a telecommunications equipment distributor that suddenly finds itself the target of a hostile takeover. Clearly, all available resources may have to be committed to challenging the takeover. The proposed project to implement an ISO 9001–based quality management system would likely be post-poned, if not canceled.

Methodologies for Designing the Processes and Outputs (Deliverables)

The tools used in designing the processes and deliverables will depend on the type of projects planned.

3. MEASURE AND MONITOR PROJECT ACTIVITY

Use tools such as cost variance analysis, milestones, and actual vs. planned budgets to monitor project activity against project plan. (Evaluate)

Body of Knowledge III.C.3

Tools for Implementing and Tracking the Project

There are both measures of the ongoing project and measures of the results of the project. With an effective tracking/monitoring, measuring, and reporting system in place, the critical performance measures of an ongoing project follow.

Timeliness. Tracking includes overall progress (such as percentage complete), status of major stages or milestones, and completion of specific activities. It is important to track both late and early variances from plan because they affect the probability of success, costs, and the status of other projects contending for the same resources.

In medium to larger projects, critical checkpoints are established in the planning stage (usually indicated on the Gantt chart). These milestones or stage gates are the points at which a check is made to ascertain progress. They are the points where key measures are taken to determine if the project is proceeding on target, and if not, decisions can be made to bring the project back on track. Adjustments may be made to increase or decrease resources and expenditures or shift resources to an activity or event on the critical path where needed. As a result of the ongoing monitoring of milestones, changes to plan may result, for example, recomputing of the critical path or revision to resource allocation plans. All changes must be documented.

While project monitoring continues at the milestone level throughout the implementation stage of the project life cycle, progress or stage/gate reviews may be targeted to key schedule dates or completion of major work packages (identified on the work breakdown structure). These reviews between the project manager, senior management, and key stakeholders evaluate the results of the project implementation to date. The reviews may include assessment of:

- Schedules against the critical path

- Expenditures against budget

- Resource utilization against plans

- Implementation results to date against plans

- Reevaluation of risks

- Major issues confronting project continuance

The outcome of the stage/gate review may be any one of these options:

- Continue on to the next stage at the approved level of funds and resources.

- Go to the next stage with new or changed objectives and plans.

- Hold off the next stage until more information is available and/or organizational conditions change.

- Postpone or cancel the project before entering the next stage.[4]

All such decisions must be documented.

Budget Variance. The project budget lays out the cash flow over the life of the project. Tracking expenditures and comparing to budget, at critical project stages, provides a basis for appropriate financial control.

A sample variance report for a partially completed project is shown in Figure 10.10.

Work package	Labor hours and costs						Suppliers' charges			Equipment charges		
	Pld hrs	Act hrs	Var	Pld $	Act $	Var $	Pld $	Act $	Var $	Pld $	Act $	Var $
Project management (QE)	25	15	10	600	375	250						
Needs analysis (QE)	24	18	6	600	450	150						
Write calibration specs (PE)	32	26	6	960	780	180						
Select suppliers (QE)	8	10	−2	200	250	−50						
Order equipment (QE)	8	8	0	200	200	0				8200	8300	1000
Order computer program (QE)	1	1	0	25	25	0						
Train QE (supplier)	24	7	16	600	200	400	5000	2500	2500			
Set up system (QE, PS)	40			1000								
Calibrate tools, equip. (QE)	240			6000								
Set calibration schedule (QE)	16			400								
Write procedures (PE, PS)	30			735								
Close-out (QE, PE, PS)	24			680								
Contingency fund				1000								
Totals	472	86		13000	2280		5000	2500		8200	8300	1000

Figure 10.10   Calibration system project—sample variance report.

The benefits/cost ratio should also be recomputed at critical stages of the project inasmuch as more of the actual costs become known and potential benefits may be clarified as the project progresses. A recomputation can signal a potential problem to address. Such changes must be documented.

Earned Value Analysis. *Earned value analysis* (EVA) methodology consists of knowing the planned value of the work to be done, the earned value of the actual work completed, and the actual costs to achieve the earned value. Two variances can then be determined: the difference between the planned and earned value of the work scheduled, and the earned value of work done compared with the actual costs to do the work. This method enables the project team to more closely monitor project performance against their scheduled plan. A scheduling system, such as CPM, is required.[4]

Resource Usage. The project plan specifies what resources (for example, facilities, human, equipment, funds, information) are required, as well as when they will be needed. Using resources owned or controlled by the organization can make the project easier to manage, but the need for special equipment or skills, or critical shortages in resources, often dictate that externally acquired resources will also be necessary. The usage of resources is reported and analyzed during the project life cycle to ensure that resources have been used wisely and that adequate resources will still be available to complete the project. Any changes must be documented.

Risk Analysis. Every project, large or small, involves some level of uncertainty. All projects that impact organizational resources involve risk. Risk assessment is an important component of project management.

Proactively identifying and mitigating potential future events, risk management may include developing contingency plans when uncertainty is identified. Properly applied, risk management may avert an undesirable event, or at least minimize its impact.

For those risks having both a high probability of occurrence and a high level of negative consequences, a strategy should be developed for offsetting the risk (for example, through the purchase of insurance or through the development of a contingency plan).

Reassessment and analysis of potential risks should be performed at critical intervals. Schedule delays, resource shortages, financial developments, competitive influences, organizational leadership changes, and external events are examples of risks that can occur after a project is under way. Documentation of the risk management plan, including any changes, provides a guide for responding to adverse events that may occur during the project. (See Chapter 8, Section 6 for more on risk management.)

Methodologies for Evaluating and Closing Out the Project

Typical end-of-project evaluation measures include:

- Objectives accomplished

- Deliverables accepted

- Financial obligations completed

- Schedule met, early or late

- Budget performance favorable

- Return on project investment (ROPI) reasonable

- Payback period achieved

- Annualized cost savings realized

- Earned value analysis favorable

- Operational measures:

  - Response time improvement

  - Waste reduction

  - Process capability improved

  - Start-up efficiencies and rates

Project Closeout Actions

The time to close down the project occurs when:

- All planned deliverables have been completed

- All project documentation has been completed, including:

  - A post-project summary review report presented to key stakeholders

  - Assessment of key stakeholders' satisfaction, feedback shared, and necessary actions taken

  - Project history (plans and decisions made) documented

- All outstanding accounts payable are resolved

- Lessons learned have been discussed and documented (see section above)

- Appropriate project closeout document has been approved

- The project team has received appropriate recognition for their accomplishments, and the team has celebrated

- Project team is officially disbanded

- The project may also be terminated because:

  - Project is no longer strategic or desirable

  - Funds or other resources are no longer available

  - Higher priorities prevail

Regardless of the project status, when closeout is to occur, the above actions must be taken. Failure to do so is one of the primary omissions in the project life cycle.

Post-Project Audit. An important aspect of the project cash/capital budgeting process is the post-audit, which compares actual results to what was predicted in the project plans, requiring explanation of any differences. For example, many organizations require their operating divisions to send a monthly report for the first six months after a project is operating, and a quarterly report thereafter until the project's results meet expectations. From then on, reports on the project are included with those of other operations.

Improved estimating can result when project managers know the results will be verified. Good decision makers systematically compare their projections to actual results to identify and eliminate conscious or unconscious biases.

Because each element of the cash flow estimate is subject to uncertainty, a percentage of all projects undertaken by any reasonably venturesome organization will be off target. This fact must be considered when appraising the performances of the operating managers who submit capital expenditure requests. At times, projects fail to meet expectations for reasons beyond the control of the project managers and for reasons that could not be realistically anticipated. Separating the operating results of one investment from those of the larger system can often be difficult. While some projects stand alone and permit ready identification of costs and benefits, the actual cost benefit from some projects can be hard to measure because of the large number of variables.

Post-Project Outcome Assessment. At some predetermined point or points in time, the ultimate outcomes of the project should be assessed and evaluated. This assessment should be both quantitative and qualitative in what it covers. Some of the areas addressed may include:

- Have the planned improvements from the project implementation been realized? For example, cycle time reduced, process capability improved, or mean time to failure increased?

- Have the planned organizational outcomes been achieved? For example, waste reduced, market penetrated, customers satisfied, employees retained, profitability increased, or organization restructured?

The assessment also typically probes the management of the project—the planning, implementation, and evaluation. Certain concepts, techniques, and tools may aid success for future projects. Identified, this information can be formulated as a guide for planning and managing projects. A goal is to not keep reinventing the project process, but to enhance it through learning from each successive project—the plan–do–study–act cycle. Applying lessons learned may be one of the most valuable outcomes from examining the processes by which a project was successful, or areas in which the project failed its objective.

4. PROJECT DOCUMENTATION

> Use written procedures and project summaries to document projects. (Apply)
>
> **Body of Knowledge III.C.4**

Part III.C.4

The job's not done until the paperwork is finished.

—Unknown

As emphasized earlier, one very important aspect in project management is documenting and sharing information with others outside of the project team to ensure that management and other stakeholders are aware of the project's status. Well-documented status reports will usually suffice.

Communicating and documenting lessons learned is important. Various channels are appropriate, including departmental meetings or time set aside specifically for shared learnings. Storing information and knowledge from projects, regardless of the degree of success, is vital to building a base for use in future project planning and estimating. (See Chapter 8, Section 7 on knowledge management.)

The details of each project should be documented utilizing the organization's preferred methodology. Such documentation will typically include:

- Project mission and/or charter statement

- Project scope

- Statement of work

- Project team members

- Stakeholder analysis

- Deliverables

- Work breakdown structure

- Gantt charts

- Time and sequence dependency diagrams (AND, CPM, PERT)

- Resource allocation matrices

- Linear responsibility matrix

- Budget

- Request for funds

- Project plan approval

- Policies and procedures affected by the project outcomes (new or revised)

- Project plan updates or revisions

- Performance results and outcomes, including financial and final benefits/cost ratio

- Project implementation sign-offs

- All changes to plans and critical decisions made

- Lessons learned

The use of formal, written communications in project management helps ensure that records are timely and complete, that background materials exist for use in future projects, and that the concerns of all parties have been addressed. Informal communications are more likely to be incomplete or misinterpreted and do not allow transfer of the methodology. Knowledge is often lost when people transfer or leave.

Many companies prefer to use a standardized project planning and management methodology. The rationale for any deviation from the standard should be documented.

The use of computer-based project management software is prevalent now that the cost and complexity in using the software have been reduced. Although a manual system has its own strengths (low cost and a hands-on feeling), a computer provides the ability to do what-if scenarios (for example, how will project timing and cost be affected by adding additional resources?) and makes it easier to create more-detailed Gantt and network charts. Computerization also permits integrating plans of multiple projects that utilize some of the same resources, making it easy to assess how a change in one project will affect others. However, it is suggested that new project planners and managers learn the basics by planning and managing a small project using manual methods.

Action Plans. Action planning, relative to deploying strategic plans, was discussed in Chapter 7. The action plan is a convenient method for planning and documenting a small project.

Figures 10.11a and 10.11b show a typical action plan form. Note that the back of the action plan form provides for an implementation schedule and is, essentially, an outline-type work breakdown structure.

Action plan

Means I.D./plan title: Description:	Plan no.:	
	Date initiated:	
	Date needed:	
	Approval:	
	Team (L):	
	Team (M):	
	Team (M):	
	Team (M):	
	Team (M):	

Major outcomes/objectives desired/required:

Scope (Where will the solution/implementation be applied? What limitations?):

By what criteria/measures will completion and success of project be measured?

Assumptions made that may impact project (resources, circumstances outside this project):

Describe the overall approach to be taken:

When should the project be started to meet the date needed/wanted?:

Estimate the resources required (time and money):

Outline the tentative *major* steps to be taken, a project *start and complete date* for each step, and the *person to be responsible* for each step. (Use the back to sketch your timeline.)

Figure 10.11a   Action plan form (front).

Source: Reprinted with permission of R. T. Westcott & Associates.

Part III.C.4

Action plan implementation schedule

Step no.	Activity/event description	Depends on step	Start date	Finish date	Person responsible

Figure 10.11b   Action plan form (back).

Source: Reprinted with permission of R. T. Westcott & Associates.

ENDNOTES

1. R. T. Westcott, *Simplified Project Management for the Quality Professional: Managing Small & Medium-Size Projects* (Milwaukee: ASQ Quality Press, 2004).
2. M. E. Porter, *Competitive Strategy: Techniques for Analyzing Industries and Competitors* (New York: Free Press, 1980).
3. Stage-gate (go/no-go) decision process is discussed in R. G. Cooper, *Winning at New Products: Accelerating the Process from Idea to Launch*, 3rd ed. (Cambridge, MA: Perseus Publishing, 2001).
4. W. Fleming and J. M. Koppelman, *Earned Value Project Management*, 2nd ed. (Newtown Square, PA: Project Management Institute, 2000).

See Appendix A for additional references for this chapter.

Chapter 11

D. Quality System

Quality may be viewed from several perspectives:

- Various meanings of "quality"
- Various characteristics of quality
- Drivers of quality
- Quality of design versus quality of conformance
- Quality planning, control, and improvement
- Little q and Big Q
- Quality is strategic

Various Meanings of Quality

The meaning of quality differs depending on circumstances and perceptions. Quality is a different concept when tangible products are the focus versus the perception of a quality service. The meaning of quality is also time-based, or situational. The new car bragged about yesterday is cursed this morning when it fails to start and an appointment is missed.

Quality is how the recipient of the product or service views it: before buying, upon delivery, and after the delivery—and use, if a product. Some of the common meanings for quality are:

Quality is conformance to requirements:

- Quality is keeping the promise made when an order is taken or a commitment is made.
- Quality means meeting the specifications.
- Quality means the product or service is free of deficiencies.

Quality is fitness for use:

- Quality means the product or service does what it is intended to do.
- Quality is what a product or service costs users if it doesn't do what it is supposed to do.

Quality is meeting customer expectations:

- Quality is satisfying the customer.

- Quality is whatever the customer says it is.

- The quality in a product or service is whatever the customer perceives it to be.

Quality is exceeding customer expectations:

- Quality is the extent to which the customers or users believe the product or service surpasses their needs and expectations.

- Quality is delighting the customer.

Quality is superiority to competitors:

- Quality is how a company's products and services compare to those of competitors or how they compare to those offered by the company in the past.

- Quality is perceived as the overall measure of goodness or excellence of a brand or supplier.

Of course, some customers may say, "Quality—I'll know it when I see it."

Examples of Quality Characteristics

Product

Performance	Serviceability	Reliability
Reasonable price	Ease of use	Maintainability
Durability	Simplicity of design	Aesthetics
Availability	Safety	Ease of disposal

Service

Responsiveness	Credibility	Availability
Reliability	Security	Safety
Competence	Understanding of customer	Accessibility
Accuracy	Completeness	Timeliness
Courtesy	Communication	

Drivers of Quality

Customers. In a customer-driven organization, quality is established with a focus on satisfying or exceeding the requirements, expectations, needs, and preferences of customers. Customer-driven quality is a common culture within many organizations.

Products/Services. A culture of product-/service-driven quality was popular in the early stages of the quality movement. Conformance to requirements and zero-defect concepts have roots in producing a product/service that meets stated or documented requirements. In some cases, product/service requirements originate from customer requirements, thereby creating a common link to customer-driven quality, but the focus of the culture is on the quality of the product/service. If the customer requirement is accurately stated and designed into the production/service delivery process, then as long as the product/service meets requirements, the customer should be satisfied. This point of view is common in supporting the ISO 9001–based quality management system.

Employee Satisfaction. This concept is that an organization takes care of employees' needs so that they can be free to care only about the customer. Employee satisfaction is a primary measure of success for this type of organization.

Organizational Focus. Some organizations tend to focus on total organizational quality, while others are quite successful at using a segmented approach to implementing quality.

Competitors. While organizations typically strive to provide products and/or services that meet or exceed the customer's expectations, competitors can leverage quality of performance to their strategic benefit. Both short- and long-term performance may be compared by the customer in terms of reliability and cost of the product/service over its lifetime, thereby affecting their selection of a supplier. This situation can cause an organization to ensure an aggressive and introspective review of its internal processes and product/service quality results.

Quality of Design versus Quality of Conformance

The organization's values, goals, mission, policies, and practices reinforce designing quality into the product or service rather than inspecting it in. Emphasis is placed on doing the right things right the first time. The organization's aim is to not only meet, to the letter, customers' requirements, but to exceed them wherever possible. This process is often called *design for Six Sigma* (DFSS). Conformance is the norm; the organization's overriding purpose should be to excite the customers with extraordinary products and service.

Quality Planning, Control, and Improvement

The focus of this perspective is for organizations to continually improve their products, services, processes, and practices, with an emphasis on reducing variation and reducing cycle time. This approach implies extensive use of the quality management tools, including cost of quality (see Chapter 13, Section 5), process management approaches (see Chapter 14), and measurement techniques (see Chapter 15).

Little q and Big Q

Organizations focusing on quality control and inspection activities (little q) will fail to see that to be fully effective they must transform their thinking to quality across the organization (Big Q).

Quality Is Strategic

Quality, or the absence of it, has a strategic impact on the organization. Consumers buy certain products and request services based on their knowledge and perception of the organization and what it provides. Few buyers knowingly buy poor quality. Accumulated experiences and perceptions of customers ultimately make or break an organization. The Baldrige Criteria does not mention the word *quality* because every activity and decision contained in the structure of the criteria must be a quality activity or decision. Under this assumption, quality is built into the very fiber of the organization—the preferred way to conduct the business of the organization.

1. QUALITY MISSION AND POLICY

Develop and monitor the quality mission and policy and ensure that it is aligned with the organization's broader mission. (Create)

Body of Knowledge III.D.1

Quality will be a focus in the organization's *strategic planning* and in its *mission statement*. The organization will have a *quality policy* to guide the organization to excellence.

Quality Function Mission

For most quality functions, the mission includes common elements to ensure that:

- Customer focus and quality are part of the organization's mission.

- All suppliers understand fundamental principles of quality.

- All employees understand fundamental principles of quality and how to apply them.

- All employees master the quality tools needed to carry out their mission within the organization.

The quality function mission is both derived from and an input into the organization's mission. Upward and downward organizational collaboration is essential in quality planning. A quality function mission can be developed in several successive steps:

1. Identify one particular service or product provided by the quality function.

2. Determine the customer(s) of that service or product.

3. Discuss with the customer(s) whether they need this service or product.

    • What attributes are valuable?

    • Which are not valuable? (Consider such attributes as speed, accuracy, schedule, packaging, or formatting.)

4. If a need exists, agree on the standard and measures applicable. If the service or product is not needed, eliminate it.

5. Quantify the gap between current practice and customer needs.

6. Define the actions for improvement of that particular service or product on the basis of resources and relative priorities.

7. Make the improvement, and track results.

8. Evaluate results, and review lessons learned.

9. Maintain the gains.

10. Do it again.

The quality function mission statement should be clear and complete so that quantitative objectives and definite plans can be developed. The quality function mission statement must be linked to the organization's mission statement. For example, if the organization's mission statement emphasizes timeliness, then perhaps the quality function mission statement should emphasize that characteristic rather than cost.

Observations Related to the Quality Function Mission. The mission of the quality function can not be developed in isolation from the overall mission of the organization. This problem occurs commonly in staff organizations. The mission of the quality function is not to produce quality in the organization's products and services and establish quality objectives; those are collaborative efforts whereby the quality function makes recommendations to and guides the operations function.

Compare the finance and quality functions. The finance function does not make the money, and it does not set the financial objectives; rather, it provides honest, trustworthy records of what is really happening so that others can make informed decisions. It also supplies various tools to enable others to meet their goals. Similarly, the quality function provides quality measures and supplies the tools needed to meet quality goals. Note: Even if the quality function responsibilities are dispersed among functions producing the product, a process for understanding quality needs and tracking performance must still be defined.

Quality is an investment, not an expense. An investment is a current expenditure that is expected to produce benefits later, enabling recovery of the initial outlay and providing a surplus. Quality does cost money, but quality expenditures can be recovered. The problem with making this distinction is that usually the accounting is done department by department, function by function, so that outlays and income are separated both in time and in space. This makes it difficult to immediately spot the positive benefits-to-cost ratio.

Organizations that focus on quality enjoy many benefits. In a study commissioned by Congress, winners of the Baldrige Award, as a group, outperformed (on paper) Standard and Poor's index of 500 leading companies in the stock market. In addition, data from Profit Impact of Market Strategy (PIMS) show that organizations that focus on quality and achieve it have higher returns on resources. They frequently are major players in their markets, and their products command a premium price.

Greater revenues and lower costs are potent inducements to consider quality. Companies that focus most on what customers need instead of what their rivals are doing enjoy higher growth rates.

Crosby claims that quality is free. This is not to say that no costs are associated with achieving quality, but rather that resources prudently allocated to quality have a positive yield that is greater than almost any other investment option the firm could explore.

If an organization strives for quality and X (whatever X might be), then it is likely to achieve both quality and X. Firms that have won the Deming Prize or the Baldrige Award report that the drive for quality is an enabler, as the struggle for quality often leads to the achievement of other business goals. However, if a firm has X for its primary goal and considers quality as an optional, secondary goal, then it is likely to achieve neither X nor quality over the long term.

Quality Function Policies, Principles, and Objectives

The formulation and deployment of quality policy, principles, and objectives is discussed in Chapter 7, Section 4, as a subset of strategic plan deployment. Of primary importance is that quality policy, quality principles, and quality objectives support the organization's strategic goals and objectives.

The quality policy and the quality principles are guidelines and, therefore, not directly measurable. The effectiveness of the quality policy and quality principles is measured, indirectly, by the quality-related objectives that are linked to the policy and principles.

Quality policies may be found in a quality manual, framed and hanging on the wall, laminated into pocket-sized cards, or passed by word of mouth in smaller organizations. The key is whether or not the policy is followed and backed by management's support as well as by the actions of all employees.

Although a quality policy is not intended to be permanent, the need for revisions should be infrequent. A serious management problem is indicated when frequent changes are made.

2. QUALITY PLANNING, DEPLOYMENT, AND DOCUMENTATION

> Develop and deploy the quality plan and ensure that it is documented and accessible throughout the organization. (Create)
>
> **Body of Knowledge III.D.2**

Quality Plans

A quality plan is a document, or several documents, that together specify quality standards, practices, resources, specifications, and the sequence of activities relevant to a particular product, service, project, or contract. Quality plans should define:

- Objectives to be attained (for example, characteristics or specifications, uniformity, effectiveness, aesthetics, cycle time, cost, natural resources, utilization, yield, dependability, and so on)

- Steps in the processes that constitute the operating practice or procedures of the organization

- Allocation of responsibilities, authority, and resources during the different phases of the process or project

- Specific documented standards, practices, procedures, and instructions to be applied

- Suitable testing, inspection, examination, and audit programs at appropriate stages

- A documented procedure for changes and modifications to a quality plan as a process is improved

- A method for measuring the achievement of the quality objectives

- Other actions necessary to meet the objectives[1]

At the highest level, quality goals and plans should be integrated with overall strategic plans of the organization. As organizational objectives and plans are deployed throughout the organization, each function fashions its own best way for contributing to the top-level goals and objectives. At lower levels, the quality plan (see earlier definition) assumes the role of an actionable plan. Such plans may take many different forms depending on the outcome they are to produce. Quality plans may also be represented by more than one type of document to produce a given outcome.

An example of this is a manufacturing company that machines metal parts. Its quality plan consists of applicable procedures (describing the production process and responsibilities), applicable workmanship standards, the measurement tolerances acceptable, the description of the material standards, and so forth. These may all be separate documents.

More variable information that pertains to a particular customer may be spelled out on individual work orders (sometimes called *travelers*). *Work orders* specify the machine setups and tolerances, operations to be performed, tests, inspections, handling, storing, packaging, and delivery steps to be followed. An operating-level quality plan translates the customer requirements (the what) into actions required to produce the desired outcome (the how) and couples this with applicable procedures, standards, practices, and protocols to specify precisely what is needed, who will do it, and how it will be done. A control plan may specify product tolerances, testing parameters, and acceptance criteria. While the terminology may differ, the basic approach is similar for service and other types of organizations.

Deployment and Documentation of Quality Plans

Quality plans result from both deployed strategic quality policies (which are linked to organizational strategic plans) and from the specific legal regulations, industry standards, organization policies and procedures, internal guidelines, and good practices needed to meet customers' requirements for products or services.

Strategic-level quality plans are developed and deployed through the strategic planning process (see Chapter 7). These broad-based quality plans become the guideline for each function's or department's supporting quality plan. Where appropriate, each function or department may develop and internally deploy operating-level quality plans.

Operating-level quality plans often are the resulting document(s) from a production scheduling function. As such, this documentation often includes blueprints, a copy of the customer's order, references to applicable standards, practices, procedures, and work instructions, and details on how to produce the specific product or service.

When the product or service is produced, the planning documents may be augmented by inspection documentation, SPC charts, and copies of shipping documents and customer-required certifications. In the process, the plans are transformed from documents to records. In a fully computerized system, the documents mentioned may well be interactive computer screens, accessed at operators' workplaces and control points. These screens, internally, become records when operators, inspectors, shippers, and others make computer entries to the screens.

A completed set of matrices, developed by a quality function deployment (QFD) process, may fulfill a component of an organization's quality plan. The purpose of QFD is to capture and deploy the customers' needs and requirements throughout the organization (see Chapter 17, Section 1).

Documenting the quality plan(s) has multiple uses, such as:

- Assuring conformance to customer requirements

- Assuring conformance to external and internal standards and procedures

- Facilitating traceability

- Providing objective evidence

- Furnishing a basis for training

- Together with multiple plans for the organization's products, services, and projects, providing a basis for evaluating the effectiveness and efficiency of the quality management system.

3. QUALITY SYSTEM EFFECTIVENESS

> Evaluate the effectiveness of the quality system using various tools: balanced scorecard, internal audits, feedback from internal and external stakeholders, skip-level meetings, warranty data analytics, product traceability and recall reports, and management reviews. (Evaluate)
>
> **Body of Knowledge III.D.3**

Tools and Metrics for Evaluating the Effectiveness of the Quality System

Balanced Scorecard. A popular method for tracking total organizational performance is to use the *balanced scorecard* (BSC) approach introduced by Kaplan and Norton.[2] This macro-level evaluation is intended to move the organizational decision makers away from considering only the financial factor. A basic approach defines metrics in four areas: customer, internal business process, learning and growth, and financial. Six common process metrics are cost, time, quality, agility (ability to adapt), capacity, and variability. The BSC approach considers metrics in multiple areas and recognizes that all are important to the organization's success.

Another method used is tracking leading indicators, which tend to be predictive of future performance, versus lagging indicators (easier to collect) that report on past successes or failures. Taking action to affect leading indicators is the secret to managing and understanding a process. Table 11.1 shows a partially completed matrix for a medium-size distributor of small household appliances. The "*" denotes those measures/indicators that are used as performance improvement drivers.

Note: A BSC can be designed with virtually any choice of categories to track, as long as the categories chosen are critical to performance and kept to a minimum number.

Using one set of factors, following are examples of supporting metrics:

- Customer

  - Market share gains and losses

  - Customer retention

Table 11.1   Example of a partial, hypothetical balanced scorecard.

Category	Strategic objective	Action plan	Measures
Customers	1. Meet customers' requirements for just-in-time (JIT) delivery 2. Etc.	1. Establish regional warehouse operations 2. Etc.	1. # JIT deliveries by region 2. Average cost per delivery 3. % improvement in CSI (customer satisfaction index)* 4. Etc.
Employees	1. Develop a core competency to support a new service category 2. Etc.	1. Design and implement program to train service personnel 2. Etc.	1. % of service personnel qualified to provide new service* 2. CSI—new service* 3. ROTI—return on training investment 4. Etc.
Shareholders	1. Acquire new business 2. Etc	1. Analyze acquisition alternatives, select investment, buy business 2. Etc.	1. ROA—return on assets 2. Dividend dollars 3. Etc.
Process	1. Reduce overall service cycle time 2. Etc.	1. Reengineer the service delivery process 2. Etc.	1. % on-time service* 2. ROPI—return on project investment 3. Cost of quality* 4. Etc.

*Leading indicators (performance drivers)

- Satisfaction survey results

- Complaints, product returns, product recalls, warranty costs

- Field service performance

- Certification by customers

- Customer recognition

- Favored supplier agreements

Part III.D.3

- Internal business practices

  - Cost of quality

  - Productivity

  - Cost reductions

  - Process cycle time

  - Continual quality improvement

  - Innovation

  - Product/service development cycle time (from concept to market)

  - Supplier performance

- Learning and growth

  - Employee retention

  - Competency level

  - Employee development

  - Knowledge management

- Financial

  - Profitability or margin

  - Cash flow

  - Return on investments

  - Return on assets

  - Liquidity ratios

Self-Assessment Documents are available from several sources to assess an organization against the Baldrige Award criteria and to assess an organization's quality management system against the ISO 9001 standard. Such assessments are typically used prior to applying for the Baldrige Award or seeking certification to the ISO 9001 standard. Contact ASQ for currently available assessment tools (800-248-1946 or www.asq.org).

Quality Audits. On the micro level, a quality audit is "a systematic and independent examination to determine whether quality activities and related results comply with planned arrangements and whether these arrangements are implemented effectively and are suitable to achieve objectives."[3]

Three principal parties are involved in a quality audit. By function, they are the:

- *Auditor.* The person(s) who plans and conducts an audit in accordance with an established standard

- *Client.* The person/organization that has been scheduled for an audit or who has requested that an audit be conducted

- *Auditee.* The organization to be audited

An audit may be classified as *internal* or *external*, depending on the interrelationships that exist among the participants. Internal audits are first-party audits, whereas external audits can be either second- or third-party audits.

- A *first-party audit* is performed within an organization to measure its strengths and weaknesses against its own procedures or methods and/or external standards adopted by the auditee organization (voluntary) or imposed on the auditee organization (mandatory). A first-party audit is an internal audit conducted by auditors who are employed by the organization being audited, but who have no vested interest in the audit results of the area being audited. The persons conducting these audits are referred to as *internal auditors*.

- A *second-party audit* is an external audit performed at a supplier's location by a customer or a contracted (consulting) organization on behalf of a customer. Typically, this is also called a *supplier audit*.

- A *third-party audit* is performed on a supplier or regulated entity by an external party other than a customer. The organization to be audited—or in some cases the client—compensates an independent party to perform an audit. For example, an auditor from the registrar for ISO 9001–based quality management systems (QMSs) performs an audit of a client's QMS and recommends, or not, the QMS for certification to the standard. The auditor is compensated by the registrar. The registrar bills and collects its fees from the client.

Quality audits can be performed on a product/service, process, or system:

- A *product quality audit* is an in-depth examination of a particular product (or service) to evaluate whether it conforms to product specifications, performance standards, and customer requirements. A product audit should not be confused with inspection, although an auditor might use inspection techniques. Product audits have a broader scope and are a sporadic method of reinspecting or retesting a product to measure the effectiveness of the system in place for product acceptance. In contrast, inspection is a regular, continual method for product approval that verifies a product's conformance to standards as stipulated by certain product characteristics.[4]

- A *process quality audit* examines a single process or activity—such as marking, stamping, coating, soldering, or welding—to verify that the inputs, actions, and outputs are in accordance with requirements established by procedures, work instructions, or process specifications.

- A *quality system audit* is "a documented activity performed to verify, by examination and evaluations of objective evidence, that applicable elements of the quality system are appropriate and have been developed, documented, and effectively implemented in accordance and in conjunction with specified requirements."[5] A system audit examines processes, products, and services as well as all the supporting groups—for example, purchasing, customer service, design engineering, and order entry—that assist in providing an acceptable product or service.[6]

- Internal audits of a quality system are conducted to determine if:

  - The system is appropriate for the organization.

  - The system design conforms to an established standard and/or accepted practices.

  - The system is properly documented.

  - There is objective evidence available that the work performed is in accordance with the documented system.

Auditing concerns the *check* and *act* stages of the PDCA cycle and consists of three stages: (1) audit preparation, (2) audit performance, and (3) audit reporting, corrective action, follow-up, and closure.

The following activities are performed during audit preparation:

- Prepare the audit plan.

- Schedule activities.

- Define the purpose of the audit.

- Establish the scope of the audit.

- Select the audit team.

- Identify resources needed.

- Identify authority for the audit.

- Identify standard(s) to be used.

- Conduct a technical review.

- Secure and review quality-related documentation.

- Develop checklists and other working papers (develop appropriate data collection methods).

- Contact auditee.

Audit performance is the actual data collection phase. The following occur during this phase:

- Hold the opening meeting.

- Employ auditing strategies to collect data.

- Verify documentation.

- Analyze data and categorize results.

- Present audit results (findings) at a closing meeting.

Once the audit performance stage has been completed, the audit team must formally report audit results to the client and/or auditee. The appropriate corrective actions, follow-up, and closure must be performed for any problem areas noted:

- Distribute formal audit report.

- Request corrective action.

- Evaluate auditee's response to corrective action requests.

- Assess the best mode for verifying corrective action.

- Close out audit once corrective action has been verified.

Figure 11.1 shows the sequence of steps performed in a typical audit.

Management by Walking Around (MBWA). Another micro-level evaluation where senior management may, in addition to more formal means for evaluating, take a periodic walk through the quality system, in its entirety or a part at a time. This may be done by following an order from receipt through to delivery. Or, the choice may be to review the quality system a function at a time, for example, order processing, or subassembly B. The observations from this informal MBWA approach are typically not formally documented; however, the observations are shared with the responsible managers and are to be taken seriously.

In one case of MBWA, the CEO, on random days of the month, parks in the back of the plant and walks through to the offices, stopping to ask questions and solicit feedback along the way. Anything critical is shared immediately, as well as outstanding performance. Other observations are saved for the weekly staff meeting.

Management Reviews. Considered micro-level, top management reviews, such as required by the ISO 9001 standard, are conducted on a schedule (bimonthly, quarterly, or annually). Key performance indicators, trends, and system problems may be reviewed, such as:

- Customer satisfaction and complaints

- Supplier performance

- Cost of quality

- Internal process/product quality indicators

- Audit results

- Effectiveness of the quality management system

Usually, formal minutes are recorded and distributed to attendees. Action items are assigned, such as corrective actions, matters to research, external contacts to be made, or critical problems. Results of action items from the previous meeting are reviewed and closed out if the issue has been resolved. If an organization is required to meet third-party quality system requirements, full evidence of the activities listed above is required to be maintained and made available for audit review.

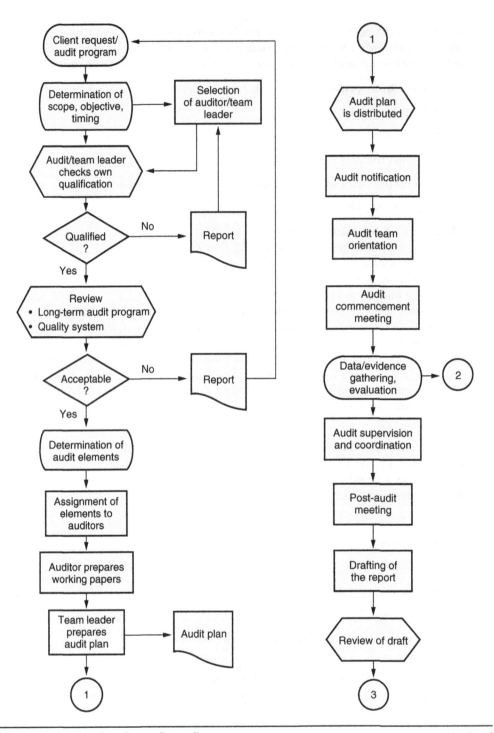

Figure 11.1 Flowchart for quality audit. *Continued*

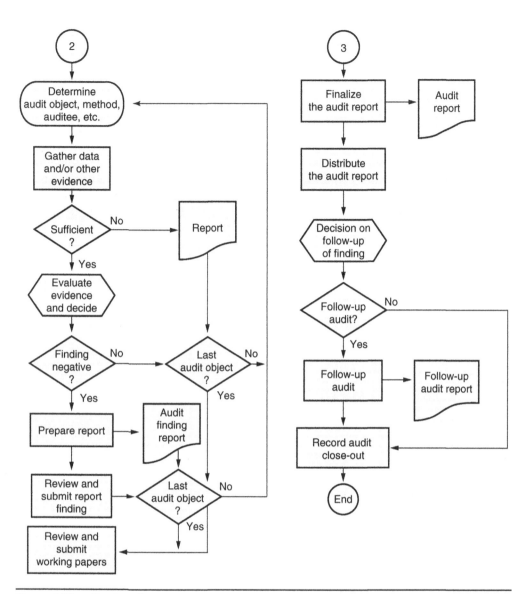

Figure 11.1   *Continued*

Skip-Level Meetings. A micro-level evaluation, skip-level meetings occur when a member of senior management meets with persons two or more organizational levels below, without in-between management being present. The purpose is to get a more grassroots perspective of the effectiveness of the quality system. Care must be taken to not appear to be circumventing the in-between management levels. The intent is to give lower-level employees opportunity to make higher management aware of system problems and needs. Skip-level meetings are often more for venting issues and concerns than for managing the operation. With the

Part III.D.3

advent of internal electronic communication and a more open culture, one-to-one contact between various organizational levels is more prevalent and follows less the chain of command.

Collecting and Analyzing Customer Feedback. Using information to evaluate and improve customer service and satisfaction is implied in all quality management systems and required in meeting certain standards, for example, ISO 9001 (see Chapter 12, Section 2). Inasmuch as the principal aim of a quality system is to be customer-focused, assessing information derived from direct customer feedback is essential. Data should include feedback from both internal and external customers. This type of analysis is also considered a micro-level evaluation.

Among the quality system effectiveness data critical to review are trends relative to:

- Customer complaints (see Chapter 17, Section 2)
- Customer orders canceled
- Warranty returns
- Product recalls, including ease of traceability and percentage recalled
- Lost customers

Data may be categorized by:

- Product or service type
- Reason for complaint, return, recall, or loss
- Quantity
- Date or time of occurrence
- Frequency of occurrence
- Reported deficiency
- Risk level of deficiency
- Customer segment (see Chapter 16, Section 3)
- Response time to customer
- Ratio of resolutions to total reported
- Cost of resolution

Collecting and analyzing employee feedback—and using the information to evaluate and improve employee response to the quality mission, policies, and the quality system, as well as employee well-being and satisfaction—is implied in any effective quality system.

Typical employee-related trends reviewed are:

- Turnover rate
- Retention rate

- Grievances by type and frequency
- Lost time by type—accident, illness, disciplinary action, personal
- Mobility—promotions, lateral transfers, demotions
- Recognition and rewards by type, reason, and frequency

Tools and Metrics

The evaluator of quality systems has a number of tools and documents available:

- Accepted auditing protocols, auditor conduct standards, and codes of conduct
- Applicable standards and guidelines (external and internal)
- The organization's policies, procedures, work instructions, workmanship standards, and forms
- Process maps (detailed flowcharts depicting the steps and decision points in the system)
- Checklists (detailed questions to ask to get responses that can be verified by objective evidence)
- Sampling techniques (to enable an auditor to reduce the number of transactions/things checked, yet get a representative view of the operating effectiveness of the system)
- Copies of prior external assessments
- Copies of previous internal audits
- Quality system records

A variety of measurement approaches and metrics enable evaluation of the effectiveness of a quality system. Fundamental metrics include:

- Cost of quality measures (see Chapter 13, Section 5), for example, ratio of prevention costs to total quality costs increasing, with failure costs decreasing
- Return on quality investment (ROQI) (see Chapter 8, Section 5, and Chapter 10, Section 3), rate of return equals or exceeds organizational norms for project investments
- Customer retention (see Chapter 17, Section 2)
- Supplier performance (see Chapter 18)
- Process measurements (see Chapter 15)
- Strategic goals, objectives, and plans (see Chapters 5, 6, and 7)
- Process benchmarking (see Chapter 12, Section 3)

Part III.D.3

ENDNOTES

1. Adapted from the American National Standard, ANSI/ASQC Q9004-1-1994, *Quality Management and Quality System Elements—Guidelines* (Milwaukee: ASQC Quality Press, 1994).
2. R. S. Kaplan and D. Norton, "The Balanced Scorecard," *Harvard Business Review* 74 (November–December 1996): 86.
3. ANSI/ISO/ASQC A8402-1-1994, *Quality Management and Quality Assurance—Vocabulary* (Milwaukee: ASQC Quality Press, 1994).
4. J.P. Russell, ed., *The Quality Audit Handbook* (Milwaukee: ASQ Quality Press, 1997).
5. ASQ Certification Department.
6. Russell, *Quality Audit Handbook*.

See Appendix A for additional references for this chapter.

Chapter 12

E. Quality Models and Theories

Throughout this book, information is presented identifying central themes and principles of total quality that provide the foundation for achieving customer satisfaction. An organization needs a well-structured system that identifies, documents, coordinates, integrates, and maintains key quality-related activities throughout all operations. Feigenbaum defined a total quality system as "the agreed companywide and plantwide operating work structure, documented in effective, integrated technical and managerial procedures, for guiding the coordinated actions of the workforce, the machines, and the information of the company and plant in the best and most practical ways to assure customer quality and economical costs of quality."[1]

The process of implementing a system for quality is somewhat simplified if organizations have a model for guiding design and implementation of quality-related processes, and a means of assessing how well actions are carried out. Awards and certification programs provide tested organizational models as well as a basis for assessing progress, achievement, and conformance. Widely used models for quality management are the United States' Baldrige Performance Excellence Program (BPEP), Japan's Deming Prize, and the worldwide ISO 9000 series standards. In addition, many states, municipalities, industry groups, and even large corporations have developed significant quality awards, thereby widening the range of organizations eligible for recognition.

1. PERFORMANCE EXCELLENCE MODELS

> Define and describe common elements and criteria
> of performance excellence models such as the
> Malcolm Baldrige National Quality Award (MBNQA),
> Excellence Canada, and European Excellence Award
> (EFQM). Describe how their criteria are used as
> management models to improve processes at an
> organization level. (Understand)
>
> **Body of Knowledge III.E.1**

In October 1982, recognizing that U.S. productivity was declining, President Ronald Reagan signed legislation mandating a national study/conference on productivity. The American Productivity Center (now the American Productivity and Quality Center) sponsored seven computer networking conferences in 1983 to prepare for an upcoming White House conference on productivity. The final report from these conferences recommended that "a National Quality Award, similar to the Deming Prize in Japan, be awarded annually to those firms that successfully challenge and meet the award requirements." The Malcolm Baldrige National Quality Award (MBNQA) was signed into law (Public Law 100-107) on August 20, 1987, and is named after President Reagan's secretary of commerce, who was killed in an accident shortly before the Senate acted on the legislation.

A *total quality management* (TQM) business approach is the basis for the MBNQA, an annual award to recognize U.S. organizations for performance excellence, under the Baldrige Performance Excellence Program (BPEP) criteria. In 1999, the criteria for performance excellence expanded to create separate but parallel criteria for education and healthcare organizations. The BPEP promotes an understanding of the requirements for performance excellence and fosters sharing of information about successful performance strategies and the benefits derived from using these strategies. The Baldrige criteria are presented from a systems perspective. Figure 12.1 shows the interrelationship of the seven categories.

Category Descriptions

An overview of the BPEP criteria categories follows.[2]

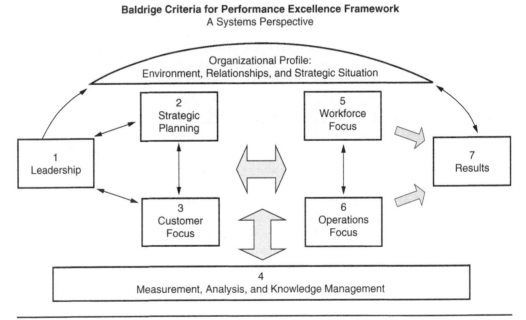

Figure 12.1   Baldrige criteria for performance excellence framework.

Preface: organizational profile. This is a snapshot of the applying organization, the key organizational characteristics, and the organization's strategic situation. The preface identifies the organization's product/service offerings, the vision and mission, a profile of its workforce, major physical assets, regulatory requirements, organizational structure, customers and stakeholders, and suppliers and partners.

1. *Leadership.* This category examines how the organization's senior leaders guide and sustain the organization, and communicate with the workforce. Also examined are the organization's governance and how the organization addresses its ethical, legal, and societal responsibilities.

2. *Strategic Planning.* This category examines how the organization develops strategic objectives and action plans. Also examined is how the chosen strategic objectives and action plans are deployed and changed if circumstances require, and how progress is measured.

3. *Customer Focus.* This category examines how the organization engages its customers for long-term marketplace success. Also examined is how the organization listens to the voice of its customers, builds customer relationships, and uses customer information to improve and identify opportunities for innovation.

4. *Measurement, Analysis, and Knowledge Management.* This category examines how the organization selects, gathers, analyzes, manages, and improves its data, information, and knowledge assets, and how it manages its information technology. Also examined is how the organization reviews its performance in order to improve.

5. *Workforce Focus.* This category examines the organization's ability to access workforce capability and capacity needs and build a workforce environment conducive to high performance. Also examined is how the organization engages, manages, and develops the workforce to utilize its full potential in alignment with the organization's overall mission, strategy, and action plans.

6. *Operations Focus.* This category examines how the organization designs, manages, and improves its work systems and work processes to deliver customer value and achieve organizational success and sustainability. Also examined is the organization's readiness for emergencies.

7. *Results.* This category examines the organization's performance and improvement in all key areas—product and process outcomes, customer-focused outcomes, leadership and governance outcomes, and financial and market outcomes. Performance levels are examined relative to those of competitors and other organizations with similar product offerings.

Using the BPEP Criteria As a Management Model

The BPEP criteria are designed to help organizations improve the value of what they offer to their customers and market, and improve their overall organizational performance. Criteria are specifically worded using nonprescriptive statements of requirements to allow for different interpretations. It is up to the organization to develop its approach to satisfy the criteria requirements that will best suit its needs. A quality management system can be designed simply by using the seven categories, although for more complex systems, the criteria identify items within the seven categories and numerous areas within the items.

The Baldrige criteria can be used as a model for planning and implementing quality management. Figure 12.1 is the model:

- Senior leaders (category 1) identify the value of their products and services to their current customers and potential customers in their market.

- Key participants develop a strategy (category 2) to satisfy the requirements and expectations of customers and markets (category 3).

- Strategic objectives from planning are turned into action plans to track the movement of the organization from where it currently is in the market to where it wants to be.

- Measurement and analysis are accomplished to recognize achievement of planned activities or to stimulate improvement opportunities (category 4).

- Employees are trained, educated, and developed (category 5) to prepare for the organization's transition from where it is to where it needs to be relative to skills and knowledge of their products and services.

- Processes are managed (category 6) to ensure that performance expectations are effective and efficient, and will satisfy the expectations and requirements of customers, markets, and regulatory agencies.

- Business results (category 7) are reported and analyzed (category 4) to determine the achievement and/or opportunity for improvement to expected outcomes as identified in strategy and action plans.

The BPEP criteria are designed to serve three purposes in building and strengthening U.S. competitiveness:

1. Helping improve organizations' performance practices, capabilities, and results

2. Facilitating communication and sharing of best practices information among U.S. organizations of all types

3. Serving as a tool for organizations' understanding and managing of performance, as well as for guiding organizational planning and opportunities for learning

As with any model for management of business, success is not a guarantee. Use of the Baldrige criteria as a management model will only increase the probability of achieving expected performance outcomes. Detailed examples of how the Baldrige criteria can be applied to an organization are available in the form of case studies used by examiners for the BPEP and many state quality award programs. Case studies can be obtained for a fee.

The Baldrige criteria booklets may be obtained from the Baldrige Performance Excellence Program (http://www.nist.gov/baldrige/) or from ASQ (http://www.asq.org)

Other Quality-Related Awards

Many states offer Baldrige criteria–type awards. A number of larger business entities have also established their own internal Baldrige-type awards.

The *European Quality Award* was initiated in 1991. This award is similar to the BPEP award in that it, too, is nonprescriptive. It is offered to four sectors: large business, operational units within companies, public sector organizations, and small and medium-size enterprises.

A Japanese award for excellence is the *Deming Prize*. It was established in 1951 to encourage and recognize quality improvement.

The *Shingo Prize for Excellence in Manufacturing* (Japan) was established in 1988 to promote lean manufacturing concepts and reduction of waste.

2. ISO QUALITY MANAGEMENT STANDARDS

> Define and describe how the ISO 9001 standards can be used to support quality management systems. (Understand)
>
> **Body of Knowledge III.E.2**

International Quality Management—ISO 9000 Series of Standards

Since their inception in 1987, the ISO 9000 quality management standards have grown to become the most widely accepted international standard. The standard is currently the national standard in 178 countries around the world, and there are over one million registered organizations.

The ISO 9000 series of quality management system standards and guidelines assists an organization in developing, implementing, registering, and sustaining an appropriate quality management system that functions independently of the specific product and/or service. They are different from the traditional notion of a standard, for example, engineering standards for measurement, terminology, test methods, or product specifications; ISO 9000 standards are based on the premise that a well- designed and carefully managed quality management system can provide confidence that the product or service produced by the quality management system will meet customer expectations and requirements. Certification of the quality management system, however, does not certify or guarantee the quality of the product or service produced.

The basic ISO 9000 series consists of three booklets.[3] They are:

- ISO 9000:2005, *Quality management systems—Fundamentals and vocabulary*, which covers fundamentals of quality management systems and terminology and definitions.

- ISO 9001:2008, *Quality management systems*, which specifies basic overall requirements for the QMS. An organization's QMS must be audited by a third party and comply with the standard to obtain certification of the QMS. This booklet covers terms and definitions, general requirements, and a model for the QMS.

- ISO 9004:2009, *Managing for the sustained success of an organization— A quality management approach*, which describes and provides guidance on the principles of quality management to enhance performance improvements.

The ISO 9001:2008 standard lays out requirements in broad, general terms. Each organization must interpret them within the context of its own business environment and develop its own quality management system to reach compliance. A brief outline of key requirements follows.

Quality management system addresses:

- Overall management system requirements

- Documentation requirements (quality manual requirements)

- Control of documents requirements

- Control of records requirements

Management responsibility addresses:

- Management commitment to the development and implementation of the QMS and to continually improving QMS effectiveness

- Management's customer focus

- Quality policy that is appropriate and includes continual improvement

- Quality objectives that are measurable and consistent with the quality policy

- Planning that helps ensure the integrity of the QMS

- Effectively communicating the deployment of the responsibilities and authority granted within the organization to ensure employees have a clear understanding

- Appointment of a management representative responsible for overseeing maintainance of the QMS and promoting awareness of customer requirements

- Internal communications to ensure appropriate communication processes and communication about the effectiveness of the quality management system

- Establishment of a management review process conducted at defined intervals to ensure that the QMS remains suitable and effective.

Resource management addresses:

- Providing adequate resources to maintain the QMS

- Ensuring that employees are competent on the basis of their education, work experience, knowledge, skills, and requisite training

- Providing suitable infrastructure (faculties, equipment, and supporting services)

- Providing a suitable work environment to achieve conformity of product

Processes realization for producing products and services addresses:

- Planning for product realization to ensure that production or service is adequately planned to meet desired results.

- Requirements for customer-related processes to ensure that customer requirements are clearly understood, with clear contractual agreement and a record of contract review

- Requirements to ensure that there is a clear plan for control over each stage of design and development. Records of design reviews, verification, and validation are required.

- The purchasing process to ensure that there is clear purchasing information, verification of purchased product, and evaluation of suppliers.

- Control of production and service to ensure that employees have a clear understanding of the work requirements: validation of all required processes, identification and traceability process, handling of customer property, and preservation of product.

- Control of monitoring and measuring equipment is required to ensure that the process is accurate. This type of equipment must be calibrated with a proper calibration status sticker, have a calibration certificate and be on a calibration schedule.

Measurement, analysis, and improvement addresses:

- General requirements for monitoring, measurement, analysis, and improvement of the QMS.

- Monitoring customer satisfaction to ensure that customer requirements are being met, and using this information to seek continual improvement.

- Internal audit to ensure that the QMS is effective and continually improved to meet the needs of the organization.

- Monitoring and measuring of the product or service to ensure that it meets the requirements. A record is required indicating the person authorizing release prior to delivery to the customer.

- Control of nonconforming product is required to ensure that any product or service that does not meet the customer's requirements is not sent out. This would also include incoming material from suppliers that is not suitable for use.

- Analysis of data to evaluate the QMS to identify improvements to processes. This analysis data would include customer satisfaction data, conformance to product requirements, characteristics and trends of process or products, and supplier data.

- Corrective and preventive action process used to take action to correct nonconformance or potential nonconformance issues.

ISO 9004:2009 includes eight principles that when followed should improve organizational performance. The essence of these principles is:

- The organization has a focus on meeting customers' requirements and exceeding customers' expectations.

- The organization's leadership develops and sustains a working environment in which people become involved in helping the organization meet its objectives.

- Throughout the entire organization, the people are enabled to utilize their abilities for the mutual benefit of the organization and themselves.

- The inputs, resources, and outputs pertaining to the organization's activities are managed as a process.

- Within the organization, relationships among the processes are managed as a system. The system supports organizational effectiveness and efficiency in meeting objectives.

- The organization fosters continual improvement in everything it does.

- The organization's people make fact-based decisions.

- Supplier relationships are mutually beneficial and value enhancing.

When using the ISO 9001 standard as a systems management model, remember the following:

- Eight quality management principles are the basis for the standard: customer focus, leadership involvement, engagement of people at all levels, process management, system approach to managing, continual improvement, fact-based decisions, and mutually beneficial supplier relationships.

- Recognize that customer requirements must drive transformation activities. This is important if an organization wants to retain customers. Management is responsible for identifying what the organization is going to do in the future and for establishing a policy for quality and the direction of the organization. Many organizations do this by creating a mission and vision statement and a quality policy.

- An organization must obtain information from the customer as to how well it has done at meeting the needs of the customer. This can be done in at least two ways. The first is to follow up with customers to see how well the organization performed. The second is to ensure that customer requirements are documented and met prior to the delivery of the product or service. Care must be taken to stay current with changing customer requirements.

- To create the capability to meet the customers' needs, the organization must have resources available to perform the processes. This includes raw materials, skills, knowledge, talent, money, time, and space. Processes are developed and documented, delineating how resources are to be planned, allocated, and managed.

- After planning activities, ensure that resources are available for required activities, and production processes are identified and documented to ensure effective and efficient utilization of the resources and product/service conformance to requirements. Contributing activities of suppliers and partners are included in the control of production activities. Inasmuch as an ISO 9001 certification of the QMS does not guarantee that the quality system works as designed, there must be a feedback mechanism indicating the quality of the output. In-process and final inspections and tests are conducted to determine the effectiveness of the inspection and test criteria, as well as to verify the conformance to customer requirements of the product or service.

- Information from production output activities and feedback from customers provide indicators of whether the system for managing quality is working as planned. Management reviews the effectiveness and efficiency of the quality system by reviewing measurements, audits, analysis, and improvement information.

- The cycle repeats itself. Results from the management review are integrated into the management of resources, production activities, and measurement activities.

- The ISO 9001 standard is considered a foundation for an effective quality management system. ISO 9004 provides guidelines to expand the potential to achieve maximum benefits (and ROI) from the QMS implementation.

There are many benefits of implementation and certification of an ISO 9001–based QMS. Some common benefits are:

- Reduction in waste, rework, and redundancy

- Reduction in potential for external failures

- Cost reductions

- Increased productivity

- Improved performance

- More orderly method of doing business

- Improved customer satisfaction

- Reduction in number of on-site customer-ordered audits

- Marketing edge over suppliers that do not have a certified QMS

- Increased employee pride in the organization and the work they do

- Greater awareness and commitment to quality throughout the organization

Comments and criticisms of the ISO 9000 series include:

- A tendency to overdo the quantity and complexity level of procedures.

- The standard makes no assurances about a company's products or services.

- Confusion when determining what a quality plan means for the organization designing a QMS: What should be included? Who will use it? How will it be used? What level of detail is necessary? What format/medium should be used?

- Uncertainty about what constitutes design and development and how it should be treated.

- Lack of understanding as to the difference between monitoring versus measuring.

- Frequent misunderstanding prevails about the difference between a correction versus corrective action versus preventive action.

- The intent and use of ISO 9004 is widely misunderstood and largely ignored by many organizations, who fail to realize that it is the key to unlock the real potential of a QMS. ISO 9001 is the basic investment. ISO 9004 guidance leads to the payoff.

- Registration (precertification audits, certification audits, and surveillance audits, costs for consultants, employee time, and documentation) can amount to a significant cost (or investment, depending on the value placed on continual improvement and compliance with customers' requirements).

Other Pertinent ISO-Related and International Standards

Following is a list of other important ISO-related standards.[4]

ISO 19011:2011 *Guidelines for quality and/or environmental management system auditing*

ISO 10012:2003 *Measurement management systems—Requirements for measurement processes and measuring equipment*

ISO 14001:2004 *Environmental management systems—Requirements with guidance for use*

ISO 22000:2005 *Food safety management systems—Requirements for any organization in the food chain*

ISO 26000:2010 *Guidance on social responsibility*

ISO 31000:2009 *Risk management—Principles and guidelines*

ISO 50001:2011 *Energy management systems—Requirements with guidance for use*

ISO 13485:2003 *Medical devices—Quality management systems— Requirements for regulatory purposes*

AS9100 Aerospace quality management system

OHSAS 18001 Occupational health and safety management system

ISO/TS 16949:2009 Automotive management system

ISO/IEC 27001:2005 *Information technology—Security techniques— Information security management systems—Requirements*

TL 9000 Telecommunication quality management system

ISO 10001:2007 *Quality management—Customer satisfaction—Guidelines for codes of conduct for organizations*

ISO 10002:2004 *Quality management—Customer satisfaction—Guidelines for complaints handling in organizations*

ISO 10003:2007 *Quality management—Customer satisfaction—Guidelines for dispute resolution external to organizations.*

Examples of Other Standards

Other industries have issued standards, such as:

- *TJC.* The Joint Commission (TJC) was created to empower a formal accreditation process for assuring safety and integrity of healthcare. During the late 1990s the commission realized the value in adapting the criteria outlined for the Baldrige Award. To date, each update of the Joint Commission standards has shown a closer linkage to the Baldrige criteria.

- *NCQA.* The National Committee for Quality Assurance (NCQA) is a not-for-profit organization that assesses and reports on the quality of managed care and health maintenance organizations. To earn this seal of approval, an organization must meet rigorous standards of confidentiality, access, customer service, and quality improvement. The mission of NCQA is to provide information about managed healthcare organizations, enabling users to make better decisions about plans based on quality.

- *CE mark.* An abbreviation of a French phrase (*conformité Européenne*), the CE mark on a manufacturer's product asserts that the product complies with the essential/safety requirements of relevant European regulations.[5]

- *Good manufacturing practices* (GMP). There are variations in the requirements for GMP, for example, medical device manufacturing and pharmaceuticals in the United States, EU directives in Europe, and others. In the United States, the U.S. Food and Drug Administration (FDA) monitors medical device problem data and inspects the operations and records of device developers and manufacturers to determine compliance with GMP.

- There are quality-related guidance and certifications in the field of computer software development. *TickIT* is a certification of quality management systems that conform to the requirements of the ISO 9001 standard.

- *SEI capability maturity model.* This model is used to determine current process capabilities and identify critical software issues for improvement.

3. OTHER QUALITY METHODOLOGIES

Describe and differentiate methods such as total quality management (TQM), continuous improvement, and benchmarking. (Apply)

Body of Knowledge III.E.3

Total Quality Management

Total quality management (TQM) is a term initially coined by the U.S. Naval Air Systems Command to describe its Japanese-style management approach to quality improvement. TQM is an umbrella methodology drawing on a knowledge of the principles and practices of the behavioral sciences, the analysis of quantitative and nonquantitative data, economics theories, and process analysis to continually improve the quality of all processes.

The principles and tools of TQM were developed over a long period of time. Some of the first seeds of quality management were planted in the 1920s as the principles of scientific management swept through U.S. industry. At that time businesses clearly separated the processes of planning and carrying out the plan, and union opposition arose as workers were deprived of a voice in the conditions and functions of their work. The Hawthorne experiments in the late 1920s showed how worker productivity could be impacted by participation.

In the 1930s Walter Shewhart developed the methods for statistical analysis and control of quality. In the 1950s W. Edwards Deming taught these methods to Japanese engineers and executives, while Joseph M. Juran taught the concepts of controlling quality and managerial breakthrough.

Armand V. Feigenbaum's 1961 book *Total Quality Control* is a forerunner of the present understanding of TQM. Likewise, Philip B. Crosby's promotion of zero defects paved the way for quality improvement in many companies.

The Japanese approach to quality management, influenced by Deming, Juran, and Feigenbaum, was promoted under several names. In 1968 the Japanese named their approach to total quality *companywide quality control*. Kaoru Ishikawa's synthesis of the philosophy contributed to Japan's ascendancy as a quality leader.

TQM is the name for the philosophy of a broad and systemic approach to managing organizational quality. Quality standards such as the ISO 9000 series and quality award programs such as the Deming Prize and the Baldrige Performance Excellence Program (BPEP) specify principles and processes that comprise TQM.

Primary Elements of TQM

The philosophy of TQM can be summarized as a management system for a customer-focused organization that engages all employees in continual improvement of the organization. It is an integrative system that uses strategy, data, and effective communications to integrate the quality discipline into the culture and activities of the organization.

• *Customer-focused.* It is fundamental to understand that the customer ultimately determines the level of quality. No matter what an organization does to foster quality improvement—training employees, integrating quality into the design process, upgrading computers or software, or buying new measuring tools—the customer ultimately determines whether the efforts were worthwhile. Chapters 16 and 17 provide further information on customer focus.

• *Total employee involvement.* Total employee involvement refers to participation of all employees in working toward common goals. Total employee commitment can only be obtained after fear has been driven from the workplace, when empowerment (see Chapter 2) has occurred, and management has provided a motivational environment. High-performance work systems integrate continuous improvement efforts with normal business operations. Self-managed work teams (see Chapter 3) are one form of empowerment often used.

• *Process-centered.* A fundamental part of TQM is a focus on process thinking. A process is a series of steps that take inputs from suppliers (internal or external) and transforms them into outputs that are delivered to customers (again, either internal or external). The steps required to carry out the process are defined, and performance measures are continually monitored in order to detect unexpected variation (see Chapter 15).

- *Integrated system.* Although an organization may consist of many different functional specialties, often organized into vertically structured departments, it is the horizontal processes interconnecting these functions that are the focus of TQM. Micro processes add up to larger processes, and all processes aggregate into the business processes required for defining and implementing strategy. Everyone must understand the vision, mission, and guiding principles, as well as the quality policies, objectives, and critical processes of the organization. Business performance must be monitored and communicated continuously. An integrated business system may be modeled after the BPEP criteria and/or incorporate the ISO 9000 or other standards. Every organization has a unique work culture, and it is virtually impossible to achieve excellence in its products and services unless a good quality culture has been fostered. Thus, an integrated system connects business improvement elements in an attempt to continually improve and exceed the expectations of customers, employees, and other stakeholders.

- *Strategic and systematic approach.* A critical part of the management of quality is the strategic and systematic approach to achieving an organization's vision, mission, and goals. This process, called *strategic planning* or *strategic management,* includes the formulation of a strategic plan that integrates quality as a core component (see Chapters 5, 6, and 7).

- *Continual improvement.* A major thrust of TQM is continual process improvement. Continual improvement drives an organization to be both analytical and creative in finding ways to become more competitive and more effective in meeting stakeholder expectations.

- *Fact-based decision making.* In order to know how well an organization is performing, data on performance measures are necessary. TQM requires that an organization continually collect and analyze data in order to improve decision-making accuracy, achieve consensus, and allow prediction based on past history (see Chapter 15).

- *Communications.* During times of organizational change, as well as in day-to-day operations, effective communication plays a large part in maintaining morale and in motivating employees at all levels. Communications involve strategies, method, and timeliness (see Chapter 9).

These elements are considered so essential to TQM that many organizations define them, in some format, as a set of core values and principles on which the organization is to operate. For example, the Baldrige criteria comprise a set of core values and concepts that define behaviors in high-performing organizations.

Benefits of TQM

Following are some of the direct and indirect benefits that may result from TQM:

- Strengthened competitive position
- Adaptability to changing or emerging market conditions and to environmental and other government regulations
- Higher productivity

- Enhanced market image
- Elimination of defects and waste
- Reduced costs and better cost management
- Higher profitability
- Improved customer focus and satisfaction
- Increased customer loyalty and retention
- Increased job security
- Improved employee morale
- Enhanced shareholder and stakeholder value
- Improved and innovative processes
- Greater emphasis on and awareness of the value of producing quality products and services

TQM Implementation Approaches

No one solution is effective for planning and implementing TQM in all situations. Each organization is unique in terms of culture, management practices, its products and services, and the processes used to create and deliver them. The TQM strategy will then vary from organization to organization; however, the key elements just mentioned should be present. Following is a generic model for implementing TQM:

1. Top management learns about and decides to commit to TQM. TQM is identified as one of the organization's strategies.

2. The organization assesses current culture, customer satisfaction, and quality management systems.

3. Top management identifies core values and principles to be used, and communicates them.

4. A TQM master plan is developed on the basis of steps 1, 2, and 3.

5. The organization identifies and prioritizes customer demands, and aligns products and services to meet those demands.

6. Management maps the critical processes through which the organization meets its customers' needs.

7. Management oversees the formation of teams for process improvement efforts.

8. The momentum of the TQM effort is managed by the steering committee.

9. Managers contribute individually to the effort through hoshin planning, training, coaching, or other methods.

10. Daily process management and standardization take place.

11. Progress is evaluated, and the plan is revised as needed.

12. Constant employee awareness through feedback on status is provided, and a recognition/reward process is established.

Following are five different strategies that may be used to develop TQM:

• *Strategy 1: The TQM element approach.* This is a TQM element-by-element approach that uses the tools of TQM to foster improvements. This method was widely used in the early 1980s as companies tried to implement parts of TQM as they learned them. Examples of this approach include quality circles, statistical process control, Taguchi methods, and quality function deployment. Some gain is achieved, but overall effectiveness is lacking.

• *Strategy 2: The guru approach.* The guru approach uses the teachings and writings of one of the leading quality thinkers as a guide with which to determine where the organization has deficiencies, then make appropriate changes to remedy those deficiencies. For example, managers might study Deming's 14 points and seven deadly diseases, or attend the Crosby College. They would then work on implementing the approach learned. This approach often ignores the values offered by gurus not selected and tends to lead to an elitist perspective (for example, "We follow the Deming teachings.")

• *Strategy 3: The organization model approach.* In this approach, individuals or teams visit organizations that have taken a leadership role in TQM and determine their processes and reasons for success. They then integrate these ideas with their own ideas to develop an organizational model adapted for their specific organization. This method was used widely in the late 1980s and is exemplified by the initial winners of the MBNQA. There is often a tendency to just copy what is learned.

• *Strategy 4: The Japanese total quality approach.* Organizations using the Japanese total quality approach examine the detailed implementation techniques and strategies employed by Deming Prize–winning companies and use this experience to develop a long-range master plan for in-house use. This approach was used by Florida Power and Light—among others—to implement TQM and to compete for and win the Deming Prize. If the approach is not integrated into the organization's culture and continually sustained, it fades away.

• *Strategy 5: The award criteria approach.* When using this model, an organization uses the criteria of a quality award, for example, the Deming Prize, the European Quality Award, or the BPEP, to identify areas for improvement. Under this approach, TQM implementation focuses on meeting specific award criteria. Although some argue that this is not an appropriate use of award criteria, some organizations do use this approach, and it can result in improvement.

What is the best approach? *The one that works best for the organization.* And that is usually an amalgam of various philosophies, theories, adaptations of successful techniques and tools used by others, all combined to address the uniqueness of the organization.

Common TQM Implementation Problems

Difficulties in implementing TQM can include:

• *Lack of management commitment.* When management talks TQM, but its actions fail to support the effort, it will ultimately fail to meet expectations. The result is cynicism and mistrust—and difficulty launching another attempt. For implementation to succeed, management must clearly and frequently communicate the reason for adopting TQM, be consistent in its application of TQM principles, and not present TQM as if it is another fad.

• *Changing organizational culture.* Changing an organization's culture is extremely difficult and time-consuming. Fear of change must be addressed, labor–management conflicts must be resolved, and the organization's focus must change from maintaining the status quo. Most employees will need to be convinced of the benefits that a TQM program will provide for them to buy into the changes. This often means that employees need to change behaviors or perform tasks in a different way than before TQM. If motivation is lacking, frustration and stress are likely. And trust is a must!

• *Preparation.* Before implementing TQM, management should strive for an organization-wide commitment, clearly communicate the organization's vision, mission, goals, and strategies, and foster open communication about the organization's changed focus.

• *Use of data.* TQM relies on data-based decision making. To succeed in building and sustaining a TQM environment, data must be accurate, timely, and reliable. The measurement process used must be valid and consistent, and data access should be efficient. Decision makers must be trained in data analysis and interpretation.

Other problems, many of which fall under the four previous categories, include, but are not limited to:

• Lack of strategic direction

• Lack of shared vision, mission, or guiding principles

• Lack of cooperation and teamwork among different work groups

• Focus on short-term profits rather than on long-term goals

• Failure to understand what teamwork entails

• Failure to focus on customers' needs and expectations

• Lack of mutual trust and respect among levels of employees

• Insufficient resources or lack of sustained commitment of those resources

• Lack of continual and effective training and education

• Management's failure to recognize and/or reward achievements

TQM, as a term, is not used as widely in the United States as it once was. Most of the concepts, principles, and methodology have been subsumed under the term *quality management.*

Continuous Quality Improvement (CQI)

The concept of company-wide continuous improvement originated with American companies (National Cash Register, Lincoln Electric Company) dating as far back as 1894. Gradually, the momentum changed from improving the workplace environment to an emphasis on productivity improvement and work simplification. Japanese companies began development of continuous quality improvement programs in the early 1950s (Toshiba, Matsushita Electric, and Toyota).

The ISO 9001:2008 standard requires continual quality improvement. The term changed from *continuous* (implying nonstop) to *continual* (meaning recurring often).

Kaizen. Kaizen is a Japanese word meaning incremental and orderly continuous improvement, and is often considered the single most significant contributor to Japanese success in the marketplace.[6] The kaizen philosophy embraces all business areas and processes. The focus is on improving the quality of people, which leads to quality of product and service.

Workers are given the quality improvement tools to expose opportunities for improvement and reduce waste. Top management supports the efforts, allocates resources, and provides reward programs that encourage improvement. Workers participate in suggestion systems and group activities. They receive training in problem solving and quality tools. Japanese organizations expect and receive an extremely large quantity of suggestions per employee, most of them small, incremental improvements costing little to implement.

A *kaizen event* (also called a *kaizen blitz*) is typically a five-day, highly intensive activity that may target eliminating waste, improving the work environment (especially safety), and reducing costs. It involves a work team focused on a specific opportunity for increased effectiveness and efficiency. Importantly, the result is not only a process improvement, but also the development of a new or revised work standard (without which the benefit of the improvement might soon dissipate). A structured approach is used for the five-day event.

A cycle time reduction team is a team comprising workers involved with a given process. They meet periodically, for example, once a week, to study the process and create innovative methods and/or use tools for shortening the process cycle time. Examples are single minute exchange of die (SMED) and other ways to reduce setup time, cellular processing, and single-piece flow (see Chapter 14, Section 3, for more on lean tools).

Six Sigma. Six Sigma: A statistical term? A methodology? A breakthrough strategy? A philosophy? It's all of these. The overall objective of a Six Sigma approach is to reduce variation and produce the product or service outputs consistently within customers' requirements. See Chapter 13, Section 3, for more on Six Sigma.

Benchmarking. Benchmarking is a process for identifying, comprehending, and adapting knowledge of exemplary practices and processes from organizations worldwide to assist an organization in improving its process or product performance. Best-in-class organizations use benchmarking as a key activity in setting goals as well as in determining how to meet them. Benchmarking assures management that chosen goals and objectives are competitive and attainable. *Benchmarks* are the measures of a best-in-class process.

Benchmarking involves identifying potential sources of best practices. First, however, it requires gaining a complete understanding of one's own process as it is impossible to do an accurate comparison to others without such an understanding. This requires knowing the boundaries of the process to be studied, the steps involved (as identified through a process map), and the current performance level of the process.

Benchmarking levels include:

1. *Internal benchmarking.* Comparing a process in one function with that of another function or comparing the same process across locations. Data are fairly easy to collect; however, focus is limited and possibly biased.

2. *Competitive benchmarking.* Comparing with direct competitors, either locally, nationally, or worldwide. The organization may not be viewed as a competitor when comparing with other organizations outside the local market area. In this case, the data can be more relevant, but difficult to collect. Typically, there will be resistance from a local direct competitor. Also, ethical and legal issues can be a concern.

3. *Functional benchmarking.* Comparing processes to other organizations with similar processes in the same function, but outside the industry.

4. *Generic benchmarking.* Finding organizations that have best-in-class processes and approaches from which one may learn and translate to improvements at one's own organization. When you think outside the box, there is a high potential for discovering innovative practices, and usually little resistance to partnering with a noncompetitor (see Table 12.1). There can be problems and high costs in translating practices learned to one's own work environment.

Many organizations conduct benchmarking studies at all four levels. Typical steps in benchmarking are:

1. Review, refine, and define existing process to be benchmarked.

2. Determine what to benchmark.

3. Form a benchmarking team.

4. Identify benchmark partners.

5. Collect and analyze benchmarking information.

6. Evaluate organization's performance versus benchmark partner.

7. Determine how upgrading practices will impact the organizations involved.

8. Establish new strategic targets.

Table 12.1   Examples for benchmarking a process.

Industry	Area—process improvement	Possible partner
Airline	Service planes quickly	Auto racing pit crews
Bandage manufacturer	Convert material to product	Auto manufacturer
Education	Teach/train students	Industry trainers
Hospital	Bill and collect payments	Credit card companies
Pizza delivery	Deploy personnel rapidly	Military, hospital emergency room
Ammunition casing	Make smooth cylinders	Lipstick manufacturer
Municipal government	Pothole repairs—time and material	Electric or gas utility
Hotel	Maintenance of public spaces	Gambling casino
Professional association	Book and product sales	Internet-based book company
On-call TV repair service On-call plumber Cable TV service Public utility	Truck stock replenishment or selection of on-board tools and equipment	Fire department Ambulance service Police department
Urban transit company	Bus/trolley car maintenance	Interstate truck stop service center
Sports arena	Processing mailed-in ticket sales	Commercial mail-order company
Metal stamping manufacturer (job shop)	Time to changeover dies for new order	Aircraft carrier—mounting weapons/ammunition on planes
Bank	Handling cash transactions	Sports arena
Assembly plant	Restocking parts just in time	Supermarket
Aerospace manufacturer	Large-project management	Major commercial building construction firm
Printer of continuous web paper products	Improving operating performance	Manufacturer of rolled metal products
Large hi-tech electronics manufacturing and assembly	Establishing customer/public tours and information center	NASA Large public utility

9. Implement improvements and a system to monitor progress.

10. Do it all over again.

Sources of organizations with which to partner in a benchmarking study can be found by examining trade publications for listings of companies deemed best in their industries, perusing best-practices databases available from major consulting firms, or talking with award-winning companies or others from whom

Figure 12.2   Sources of benchmarking information.

it is expected that significant learning can occur. The internet is a widely used resource for benchmarking, although the reliability of the information should be confirmed (see Figure 12.2 for a hierarchy of resources).

If process results or outcomes are all that are needed, then available performance figures might be sufficient and no further analysis necessary. If the process that achieves those results is to be benchmarked, however, then a visit to the benchmarking partner can be arranged. Once performance data have been analyzed, the project team can determine how the partner is achieving that performance and then develop objectives and an action plan to achieve similar or greater success.

The process of benchmarking can become so large that it becomes an entity in its own right. Before using it as a key decision-making tool, an organization should determine whether benchmarking is the best use of its resources. A benchmarking effort might initially be limited to discovering whether anyone has overcome the same or similar constraints as the organization is experiencing. If so, the benchmarking team can decide whether benchmarking is required in order to learn from the partner's success. Sponsorship and substantial support of management is mandatory when process benchmarking is to be done.

When done correctly, benchmarking offers many benefits. It allows the team to look beyond its own organization and even its industry. Looking beyond normal, everyday boundaries allows new ideas to emerge. In addition, a successful relationship with a benchmarking partner can create a mutually beneficial sales tool for both organizations. Significant research and development resources can be saved when mistakes are avoided. Finally, benchmarking can allow an organization to gain ground on the competition in a very short time.

Successful benchmarking includes:

- Having the right and best people on the team

- The ability to successfully break a process into its components

- Avoiding taking on too large a process for the resources available

Part III.E.3

- A long-term management commitment

- Focusing on a process rather than on just performance metrics

- Integrating the benchmarking initiative with broader goals

- Realizing that differences in culture, the portfolio of processes, and skill levels will likely make just copying a process from one organization into another ineffective

- Awareness of and diligent concern for proprietary and ethical issues

See Figure 12.3 for a benchmarking code of conduct.

Organizations that already have effective quality systems in place and are among the high-level profit producers for their size and type of business will probably benefit most from benchmarking. Mid-level profit producers can gain valuable insights, but may get a better return on their investment by first getting their own organization's processes in better shape. Lower-level profit producers, with few or no quality systems in place, may become frustrated with the gap between their practices and a best-in-class producer and have difficulty finding a benchmarking partner. (A benchmarking partner expects new partners to bring something to share and not expect to be educated on basic knowledge.)

Examples of what to benchmark include systems, processes, or practices that:

- Incur the highest costs

- Have a major impact on customer satisfaction, quality, and process cycle time

- Strategically impact the business

- Have the potential for high impact on competitive position in the marketplace

- Present the most significant area for improvement

- Have the highest probability of support and resources if selected for improvement

Examples of some of the areas for which benchmarking studies have been done include:

- Accounting systems

- Compensation systems

- Purchasing practices, for example, supplier selection

- Manufacturing and distribution processes

- Customer service practices

- Customer database design

- Cost of quality

- Capital investments, for example, selection criteria

Preamble—To guide benchmarking encounters and enhance the professionalism and effectiveness of benchmarking, many organizations have adopted this common Code of Conduct. All organizations are encouraged to abide by this Code of Conduct. Adherence to these principles will contribute to efficient, effective, and ethical benchmarking.

1. Principle of Legality.
   - If there is any potential question on the legality of an issue, don't do it.
   - Avoid discussions or actions that could lead to or imply an interest in restraint of trade, market, and/or customer allocation schemes, price fixing, dealing arrangements, bid rigging, or bribery. Don't discuss costs with competitors if costs are an element of pricing.
   - Refrain from the acquisition of trade secrets by any means that could be interpreted as improper, including the breach or inducement of a breach of any duty to maintain secrecy. Do not disclose or use any trade secret that may have been obtained through improper means or that was disclosed by another in violation of a duty to maintain secrecy or limit its use. Do not, as a consultant or client, extend one benchmarking effort's findings to another company without first obtaining permission from the parties of the first effort.

2. Principle of Exchange.
   - Be willing to provide the same type and level of information that you request from your benchmarking partner to your benchmarking partner.
   - Communicate fully and early in the relationship to clarify expectations, avoid misunderstanding, and establish mutual interest in the benchmarking exchange. Be honest and complete.

3. Principle of Confidentiality.
   - Treat benchmarking interchanges as confidential to the individuals and companies involved. Information must not be communicated outside the partnering organizations without the prior consent of the benchmarking partner who shared the information.
   - A company's participation in a study is confidential and should not be communicated externally without its prior permission.

4. Principle of Use.
   - Use information obtained through benchmarking only for purposes of formulating improvement of operations or processes within the companies participating in the benchmarking effort.
   - The use or communication of a benchmarking partner's name with the data obtained or practices observed requires the prior permission of that partner.
   - Do not use benchmarking as a means to market or sell.

5. Principle of First-Party Contact.
   - Initiate benchmarking contacts, whenever possible, through a benchmarking contact designated by the partner company.
   - Respect the corporate culture of partner companies and work within mutually agreed-on procedures.
   - Obtain mutual agreement with the designated benchmarking contact on any hand-off of communication or responsibility to other parties.

6. Principle of Third-Party Contact.
   - Obtain an individual's permission before providing his or her name in response to a contact request.
   - Avoid communicating a contact's name in an open forum without the contact's permission.

7. Principle of Preparation.
   - Demonstrate commitment to the efficiency and effectiveness of benchmarking by completing preparatory work prior to making an initial benchmarking contact, and follow a benchmarking process.
   - Make the most of your benchmarking partner's time by being fully prepared for each exchange.
   - Help your benchmarking partners prepare by providing them with an interview guide or questionnaire and agenda prior to benchmarking visits.

Figure 12.3   Benchmarking Code of Conduct.

Source: American Society for Quality, Quality Management Division, Benchmarking Committee. See the Fall 1997 issue of *The Quality Management Forum* for additional information on ethics and etiquette and benchmarking protocol.

- Techniques and tools
- Facility size, layout, decor
- Staffing practices, for example, size of departments, hiring criteria, training programs
- Employee involvement, empowerment, and recognition
- Marketing and promotion practices
- Knowledge management approaches
- Innovative usage of information technology
- Services and products offered
- Customer acquisition and retention approaches
- Customer satisfaction practices
- Overall operation, for example, building the organization's image, hours of operation
- Special practices and incentives

It is crucial to understand that benchmarking *is not*:

- Industrial spying
- Competitive analysis
- Industrial tourism
- Focused only on numbers, but mostly on the processes that produce the numbers
- Effectively planned and initiated unless there are significant potential gains expected
- A quick or inexpensive process when properly executed
- For organizations that are unwilling to make the effort to learn and measure what they are presently doing
- Appropriate without proper protocol and legal considerations
- Worth initiating unless your organization is prepared to make changes resulting from what's learned
- Easily accomplished if you have nothing to trade in your partnering arrangement
- Usually a one-shot process

In a 1944 interview, Juran told about German generals in the early 1900s who came to the United States to follow an American circus around.[7] The circus performed in tents, monstrous things to set up and take down. The circus moved from city to city on very short notice, which was a complicated process involving animals, people, equipment, food, and housing. To do this they had special railway cars designed. They were very proficient at handling every little detail.

The generals had a situation, but one that seemed to be far from that of a circus, or so they thought until they looked at the similarities. They had people, horses, ammunition, food for both humans and animals, and tons of equipment. And they, too, were faced with the need for setting up and dismantling their camps on very short notice. These generals learned about deployment from observing a circus, which, at first, appeared to have no relation to their army. This was a classical case of functional benchmarking.

4. QUALITY PHILOSOPHIES

> Describe and apply basic methodologies and theories proposed by quality leaders such as Shewhart, Deming, Juran, Crosby, Feigenbaum, and Ishikawa. (Apply)
>
> **Body of Knowledge III.E.4**

Theories of Major Contributors to Quality

Many theorists contributed to the philosophies and methods supporting TQM. Following are brief summaries of some of the work of the more widely known quality gurus.

Walter A. Shewhart. Shewhart is referred to as the father of statistical quality control because he brought together the disciplines of statistics, engineering, and economics. Shewhart worked at Bell Laboratories, who pioneered the quality discipline and gave the profession some of its most capable experts. A mentor of both Juran and Deming, Shewhart did extensive research in statistics and probability. He described the basic principles of the new discipline in his book *Economic Control of Quality of Manufactured Product*, the first statistics text focused on quality.

In his book he first proposed that there are two types of variation in a process—*chance causes* and *assignable causes*—and pointed out that assignable causes can be searched out and removed. He then presented a theory of charting data from the process, using statistically based control limits as a means of differentiating between the two types of causes. The use of lot-by-lot inspection and understanding the relationship between process variation and specifications were also spelled out. Shewhart's focus was on finding economic ways to reduce costs by identifying problems sooner in the process and by reducing the cost of inspection. See Chapter 15 for more on statistical techniques.

Shewhart created the concept of plan–do–check–act, which Deming later adapted.

W. Edwards Deming. Deming saw quality as the primary driver for business and societal success, and communicated the philosophy as a chain reaction. The premise is that if one improves quality, then costs will be lowered and resources better utilized. This increase in productivity will then allow the company to capture market share due to both higher quality and lower price, which will allow the organization to stay in business and to provide more jobs (known as the *Deming chain reaction*).

Deming's best known contribution was his 14 points for transformation of Western management:

1. Create constancy of purpose for improving products and services.

2. Adopt the new philosophy.

3. Cease dependence on inspection to achieve quality.

4. End the practice of awarding business on price alone; instead, minimize total cost by working with a single supplier.

5. Improve constantly and forever every process for planning, production, and service.

6. Institute training on the job.

7. Adopt and institute leadership.

8. Drive out fear.

9. Break down barriers between staff areas.

10. Eliminate slogans, exhortations, and targets for the workforce.

11a. Eliminate numerical quotas for the workforce.

11b. Eliminate numerical goals for management.

12. Remove barriers that rob people of pride of workmanship, and eliminate the annual rating or merit system.

13. Institute a vigorous program of education and self-improvement for everyone.

14. Put everybody in the company to work accomplishing the transformation.

Deming also defined *seven deadly diseases* that he believed to be the major barriers to business success:

1. *Lack of constancy of purpose.* A company without constancy of purpose has no long-range plans for staying in business. Management is insecure, and so are employees.

2. *Emphasis on short-term profits.* Looking to increase the quarterly dividend undermines quality and productivity.

3. *Evaluation by performance, merit rating, or annual review of performance.* The effects of these are devastating—teamwork is destroyed, rivalry

is nurtured. Performance ratings build fear and leave people bitter, despondent, and beaten. They also encourage defection in the ranks of management.

4. *Mobility of management.* Job-hopping managers never understand the companies they work for and are never there long enough to follow through on long-term changes that are necessary for quality and productivity.

5. *Running a company on visible figures alone.* The most important figures are unknown and unknowable—the multiplier effect of a happy customer, for example.

6. *Excessive medical costs for employee healthcare.* These increase the final costs for goods and services.

7. *Excessive costs of warranty.* These are often fueled by lawyers who work on the basis of contingency fees.

Deming emphasized that transformation of organizations begins with the individual and that this comes from their gaining a different understanding of self and the world in which he or she lives. This will require understanding the *system of profound knowledge*, which consists of four major components:

1. *Appreciation for a system.* An organization is a system of interrelated components with a common purpose. Changing one part of the system affects other parts.

2. *Knowledge about variation.* Everything varies, but understanding whether the variation is due to chance cause or random cause will determine what action should be taken, if any.

3. *Theory of knowledge.* No learning has occurred if there is no theory that allows prediction. Operational definitions are necessary in order to allow theories to be useful to many.

4. *Psychology.* We all want to be appreciated. People have different needs, however, and what will make one happy might negatively impact another.[8]

Deming adapted Shewhart's plan–do–check–act cycle to plan–do–study–act (with proper attribution to Shewhart) to better reflect the actions of this process. PDCA is the term more often used, and often incorrectly attributed to Deming.

Joseph M. Juran. Joseph M. Juran pursued a varied career as an engineer, executive, government administrator, university professor, labor arbitrator, corporate director, and consultant. Specializing in managing for quality, he is the editor of *Juran's Quality Handbook* (with A. Blanton Godfrey).[9]

Juran defines quality as consisting of two different, but related concepts:

1. One form of quality is income oriented and consists of those features of the product that meet customer needs and thereby produce income. In this sense, higher quality usually costs more.

2. A second form of quality is cost oriented and consists of freedom from failures and deficiencies. In this sense, higher quality usually costs less.

He defined three basic managerial processes required for quality, called the *Juran trilogy*. The processes are quality planning, quality control, and quality improvement, which, he noted, parallel the processes traditionally used to manage finance.

Juran's quality planning road map consists of the following steps:

- Determine quality goals.

- Identify customers.

- Discover customers' needs.

- Translate customer language into products having desired features.

- Develop processes able to produce the product.

- Transfer the process, with appropriate controls, to operations.

Control takes place at all levels, from the CEO down to the workers, and all use the same feedback loop, which is the following:

- Measure performance of the process.

- Compare performance to the goal.

- Take action if there is a gap.

The goal of management should be to achieve what Juran calls *self-control* in all processes, wherein the person performing the process is capable of making all adjustments necessary to maintain control. Planning for control is part of the function of designing the process.

Juran presented a structured approach for improvement in his book *Managerial Breakthrough* (1964) and included a list of responsibilities that upper managers should not delegate:

- Creating awareness of the need and opportunity for improvement.

- Making quality improvement a part of every job description.

- Creating an infrastructure—a quality council who selects projects for improvement and establishes teams.

- Providing training in quality improvement methods.

- Regularly reviewing improvement progress.

- Giving recognition to improvement teams.

- Using the results to spread the word on the power of the efforts.

- Revising the reward system to enforce the rate of improvement.

- Maintaining momentum by enlarging the business plan to include goals for quality improvement.

Juran also defines three levels of quality management:

1. *Strategic quality management,* which concerns itself mostly with policies

2. *Operational quality management,* which concerns itself with process management

3. *The workforce,* which concerns itself with specifications and work procedures

Juran defines TQM as a collection of certain quality-related activities:

- Quality becomes a part of each upper management agenda.

- Quality goals enter the business plan.

- Stretch goals are derived from benchmarking; focus is on the customer and on meeting competition, and there are goals for annual quality improvement.

- Goals are deployed to the action levels.

- Training is done at all levels.

- Measurement is established throughout.

- Upper managers regularly review progress against goals.

- Recognition is given for superior performance.

- The reward system is revised.

Juran expressed what he termed a universal sequence, described in two journeys. A *diagnostic journey* goes from symptom to cause. This includes analyzing symptoms, theorizing causes, testing theories, and establishing causes. A *remedial journey* moves from causes to remedy. The activities included are developing remedies, testing remedies, proving remedies under operating conditions, dealing with resistance to change, and establishing controls to maintain the gains.

Philip B. Crosby. Crosby defines quality as conformance to requirements; therefore, quality is measured by the cost of nonconformance. Using this approach means that one arrives at a performance goal of zero defects. Quality management means prevention, so inspection, testing, checking, and other non-preventive techniques have no place in quality management. Crosby believed that statistical levels of compliance set people up for failure.

Crosby defined what he called *absolutes of quality management*:

1. Quality means conformance, not elegance.

2. There is no such thing as a quality problem.

3. There is no such thing as the economics of quality; it is always cheaper to do the job right the first time.

4. The only performance measurement is the cost of quality.

5. The only performance standard is zero defects.[10]

Part III.E.4

Crosby maintains that absolutely no reason exists for having errors or defects in any product or service, and that companies should adopt a quality "vaccine" to prevent nonconformance. The three ingredients of this vaccine are determination, education, and implementation. Quality improvement is a process, not a program; it should be permanent and lasting. He also has 14 steps he believes necessary for improvement:

1. Make it clear that management is committed to quality.

2. Form quality improvement teams with representatives from each department.

3. Determine how to measure where current and potential quality problems lie.

4. Evaluate the cost of quality and explain its use as a management tool.

5. Raise the quality awareness and personal concern of all employees.

6. Take formal actions to correct problems identified through previous steps.

7. Establish a committee for the zero defects program.

8. Train all employees to actively carry out their part of the quality improvement program.

9. Hold a zero defects day to let all employees realize that there has been a change.

10. Encourage individuals to establish improvement goals for themselves and their groups.

11. Encourage employees to communicate to management the obstacles they face in attaining their improvement goals.

12. Recognize and appreciate those who participate.

13. Establish quality councils to communicate on a regular basis.

14. Do it all over again to emphasize that the quality improvement program never ends.

Armand V. Feigenbaum. Total quality control uses quality as a strategic business tool that requires awareness by everyone in the organization (just as cost and schedule are regarded in most organizations). Quality reaches far beyond defect management on the shop floor: it is a philosophy and commitment to excellence.

Quality is a way of corporate life—a way of managing. Total quality control has an organization-wide impact that involves implementation of customer-oriented quality activities. This is a prime responsibility of general management as well as marketing, engineering, production, industrial relations, finance, and service, and of the quality function itself. Feigenbaum defines total quality control as excellence driven rather than defect driven, and suggests that the quest consists of three elements: quality leadership, quality technology, and organizational commitment.

Continuous leadership emphasis must be placed on quality, which must be thoroughly planned in specific terms. The establishment of a quality circle program or a corrective action team is not sufficient for ongoing success.

The traditional quality department can not resolve 80 percent to 90 percent of quality problems. In a modern setting, all members of the organization must be responsible for the quality of their product or service. This means integrating office staff into the process, as well as engineers and shop floor workers. Error-free performance should be the objective. New techniques must be evaluated and implemented as appropriate. What might be an acceptable level of quality to a customer today might be unacceptable tomorrow.

For quality to be achieved, continuous motivation is required. Training that is specifically related to the task at hand is of paramount importance. Quality should be considered a strategic element of business planning.

Feigenbaum defined four management fundamentals of total quality:

1. Competition means there's no such thing as a permanent quality level. Continuous improvement is necessary if one is to stay competitive.

2. Good management involves personally leading the effort by mobilizing the organization's quality knowledge, skill, and attitudes such that everyone realizes that improvement in quality makes everything better.

3. Successful innovation requires high quality to support it, especially where it enables new products to be designed and launched quicker and more effectively.

4. Cost and quality are complementary rather than conflicting objectives.[11]

Kaoru Ishikawa. Ishikawa was an early student of Deming and a member of the Union of Japanese Scientists and Engineers (JUSE). He authored the *Guide to Quality Control* to help in the training of foremen and middle managers in Japan for the operation of quality circles. In his book *What Is Total Quality Control? The Japanese Way,* he discusses the following aspects of total quality control:

- *Quality control* (QC) is the responsibility of all workers and all divisions.

- *Total quality control* (TQC) is a group activity and can not be done by individuals. It calls for teamwork.

- TQC will not fail if all members cooperate, from the president down to line workers and sales personnel.

- In TQC, middle management will be frequently talked about and criticized—be prepared.

- QC circle activities are a part of TQC.

- Do not confuse objectives with the means to attain them.

- TQC is not a miracle drug; its properties are more like those of Chinese herbal medicine.

To achieve total quality control, a thought revolution must occur:

Part III.E.4

- Quality first—not short-term profit first.
- Consumer orientation—not producer orientation. Think from the standpoint of the other party.
- The next process is your customer—break down the barrier of sectionalism.
- Use facts and data to make presentations—utilize statistical methods.
- Respect for humanity as a management philosophy—full participatory management.
- Cross-functional management.

Ishikawa advocated four types of audits:

1. Audit by the president
2. Audit by the head of the unit (for example, division head or branch office manager)
3. QC audit by the QC staff
4. Mutual QC audit

The concept of quality circles is attributed to Ishikawa. He also introduced the cause-and-effect diagram and variations of the check sheet.[12]

Genichi Taguchi. Taguchi is best known in the United States for the *Taguchi methods*, which involve the efficient use of design of experiments for identifying the major contributors to variation (parameter design), for setting tolerances based on inherent statistical variation (tolerance design), and for designing robust products and processes. Taguchi maintains that the goal is the most robust combination of product and process. That is, the product that best meets the customers' requirements by being most consistently produced by the process.

He defines quality of a product as "the (minimum) loss imparted by the product to society from the time the product is shipped." From this, he designed the *Taguchi loss function*, which translates any deviation of a product from its target parameter into a financial measure (see Figure 12.4). The Taguchi loss function is a driver for continuous improvement.

ENDNOTES

1. A. V. Feigenbaum, *Total Quality Control*, 3rd ed. (New York: McGraw-Hill, 1991).
2. The content wording of the BPEP criteria is subject to change from year to year. Also, the wording in the criteria for education and for healthcare differs from the "all other" criteria shown here.
3. The ISO 9000 series (three booklets) is available through ASQ (800) 248-1946.
4. Most of these standards may be obtained through ASQ at (800) 248-1946 or the ASQ Quality Press Bookstore at www.asq.org/quality-press.
5. P. Brooks, "The Global Marketplace and CE Marking: If You Want to Sell in Europe, Here's What You Need to Know," *Quality Digest* (July 2002): 44–47.

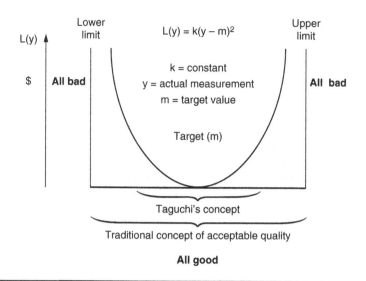

Figure 12.4   The Taguchi loss function.

6. M. Imai, *Kaizen: The Key to Japan's Competitive Success* (New York: Random House Business Division, 1986).
7. J. M. Juran, ed., *A History of Managing for Quality* (Milwaukee: ASQC Quality Press, 1995).
8. W. E. Deming, *The New Economics*, 2nd ed. (Cambridge, MA: MIT Center for Advanced Educational Studies, 1994).
9. J. M. Juran, *Juran's Quality Handbook*, 5th ed. (New York: McGraw-Hill, 1999).
10. P. B. Crosby, *Quality Is Free* (New York: Mentor Books, 1979).
11. A. V. Feigenbaum, *Total Quality Control*, 3rd ed. (New York: McGraw-Hill, 1991).
12. Ishikawa, *Guide to Quality Control* (Tokyo: Asian Productivity Organization, 1982).

See Appendix A for additional references for this chapter.

Part III.E.4

Part IV

Quality Management Tools

The significant problems we face cannot be solved at the same level of thinking we were at when we created them.

—Albert Einstein

The systems perspective tells us that we must look beyond individual mistakes or bad luck to understand important problems.

—Peter Senge

Defects are not free. Somebody makes them, and gets paid for making them.

—W. Edwards Deming

Part IV

Chapter 13

A. Problem-Solving Tools

R egardless of the current level of organizational performance, room for improvement always exists. Project-by-project problem solving and process improvement has become a basic practice for managing any organization. In order for improvement efforts to be effective, however, a systematic approach must be used to identify, understand, and address the opportunities.

Analyzing a process in order to identify factors needing to be changed involves the use of data or ideas. Such information needs to be presented in a way that allows ease of interpretation. Visual representation of processes and information is one way of accomplishing this, and tools such as flowcharts and Pareto charts have therefore become widespread in their use. Since solutions often call for outside-the-box thinking, additional tools have been developed to help increase creativity.

Often, what is initially determined to be causing a problem or defect (for example, a specific machine, department, component, or person) may simply be a symptom of a much larger difficulty. Problems are also often caused by a combination of factors that require in-depth searches for root causes. In addition, what may appear to be a problem may be just the result of random variation of a process. Punishing or rewarding people for random swings in a process is a sure way for management to lose credibility.

Just as auto mechanics need to accurately diagnose and quickly fix engine problems (rather than simply replacing components until the problem part is found—a lengthy and costly method), process improvement efforts need to follow a systematic approach. A systematic approach, carried out on a project-by-project basis, works for several reasons:

- Focused allocation of resources improves the chances of success by preventing spreading those resources too thinly.

- The use of facts and data improves problem-solving efficiency and effectiveness by ensuring that improvement efforts are objective and focus on the proper causes.

- A systemwide view may allow other areas of the organization to benefit.

Some reasons a problem-solving process often fails are:

- Jumping from analysis to a solution too quickly

- Using data that are inaccurate or biased

- Failing to test a solution before implementing it

- Mistaking a symptom for the root cause of the problem

- Failing to include the right people in the problem-solving process

- Failing to evaluate the potential benefits and costs of the chosen solution

Many methods and associated tools can be used to improve organizational processes. The focus of this chapter is on the tools typically used to reduce process variation. Chapters 14 and 15 will present some additional methods used for continual improvement, and Chapter 3 discusses the methods for ensuring that teams are effectively organized and managed.

Finally, it is important that improvement efforts not simply be a hodgepodge of seemingly random projects. Organizations need to have a process for identifying the most significant improvement opportunities, and must also track the progress of efforts. *Cost of quality* is a tool that can be used to look at an organization's financial information in such a way as to highlight opportunities for quality improvement.

1. THE SEVEN CLASSIC QUALITY TOOLS

Select, interpret, and evaluate output from these tools: Pareto charts, cause and effect diagrams, flowcharts, control charts, check sheets, scatter diagrams, and histograms. (Evaluate)

Body of Knowledge IV.A.1

Part IV.A.1

Flowchart (1)

A *flowchart* is a map of the sequence of steps and decision points in a process. An example of a flowchart is shown in Figure 13.1. Flowcharting a process is a good starting point for a team, as it helps the group gain a common understanding of the process flow. Each team member typically has a perspective based on his/her own role, but may not have a full understanding of the entire process. A flowchart can also reveal missing, redundant, or erroneous steps.

In addition to providing basic information, flowcharts may contain additional items depending on the purpose of the project, such as times, tools, and

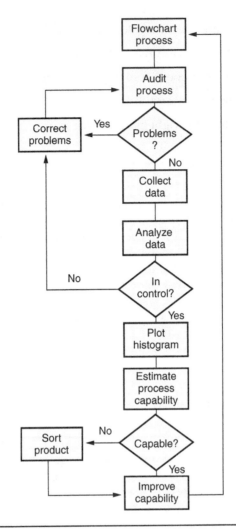

Figure 13.1 Flowchart example.

responsibilities. For example, a *deployment flowchart*, sometimes called a *swim-lane chart* (Figure 13.2), is likely to be used for a larger process where multiple departments have responsibility.

A flowchart may be used to:

- Document the as-is condition of a process

- Reflect changes that are to be made to a process

- Design an entirely new process

- Fulfill the ISO 9001 standard's requirement to identify and document the organization's processes and the sequence and interaction of these processes

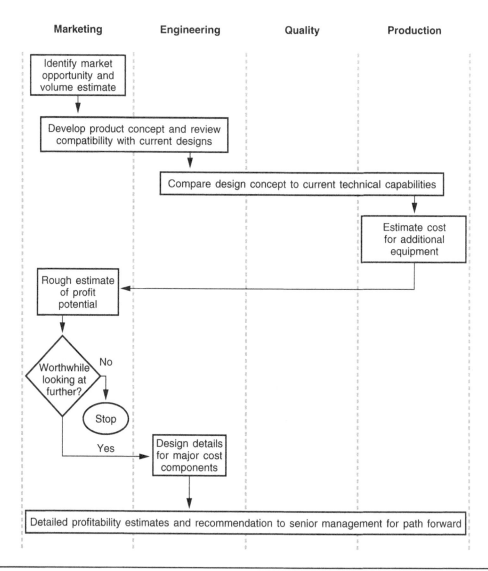

| Marketing | Engineering | Quality | Production |

Figure 13.2   Deployment flowchart example (also called a swim-lane chart).

Check Sheet (2)

The *check sheet* (sometimes called a *tally sheet*) is used for gathering information to analyze. As with most of the tools, it facilitates the use of facts, rather than just opinions, in talking about and solving problems. Check sheets are used to gather data on frequency of occurrence (see Figure 13.3). Data from several check sheets can be organized into a Pareto chart for final analysis.

In some applications a more visually oriented data collection device may be desired. For example, in order to record the location of defects in a printing process, a sample of the product being printed could be given to individuals who are

Switch Assembly Op 236 Plastic footer Operator_____						
Chart began _July 12, 2013_						
Week 1						**Totals**
Burns	III	JHT				
Misrun		III	II			
Bad finish	JHT					
Porosity		I				
Flash	JHT JHT I	IIII I				
Color						

Figure 13.3   Check sheet example.

to collect the data. They could then simply mark on the printout where each of the defects is located on the inspected products. Clusters indicating the biggest problem areas would quickly become apparent. (This type of check sheet is sometimes called a *measles chart* or a *defect data check sheet*.)

Cause-and-Effect Diagram (3)

The *cause-and-effect* (C-E) diagram (also called an *Ishikawa diagram* after its developer Kaoru Ishikawa, or alternatively called a *fishbone diagram*) provides a way of collecting and organizing what may be a long list of potential causes that might contribute to a particular problem. In a C-E diagram, the problem (the effect) is stated in a box at the right side of the chart, and likely causes are listed under major categories that can lead to the effect. The *four M's* (manpower, machinery, methods, and materials) are categories of problem sources typically used for manufacturing problems, although other headings such as *environment* and *measurements* are sometimes added. For service processes, the *four P's* (people, policies, procedures, and plant) are often used. Figure 13.4 shows a C-E diagram of some of the reasons that outpatient clients may not be able to locate the X-ray department in a hospital.

The items for the diagram may be created through a brainstorming session or by a review of the relevant process flowchart to explore what can go wrong at each step. Once the C-E diagram is completed, the potential causes should be organized and ordered so that internal and external relationships are clear. The *affinity diagram* is one way to do this. Data must be gathered to determine which of the causes or groups of causes is (are) most likely to be acting on the problem being studied.

Pareto Chart (4)

Vilfredo Pareto, an 1800s Italian economist, noted that 80 percent of the wealth in Italy was held by 20 percent of the population. Juran later applied the Pareto

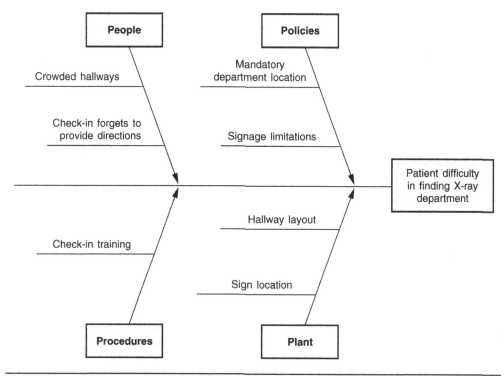

Figure 13.4   Cause-and-effect diagram example.

principle for other applications, pointing out that 80 percent of the variation in a process is caused by roughly 20 percent of the variables; he labeled these variables the *vital few*, as opposed to the *trivial many* (changed later to *useful many*) that had much less overall impact.

Figure 13.5 is an example of a *Pareto chart* that indicates how much each work center contributes to quality costs. Pareto analysis could also be used by a supervisor within each of the higher-cost work centers to pinpoint the particular machines that are the primary sources of trouble. Note that although the *y*-axis of a Pareto chart often represents the frequency of a problem, it is also important to do a similar analysis based on costs, since not all problems have equal financial impact. The right side of Figure 13.5 includes another feature, cumulative percentage.

Control Charts (5)

Control charts are a refinement of the original *run chart*, which does not include control limits. A control chart serves two vital purposes as a data-gathering tool: (1) it shows when a process is being influenced by special causes, creating an out-of-control condition, and (2) it indicates how a process behaves over time.

Control charts should be examined for nonrandom patterns of data points; such an analysis of patterns can indicate what source of variation is most likely creating the condition (for example, which of the causes in the C-E diagram is most likely influencing the process). Patterns could reflect wildly fluctuating values,

Part IV.A.1

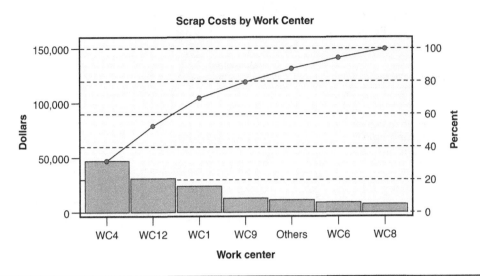

Figure 13.5   Pareto chart example.

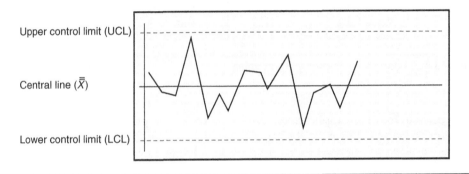

Figure 13.6   Control chart example.

sudden process jumps or shifts, a gradual trend, or increased variation. Each of the causes in the C-E diagram is likely to create only a particular type of pattern, making the control chart a valuable diagnostic tool. The pattern might also reveal improvement in a process, indicated by decreased variation. Investigating this change to find the cause may provide deeper learning.

A control chart is shown in Figure 13.6. See Section 3 of this chapter for more on control charts.

Histograms (6)

While control charts allow seeing how a process performs over time, a *histogram* provides a graphical picture of the frequency distribution of the data. The histogram allows detection of distributions that do not demonstrate a typical bell-shaped curve, and shows how the process spread and central tendency relate to process specifications. A histogram is shown in Figure 13.7.

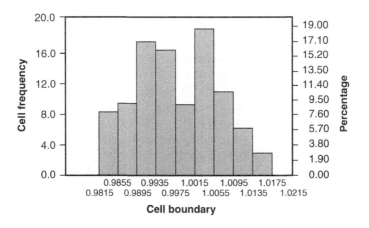

Figure 13.7   Histogram example.

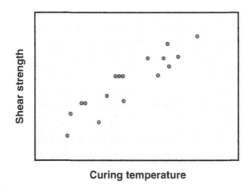

Figure 13.8   Scatter diagram example.

For a normal (bell-shaped) distribution, the most frequently appearing value (mode) is centered, with data appearing equally on either side. If data extend beyond the specification limits, the process or product is out of tolerance. Additionally, the histogram may also point out that there are actually two different distributions at work (as shown in Figure 13.7) in the process (for example, differing impact of the same raw material purchased from two different suppliers).

Scatter Diagrams (7)

A *scatter diagram* shows whether or not there is a correlation between two variables. Correlation does not necessarily mean a direct cause-and-effect relationship, however. If it appears that values for one of the variables can be predicted based on the value of another variable, then there is correlation.

In the example in Figure 13.8, the curing temperature of a glue joint has been plotted along the *x*-axis and the shear strength along the *y*-axis. In this example, the shear strength of the joint increases with an increase in cure temperature, within the normal processing limits. If the data points were to fall along a single, straight line, the variation in glue strength would be fully explained by the value of the cure temperature. In most cases, there is deviation from a straight line, indicating the existence of other sources of variation in the process.

If the slope of the plots is generally upward, as in this example, it is said that a *positive correlation* exists between the variables. That is, as one increases, the other also increases. Other possible measures of correlation are negative, weak, or none. A *negative correlation* exists if the line slopes downward, meaning that as one variable increases in value, the second decreases. If no visible pattern appears to exist in the plotted points, the two variables are not correlated. A numeric value called the correlation coefficient (r) can also be calculated, with values approaching +1 or –1 indicating high positive or negative correlation, respectively, and a value near zero indicating no correlation.

Some additional factors should be considered when using the scatter diagram. First, not all relationships between variables are linear. If the range of temperatures were extended in Figure 13.8, it is likely that a peak strength in the glue joint would be reached, after which increasing the cure temperature would damage the joint and reduce its strength. Therefore, the relationship between the two variables is not really a straight line, but rather a curve that climbs upward, peaks, and then descends.

A second consideration is that the visual slope of the line does not provide any information about the strength of correlation since the scales of the graph can be expanded or compressed on either axis. The third consideration, and probably the most important, is that a direct and strong correlation does not necessarily imply a cause-and-effect relationship. An example is that the volume of ice cream sold per day is strongly correlated to the daily number of fatalities by drowning. Obviously, neither of these variables is the cause of the other, and the most likely explanation is that each of these variables is a result of and is, therefore, strongly correlated to a third variable, such as the outside temperature.

While correlation does not prove causality, the lack of correlation may indicate that no cause-and-effect relationship exists. (For more information on correlation, see "Advanced Statistical Methods, Linear Regression" in Chapter 15, Section 3.)

2. BASIC MANAGEMENT AND PLANNING TOOLS

Select, interpret, and evaluate output from these tools: affinity diagrams, tree diagrams, process decision program charts (PDPCs), matrix diagrams, prioritization matrices, interrelationship digraphs, and activity network diagrams. (Evaluate)

Body of Knowledge IV.A.2

Part IV.A.2

While the QC tools in the previous section are typically used by employee teams to analyze and improve processes, the tools presented in this section are more often used by managers or knowledge workers to organize concepts, ideas, and words. These tools are also known as the *new QC tools*, and are oriented more toward facilitating management and planning activities. The seven tools are the activity network diagram, affinity diagram, interrelationship digraph, matrix diagram, priorities matrix, process decision program chart, and tree diagram. In addition to these seven tools, the Gantt chart is added for project task monitoring and control.

Activity Network Diagram (1)

The *activity network diagram* (AND) is an umbrella term that includes the *critical path method* (CPM) and the *program evaluation and review technique* (PERT). The AND is used when a task is complex and/or lengthy and, because of schedule constraints, it is desirable to determine which activities can be done in parallel. The AND is used often as a planning aid for construction projects and for large manufacturing contracts that are best handled as projects. The AND shows who is going to do what and when, and arrows are drawn to show what must be done in series and what can be done in parallel so that action can be taken if the overall time estimate is too high to meet goals.

In the AND shown in Figure 13.9, each numbered node represents one task that must be completed as a part of a project. The numbers shown between nodes are estimates of the number of weeks to complete the work in a given activity. The critical path can then be computed. The *critical path* is the longest path in the series of activities—those activities that must be completed on time to meet the planned project completion date. This diagram is often created via a project

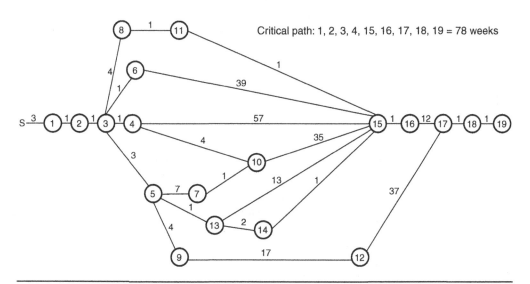

Figure 13.9   Network diagram example (activity on node).

Part IV.A.2

management software package. Chapter 10, "Project Management," discusses more on CPM and PERT. For control of scheduling simpler projects or where clarity of monitoring and communication of status is desired, the Gantt chart may be used. (See section below on Gantt charts.)

Affinity Diagram (2)

The *affinity diagram* is a method used to organize a large group of items into smaller chunks that are easier to understand and deal with. It is often used after a brainstorming process (discussed later in this chapter) to organize the ideas that were listed. It can be done by first creating categories into which ideas will be placed, or all ideas can first be grouped into what appear to be similar categories that will be named after all grouping is completed. The process can be aided by writing each idea on a sticky note and having members of the group move the notes around until they are satisfied with the groupings. Some items may also be placed in multiple groups when deemed useful.

A major benefit of the affinity diagram is that it creates a discussion on what the various ideas mean to each individual, and the resulting diagram is a jointly created mental model of the situation being analyzed. Figure 13.10 is an example of a simple affinity diagram.

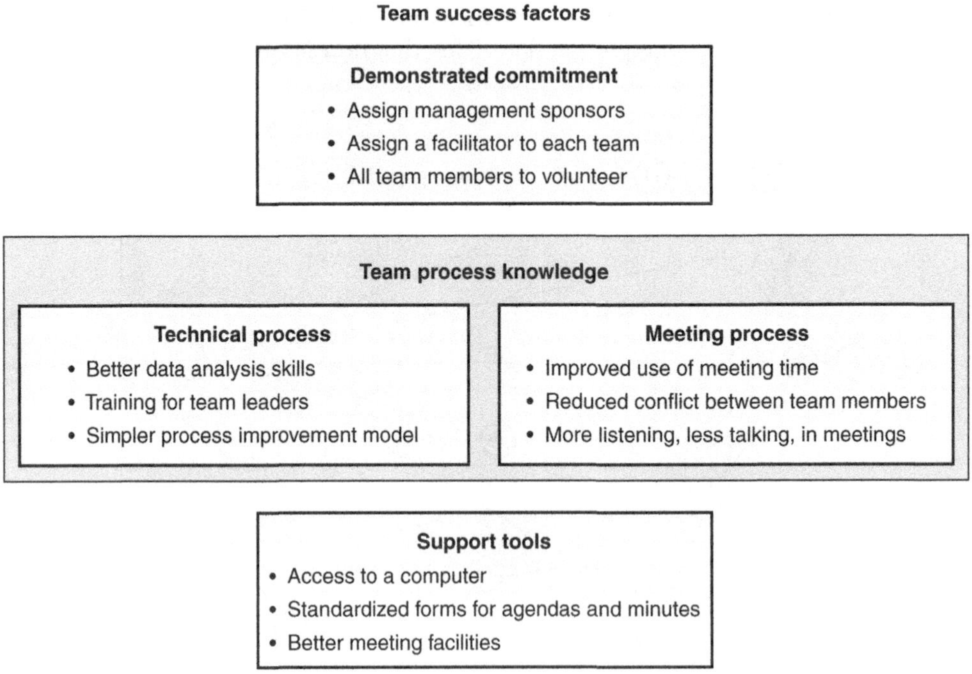

Team success factors

Demonstrated commitment
- Assign management sponsors
- Assign a facilitator to each team
- All team members to volunteer

Team process knowledge

Technical process	**Meeting process**
• Better data analysis skills	• Improved use of meeting time
• Training for team leaders	• Reduced conflict between team members
• Simpler process improvement model	• More listening, less talking, in meetings

Support tools
- Access to a computer
- Standardized forms for agendas and minutes
- Better meeting facilities

Figure 13.10   Affinity diagram of "methods to improve team performance."

Interrelationship Digraph (3)

While the affinity diagram organizes and makes visible various ideas about a project, the *interrelationship digraph* (or *relationship diagram*) pinpoints logical cause-and-effect relationships between ideas. The interrelationship digraph is often constructed using the components of an affinity diagram by asking, "If this category were changed, would it impact each of the other categories?" When the answer is yes for any pair of categories, an arrow is drawn from the first to the second, showing the cause-and-effect relationship.

A completed interrelationship digraph is shown in Figure 13.11. It shows the various issues that can impact the results of a team-based continual improvement effort and how they are interconnected. This diagram could be used to identify which components of the team process in an organization may not be working sufficiently well, or how there may be a lack of alignment between them. It may also be used to distinguish processes that are primarily drivers from processes that are primarily driven.

Matrix Diagram (4)

The *matrix diagram* answers two important questions when sets of data are compared: Are the data related, and if so, how strong is the relationship? A matrix

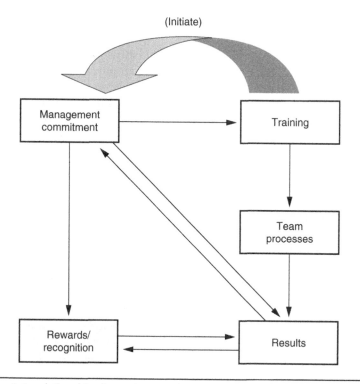

Figure 13.11   Interrelationship diagraph example.

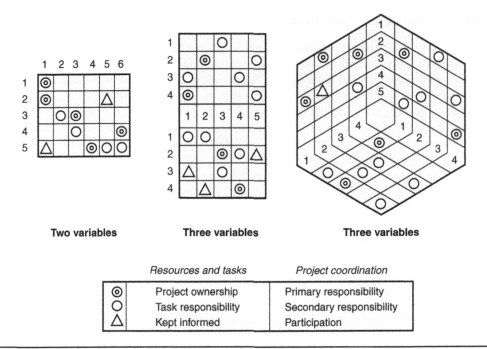

Figure 13.12   Matrix diagrams at various stages of completion.

diagram can be used to analyze the relationships between variables in an affinity diagram as part of the process in creating an interrelationship digraph. In this way the matrix diagram promotes systems thinking.

Another use of the matrix diagram is when an organization is faced with a large and complex project requiring the integration of activities carried out by resources from multiple departments. The horizontal axis of the matrix diagram would represent the tasks required, and the vertical axis the departments available to perform the work. For each of the required tasks, the matrix diagram shows which departments are in charge, which have some involvement, and which have no involvement in the performance of the tasks. Figure 13.12 shows different ways to show relationships between up to three variables in a matrix diagram.

Priorities Matrix (5)

The *priorities matrix* assists in choosing between several options that have many useful benefits, but where not all of them are of equal value. The relative merit of each available course of action and the related effects creates a complicated picture that is difficult to prioritize in one's mind. For example, how does a person choose between two automobiles, one of which offers average gas mileage, four-wheel drive, and a fully automated set of window and seat controls, and another that has a superior sound system, a significantly smoother ride, and better fuel economy? For one driver, four-wheel drive might be a must-have option that dominates all other considerations, but another driver might value fuel economy above all other options.

A priorities matrix is created and used according to the following steps:

- A matrix is created to compare all criteria to be used in making the choice (see Figure 13.13a). All criteria are listed on both the horizontal and vertical axes, and are then compared and assigned a weighted score (relative row percentage) on the basis of the perceived importance of each criterion relative to each other.

- Once criteria have been weighted, then all possible choices (items from which selection will be made) are rated on how well they compare based on each criterion. A new matrix is required to evaluate the options against each criterion (for example, Figure 13.13b only evaluates the choices based on one of the four criteria that are to be used).

	Handling	Acceleration	Comfort	Price	Row total	Row %
Handling		1	10	5	16.0	42.3
Acceleration	1		10	5	16.0	42.3
Comfort	1/10	1/10		1/5	.4	1.1
Price	1/5	1/5	5		5.4	14.3

10	Overwhelmingly more important	**Total**	**37.8**
5	More important		
1	Equal		
1/5	Less important		
1/10	Overwhelmingly less important		

Figure 13.13a   Priorities matrix—evaluating relative importance of criteria.

	Auto 1	Auto 2	Auto 3	Auto 4	Row total	Row %
Auto 1		5	1/10	1/10	5.2	10.2
Auto 2	1/5		1/5	1/10	.5	1.0
Auto 3	10	5		1/10	15.1	29.7
Auto 4	10	10	10		30	59.1

10	Overwhelmingly better	**Total**	**50.8**
5	Somewhat better		
1	Same		
1/5	Somewhat less good		
1/10	Overwhelmingly less good		

Figure 13.13b   Priorities matrix—comparing objects based on one criterion (acceleration).

Part IV.A.2

	Handling	Acceleration	Comfort	Price	Row total	Row %
Auto 1	(Criteria row total × Option row total)	(42.3 × 10.2) 431				
Auto 2		(42.3 × 1.0) 42				
Auto 3		(42.3 × 29.7) 1256				
Auto 4		(42.3 × 59.1) 2500				

Figure 13.13c   Priorities matrix (partial)—evaluating all objects against criteria.

- A final matrix compares the possible choices on the left axis and the decision criteria along the top. The appropriate weighted scores from the other matrices are inserted and multiplied to get a score for each option for each criterion. Figure 13.13c shows the beginning of this matrix based on information gained from Figures 13.13a and 13.13b. The option achieving the highest row total is then considered the best overall choice.

The priorities matrix can add objectivity to what might otherwise be an emotional decision. When numerous possibilities exist, and the selection criteria are many and complicated, this tool permits a group to systematically discuss, identify, and prioritize the criteria that should have the most influence on the decision, and to then evaluate all the possibilities while keeping a complete picture in mind.

Process Decision Program Chart (6)

No matter how well planned an activity is, things do not always turn out as expected. The *process decision program chart* (PDPC), similarly to fault tree analysis, can be used to identify contingency plans for several situations that might contribute to failure of a particular project. The tasks to be completed for the project are listed, followed by a list of problems that could occur. For each problem, a decision can be made in advance as to what will be done if each problem does occur. The contingency plan should also include ensuring availability of the resources needed to take the action. Figure 13.14 shows a process decision program chart, a tool that is especially useful when a process is new, meaning there are no previous data on types and frequencies of failure.

Tree Diagram (7)

The *tree diagram* breaks down an objective into the more detailed steps that must be carried out in order to achieve the objective. It begins with the broad objective and becomes more specific at each level. A tree diagram, shown in Figure 13.15, is similar to the work breakdown structure used in project management.

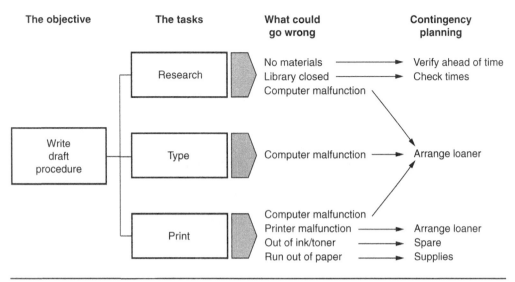

Figure 13.14   Process decision program chart example.

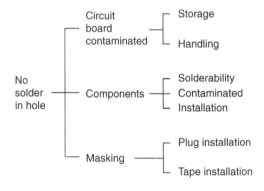

Figure 13.15   Tree diagram example.

Gantt Chart

When simple projects need to be scheduled and monitored, or when a simple means of communicating project status is desired, a Gantt chart is often used. A Gantt chart uses horizontal bars on a time scale to show project activities, when each starts and ends, how the actual time used compares to the planned time, and may also show who is assigned to each activity. Each horizontal bar is an activity; which activities depend on others is not shown.

The methodology for the Gantt chart is as follows:

1. Identify the activities that need to be done for the project, the sequence in which the activities need to be completed, and the key project milestones. Some activities may be run concurrently.

2. Determine the time needed to complete each activity and how the activities relate to the milestones. Determine the required completion date for the project.

3. Draw a horizontal time axis, usually across the top of the page. Mark off days or weeks as needed, running from the start to the required completion date. At the left side, list the identified activities in order. Fill in the time required for each activity; some may be represented by a single mark, others by horizontal bars showing start to finish. Fit the activities between the required completion date and the start time so that the schedule is met and activities do not overlap inappropriately. Some overlap is common.

4. To shorten activity timelines to meet the required project completion date, consider adding resources.

5. As activities progress, mark a second horizontal bar showing actual times under the planned times for each activity. Mark the current date on the chart. Late completions or behind-schedule activities are usually highlighted. (See Chapter 10, Section 2, Figure 10.6 for a sample Gantt chart.)

3. PROCESS IMPROVEMENT TOOLS

> Select, interpret, and apply tools such as root cause analysis, PDCA, six sigma DMAIC (define, measure, analyze, improve, control), and failure mode and effects analysis (FMEA). (Evaluate)
>
> **Body of Knowledge IV.A.3**

Root Cause Analysis

Although an effort to solve a problem may utilize many of the tools, involve the appropriate people, and result in changes to the process, if the order in which the problem-solving actions occur isn't logically organized and methodical, much of the effort is likely to be wasted. In order to ensure that efforts are properly guided, many organizations create or adopt one or more models—a series of steps to be followed—for all such projects.

Seven-Step Problem-Solving Model. Problem solving is about identifying root causes that have caused the problem to occur and taking actions to alleviate those causes. Following is a typical problem-solving process model and some possible activities and rationale for each step:

1. *Identify the problem and the process.* This step involves making sure that everyone is focused on the same issue. It may involve analysis of data to determine

which problem should be worked on, and writing a problem statement that clearly defines the exact problem to be addressed and where and when it occurred. A flowchart might be used to ensure that everyone understands the process in which the problem occurs.

2. *List possible root causes.* Before jumping to conclusions about what to do about the problem, it is useful to look at a wide range of possibilities. Brainstorming and cause-and-effect analysis are often used.

3. *Search out the most likely root cause.* This stage of the process requires looking for patterns in failure of the process. Check sheets might be used to record each failure and supporting information, or control charts may be used to monitor the process in order to detect trends or special causes.

4. *Identify potential solutions.* Once it is fairly certain that the particular root cause has been found, a list of possible actions to remedy it should be developed. This is a creative part of the problem-solving process and may rely on brainstorming as well as input from specialists who may have a more complete understanding of the technology involved.

5. *Select and implement a solution.* After identifying several possible solutions, each should be evaluated as to its potential for success, cost and timing to implement, and other important criteria. Simple processes such as ranking or multivoting, or more scientific analysis using a matrix, are likely to be used in the selection process.

6. *Follow up to evaluate the effect.* All too often, problem-solving efforts stop after remedial action has been taken. As with any good corrective action process, however, it is necessary that the process be monitored after the solution has been implemented. Control charts or Pareto diagrams are tools used to determine whether the problem has been solved. Possible findings might be that there was no effect (which may mean the solution wasn't properly implemented, the solution isn't appropriate for the root cause, or the real root cause wasn't found), a partial effect, or full resolution of the problem. If there was no effect, then the actions taken during the previous steps of the problem-solving model need to be reviewed in order to see where an error might have occurred.

7. *Standardize the process.* Even if the problem has been resolved, there is one final step that needs to occur. The solution needs to be built into the process (for example, poka-yoke, training for new employees, updating procedures) so that it will continue to work once focused attention on the problem is gone. A review to see what was learned from the project is also sometimes useful.

PDCA/PDSA Cycle

The problem-solving model presented above is actually nothing more than a more detailed version of a general process improvement model originally developed by Walter Shewhart, the *plan–do–check–act* (PDCA) *cycle*, which was adapted by W. Edwards Deming as the *plan–do–study–act* (PDSA) *cycle*, emphasizing the importance of learning from improvement. In both cases action is initiated by developing a plan for improvement, followed by putting the plan into action.

In the next stage the results of the action are examined critically. Did the action produce the desired results? Were any new problems created? Was the action worthwhile in terms of cost and other impacts? The knowledge gained in the third step is acted on. Possible actions include changing the plan, adopting the procedure, abandoning the idea, modifying the process, amplifying or reducing the scope, and then beginning the cycle all over again. Shown in Figure 13.16, the PDCA/PDSA cycle captures the core philosophy of continual improvement.

SIPOC Analysis

Problem-solving efforts are often focused on remedying a situation that has developed in which a process is not operating at its normal level. Much of continual improvement, however, involves improving a process that may be performing as expected, but where a higher level of performance is desired. A fundamental step to improving a process is to understand how it functions from a process management perspective. This can be seen through an analysis of the process to identify the supplier–input–process–output–customer (SIPOC) linkages (see Figure 13.17).

It begins with defining the process of interest and listing on the right side the outputs that the process creates that go to customers, who are also listed. Suppliers and what they provide to enable the process (the inputs) are similarly shown

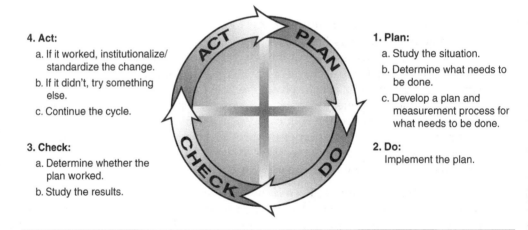

4. Act:
a. If it worked, institutionalize/ standardize the change.
b. If it didn't, try something else.
c. Continue the cycle.

3. Check:
a. Determine whether the plan worked.
b. Study the results.

1. Plan:
a. Study the situation.
b. Determine what needs to be done.
c. Develop a plan and measurement process for what needs to be done.

2. Do:
Implement the plan.

Figure 13.16   PDCA/PDSA cycle.

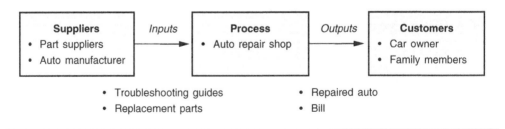

Suppliers	*Inputs*	**Process**	*Outputs*	**Customers**
• Part suppliers • Auto manufacturer		• Auto repair shop		• Car owner • Family members

• Troubleshooting guides   • Repaired auto
• Replacement parts   • Bill

Figure 13.17   SIPOC diagram example.

on the left side. Once this fundamental process diagram is developed, two additional items can be discussed—measures that can be used to evaluate performance of the inputs and outputs, and the information and methods necessary to control the process.

Six Sigma and the DMAIC Model

In process improvement language, *sigma* is a term indicating to what extent a process varies from perfection. The quantity of units processed divided into the number of defects actually occurring, multiplied by one million, results in defects per million. Adding a 1.5 sigma shift in the mean, results in the following number of defects per million:

1 sigma = 690,000 defects per million

2 sigma = 308,000 defects per million

3 sigma = 66,800 defects per million

4 sigma = 6210 defects per million

5 sigma = 230 defects per million

6 sigma = 3.4 defects per million

The definition of *sigma* is different in statistical analysis, where the term *sigma* refers to a calculated measure of variability called *standard deviation of the sample*.

While much of the literature refers to defects relative to manufacture, six sigma may be used to measure material, forms, a time frame, distance, computer program coding, and so on. For example, if the cost of poor quality, at a four sigma level, represented 15 percent to 20 percent of sales revenue, an organization should be concerned.

Six Sigma, as a philosophy, translates to the organizational belief that it is possible to produce totally defect-free products or services—albeit more a dream than a reality for many organizations. For organizations operating at about three sigma or below, getting to perfection leaves much work to be done.

Motorola initiated the Six Sigma methodology in the 1980s. General Electric's CEO launched their Six Sigma initiative in 1995. Six Sigma constitutes an evolving set of principles, fundamental practices, and tools—a breakthrough strategy.

The evolving Six Sigma principles are:

1. Committed and strong leadership is absolutely essential—often, this is a major cultural change.

2. Six Sigma initiatives and other existing initiatives, strategies, measures, and practices must be integrated—Six Sigma must be an integral part of how the organization conducts its business.

3. Quantitative analysis and statistical thinking are key concepts—it's data-based managing.

4. Constant effort must be applied to learning everything possible about customers and the marketplace—intelligence gathering and analysis is critical.

5. The Six Sigma approach must produce a significant payoff in a reasonable time period—real, validated dollar savings is required.

6. A hierarchy of highly trained individuals with verified successes to their credit, often referred to as Master Black Belts, oversee the Black Belts and Green Belts that are needed to extend the leadership to all organizational levels.

7. Performance tracking, measuring, and reporting systems are needed to monitor progress, allow for course corrections as needed, and link the Six Sigma approach to the organizational goals, objectives, and plans. Very often, existing performance tracking, measuring, and reporting systems fail to address the level where they are meaningful to the people involved.

8. The organization's reward and recognition systems must support continual reinforcement of the people, at every level, who make the Six Sigma approach viable and successful. Compensation systems, especially, need to be reengineered.

9. The successful organization should internally celebrate successes frequently—success breeds success.

10. To further enhance its image, and the self-esteem of its people, the successful organization should widely publicize its Six Sigma accomplishments, and to the extent feasible, share its principles and practices with other organizations—be a member of a world-class group of organizations that have committed their efforts to achieving perfection.

The following list contains fundamental Six Sigma practices—and some of the applicable tools—commonly known by the mnemonic DMAIC, which stands for:

Define the customer and organizational requirements.

- Data collection tools—check sheets, brainstorming, and flowcharts (see Section 1, this chapter).

- Data analysis tools—cause-and-effect diagrams, affinity diagrams, tree diagrams, root cause analysis (see Section 1, this chapter).

- Customer data collection and analysis—QFD, surveys (see Chapter 15, Section 9, and Chapter 17).

Measure what is critical to quality, map the process, establish measurement system, and determine what is unacceptable (defects).

- Process control tools—control charts (see Section 1 above).

- Process improvement tools (see Chapter 13, Section 3).

Analyze to develop a baseline (process capability) (see Chapter 15, Section 7).

- Identify root causes of defects (see Chapter 13, Section 3).

- Pinpoint opportunities and set objectives (see Chapter 13, Section 3).

Improve the process.

- Project planning and management (see Chapter 10).
- Training (see Chapter 19).

Control the system through an established process.

- Post-project audits (see Chapter 10, Section 3).
- Process control tools (see Chapter 14).

Failure Mode and Effects Analysis

Failure mode and effects analysis (FMEA) has been in use for many years and is used extensively in the automotive industry. FMEA is used for analyzing designs or processes for potential failure. Its aim is to identify and reduce risk of failure. There are two types in general use: the *design* FMEA (DFMEA) for analyzing potential design failures, and the *process* FMEA (PFMEA) for analyzing potential process failures.

For example, a small organization engaged in bidding on military contracts for high-tech devices successfully used a DFMEA to identify and assess risks for a product never made before. The DFMEA aided in evaluating design inputs, assured that potential failure modes were identified and addressed, provided for the identification of the failure modes' root cause(s), determined the actions necessary to eliminate or reduce the potential failure mode, and added a high degree of objectivity to the design review process. The DFMEA also directed attention to design features that required additional testing or development, documented risk reduction efforts, provided lessons-learned documentation to aid future FMEAs, and assured that the design was performed with a customer focus.

The basic FMEA methodology is:

1. Define the device design inputs or process functions and requirements.

2. Identify a failure mode (what could go wrong) and the potential effects of the failure.

3. Rank the severity of the effects using a 1–10 scale, where 1 is minor and 10 is major (and without warning).

4. Establish what the root cause(s) could be.

5. Rate the likelihood of occurrence for the failure using a 1–10 scale.

6. Document the present design or present process controls regarding prevention and detection.

7. Rate the likelihood of these controls detecting the failure using a 1–10 scale.

8. Compute the risk priority number (RPN = Severity × Occurrence × Detection). Using the RPN, rank-order items, the worst at the top.

9. Recommend preventive/corrective action (what action, who will do it, when). Note that preventive action is listed first when dealing with the

design stage, and corrective action first if analyzing potential process failures.

10. Return to number 2 if other potential failures exist.

11. Build and test a prototype.

12. Redo the FMEA after test results are obtained and any necessary or desired changes are made.

13. Retest and, if acceptable, place in production.

14. Document the FMEA process for the knowledge base.

The collaboration of employees who have been involved in design, development, production, and customer service activities is critical because their knowledge, ideas, and questions about a new product design will be based on their experience at different stages of product realization. Furthermore, if your employees are also some of your customers (end users), obtaining and documenting the employees' experience is most useful.

This experiential input, along with examinations of similar designs (and their FMEAs, nonconforming product and corrective action records, and customer feedback reports), is often the best source for analysis input. Figure 13.18 shows a sample PFMEA.

Process Improvement Model

As not all improvement projects involve root cause analysis, a more general model for continual process improvement is also useful. Following is one example:

1. *Select the process to improve.* This is done through analysis of feedback from customers (external or internal), as well as identifying those processes that are critical to improvement.

2. *Review current performance.* Current performance measures are reviewed to ensure that they are adequate and appropriate, and compared to expectations or needs.

3. *Identify improvement needs or opportunities.* Areas of the process where improvement would be most beneficial are selected, and the process analyzed to determine what could be changed to improve it.

4. *Implement process changes.* A plan is developed and communicated regarding changes in the process steps, and may be piloted on a small scale before full implementation.

5. *Evaluate progress.* Process performance is again reviewed to see whether the desired impact was achieved. If so, the change is standardized, and a new process or opportunity for improvement is selected. Many organizations also include celebrations and sharing of learning as part of wrapping up each improvement effort.

Although using the appropriate steps for problem solving and process improvement will enhance the probability of success, a set of guiding principles used to

Item/change level: EVN-7823/C
Process responsibility: Housing assembly
Team members: J. White, S. Burns, C. Smith

FMEA no. 10554
Page 1 of 1
Prepared by J. White
Date 4/3/13

Operation no. / Process function and/or requirements	Potential failure mode	Potential effect(s) of failure	Severity	Class	Potential cause(s) of failure	Occurrence	Current controls prevention	Current controls detection	Detection	RPN	Recommended actions	Responsible and target completion date	Action results — Actions taken	S	O	D	RPN
40 Press bearing into housing	Bearing not fully seated	Insufficient support for outer race, noisy gear	7		Improper setup of press	5	First-piece approval / Machine setup training	Depth check by operator	7	245	Add auto depth check to force electronics	J. White 5/10/13		7	5	2	70
	Assemble wrong bearing	Bearing moves up when nut on mating shaft is torqued, bearing failure	9	X	Operator loaded wrong bearing to chute	8	Push-in force measurement	Daily inventory balance of bill of materials	2	144	None						

Part IV.A.3

Figure 13.18 Process FMEA example.
Used with permission of APLOMET.

shape all such efforts is often useful. These principles can be used by the steering committee, a process improvement team, or a team facilitator as a tool for helping identify barriers to improvement progress. The steps are:

- *Leadership.* Senior executives should oversee the process of continual improvement.

- *Strategic.* Improvements should be targeted primarily at those processes that will provide a strategic gain or advantage; they should impact the bottom line.

- *Customer.* Process changes should be based on and/or take into account customer feedback, needs, and potential impact.

- *Involvement.* Because of their knowledge and responsibility, people who actually carry out the process to be improved should be the ones who are involved in making the decisions and implementing change.

- *Process.* Approach all projects from the view that what is to be improved is a process that transforms inputs (from suppliers) into outputs (for customers).

- *Data.* Decisions such as what processes to improve and what to change to make them better should be based on data, when possible.

- *Prevention.* Because the idea is to create processes that are able to meet or exceed requirements, actions taken should keep process problems from occurring or recurring.

4. INNOVATION AND CREATIVITY TOOLS

Use various techniques and exercises for creative decision-making and problem-solving, including brainstorming, mind mapping, lateral thinking, critical thinking, the 5 whys, and design for six sigma (DFSS). (Apply)

Body of Knowledge IV.A.4

Creative Thinking versus Analytical Thinking

The process of improvement often requires analysis of the process, breaking it down into discrete parts, and understanding how each part contributes to the overall process. Many of the tools presented in this chapter provide a means of performing this analysis, either by representing the process (for example, through a flowchart or cause-and-effect diagram) or showing how it is currently performing (for example, through a Pareto chart of the problem or a control chart of trends). Therefore, analytical thinking is an important part of process improvement.

Equally important is the part of improvement that requires identifying new ideas and deciding which of those ideas will be used to take action. For example, brainstorming possible causes of a problem before determining what is actually the cause, or identifying potential solutions to a problem before settling on one to try is not an analytical process; it's creativity and openness.

Analytical and creative thinking are sometimes seen as opposites because a person can not do both at the same time. Because an individual usually has a dominant way of thinking, it is sometimes a challenge to get both the analytical and creative processes to work within the same group. There are, however, tools designed specifically to help facilitate the creative and group decision-making processes.

As with analytical thinking, creativity also has stages that can be followed in order to improve outcomes. One model is:

- *Generate.* Create a list of as many ideas as possible, regardless of how wild some of them may be.

- *Percolate.* Allow time to think over these and other ideas. A few days away from the problem allows the subconscious mind to continue working, and often many new ideas will occur.

- *Illuminate.* Return to the list and discuss what has been discovered since the last meeting. Add, delete, combine, or otherwise modify items on the list.

- *Substantiate.* Test out and verify some of the ideas that appear more feasible.

Brainstorming

Brainstorming is a simple way for a group to generate multiple ideas, such as possible solutions to a known problem. A brainstorming session proceeds as follows:

- The brainstorming topic is agreed on and written in clear terms in view of the group.

- The leader/facilitator asks for ideas from the group.

- Each idea is written down without discussion, analysis, or criticism.

- The process is continued until the flow of ideas stops, or time runs out.

The list of ideas is then reviewed to ensure that everyone understands the ideas, and is then processed by combining similar ideas, eliminating some, or adding something forgotten to produce a smaller set from which a final selection will be made.

Brainstorming can also be more structured. A *round-robin* approach involves asking each person in the group to state one idea. If they have none, they simply pass. The next person is asked for one idea, then the next, and so on. When everyone has passed on a final round, the brainstorming session is complete. A similar process can be used where several sheets of paper (for example, flip charts) are posted around the room, with a particular topic or problem written at the top of each one. Team members simply move from sheet to sheet, writing down ideas that come to mind. Other groups have simply rotated sheets of paper around the table to accomplish the same result.

A final method of brainstorming is especially useful when the topic with which the team is dealing is particularly sensitive or when the team may not yet have a high level of trust. This method, called *Crawford slip*, asks each person to create his or her own list of ideas on a slip of paper, and the slips are subsequently given to a trusted individual who compiles them into a single list. The anonymous nature of this method allows people to feel freer to provide their ideas, and the team will often find that several people have the same idea, which begins to build common ground.

Mind Mapping

When trying to improve a process, an individual or group must think through many different issues, and keeping them all in mind simultaneously is difficult. A mind map creates a visual representation of many issues and can help a group get a more complete and common understanding of a situation.

A mind map is created by first listing the primary objective or topic in the center, then listing major related issues around it. Each of these issues will then bring other issues to mind, which are added to the map wherever logical. As a creative process, it can be useful to use symbols or photos rather than words in creating the map.

Figure 13.19 is a mind map created by a school board that was trying to decide how to improve the safety of a specific school crossing. The map helped the board look at the wide range of issues to consider, which meant members were more

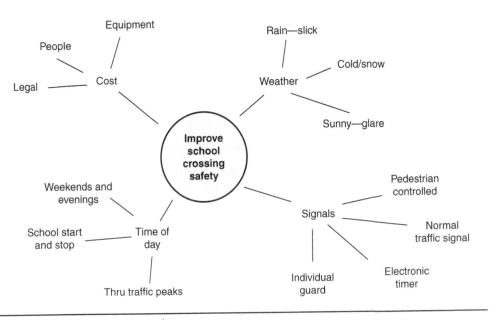

Figure 13.19   Mind map example.

likely to make a decision to which all agreed and would be willing to express to the public, and was the best for the situation.

Analogies

Innovation is about coming up with new ideas that don't fit the norm. One way to help accomplish this is to come at a problem or situation from a completely different viewpoint. Using words or ideas that are seemingly unrelated to the problem can help an individual or group to develop a perspective from which they are likely to see the situation differently.

Consider the example of an organization that wants to make and sell a new gardening tool used to remove weeds. In order to come up with a unique perspective to guide the design and marketing processes, the group randomly selects the phrase "soaring like an eagle" to help them. They then list ideas that come to mind when they think of this phrase, and ask, "How do these ideas apply to a gardening tool?" Figure 13.20 shows the results, which can be used to help ensure that the new tool will be designed and marketed based on what customers would perceive as being as pleasurable as soaring like an eagle.

The words or phrases used for this process can be completely randomly selected. For example, simply opening a newspaper or looking at an object nearby might work. If a particular selection doesn't help, then the group simply selects another word or phrase.

Nominal Group Technique

One popular way of processing brainstormed ideas is the *nominal group technique* (NGT), which consists of applying the following steps to a list of ideas from which a small number is to be selected:

1. Discuss the ideas and simplify/combine those where it makes sense in order to make the list complete and clear, but not repetitive.

2. Ask each participant to rank the items in numerical order (for example, 1 is best to 8 is worst in a list of eight items).

3. Record the ranks of all participants beside each item.

Eagle description	Would equate to
Sharp eyes	Seeing ways to reduce the time required to weed
Weightless	Wouldn't be tired after weeding
Automatic, air does the work	Very easy to use, doesn't require bending/stooping
Wide view	Can cover a lot of ground
Kills rodents	Gets weeds out by the roots so they don't come back

Figure 13.20   Use of analogies for a gardening tool.

Part IV.A.4

4. Total the rankings for each item. Those with the lowest totals are the preferred options.

Figure 13.21 shows a simple example of the nominal group technique applied by a group of course participants to decide where they wanted to go for lunch. Out of four choices, Marlow's received the lowest total (highest priority), becoming the first choice.

Multivoting

Another way to reduce a long list of items to fewer items is to have the group select those that they prefer. The number they select is often approximately one-half of the beginning number. After all participants have made their selections, the facilitator goes down the list and asks how many participants have voted for each option. The Pareto principle will most likely apply, with several of the options getting none or a very few votes, and they are dropped from the list. The process of voting is then repeated (for example, vote for approximately one-half of the number left on the list) until a workable number of items are left. Figure 13.22 shows repetitive multivoting for a larger number of possible selections.

Restaurant	Individuals and rankings					
	Tom	Joe	Mary	Sue	Terry	Total
Marlow's	1	2	3	1	2	9
Grunge Café	3	1	1	2	3	10
Stew & Brew	2	4	2	4	4	16
Fancaé	4	3	4	3	1	15

Figure 13.21 Nominal group technique ranking table.

Restaurant	First vote (Select 4)	Second vote (Select 3)	Third vote (Select 1)
Pizza R Us	2		
Marlow's	4	8	
Alice's Restaurant	1		
Grunge Café	5	5	④
Mom's Diner	0		
Stew & Brew	3	2	
Fancaé	5	5	1

Figure 13.22 Multivoting example.

Lateral and Parallel Thinking

The concept here is that the mind acts as a system of patterns. When these patterns are continually reinforced, mainstream patterns form. As these patterns grow deeper (like a rut), these perceptions are harder to ignore or discard. *Lateral thinking* is a process that includes recognizing the patterns and becoming unencumbered with old ideas while creating new ones. Or, as Dr. deBono, the originator of the term, described it, "pattern switching in an asymmetric patterning system."[1] Dr. deBono asserts that one can get only so much from the traditional tools and approaches. There comes a time when creativity is needed to go further.

With *parallel thinking*, Dr. deBono proposes a concept that is more constructive than traditional argument-type thinking. He uses the *six thinking hats* to enable participants to try one role at a time and to ultimately map a preferred style of thinking. The six roles he calls *hats* are:

Color	Characteristics
White	Just the facts, figures, or information. Neutral
Red	Emotions and feelings predominant. Intuitive
Black	Brings out the negative viewpoint
Yellow	Optimistic, proactive, and constructive—makes it happen
Green	Creative. Looks for alternatives. Moves forward
Blue	Controlled. Focused. Summarizes. Ensures rules are followed

Critical Thinking

Critical thinking relies on careful analysis, evaluation, and reasoning (both deductive and inductive), and clear thinking (analytical as well as systems thinking).
Critical cognitive skills for critical thinkers are:

- Interpret
- Analyze
- Evaluate

- Infer
- Explain
- Self-regulate

Critical thinkers are:

- Inquisitive
- Judicious
- Truth seeking
- Confident in reasoning

- Open-minded
- Analytical
- Systematic

Five Whys

Throughout most problem solving activities there is usually a significant amount of effort expended in trying to understand why things happen the way they do.

Root cause analysis requires understanding how a system or process works, and the many complex contributors, both technical and human

One method for getting to root causes is to repeatedly ask, "why?" For example, if a car doesn't start when the key is turned, ask, "why?" Is it because the engine doesn't turn over, or because when it does turn over, it doesn't begin running on its own? If it doesn't turn over, ask, "why?" Is it because the battery is too weak or because the starter is seized up? If it's because the battery is too weak, ask, "why?" Is it because the temperature outside is extremely cold, the battery cables are loose, or an interior light was left on the previous evening and drained the battery? Although this is a simple example, it demonstrates the process of asking *why* until the actual root cause is found. It is called the *five whys* tool since it will often require asking *why* five times or more before the actual root cause has been identified. The use of data or trials can help determine answers at each level. Figure 13.23 is adapted from a healthcare facility application.

Design for Manufacturing Ability and Design for Six Sigma

Design for manufacturing ability (DFMA), also called *design for manufacture/ manufacturing and assembly*, sometimes aims to create a design at its utmost level of

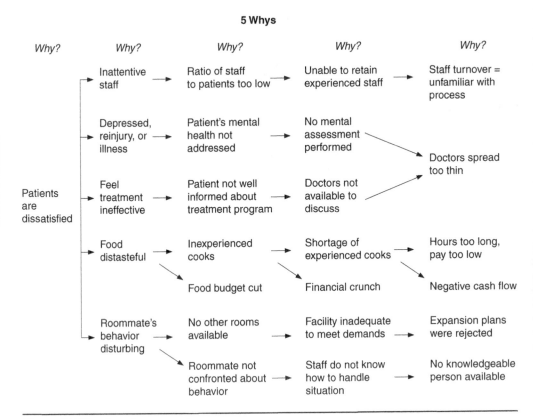

Figure 13.23   Five whys example.

simplicity. Intended to develop an awareness of the need for concurrent product/process development, DFMA focuses on preventing design changes during production. It also emphasizes decreasing the number of parts required and the specification of new but similar parts. DFMA standardizes and simplifies, for example, setting design tolerances based on previous process capability instead of engineering's frequent emphasis on close tolerance for every part.

Design for Six Sigma (DFSS) adds statistical techniques to the DFMA principles, including analysis of tolerances, mapping of processes, development of a product scorecard, design to unit production costs (DTUPC), and design of experiments (DOE). DFSS aims to design products and services so that they can be produced and delivered with Six Sigma quality. Focused on new product development, DFSS provides additional structure and better methods for managing the deliverables.

DFSS is a strategy that uses tools that are not always new. The strength of DFSS is the organization of the tools, and their integration with and alignment to the new product design process. A key to the effective use of DFSS is the selection process used to determine the probability of commercial and technical success of the ultimate product. Mader outlines a 12-step method.[2]

TRIZ

TRIZ is a Russian acronym—translated it is *the theory of the solution of inventive problems.*[3] Under development and testing for over 50 years, TRIZ evolved into a structure for the deployment of innovative and creative problem solving.

TRIZ comprises a set of analytical and knowledge-based tools that are typically hidden, subconsciously, in the minds of creative inventors. Ask an inventor what process he or she uses and the answer is vague or "Don't really know." Genrich Altshuller (the inventor of TRIZ) has succeeded in identifying the mystifying process of invention. Using TRIZ, persons of average intelligence can access a huge quantity of inventive knowledge. With that knowledge, they can, using analogic analysis, produce outside-the-box solutions.

TRIZ has been refined from the output of some of the world's best inventors. The result is a large collection of knowledge-based tools and 40 principles. The principles are:

- Segmentation
- Extraction
- Local quality
- Asymmetry
- Consolidation
- Universality
- Nesting
- Counterweight
- Prior counteraction

- Prior action
- Cushion in advance
- Equipotentiality
- Do it in reverse
- Feedback
- Mediator
- Self-service
- Copying
- Dispose
- Spheroidality
- Dynamicity
- Partial or excessive action
- Transition into a new dimension
- Mechanical vibration
- Periodic action
- Continuity of useful action
- Rushing through
- Convert harm into benefit
- Replacement of mechanical systems
- Pneumatic or hydraulic construction
- Flexible membranes or thin films
- Porous material
- Changing the color
- Homogeneity
- Rejecting or regenerating parts
- Transformation of properties
- Phase transition
- Thermal expansion
- Accelerated oxidation
- Inert environment
- Composite materials

SCAMPER

Using this method, seven questions are used by a team to stimulate creativity:

- What can be used as a *substitute*?

- What can be *combined* with _____?

- How can _____ be *adapted*?

- How can _____ be *modified*?

- How can _____ be *put* to other uses?

- How can _____ be *eliminated*?

- What if _____ were *reversed* (or *rearranged*)?

Storyboard

The *storyboard* technique is used in a team context to build the key ideas and the relationship of those ideas to the problem. It is a visual display of thoughts. As scriptwriters for a film would do, a storyboard introduces the physical setting and a two-dimensional view of the product, process, or action being discussed, usually in step-by-step or scene-by-scene views, as the team progresses through the problem-solving process. Ideas are generated through brainstorming and captured in words and pictures on sticky notes, and posted under major topical headings. Ideas are added and deleted, and the notes moved around to relate the ideas in various configurations in search of the best alignment. When the ideas (pictures) finally appear to fit together, the storyboard displays the problem solution in a desired sequence for further action. Nancy Tague, in *The Quality Toolbox*, provides more-detailed process steps for this tool (see references in Appendix A for Part IV.)

Other Creativity Tools

Other tools for stimulating creativity include:

- Brainwriting—same as Crawford slip method

- Imaginary brainstorming—breaks traditional thinking patterns

- Knowledge mapping—visual thinking, similar to mind mapping

- Morphological box—developing the anatomy of a solution

- Picture association—using pictures to generate new perspectives

- Purpose hierarchy—identifies all potential purposes of an improvement intervention

- TILMAG—stimulates ideal solutions using associations and analogies

- Who, what, where, when, why, and how questions
- Is–is not question

5. COST OF QUALITY (COQ)

> Define and distinguish between prevention, appraisal, internal, and external failure cost categories and evaluate the impact that changes in one category will have on the others. (Evaluate)
>
> **Body of Knowledge IV.A.5**

Cost of quality is a method used by organizations to show the financial impact of quality activities. Attaching a dollar amount to quality-related activities clarifies where there may be significant opportunities for quality improvement. Once recognized, process improvement efforts can be focused on those with the higher potential payoff.

In the 1950s Armand Feigenbaum saw value in a management reporting system focusing on quality costs, their causes, and their effects. During this time it was recognized that costs buried in standards and buried in overhead rates were not addressed. During the same period Joseph Juran wrote of the importance of measuring quality in terms best understood by upper management: dollars. These concepts were the basis of what has evolved into cost of quality programs. No one method exists for collecting and reporting an entity's quality cost drivers because each company's accounting system collects and reports costs differently. By applying the concept of cost of quality, however, any accounting or quality manager can design a meaningful measurement tool that can be used to report on and highlight quality issues, and that will help the company undertake meaningful quality improvement activities.

By the 1980s the costs of quality were categorized: failure costs (internal and external), prevention costs, and appraisal costs. In the efforts to learn more about and attempt to control the true costs of quality, certain facts became evident:

- Most quality costs are not identified in the financial records and statements of the organization.
- Most organizations were not aware of the cost to produce poor quality.
- Increasing sales does not decrease the cost of poor quality.
- The focus should really be on cost of poor quality and its impact on the organization (financial, competitiveness, customer retention and satisfaction, employee motivation).

Because it is measuring dollars, cost-of-quality reporting is one of the best tools available to raise an organization's awareness of quality issues. Some basic education on the concept and methods of cost of quality must be done, with an initial focus on top management. The educational process might also be deployed to other levels, however, as workers who understand how costs are collected and reported are more likely to understand how their work influences the company's performance.[4]

Categorizing Quality Costs

There are three major categories of quality costs: *appraisal*, *prevention*, and *failure*. In his book *Quality Is Free* Phil Crosby asserts that quality does not cost money; rather, it is the absence of quality (the nonconformances and failures) that increases total costs. Crosby popularized the terms *cost of poor quality*, or *cost of non-quality*, emphasizing that to avoid these bad costs, money would have to be spent up front on prevention and appraisal.

When designing a cost-of-quality program and setting up accounts to track the elements, attention must be given to the three categories of quality cost typically used: prevention, appraisal, and failure (internal and external). Because the total cost of quality can often be 10 percent to 15 percent of sales, these dollars must be traced to their sources to understand their cause-and-effect relationships:

- *Internal failure costs* occur before the product is delivered to the customer. Examples are costs of rework and repair, reinspecting and retesting of product, material downgrading, inventory shrinkage, unscheduled downtime, and internal miscommunications that result in delays.

- *External failure costs* occur after the delivery of product or while furnishing a service to the customer. Examples include the costs of processing customer complaints, field service, customer returns, warranty claims, product recalls, and product liability lawsuits.

- *Appraisal costs* are costs associated with measuring, evaluating, or auditing products or services to ensure conformance to quality standards and performance requirements. They include the costs of incoming and source inspection/test of purchased materials; validation, verification, and checking activities; in-process and final inspection/test; product, service, or process audits; and calibration of measuring and testing equipment, including associated supplies, materials, and external services.

- *Prevention costs* are costs incurred in minimizing failure and appraisal costs throughout the entire organization's processes. Examples include new-product design reviews, quality planning, supplier quality surveys, process capability evaluations, quality improvement team meetings, and quality education and training.

- *Total cost of quality* is the sum of all failure costs + appraisal costs + prevention costs.

Following is an example of quality cost categorization: The total cost of quality, before improvement, was 15 percent of sales, broken down into internal failures at 45 percent, external failures at 30 percent, appraisal costs at 20 percent, and prevention costs at 5 percent. Once known, these were unacceptable. The organization's objective is to reduce the total costs by decreasing failure costs, minimizing appraisal costs, and increasing prevention costs only to the extent necessary to achieve the failure and appraisal cost decreases.

The objective for the cost-of-quality improvement initiative is total costs of quality reduced to 3 percent of sales, broken down into internal failures at 20 percent, external failures at 5 percent, appraisal costs at 25 percent, and prevention costs at 50 percent.

Quality costs apply to all departments and should not be confined to just those associated with production. The costs generated within support functions often represent a significant portion of total quality costs and may be hidden within standard costs. In addition, labor expenses might be reported with an overhead allocation that includes benefits and other indirect expenses. These issues require care in properly determining true and comparable costs.

The cost-of-quality categories also apply equally well to nonmanufacturing situations. Consider the training conducted in a restaurant to help ensure that food and service quality are maintained (prevention), as well as the sampling done by the cook, and customer feedback cards used to measure quality (appraisal). Internal failure costs are incurred if food must be returned to the kitchen due to inadequate preparation or if the customer refuses to tip based on poor service. In this case, as is true with many service processes, direct external failure costs are absorbed by the customer, who ends up with indigestion or food poisoning, but the loss of future business (and perhaps litigation) is incurred by the restaurant.

Other service examples include:

- *Prevention costs.* Time and expenses related to an accounting firm learning about changes in tax laws

- *Appraisal costs.* Screening of baggage by an airline

- *Internal failure costs.* Incurred when a technician in a hospital must repeat a chest X-ray because the first one was not clear

- *External failure costs.* Correction of an error found by a customer in their banking statement

Initiating a Cost-of-Quality Program. For an organization that has not used cost-of-quality measurement before, education of senior management in the methods for and benefits of such a program must be done first. Once management has agreed to implement cost of quality, a pilot program can then be used to help demonstrate the process and benefits without fully involving the entire organization and extensive resources. For example, a product line where there are obvious opportunities for improvement, but where the improvements are not expected to be overly complex to attack, might be a good place to start.

Key management/supervisory personnel from the pilot area should be involved in estimating the cost of quality, working with accounting and quality personnel. A rough estimate may be all that is required to show the opportunities, which can then be addressed through either a process improvement team or other organized method for improvement.

Establishing and Tracking Measurements. Once the organization is convinced and committed to using cost of quality, a more detailed cost-of-quality baseline should be established that allows the organization to know where it is and will allow tracking of overall improvement. In developing the details of the quality cost system, there are two important criteria to follow: (1) recognize that quality cost is a tool to justify improvement actions and measure their effectiveness, and (2) realize that including insignificant activities is not essential.

Several methods are available for measuring cost of quality. One method often used in manufacturing organizations is to analyze the company's chart of financial accounts. If the accounting manager and quality manager were to review the accounts on the expense side, they would quickly find that some contain expenses obviously related to quality (for example, salary of the quality manager and metrology technicians, scrap of nonconforming material, travel expenses to visit customers when problems occur), while others have no or very few quality-related expenses (for example, tooling and accountant's salary).

The accounts that do contain quality expenses can then be pulled out separately and categorized as to whether they contain prevention, appraisal, internal failure, or external failure costs. The proportion of each account that should be allocated to each cost-of-quality category can then be estimated, and a rough estimate of cost of quality obtained by totaling the actual expenses for the last year as indicated by the allocations.

The total then needs to be normalized to adjust for changes in volume of business. Reporting cost of quality as a percentage of a commonly used internal volume measure is typical.

Another method is simply to do an activity assessment of the organization. By listing the activities that fit into the cost-of-quality categories and estimating the amount of time invested in each activity, a rough calculation of cost of quality can be obtained. This process could be used more accurately at the department level, although it must be understood that failures may be created in one part of the organization, but found in another.

Some organizations also elect to measure only failure costs. Depending on where they are in their quality journey, this may be sufficient to provide the incentive to move forward with continual improvement and to see the benefits. For organizations that are using activity-based costing/management (ABC/M), quality cost dollar amounts are more easily obtained. Activity-based costing allocates overhead expenses to the activities based on the proportion of use rather than proportion of costs.

Institutionalizing Cost of Quality. Once an organization is comfortable with the concept and usefulness of cost of quality, a formal reporting process needs to be developed. Quality costs should be a performance measure used for decision making for continuous improvement and strategic planning. Responsibilities for and the format for collecting and reporting the information must be defined, as well as the frequency and agenda where it will be used for decision making.

Education of the workforce—whether just before beginning a cost-of-quality-driven improvement project in a particular area, or having everyone learn about cost of quality—can help the organization to make a permanent connection between quality performance and cost performance.

Part IV.A.5

Activity-Based Costing. The objective of *activity-based costing* (ABC) is to improve the organization's effectiveness through the identification of quality costs associated with specific activities, analysis of those costs, and implementation of means to lower total costs. Under the ABC approach, costs of resources used are allocated in proportion to the use of the resource for given activities.

ABC contrasts with traditional cost accounting whereby costs were allocated based on some arbitrary percentage of direct labor. With direct labor becoming a smaller portion of the cost of producing a specific product or service, this approach is no longer viable for many organizations.

Employing ABC, some organizations have identified and discontinued producing unprofitable products. Before ABC, they hadn't realized the extent to which such products were eating their profits.

ENDNOTES

1. E. DeBono, *Six Thinking Hats* (Boston: Little, Brown and Company, 1985), 141.
2. D. P. Mader, "Selecting Design for Six Sigma Projects," *Quality Progress* (July 2004): 65–70.
3. S. F. Ungvari, "TRIZ," in *Manufacturing Handbook of Best Practices: An Innovation, Productivity, and Quality Focus*, ed. J. B. ReVelle (Boca Raton, FL: CRC Press, 2002), 399–425.
4. ASQ Quality Management Division, *Principles of Quality Costs: Financial Measures for Strategic Implementation of Quality Management*, 4th ed., ed. D. C. Wood (Milwaukee: ASQ Quality Press, 2013).

See Appendix A for additional references for this chapter.

Chapter 14

B. Process Management

A process is a series of interrelated actions taken to transform a concept, a request, or an order into a delivered product or service. A process is an activity or group of activities that takes an input, adds value to it, and provides an output to an internal or external customer. This is often visualized by the use of a SIPOC diagram. SIPOC stands for *supplier, input, process, output,* and *customer* (see Chapter 13).

The terms *process* and *system* are often used interchangeably, causing some confusion (for example, is a process part of a system, or is a system part of a process?). A *system* may be defined as a network of connecting processes that work together to accomplish the aim of the system. When viewing the total organization as a system:

- There will be subsystems (for example, a payroll system, accounting system, management information system).

- There will be processes (for example, manufacturing process, accounting process).

- There will be subprocesses (for example, design process, field service process).

- There may be supporting systems (for example, calibration system, activity-based costing system, inventory management system, fleet scheduling system, production scheduling system).

- Within these supporting systems there will be processes (for example, data entry process, data analysis process, report generation process, error alert process).

The distinction appears to be that a system has its own self-serving objective. A process aims at transforming inputs into outputs to achieve (ultimately) the strategic objectives of the organization. Thus, an accounting system might achieve its own purpose of processing numbers in accordance with the parameters set for the system, but could fail to meet the needs of management in managing the entire organization.

Process management is using a collection of practices, techniques, and tools to implement, sustain, and improve process effectiveness. Process management includes planning and setting goals, establishing controls, monitoring and measuring performance, documenting, improving cycle time, eliminating waste, removing constraints, eliminating special causes of variation, maintaining the gains, and continually improving. Figure 14.1 is a *process management maturity assessment* tool for assessing an organization's process management maturity level relative to six criteria.

The American Productivity and Quality Center (APQC), Houston, Texas, is a member-based nonprofit serving organizations in all sectors of business, education, and government. As an aid to their members and the public, APQC has created the *APQC Process Classification Framework* (PCF) as an open standard to facilitate improvement through process management and benchmarking regardless of industry, size, or geography. The PCF is available for download at http://www.apqc.org/process-classification-framework. Readers will find the PCF helpful in visualizing the processes and activities that may comprise an organization. The PCF is updated periodically.

1. PROCESS GOALS

> Describe how process goals are established, monitored, and measured and evaluate their impact on product or service quality. (Evaluate)
>
> **Body of Knowledge IV.B.1**

To begin, let's look at how process goals and process objectives are related:

- Process goals are aims, intents, targets, or ends.[1]

- Process goals are supported by measurable objectives.

- Process goals are linked to the strategic plan of the organization.

- Process objectives represent the intended actions that are needed to achieve the process goals.

- Process objectives are measurable (see the S.M.A.R.T. W.A.Y. structure for setting objectives in Chapter 5).

- Process objectives may be supported by product or service specifications, work orders, and so on.

- Process objectives may also be based on maintaining the gains in a stable process, or the objectives may support the resolution of a previous performance problem or deficiency.

Figure 14.2 is an example of the deployment of strategic goals and objectives to process goals and objectives.

Process goals, derived from strategic goals, interpret and expand the top-level goals and objectives for use at the operational level. Each organization, no matter

Level		Assessment criteria					
		Activities	Metrics	Ownership	Interconnections	Improvement	Changes
Improved	5	Process activities are continually improved.	Metrics are altered as necessary to identify new opportunities. Leading metrics are used where feasible.	Process owners place high value on ensuring that all employees have ownership of processes.	Internal customers and suppliers work together on improvement projects.	Processes have been continually improved in line with business objectives and desired outcomes.	The method for changing processes is continually upgraded to provide rapid and effective response to changing needs.
Managed	4	Process activities are reviewed for acceptable performance.	Metrics are reviewed regularly to provide feedback and improve.	Process owners regularly discuss process performance with team members.	Discussions between internal customers and suppliers have resulted in process changes.	Process improvement is regularly carried out, but may not impact business performance.	Process changes are evaluated, validated, and documented.
Standardized	3	Process is documented and personnel trained to follow it.	Standard metrics are in place for most processes, but do not impact performance.	An owner has been identified for most processes.	Regular feedback exists between internal customers and suppliers.	A standard process improvement methodology exists.	A process for reviewing and approving process changes exists.
Repeated	2	Personnel try to replicate actions each time.	Processes are measured when there are problems.	Individuals are responsible for certain portions of processes.	Discussions occur between members of related processes when there are problems.	Attempts are made to improve processes when there are significant problems.	Sketchy records are kept of process changes.
Unmanaged	1	Processes are carried out as each person sees fit.	Performance of processes is not measured.	Anyone or no one may claim to own a process.	Interconnection of processes has not been discussed.	Processes are seldom improved.	Anyone can make a process change.

Figure 14.1   Process management maturity assessment.
Source: Adapted from the Capability Maturity Model Integration (CMMI). Reprinted with permission of APLOMET.

Part IV.B.1

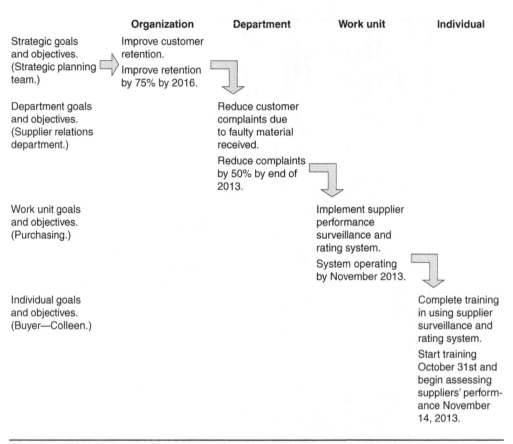

	Organization	**Department**	**Work unit**	**Individual**
Strategic goals and objectives. (Strategic planning team.)	Improve customer retention. Improve retention by 75% by 2016.			
Department goals and objectives. (Supplier relations department.)		Reduce customer complaints due to faulty material received. Reduce complaints by 50% by end of 2013.		
Work unit goals and objectives. (Purchasing.)			Implement supplier performance surveillance and rating system. System operating by November 2013.	
Individual goals and objectives. (Buyer—Colleen.)				Complete training in using supplier surveillance and rating system. Start training October 31st and begin assessing suppliers' performance November 14, 2013.

Figure 14.2   Deployment of strategic goals and objectives to process goals and objectives.

the industry, will have its own set of process goals; however, some generic topical areas may be addressed, such as:

- Meeting or exceeding customer requirements for the product/ service

- Ensuring that the process makes a contribution to the organization's profits (or cost containment)

- Ensuring that the product or service design and execution follows good practices to ensure users' safety, including unintended use

- Ensuring that the product or service produced does not present a hazard to users or the environment for the life of the product or service

- Ensuring the safety, security, and well-being of employees

- Meeting or exceeding industry-accepted practices for a good working environment

- Continually improving the process through elimination of non-value-added product/service features, process steps, and materials

- Continuing the quest to reduce cycle time

Goals may involve making changes or maintaining a specific target level. How the process goal is defined depends on the strategic direction of the organization and the level of the process being addressed (for example, from order entry through design, production, and shipping; or just the subprocess of accepting and entering a customer's order).

For example, a process goal for Family Cleaners, which handles an average of 158 customer orders per day, is "Family Cleaners will ensure that all customers receive high-quality cleaning services." This goal is then translated into a process objective: decrease disputes and rework due to receiving errors from 12 per week to one per week within six months. The objective is supported by a procedure, which outlines the receiving clerk's responsibilities:

1. Before accepting customer items, examine each with the customer and determine the type of cleaning service required, level of warranty (standard or premium), price, and delivery date.

2. Determine, based on training, experience, or approval of the manager, whether any questionable item can be properly cleaned by Family Cleaners. If not, provide the customer with an explanation and return the item to the customer. Should the customer opt to waive the information provided, prepare a waiver form and obtain the customer's signature.

3. Prepare and present to the customer a claim check (yellow copy of cleaning order) identifying the items received for cleaning, warranty level, the price for each, and the agreed date available for pickup.

4. Bundle the items received with the cleaning order (white original) in a receiving basket and place basket on conveyor.

How Are Process Objectives Monitored, Measured, and Reported?

Process objectives are monitored, measured, and reported for decisions as to actions needed. In the previous example, when the customer picks up the cleaning, any disputes and rework due to receiving errors are recorded by the pickup clerk on the original work order. The completed work orders are processed weekly. The total of disputes and rework are measured against the standard (no more than one occurrence). If more than one, the manager reviews the case(s) with the receiving clerk to determine the cause and any corrective or preventive action necessary.

Guidelines for monitoring, measuring, and reporting include:

- It must be known what value is desired, what to measure, how to measure it, unit of measure, device/method to be used, frequency of measure/analysis, and priority of the objective.

- How objectives are monitored is a function of who does it, how often it is to be done, and to whom information is distributed for analysis.

- Objectives are monitored through minute-to-minute, day-to-day, month-to-month, and year-to-year analysis by individuals, teams, departments, the management group, and executive staff.

In more complex situations, a more extensive system for monitoring, measuring, analyzing, and reporting results versus objectives would be necessary, but the principles remain the same.

2. PROCESS ANALYSIS

> Use various tools to analyze a process and evaluate its effectiveness on the basis of procedures, work instructions, and other documents. Evaluate the process to identify and relieve bottlenecks, increase capacity, improve throughput, reduce cycle time, and eliminate waste. (Evaluate)
>
> **Body of Knowledge IV.B.2**

There are many reasons for examining and documenting the steps in a process. Several examples are:

- When designing a new process or a change to a process

- To prepare for an audit/assessment of a process or system

- As part of the building project plans for a new facility

- To aid in planning a preventive action

- As a diagnostic technique for locating possible problem areas

- As a tool for identifying non-value-added steps and bottlenecks in an effort to increase capacity, improve throughput, reduce cycle time, and eliminate waste

- As a technique for comparing before and after changes to a process

- To aid in developing a quality system's documentation (often including both text and process maps)

- As a technique for helping quality improvement teams to understand a process

- As a training aid for understanding the process for which training is being given

- As a technique to help strategic planners understand the interrelationships of existing processes

While there are a number of tools and techniques used in understanding and analyzing processes, the basic flowchart/process map is the predominant tool used.

Flowcharting/Process Mapping

Flowcharting is briefly discussed in Chapter 13 as one of the seven classic quality tools. A *process map* is a more detailed process flowchart. Process mapping is a technique for designing, analyzing, and communicating work processes. A process map may often show the tasks, activities, functions, and/or decisions that must be performed in a particular process and, where applicable, by whom (participants).

Process mapping is used:

- To communicate and create understanding of a process flow

- To identify non-value-added steps for potential elimination or modification

- To serve as a procedure on how to perform a task or job

- To serve as part of the instructional material used in training a new performer

- To envision the flow of a new or redesigned process

- To support a planning exercise for a team to map what members perceive the process flow to be

- To serve as a simulation tool for a hypothetical walk-through of a process (for example, to look for possible redundancies, disconnects, dead ends, and other anomalies)

Depending on needs identified from the previous list, process mapping may be done by a:

- Current process owner

- Potential process owner

- Quality/process improvement team

- Reengineering team

- Strategic planning team

- Trainer

- Trainee

- Technical writer

Process mapping is usually iterative because to get it right may take a number of PDCA-type cycles. The methodology depends on the purpose and style of the map, where in the sequence of mapping steps the map is being created, and the competency of the mapper. A generic sequence of mapping steps is:

1. Select the process to be mapped.

2. Define the purpose for the map.

3. Select the style of map to be produced.

4. Define the process to be mapped:

    • Inputs and outputs

    • Users/customers to whom outputs are directed

    • Requirements of users/customers

    • Titles of persons involved in the process

    • Title of process owner

    • Titles of other stakeholders (not including suppliers)

    • First and last step in the process

    • Suppliers and their inputs

    • Constraints (for example, standards and regulations)

5. Map out the principal flow (main flow without exceptions).

6. Add the decision points and alternative paths.

7. Add the check/inspection points and alternative paths.

8. Do a desktop walk-through with persons who know the process.

9. Modify the map as needed (and as it will be).

10. Review changes and obtain approval.

11. Use map for purpose intended.[2]

Whether the process mapper uses pencil and paper or a computer software product to produce the process map depends on the stage in the mapping process and the desired end result. Unless the mapper is also the process owner, one or more persons usually have to be queried as to what they do and how they do it. The approach can be as simple as taking pencil and paper notes in a one-to-one off-site interview to collecting data on-site from the work unit performers, using note taking, or videotaping the performers. The mapper, unless very experienced, will probably sketch, freeform, the process steps using paper and pencil. When reasonably satisfied that the process sketched is correct, it may be more formally drawn in pen and ink, or with a software product.

Process Mapping Methods. Traditional process mapping symbols are shown in Figure 14.3. A sample process map (incomplete) is shown in Figure 14.4.

Organizational processes usually involve two or more participants (individuals and/or groups, such as a department or organizational unit). There is then an advantage if the process map indicates who is responsible for actions depicted

Symbol	Descriptor	Comments
(oval)	Terminal symbol	Shows beginning and ending points. Usually labeled *start* or *begin* or *stop* or *end*.
(rectangle)	Activity symbol	Shows any single step in the process. A brief description of the activity appears inside the rectangle.
(diamond)	Decision symbol	Shows the decision point at which the process branches into two or more paths. A question appears within the diamond, and the path taken depends on the answer to the question.
(arrows)	Flow line	Connects steps and shows the direction of process flow from one activity to the next in a sequence. The arrowhead on a flow line shows the direction of the process flow.
(D shape)	Delay or wait symbol	Shows a bottleneck or holding point, which is an opportunity for time reduction. A brief description of the delay appears inside the symbol.
(circle)	Link symbol	Used to show the beginning and the end of a page or column break in the drawing of the process flow. Usually the *from* and *to* circles are labeled with a letter.
(parallelogram)	Input or output symbol	Identifies either current or expected inputs and outputs within the process flow. A brief description of the item appears inside the symbol.
(document shape)	Document symbol	Identifies either the input or the output as a document. The title of the document may appear inside the symbol.

Figure 14.3   Traditional process mapping symbols.

in the process. Figure 14.5 shows the process flow in a grid format (also called a *swim-lane chart*) that lays out the map in columns representing each department. This type of chart is also called a *cross-functional flowchart* or *deployment chart*.

What to Look for in the Process Map. The mere action of process mapping will often surface situations that may be the cause of current problems, or identify potential areas for improvement. Some of these situations are:

- Branching steps exceed the number of steps in the main flow.
- Checking/inspection steps are missing or excessive.
- Steps take the process flow back and forth between different work units.
- Important steps are missing.
- There are steps that add no value to the end product or service.
- There are redundant steps.

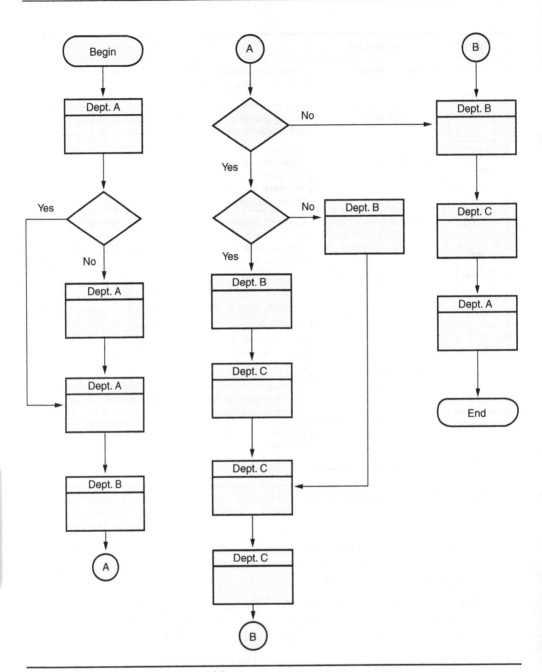

Figure 14.4   Process map–non-grid format.

- Steps may need to be decomposed into several steps.
- There are dead ends.
- There are disconnects (for example, a *go to* but no *from* circle).
- Flow is difficult to understand, confuses performers.

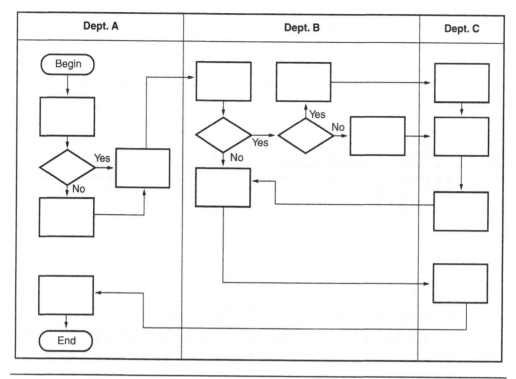

Figure 14.5   Process map–grid format.

- Too much detail is shown:
  - Map appears to be overdone.
  - Map is a jumbled mass of data.
- Too little detail is shown:
  - Too skimpy for purpose intended.
  - Complexities masked by macro-level steps.
  - Detail expected is omitted, for example, duration of steps, responsibility, number of operatives.
- Misses the point of the purpose for mapping the process.
- Fails to present the process map in the most advantageous style or format wanted.

Common problems with developing effective process maps include the following:

- Difficulty in identifying processes and subprocesses from beginning to end. Often lacking is a common understanding of what a process consists of and what the parameters of the processes are in the context of the work environment.

- Difficulty in identifying alternative paths, inspection points, and ways to improve a process.

- Difficulty in applying principles and techniques for effective communication regarding quantity of information, formats, styles, layout, wording, and titles to the process map.

Procedures and Work Instructions

Many organizations have been in existence for decades, managing their processes without much, if any, formal documentation and yet continue to ship products that meet customers' specifications. Today, however, major changes are impacting all organizations, for example, global marketing, mergers and sellouts, cultural norms, population movement, and time pressures. These types of changes are causing organizations to document their systems, processes, and practices. In many cases they may be forced to do so to remain competitive. In formally documenting processes, organizations are realizing the following internal advantages. The documentation:

- Identifies the preferred/required approach to be followed

- Provides a basis for measuring/assessing performance

- Emphasizes a consistent method of doing work

- Supports training

- Captures the one best way as a synthesis of methods used by experienced people

- Serves as a job aid guiding/refreshing the trained performer

- Provides a baseline for assessment and improvement

One model for structuring the quality management system documentation is shown in Figure 14.6. As implied by the pyramidal structure, each level in the

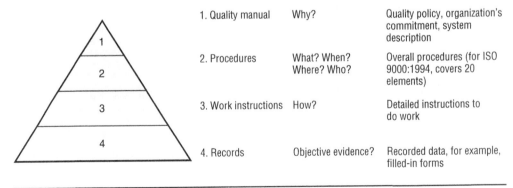

1. Quality manual	Why?	Quality policy, organization's commitment, system description
2. Procedures	What? When? Where? Who?	Overall procedures (for ISO 9000:1994, covers 20 elements)
3. Work instructions	How?	Detailed instructions to do work
4. Records	Objective evidence?	Recorded data, for example, filled-in forms

Figure 14.6   A quality management system documentation hierarchy.

structure interlocks with and supports a higher level. For example, the description of the system in level 1 references the supporting procedures in level 2, level 2 procedures reference work instructions, and records are referenced in both level 2 and 3 documents.

In documenting procedures and work instructions, ensure that the following questions are addressed:

- If the documentation is to conform to a standard, does it?

- Is the documentation appropriately deployed and kept up to date?

- Is the documented system being followed by the people who produce the work?

- Are the required records kept?

- Is the documentation system periodically assessed for effectiveness?

Excepting standards that an organization may self-impose, there are no prescribed standards for composing or formatting a documented system. Variations include:

- Outline with bulleted text

- Process map with annotations

- Process map with adjacent outline text

- Photographs depicting different stages in the process with outline text

- Checklists

Organizations choose their own approach to documentation unless they are required to conform to a specific standard. Some examples of the media on which procedures and work instructions may be presented are:

- Hard copy (paper or like material)

- Computer screen at workstation

- Video (stream or clips)

- Instructions embedded in a work order/traveler

- Process map displayed in work area

- Handheld electronic display

- Intranet (internal organization's own internet)

- Job aids:

  – Samples or photos of product in various stages of manufacture

  – Painted color-coded work areas and tool boards (for placement of tools)

  – Signage to designate specific areas for materials and scrap

- Forms annotated with brief instructions for completion

- Laminated cards/tags displayed at workstation

Control Plans

Control plans typically address product/service plans: identifying, classifying, and weighting the characteristics for quality, as well as tolerances, applicable measurements, and methods of control.

A control plan does not replace the details required in specific operator instructions. Typically, each item in the control plan is supported by procedures and/or work instructions. For example, the overall standard for packaging and delivery may be supported by a shipping manual giving specifications for packaging different types, sizes, and weights of product, and the type of carrier to use. In the case of a project-oriented organization where every project is unique, the control plan is specific to each project. Note: Specific customer requirements could, in case of conflict, override the organization's control plan when mutual agreement has been obtained up front. Figure 14.7 shows a partial sample of one type of detailed control plan.

Industry-Specific Documentation

The automotive industry standard (ISO/TS 16949) requires the following from its suppliers:

- Advanced product quality planning (APQP) and control plan are used to guide the process of developing and launching a new product and/ or process.

- Production part approval process (PPAP) is used to document the findings of the new process.

- Failure mode and effects analysis (FMEA) is used to evaluate risks related to product and process design.

- Measurement systems analysis (MSA) and statistical process control (SPC) are used to evaluate the ability of measurement devices and processing equipment to meet capability requirements.

Other industries may require specific instructional documentation.

Eliminating Waste

Waste is anything that does not add value. Waste is frequently a result of how the system is designed. The Japanese word for waste is *muda*.

The seven types of waste, with examples, are:

1. Overproduction

- Enlarging the number of requirements beyond customers' needs

- Including too much detail or too many options in designs

Control Plan

Control Plan Number	10233	Key Contact/Phone	John White/423-555-1212	Date (orig)	01/09/13	Date (rev)	07/13/14
Part Number/Latest Change Level	EVN-7823/C	Core Team	JWhite, SBurris, CSmith	Customer Engineering Approval/Date (if req'd)			
Part Name/Description	Outer Housing Assembly	Supplier/Plant Approval/Date	03/05/13	Customer Quality Approval/Date (if req'd)			
Supplier/Plant	XYZ Company, Anywhere USA	Other Approval/Date (if req'd)		Other Approval/Date (if req'd)			

Part/ process number	Process name/ operation description	Machine, device, jig, tools for mfg.	Characteristics			Special char. class	Specification/ tolerance	Methods				Reaction plan
			No	Product	Process			Evaluation measurement technique	Size	Freq.	Control method	
10	Receive and verify	N/A	A	Chemistry			Spec 0143	Compare COA	1	Lot	Accept/reject, lot acceptance report	Return to vendor
20	Machine complete	Mazak	B	Bearing diameter		X	23.00 ± .01mm	CMM	3	2 hrs	x-bar/R chart	Change tool, scrap bin
		BV-120.1 bore tool										
30	Impregnate	Vacufill tank			Temperature		90–100 C	Temp chart	1	Batch	Batch signoff sheet	Reprocess once, then return to vendor
					Vacuum		12 mm	Vacuum chart	1	Batch	Batch signoff sheet	Reprocess once, then return to vendor
					Viscosity		100–120 mpoise	Viscon meter	1	Batch	Batch signoff sheet	Reprocess once, then return to vendor
			C	Leakage		X	2cc/min max @ 60 PSI	Aircheck M/C	5	Batch	Batch signoff sheet	Reprocess once, then return to vendor
40	Assemble bearing	Bearing press			Force required	X	150–220 N	Load cell	100%	100%	Machine accept/reject, production log	Scrap part
			D	Flush to surface			.2 mm max above	Caliper	2	Hour	Production log	Scrap part

Figure 14.7 Portion of a sample control plan.

Source: Used with permission of APLOMET.

Part IV.B.2

- Specifying materials that require sole-source procurement or that call for seeking economy-of-scale-oriented procurement

- Requiring batch processing, lengthy and costly setups, or low-yield processes

2. Delays, waiting

- Holdups due to people, information, tools, and equipment not being ready

- Delays waiting for test results to know if a part is made correctly

- Unrealistic schedules resulting in backups in manufacturing flow

- Part improperly designed for manufacture, design changes

3. Transportation

- Non-value-added transport of work in process

- Inefficient layout of plant causing multiple transports

- Specifying materials from suppliers geographically located a great distance from manufacturing facility, resulting in higher shipping costs

4. Processing

- Non-value-added effort expended.

- Designers failed to consider production process capabilities (constraints, plant capacities, tolerances that can be attained, process yield rate, setup time and complexity, worker skills and knowledge, storage constraints, material handling constraints).

- Designs too complex.

- Pulse (takt time) of production flow too high or too low in relation to customer demand.

5. Excess inventory

- Stockpiling more materials than are needed to fulfill customer orders

- Material handling to store, retrieve, store as part proceeds in the process

- Unreliable production equipment necessitating safety stock

6. Wasted motion

- Non-value-added movements, such as reaching, walking, bending, searching, sorting

- Product designs that are not manufacturing-friendly

- Requirements for lifting cumbersome and/or heavy parts

- Manufacturing steps that require frequent repositioning

7. Defective parts

- Corrective actions, looking for root cause

- Scrap

- Downgrading defectives (reducing price, seeking a buyer) in order to recover some of the cost of manufacture

- Faulty design causing defects

- Excessive tolerances creating more defectives

Inventories (buffer stock and batch and queue processing) can be a huge waste. Consider this example: The order is for 200 pieces. The process consists of three operations of 10 seconds each. If the 200 pieces are processed as a batch, the total cycle time is 6000 seconds (200 × 30 seconds). However, in a single-piece flow mode, there is no accumulation of material between steps. Cycle time is 30 seconds for a single piece and approximately 2000 seconds total for the lot of 200 (each completed piece is coming off the line at 10 second intervals × 200 pieces) The reduction in total cycle time (6000 seconds – 2000 seconds = 4000 seconds / 6000 = 67 percent reduction. Work in process (WIP) has also been reduced to 3 pieces, from all 200 waiting at step 2 and then again at step 3. Aside from reducing the cycle time by single-piece flow, if any problem occurs during processing it is more likely to be detected early in the process, reducing scrap and the potential for shipping defective product.

Analyses of processes for waste usually involve diagrams that show the flow of materials and people, and documenting how much time is spent on value-added versus non-value-added activity. Cycle time is affected by both visible and invisible waste.

Examples of *visible waste* are:

- *Out-of-spec incoming material.* For example, an invoice from a supplier has incorrect pricing, or aluminum sheets are the wrong size.

- *Scrap.* For example, holes are drilled in the wrong place, or shoe soles are improperly attached.

- *Downtime.* For example, school bus is not operable, or process 4 can not begin because of a backlog at process 3.

- *Product rework.* For example, failed electrical continuity test, or customer number is not coded on invoice.

Examples of *invisible waste* are:

- *Inefficient setups.* For example, a jig requires frequent retightening, or incoming orders are not sorted correctly for data entry.

Part IV.B.2

- *Queue times of work in process.* For example, an assembly line is not balanced to eliminate bottlenecks (constraints), or an inefficient loading zone protocol slows school bus unloading, causing late classes.

- *Unnecessary motion.* For example, materials for assembly are located out of easy reach, or workers need to bring each completed order to dispatch desk.

- *Wait time of people and machines.* For example, a utility crew (three workers and truck) waiting until a parked auto can be removed from the work area, or planes are late in arriving due to inadequate scheduling of available terminal gates.

- *Inventory.* For example, obsolete material returned from a distributor's annual cleanout is placed in inventory anticipating the possibility of a future sale, or, to take advantage of quantity discounts, a year's supply of paper bags is ordered and stored.

- *Movement of material, work in process, and finished goods.* For example, in a function-oriented plant layout, WIP has to be moved from 15 to 950 feet to the next operation, or stacks of files are constantly being moved about to gain access to filing cabinets and machines.

- *Overproduction.* For example, because customers usually order the same item again, an overrun is produced to place in inventory just in case, or extras are made at earlier operations in case they are needed in subsequent operations.

- *Engineering changes.* For example, problems in production necessitate engineering changes, or failure to clearly review customer requirements causes unnecessary changes.

- *Unneeded reports.* For example, a report initiated five years ago is still produced each week even though the need was eliminated four years ago, or a hard copy report duplicates the same information available on a computer screen.

- *Meetings that add no value.* For example, a morning production meeting is held each day whether or not there is a need (coffee and Danish are served), or 15 people attend a staff meeting each week where one of the two hours is used to solve a problem usually involving less than one-fifth of the attendees.

- *Management processes that take too long or have no value.* For example, all requisitions (even for paper clips) must be signed by a manager, or a memo to file must be prepared for every decision made between one department and another.

3. LEAN TOOLS

> Identify and use lean tools such as cycle-time
> reduction, 5S, just-in-time (JIT), kanban, value
> stream mapping, single-minute exchange of
> die (SMED), poka-yoke, kaizen, and overall
> equipment effectiveness (OEE). (Apply)
>
> **Body of Knowledge IV.B.3**

Lean tools are used to identify non-value-added steps and bottlenecks in an effort to increase capacity, improve throughput, reduce cycle time, and eliminate waste.

Cycle-Time Reduction

Cycle time is the total amount of time required to complete a process, from the first step to the last. Today's methods for cycle-time reduction came about through Henry Ford's early focus on minimizing waste, traditional industrial engineering techniques (for example, time and motion studies), and the Japanese adaptation of these methods (often called the Toyota Production System [TPS]) to smaller production run applications.

Although cycle-time reduction is best known for its application to production operations, it is equally useful in nonmanufacturing environments, where person-to-person handoffs, queues of jobs, and facility layout affect the productivity of knowledge workers.

To be able to select where best to implement cycle-time reduction requires a high-level system analysis of the organization to determine where current performance deficits or bottlenecks are located. The organization's overall system has a *critical path* (the series of steps that must occur in sequence and take the longest time to complete). Clearly, improving a process that is not on the critical path will have no real impact on cycle time.

Typical actions to shorten the cycle time of processes include:

1. Removing non-value-adding steps.

2. Speeding up value-adding steps.

3. Integrating several steps of the process into a single step; this often requires expanding the skill level of employees responsible for the new process and/or providing technical support such as a computer database.

4. Breaking the process into several smaller processes that focus on a narrower or special product. This *work cell* or *small business unit*

concept allows employees to develop customer product–focused skills and usually requires colocating equipment and personnel responsible for the cell.

5. Shifting responsibility to suppliers or customers, or taking back some of the responsibility currently being performed by suppliers or customers. The practice of modular assembly is a typical example of this process.

6. Standardizing the product/service until as late as possible in the process, then creating variations when orders are received; this allows the product to be partially processed, requiring only completion before shipment (for example, the practice of producing only white sweaters, then dyeing them just prior to shipment).

Other ways of improving cycle times include improving equipment reliability (thereby reducing non-value-added maintenance downtime), reducing defects (that use up valuable resource time), and reducing unnecessary inventory. Another fundamental process for improving cycle time is that of simply better organizing the workplace (see the *five S* tools discussed later).

Reducing cycle time can reduce work in process and finished goods inventories, allow smaller production lot sizes, decrease lead times for production, and increase throughput (decrease overall time from start to finish). Also, when process steps are eliminated or streamlined, overall quality tends to improve. Because many opportunities might be identified when beginning the effort to reduce cycle time, a Pareto analysis (see Chapter 13, Section 1) can be performed to decide which factors demand immediate attention. Some problems might be fixed in minutes, whereas others might require the establishment of a process improvement team and take months to complete.

A *work cell* is a self-contained unit dedicated to performing all the operations to complete a product or a major portion of a production run. Equipment is configured to accomplish:

- Sequential processing

- Counterclockwise flow to enable operators to optimize use of their right hands as operators move through the cell (moving the part to each subsequent operation)

- Shorter movements by close proximity of machines

- Positioning of the last operation close to the first operation for the next part

- Adaptability of the cell to accommodate customers' varying demands

The most prevalent layout is a U shape (see Figure 14.8), although L, S, and V shapes have been used. Product demand, product mix, and constraints (such as that monument management just won't dispose of) are all considerations in designing a work cell.

Although lean production is based on basic industrial engineering concepts, it has been primarily visible to U.S. companies as the Toyota Production System.

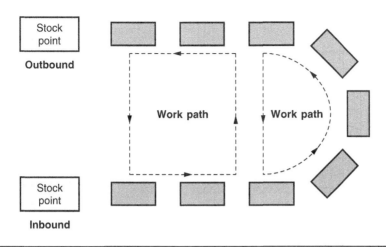

Figure 14.8   Typical U-shaped cell layout.

The basic premise is that only what is needed should be produced, and it should only be produced when it is actually needed. Due to the amount of time, energy, and other resources wasted by the way processes and organizations are designed, however, organizations tend to produce what they think they might need (for example, based on forecasts) rather than what they actually need (for example, based on customer orders).

Five S

The Japanese use the term *five S* for five practices for maintaining a clean and efficient workplace:

1. *Seiri* (sort). Separate needed tools, parts, and instructions from unneeded materials, and remove the latter.

2. *Seiton* (set in order). Neatly arrange and identify parts and tools for ease of use.

3. *Seiso* (shine). Conduct a cleanup campaign.

4. *Seiketsu* (standardize). Conduct *seiri*, *seiton*, and *seiso* at frequent intervals to maintain a workplace in perfect condition

5. *Shitsuke* (sustain). Form the habit of always following the first four S's.

Far more than just good things to do, five S can:

• Build awareness of the concept and principles of improvement

• Set the stage to begin serious waste reduction initiatives

Part IV.B.3

- Break down barriers to improvement, at low cost

- Empower the workers to control their work environment

In step 2 (seiton), visual management is used to arrange the workplace—all tools, parts, and material, and the production process itself—so that the status of the process can be understood at a glance by everyone. Further, the intent is to furnish visual clues to aid the performer in correctly processing a step or series of steps, reduce cycle time, cut costs, smooth work flow, and improve quality. By seeing the status of the process, both the performer and management have an up-to-the-second picture of what has happened, what's presently happening, and what's to be done. Advantages of visual management are:

- It catches errors and defects before they can occur.

- Quick detection enables rapid correction.

- It identifies and removes safety hazards.

- It improves communications.

- It improves workplace efficiency.

- It cuts costs.

Examples of visible management include:

- Color-coded sectors on meter faces to indicate reading acceptance range, and low and high unacceptable readings

- Electronic counters mounted over a work area to indicate the rate of accepted finished product

- Work orders printed on colored paper where the color denotes the grade and type of metal to be used

- Lights atop enclosed equipment indicating the status of product being processed

- Slots at the dispatch station for pending work orders, indicating work to be scheduled (and backlog) and when the work unit(s) will become idle

- Painted floor and/or wall space with shadow images of the tool, die, or pallet that usually occupies the space when not in use

Just-in-Time

Just-in-time (JIT) is a material requirement planning system that provides for the delivery of material or product at the exact time and place where the material or product will be used. Highly coordinated delivery and production systems are required to match delivery to use times. The aim is to eliminate or reduce on-hand inventory (excessive buffer stock) and deliver material or product that requires no or little incoming inspection.

Kanban

This method is used in a process to signal an upstream supplier (internal or external) that more material or product is needed downstream. Originally, it was just a manual card system but has evolved to more-sophisticated signaling methods in some organizations. It is referred to as a *pull* system because it serves to pull material or product from a supplier (or previous work unit) rather than relying on a scheduling system to push the material or product forward at predetermined intervals. It is said that the kanban method was inspired by Toyota executive Taiichi Ohno's visit to a U.S. supermarket.

Value Stream Mapping

Value stream mapping (VSM) is charting the sequence of movements of information, materials, and production activities in the value stream (all activities involving the designing, ordering, producing, and delivering of products and services to the organization's customers). An advantage to this is that a "before action is taken" value stream map depicts the current state of the organization and enables identification of how value is created and where waste occurs. Plus, employees see the whole value stream rather than just the one part in which they are involved. This improves understanding and communication, and facilitates waste elimination.

A VSM is used to identify areas for improvement. At the macro level, a VSM identifies waste along the value stream and helps strengthen supplier and customer partnerships and alliances.

At the micro level, a VSM identifies waste—non-value-added activities—and identifies opportunities that can be addressed with a *kaizen blitz*.

Figures 14.9 and 14.10 are sample value stream maps (macro level and micro level).

Single-Minute Exchange of Die

The long time required to change a die in a stamping operation meant that a longer production run would be required to absorb the downtime caused by the changeover. To address this, the Japanese created a method for reducing setup times called *single-minute exchange of die* (SMED), also referred to as *rapid exchange of tooling and dies* (RETAD). Times required for a die change were dramatically reduced, often reducing changeover time from several hours to minutes.

To improve setup/changeover times, initiate a plan–do–check–act approach:

1. Map the processes to be addressed. (Video recording the setup/changeover process is a useful means for identifying areas for improvement.)

2. Collect setup data times for each process.

3. Establish setup time reduction objectives.

4. Identify which process is the primary overall constraint (bottleneck). Prioritize remaining processes by magnitude of setup times, and target next process by longest time.

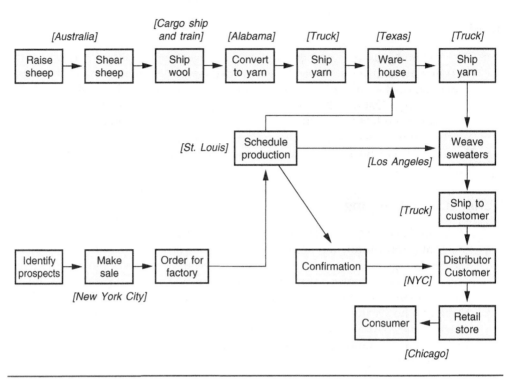

Figure 14.9   Value stream map—macro level (partial).

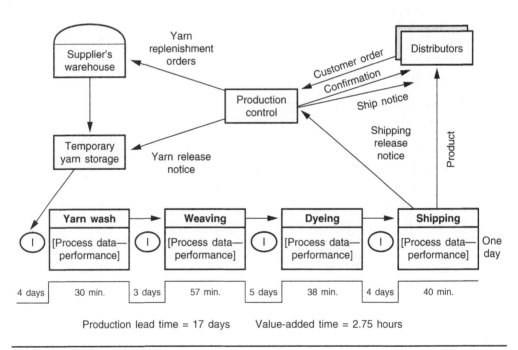

Figure 14.10   Value stream map—plant level (partial).

5. Remove non-value-adding activities from the targeted process (for example, looking for tools required for the changeover). Trischler (see additional resources) lists dozens of non-value-added activities, most of which are applicable in a variety of industries and processes. Note that there are some steps that fit the non-value-added category that can not actually be removed, but can be speeded up.

6. Identify setup steps that are internal (steps the machine operator must perform when the machine is idle) versus steps that are external (steps that can be performed while the machine is still running the previous part. For example, removing the fixture or materials for the next part from storage and locating them near the machine).

7. Focus on moving internal steps to external steps where possible.

8. Identify setup activities that can be done simultaneously while the machine is down (the concept of an auto racing pit crew).

9. Speed up required activities.

10. Standardize changeover parts (for example, all dies have a standard height, all fasteners require the same size wrench to tighten).

11. Store setup parts (dies and jigs) on portable carts in a position and at the height where they can be readily wheeled into place at the machine and the switchover accomplished with minimum movement and effort.

12. Store all setup tools to be used in a designated place within easy reach (for example, visual shadow areas on a portable tool cart).

13. Error-proof the setup process.

14. Evaluate the setup/changeover process and make any modifications needed.

15. Return to step 4 and repeat the sequence until all setup times have been improved

16. Fully implement setup/changeover procedures.

17. Evaluate effectiveness of setup/changeover time reduction efforts against objectives set in step 3.

18. Collect setup time data periodically and initiate improvement effort again; return to step 1.

Poka-Yoke or Mistake-Proofing

Mistake-proofing originated in Japan as an approach applied to factory processes. It was perfected by Shigeo Shingo as *poka-yoke*. It is also applicable to virtually any process in any context. For example, the use of a spell checker in composing text on a computer is an attempt to prevent the writer from making spelling errors (although we have all realized it doesn't catch every mistake).

This analytical approach involves probing a process to determine where human errors could occur. Then each potential error is traced back to its source. From these data, consider ways to prevent the potential error. Eliminating the step is the preferred alternative. If a way to prevent the error can not be identified, then look for ways to lessen the potential for error. Finally, choose the best approach possible, test it, make any needed modifications, and fully implement the approach.

Mistakes may be classified into four categories:

- Information errors:
  - Information is ambiguous.
  - Information is incorrect.
  - Information is misread, misinterpreted, or mismeasured.
  - Information is omitted.
  - There's inadequate warning.
- Misalignment:
  - Parts are misaligned.
  - A part is misadjusted.
  - A machine or process is mistimed or rushed.
- Omission or commission:
  - Material or part is added.
  - Prohibited and/or harmful action is performed.
  - An operation is omitted.
  - Parts are omitted, so there's a counting error.
- Selection errors:
  - A wrong part is used.
  - There is a wrong destination or location.
  - There's a wrong operation.
  - There's a wrong orientation.

Mistake-proofing actions are intended to:

- Eliminate the opportunity for error.
- Detect potential for error.
- Prevent an error.

Let's look at some examples. In the first situation, a patient is required to fill out forms at various stages of diagnosis and treatment (the ubiquitous "clipboard treatment"). The patient is prone to making errors due to the frustration and added anxiety of filling out multiple forms.

After analyzing the situation, the solution is to enter initial patient data into a computer at the first point of the patient's arrival, adding to the computer record as the patient passes through the different stages with different doctors and services. When referrals are made to doctors outside the initial facility, send an electronic copy of the patient's record (e-mail) to the referred doctor. Except to correct a previous entry, the intent is to never require the patient to furnish the same data more than once.

Considering the four types of mistakes, we can see that information was omitted or incorrectly entered at subsequent steps. The solution eliminates resubmitting redundant data.

In the second example, a low-cost but critical part is stored in an open bin for access by any operator in the work unit. While there is a minimum on-hand quantity posted, and a reorder card is kept in the bin, the bin frequently is empty before anyone takes notice. The mistake is that there's inadequate warning in receiving vital information.

The solution is to design and install a spring-loaded bin bottom that is calibrated to trigger an alarm buzzer and flashing light when the minimum stock level is reached. The alarm and light will correct the mistake.

In the final example, there is a potential to incur injury from the rotating blades when operators of small tractor-mowers dismount from a running tractor. The solution is to install a spring-actuated tractor seat that shuts off the tractor motor as soon as weight is removed. Using this tractor seat will prevent a harmful action.

Careful elimination, detection, and prevention actions can result in near 100 percent quality. Unintended use, ignorance, or willful misuse or neglect by humans may still circumvent safeguards, however. For example, until operating a motor vehicle is prevented before all seatbelts are securely fastened, warning lights and strict law enforcement alone won't achieve 100 percent effectiveness. Continually improve processes and mistake-proofing efforts to strive for 100 percent.

Kaizen

Kaizen is a Japanese word (*kai* means *change* or *school*, *zen* means *good* or *wisdom*). It has come to mean a continual and incremental improvement (as opposed to reengineering, which is a breakthrough, quantum-leap approach). A *kaizen blitz*, or *kaizen event*, is an intense process often lasting three to five consecutive days. It introduces rapid change into an organization by using the ideas and motivation of the people who do the work. It has also been called *zero investment improvement* (ZII).

In a kaizen event/blitz, a cross-functional team focuses on a target process, studies it, collects and analyzes data, discusses improvement alternatives, and implements changes. The emphasis is on making the process better, not necessarily perfect. Subprocesses that impact cycle time are a prime target on which to put the synergy of a kaizen team to work.

The typical stages of a kaizen event are:

- Week before blitz:

  - *Wednesday.* Train three or four facilitators in kaizen blitz techniques and tools, and enhance their facilitation skill level.

  - *Thursday.* Target the process to be addressed.

  - *Friday.* Gather initial data on the present targeted process.

- Blitz week:

  - *Monday.* Train the participants in kaizen blitz techniques and tools.

  - *Tuesday.* Train (a.m.), create process map of present state (p.m.).

  - *Wednesday.* Create process map of future state. Eliminate non-value-added steps and other waste. Eliminate bottlenecks. Design new process flow.

  - *Thursday.* Test changes, modify as needed.

  - *Friday.* Implement the new work flow, tweak the process, document the changes, and be ready for full-scale production on Monday. Prepare follow-up plan.

- Post blitz:

  - Conduct follow-up evaluation of change (at an appropriate interval).

  - Plan the next blitz.

Overall Equipment Effectiveness

Overall equipment effectiveness (OEE) is a method for measuring the efficiency and effectiveness of a process by breaking it down into three constituent components: availability, performance, and quality. *Availability* takes into account *downtime loss,* or events that stop planned production for an appropriate amount of time, such as setups, adjustments, and breakdowns. *Performance* takes into account *speed loss,* or factors that cause the process to operate at less than the minimum possible speed, when running. *Quality* takes into account *quality loss,* or parts that do not meet quality requirements, such as startup rejects or production rejects. The three components are calculated as:

- Availability = Operating time / Planned production time

- Performance = Ideal cycle time / (Operating time / Total pieces) or (Total pieces / Operating time) / Ideal run rate

- Quality = Good pieces / Total pieces

- OEE = Availability × Performance × Quality

See OEE website for more information at http://www.oee.com.

Pitfalls to Avoid in Achieving Cycle-Time Reduction

Any time an organization applies lean tools there can be problems. Common pitfalls include:

- Creating a bottleneck.

- Focusing on a portion of the system that is not on the critical path. Bottleneck operations in a production process must be recognized and addressed first.

- Failing to attend to the social aspects of any change.

- Failing to give attention to other issues. For example, in and of itself, cycle-time reduction might not result in an improved product or service. It must be studied to ensure that it does not adversely affect quality or other processes or resources. Also, expectations need to be examined to determine whether they are realistic. Finally, remember that absence or misinterpretation of data can lead to unexpected results. Establishing times for and determining the true sequence of events is important to the improvement process. (Video recording of activities for review by the cycle time improvement team is an excellent technique for doing this.)

Table 14.1 includes some of the techniques and tools that are used in applying lean methods. Note: The table mentions tools that are not discussed in the preceding text.

4. THEORY OF CONSTRAINTS (TOC)

Define key concepts of TOC: systems as chains, local vs. system optimization, physical vs. policy constraints, undesirable effects vs. core problems, and solution deterioration. Classify constraints in terms of resources and expectations as defined by measures of throughput, inventory, and operating expense. (Understand)

Body of Knowledge IV.B.4

Most organizations have strategies, goals, objectives, and plans to do more with less. They usually have finite resources available, which tends to conflict with ever-increasing expectations from stakeholders. Traditional process improvement methods—for example, to reduce cycle time and get more done with less—have focused on Pareto analysis to pinpoint what process or problem area to tackle first. The resulting fragmented approach has often led to improving the target processes at the expense of the whole organization (suboptimization).

Table 14.1   Techniques, methodologies, and tools applicable to process management.

Technique/ Methodology/Tool	Chap	Explanation/Purpose
Action plan	7.1 10.4	A mini project plan. Describes action to be taken, responsibility, start and end dates, applicable standards and constraints, resources, and steps to be taken.
Activity-based costing (ABC)	13.4	Accounting system that allocates cost to products based on resources used to produce the product.
Activity network diagram (AND)	13.2	Diagram showing the flow of activities in a process/project and the dependencies among activities.
Affinity diagram	13.2	A method to organize a large number of items into smaller chunks/clusters.
Andon board		Electronic device to display status alerts to operators.
Advanced product quality planning (APQP)	14.2	Methodology used to guide the process of developing and launching a new product/process (automotive industry). Defines the phases: conceptualize, design, develop, validate, and launch new product and process designs.
Autonomation (*jidoka*)		Specially equipped automated machines capable of detecting a defect in a single part, stopping the process, and signaling for assistance.
Batch-and-queue	14.2	Scheduling large batches of product that must wait in a queue between each step in the process.
Brainstorming	13.4	Team technique to generate ideas, for example, on how to reduce cycle time.
Cause-and-effect (fishbone) diagram	13.1	Diagramming technique to identify causes and subcauses leading to an effect. Aids in analyzing the root cause of how a situation came to be.
Cell (typically U-shaped)	14.3	Configuration of machines of varying types, arranged so that operations occur in sequence, permitting single-piece flow and flexible use of cross-trained operators.
Chaku-chaku (load-load in Japanese)		Within a cell, operator removes a part from one machine and loads it into the next machine, continuing the sequence until the part has been through all the steps needed for completion. As one part is removed from a machine, another is started through, thus enabling one-piece scheduling.
Changeover		Changing machine from one part number (for example, product) to another.
Check sheet	13.1	Tool for tallying frequency of occurrences, over time, for several items being tracked.
Control charts	13.1 13.3	Charts used to identify special cause variation, or that a process is out of control.

Continued

Table 14.1   *Continued.*

Technique/ Methodology/Tool	Chap	Explanation/Purpose
Control plan	14.2	Document(s) that may include the quality characteristics of a product or service, measurements, and methods of control.
Cost of quality (COQ)	13.5	A method used by organizations to show the financial impact of quality activities.
Cycle time	14.3	The total time to complete one cycle in an operation.
Design for Six Sigma (DFSS)	13.4	DFSS is used to design products and services so that they can be produced and delivered with Six Sigma quality.
DMAIC	13.3	*Define* the customer and organizational requirements. *Measure* what is critical to quality, map the process, establish measurement system, and determine what is unacceptable (defects). *Analyze* to develop a baseline (process capability), pinpoint opportunities and set objectives, identify root causes of defects. *Improve* the process. Establish a system to *control* the process.
Eliminate non-value-added steps in the process	14.3	Reduce waste and cut costs.
Eliminate or reduce buffer stocks and inventories	14.3	Smooth process flow, reduce costs, improve quality, and increase customer satisfaction.
Failure mode and effects analysis (FMEA)	13.3	Used to develop a preventive strategy, based on risk analysis, with identification of corrective or preventive actions to be taken. Applicable to designs, processes, support services, suppliers, etc.
Five S	14.3	(Japanese) methods to make everything about the workplace orderly and clean, and keep it so. Conveys message that quality starts with the people, and ultimately reflects in lower costs, increased customer satisfaction, and pride in work.
Five whys	13.4	Probing method of repeatedly asking "why?" until reaching the root cause of a situation or problem.
Flexibility/agility		Concept and practice of configuring facilities, equipment, people, and support services to cope with inevitable change. Enables organization to reduce costs, respond more effectively to marketplace demands, withstand economic fluctuations, and facilitate continual improvement.

Continued

Part IV.B.4

Table 14.1   *Continued.*

Technique/ Methodology/Tool	Chap	Explanation/Purpose
Flowchart	13.1 14.2	Step-by-step diagram of a process flow. Helps in understanding the process, identifying bottlenecks, and eliminating non-value-added steps.
Gemba (Japanese for *workplace*)		Management is urged to go to gemba, to get out to where the work is being done to better understand a problem and appreciate the process involved in making the product or delivering the service.
Histogram	13.1	Diagram showing the frequency distribution of data.
Interrelationship digraph	13.2	Tool to examine the relationships of a category/item to each of the other categories being examined.
Just-in-time (JIT)	14.3	An approach that allows the matching of material deliveries to the right time and place in the manufacturing process. Concept is applicable elsewhere, for example, JIT training (training delivered in the exact time and place needed).
Kaizen blitz/event	14.3	In a kaizen event a cross-functional team focuses on a target process, studies it, collects and analyzes data, discusses improvement alternatives, and implements changes. The intense event may consume three to five consecutive days.
Kanban	14.3	Signaling method to alert an upstream process that more material/product is required; the pull method. Signal may be a card, ticket, empty bin, and so on.
Line balancing	14.3	The process of distributing work and performers evenly to meet takt time and smooth workflow.
Matrix diagram	13.2	Diagram showing relationships between variables.
Mind mapping	13.4	A mind map creates a visual representation of many issues and can help a group get a more complete and common understanding of a situation.
Monument		Point in a process where the product must wait in a queue before processing, for example, a large, expensive machine purchased with the aim of achieving economy of scale.
Muda (Japanese for *waste*) (seven classes of waste)	14.3	Non-value-added activity that consumes resources. • Overproduction • Delays • Transportation • Processing • Excess inventory • Wasted motion • Defective parts

Continued

Part IV.B.4

Table 14.1   *Continued.*

Technique/ Methodology/Tool	Chap	Explanation/Purpose
Objectives, setting of	5	(S.M.A.R.T. W.A.Y.)
Overall equipment effectiveness (OEE)	14.3	Method for measuring effectiveness and efficiency of processes.
Pareto chart	13.1	Diagram that ranks causes of cycle time delays, causes of problems, and so on. Used to visualize the relative magnitude (hence priority) of charted items.
PDCA cycle	13.3	A tool for planning and analyzing a continual improvement: *P* Plan *D* Do *C* Check (or Study) *A* Act
Poka-yoke (error-proofing)	14.3	Methods for mistake-proofing a process to prevent a defect from occurring, cut costs, improve/decrease cycle time, improve quality, and improve safety.
Priorities matrix	13.2	A tool to compare all criteria to be used in making a choice, assigning weights to the choices, and scoring to identify the priorities of the choices.
Problem-solving model—seven steps	13.3	1. Identify the problem. 2. List possible root causes. 3. Search out the most likely root cause. 4. Identify potential solutions. 5. Select and implement a solution. 6. Follow up to evaluate the effect. 7. Standardize the process.
Procedures, work instructions	14.2	Documentation for the quality management system.
Process decision program chart	13.2	A tool for breaking down a decision into tasks with outcomes and contingency plans.
Process map	14.2	A more detailed process flowchart used for designing, analyzing, and communicating information about work processes.
Process reengineering	14.3	A "start from scratch" breakthrough strategy aimed at eliminating non-value-added operations, reducing cycle time, cutting costs, and so on. May be applied to an organization as a system, or to specific processes.

Continued

Part IV.B.4

Table 14.1   *Continued.*

Technique/Methodology/Tool	Chap	Explanation/Purpose
Process village		Machines grouped in one area by the type of operation/function they are used for; a batch-and-queue arrangement.
Production part approval process (PPAP)	14.2	Documents used to demonstrate to the customer that the new product/process is ready for full-blown production and to obtain approval to release it for production (automotive industry).
Quality manual	14.2	A document that may include description of the organization's policies, practices, processes, procedures, responsibilities, and so on, pertaining to the quality management system.
Root cause analysis	13.3	Use of one or more tools to locate the real cause of a problem or situation.
Sales leveling	18.E	Establishing long-term relationships with customers that lead to fixed-amount, fixed-delivery-date contracts to enable smoothing the production flow and eliminate surges.
Scatter diagram	13.1	Tool used to show if there is a correlation between two variables.
Single minute exchange of die (SMED)	14.3	A term used to indicate rapid setup changeover to the next type of product.
Single-piece flow	14.3	Product proceeds through the sequence of operations, one piece at a time, without interruption, backflows, or scrap.
SIPOC analysis	13.3	*S* Suppliers *I* Inputs *P* Process A tool for analyzing a process. *O* Outputs *C* Customers
Six Sigma approach	12.3 13.3	A process improvement initiative that uses a variety of techniques and tools all focused on producing defect-free products and services.
Spaghetti map		A "before lean" map of the physical flow and the interrelationships in the existing process. The map may resemble a bowl of spaghetti, as it shows poor layout, redundant steps, unnecessary storage, and so on.
Takt time	14.3	Available production time divided by the rate of customer demand. Takt time sets the production pace to match the rate of customer demand—the lean system's heartbeat.
Theory of constraints (TOC)	14.4	A methodology aimed at improving system performance by eliminating the constraint (weakest link in the process).
Throughput time	14.4	Total time required (processing + queue) from concept to launch, order to delivery, raw material to customer.

Continued

Table 14.1   *Continued.*

Technique/ Methodology/Tool	Chap	Explanation/Purpose
Total productive maintenance (TPM)		Methods to reduce downtime, reduce service/process interruptions, reduce waste, cut costs, prolong life of facilities, vehicles, and equipment, and improve quality and customer satisfaction.
Tree diagram	13.2	Tool for breaking down an objective into more-detailed steps.
TRIZ	13.3	Russian acronym—translated it is *the theory of the solution of inventive problems.*
Value stream map	14.3	A map of all process activities needed to provide specific products/services to the customer. The map shows metrics related to each process step (for example, cycle time, equipment downtime, quality performance, number of operators, WIP).
Visual control	14.3	Positioning all tools, parts, production activities, and performance indicators so that the status of a process can be seen at a glance. Purpose is to provide visual clues to aid the performer in correctly processing a step or series of steps, reduce cycle time, cut costs, smooth work flow, and improve quality.

Among a new group of thinkers promulgating the concept of thinking of organizations as systems is Eliyahu Goldratt. Goldratt's principles in the *theory of constraints* (TOC) are:[3]

- The whole organization must be treated as a system.

- Systems thinking is favored over analytical thinking for managing change and problem solving.

- Over a period of time, the optimal system solution degenerates as changes occur in the environment. Continual improvement is necessary to refresh and sustain the system's effectiveness.

- Optimum performance of a system means that only one part of the system is performing as well as it can. Optimum system performance is not the aggregate of all the local optima.

- Success or failure is dictated by how well the several processes within the system affect one another.

- The system, much like a chain with individual links connecting the whole, is only as strong as its weakest link.

- Little improvement occurs until the improvement of the weakest link is addressed.

- The weakest link is the system's *constraint.*

- A few core problems constitute the majority of the unwanted effects within a system.

- Linking *undesirable effects* (UDEs) by cause and effect helps surface core problems that are not apparent.

- Solving individual UDEs and neglecting the core problems leads to short-duration solutions.

- Obscure underlying conflict tends to perpetuate core problems. Solution involves addressing the conflicts and abolishing at least one such conflict.

- The system's current reality must be understood, and the difference between it and the goal, including the magnitude and direction.

- To improve the overall system, increase throughput, decrease inventory and operating expenses (terms are modified for the not-for-profit sector).

- Continual improvement can be thwarted by inertia. Solutions may appear to reject further change.

- Coming up with an idea is not coming up with a solution.

How TOC Treats the Flow of Money

Let's begin with some definitions:

- *Throughput* (T) is the rate at which the entire system generates money through sales of product or service (money coming in).

- *Inventory* (I) is all the money the system invests in things it intends to sell (money tied up inside the organization).

- *Operating expense* (OE) is all the money the system spends turning inventory into throughput (money going out).

So, to figure out key measures, use these equations:

$$\text{Profit} = T - OE$$

$$ROI = \frac{T - OE}{I}$$

$$\text{Productivity} = \frac{T}{OE}$$

$$\text{Inventory turns} = \frac{T}{I}$$

To focus improvement on the part of the process most capable of producing a positive impact on the system:

1. Locate the weakest link in the system and identify whether it is physical or a matter of policy constraint.

2. Determine what can be done to squeeze more capability from the constraint without having to undergo expensive changes.

3. Unless step 2 eliminated the constraint, adjust the system so that the constraint can function at its greatest effectiveness.

4. If steps 2 and 3 were not sufficient, consider making major changes to eliminate the constraint.

5. When either step 3 or 4 has eliminated the constraint, the steps must be repeated in order to deal with the next constraint. This is a never-ending cycle.[4]

Tools Used in TOC

There are a variety of diagrams used in TOC. They are:

- *Current reality tree.* A root cause analysis method to identify undesirable effects by working backward from the undesirable effect to identify the core problem.

- *Future reality tree.* A picture of the changed process identifying the desirable effects (used to show what to change and to identify any new unfavorable aspects to be addressed before implementing change).

- *Prerequisite tree.* Identifies obstacles to implementation by creating a sequence of events and potential obstacles.

- *Transition tree.* Details for implementing change, including a step-by-step action plan.

- *Conflict resolution diagram.* Described by Goldratt as an "evaporating cloud." As the name implies, this method aids in the resolution of conflicts. This includes identifying assumptions that appear valid but are suspect and can be eliminated as a conflict.[5]

Constraints are categorized as *physical* or *policy* constraints. Physical constraints are the easiest to identify and eliminate. Policy constraints are more difficult, but their elimination usually means a higher degree of system improvement.

All resources (raw material availability, equipment capacity, workforce, number of hours in the day, cash) are finite or limited. Exceeding the limit causes a constraint. What often drives these resources to the limit are increased expectations of the marketplace, customers, and management.

ENDNOTES

1. Throughout this book, the editor positions a *goal* as the higher-level intent and *objective* as the measurable action needed to achieve the goal. Ergo, a goal is measured by the attainment of the objectives supporting the goal.

Part IV.B.4

2. D. Galloway, *Mapping Work Processes* (Milwaukee: ASQC Quality Press, 1994).

3. E. Goldratt and J. Cox, *The Goal: A Process of Ongoing Improvement*, 2nd rev. ed. (Croton-on-Hudson, NY: North River Press, 1992).

4. H. W. Dettmer, *Goldratt's Theory of Constraints: A Systems Approach to Continuous Improvement* (Milwaukee: ASQ Quality Press, 1997).

5. Goldratt and Cox, *The Goal*.

See Appendix A for additional references for this chapter.

Chapter 15

C. Measurement: Assessment and Metrics

E
ffective management of an organization depends on defining, gathering, and analyzing information that provides feedback on current performance as well as projects future needs. This concept is embodied in *management by fact*, a core value of the Baldrige Performance Excellence Program.

Most organizations have massive amounts of data available. Much of it, however, may have little value or may even pose a risk if it is not accurate, timely, and properly analyzed, or is measuring the wrong things. Deming's famous red bead experiment demonstrated how improper responses to data could undermine employee morale while resulting in no improvement to the system.[1]

Statistics is the science of turning data into information. Many statistical techniques are simple yet powerful, such as looking at how data from a process vary over time. For example, a change could consist of a gradual increase or decrease in the relative value or average, or could involve rapid but short-term changes in the range or variance of the data.

Ensuring that the data measure what is intended requires understanding the purpose of the data (for example, what decisions are to be made based on them?) and making sure that the measurement system will repeatedly produce the same data in increments appropriate for the purpose. This involves calibrating and verifying the capability of the data source. It is also possible that the process being measured was not properly designed to be able to produce the desired results and will, therefore, require more than monitoring to meet requirements.

Data can be past or future oriented. They can indicate what has happened and help project what may happen.

Much of the data used by organizations is *quantitative*, meaning that it comes from simply counting something (for example, number of customers who complain) or a physical measurement (for example, temperature of a heat-treat oven). Sometimes, however, the most useful information is *qualitative*, for which special methods for gathering and analysis have been developed.

1. BASIC STATISTICAL USE

> Use techniques such as the goal-question-metric (GQM) model and others to identify when, what, and how to measure projects and processes. Describe how metrics and data gathering methods affect resources and vice-versa. (Apply)
>
> **Body of Knowledge IV.C.1**

Techniques and Tools to Measure Processes

To begin, go over a checklist for developing measures. Ask:

- Are measures simple to understand and easy to use?

- Do they have adequate and appropriate meaning to stakeholders?

- Is the definition clear?

- Are the data economical to gather and analyze?

- Are the data verifiable and repeatable?

- Does the measure make sense to those who must use it?

- Is the message conveyed by the measure consistent with the organization's values, vision, mission, strategy, goals, and objectives?

- Does the measure indicate trends?

- Will the use of the measure cause the correct actions?

- Does the measure achieve the stated purpose?

Goal–question–metric (GQM) is a method used to define measurement of the project, process, and product in such a way that:

- Resulting metrics are tailored to the organization and its goal.

- Resulting measurement data play a constructive and instructive role in the organization.

- Metrics and their interpretation reflect the values and the viewpoints of the different groups affected (for example, developers, users, and operators).

GQM defines a measurement model on three levels:

- *Conceptual level (goal).* A goal is defined for an object—for a variety of reasons—with respect to various models of quality, from various points of view, and relative to a particular environment.

- *Operational level (question).* A set of questions is used to define models of the object of study and then focuses on that object to characterize the assessment or achievement of a specific goal.

- *Quantitative level (metric).* A set of metrics, based on the models, is associated with every question in order to answer it in a measurable way.

Although originally used to define and evaluate a particular project in a particular environment, GQM can also be used for control and improvement of a single project within an organization running several projects.

The development of metrics can vary from one organization to another and depends on the project or process involved. An example of the steps in development is:

- Determine how to plan a good measurement program.

- Determine how to define goals, questions, metrics, and hypotheses for related processes.

- Collect data.

- Analyze and interpret the results, and present the results.

Using the GQM technique benefits the organization because writing goals, defining questions, and showing the relationships between goals and metrics helps it focus on important issues. Plus, GQM techniques provide the organization with flexible means to focus the measurement system on its particular need. Another advantage of using GQM is that it aids in reducing costs and cycle time, increasing efficiency, understanding risk, and overall quality improvement.

Measuring Independent Process Variables

It is important to determine the process parameters that are the real drivers of process performance. Most process output measures can not be directly changed because they respond to other variables within the process. In this case, the independent variables must be changed before the response-type variables. Consider an example.

A hospital pharmacy's management wants to improve the time from receipt of paper script (order for medicine) to delivery of the prescribed medicine to the nurses' station where the medicine will be dispensed. A simple cycle time measure would record the time elapsed in filling and delivering the order (response-type measure), but would shed little light on the process delays. These are independent variables such as availability of requested medicine in proper strength and quantity, adequacy of pharmacy staffing to meet the demand, delivery schedule, and communication-related questions that arise, for example, incorrect patient identification, illegible writing, and questionable dosage instructions. Measures would be needed for all of the independent variables, or a Pareto analysis could be used to select one or two of the independent variables that incur the largest number of problems.

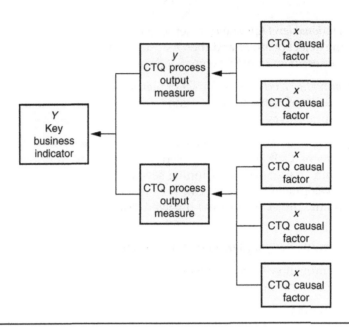

Figure 15.1   Causal relationship in developing key process measurements.

In the realm of Six Sigma methodology, there is a tool for displaying the causal relationship between the key business indicators (labeled as Y), the *critical-to-quality* (CTQ) process outputs (labeled y) that directly affect the Y's, and the causal factors that affect the process outputs (labeled as x). For example, one key business indicator (an outcome, a dependent variable) is *customer retention* (Y). CTQ outputs are *services delivered on time* (y), *services delivered correctly* (y), and *customer satisfied* (y). Factors affecting outputs (independent variables) are scheduling/dispatch system (x); training of service personnel (x); supplies, vehicles, tools, and equipment (x); and time to complete service properly (x). See the relationship of x to y and y to Y in Figure 15.1.

The selecting of the key metrics to be included in the balanced scorecard (discussed in Chapter 11, Section 3) is illustrative of how key indicators are established. The top-level metrics of the scorecard (typically four) are the ones executives use to make their decisions. Each of these top-level metrics (dependent variables) is backed up by metrics on independent variables. Thus, if the marketing vice president wants to know the cause for a negative trend in the customer metric of the scorecard, the vice president can drill down to the variable affecting the negative trend.

Establishing Process Measures

Four steps are needed to establish process measures:

1. Identifying and defining the critical factors impacting the customers:

   • Timing

- Availability

- Cost to purchase

- Product quality

- Product reliability and usability

- Life cycle of product

- Safety and environmental safeguards

2. Mapping the process across all applicable functions.

3. Identifying and defining the critical tasks and resources (including competencies) required.

4. Establishing the measures that will be used to track and manage the required tasks and resources.

Techniques and Tools for Measuring Projects

It is important to remember that there is a minimum of two processes involved: the *project planning and management* process and the *deliverables* process for which the project is initiated. Within the context of the project planning and managing process, measurements are applied during all phases of the project implementation as well as after the project is completed. Measuring the deliverables process commences when there are outputs delivered, and for some reasonable period thereafter.

Project planning and management measurements may include:

- Schedules met

- Resources used

- Costs versus budget

- Earned value analysis (EVA)

- Risks identified and eliminated or mitigated

- Project objectives met

- Safety and environmental performance

- Project team effectiveness

Project deliverables measurements may include:

- Targeted outcomes achieved

- Additional unplanned benefits obtained

- Return on investment

- Customer satisfaction (internal and/or external)

Chapter 10 discusses project management in more detail.

Part IV.C.1

How Metrics and Data-Gathering Methods Affect Some People

Some negatives to managing projects can be:

- Performers often perceive excessive data collection and creation of a plethora of metrics as management's obsession with the numbers rather than as being helpful in producing a better product or service. A major concern in many organizations is the number of measures it is attempting to monitor. In extreme cases this can result in rooms displaying wall-to-wall and ceiling-to-floor charts. This presents a problem of keeping the charts up to date and keeping the data flow accurate, as well as how effectively the charts can be used.

- Performers doing the work often don't understand the connection between what they produce and the metrics by which management assesses their performance. Without seeing the connection, the performers may feel unappreciated, unmotivated, and unfairly treated.

- When performers receive criticism or a disciplinary action because they are considered the cause of a negative event or trend in the metrics, they are likely to perceive the metrics as the cause of their discomfort. The performer's resulting reaction may be adopting a "don't care" attitude, finding a way to fudge the numbers, bad-mouthing management, initiating a grievance, purposely causing defects, or quitting the job.

- Performers are asked to do A, but recognition and reward (and measurement) relate to doing B.

- If management views the use of metrics primarily as a means for controlling those beneath them in the hierarchy, management demonstrates a misguided strategy. Metrics should be focused on surfacing areas for continual improvement.

- People, especially skilled workers, tend to resent the paperwork (or computer data entry work) usually required for their job positions. They often feel that the systems in which they work put greater emphasis on gathering data than on performing their tasks. They feel particularly resentful when they can see no logical reason for the data collected and/or how or whether it is used.

Well-intended and well-designed metrics can positively impact performers when the metrics:

- Provide a means for the performer to measure her or his own performance against a standard, objective, or customers' requirements. How effective this feedback is depends on:

  - The performer being aware of the basis for measurement

- How meaningful and understandable the metric is to the performer prior to the work being performed

- The frequency of the feedback

- The presentation of the feedback (simple graphics usually preferred)

- Whether the performer participated in the development of the metric

- Whether oral discussion with the boss accompanies the visual feedback, and whether the oral feedback is constructive and reinforces positive actions of the performer

- Whether the metrics presented clearly indicate a linkage with the higher-level organizational metrics (the strategic plan, the big picture)

- Whether the metrics are generally perceived as beneficial and the basis for improvement rather than just another management effort to control

- Whether the metrics support or conflict with delivered rewards and formulated strategy

• Create a work environment in which the performer feels motivated to improve, including:

- Feeling good about achieving the objectives and meeting the expectations, or feeling good about the progress made since the last feedback.

- Making suggestions for improving the process being measured.

- Making suggestions for improving the metric(s) by which the process is measured.

Measurement data also must be reliable, accurate, and accessible to the right people at the right time in order to be useful in detecting a need for corrections. Personnel who are responsible for analyzing data and taking action should be trained to do so to reduce the likelihood of human errors in judgment "Quality control is greatly simplified when operating people are in a state of self-control. . . . Ideally, the quality planning for any job should put the employee into a state of self-control. When work is organized in a way that enables a person to have full mastery over the attainment of planned results, that person is said to be in a state of self-control and can therefore properly be held responsible for the results. . . . To put people into a state of self-control, several fundamental criteria must be met. People must be provided with:

• Knowledge of what they are supposed to do (for example, the budgeted profit, the schedule, and the specification).

• Knowledge of what they are doing (for example, the actual profit, the delivery rate, the extent of conformance to specification)

Part IV.C.1

- Means for regulating what they are doing in the event that they are failing to meet the goals. These means must always include the authority to regulate and the ability to regulate by varying either (a) the process under the person's authority or (b) the person's own conduct."[2]

Three Timely Tenets

Whether you are measuring a process or a project, remember these tenets:

1. Never design and institute a measurement without first knowing:

   - What data you need

   - Who will supply the data

   - How the data will be transformed into information

   - How the information will be used and for what purpose

   - How you will communicate this information to all applicable stakeholders

   - How cost-effective taking the measurement will be

2. Always involve the people doing the work in helping in the design of the measurement.

3. Establish a rule that the primary reason for the measurement is to improve the process, project, or product. There may be other secondary reasons.

2. SAMPLING

> Define and describe basic sampling techniques such as random and stratified. Identify when and why sampling is an appropriate technique to use. (Understand)
>
> **Body of Knowledge IV.C.2**

Determining the process for acquiring data is an important part of any measurement process. Whether it's selecting the number of customers to survey or the process of taking samples from a moving conveyor, the sampling process will depend on the purpose, desired statistical confidence, and economics.

Whether or not sampling is needed is an important determination. Some of the reasons for not using sampling include:

- The customer's requirement is for 100 percent inspection of entire shipment.

- The number of items or services is small enough to inspect the entire quantity produced/delivered.

- The cost of sampling is too high relative to the advantages gained from sampling.

- Self-inspection by trained operators is sufficient for the nature of the product produced.

- The inspection method is built in, or the process is mistake-proofed so that no defectives can be shipped.

- Product is low cost and/or noncritical (wide or no specification range) to customer so that the producer can risk not sampling. (For example, delivering the fill to bring a building lot up to grade level to meet town height requirements.)

Acceptance Sampling Methods

Assuming sampling is needed, the intended purpose helps in deciding whether the sample should be randomly selected or stratified. *Random sample* selection is similar to pulling a number out of a hat (although a random sample number generator or table of random numbers is more likely used) and helps ensure that data will not be biased toward one particular portion of the population. It is expected that the sample will truly represent the range and relative distribution of characteristics of the population. In some cases, however, it may be desired that only a particular portion of the population be evaluated, which means that a *stratified sample* will be set up to create the desired distribution within the sample.

Sample size is dependent on the desired level of statistical confidence and the amount of difference between samples that one is trying to detect. For a given difference (for example, between means of two groups of data), testing at a statistical probability of .01 (a one percent chance the result will be labeled as significant when it is not), a larger sample size will be needed than if a probability of .05 is acceptable. The cost of selecting the samples and collecting the information also enters into this decision.

An additional sampling issue, *rational subgrouping*, must be considered for control charts. A chart meant to detect a shift in the mean will be more sensitive if variability within subgroups is minimized. This means that all samples within a subgroup should consist of parts taken within a relatively short time as compared to the time between subgroups. In addition, a subgroup should consist of a single process stream rather than mixing products from different streams (for example, two cavities in the same mold).

Systematic sampling is where every *n*th item is selected, for example, every tenth item. *Cluster sampling* is where a random sample is taken from within a selected subgroup. *Best judgment sampling* is when an expert's opinion is used to determine the best location and characteristics of the sample group.

Acceptance sampling is the process of sampling a batch of material to evaluate the level of nonconformance relative to a specified quality level. It is most frequently applied to decide whether to move material from one process to another or to accept material received from a supplier. Many sampling processes are based on the work of Dodge and Romig and standards such as ANSI/ASQ Z1.4 and ANSI/ASQ Z1.9.

Sampling assumes that nonconformances randomly occur throughout a lot and that a random sample can determine whether a given level of nonconformance is exceeded. Whether sampling is the best technique for assessing a product depends on the lot size, frequency of production/receipt, typical level of nonconformance, and acceptable level of risk. For example, pencils received from an office supply house are normally not sampled because the risk associated with defective pencils is minimal. In contrast, medical devices might be subjected to extensive sampling or even 100 percent inspection because of the consequences of failure.

When properly applied over time, sampling can keep nonconformances below a predetermined level called the *average outgoing quality limit* (AOQL). Compared with 100 percent inspection, sampling is more economical, requires less handling of the product, and is often more accurate since there is less fatigue. Sampling plans do have drawbacks: they may be used to avoid adequate process control, they are less economical than process control, and they yield less information on the true state of nonconformance than do 100 percent inspection or statistical analysis. *No sampling plan yields 100 percent detection of nonconformances.* Because of this and possible legal or political issues, some industries do not use sampling. For example, a U.S. population census conducted by sampling might be believed to result in misleading allocation of tax funds.

Risks in Sampling

Two types of errors can occur in sampling. The alpha (α) or *producer's risk* refers to the possibility that good product will be rejected (a *type 1 error*). The beta (β) or *consumer's risk* refers to the possibility that bad product will be accepted (a *type 2 error*). The *operating characteristic* (OC) curve for a particular sampling plan indicates the probability of accepting a lot based on the sample size to be taken and the fraction defective in the batch. Producer's risk is often set at .05 (acceptance probability of .95) and consumer's risk at .10. Consumer's risk is also frequently called *lot tolerance percent defective* (LTPD). Figure 15.2 shows the OC curve for two sampling plans with different sample sizes. In both cases the acceptance number is zero ($c = 0$).

When sampling is to be used, the decision must be made as to which family of sampling plans and which table within that family will be applied. The *acceptable quality limit* (AQL) must be determined and is often spelled out in a specification or contract. AQL is associated with the point on the curve correlated to the producer's risk. ANSI/ASQ Z1.4 (2008) perceives AQL as the worst tolerable process average when a continuing series of lots is submitted for acceptance sampling. Inasmuch as AQL goes against the philosophy of zero defects, it is useful to ensure that all parties involved understand why a particular AQL has been chosen.

Sampling can also be done based on a single sample or multiple samples. In *single sampling*, lots are inspected, and the decision to accept or reject is based on the acceptance number c for the sample size n. In *double sampling* (see Figure 15.3), lots are inspected and the decision to accept or reject is based on the acceptance number c for the combined sample size ($n1 + n2$). In double sampling plans, the first sample will have an acceptance number, a zone of continuing sampling, and

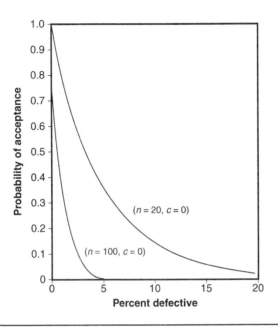

Figure 15.2   OC curves.

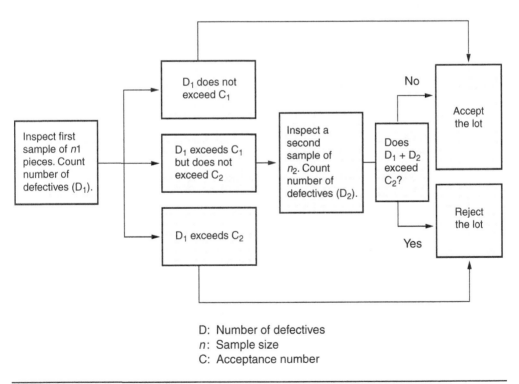

D: Number of defectives
n: Sample size
C: Acceptance number

Figure 15.3   Sampling decisions.

a reject number. If process quality is good, most lots will be accepted on the first sample, thereby reducing sampling cost. The inspector also can feel that the lot is being given a second chance if a second sample must be drawn.

In *multiple sampling*, lots are inspected, and the decision to accept or reject is based on a maximum of seven samples of *n*. Multiple plans work the same as double plans but use as many as seven draws before a final decision is made. This is the most discriminating of plans, but also the most susceptible to inspector abuse.

Zero acceptance number plans are useful in emphasizing the concept of *zero defects* and in product liability prevention. The concept is that if no defects are found in a sample, there are no defects in the remaining lot. Conversely, if a defect is found in the sample, the whole lot is considered defective. *Juran's Quality Handbook*, Fifth Edition, Section 46, discusses acceptance sampling.

3. STATISTICAL ANALYSIS

Calculate basic statistics: measures of central tendency (mean, median, mode), and measures of dispersion (range, standard deviation, and variance). Identify basic distribution types (normal, bimodal, skewed) and evaluate run charts, statistical process control (SPC) reports, and other control charts to make data-based decisions. (Evaluate)

Body of Knowledge IV.C.3

Simple Statistics Used to Analyze Groups of Data

Some measures of central tendency are:

- *Average.* Also called the *arithmetic mean*, it is the sum of the individual data values ($\sum x$) divided by the number of samples (n).

- *Median.* If data are arranged in numeric order, the median is the center number. If there is an even number of data points, the median is the average of the two middle numbers.

- *Mode.* Another measure of central tendency, mode is the number in the data set that occurs most often.

The *spread* of a sample group of data (also called *dispersion* or *variation*) is:

- *Range (R).* The arithmetic difference between the largest and smallest number in the data—a measure of spread, dispersion, or variation.

- *Standard deviation.* The standard deviation of a sample of data is given as:

$$s = \sqrt{\frac{\sum (X - \bar{X})^2}{n - 1}}$$

- *Variance.* Another measure of dispersion, the standard deviation squared.

If variance is the same as the standard deviation squared, why does it exist? The standard deviation is in the same units as the mean or average, the units of the measurement. This allows a clear representation of both the central tendency and the variability. If there are multiple sources of variability (such as tool choice and material choice), there would be several components of variability that are added to make the total. Standard deviations from multiple sources can not be added, but the square of the standard deviation components (that is, the variances) may be added.

Two sets of data could be analyzed simply by comparing their central tendencies and spread. For example, standardized test scores for groups of students who attend two different schools could be compared to try to determine whether the scores are higher (average, median, or mode) or more consistent (range or standard deviation) at one school versus the other. (Note: Making decisions based solely on these rough comparisons would of course be dangerous due to the large number and the interactive nature of the variables that could contribute to differences.)

Another way to analyze two comparable data sets is to create a histogram (see Chapter 13, Section 1) to see how their distributions compare. (Care must be taken to use the same *x*- and *y*-axis scales).

Probability Distributions. Comparisons that take into account statistical probability can be done using tests for significance such as the *F*-test to compare standard deviations and the *t*-test to compare means. *Juran's Quality Handbook* contains a table to help in selecting these and other test statistics. Advantages of this approach include compensating for sample size differences (by adjusting based on the degrees of freedom) and basing the decision on whether observed differences are actually statistically significant.

Although the normal distribution may be more common, there are several different shapes that probability distributions can take, depending on the type of data (for example, discrete versus continuous data) and characteristics of the process that produces the data. Following are some of the more widely used distributions; Figure 15.4 depicts them graphically:

- *Normal.* A bell-shaped distribution for continuous data where most of the data are concentrated around the average (approximately two-thirds are within ±1 standard deviation) and it is equally likely that an observation will occur above or below the average. This distribution especially applies to processes where there are usually many variables that contribute to the variation. This is one of the most common distributions.

- *Exponential.* A continuous distribution where data are more likely to occur below the average than above it (63.2 percent and 36.8 percent respectively, compared to 50 percent/50 percent for the normal distribution). Typically used to describe the break-in portion of the failure bathtub curve.

Juran's Quality Handbook, Chapter 48.5, discusses the *bathtub curve* for predicting reliability of a product over its lifetime. There would be a high incidence of failures during the product's "infant mortality" phase, random failures during the period of normal use, and an increase in wear-out failures toward the

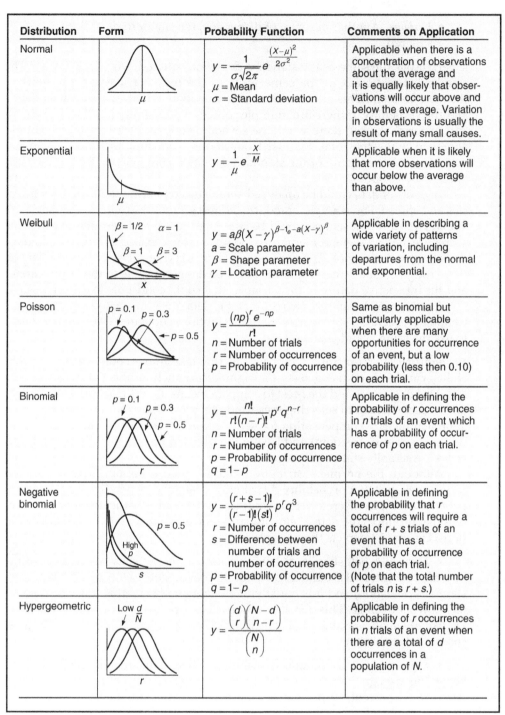

Distribution	Form	Probability Function	Comments on Application
Normal		$y = \dfrac{1}{\sigma\sqrt{2\pi}}e^{\frac{(X-\mu)^2}{2\sigma^2}}$ μ = Mean σ = Standard deviation	Applicable when there is a concentration of observations about the average and it is equally likely that observations will occur above and below the average. Variation in observations is usually the result of many small causes.
Exponential		$y = \dfrac{1}{\mu}e^{\frac{X}{M}}$	Applicable when it is likely that more observations will occur below the average than above.
Weibull	$\beta = 1/2 \quad \alpha = 1$ $\beta = 1 \quad \beta = 3$ X	$y = a\beta(X-\gamma)^{\beta-1}e^{-a(X-\gamma)^\beta}$ a = Scale parameter β = Shape parameter γ = Location parameter	Applicable in describing a wide variety of patterns of variation, including departures from the normal and exponential.
Poisson	$p = 0.1$ $p = 0.3$ $\leftarrow p = 0.5$ r	$y = \dfrac{(np)^r e^{-np}}{r!}$ n = Number of trials r = Number of occurrences p = Probability of occurrence	Same as binomial but particularly applicable when there are many opportunities for occurrence of an event, but a low probability (less then 0.10) on each trial.
Binomial	$p = 0.1$ $p = 0.3$ $p = 0.5$ r	$y = \dfrac{n!}{r!(n-r)!}p^r q^{n-r}$ n = Number of trials r = Number of occurrences p = Probability of occurrence $q = 1-p$	Applicable in defining the probability of r occurrences in n trials of an event which has a probability of occurrence of p on each trial.
Negative binomial	$p = 0.5$ High p s	$y = \dfrac{(r+s-1)!}{(r-1)!(s!)}p^r q^3$ r = Number of occurrences s = Difference between number of trials and number of occurrences p = Probability of occurrence $q = 1-p$	Applicable in defining the probability that r occurrences will require a total of $r + s$ trials of an event that has a probability of occurrence of p on each trial. (Note that the total number of trials n is $r + s$.)
Hypergeometric	Low $\dfrac{d}{N}$ r	$y = \dfrac{\dbinom{d}{r}\dbinom{N-d}{n-r}}{\dbinom{N}{n}}$	Applicable in defining the probability of r occurrences in n trials of an event when there are a total of d occurrences in a population of N.

Figure 15.4   Probability distributions.

end of the product's life cycle. The chart of the distribution appears to resemble a bathtub.

- *Weibull.* A distribution of continuous data that can take on many different shapes and is therefore used to describe a variety of patterns, including distributions similar to but slightly different from the normal and exponential.

- *Binomial.* Defines the probability for discrete data of r occurrences in n trials of an event that has a probability of occurrence of p for each trial. Used when the sample size is small compared to the population size and when proportion defective is greater than 0.10.

- *Poisson.* Also used for discrete data and resembles the binomial. It is especially applicable when there are many opportunities for occurrence of an event, but a low probability (less than 0.10) on each trial.

- *Hypergeometric.* A discrete distribution defining the probability of r occurrences in n trials of an event when there are a total of d occurrences in a population of N. It is most applicable when the sample size is a large proportion of the population.

Advanced Statistical Methods

More-complex analysis of process variables can be done with advanced statistical methods such as *regression, analysis of variance* (ANOVA), and *response surface.* Such experimental design techniques are used for two primary purposes: (1) screening, or trying to find which independent variables have the greatest impact on results, and (2) optimization, or finding the level and combination for each independent variable that will provide the best overall performance.

Design of experiments (DOE) looks at interrelationships between many variables at one time. Replication of runs at particular levels is used to reduce the amount of experimental error, and designs include techniques such as blocking, nesting, and fractional factorials to gain maximum useful information with a minimum amount of testing.

Linear regression is a mathematical application of the concept of a scatter diagram (see Chapter 13, Section 1), but where the correlation is actually a cause-and-effect relationship. The analysis provides an equation describing the mathematical relationship between the two variables, as well as the statistical confidence intervals for the relationship and the proportion of the variation in the dependent variable that is due to the independent variable. Regression can also be applied to nonlinear relationships by transforming the data (for example, performing a mathematical conversion such as squaring each value of the independent variable), as well as to situations where there are multiple independent variables (called *multiple regression*).

Analysis of variance (ANOVA) is similar to performing a t-test, but allows looking at the differences between multiple distributions. It tests the statistical significance by looking at how much the average of each factor being tested varies from the overall average of all factors combined. The ANOVA table then provides an f value for which statistical significance can be determined.

Response surface is the process of graphically representing the relationship between two or more independent variables and a dependent variable. A response surface often looks similar to a topographic map, which uses lines to indicate changes in altitude at various latitudes and longitudes. *Evolutionary operation* (EVOP) is the process of adjusting variables in a process in small increments in a search for a more optimal point on the response surface.

Statistical Process Control (SPC)

Simply comparing the results of a process to itself over time is not sufficient in an environment where external competitive pressures and an internal desire for continual improvement exist.

The focus of this section is on how to effectively analyze information to enable the organization to manage and improve processes—whether at the strategic or operational level. Let's look at a simple example: Three people—a manager, a computer technician, and a staff analyst—each review the same data on downtime of a particular computer (see Table 15.1). What conclusions might each come to?

The manager might total up the amount of lost time and convert it to average daily dollars in lost productivity. The technician might notice times when the downtime appeared excessive compared to other machines for which she is also responsible, and that the last six days have been better than any other period, indicating improvement. The analyst (the user of the machine) might point out that problems occur with the computer nearly every day.

Another way to look at the data is to use a control chart (see Figure 15.5). If these same three individuals understand this simple statistical tool, they are likely to agree that (1) the computer is down an average of 10 minutes per day, (2) there were four days where downtime was, statistically, significantly higher, and (3) there is insufficient data to confirm a trend at the end of the month.

Other questions could be asked about the raw data themselves, such as:

- Was the computer being used the full 24 hours of each day, or might days when downtime was lower have been during periods when it was not used on all shifts?

- Who recorded the data (for example, one person or several) and was the same definition of downtime used by all? Did they measure the downtime in the same way? For example, if the computer went down five minutes before midnight and was down a total of 12 minutes, did this count as five minutes one day and seven the next, or were all 12 minutes recorded for the first day or for the second day?

- What other information might be necessary in order to make sense of the data? For example, if the day of the week was also included in the log, it would be more readily apparent that there is a pattern of high downtime every seven days, when the system backup is done.

- Should the data be separated into groups by cause of downtime (for example, backups, printer, and cable, or an actual failure versus intentional downtime) in order to more easily identify and remedy root causes?

Table 15.1   Computer downtime log.

Date	Downtime (Minutes)	Causes	Date	Downtime (Minutes)	Causes
4/1	0	—	4/16	12	Printer
4/2	2	—	4/17	33	Backup
4/3	18	Backup	4/18	6	Locked up
4/4	11	Cable damaged	4/19	6	Printer
4/5	7	Power failure	4/20	17	Cable damaged
4/6	4	Locked up	4/21	1	—
4/7	4	Locked up	4/22	0	—
4/8	5	—	4/23	13	Upgrading software
4/9	10	Unknown	4/24	22	Backup
4/10	25	Backup	4/25	8	Locked up two times
4/11	8	Locked up two times	4/26	6	Swap out display
4/12	12	Printer	4/27	2	—
4/13	3	Locked up	4/28	0	—
4/14	0	—	4/29	4	—
4/15	63	Unknown, reload TCP/IP	4/30	2	Locked up

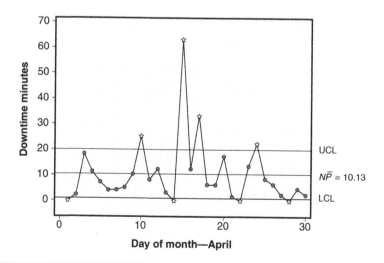

Figure 15.5   Control chart for computer downtime.

- Is one month's data sufficient for making a decision, or might there have been something different about this month versus previous months?

- How much downtime can be incurred before the quality or output of the process for which the computer is used is affected?

- How does downtime for this computer compare to other computers used within the same location, to similar computers used at other locations, and different brands of computers?

As the previous example shows, tabular data do not as easily lend themselves to consistent interpretation. The power of statistics is that it can reduce the amount of data to be interpreted and also help to point out specific issues that may be more important. Simple statistics used to analyze groups of data are discussed earlier in this section.

Types of Control Charts. A control chart is used to determine whether or not a process is *stable*, which means that it has predictable performance. By monitoring the output of a process over time, a control chart can be used to assess whether the application of process changes or other adjustments has resulted in improvements. If the process produces measurable parts, the average of a small sample of measurements, not individual measurements, should be plotted.

There are several software packages that assist in control chart creation and maintenance. Care should be taken in using these that the fundamental process of control charts is understood. For example, most of these software packages allow the instant recalculation of the control limits as new data are added to the chart. This is a feature to aid in the creation of the control system. If this feature is not disabled after the control limits have been set from an in-control data set, the process will never leave the control region. Thus, the purpose of the control chart will be lost.

There are many different types of control charts, each of which applies to either variables data (continuous or measured) or attributes data (discrete or counted). Variables-type control charts include:

- Charts for average and range (x-bar and R chart)

- Charts for averages and standard deviation (x-bar and s chart)

- Chart used to detect very small changes that occur over time (CUSUM chart)

Attributes-type control charts include:

- Chart used to chart number of defective units where sample size is constant (np-chart)

- Chart used for tracking fraction of units defective, where sample size is not constant (p-chart)

- Chart used to chart number of defects in a constant sample size (c-chart)

- Chart for number of defects where sample size is changing (u-chart)

There are other less common charts; however, understanding those above should suffice for managing operations. Additional detail can be found in the references for this chapter.

Although control limits are usually set at ±3 sigma using data from when the process is in control, in some applications they may be set tighter (for example, ±2.5 sigma) if one desires a quicker response to an out-of-control situation; however, this increases the probability of reacting when the process is actually in control. The inverse is also true: control limits can be loosened in order to reduce the frequency of looking for a change in variation, but this also means there is an increased chance of not reacting when the process has actually changed.

Four guidelines are used as a basic test for randomness in control charts:

- The points should have no visible pattern.

- Approximately two-thirds of the points should be close to the centerline (within ±1 standard deviation).

- Some points should be close to the outer limit (called *control limits* in statistical process control).

- An approximately equal number of points should fall above and below the centerline.

If all four criteria are met, then the process is likely to be in control.

Control charts are based on the concept of statistical probability, but are used for time-ordered data. The theory is that if the process from which the data are collected is a stable one (in control), then future values of data from the process should follow a predictable pattern. The probability limits (control limits) are based on the distribution for the type of data being analyzed. For example, the control limits for an x-bar and R chart are based on the normal distribution since it is known that averages will tend to create a normal distribution regardless of the shape of the underlying distribution from which the individual values were taken. (Note: There is a test for normality called the Chi-square test. See references for this chapter.)

Control charts can be used for both analysis of a process (for example, for improvement purposes) and maintaining control of a process. For process control purposes, an alternative to control charts, pre-control, can sometimes be used.

Pre-Control

Pre-control is an alternative to statistically based control charts, and involves dividing the specification range into four equal zones. The center two zones are the green (good) zone, the two areas on the outside of the green zone (which are still within spec) are considered the yellow (caution) zone, and the area outside specification is considered the red (defect) zone.

Decisions about the process are made according to the particular zone into which process output falls. For example, the red zone indicates that the process has probably shifted, while the green zone indicates that everything is OK. If output falls into the yellow zone, another reading is taken. If both readings are in the same yellow zone, it is assumed that the process has shifted, while if they are in opposite yellow zones, it is assumed that there is abnormal variation in the process that must be investigated. An example from one organization uses the same concept with the four bands, but in a slightly different manner:

- The green zone is set to ± 50% of the tolerance (to simulate 95.4% within ± 2 sigma)

- The yellow zone is within the 2 to 3 sigma range or the 50%–75% range of the tolerance (to simulate 99.7% within ± 3 sigma)

- The red zone is just *before* the spec limit at the 75%–100% range of the tolerance (to simulate 4 sigma for a coverage of 99.997).

Following the same reaction plans for points in the yellow and red zones, and utilizing proper sampling and operator responsiveness, can usually enable a process to achieve a 1.33 C_{pk}. In this case, if a point occurs within the red zone, the product would be in specification, but the process is likely out of control. Containment/rework should not be necessary, but preventive process adjustment would be. In the original definition, if the red zone were set beyond the specification limit, then a C_{pk} of 1 could likely be enabled, and defective process results could inadvertently be passed on to the customer.

Pre-control is often used when a process is just being started, and can be especially useful when there is not yet sufficient data to develop statistically based control limits. The rules for pre-control include both sampling frequency and actions to take, with the sample frequency being varied according to how well the process appears to be working.

4. MEASUREMENT SYSTEMS ANALYSIS

> Define basic measurement terms: accuracy, precision, bias, and linearity. Understand the difference between repeatability and reproducibility in gage R&R studies.
> (Understand)
>
> **Body of Knowledge IV.C.4**

Another measurement validation process is that of *gage repeatability and reproducibility* (gage R&R) studies. The purpose of an R&R study is to determine how much variation exists in the measurement system, which includes variation in the product, the gage, and the individuals using the gage. The desire is to have a measurement system whose error does not take up a large proportion of the product tolerance. *Repeatability* is the variation in results on a single gage when the same parts are measured repeatedly by the same person, while *reproducibility* is the variation from person to person using the same gage.

Calibration is a process used to maintain the performance of a measurement system. For physical measurement devices this involves determining whether, under a predefined set of conditions, the values indicated by the instrument agree with the results obtained for a standard that has been independently tested. The standards used for calibration are typically traceable back to an organization such as the National Institute of Standards and Technology (NIST) in the United States.

The terms *accuracy* and *precision* are most often used to discuss physical measurement devices, where accuracy is equivalent to *validity* (the correct value) and precision is how well the device can reproduce the same results when measurements are taken repeatedly (*reliability*).

Calibration programs typically consist of the following general requirements:

- Identify all equipment that is used for measuring product quality or controlling important process variables.

- Ensure that the equipment is capable of the accuracy and precision necessary for the tolerance to be measured.

- Give each piece of equipment a specific identification number, and establish a frequency and method for calibration.

- Calibrate the equipment using traceable or otherwise documented standards.

- Perform the calibrations under known environmental conditions.

- Record the calibration findings, including as-found and after-correction data.

- Investigate any possible problems that may have been created by an out-of-calibration device.

- Identify or otherwise control any devices that have not been calibrated or are otherwise not for use.

The principle of calibration can also be applied to nonphysical measurement applications. For example, if several people are to conduct separate interviews on the same subject, in order to calibrate all the interviewers, a set of definitions is usually developed and documented, and interviewers are trained to ensure consistent understanding and use of the terms.

(See Section 8 of this chapter for a discussion of reliability and validity.)

5. TREND AND PATTERN ANALYSIS

> Interpret graphs and charts to identify cyclical, seasonal, and environmental data trends.
> Evaluate control chart patterns to determine shifts and other trend indicators in a process.
> (Evaluate)
>
> **Body of Knowledge IV.C.5**

Trend analysis is the process of looking at data over time in order to identify, interpret, and respond to patterns. A desired trend may be a continuous upward movement (for example, in gross sales or net margin), a continuous downward movement (for example, in customer complaints), or a sustained level of performance (for example, holding nominal specification).

Before conducting trend analysis, one must ensure that the correct things are being measured and that the measurements are accurate and able to discriminate at the desired level. Trend data must also sometimes be normalized to compensate for changes in other parameters that impact the measure being tracked. For example, tracking scrap dollars in absolute terms is not the same as tracking it as a percentage of cost of goods sold.

By themselves, measurement data do not result in continual improvement, but having data organized in a manner that supports analysis is vital.[3] Analytical tools that organize data and are helpful in trend analysis include Pareto charts, check sheets, histograms, control charts (all discussed in Chapter 13, Section 1), and run charts that simply show data arranged chronologically. In analyzing a trend, it is important to distinguish a trend from a cyclic pattern and from changes in variation. Figure 15.6 portrays the distinction.

Having a clear understanding of the purpose of the data being used for trend analysis is most necessary. "A further distinction in controls is whether they provide information before, during, or after operations."[4] Leading indicators are measures that can be used to predict the outcome of future events on the basis of analysis of past and current results. For example, market research to ascertain customer wants and needs, as well as what competitors are doing, might precede the determination to develop a new product. Lagging indicators depict actual trends versus expected performance levels, such as warranty claims. "A well-balanced system of executive reports makes use of leading indicators as well as indicators that lag behind operations."[5]

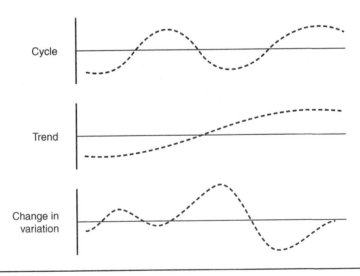

Figure 15.6   Run chart patterns.

Long-Term versus Short-Term Trend Analysis

Long-term trend analysis is the examination and projection of company-level data over an extended period of time. It is used primarily for planning and managing strategic progress to achieve organization-wide performance goals.[6] At the organization level, data—including corporate summaries of financial and nonfinancial measures—are analyzed to help management understand the company's performance and prioritize improvement actions. Performance trends can also be compared to those of competitors.

Various forms of trend charts are used to trigger process adjustments or systems improvements when conducting short-range trend analysis at the process level or the work unit level.[7]

At the process level, analysis of measurement data provides both departmental and cross-functional understanding of the system's performance over time. Often, company policy defines the frequency for the trending and reporting of performance results, along with criteria that define what are considered adverse trends and the appropriate actions to take to establish or regain control.

At the work unit level, the process operator analyzes measurement data and adjusts the process to eliminate special causes of variation. To accomplish this, the operator might use a control chart to help determine what constitutes a trend. This type of trending is based on the interpretation of a series of events that are closely related in time, with the objective of sustaining process control.

Through the use of quality control tools incorporated into work processes, process operators are able to monitor the performance of key process characteristics. Work instructions for measuring data, analyzing trends in data, and making and recording process adjustments are documented as part of the quality system.

Patterns in Trend Analysis

As previously mentioned, it is typically expected that trended data will show a continual increase or decrease, or will maintain a consistent level. Some data, however, will exhibit other particular patterns that indicate that the process being measured is working as desired or has encountered an unexpected factor. Two other patterns that may be superimposed on the three basic trends are:

- *Cyclical.* Some businesses or processes are affected by seasonal or other factors that cause the output to gradually increase (or decrease), then gradually return to approximately the original level. For example, the quality of product produced in a plant that is not temperature-controlled might be impacted by seasonal changes in outdoor temperatures.

- *Shifts.* An abrupt change in an important variable (for example, a new sales initiative or change in raw material suppliers) may cause an output measure to suddenly increase or decrease. For example, facilities that operate three work shifts and do not have adequate standardization of operational methods often see significant differences in process performance at shift changeovers.

Tabular Data

Although run charts and other graphical displays of information are preferable, data are sometimes organized in tables for presentation. When tables are used, the following are a few simple rules that can help make interpretation of the data easier and more accurate:

- Organize the data so that they flow down, then across; it is generally easier to compare numbers in a column than across rows.

- Keep the number of digits to the right of the decimal point constant so that numbers are properly aligned; this helps highlight differences in magnitude of numbers.

- Use clear column titles and row headings, and keep the groupings consistent throughout the table.

- The length of a column before beginning a new one on the same page should encompass a logical block of data (for example, all data for a particular week or state should be in the same column if comparison of weeks or states is of interest).

Tabular data are more likely to be analyzed correctly if analysis is done using statistical methods. However, visual scanning of tables can sometimes identify patterns that might be investigated by simply circling the larger and/or smaller numbers.

Data Mining

Data mining began as a marketing process used to surface previously unknown linkages between variables in mammoth data sets, for example, mining the data collected by computerized checkout registers in retail stores. Its advantage is that it brings to light patterns of influence on quality that heretofore would have appeared impossible to detect.

Data mining technologies include:

- *Neural networks.* Using a computer with its architecture patterned after the neurons of a human brain, the computer's web of electronic neurons send signals to each other over thousands of connections. A neural network is capable of simple learning.

- *Decision trees.* This technology uses a tree-shaped structure representing sets of decisions used to predict which records in an uncategorized data set will yield a stated outcome.

- *Rule induction.* This method is the finding of useful if/then rules within the data, based on statistical significance.

- *Genetic algorithms.* This method applies optimization techniques derived from the concepts of genetic combination, mutation, and natural selection.

- *Nearest neighbor.* This technique classifies each record based on other records that are most similar.

- Other pattern recognition techniques:

  - Linear models

  - Principal component analysis

  - Factor analysis

  - Linear regression

- Other methods:

  - Hotelling's *t*-squared statistic

  - Forecasting

  - Clustering

One of data mining's strengths is the capability to uncover an optimum combination of factors that can be used for *design of experiments* (DOE). Another advantage is that data mining and a geographic information system can be combined to produce smart maps.

Geographic Information System

A *geographic information system* (GIS) is especially useful in looking at markets, customer clusters, and social/economic/political data—before change and after change. GIS is a specialized type of software that depicts patterns, and runs on personal computers. It resembles a database program in that it analyzes and relates stored records, with some major differences—the GIS database contains information used to draw a geometric shape. That shape represents a unique place on earth to which the data correspond. Fields of special data enable the program to draw the shape of the information.

GIS is more than a program for drawing maps; it is a system for mapping and analyzing the geographical distribution of data. There is a big difference between viewing data in tabular form and seeing it presented as a map. Because of the human ability of *pattern recognition,* the way one sees the data has a huge effect on the connections and conclusions one derives from the mapped data.

GIS is an extremely useful tool for trend analysis, providing "before" and "after" maps of data from a targeted population or area of investigation.

Barriers to Successful Trend Analysis

Some common barriers to successful trend analysis include lack of:

- Timely access to data required in order to maintain a state of control or to prevent nonconformances

- Knowledge of how to interpret the data

- Knowledge or authority to respond to trends

- Understanding of the theory of variation (see Section 6), leading to poor decisions when evaluating alternatives and projecting results

In *The Fifth Discipline*, Senge discusses the difficulties corporations have related to trend analysis, and how this threatens their survival. He believes that managers often are so concerned with individual events that they are precluded from recognizing longer-term patterns (or trends) of change that lie behind the events and from understanding the causes of the patterns. Senge uses the parable of the boiled frog to illustrate this lack of managerial self-control in being able to recognize and respond to gradual changes that often pose the greatest threats to survival:

> *If you place a frog in a pot of boiling water, it will immediately try to scramble out. But if you place the frog in room temperature water, and don't scare him, he'll stay put. Now, if the pot sits on a heat source, and if you gradually turn up the temperature, something very interesting happens. As the temperature rises from 70 to 80 degrees F, the frog will do nothing. In fact, he will show every sign of enjoying himself. As the temperature gradually increases, the frog will become groggier and groggier, until he is unable to climb out of the pot. Though there is nothing restraining him, the frog will sit there and boil. Why? Because the frog's internal apparatus for sensing threats to survival is geared to sudden changes in his environment, not to slow, gradual changes.*[8]

Senge then describes how the U.S. automobile industry succumbed to this phenomenon when it did not view Japanese automakers as a threat when the Japanese had less than 4 percent of the market. It was not until the 1980s that attention was given to the trend, which by then had reached a 20 percent market share—and the trend continued to increase, spreading to other Asian countries.

Another difficulty in trend analysis is that attempts to fix one problem often trigger another one. It is often difficult to identify this sort of pattern since consequences of an action are not immediately apparent and may only be visible in another part of the system.

Organizations should constantly be on the watch for both short- and long-term trends. Responses should be made according to company policy, objectives, and strategic plans. When the plan–do–check–act (PDCA) cycle is not executed at all levels within a company, nonsystemic and non-fact-based decision making occurs.

6. PROCESS VARIATION

> Analyze data to distinguish between common and special cause variation. (Analyze)
>
> Body of Knowledge IV.C.6

Variation is inherent; it exists in all things. No two entities in the world have exactly the same measurable characteristics. The variation might be small and unnoticeable without the aid of precise and discriminative measuring instruments, or it might be quite large and easily noticeable. Two entities might appear to have the same measurement because of the limitations of the measuring device.

Factors Affecting Variation

Everything is the result of some process, so the chance for some variation in output is built into every process. Because material inputs are the outputs of some prior process, they are subject to variation, and that variation is transferred to the outputs. Variation will exist even in apparently identical processes using seemingly identical resources. Even though a task is defined and performed in the same manner repeatedly, different operators performing the same task or the same operator performing the same task repeatedly introduce variation. The precision and resolution of the measuring devices and techniques used to collect data also introduce variation into the output data.

Variation can result from changes in various factors, normally classified as follows:

1. People (worker) influences

2. Machinery influences

3. Environmental factors

4. Material influences

5. Measurement influences

6. Method influences

The resulting total variation present in any product is a result of the variations in these six main sources. Because the ramifications of variation in quality are enormous for managers, knowing a process's capabilities (see Section 7) prior to production provides for better utilization of resources. Operating costs are reduced when inspection, rework, safety stock storage, and troubleshooting are eliminated. Proper management requires a deep appreciation of the existence of variation, as well as an understanding of its causes and how they can be corrected.

Types of Variation

Walter Shewhart, the father of modern quality control, was concerned with the low-cost reduction of variation. Shewhart distinguished two kinds of processes: (1) a stable process with "inevitable chance variation" and (2) an unstable process with "assignable cause variation." If the limits of process variation are well within the range of customer tolerance (specification), then the product can be made and shipped with reasonable assurance that the customer will be satisfied. If the limits of process variation just match the range of customer tolerance, then the process should be monitored closely and adjusted when necessary to maximize the amount of satisfactory output. If the limits of process variation extend beyond the range of customer tolerance, output should be inspected to determine whether it meets customer requirements.

When the amount of variation can be predicted with confidence, the process is said to be in a state of *statistical control* (*stable*). Although a singular value can not be predicted exactly, it can be anticipated to fall within certain limits. Similarly, the long-term average value can be predicted.

In an unstable process, every batch of product is a source of excitement! It is impossible to predict how much, if any, of the product will fall within the range of customer tolerance. The costs necessary to produce satisfactory product are unknown because the organization is forced to carry large quantities of safety stock, and bids for new work must include a safety factor.

Shewhart developed simple statistical and graphical tools to inform operators and managers about their processes and to detect promptly when a stable process becomes unstable and vice versa. These tools, called *control charts*, come in various forms depending on whether measures are attributes or variables, and whether samples are of constant size or not (see Section 2 on sampling and Section 3 on statistical process control). Deming also recognized Shewhart's two sources of variation, calling them *common causes* and *special causes*. He also distinguished between the duties of those who work in the process and the managers who work on the process.

Common Causes. Variation that is always present or inherent in a process is called *common cause variation*. It occurs when one or more of the six previously mentioned factors fluctuate within the normal or expected manner and the process can be improved only by changing a factor. Common causes of variation occur continually and result in controlled variation. They ensue, for example, from the choice of supplier, quality of inputs, worker hiring and training practices, equipment selection, machinery maintenance, and working conditions. If the process variation is excessive, then the process must be changed.

Eradicating these stable and predictable causes of variation is the responsibility of the managers of the process. Common causes are beyond the control of workers, as was demonstrated by Deming's famous red bead experiment.[9] In that experiment, volunteers were told to produce only white beads from a bowl containing a mixture of white and red beads. Monitoring or criticizing worker performance had no effect on the output. No matter what the workers did, they got some red beads (representing common cause variation)—sometimes more, sometimes less—but always some because the red beads were in the system.

Deming estimated that common causes account for 80 percent to 95 percent of workforce variation. This is not the fault of the workers, who normally do their best even in less-than-ideal circumstances. Rather, this is the responsibility of the managers, who work on, not in, the process.

Management decides how much money and time is to be spent on designing processes, which impacts the resources and methods that can be used. It is the design of the process that impacts the amount of common cause variation.

Special Causes. When variation of one or more factors is abnormal or unexpected, the resultant variation is known as *special cause variation*, or *assignable cause variation*. This unexpected level of variation that is observed in an unstable process is due to special causes that are not inherent in the process. Special causes of variation are usually local in time and space, for example, specific to a change in a particular machine or a difference in shift, operator, or weather condition. They appear in a detectable pattern and cause uncontrolled variation. Special causes of variation often result in sudden and extreme departures from the normal, but can also occur in the form of gradual shifts (or drifts) in a characteristic of a process. When a control chart shows a lack of control, skilled investigation should reveal what special causes are affecting the output. The workers in the process often have the detailed knowledge necessary to guide this investigation.

Structural Variation. Structural variation is inherent in the process;[10] however, when plotted on a control chart, structural variation looks like a special cause (blip), even though it is predictable. For example, a restaurant experiences a high number of errors in diners' orders taken on Saturday nights. The number of diners increases by 50 percent or more on every Saturday night, but they are served by the same number of waitpersons and chefs as on other nights.

Achieving Breakthrough Improvement

Building on Shewhart's notions of developing a systematic method for improvement, Juran distinguished between sporadic and chronic problems in *quality improvement projects* (QIPs). Starting from a state of chaos, a QIP should first seek to control variation by eliminating sporadic problems. When a state of controlled variation is reached, the QIP should then break through to higher levels of quality by eliminating chronic problems, thereby reducing the controlled variation. The notions of control and breakthrough are critical to Juran's thinking.

The following scenario demonstrates this concept: A dart player throws darts at two different targets. The darts on the first target are all fairly close to the bull's-eye, but the darts are scattered all over the target. It is difficult for the player to determine whether changing stance (or any other variable) will result in an improved score. The darts thrown at the second target are well off target from the bull's-eye, but the location of the darts is clustered and therefore predictable. When the player determines what variable is causing the darts to miss the bull's-eye, immediate and obvious improvement should result.

The impetus behind Juran's work was to achieve repeatable and predictable results. Until that happens, it will be almost impossible to determine whether a quality improvement effort has had any effect. Once a process is in control, breakthroughs are possible because they are detectable.

The following points are essential to an understanding of variation:

- Everything is the result or outcome of some process.

- Variation always exists, although it is sometimes too small to notice.

- Variation can be controlled if its causes are known. The causes should be determined through the practical experience of workers in the process as well as by the expertise of managers.

- Variation can result from special causes, common causes, or structural variation. Corrective action can not be taken unless the variation has been assigned to the proper type of cause. For example, in Deming's bead experiment (white beads = good product, red beads = bad product) the workers who deliver the red beads should not be blamed; the problem is the fault of the system that contains the red beads.

- Tampering by taking actions to compensate for variation within the control limits of a stable process increases rather than decreases variation.

- Practical tools exist to detect variation and to distinguish controlled from uncontrolled variation.

Variation exists everywhere (even the earth wobbles a bit in its daily rotation on its axis). So too, variation exists at an organizational level—within management's sphere of influence. The organization as a system is subject to common cause variation and special cause variation. Unfortunately, members of management in many organizations do not know about or understand the theory of variation. As a result of this, management tends to treat all anomalies as special causes and therefore treats actual common causes with continual tampering. Three examples follow:

- A donut shop, among its variety of products, produces jelly donuts. The fruit mix used to fill the jelly donuts is purchased from a longtime, reliable supplier. From time to time, a consumer complains about the tartness of the donut filling (nature produces berries of varying degrees of sweetness). The shop owner complains to the jelly supplier, who adds more sugar to the next batch (tampering). Several consumers complain about the overly sweet donut filling. The shop owner complains to the supplier, who reduces the amount of sugar in the next batch (tampering). More consumers complain about tartness, and so it goes. (Then there is the common example of an office building's occupants and their ongoing up-and-down interaction with the air conditioning and heating system.)

- Susan, a normally average salesperson, produces 10 percent fewer sales (number of sales, not dollar value) this month. The sales manager criticizes Susan for low sales production and threatens her with compensation loss. Susan responds with an extra effort to sell to anyone who will buy the service, regardless of the dollar volume of the sale (tampering). The sales manager criticizes Susan again, pointing out that dollar volume is more important than number of sales made. Susan concentrates on large-dollar buyers, which take several months to bring to fruition. Susan's monthly figures show a drastic drop and she is severely criticized for lack of productivity. Susan leaves the company and takes the large-dollar prospects with her to a competitor. The system failed due to tampering, but the worker was blamed.

- A VP of finance of a widely known charity continually tinkers with the organization's portfolio of investments, selling or buying whenever a slight deviation is noted, resulting in suboptimal yield from the portfolio.

An organization must focus its attempts at reducing variation. Variation does not need to be eliminated from everything; rather, the organization should focus on reducing variation in those areas most critical to meeting customers' requirements.

Six sigma is a term indicating the extent a process varies from being perfect. Six sigma is discussed in Chapter 13, Section 3.

7. PROCESS CAPABILITY

> Recognize process capability (C_p and C_{pk}) and performance indices (P_p and P_{pk}). (Understand)
>
> **Body of Knowledge IV.C.7**

Process capability is the range within which a process is normally able to operate given the inherent variation due to design and selection of materials, equipment, people, and process steps. Knowing the capability of a process means knowing whether a particular specification can be held *if* the process is in control.

If a process is in control (see control charts, Section 3) one can then calculate the process capability index. Several formulae are used to describe the capability of a process, comparing it to the specification limits; the two most popular indexes are C_p and C_{pk}. C_p indicates how the width of the process compares to the width of the specification range, while C_{pk} looks at whether the process is sufficiently centered in order to keep both tails from falling outside specification. Following are the formulae:

$$C_p = \frac{\text{Specification range}}{\text{Process range}} = \frac{\text{Upper spec} - \text{Lower spec}}{6\sigma}$$

$$C_{pk} = \frac{|\text{Upper spec} - \text{Average}|}{3\sigma} \ \text{(or)} \ \frac{|\text{Lower spec} - \text{Average}|}{3\sigma}, \ \text{whichever is smaller.}$$

Note that the sigma used for this calculation is not the standard deviation of a sample. It is the process sigma based on time-ordered data, such as given by the formula $R\text{-bar}/d_2$.

Initial process capability studies are often performed as part of the process validation stage of a new product launch. Since this is usually run on a smaller group of parts (a few hundred, or so), it does not include the normal variability that may be seen in full production, such as changes in material lots, operators, tooling changes, seasonality, and so on. In this case, this study is called a *potential process capability*, with the symbol C_{pk} used instead of P_{pk}. To compensate for the reduced variability at the initial analysis, the decision points are typically set at:

$C_{pk} > 1.67$ (capable)

$C_{pk} = 1.33 - 1.67$ (capable with tight control)

$C_{pk} < 1.33$ (not capable)

Capability is often studied soon after production release and again on an as-needed basis during normal production. The symbol P_{pk} is used instead of C_{pk}. *(In industry, though, the term C_{pk} may be used interchangeably by customers to denote both long- and short-term capability).* Changes to the process due to engineering changes or as part of continuous improvement should also be evaluated for their impact on process capability. Following are the rules often used to determine whether a long-term process is considered capable:

$$P_{pk} > 1.33 \text{ (capable)}$$

$$P_{pk} = 1.00 - 1.33 \text{ (capable with tight control)}$$

$$P_{pk} < 1.00 \text{ (not capable)}$$

Note that a long-term P_{pk} of 1.00-1.33 may not be satisfactory for a safety-based feature. If process capability is found to be unsatisfactory, the following may be considered:

- Ensure that the process is centered.

- Initiate process improvement projects to decrease variation.

- Determine if the specifications can be changed.

- Do nothing, but realize that a percentage of output will be outside acceptable variation.

When using statistical software programs to evaluate process capability, it is important that the user understand the specific terminology used by the programmers. Although the same concepts may be used, different symbols or formulae may be used.

8. RELIABILITY TERMINOLOGY

Define and describe basic reliability measures: mean time between failures (MTBF) and mean time to repair (MTTR). Understand the value of reliability for estimating the probability of being able to meet requirements or specifications, typically for a specific period of time. (Understand)

Body of Knowledge IV.C.8

Product Reliability

Reliability refers to the probability that a product can perform its required functions for a specified period of time under stated conditions. Consistent repeatability during the useful life of the product is the objective. Important concepts are:

- A product's failure conditions must be clearly stated, including its decreasing degree of performance over time.

- A time interval is specified using metrics such as hours, cycles, miles, and so on, in defining the life cycle of the product.

- Some products are for one-time use, such as the ignition device for a rocket. Such devices operate only when initiated or triggered, and are measured as *worked as planned* or *failed*.

Reliability engineers are concerned with how a product fails so they can compute, predict, and improve the product's reliability. One reliability model is referred to as the *bathtub curve* (also called *life-history curve* or *Weibull curve*) because graphically it resembles a bathtub (see Figure 15.7). Plotting the failure rate over the life cycle of a product (left to right), the stages are:

- *Infant mortality* (burn-in period). The failure rate decreases as the next stage is reached.

- *Random failure* (useful life period). Stable failure rate during normal use.

- *Wear-out.* The failure rate increases until the product is no longer useful as intended.

Some methods for consideration to reduce the burn-in period are:

- Stringent supplier certification

- Production and quality engineers participating in design reviews

- Appropriate acceptance sampling

- Application of process failure mode and effects analysis (PFMEA)

- Use of statistical process control methodology

- Application of design for manufacturability and assembly (DFMA)

A key point to consider is that the life cycle of the entire product is dependent on the failure of the weakest (most failure-prone) element or part within the product, for example, the material used, the process used, the robustness of the design,

Part IV.C.8

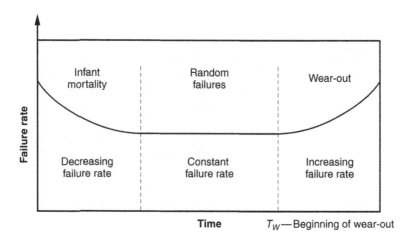

Figure 15.7   Bathtub curve.

or the unexpected, unintended improper use of the product by the buyer, the environment in which the product is used, or even regulatory restrictions not anticipated.

Mean Time to Failure (MTTF)

This is a basic measure of reliability for non-repairable product and is computed as the total number of delivered products divided by the total number of failures within a population receiving the product, during a discrete measurement interval and under stated conditions. MTTF should not be confused with MTBF.

Mean Time between Failures (MTBF)

This is a basic measure of reliability for repairable product and refers to the mean (average) number of products in which all elements or parts of the product perform within their specification limits during a discrete measurement interval under stated conditions.

Other Measures of Reliability

Maintainability is the ability of a product to be retained in, or restored to, a state in which it can meet the service or intent for which it was designed. The focus is on reducing the duration of downtime. Maintainability would be a factor to consider during the early stages of product development.

Mean time between maintenance actions (MTBMA) is a measure related to demand for maintenance personnel. It is computed as the total number of system product units divided by the total number of preventive and corrective maintenance actions during a stated time period.

Mean time to repair (MTTR) is another basic reliability measure. It is calculates by dividing the sum of corrective maintenance actions at any specific level of repair by the total number of failures within an item repaired at that level during a specific time interval under stated conditions.

Availability is the probability that a unit will be ready for use at a stated time, or over a stated time period, based on the combined aspects of reliability and maintainability. Three types of availability are identified:

1. *Inherent availability* is a function of reliability (MTBF) and maintainability (MTTR). To calculate inherent availability:

$$(A_I) = \text{MTBF}/(\text{MTBF} + \text{MTTR})$$

2. *Achieved availability* includes the measure of preventive and corrective maintenance. To calculate achieved availability:

$$(A_A) = \text{MTBMA}/(\text{MTBMA} + \text{MMT})$$

Where MMT = mean maintenance time = the sum of preventive and corrective maintenance times divided by the sum of scheduled and unscheduled maintenance events during a stated period of time.

3. *Operational availability* includes both the inherent and achieved availability and also logistics and administrative downtime. To calculate operational availability:

$$(A_O) = \text{MTBMA}/(\text{MBTMA} + \text{MDT})$$

Where MDT = mean maintenance downtime, which includes supply time, logistics time, administrative delays, active maintenance time, and so on.

Effective process management and continual improvement rely on data to help ensure that decisions are made based on facts rather than just opinions. Data on customer satisfaction, cost of quality, product quality levels, process capability, and many other performance measures are continually being gathered, analyzed, and reported in order to support quality planning, control, and improvement. Another level of quality is then also important—quality of the data being used to make decisions. Two specific measures of data quality are typically used: reliability and validity.

Reliability is a measure of the repeatability of the data. That is, if the same measurement were made over and over, would the same results be obtained? In the field of instrumentation this is called *precision* and reflects the amount of spread in the data if the same measurement is repeatedly made.

Validity is the accuracy of the data—how close it is, on average, to the real value. In instrumentation this is known as *accuracy*, or amount of inherent bias in the device. Figure 15.8 visually demonstrates the concepts of reliability and validity.

Reliability and validity can be impacted by the design of the measurement device (for example, how a survey question is written, what training is provided for interviewers, or how a piece of equipment used for physical measurement is handled), how the sample is chosen, and how the data are interpreted. For example, if an incorrect word is used in a questionnaire, the answers may be invalid. If a word is correct but does not mean the same thing to all respondents (or to different researchers), reliability will be impacted.

Part IV.C.8

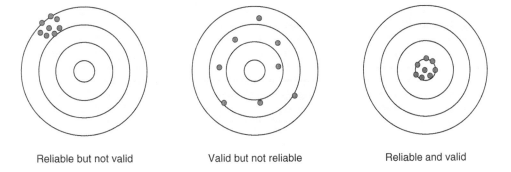

Reliable but not valid   Valid but not reliable   Reliable and valid

Figure 15.8   Reliability and validity.

When measuring validity, consider these issues:

- *Face.* An instrument may be said to have face validity to the extent that the distinctions it provides correspond with those that would be made by most observers without the aid of the instrument.

- *Criterion.* A criterion-related strategy looks at how well the performance of one measure can predict performance of a particular variable to be impacted. For example, if a written test on troubleshooting techniques is given to people who are studying to learn computer repair, how well do the results predict who is more likely to be able to solve real computer problems quickly? In this case the criterion for success is the ability to solve real problems, and if the written test is able to predict success, then it is considered a valid test.

- *Construct.* Construct-related validity also uses one variable to predict another, but does so using a pseudo variable (a construct one believes to be related) as the predictable variable. If a company wanted to measure the level of customer satisfaction by simply observing customers as they were shopping, they might choose to use how much customers smiled as they looked at products as a predictive measure of satisfaction. If they find that those who smiled more were, in fact, more satisfied with their shopping experiences (for example, based on a sample of shoppers who were both observed and interviewed), then *smiling* has construct validity. If, however, it was found to not be a good predictor, then it is not valid.

- *Content.* Content-related validity is concerned with how well a measure predicts the full range of performance measures for which it might be used. For example, the written troubleshooting test might be a valid predictor of whether the individual would be a good hardware troubleshooter, but not a valid predictor of their ability to correct software problems.

Reliability and validity are often controlled by using data collection devices that have already been proven instead of designing a new one. Contract test labs and firms that specialize in customer satisfaction measurement attest to the costs that can be incurred in developing new measurement systems. When it is necessary to develop a new measurement device, it must first be calibrated by comparing it to one of known reliability and validity.

9. QUALITATIVE ASSESSMENT

Identify subjective measures such as verbatim comments from customers, observation records, and focus group output. Describe how they differ from objective measures, and determine when measurements should be captured in categories rather than numeric values. (Analyze)

Body of Knowledge IV.C.9

Much of the information used by organizations to measure and track performance consists of quantitative data. Figures such as sales of a particular product, on-time delivery of suppliers, average length-of-stay in a hospital, or percentage of college entrants who graduate are easily measured or counted.

Qualitative information is also important for organizational decision making. Examples could be how satisfied customers are with a new product, employee opinion about the value of a new benefits package, or consistency of leadership practices with stated organizational principles. Qualitative data are expressed using words (opinions, beliefs, feelings, attitudes)—things that are not really measurable per se.

Qualitative data add complexity to the assessment process due to the subjectivity of what is being studied. What information can be gathered that will reflect the parameter(s) of interest? This is usually addressed by creating a series of questions to be answered, or by gathering information that is already available and grouping the findings into categories believed to be related to a question of interest.

Qualitative assessments are frequently conducted using one of the following techniques:

- Written surveys or questionnaires that are mailed (or e-mailed) to target groups or are available as part of a business interaction (for example, the feedback card at a restaurant table)

- One-on-one interviews (in person or by phone) or group interviews (focus groups)

- Observation of actual behaviors (for example, mystery shoppers who study how they are treated during transactions)

- Content analysis conducted by reviewing memos or other normal business processes to determine what events occur (or do not occur)

In order for qualitative data to be analyzed, they are usually gathered as or converted to a numeric format either by using frequencies of occurrence or through the use of scales (for example, a Likert-format scale including the categories *strongly agree, agree, neutral, disagree, strongly disagree*). If the information is narrative, it can be analyzed by looking for particular words, phrases, or contexts that occur repeatedly. The information can also be organized into an affinity diagram (see Chapter 13, Section 2) to help indicate common areas.

Qualitative data, when transformed through analysis into information, are used to examine the depth of motivations, values, attitudes, perceptions, and emotions. Quantitative data, in contrast, are better used for developing information about the breadth of information—how many and how much. See Chapter 17, Section 2, for the use of qualitative assessments relative to customer satisfaction and loyalty.

Survey Analysis and Use

Surveys typically require a significant investment of time and resources, but if effectively analyzed and used, can drive and monitor continual improvement efforts. Following are suggested actions:

1. Analyze the raw data:

   - Compute average, range, and standard deviation for each question and for each category/topic for which questions were designed to study. Where there are large ranges, go back and review the raw data and the data entry process to check for errors.

   - Rank the findings (answers to questions) in order of high to low outcomes. What does this say about particular topics?

   - Look for correlation between questions. Do multiple questions designed to assess the same topic agree or disagree?

   - Segregate the data based on demographic, market, or other groups within the study population. Look for differences based on product line, geographic location, and so on.

2. Compare the data to other information:

   - Compare findings to those of previous surveys. Does it show expected/desired changes? If not, why?

   - Compare findings to other internal and external data. Do they agree, or do anomalies exist that should be further investigated?

3. Communicate the information to decision makers:

   - Give the data to those who had originally planned to use it. Also consider openly sharing the findings with others who may be able to learn from them. (Caution: This sharing may exclude competitors.)

   - Do not be selective in communicating the information. Do not hide findings where results were undesired or are uncomfortable to deal with.

4. Use the information and verify results:

   - Where significant needs or opportunities for improvement are indicated, find ways to confirm understanding or get more detailed information to guide changes.

   - Do a follow-up survey after improvements have been implemented to determine how effective they have been.

ENDNOTES

1. W. E. Deming, *The New Economics* (Cambridge, MA: MIT Center for Advanced Educational Services, 1994), Chapter 17.
2. J. M. Juran and F. M. Gryna, eds., *Juran's Quality Control Handbook*, 4th ed. (New York: McGraw-Hill, 1988), 6.19, 6.32.
3. ASQ Quality Management Division, *Principles of Quality Costs: Financial Measures for Strategic Implementation of Quality Management*, 4th ed., ed. D. Wood (Milwaukee: ASQ Quality Press, 2013).
4. Juran and Gryna, *Quality Control Handbook*, 8.11.

5. Ibid.

6. ASQ Quality Management Division, *Quality Costs*, 28.

7. Ibid.

8. P. Senge, *The Fifth Discipline: The Art & Practice of the Learning Organization* (New York: Doubleday, 1990), 22.

9. W. E. Deming, *Out of the Crisis* (Cambridge, MA: MIT Center for Advanced Educational Services, 1986).

10. ASQ Statistics Division, *Improving Performance Through Statistical Thinking* (Milwaukee: ASQ Quality Press, 2000).

See Appendix A for additional references for this chapter.

Part IV.C.9

Part V

Customer-Focused Organizations

There is only one boss—the customer. And he can fire everybody in the company—from the chairman on down—simply by spending his money somewhere else.

—Sam Walton

Marketing and customer service research studies have shown that it is more cost-effective to win and keep a customer than to move through a customer life cycle of acquiring, losing, and reacquiring a customer. Hence, the emphasis here on the importance of becoming a customer-focused organization.

—ASQ's Certified Manager of Quality/
Organizational Excellence Program

Real profits are generated by loyal customers—not just satisfied customers.

—Rafael Aguayo

When a customer complains, consider getting down on your knees to offer profuse gratitude because that person has just provided you with priceless advice—free of charge.

—Owen Harari

Part V

Chapter 16

A. Customer Identification and Segmentation

Virtually all quality management approaches focus on the customer. The first step in all quality planning is the identification of customers. Correctly identifying customers is essential because all activities are based on the fulfillment of customers' needs or requirements. Today, most quality professionals consider the customer to be any individual or group that receives and must be satisfied with the service, work product, or output of a process. In other words, the customer is the individual or group whose requirements a process is intended to fulfill. This, however, is a fairly narrow definition of the term. Gryna broadly describes a customer as "anyone who is affected by the product or process."[1] Clearly, this definition includes more than just those who receive the output of a process.

The quality professional must realize that a process and its output touch many people both within and beyond organizational boundaries. Whether or not an organization's definition of *customer* encompasses all stakeholder groups, it is important to recognize that all of them might have requirements to be satisfied.

Overview of Customer Types

Harrington, in *Business Process Improvement*, discussed five types of customers.[2] Other types have also been identified. Customers can be in more than one of these categories:

- *Primary customer.* A primary customer is the individual or group who directly receives the output of a process. For a bank loan officer, the primary customer is the individual or organization that is requesting a loan. For a test laboratory, it is the individual or department who needs the requested test results in order to make a decision. The primary customer is a major source of product and process requirements, and is sometimes referred to as a *direct customer.*

- *Secondary customer.* Secondary customers are those individuals or groups from outside of the process boundaries who also receive process output, but who are not the reason for the process's existence. For example, a business process that produces invoices for an organization's primary customer might also send copies of those invoices to an internal department for sales analysis and reporting. In this case, the internal department is a secondary customer.

- *Indirect customer.* Like secondary customers, indirect customers are within the organizational boundaries. They do not receive process output directly, but are affected if the process output is incorrect or late. The output passes through other steps before leaving the organization. For example, the delivery function of a wholesale grocery distributor is not the final user of the grocery order, but is still affected if the packed order is late in arriving on the shipping dock and delivery is delayed.

- *External customer.* External customers are located outside the organizational boundaries and receive the end product or service, but might not be the actual user. For example, an award-winning company makes power supplies for computers, copiers, and other business machines. The company's external customers are companies such as computer equipment and camera manufacturers; however, these customers are not the final users of the power supplies.

- *Consumer/end user.* Consumers, also called *end users*, are the final users of a product or service. This term describes where a product or service is finally used or consumed. Sometimes the external customer and the end user are the same, but more often products and/or services are delivered to a distributor, representative, or retailer that sells the product to the consumer.

- *Intermediary.* An intermediary may exist to perform tasks not always visible to the consumer/end user, for example, the owner of the boxcar containing the consumer's product and the several different rail carriers that handle the boxcar during shipment.

- *False customer.* A false customer is an individual or group within a process that performs activities that do not add value to the product or service. Obviously, an objective of process improvement projects is to identify and eliminate as many false customers as possible. Examples of false customers include an inspector who monitors 100 percent of process output because of poor up-front quality planning, a manager who edits all memos written by all of his or her employees before they can be distributed, and a process or business function that can not identify its customer. "If a function or process does not seem to have a real customer, then that function should be reevaluated. The function may be unnecessary, or it may simply be part of a larger process."[3] When a function does not add value, it should be eliminated unless mandated.

- *Internal customer.* The term *internal customer* has come into popular use to generally refer to individuals or groups within a process who are inside the organizational boundaries. It is used to refer to the idea that everyone who works in a process has a customer and that their objective is to identify and meet their internal customer's requirements. This concept has value in process management; however, some companies have discovered that the term often lessens the focus on the external customer and consumer. To avoid confusion and ensure a customer focus, one company refers to these individuals or groups as *process partners*. Others refer to *service providers* and *service receivers*. A company that chooses to use the internal customer label must be sure that all employees recognize that the company's ultimate responsibility and the intent of the process is to serve the external customer.

Part V.A

Importance of Identifying Customer Types

There are a number of reasons for knowing an organization's customer types:

1. Identifying and defining customer types is an important part of service and process management and improvement:

   - Defining a process through documentation and process mapping requires that process owners and improvement teams identify every customer type and source of process and service/product requirements.

   - Measuring service/process effectiveness also requires customer input.

2. Generally, customer satisfaction research is performed among the end users of an organization's products or services.

3. When an organization performs market research, it should look beyond its current customers. Surveying lost customers, prospective customers, and competitors' customers can also provide useful insights as to what satisfies customers. Such research can also provide information as to what new or improved products, services, or processes might fulfill the customer's requirements and result in satisfaction. Methods used to gather customer satisfaction data are discussed in Section 2.

Figure 16.1 depicts a greatly simplified hypothetical product/service flow, through several types of customers, for a consumer product sold via an internet web page:

- Consumer (external customer) accesses the web via an external provider.

- Consumer searches for desired product, accessing various product sellers.

- Consumer places the order electronically through selected seller's website.

- Seller places/forwards the order to the publisher. (Seller is external customer of publisher).

- Publisher notifies seller, who notifies consumer that order is confirmed.

- Publisher transmits pick order to warehouse (not shown), which picks product from shelf and sends to shipper. (Warehouse is internal customer of order service.)

- Shipper delivers product to consumer. (Shipper is an intermediate customer of warehouse; consumer is an external customer of shipper.)

- Warehouse notifies billing. (Billing is an internal customer of warehouse.)

- Billing bills consumer. (Consumer is external customer of billing.)

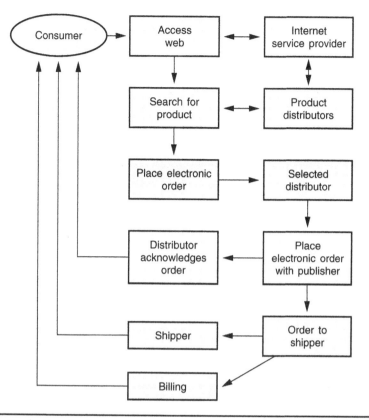

Figure 16.1   Product/service flow.

1. INTERNAL CUSTOMERS

> Define and describe the impact an organization's treatment of internal customers will have on external customers. Develop methods for energizing internal customers to improve products, processes, and services and evaluate the results. (Evaluate)
>
> **Body of Knowledge V.A.1**

Internal customers are found within an organization. Who are they? How can an organization work with internal customers to effectively improve processes and services? How does an organization's treatment of its internal customers influence its processes for external customers?

Bhote discusses the term *next operation as customer*.[4] Every function and work group in an organization is both a receiver of services and/or products from internal and/or external sources as well as a provider of services and/or products to internal and/or external customers. These interfaces between provider and receiver may be one to one, one to many, many to one, or many to many. Each receiver has needs and requirements. Whether the delivered service or product meets these needs/requirements impacts the customer's effectiveness and the quality of service/product to their customers, and so on. Examples include:

- If A delivers part X to B one hour late, B may have to apply extra effort and cost to make up the time, or else perpetuate the lateness in delivering to the next customer.

- Engineering designs a product based on the salesperson's understanding of the external customer's need. Production produces the product, expending material, personnel, and other costs. The external customer rejects the product because it fails to meet its needs. The provider reengineers the product; production makes a new one that the customer accepts, late. Possibly the last order from this customer.

- Computer services delivers copies of a production cost report (average of 50 pages of fine print per week) to six internal customers. Computer services has established elaborate quality control of the accuracy, timeliness, and physical quality of the report. Of the six report receivers, however, only two need information of this type any longer. Neither of these two find the report directly usable for their current needs. Each has assigned clerical people to manually extract pertinent data for their specific use. All six receivers admit diligently storing the reports for the prescribed retention period.

- Production tickets, computer-printed on light card stock, are attached by removable tape to each module. When the module reaches the paint shop, it is given an acid bath, a rinse, high-temperature drying, painting, and high-temperature baking. Very few tickets survive intact and readable. The operation following the paint shop requires attaching other parts to the painted modules, depending on information contained on the ticket. Operators depend on their experience to guess which goes with what. Ninety-five percent emerge from this process correctly, a lower percentage when variations go down the line or when an experienced operator is absent.

In order to improve internal processes and services, the approach is to:

1. Identify internal customer interfaces (providers of services/products and receivers of their services/products).

2. Establish internal customers' service/product needs/requirements.

3. Perform a gap assessment to identify areas for improvement.

4. Set improvement objectives and measurements.

5. Modify processes where needed.

6. Implement systems for tracking and reporting performance and for supporting the continual improvement of the process.

7. Document *quality-level agreements* between provider and receiver.

Quality-Level Agreements

Quality-level agreements (QLAs), also called *service-level agreements*, can be implemented on a gradual basis, starting with the most critical deliverables first.[5] QLAs aid employees' understanding and recognition of the importance of internal customer/receiver requirements, from the receiver's perspective. Employees can also gain insights into the potential impact of their contribution on the business process in which they play a part. QLAs and the documented performance achieved show the objective evidence that providers comply with their receiver/customer requirements, thus linking internal product/service quality with the quality management system, and ultimately with external customers' requirements. QLAs provide a natural extension of documented quality management systems by providing the basis for working-level performance measurement and review, leading to continuous improvement. QLA content data will vary according to the needs of the providers and receivers of the products/services and their organization.

Initiating QLAs increases understanding and collaboration between providers and receivers. A QLA should remove all doubt as to what a receiver expects from a service or product received from their provider. It should eliminate needless controversy and confusion if expectations are not met. The QLA can offer a sound basis for performance measurement, evaluation, and continual improvement. A QLA deploys the voice of the internal customer. Figure 16.2 is a sample QLA.

Three Timely Tenets

1. Basically, valid requirements for the service/product to be delivered by the providers are the requirements the receivers have provided, have agreed to, and that meet the receivers' needs.

2. A valid measurement of the quality of the service/product delivered is the level of the receiver's satisfaction.

3. All internal customer requirements must be consistent with the external customers' requirements.

How Treatment of Internal Customers Influences Processes for External Customers

Careless behavior of management (and management's systems) toward internal customers (for example, poor tools and equipment, defective and late material input from previous operations, incorrect/incomplete instructions, ineligible work orders or prints, circumvention of worker safety procedures and practices,

Part V.A.1

Panacea, Inc. Quality-Level Agreement		
Services/product receiver: Dept./function Contact name: Title: Contact no.		QLA no.: Original issue date: Date last revision: Current date:
Description of service/product:		Identifiers: Part nos.: External customer:
Specific requirements: 1 2 3 4		Measurements: 1 2 3 4
Conditions that may impact achieving agreed quality level:		Relative to requirement no.:
Report quality level agreement failure to: Name: Title: Contact no.:		Comments:
Agreed for receiver/customer: Name: Title: Contact no.:		Date: Signature: _____
Agreed for provider: Name: Title: Contact no.:		Date: Signature: _____
Approval (if required) for receiver/customer: Name: Title: Contact no.:		Date: Signature: _____
Approvel (if required) for provider: Name: Title: Contact no.:		Date: Signature: _____
This agreement relates to:		Procedure nos.: Work instruction nos.:

Figure 16.2   Quality–level agreement.

Source: Reprinted with permission of R. T. Westcott & Associates.

unhealthy work environment, disinterest in internal complaints, disregard for external customer feedback) may engender careless or indifferent treatment of external customers. Continued, this indifference could generate a downward spiral that can adversely affect an organization's outcomes. Ignoring regard for the needs of internal customers makes it very difficult to instill employees' intent to care for the needs of external customers.

So many organizations fail to learn, or may ignore, the internal customers' needs and wonder why their management's exhortations fail to stimulate internal customers to care about how and what they do for external customers. The surly and uncooperative sales representative, waitperson, housekeeping employee, delivery person, and customer service representative usually reflect lack of caring for internal customers behind the scenes.

Organizations must work constantly to eliminate the internal customers' lament: "How do you expect me to care about the next operator, or external customer, when no one cares whether I get what I need to do my job right?"

Methods to Energize Internal Customers

The organization should consider all or several of the following methods to energize internal customers to improve products, processes, and services:

- Ensure that all employees understand who the external customers are and what the customers need and want.

- Ensure that employees know what the organization expects of them and what boundaries pertain to what they can do to satisfy the external customer.

- Involve employees in designing and implementing strategies, procedures, and tools that will facilitate customer satisfaction.

- Ensure that employees have the information, training, time, and support they need to meet external customer needs, wants, and satisfaction.

- Ensure that employees have the tangible things they need to serve customers well, for example, supplies, tools, working equipment, clean work space, safe workplace, appropriate policies and procedures.

- Demonstrate through words and actions the commitment the organization has to serving its customer to the best extent possible.

- Ensure that the recognition and reward systems are supportive of the internal customer satisfaction focus.

- Provide positive reinforcement to employees who are, or are trying, to do their best to satisfy external customers.

- Provide employees with substantive performance feedback and assist in continual improvement.

Part V.A.1

2. EXTERNAL CUSTOMERS

> Define external customers and describe
> their impact on products and services.
> Develop strategies for working with them
> and integrating their requirements and needs
> to improve products, services, and processes.
> (Evaluate)
>
> **Body of Knowledge V.A.2**

Types of External Customers

The following is a list of many types of external customers and some of the influences these customers have on the products and services provided.

- *Wholesale buyer.* Wholesalers buy what they expect they can sell. They typically buy in large quantities. They may have little direct influence on the product design and manufacture, but do influence the providers' production schedules, pricing policies, warehousing and delivery arrangements, and return policies for unsold merchandise.

- *Distributor.* A distributor is similar to a wholesaler in some ways, but differs in the fact that they may stock a wider variety of products from a wide range of producers. What they stock is directly influenced by their consumers' demands and needs. Their customers' order quantities may often be small and for diverse products. The distributor's forte is stocking thousands of catalog items that can be picked and shipped on short notice at an attractive price. Distributors stocking commodity-type items (for example, sheet metal, construction materials, mineral products, stationery items, and so on) are mainly influenced by customers seeking an industry level of quality, at a good price, and immediately available. For example, to reduce the buyer's cost and enable the supplier's efficiency, orders for some types of materials might be for a yearly quantity delivered in partial shipments throughout the year (called *blanket orders*).

- *Retail chain buyer.* Buyers for large retail chains, because of the size of their orders, place major demands on their providers. For example, pricing concessions, very flexible deliveries, requirements that the provider assume warehousing costs for already purchased product, special packaging requirements, no-cost return policy, or a requirement that the provider be able to accept electronically sent orders.

- *Other volume buyers.* Government entities, educational institutions, healthcare organizations, transportation companies, cruise lines, hotel chains, and restaurant chains all represent large-volume buyers who provide services to customers. Each of these organizations has regulations governing their services. Each requires a wide range of products, material, and external services in delivering their services, much of which is transparent to the consumer. Each requires high quality, and each has tight limitations on what they can pay (for example, based on appropriations, cost-control mandates, tariffs, heavy competition). Each such buyer demands much for their dollar, but may offer long-term contracts for fixed quantities. The influences on products required are frequently generated by the buyer organizations' internal customers. Inasmuch as price and delivery are often the prevailing considerations, feedback to the providers relative to end user satisfaction with the products or services delivered, if feedback is available at all, travels a slow and convoluted path.

• *Service providers.* The diversity of service providers buying products and services from other providers is mind-boggling. These buyers include the plumber, public accountant, dentist, doctor, building contractor, cleaning service, computer programmer, website designer, consultant, manufacturer's rep, actor, and taxi driver. This type of buyer, often self-employed, buys very small quantities, shops for value, buys only when product or service is needed, and relies on high quality of purchases to maintain its customer's satisfaction. Influences on products or services from providers to this type of buyer range from being able to furnish service and/or replacement parts for old or obsolete equipment, or being able to supply extremely small quantities of an extremely large number of products (for example, such as supplied by a hardware store, construction materials depot, medical products supply house, and so on), to having product knowledge that extends to knowing how the product is best used.

• *Retail buyer.* The retail buyer influences the design and usability of product features and accessories based on volume purchased. Consumer product watch organizations warn purchasers of potential problems. (For example, in the late 1990s a fake fat substance was introduced in a number of food products as a boon to health-conscious people. These products didn't taste good and were found to have harmful side effects. Many buyers stopped buying those products.) Features important to these buyers, depending on type of product, are reasonable price, ease of use, performance, safety, aesthetics, and durability. Other influences on product offerings include installation, instructions for use, post-purchase service, warranty period, packaging, and brand name.

• *Discount buyer.* The discount buyer shops primarily for price, is more willing to accept less well-known brands, and is willing to buy quantities in excess of immediate needs. These buyers have relatively little influence on the products, except for, perhaps, creating a market for off-brands, production surpluses, and discontinued items.

• *Employee buyer.* The employee buyer purchases their employer's products, usually at a deep discount. Often being familiar with, or actually a contributor to the products bought, this buyer can provide valuable feedback to the employer (directly through surveys, indirectly through volume and items purchased). A useful question is, "Would the salespersons who sell an organization's product buy and use it themselves?"

• *Service buyer.* The buyer of services (for example, TV repair, dental work, tax preparation) often buys by word of mouth. Word of good or poor service spreads rapidly and influences the continuance of the service provider's business.

Organizations have created lists, accessed through a website, to furnish feedback from former service buyers to prospective service buyers to help guide them in their selection of a service provider.

• *Service user.* A captive service user (electricity, gas, water, municipal services, schools) generally has little influence as to from whom it receives services. In recent times, more choices are available, but customers are still limited to a small number of providers. Until more competition is introduced, there is little incentive to providers to vary their services.

• *Organization buyer.* Buyers for organizations that use a product or service in the course of their business or activity can have a significant influence on the types of products offered them, as well as the organization from which they buy. Raw materials or devices that become a part of a manufactured product are especially critical in sustaining quality and competitiveness for the buyer's organization (for example, performance, serviceability, price, ease of use, durability, simplicity of design, safety, and ease of disposal). Other factors include flexibility in delivery, discounts, allowances for returned material, and extraordinary guarantees.

Factors that particularly pertain to purchased services include reputation and credibility of provider, range of services offered, degree of customization offered, timeliness, and fee structure.

3. CUSTOMER SEGMENTATION

> Define and describe the process of customer segmentation and its impact on aligning service and delivery to meet customer needs. (Evaluate)
>
> **Body of Knowledge V.A.3**

The Shift to Customer Segmentation

One key legacy of the industrial age was the trend of mass production. Henry Ford said the following about the people waiting to buy his company's Model T's: "Any customer can have a car painted any color that he wants so long as it is black." In reality, not every customer would have wanted to purchase a black car, but this was the only choice, given Ford's initial concept of mass production (and the fact that black paint was the only color that would dry fast enough). For many decades the idea of mass production was associated with the concept of mass markets.

Market segmentation has its roots in the marketing concept, generally attributed to Philip Kotler. The basic premise of the marketing concept is that a company should determine what consumers need and want, and then try to satisfy those wants and needs, provided that (1) doing so is consistent with the company's, strategy and (2) the expected rate of return meets company objectives.[6] By encouraging organizations to structure products and services around customer needs and wants rather than being driven strictly by technological capability, organizations move from a product-driven approach toward a market- or customer-driven emphasis.

Alvin and Heidi Toffler offer clues on trends relating to mass production, mass markets, and the changing workplace. They used the term *demassification* to describe these changes, including a trend where organizations' homogeneous customer groups begin to splinter into many groups with unique needs and expectations.[7] In his keynote address at the 50th Annual Quality Congress in 1996, Alvin Toffler used the term *mass customization* to further characterize this trend, suggesting that nearly every customer has unique requirements that product and service providers need to address on a customer-by-customer basis.

The implication of such a trend is staggering for many organizations, especially in view of their current practices used to serve their customers. Organizations that surpass competitors in serving key market segments should find themselves in a commanding position in the marketplace. The challenge to an organization is to clearly know its customers and their unique requirements and expectations. This new way of thinking has come to be known as *customer relationship management* (CRM) or *one-to-one marketing*.

"The biggest single barrier to the development of an effective corporate strategy is the strongly held belief that a company has to appeal to the entire market."[8] Organizations can often realize more efficient returns on their marketing resources when they narrow the scope of their focus. This section discusses some of the ways to identify and segment particular customers or markets.

Customer Segmentation

The identification of customers is straightforward for some organizations and very difficult in others. When the supplier and customer have a direct relationship, identifying customers and their requirements is a relatively simple task. For example, new car dealers have detailed information on the purchasers of new cars and frequently provide post-purchase service and support. When the supplier and end user never come into direct contact, however, it is much more difficult for the product or service provider to identify the customer and his or her unique needs. For example, manufacturers of consumer products distributed through various retail outlets rarely have detailed information about end users unless these customers return warranty registration cards, submit complaints, or respond to special offers. In any case, the product or service provider might speculate on the requirements of the key customer segment(s) served, but knowing the actual identity of the customer (as in the case of the automobile dealership) enables the provider to collect information and make special offers to that customer or customer segment.

An organization must be able to meet or exceed the needs of key customers or customer groups. If product features and service delivery processes are designed to satisfy needs and expectations of one homogeneous group, some customer groups will be satisfied; however, many other groups may be very disappointed. An organization that neglects to explore the ways in which customer needs or wants vary across market segments misses an opportunity to maximize customer satisfaction in segments vital to the organization's well-being. Scarce service delivery resources might be allocated in a manner that maximizes satisfaction among the key business segments once the needs and expectations of these core customer groups are determined.

Core/key customers typically are those customers most vital to the organization's economic success. These can be high-volume customers, customers from selected industries, customers with the greatest impact on the organization's profitability, or customers deemed most likely to have significant impact on the firm's future viability.

A company can identify its core customers by doing a detailed analysis of their financial performance, as well as by creating a possible scenario for the future to decide whether they really are key customers. Core customers are often willing and eager to enter into partnerships or other forms of strategic alliances with a business so that both companies can grow and be more profitable.

Noncore customers may or may not have requirements unique from those of core customers. Whether an organization chooses to serve these customers should be contingent on an evaluation of the cost of service versus the economic benefit. Cost of service can vary depending on whether the same service delivery process (resources) is used for both core and noncore customer segments, and on whether the noncore segment requires or justifies its own service delivery system.

Potential customers are not currently on the customer list, but could use the product or service offered. A strategy to reach appropriate segments of potential customers needs to be developed and implemented as the business grows.

The Process of Segmenting Customers

The term *market segments* refers to the concept that there are groups of potential customers sharing particular wants or needs (rather than simply one large homogeneous market) and that these groups are objectively identifiable.[9]

Segmentation differentiating factors can be considered in creating customer or market segments. Examples of some commonly used differentiators are:

- *Purchase volume.* Some organizations split their customer base into two or more groupings on the basis of volume. High-volume customers are often thought of as core customers, and might account for only 10 percent of the customer base, but as much as 90 percent of the total business volume.

- *Profitability.* Profitability segmentation can yield different results than volume segmentation. The key distinction is that the criteria would be based on the profit from customer segments rather than on purchase volume.

- *Industry.* One common basis of segmentation in business-to-business markets is identifying that customers from different industries have unique requirements that determine the value they receive from products and services. For example, customers in the energy utility business might differ from customers buying from organizations offering products on the internet in terms of their requirements for telecommunications services.

- *Type of organization.* Segments could include: original equipment manufacturer (OEM), distributor, retailer, wholesaler, repackager, and so on.

- *Purchasing organizations' size.* Size of the buyers may be a useful segmentation strategy for some organizations.

- *Type of purchases made.* Segmentation could include raw materials for conversion into product, facility maintenance supplies, calibration services, hazardous waste disposal services, and so on.

- *Buyers' organizational structure.* Differentiating by type of organizational structure, such as sole proprietorship, partnership, corporation, and joint venture, may constitute a useful segmentation strategy.

- *Geographic.* Customers and markets are often segmented geographically, but usually this is a method of allocating resources (for example, sales and field support) to a region rather than being driven by unique customer requirements. An exception would be when buying habits for certain types of products or services differ by geographic region (for example, due to a predominant culture).

- *Demographic.* Examples of demographic-based segments include groupings based on any combination of factors such as age, income, marital status, education, and gender. Sometimes, demographic characteristics are combined. For example, family life cycle usually combines head-of-household age, marital status, and a factor indicating both the presence and the ages of children living at home to determine a resulting segment. Some of the unique resulting segments include single adult head of household, young married couples with no children, households with young children, households with teenagers, same-sex partners, empty nest (working age, but children have left home), and retired. Marketers have long used these kinds of segments to identify and characterize key target markets. Certain products/services (for example, diapers and educational software) appeal to or are best suited for one or more demographic segments.

- *Psychographic.* Segmentation leads to groupings based on values, attitudes, and beliefs. Insurance marketers might want to target consumers with a balanced, healthy lifestyle as manifested by attitudes. For example, a key target segment might include individuals who believe that smoking is unhealthy and that a good diet, a regular exercise regimen, and getting plenty of rest are all important. Strong religious beliefs of a group could identify a segment.

- *Language spoken.* Segmentation groups customers into clusters based on the buyers' language in common use. Care must be taken that the data for making this determination are factual. For example, it would not be useful to presume that every customer with a Spanish-sounding or -spelled name speaks Spanish and others do not.

- *Decision maker.* Segmentation requires factual data that identify the decision maker in a purchase. This means that other data that are pertinent are correctly linked with the decision maker.

- *Occasion for purchase.* Segmenting customers by the event or reason for the purchase and for whom the purchased product or service is intended.

Part V.A.3

- *Potential or past customers.* This can constitute a segment, providing the data are available. Data for the potential customers would be drawn from outside the organization's customer database. Data for past customers may still reside in the customer database or in archived files.

Segmentation Concepts

Key segmentation concepts are depicted in Figure 16.3.[10] These concepts are:

- *No segmentation.* In Figure 16.3a customers are completely undifferentiated; all customers are perceived as having the same expectations. Uniform quality is the goal, and mass marketing is used.

- *Complete market segmentation.* Each customer in Figure 16.3b has a unique set of requirements. The quality requirements are set by each customer's individual demands, and customized marketing is used.

- *Segmentation by a single criterion.* Figures 16.3c and 16.3d show segmentation based on a single differentiating factor (income or age). Each distinct class requires a different marketing approach, and quality requirements may differ for each class.

- *Segmentation by multiple criteria.* Two differentiating factors (income and age) are used in Figure 16.3e. Customers are classified according to both factors. Marketing strategy and quality requirements can vary for each class identified.

a. No market segmentation   b. Complete market segmentation

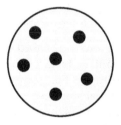 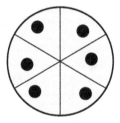

c. Segmented by income   d. Segmented by age classes   e. Segmented by income–
classes 1, 2, and 3   A and B   age class

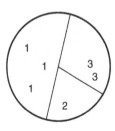 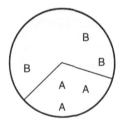 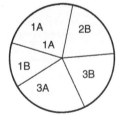

Figure 16.3   Preference segment patterns.

- *Patterns of segmentation.* Customers are often segmented by demographic (for example, age and income) or psychographic (lifestyle and attitudes) criteria, but segmentation by product attributes is especially helpful to quality managers. Customers' likes and dislikes indicate their preferences. Three broad preference patterns are shown in Figure 16.4.

- *Homogeneous preferences.* Customers with homogeneous preferences have roughly the same preferences. In Figure 16.4 (left) the two product attributes (quality and price) graphed do not appear to cause a natural segmentation. Competing brands are likely to be similar and located near the center.

- *Diffused preferences.* In Figure 16.4 (middle) no natural segments exist, but customer preferences vary greatly. Competitors would be expected to offer dissimilar products in response to customer preferences.

- *Clustered preferences.* Natural market segmentation occurs in Figure 16.4 (right). Distinct preference clusters exist, and competing products are expected to be dissimilar between clusters and similar within clusters.

Market segmentation must be based on sound statistical techniques that ensure that samples taken represent the market as a whole, as well as the individual segment being studied. This aids in the identification of key segments of potential customers. *Cluster analysis* is a multivariate technique that creates groupings on the basis of minimizing variation within groups and maximizing variation between groups, according to a list of variables or criteria. *Factor analysis* is sometimes used to map the perceptual space of customer needs and wants for a market for a particular good or service. Used together, the resulting perceptual maps identify both the location of segments and the market perceptions of competitors in meeting key needs and wants. For example, creation of multiple fragrances of

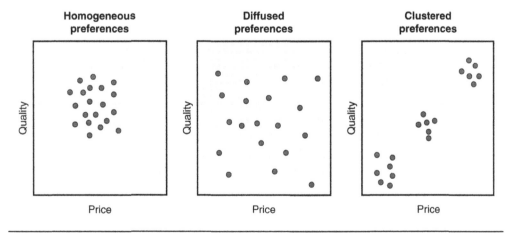

Figure 16.4   Segmentation concepts.

Part V.A.3

cleaning products was based on research that identified market segments with the requirement of something other than lemon or pine fragrances for cleaning products. As none of the existing brands were positioned to meet these requirements, fragrances such as Sea Breeze, Spring Rain, and Mountain Fresh were created and marketed specifically to meet those needs.

To aid in discerning discrete customer patterns, population mapping using geographic information systems (GIS) is frequently used (see Chapter 15, Section 5). Uncovering relationships from a vast amount of customer data is the aim of data mining the customer database (see Chapter 15, Section 5).

Choosing a Segmentation Strategy

Identifying customers and providing benefits targeted to meet or exceed their unique requirements is a prescription leading to extraordinary levels of customer satisfaction, loyalty, and profitability. The principal reasoning behind this axiom is that a market includes individuals and organizations from all circumstances. If all individuals and organizations had the same needs and expectations, it would be easy to standardize product features and service delivery processes to maximize the value that each desired.

In reality, however, the marketplace is far more complex. Many subsets of customer needs and requirements (segments) exist. An organization attempting to appeal to the needs of everyone in the market might actually fail to deliver the value expected by any of its segments. The key is to identify the segment(s) that should be the strategic focus of the organization. High rates of market segment penetration are likely when product features and service processes are in alignment with customer requirements.

Best practices in customer identification and segmentation include the following:

- Creating and maintaining a customer information system to provide data on customer identity, potential segmentation criteria, and, if possible, data on customer needs and requirements. If a comprehensive customer database is not feasible, market research can be used to characterize customer segments.

- Using SWOT analysis (see Chapter 6, Section 1) as a preliminary indication of competitive position. Segmentation strategies that offer the most leverage for building on current strengths and minimizing current weaknesses should be explored.

- Using customer and market surveys to evaluate customer and market perceptions of the organization and compare these perceptions to those held toward others in the business. This information can be used to identify current position (in the minds of both customers and noncustomers) relative to current and potential market opportunities.

- Choosing a segmentation strategy that fits the organization's strategic intent in the context of opportunity. Segmentation can be integrated into strategic planning, marketing planning, and quality and service process improvement plans.

An organization's marketing strategy must take into consideration whether the organization is interested most in pursuing more customers or in targeting the right customers. Effectively targeting a market requires a clear understanding of the current customer strata and how each contributes to revenue and profit. Anthony suggests a focused approach for developing the right customers:

- Direct the marketing efforts precisely (focus to avoid undisciplined expansion).

- Tailor marketing plans/campaigns (and service delivery processes) to meet the needs of core customer segments. This translates into properly allocating marketing resources across segments, as underfunding efforts directed at core segments could result in lost opportunities.

- Use appropriate marketing performance indicators to monitor and guide the relative success of segmentation initiatives. Move away from indicators such as number of customers and gross sales in favor of cost of sales, cost of retention (a cost-of-quality component), potential for expansion, and customer profit contribution.[11]

Considerations for effective customer identification and segmentation are:

- Make the effort to identify customers.

- If an organization sells through wholesalers and retailers and has no idea of the identity of its customers, it can build a segmented customer database through product registrations and warranty work, or conducting market research.

- When an organization believes it knows its customers, the evidence might be anecdotal and unsupported by hard data. Effective segmentation requires metrics to classify customers into groups, as well as to evaluate their value to the organization (for example, sales revenue and profit contribution).

- A segmentation initiative generally emanates from the marketing side of the organization, supported by the organization's strategy. However, stakeholders in quality and operations planning need to integrate the thinking and systems of the organization to align service delivery processes and quality with the customer requirements dictated by the segmentation strategy.

There are some cautions when following a segmentation strategy. For example, be careful that the segmentation strategy is not actually a ruse, or can be misinterpreted as such, for example, charging a higher late-payment fee to delinquent buyers from low-income families. And, if using segmentation concepts and practices with internal customers, be mindful of any potential for violating a management–labor contract in effect, for example, arbitrarily tailoring employee benefits according to employee gender, age, or other demographic or psychographic factor.

When an organization adopts a segmentation strategy, it is tempting to optimize the service delivery system to maximize customer satisfaction for the core customers or the strategically most significant segment. Sometimes a separate service delivery process is created to serve noncore segments. This may entail duplication of whole systems internally, for example, call centers, distribution facilities, and staff functions such as sales, technical support, and installation and repair personnel.

Process for Working with External Customers

The following process is an approach to working with external customers to improve products, services, and internal processes:

1. Identify who the customers are:

   - Define and prioritize the customer segments the organization serves.

   - Determine whether the types of customers served represent the right segment mix to support the organization's strategic objectives.

   - Conduct a gap analysis to highlight types of customer segments that should be added, phased out, or realigned to meet strategic objectives.

2. What do the customers in the key segments to be served need/want?

   - Use techniques and tools to capture the voices of the key customer segments (see Chapter 17, Section 1).

   - Conduct a gap analysis to identify opportunities for adding to, discontinuing, or modifying the present product and service portfolio.

3. What internal processes would need change?

   - Examine internal processes for their capability to meet the new needs resulting from the two gap analyses.

   - Perform a feasibility study of each recommended change.

   - Perform a risk analysis of each recommended change.

4. Establish action plans and implement the feasible changes to internal processes.

5. Test-market the changes and make necessary corrections.

6. Roll out the full-scale changes.

7. Evaluate the effectiveness of implemented changes.

ENDNOTES

1. F. M. Gryna, "Market Research and Marketing," in *Juran's Quality Handbook*, 5th ed., ed. J. M. Juran and A. B. Godfrey (New York: McGraw-Hill, 1999), 18.11.

2. H. J. Harrington, *Business Process Improvement: The Breakthrough Strategy for Total Quality, Productivity, and Competitiveness* (New York: McGraw-Hill, 1991).
3. J. L. Hradesky, *Total Quality Management Handbook* (New York: McGraw-Hill, 1995), 29.
4. K. R. Bhote, *Strategic Supply Management* (New York: AMACOM, 1989).
5. R. T. Westcott, "Quality-Level Agreements for Clarity of Expectations," *The Informed Outlook* (December 1999): 13–15.
6. T. Levitt, *The Marketing Imagination* (New York: The Free Press, 1983), 216–17.
7. A. Toffler and H. Toffler, *Powershift: Knowledge, Wealth, and Violence at the Edge of the 21st Century* (New York: Bantam, 1990).
8. A. Ries, *Focus: The Future of Your Company Depends on It* (New York: HarperCollins, 1996), 128.
9. Levitt, *Marketing Imagination*, 217.
10. T. J. Pyzdek, *The Complete Guide to the CQM* (Tucson: Quality Publishing, 1996), 299–302.
11. M. Anthony, "More Customers or Right Customers: Your Choice," *Marketing News* (August 31, 1998): 13.

See Appendix A for additional references for this chapter.

Part V.A.3

Chapter 17

B. Customer Relationship Management

C hapter 16 defined types of customers. This chapter focuses on the most important customer type, the primary customers. The *primary customer* is almost always an external customer and is frequently the consumer, or end user, of the organization's product or service.

Defining Customer Focus

Organizations that recognize the importance of customers and focus on their wants and needs are commonly referred to as being *customer focused* or *customer driven*. In business literature, the terms *customer driven* and *market driven* are often used interchangeably; however, a customer-driven organization focuses more on the care and retention of existing customers, whereas the market-driven organization is more attuned to attracting new customers.

In best-in-class organizations, virtually every activity is undertaken with the customers' interests in mind. Note that this does not imply that an organization should do so at a financial loss. Organizations that are not profitable ultimately cease to do business.

Many customers express requirements in value terms—the components that influence the buy decision, for example, price, product quality, innovation, service quality, provider's image, and reputation.

Managing Customer Relationships

Customer relationships, in their most advanced form, become supplier–customer partnerships or alliances (see Chapter 18). Although partnerships or alliances are not always the ultimate objective of a customer relationship, an effective relationship exists when a customer has a strong preference for a particular supplier. This may be based on any of a number of factors, such as performance history or experience, responsiveness, flexibility, trust, and other aspects that lead to value for the customer. The practice of *customer relationship management* (CRM) is most appropriate with those customers who can most affect a company's future.

CRM is a relatively new way of thinking about marketing and doing business. The CRM strategy aims to learn, in depth, about the customers' needs, values, and behaviors. A supplier organization collects and coordinates customer information, sales information, marketing effectiveness, responsiveness to customers, and market trends. It helps in maintaining satisfactory relationships with customers, and requires the commitment of both management and the entire workforce. Also referred to as *relationship marketing* or *one-to-one marketing*, CRM is a concept profoundly influenced by Peppers, Rogers, and Dorf.[1] McKenna offers the following perspective:

> *Differentiation, from the customer's viewpoint, is not something that is product or service related as much as it is related to the way you do business. In the age of information, it is no longer possible to manufacture an image. The distinction between perception and reality is getting finer. Further, in a world where customers have so many choices, they can be fickle. This means modern marketing is a struggle for customer loyalty. Positioning must involve more than simple awareness of a hierarchy of brands and company names. It demands a special relationship with the customer and infrastructure of the marketplace.[2]*

1. CUSTOMER NEEDS

> Use quality function deployment (QFD) to analyze customer needs in relation to products and services offered. Use the results of the analysis to prioritize future development in anticipation of changing customer needs. (Analyze)
>
> **Body of Knowledge V.B.1**

Anticipating Customer Expectations and Needs

Anticipating customer expectations can occur at two levels: from analyzing markets and observing social trends (see Chapter 6, Section 2), and from contacts with customers and suppliers. At the first level, it's staying current with or ahead of emerging trends. Contributors to potential future expectations are market researchers, social psychologists, and future-oriented societies dedicated to analyzing a wide range of prognostications.

At the customer contact level there are two aspects to address: analysis of how customers feel current products meet their expectations, and what customers foresee as future wants and needs. Customer expectations vary depending on whether there are suppliers already providing the type of product or service required by the customer or whether there is a probability that known suppliers can develop the product or service needed. Organizations that introduce a new product or service into the marketplace are not initially responding to a customer's expectations; they are concerned with building a demand for their offerings.

Data about customer needs can be found within and outside of the organization. Data found within the organization include:

- Customer complaints
- Past records of claim resolutions

Part V.B.1

- Warranty and guarantee usage
- Service records—product failure, product maintenance
- Customer contact personnel
- Listening post data
- Customer satisfaction surveys or other feedback
- Market research

Data obtained from outside the organization include:

- Data about competitors' customers
- Research—magazine and newspaper articles, information from trade journals
- Public information, for example, customers' and competitors' annual reports
- Advertising media—brochures, TV and radio, websites
- Industry market research

Read the following three scenarios and, from a customer's perspective, ask what factors or features:

- May be satisfiers?
- May be dissatisfiers?
- Would meet my priorities?
- Would just meet my needs?
- Would truly excite or delight me?

In the first scenario, Alpha is a distributor of replacement parts for household appliances. Alpha's perception of customers' expectations is as follows: the part needed is in stock, the part needs to work as intended, the part needs to be the same or higher quality as the part it replaces, there is a very short waiting time, courteous treatment is given, supplier offers some instruction on how to install the part, and the price for the part is fair.

In the second scenario, Beta, a manufacturer of toy action figures, is launching a new action figure. Beta's customers are toy distributors who expect, for example, that Beta has made a sound judgment that the new action figure will rapidly become a high-demand item, quality of product will be the same or higher compared to previous products from Beta, delivery will be on time to meet the holiday market (assuming the demand will build), and Beta is prepared to manufacture and ship additional product to distributors on short notice if demand exceeds original projections.

Epsilon, a department store, buys an initial shipment of the new toy from its toy distributor. Epsilon expects that Beta will heavily promote the item, that the toy will generate interest and demand, and that Epsilon will make a profit. It also expects the distributor to be able to deliver rush orders if demand exceeds original estimates.

One of Epsilon's customers is Peggy, the mother of seven-year-old Billy. Peggy expects to find something new and different to buy for Billy, something that costs less than $25, and is not too heavy to carry. Peggy is shopping in the first week of December. Searching the toy department she sees several items that may meet her needs. Several action figures look familiar, probably from last year's promotions. One item, Captain Saturn, appears to be new and is unknown to her. It is selling for $19.95 and weighs only a couple of pounds. But will Billy want that? The parking meter is about to expire, so she leaves without buying anything.

A couple of weeks pass. Billy has been avidly following the TV adventures of Captain Saturn. He has taken much notice of the advertisements for the new action figure now available. Desire builds, and Billy pesters his mother for the toy.

A week before the holiday, Peggy ventures into the horde of holiday shoppers in search of Captain Saturn. She expects to find the toy, and at the same price as before. A mob of angry shoppers surround a large sign notifying potential buyers that the Captain is presently sold out. Orders are being taken on a first-come basis, at a price of $34.95, with no guarantee the item will be delivered before the holiday. Peggy quits, empty-handed.

A block away, a street vendor is offering "Captain Saturn in the original carton" for $50, cash only, no returns. Frustrated, Peggy buys one. The toy survives only two hours of Billy's vigorous play. It was a knock-off, not the authentic Beta model.

In our third scenario, Omega College, a small, privately endowed institution, offers associate and bachelor's degrees in business. Following its strategic planning goals, Omega has decided it must offer a new degree program to address the local business need for management candidates with an emphasis on quality management. The new program will be offered on an accelerated basis, with all of the students' work done online. This is to accommodate employed people who normally couldn't attend either a full daytime or an evening program. Omega expects that its projected enrollment will more than support the costs of launching the new program, including hiring faculty.

Susan and the 11 other students enrolled in the first class of the new program expect to learn material that will qualify them for good-paying management positions upon graduation. They speculate that the teachers from the business world will be more interesting, realistic, and up to date than typical college professors. These students expect a more practical education than theoretical. The degree program will cost more than the traditional business degree program.

These scenarios emphasize the importance of identifying who the customers are, and then, what expectations need to be considered. Should Alpha be concerned if its supplier produces parts made from inferior materials? Should Beta be concerned whether the TV network has plans to renew Captain Saturn for another season? Why should the Omega College administrators be concerned about the job market for quality-educated managers three years from now?

These questions, and more, are valid considerations as an organization supplying products and services anticipates and projects future needs and priorities. Thought must be given to whether the product or service offered only marginally

Part V.B.1

satisfies a customer or has the potential for generating real excitement. What are the possibilities for disappointing the customer? How will the customers' expectations, priorities, and needs fit with the supplier's priorities and needs?

Insofar as feasible, start with data from customers (gathered with one or more of the tools discussed later). One method for transforming these data into information is to document and assess these answers and the impact on the supplier's organization using the quality function deployment matrix.

Quality Function Deployment

Quality function deployment (QFD), also known as the *house of quality*, is a relationship matrix technique used to systematically translate a customer's requirements/ wants into operational requirements, and communicate the customer's voice, in understandable terms, downward through the organization. QFD translates the customers' voice into product or service characteristics that when present can affect customer satisfaction. Viewing Figure 17.1, we see that:

- Data for section A, the customers' wants and needs, is obtained from several sources, for example, customer listening systems, surveys, and customer focus groups.

- Each listed customer want is given an importance weighting in section B.

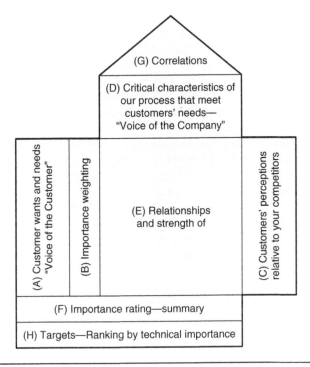

Figure 17.1   Quality function deployment matrix "house of quality."

- Through research, interviews, focus groups, and so on, data are obtained in order to rate customers' perceptions, in section C, of the wants listed in section A relative to your competitors' products/services (the horizontal connection between A and C).

- "How things are done"—the critical characteristics of your process that meet the customers' needs (the voice of the company)—is shown in columns in section D of the matrix.

- In the cells of the relationships section of the matrix, section E, where the rows and columns of the matrix intersect, relationship codes are inserted. Usually, these codes are classified as 9 = strongly related, 3 = moderately related, or 1 = weakly related.

- Section F shows totals of the vertical columns, representing the sums of the weighted totals of the relationships (where coded) between the customers' wants and the organization's voice of the company (characteristics of the process).

- The house of quality is completed by adding a roof, section G, which is a matrix to correlate the interrelationship between company descriptors. Code symbols depict the strength of the correlated relationships. See a completed sample QFD in Figure 17.2.

The QFD matrix may be changed and/or expanded according to the objectives of the analysis. If desired, customer requirements can be prioritized by importance, competitive analysis, and market potential by adding an additional matrix to the right-hand side of the QFD matrix. The company descriptors can be prioritized by importance, target values, and competitive evaluation with a matrix added to the bottom of the QFD matrix. To summarize, the QFD approach and deployment steps are:

1. Plan—determine the objective(s), and determine what data are needed.

2. Collect data.

3. Analyze and understand the data using the QFD matrix to generate information.

4. Deploy the information throughout the organization (depending on the objectives).

5. Employ the information in making decisions.

6. Evaluate the value of the information generated, and evaluate the process.

7. Improve the process.

The completed QFD matrix can also indicate which activities for problem solving or continual improvement should be given the highest priority. This graphical representation helps management and personnel involved in an improvement effort understand how an improvement will affect customer satisfaction, and helps prevent deviations from that objective. See Figure 17.3 for a diagram of the cascading

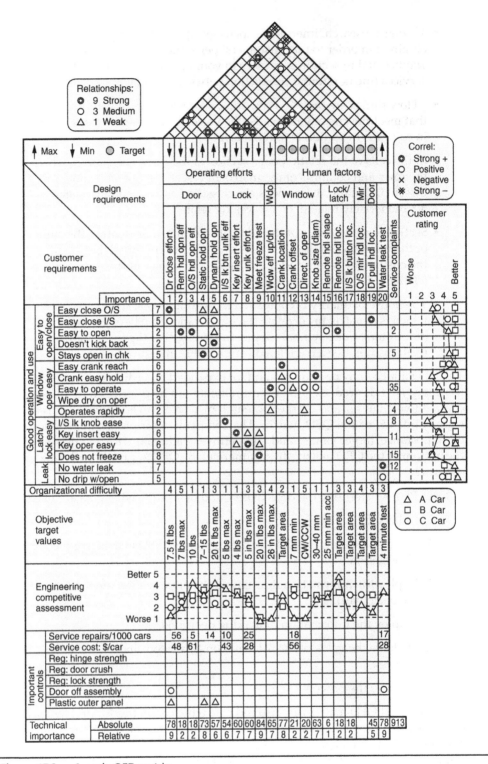

Figure 17.2   Sample QFD matrix.

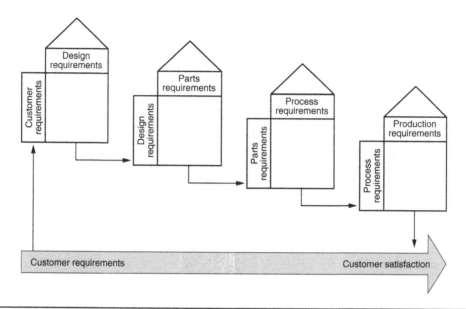

Figure 17.3   Voice of the customer deployment.

matrices involved in the deployment of the voice of the customer through design, parts planning, process planning, and production.

QFD has been used to develop products that delight the customer by providing features that are beyond their stated requirements. In many cases, the customer did not know that these options were possible, so they were not on a list of needs or priorities. By comparing the customer's requirements to product and service features, the company typically focuses on identifying and prioritizing the agreements and gaps. From this analysis, innovative new offerings are more likely to become apparent. These can provide a greater probability of moving the company into the "delighting" quality level. Findings from a competitive analysis may also identify opportunities for significant improvement.

A simpler but less comprehensive analysis may be done using a kind of priority matrix for each unique product and service offered, for each type of customer. To set up a sample priority matrix, title a spreadsheet with the name of the product or service and the type of customer. Label seven columns, reading left to right:

 a. Product/service factor/feature

 b. Potential to satisfy customers (brief commentary)

 c. Estimated rating of customers' perception of value (scale: 0 = none, 1 = low to 5 = high)

 d. Potential to dissatisfy customers (brief commentary)

 e. Estimated rating of customers' negative perception (same scale, only with minus prefix for any 1's through 5's)

 f. Estimated overall rating of impact on customers (arithmetic sum of the two ratings from c and e above)

g. Comments about increasing, sustaining, decreasing, or eliminating the factor/feature from the suppliers' perspective

List every factor/feature of the organization's products and services, including those already perceived as negative. For each line, rate the positive value perceived by the customer and the negative value perceived, with comments about each. Sum the two ratings and make comments about the impact on the organization if the feature/factor was increased, sustained, decreased, or eliminated, based on the perceptions of the customers.

A glance at the completed table provides a perception of how customers may rate present expectations, needs, and value of the organization's products or services. Creating the same type of table for a new product or service and using data from focus groups or other sources can help head off a potentially disastrous product/service launch. Likewise, using this approach with competitor data may yield valuable insights as to what the organization must do to meet or exceed the competition.

Other Models for Gathering and Deploying Voice of the Customer Information

Juran on Planning for Quality details a process for optimizing product design.[3] Juran's model uses a spreadsheet (matrix) approach, the concepts of which could be adapted to the measurement and analysis of customer satisfaction.

GOAL/QPC's voice of the customer research report describes a structured approach for gathering, analyzing, and deploying the voice of the customer, which, if desired, can be linked with QFD.[4]

Criteria category 3.2 of the Baldrige Performance Excellence Program (BPEP) examines "How do you engage customers to serve their needs and build relationships?" Readers are encouraged to obtain a copy of the Criteria and become acquainted with its entire contents. (See Chapter 12.1 for more BPEP detail.)

2. CUSTOMER SATISFACTION AND LOYALTY

> Develop systems to capture positive and negative customer perceptions and experiences, using tools such as voice of the customer, listening posts, focus groups, complaints and warranty data, surveys, and interviews. Use customer value analysis to calculate the financial impact of existing customers and the potential results of losing those customers. Develop corrective actions and proactive methods to improve customer satisfaction, loyalty, and retention levels. (Create)
>
> **Body of Knowledge V.B.2**

Determining Customer Satisfaction Levels

Customer satisfaction levels are impossible to assess unless customers' expectations, priorities, and needs have been determined. This is known as "listening to the voice of the customer." See Section 1 about QFD.

Leading organizations have measured and tracked customer satisfaction levels for decades. Results are used to identify problems and opportunities, measure the performance of managers and executives, and reveal relative competitive performance. These organizations have also integrated findings (from customer surveys and other means) into their corporate strategies, new product development, manufacturing quality, product and service delivery, and competitive positioning. Marketing decisions are made on the basis of statistical analysis that shows which factors are most important in their customers' buying decisions.

Customer satisfaction measurement has become an integral part of the quality management process as companies use customer satisfaction information to drive improvement initiatives. Figure 17.4 outlines a system for utilizing customer feedback. Leading-edge customer satisfaction systems include several key elements:

- There are formal processes for collecting and analyzing customer data and for communicating results to the appropriate business functions for action. Data can be used for company or market segment analysis to develop marketing strategies, or used at the account level to gain an understanding of the customer's opinion of the company.

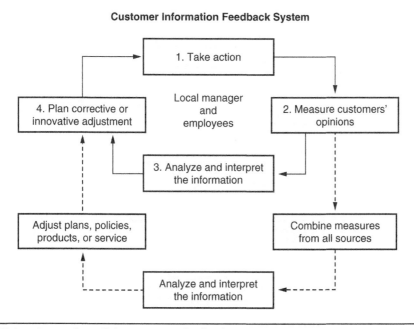

Customer Information Feedback System

Figure 17.4   System for utilizing customer feedback.

Part V.B.2

- Feedback on how well an organization is meeting requirements is gathered by using some combination of the methods listed and described below. Most companies use several formal methods for collecting customer satisfaction data. By using several sources, the companies are better able to validate results and increase their credibility.

- Because each method of gathering customer feedback has its benefits, disadvantages, and specific applications, most companies choose a combination of methods to get a more complete picture. Once information has been gathered, sophisticated techniques can be used to analyze the information.

- To be useful, data and the information derived from data must be stored appropriately and made available to those who need it.

Analyzing Customer Satisfaction Data

Kano Model. One method used to analyze customer satisfaction data is the *Kano model* (Figure 17.5). The model was developed by Noriaki Kano to show the relationship between three types of product characteristics, or qualities. These include qualities that *must be* present, those that are *one-dimensional*, and those that

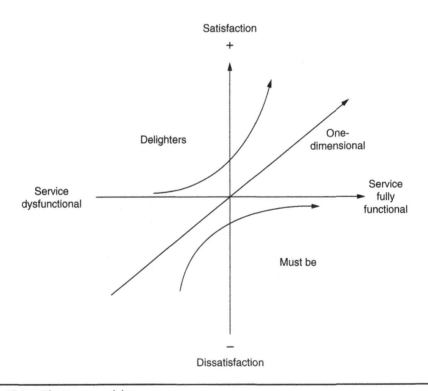

Figure 17.5   The Kano model.

are *delighters*. The presence or absence of *must-be* characteristics is shown by the curved line in the lower-right quadrant. When a must-be characteristic is not present or is not present in sufficient quantity, dissatisfaction exists. As the characteristic becomes more available or of a higher quality, customer satisfaction increases, but only to a neutral state, represented by the horizontal line. In other words, the factor can only satisfy, not delight, the customer.

One-dimensional factors drive satisfaction in direct relationship to their presence, and thus they are represented by a straight line. For example, as the interest rate on a savings account rises, so does satisfaction.

The curved line in the upper left to center area represents *delighters*. If absent, these factors have no impact on satisfaction. When present, however, these features delight the customer. An example would be automobile cup holders. When first introduced, cup holders were delighters. This example also demonstrates an important point about delighters. As they become more available, they tend to move from the upper-left side of the model to the lower left. Today, an automobile without cup holders would not be well received in the market. Cup holders have become a *must-be* feature.

Listening Post Data. Many organizations have many people within who periodically or occasionally interact with customers, for example, company engineer to customer's engineer, salesperson to salesperson, CEO to CEO, and delivery person to customer's receiving person. In many of these interactions, the customers' employees express opinions, suggestions, complaints, or compliments about the supplier's organization, the products/services' quality, delivery, price—even about the personal attention they receive (or don't). Excepting severe negative expressions, these comments, casually and informally made, are seldom captured. By not having a formal process for collecting and analyzing these data (for example, trending), an organization is unable to spot the early stage of an eventual customer problem. They also miss compliments that should get back to the responsible people as positive feedback. LCALI, a process that does just this, is discussed next.

Listen–Capture–Analyze–Learn–Improve (LCALI). This is a listening post process to capture and use the casual remarks often mentioned in conversations with customers. These remarks are usually forgotten once mentioned, yet they may be the spark of new needs or wants, or hint that a problem may be brewing. Westcott says, "Most companies have no systematic way to actively listen to customers, record what they hear, analyze the data, disseminate the information internally, and act on the information."[5] Without a process like LCALI, opportunities are lost, such as:

- An idea for a new product or service

- A suggestion for improvement of an existing product or service

- Displeasure with some feature or aspect of an existing product or service

- An observation about packaging, the delivery process, or company image

Part V.B.2

- Comments about the seller's sales approach, customer service, or inquiry handling

- Minor annoyances (long wait times, inconvenient parking, business hours)

- Actions of the seller's personnel that pleased the customer

- Comments about a competitor's product or service

- Hints that the customer may soon leave

These are but a few of the possible types of comments that may casually come up during the course of communication between the seller and the buyer (between the producer's personnel and buyer's personnel or the actual consumer). The key is to:

- Train the seller organization's personnel to tune into these remarks and know what requires immediate action (requires corrective action) versus what is casual commentary.

- Have a process for recording the casual remarks, collecting them, and analyzing them (for example, trending, severity prioritizing).

- Get the information learned to the right people in the organization to take action.

When casual customer information is captured, categorized, and trended over time, patterns evolve that can materially affect your product and service design, production, and delivery, and customer satisfaction. For example, a CEO of an engineering consulting firm, after an introduction to the LCALI process, admitted that had his firm used the process earlier, the firm could have saved over a million dollars. Four months prior, the firm's project manager was talking on the phone to the customer's engineer and heard that the engineer was looking around for another job because he could "see the handwriting on the wall." The consulting engineer, feeling that the customer's engineer's problem was not his concern (not in his job description) did nothing with the information.

Shortly thereafter, the customer's organization was bought out by a conglomerate in another part of the country. The remnants of the business the buyer wanted from the sale were moved across the country. All projects under way were abandoned. Only three people were relocated; the rest were terminated.

The engineering consulting firm had invested (consulting time and travel expenses) over a year on a project with the customer, very heavily in the last two months. Expensive tools and equipment belonging to the firm were lost when the customer's operation closed. Costly legal actions were under way to attempt to recoup some of the engineering consulting firm's losses (over a million dollars projected).

In another situation, a pharmaceutical company's delivery driver heard from a customer's receiving clerk that the customer's warehousing supervisor was upset with the way the product came in shrink-wrapped. Slow-moving product, within unopened shrink-wrapped pallets, tended to develop condensation (sweat), causing some of the product to become unusable. The warehouse supervisor hadn't complained to anyone in his company because he didn't want to cause a problem. Lately, however, the supervisor had been criticized about the amount of product scrapped before its normal expiration date. He had casually griped to the receiving clerk, who passed on the gripe to the delivery truck driver.

The truck driver, trained to tune into such comments, duly recorded the information he had heard and turned in the record to the official listening post person at the pharmaceutical company. The listening post person took the following actions: She officially informed the shipping department of the problem by initiating a corrective action request. She reported the comment to the organization's person in charge of analyzing such comments. He found that similar comments had been rumored previously from other customers. He initiated a preventive action request to review the packaging procedure. He informed the sales rep for the customer's account so that the customer could be informed that a potential problem has been noted and action was being taken. He updated the listening post person on the actions taken. He informed the truck driver's supervisor of the actions being taken so that the driver could be recognized for his contribution.

Figure 17.6 shows a sample form used in the LCALI process.

Focus Groups. Customer focus teams improve the ability of an organization to execute the strategies of customer relationship management. Often, these teams provide a point of focus for customers that cut across different functions. Typical team composition includes an account manager, customer service representative, field engineer/tech support, and plant representatives. The purpose of the customer focus team is to provide a near-seamless interface in the customer relationship. Further, it ensures that all the key stakeholders in the supplying organization are in alignment on strategy and actions on behalf of the customer.[6]

Focus groups are qualitative group discussions, usually with eight to 10 participants generally recruited based on segmentation criteria, such as level of product use, age, income, and gender. A discussion guide that outlines questions is prepared in advance. The questions are asked and facilitated by a focus group moderator. Depending on the research design, between two and 10 groups will be conducted with different customer segments in different geographic areas. Focus groups can identify important recurring themes with regard to product or service likes and dislikes, important service factors (customer requirements), and performance and product/service improvement opportunities.

The focus group has many of the benefits and uses of the in-person interview and the added benefit of a group's synergy at a lower cost per response. Focus groups are often used as a first step in developing surveys, and also used to get customer insight on sales and marketing programs. Focus groups of internal customers can provide input to improve business, manufacturing, development, administrative, and even sales processes.

External customer focus groups are usually conducted in specialized facilities. Typically, focus groups require a skilled facilitator to ensure that the sessions stay on track and are not unduly influenced by a few participants.

Part V.B.2

Customer/Client Contact Record (CCR)   [CCR no.]

A. Identification   [Cust./client no.]

Contact from:	[Person's name]		[Title]
	[Location]		[Phone]
	[Customer/client's name]		[Fax]
	[Address]		[E-mail]
	[City]	[State/province]	[Country]

Field listener:	[Name]		[Position]
	[Dept./location]	[Mail stop]	[Phone]
	[Supervisor's name]		[Title]

B. Context/situation/place of contact

❑ Complaint   ❑ Compliment   ❑ General observation *[What?]*
❑ Letter: *[Date]*   ❑ Phone call: *[Date]*   ❑ Face-to-face: *[Date]*   ❑ Other: *[Date]*
[Describe context in greater detail if "other" is checked:]

C. Quote or best recollection of words from customer/client and nature of the contact

❑ Related to specific order/product: *[Order no.]*   *[Date]*   *[Product]*
❑ Related to specific representative of this organization: *[Who]*   *[Date]*
[Record words used by customer/client's contact. If a direct quote, use quotation marks.]

[Describe any details that will make the understanding of the customer/client's perspective clear to persons reading this CCR. Note if customer/client specifically requested notification of resolution or other feedback. Use back of form if needed.]

[Field listener's commentary (viewpoint, opinion, interpretation)]

D. Action activity

Triage: ❑ Action needed now   ❑ Investigate further   ❑ Watch trend
              (Corrective action)   (Preventive action)

Action assigned to:	[Name]	[Location]	[Phone]	[Date]	
Follow-up:	[How?]	[Date]	[Date]	[Date]	[Date]
Status reports:	[How?]	[Date]	[Date]	[Date]	[Date]

E. Resolution and closeout

[State how problem/question was resolved:]   *[By whom]*   *[Date]*

[Corrective action no.]   *[Preventive action no.]*   *[Returned material auth. no.]*   *[Other?]*

[Procedure/work instruction affected]   *[Date to be changed]*   *[By whom]*

[Forms/computer programs affected]   *[Date to be changed]*   *[By whom]*

[Status/feedback to be provided—how?]   *[To whom]*   *[By whom]*   *[By date]*

[Closeout code] [Closed by:—print]   *[Signature]*   *[Date]*

Figure 17.6   A customer/client contact record, a sample LCALI form.
Source: Reprinted with permission of R. T. Westcott & Associates.

Part V.B.2

Complaint Handling

Empirical data available from Consumer Complaint Handling in America, an Update Study, shows the importance of effective complaint handling systems. The data show the importance of making it easy and convenient for customers to complain when they experience problems, and for complaint handling to be effective and efficient as well. For example, for a product costing over $100, the research results show that 9.5 percent of non-complainants experiencing problems would repurchase. Repurchase intent increases to 19 percent for complainants whose issues are unresolved and jumps to 54.3 percent when complaints are resolved satisfactorily. Additional research by the U.S. Office of Consumer Affairs/Technical Assistance Research Programs (TARP) shows that the speed of complaint resolution also affects repurchase intent, which is significantly higher when resolution is achieved quickly.[7]

Capturing, Differentiating, and Using Data from Customers

A study indicated that a majority of surveyed firms rely on reactive feedback methods (complaint monitoring, toll-free call centers, and warranty systems) to bring the voice of the customer into their organization. Less commonly used are proactive feedback methods, such as written surveys, telephoning, and visiting customers. Proactive methods, such as customer surveys, are increasingly prominent. Competitive and financial performance pressures have encouraged many organizations to strive to improve performance and increase customer satisfaction.

Businesses collect customer data using many tools and from many parts of the organization. The organization's systems for gathering data, as well as for analyzing and disseminating this information, are key to an effective use of customer data.

Customer data that can be useful in determining customer satisfaction may be from:

- Product warranty registrations
- Complaints, when logged and tracked
- Customer surveys
- Transaction data
- Data from established listening posts
- Lost-customer analysis

When integrated and analyzed, this information is extremely valuable to the organization. Unfortunately, individual departments may feel that they own this information and may not share it with others who could benefit. Regarded separately, the data streams might suggest one course of action, but if considered collectively could suggest another course. Organizations need to integrate, process, and trend data, and then disseminate the resulting information in a manner that facilitates the maximum positive impact on the organization.

Part V.B.2

Techniques and Tools Used to Collect the Data

Survey Research. Some of the most common applications of surveys include satisfaction surveys, customer satisfaction tracking, and lost-customer surveys. Quantitative research provides empirical data from which statistical inferences can be drawn and extrapolated to the population at large. Typically, rating scale questions and multiple-choice questions are thought of as quantitative. If not a census of everyone, a sample for quantitative research must be random and large enough to draw statistical inferences. (See Chapter 15, Section 9 for more on the analysis and use of survey data.)

Qualitative research is very useful in identifying key themes related to the research issues and in capturing affect (likes, dislikes, and preferences). Qualitative research, however, does not allow for statistical inferences that can be projected back to the population.

Survey Methods. There are a variety of survey methods, including:[8]

• *Written/mail surveys.* The most common survey method is the written customer satisfaction or mail survey. Many companies periodically mail out companywide surveys, tabulate the results, and provide the feedback to all areas of the organization. Some companies survey their customers annually; others send out questionnaires monthly to a random sample of customers.

Mail surveys take longer to implement than phone surveys and some in-person interviews but are the least obtrusive of all survey techniques because respondents can complete the survey at a time of their own choosing. Mail surveys are less expensive than personal interviews, and are usually less expensive than telephone surveys.

Maximizing the response rate of a mail survey is a key concern. Prior notification, a well-written cover letter, and a follow-up survey mailing to nonrespondents in the sample are some of the most effective tactics to boost response rates. (The follow-up only works if the organization can identify who did and who didn't respond.) With customer satisfaction surveys, response rates between 30 percent and 50 percent are attainable.

Mail surveys often have a low cost per response. Mail surveys can include both quantitative and qualitative questions, but the quality of open-ended qualitative data is not as good as that of telephone and in-person surveys because there is no interviewer to probe or clarify incomplete or vague responses. Mail surveys tend to produce a low response rate, in general.

To be effective, written surveys must be relatively short. This limits the number of questions dedicated to specific areas of the business and minimizes the recipient's desire to throw away the survey. The responses to written surveys are not random, as the least and most satisfied customers tend to respond more frequently than those who do not have strong feelings (the vast number of individuals in the center of the survey group). To overcome this problem, leading companies are using telephone surveys to contact a random sampling of their customers to measure and correct the bias in their written survey results.

A variation on the use of the mailed survey is the captive audience survey. In this approach, an audience of customers, or potential customers, is present for another purpose, for example, a new product demonstration or training in product use. As part of the program, the audience is asked to complete a survey. A small incentive may be offered. A high response rate is usually achieved. The question is, how representative of the customer base is the audience that took the survey?

• *Telephone surveys.* Many companies use telephone surveys to supplement or even replace written surveys. Phone surveys can be effective for collecting information about the organization as a whole or about functional areas such as sales and services. Interviewers call customer decision makers and influencers directly to find out how well their requirements are being met. The survey can be conducted and the findings made available more quickly. Phone surveys are subject to fewer nonresponse biases than mail surveys.

Because response rates tend to be higher, phone survey results can more accurately be focused on a targeted customer segment. Sample sizes can be smaller, and the company knows for sure who answered the survey questions. Phone surveys also offer more flexibility than do written surveys because an experienced interviewer can deviate from a prepared call guide to pursue specific areas of customer interest. The quality of open-ended comment data is good given adequate interviewer training and documentation, and supervision. Care must be taken with phone surveys to ensure that all interviewers conduct surveys in a consistent manner to minimize potentially biased interviewer effects. It is more difficult to ask respondents to evaluate complex concepts by phone than it is by mail or in person because visual props are not available.

There is a practical time limit for telephone calls; however, maximum survey length is generally longer than that for mail surveys but shorter than that for in-person interviews. Phone surveys have a higher cost per response than well-executed written surveys, but are less expensive than in-person interviews. Also, telephone calls are interruptive by nature, and there is an increasing resistance to them, especially when consumers are called during their mealtime! Widespread adoption of voice mail and answering machines has necessitated that numerous attempts be made to attain reasonable survey response rates. Finally, in many consumer markets, customers have unlisted telephone numbers, cell phones, or no phone service. Even with these disadvantages, however, the telephone survey continues to grow in popularity and is an excellent source of input for the quality improvement process in sales and customer service.

There are negatives to telephone surveys: Many customers resent the intrusion of organizations seeking survey responses and the increase in the number of survey requests. With *caller identification*, the recipient can eliminate the call before any contact is made. Further, without eye contact and with less guilt, many potential respondents will either cut the call short or just hang up when they detect a survey request. Surveys may be especially annoying to any cell phone users who may have to pay for incoming calls.

There is a growing trend for which the results are not yet available: fully automated telephone surveys using a recorded sender and the push buttons on the receiver's phone for responses.

• *Website and e-mail surveys.* Some organizations find that including a survey on their website is useful in collecting customer feedback. A small incentive is sometimes offered, for example, entry into a contest or drawing, or a redeemable coupon. If the survey is not for the general public but it is not programmed to be for customers only, the organization is apt to be swamped with entries. Without categorization or segmentation, such submissions may prove to be unusable. The response can be low inasmuch as the potential survey taker has to act to access the website and then take time to complete the survey. This can irritate the user when their intent was to get information from the website, not give information to the website.

Similarly, many organizations send out periodic surveys to their customers via e-mail. Careful planning is needed to be reasonably sure the survey reaches the intended customers and doesn't end up as trash (spam). Again, the receiver has to somehow be motivated to complete the survey—few receivers have the time and inclination to take a survey without a viable reason to do so.

Some e-mail services block attachments to e-mails, especially when sent to multiple addresses (security and virus protection). And some services will treat the e-mail as spam.

- *In-person interviews (one-to-one).* The face-to-face interview is one of the most powerful information-gathering techniques. It can be used to identify the issues that are most important to customers so that these issues can then be addressed in preparing written or telephone surveys. The in-person interview is also an effective stand-alone method for gathering qualitative as well as quantitative information. A skilled interviewer can quickly elicit information critical to improving the sales process. The interviewer can pursue the areas of greatest importance, probe for details, and discuss new ideas and approaches. The in-person interview is an excellent tool for getting input from both external and internal customers.

The cost of conducting a large number of in-person interviews virtually precludes the value of this technique to gather statistically significant data. This is especially true if the company has a large number of customers or if customers are widely dispersed, as scheduling logistics and geography tend to magnify costs and time requirements. The technique also requires the use of skilled, unbiased interviewers. This often means using outside contractors.

In-person interviews do have other advantages. If a sufficient number of surveys are conducted, quantitative results can be carefully extrapolated to the target population. In addition, these types of surveys allow for the longest interviews with minimal respondent fatigue. Unlike with focus groups, the attitudes expressed are truly owned by the respondent and not in any way influenced by groupthink or a dominant participant.

- *Comment cards/suggestion boxes.* Comment cards and suggestion boxes are often used on premises (for example, at fast food restaurants, hotels, and doctors' offices) to gather customer feedback. The formats are almost always very brief and provide the benefit of fostering communications with customers from whom the organization most needs to hear. They give dissatisfied customers an opportunity to vent, and the organization an opportunity to make amends (often building loyalty). Customers who receive astonishing service often find themselves compelled to tell management about their wonderful experiences. The main problem with this survey method is that it is often ignored by a majority of customers, resulting in substantial bias due to nonresponse. Many customers will not volunteer their time to answer a questionnaire unless they receive something in the mail, are contacted by phone, or are approached in person as they are leaving the establishment. Therefore, results might be useful in identifying sources of problems or causes that drive customer delight, or a major deficiency, but would be woefully inadequate in describing an average customer's experience.

• *Observation. Murmurs*, a technique with origins in Japan, is used to gather information on customer behavior. In the late 1980s Honda dispatched a team of engineers to the parking lots of Disney's theme parks to discover customers' requirements for their car trunks. The engineers reportedly watched people drive into the theme parks and unload their trunks. On departure, the engineers observed how people packed and loaded their gear into the trunks. As a result, many new design ideas were integrated into future Honda trunks to add benefits and make them easier for customers to use.

• *Mystery shoppers.* This method can be very useful in monitoring the effectiveness of policy deployment, training, and new product/program launches. Shoppers (either internal or third-party employees) pretend to be customers with specific needs, with the aim to get a bird's-eye view of the service process in action (not just the way it is supposed to work). Mystery shoppers can be trained to minimize personal biases and focus performance ratings on the basis of carefully defined (objective) service levels. However, high shopper scores do not imply that the organization's performance is universally aligned with customers' needs and expectations. When this method uncovers actions of store personnel that should be in wide use throughout the store (or chain of stores), or when a serious deficiency is noted that should be addressed, the management of the organization sponsoring the mystery shopping has cause to take appropriate action. This method is used to verify that sales personnel are properly trained and demonstrate that they have been taught the organization's policies and practices.

• *Internet.* Finch suggests a six-step process for gathering customer information from internet conversations. He says, "Anyone with internet access, even the novice, can locate and extract conversational information related to product quality issues."[9]

• *Customer councils.* Also called a *customer advisory board*, many companies have established customer councils that meet periodically to discuss common issues and concerns. These councils are an excellent way to develop supplier partnerships. Council meetings provide a forum for in-depth discussions of the organization's sales process and for identifying ways in which sales can add value to the products and services. Because council members usually come from the organization's largest and best customers, their input might not represent the attitudes of all customers. Therefore, customer councils should not be the only source of customer input.

• *Panels.* A panel is a group of customers recruited by an organization to provide ad hoc feedback on performance or product development ideas. Panel composition can vary depending on strategic intent. Panels frequently include customers who are strategic business partners, are accustomed to communicating openly, and are familiar with the sponsoring organization's business practices and technical capabilities. Like focus groups, data gathered from panels should not be extrapolated to the total population of customers.

Part V.B.2

- *Joint planning meetings.* One of the most effective ways to identify customer requirements and gather satisfaction feedback is by conducting joint planning meetings. Although joint planning meetings are known by many names, and the process might vary slightly, common characteristics exist. Joint planning meetings begin with a meeting between representatives of a key customer and the sales and service team for that account. The meeting objective is to determine how the organization can better meet the customer's requirements and expectations. A skilled facilitator leads the participants through a planning process to create a prioritized list of improvement activities. At follow-up meetings, the customer provides feedback on how well the improvements worked, and the participants work together to identify more areas on which to focus. The organization consolidates input from all the joint planning sessions to identify common issues that can be addressed on a companywide basis.

This method is most useful when salespeople or teams support one or a few large customers. Importantly, the objective of these planning meetings is improvement; customers must never perceive that the intent is to gain additional business. Users of the method do report, however, that it can identify additional business opportunities.

The discipline of customer relationship management forces an organization to reevaluate its methods of measuring the satisfaction of the targets of its initiatives. Satisfaction surveys conducted only with purchasing customers can be too limited in these enhanced business relationships. The nature of the customer/supplier interface will be dramatically expanded from the traditional seller/purchaser relationship to include cross-functional teams from both organizations. As a result, surveys will increasingly need to examine the needs of a cross-section of stakeholders from the customer's organization. In addition, organizations will be increasingly likely to implement internal satisfaction measurement systems, using in-person surveys as a vehicle to improve communications and customer satisfaction and to strengthen relationships with core customers.[10]

Customer Value Analysis. Gale and Wood describe seven tools of customer value analysis:

1. The *market-perceived quality profile* is an "indicator of how well you are performing overall for customers in your targeted market."

2. The *market-perceived price profile* is a weighted indicator of how customers perceive different competitors' performance on given price attributes.

3. The *customer-value map* is a map that reveals any significant cluster of business units receiving premium prices that are not fully supported by superior perceived quality.

4. The *won/lost* analysis is an analysis of those factors that won the sale or lost the sale.

5. The *head-to-head area chart of customer value* is a "chart of customer value displaying where you are doing well and where you do worse against a single competitor."

6. The *key events timeline* is a chronological list of the events that changed the market's perception of performance on each quality attribute, yours and your competitor's.

7. A *what/who matrix* is a method for tracking who's responsible for the actions that will make success in customer value possible.

Using these tools will "enable an organization to navigate strategically even in confusing times."[11]

Numerous factors represent value to different customers under a variety of situations. The characteristics shown in Table 17.1 illustrate different perspectives on what the customer considers important.

Unconditional Guarantees. Unlike warranties, which are conditional (time limited, conditions of use, period of use), an unconditional guarantee informs the customer that:

1. If a product fails, it will be replaced with an item of the same or equivalent value, or money will be refunded, or the item will be repaired, and/or any damage or inconvenience to the customer will be rectified or reimbursed.

2. If a service is substandard, the work performed will be redone or money will be refunded, and/or any damage or inconvenience to the customer will be rectified or reimbursed.

3. The customer will not be challenged about the claim.

4. The customer will receive a sincere apology.

5. The settlement will be quick and fair.

Unconditional guarantees provide a unique opportunity to demonstrate the application of your organization's policy, restore/enhance customer loyalty, foster stories of positive experiences, gather detailed customer data, and sell additional

Table 17.1   Perspectives of value to customers.

Characteristics—Product (examples)	Performance Reasonable price Durability Safety	Serviceability Ease/flexibility of use Simplicity of design, aesthetics Ease of disposal
Characteristics—Service (examples)	Responsiveness Reliability Competence Access Courtesy Communication (sensitivity, genuine interest/concern)	Credibility/image Confidentiality/security Understanding the customer Accuracy/completeness Timeliness

products/services. Also, the guarantee conveys the belief that your organization is sufficiently confident of your product or service quality to offer such a guarantee.

Data Mining. Data mining is a computer search of a large customer database to seek patterns of heretofore undetected relationships and correlations among the data stored in the records. As noted in Chapter 15, Section 4, geographical information systems as an output when combined with data mining can produce smart maps.

Other. A variety of other sources of valuable information exist about current and potential customers. Some of these are product/warranty registration cards, call center data, complaint systems, customer databases, and data generated from the sales force's customer visits.

Each of these sources has useful applications in terms of generating customer satisfaction metrics, as well as providing input for strategic planning, process improvement, and corrective action. Today's organizations increasingly have information about their customers—problems experienced, needs and wants, as well as competitive intelligence from many sources. It is important that each data stream be considered for the value it might hold for various stakeholders throughout the organization.

Corrective and Preventive Action

Collecting data without doing something with it is waste. Data have to be processed in some way before they become actionable information. Each of the tools and techniques discussed involve manipulation and analysis of the data produced. Much as the data from the tracking of nonconforming product detected in manufacturing processes are captured, analyzed, and targeted for corrective and/ or preventive action, customer data should be treated similarly. In the listening post approach described earlier, trended data, as appropriate, become the basis for a corrective and/or preventive action. Data gathered by the other tools also form the basis for actions to make changes and improvements.

Just as it is important to select appropriate customer data–gathering tools and techniques, it is also important to establish the processes by which the data will be recorded, monitored, collected, manipulated (sorted, collated, categorized), analyzed, correlated, measured, summarized, and reported. Many organizations have implemented customer satisfaction measurement and reporting systems. These systems alert management to critical failures in satisfying customers. They also provide information to management in deciding whether a negative trend is developing. The information can assist management in determining whether efforts should be made to ratchet up the quality of its products/services to meet ever changing customers' perceptions of satisfaction.

Computer software providers have produced a number of products for use in collecting customer data, processing them, and reporting out either detailed customer information or a synthesis of customer information. Typically, many of these programs are focused on areas where large volumes of data are to be processed, for example, from large surveys, from product registration cards, or from a complaint desk function.

Pitfalls Encountered in Determining Customer Satisfaction

The common mistake most often made by organizations is assuming that they know how satisfied the customers are and what the customers want. This perception is usually based on the existence of a long-term relationship and/or on the absence of complaints.

Another mistake is designing surveys using questions that the organization wants the customer to answer. Better survey design suggests that the customers be asked what is most important to them. Then consider what they want in creating the survey questions. (Focus groups, discussed earlier, are often used to obtain the customer perspective.) As a quality vice president from a Baldrige Award winner once said, "We tended to include survey questions to which we already knew the answers." A similar mistake is developing the survey questions in such a way as to lead the customer to answer the way the organization wants. The design of unbiased and intelligent survey questions is paramount. Another common mistake is to survey samples of customers that are neither random nor representative. This results in responses that are not statistically valid. This can also happen when customers are surveyed by mail, and the responses from the 30 percent of customers who sent back the form are analyzed. The problem is that customers at the extremes of satisfaction or dissatisfaction frequently respond to surveys more than the majority who are in the middle.

Poor question definition and invalid statistical samples can cause the organization to focus its improvement efforts in the wrong area or on areas that are not important to the customer. This wastes resources without achieving improved customer satisfaction or competitive position.

Relying too heavily on reactive data (such as complaint data) is a common mistake. The problem is that complaint data (and other reactive techniques) can not usually be used to estimate the reactions of the total population. For example, complaints might help identify key problems that need to be addressed, but they fail to quantify the true frequency at which a problem occurs. Typically, 25 to 50 times more customers experience a problem than those who bother with, or succeed in, registering a complaint with management.[12]

A failure to use the customer's language is another deficiency: Often the constructs evaluated in surveys are generated internally. It is common for these constructs to be worded differently than they would be if they were in the customers' language. The likely result is that the customers' understanding of the questions may differ from the organization's intent, and survey validity is compromised.

Organizations also, unfortunately, use poor research design. Often, survey objectives (problem statements) are not well thought out. It is very important to consider how the information will be used and what decisions will be made on the basis of the results. Every question to be included should meet the "need to know" rather than just "nice to know" test. Scrutinizing every question by asking, "Why are we asking this?" helps prevent the inclusion of questions of limited value.

Once they receive results from the research, some companies use it ineffectively. Another frequent barrier is that good information is not always acted on by the organization. It is fairly common for an organization to conduct surveys but fail to integrate the results into the strategic planning, continual improvement, and corrective and preventive action processes. A failure to disseminate the right information to the right person(s) in the organization (for example, process owners) is the most common reason for this type of breakdown. Other common reasons for ineffective survey use include a failure by leadership to set expectations for action, as well as a lack of discipline in applying a rigorous plan–do–check–act (PDCA) cycle to the survey process.

Customer Retention/Loyalty

Customer-driven organizations that address the importance of the customer relationship enjoy significant competitive advantages. Several well-known companies, such as L. L. Bean and Nordstrom, are frequently cited for their outstanding customer service—and enjoy the benefits afforded by greater than usual customer loyalty.

Operating a customer-focused organization implies there is an integrated system of plans, processes, and practices designed to deliver the organization's services and products in a way that creates retained and committed customers, at a profit. Customer satisfaction is the focus of the entire organization. Can you identify the satisfaction level of your customers (individually or by segment)?

Look at Table 17.2[13] and assume that having most customers at level 4, with many at level 5, is desirable. The extent to which everyone is focused on the customers, in thought and action, is critical. For example, applying the concept of open-book management:[14]

- Do employees know the costs of delivering less than exemplary service and products?

- How many level 1's have been lost in the past year?

- How many level 2's come and go?

- How many level 3's are there in the customer base?

- What does it cost to bring in new customers to replace departed customers?

- What are restitution costs when the customer is dissatisfied?

- Does this customer ever come back?

Table 17.2   Levels of customer satisfaction.

Level	Is your customer	Then your customer
1	Dissatisfied	Has probably departed forever
2	Marginally satisfied	Is casual (any supplier will do)
3	Basically satisfied	Is borderline, uncommitted
4	Delighted	Is a return customer (retained)
5	A committed advocate	Is loyal, appreciates what you do, and tells others

Source: Reprinted with permission of R. T. Westcott & Associates.

- What is it costing the company when your competitors cut into your share of the market?

- What is lost when delivery dates are missed?

- If the company is doing well now, how much better might profits be if there was greater customer focus—more level 4's and 5's?

Information is vital. The *voice of the customer* (VOC) is critical in a competitive environment. Typically, companies have no systematic way to actively listen to customers, record what has been heard, and analyze, distribute, and act on the information. In his book *Moments of Truth,* Jan Carlzon talks about the often unrecognized myriad opportunities all employees have for gathering customer information.[15] Karl Albrecht further defines the moment of truth as "any episode in which the customer comes in contact with any aspect of the organization and gets an impression of the quality of its service. A moment of truth is typically neither positive nor negative in and of itself. It is the outcome that counts."[16]

Without a system (including training employees to listen to the VOC) for collecting, analyzing, and disseminating the information, and taking action, the organization is operating blindly. Without a measure, or at least a sense, of how satisfied customers are, the door is open to the competition. Investigating reasons for returned product is but a small part of the picture. A customer's offhand remark to the company's salesperson or delivery person can appear insignificant in itself. These comments, however, heard as a moment of truth, can alert the company to a potential problem before it turns into a formal complaint. A call requesting clarification from a customer's engineer to your company's engineer can indicate present or potential shortcomings in identifying customer requirements. Scattered remarks from a variety of customers' personnel to several different people in your company, while not appearing important when looked at individually, can, when collected and analyzed, form a pattern pointing to needed preventive action. Earl Naumann, in *Creating Customer Value,* says, "A firm that has no customer satisfaction program and no interest in starting one should be the delight of the firm's competitors."[17] To protect their customer base, organizations may:

- *Reward usage.* This can take the form of discount coupons, provided inside a product pack, for buying additional quantities of the same product.

- *Reward loyalty.* Airlines' frequent flyer programs are an example of this phenomenon.

- *Provide unpaid services.* Some organizations offer free lessons on how to use their products.

- *Establish personal relationships.* Publicly honoring loyal customers during company events, greeting them on their birthdays and anniversaries, and giving them preferential treatment (for example, upgrading economy class fliers to business class when space is available) are examples of ways in which organizations build personal relationships with customers.

Part V.B.2

Retaining customers costs money, but is still much less expensive than going after new customers. Reichheld discusses how to put a dollar value on retained customers. Factors such as acquisition cost, base profit, revenue growth, operating costs, referrals, and price premium are considerations mentioned.[18]

Take a look at the following from a lost-customer perspective: Ms. A (a patron of ShopBetter supermarket, representing a segment of the customer base containing married buyers who own their home and have one or two children) spends an average of $125 per week at the store. That's $6500 a year. Extend that to five years (the average length of time a customer stays in the area), and it means that the potential loss of Ms. A could be $32,500. That's only one customer in one segment of the customer base.

If ShopBetter is the only supermarket that is geographically close, there may be less likelihood of a lost customer. But, add to the equation the potential opening of a new supermarket less than a mile away, and the chance of loss becomes very real.

Now, compare the cost of a lost customer with the cost of acquiring a new customer. In many industries, the cost of obtaining a new customer will substantially exceed the value of the retained customer.

Customer Value Analysis

Understanding and responding to the customers' perception of value received is a key to retention. Value may comprise perceptions of:

- The customer's basic ability to afford the product or service
- Trade-offs, or what the customer must forgo to afford the product or service
- Whether the product or service is worth the price charged
- Favorable experience with seller's products or services
- Other factors important to the customer, such as:
  - Fast delivery
  - Incentive for buying
  - Warranty or unconditional guarantee
  - Deferred payment plan
  - Product or service options available
  - Future upgrade possible (possibly at a discount)
  - Length of time product will remain in stock (in case of future need for replacement or to add another exact duplicate)
  - Prestige in owning the product or obtaining the service

From surveys, interviews, and focus groups, data can be collected to create a *customers' perceived value matrix* (CPVM). With the CPVM, weight the relevant customers' perceived values of several brands of a similar product against value factors such as those just listed. The CPVM allows management to determine where to apply resources to increase customers' perceived value or where to build on already high perceived value. A cautionary note is that the CPVM data may not exactly correlate to customers' buying habits depending on the validity of the data gathered.

Organizations protect their customer base by building an organization-wide focus on retention. They must first design appropriate metrics, for example, the percentage of revenue from repeat purchases or percentage of memberships into their third year of renewal. Then, data must be collected and analyzed as to how well the organization is meeting the objectives for retention.

Common mistakes leading to poor service and ultimately to lost customers include:

- Failure to listen

- Apathetic employees

- Negative attitudes

- Poor complaint handling

- Lack of understanding of customers' needs

- Viewing complaints or customer dissatisfaction as negative feedback

- Ignoring customer complaints (a second opportunity to delight the customer, a second opportunity to retain the customer's business, and a second opportunity to develop stronger customer loyalty)

- Introducing dimensions of quality that are unimportant to the customer

3. CUSTOMER SERVICE PRINCIPLES

> Develop and deploy strategies that support customer service principles: courtesy, politeness, smiles, cheerfulness, attention to detail, active listening, empathy, rapid response, and easy access for information and service. (Apply)
>
> **Body of Knowledge V.B.3**

Creating a Customer Service–Oriented Organization

Customer service is much more than just delivering what the customer wants. Customer service, when fully embraced by an organization, involves not only delivering what was ordered, but also truly caring about the customer. *Caring* is about customers' perceptions of your organization—its products and services, its people, its reputation. Caring is about the customers' well-being—health, safety, security. Caring is also understanding as much as possible about what the customer needs and wants, even their future needs.

The trend continues toward ultimately serving the unique needs of one customer. The organization that is most successful in achieving that end, to the mutual advantage of both the customer and the organization, usually wins the privilege of keeping that customer.

In the eyes of today's customer, customer service transcends the product or service an organization provides. It is a predominant factor in the buying decision, often overriding price. It is a primary factor that distinguishes one organization from another. In many cases, superior customer service justifies an organization charging higher prices.

Customers fall into a number of different categories (Chapter 16), yet there are no organizations without customers. And, since all organizations (for-profit and not-for-profit) have customers, a primary focus of any organization must be on providing satisfactory to exemplary service to those customers. Many organizations in classifications other than service mistakenly believe and wrongly act as if their business does not involve serving customers.

Following are some of the first key steps to improving customers' perceptions of quality customer service:

1. The top management of the organization sets the tone and the pace. There must be visible personal involvement of the senior leaders in championing exemplary customer service. Employees, or volunteers, depending on the organization, must see their leaders supporting customer service excellence—in words, in actions, and with appropriate funding. In spite of the hundreds of articles, the extensive advertising campaigns, and other media hype, there is still more talking than walking.

2. Top management's commitment is expressed in the organization's vision and/or mission statement. This statement clearly positions customers and service to customers as the primary reasons for being.

3. The organization's strategic goals and objectives reinforce the vision and mission. These plans, cascaded downward through the organization, are translated into actions to support the goals and objectives.

4. The organization's system of tracking, measuring, analyzing, reporting, and reacting ensures that actions supporting the strategic plans are measured. The means for collecting, analyzing, and disseminating the voice of the customer is integral to the achievement of the strategic goals. Both customer service initiatives and the processes for achieving the plans are continually examined for opportunities to improve.

5. The concepts and practices of superior customer service start within the organization. When internal customers receive quality service from internal providers, the beneficial results can be more easily related to external customers.

6. The organization's leadership involves its members/employees in shaping external customer service excellence. Management style evolves toward empowering the people in the organization to act in providing the best service possible. Management's role is to support, conceptually turning the organization's structure upside down from its traditional pyramidal shape (see Chapter 2, Section 5).

7. The organization employs multiple means for obtaining customer feedback. It collects, correlates, analyzes, and disseminates crucial information for management's action. Complaints are actively solicited and acted on.

8. The organization dedicates itself to training of its people. Everyone is educated in the products and services provided by the organization. They not only understand what these products and services are, but why and how the customer uses them. Everyone in the organization is trained in customer service practices, including interpersonal skills (basic courtesy, politeness, pleasantness, and conflict resolution), problem solving, and customer inquiry and complaint response techniques. Every individual in the organization is made aware of their role in the customer service process and treated as an important owner of the process. Every individual is kept well informed as to how the organization is doing in achieving its customer service objectives. Exemplary customer service performance is recognized and rewarded, frequently.

9. The organization establishes a benchmarking process. It seeks out others who are perceived as best in class for specific processes. It charters benchmarking teams to learn about how these other organizations achieve their results and help translate these finding into improvements within their own organization.

10. The organization, once it has achieved a level of excellence recognized by its customers, adopts an unconditional guarantee policy. It places the very existence of the organization on the line. And it states its policy for all to hear and see—an irreversible commitment to quality customer service.

All organizations occasionally encounter an unhappy customer. Making the effort to successfully resolve customer complaints shows the customer that you care, and can be used as a continual improvement tool. Here is a five-step recovery program:

1. *Apologize.* First and foremost, say that you are sincerely sorry for the inconvenience the customer has experienced. Also, personally accept responsibility for the problem and its resolution.

2. *Restate.* Restate the problem as the customer described it to you to make certain that you understand exactly what the customer means. Then tell or show the customer that you will do everything possible to solve the problem and resolve the complaint as soon as feasibly possible.

3. *Empathize.* Make certain that you communicate clearly to your customers so that they understand that you know how they feel.

4. *Make restitution.* Not only tell your customers that you will take immediate action to resolve their complaints (for example, refunding their money), but tell and show them that you will make it up to them in some special way. For example, provide a free gift or a discount on their next purchase.

5. *Follow up.* Later, check to see whether your customers are now satisfied. This area is where most programs fail.

Training customer service representatives (CSRs) is vital to building and retaining customers. The organization's principles, policies, and the CSR skills needed are exemplified in the following checklist.

Will the action I take:

- Meet the customer's need?

- Save the customer time and/or money?

- Earn my organization the customer's loyalty?

- Help obtain future business?

Do I treat customers as people? Have I:

- Looked at the situation/transaction from the customer's perspective?

- Been objective and calm?

- Listened carefully and been responsive and efficient?

- Taken the time and made the effort to get all the information needed to serve the customer?

- Been sensitive to the customer's unspoken needs and alert to the customer's disagreement and/or disappointment?

- Confirmed that I heard and understand the message from the customer?

- Made the effort to know my organization's products, services, processes, and procedures to maximize my ability to assist the customer?

- Carefully avoided making excuses when a problem affects the customer?

- Been clear that I share the customer's need to resolve any problem, real or imagined, that concerns the customer about my organization or what it offers?

- Been helpful and informative, letting the customer know what I will do to rectify the problem?

- Asked the customer whether what I propose to do will satisfy the customer's needs and wants?

- Taken the appropriate action in a timely manner?

Have I:

- Checked back with the customer to see if the action I took resolved the problem and that the customer is satisfied with the response?

- Thanked the customer for bringing the problem to my attention and allowing me to respond?

- Communicated the problem and the solution to appropriate persons in my organization to facilitate preventing the recurrence of the problem?

4. MULTIPLE AND DIVERSE CUSTOMER MANAGEMENT

> Establish and monitor priorities to avoid or resolve conflicting customer requirements and demands. Develop methods and systems for managing capacity and resources to meet the needs of multiple customers. Describe the impact that diverse customer groups can have on all aspects of product and service development and delivery. (Evaluate)
>
> **Body of Knowledge V.B.4**

Managing Multiple Customers

Most businesses have more than one external customer, each with their own needs/expectations for the product or service being purchased (see Chapter 16, Section 2). To meet the needs/expectations of its customers, an organization must first understand its own business. This begins with knowing what it takes, including costs, to produce the product or provide the service being offered. Next, the organization needs to determine the needs and expectations of specific customers or customer segments. This can be done by studying the industry, for example, by forming focus groups in which industry representatives express their needs. An organization should be aware that customers purchasing the same product might have very different needs.

As an example, the supplier of bookkeeping computer software could have customers from the medical device manufacturing industry, nonprofit foundations, and educational institutions. Each of these types of customers will obviously have different requirements, even though certain features of the software product might perform well in most industry categories. The medical device manufacturers would have special product traceability requirements to consider. The not-for-profit foundation needs complete security over sources of contributions. Educational institutions require features to manage their costs and delayed revenue related to student loans.

In addition to different product requirements, customers might have varying delivery requirements. Some customers might need truckloads of product but are flexible with delivery lead times, whereas others might want small volumes of material delivered just in time. A supplier must weigh these types of logistical problems and consider the additional costs that could be incurred in either case. Other customers might require the same product, but at different stages of completion. For example, one customer might prefer to purchase material that is less finished, lower in purity, and so on, because these materials meet its needs at the best value. When selling partially finished product, suppliers might find it necessary to modify their pricing structure to prevent others from buying and finishing the product and becoming strong competitors.

Organizations need to evaluate each potential sales opportunity to make an informed decision as to whether it is worthwhile business to pursue. Specifically, they should ask, "Does this potential customer fit well with our existing service processes and capabilities?" Once management has decided on which areas to focus, customers can be ranked so that research efforts can anticipate the needs of key customers. Generally, key customers are those that generate the most profits or have a high potential for generating profits, and/or are high-visibility organizations. The value of a customer should be projected over the long term because business with a customer can lead to other business with that customer or to a referral of a new customer.

Resolving Conflict

Many times, potential or real conflicts arise between organizations and their customers. Having multiple customers who compete with one another can also present special challenges for a supplier. Conflicts can result when delivery schedules overlap or when material or other resources are in short supply.

Consider this example: A supplier of products to more than one automotive customer may find it has to take special precautions. For each such customer it has to carefully train its people and segregate product during processing in order to maintain the level of security imposed by each competing customer.

Establishing a relationship based on trust is critical to avoiding or resolving conflict with a customer. A customer must know that confidential or proprietary information is safeguarded from competitors. A supplier should have procedures for protecting proprietary information, such as by limiting access to drawings and specifications and restricting competitors' access to a customer's product. An organization without these provisions faces legal liability from patent or copyright infringement or violations of a contract with the customer.

Beyond safeguarding proprietary or protected information, however, there is an economic aspect to managing customer conflict. If the systems and resources required to resolve conflict with a demanding customer exceed the economic benefit of meeting the customer's needs and resolving the conflict, it might appear to be more expedient to take no steps to resolve the conflict and let that customer go to a competitor. When making such a decision, the intangible impact should be considered. A supplier needs to consider how the loss of that customer will affect business. Unhappy customers talk about their experience with many more people than do satisfied ones, and this needs to be considered when dealing with customers. In some industries, ceasing to do business with a customer (sometimes referred to as "firing the customer") might not have adverse effects, but in a small retail company that is heavily dependent on word of mouth for its reputation and future business, this solution could be disastrous.

When conflicts arise, high priority should be given to communicating with the customer in a calm manner, conducting root cause investigations, and implementing corrective action. Results of corrective action should be fed back to the customer, and response action should not be discontinued until both parties are satisfied that the conflict has been resolved. Customer service representatives should be trained to deal with irate customers and also need to be given the information and authority to solve or resolve customer problems immediately. Passing problems along to others does not help relieve the customer's concern—the faster the problem can be dealt with, the happier (or less disturbed) the customer will be.

Resolving conflict with a customer helps establish trust and promotes a long-term relationship. This is a competitive advantage in industries in which customers are reducing supply bases to deal with fewer suppliers. A supplier should develop a relationship with its customers and clearly understand their needs. When conflicts arise, the supplier should try to understand the customer's point of view and negotiate a resolution.

The biggest mistake a supplier can make is taking the position that the customer is unreasonable and, therefore, not react to resolve the conflict, or make a halfhearted attempt at conflict resolution. Many times, this lack of action is rooted in the supplier's focus on optimizing their internal processes even if these processes do not serve the customer well. Conflict resolution is seldom possible in an environment in which the supplier tells the customer, "That's the way we do it, take it or leave it." Unfortunately, this scenario is still all too common.

The most important criterion for both multiple customer management and resolving conflict is excellent interpersonal relations. That means management's commitment to training and support. For example, an organization that responds quickly, pleasantly, and professionally to a customer's complaint can often demonstrate its policy of exemplary customer service and can turn an irate customer into a good repeat customer who will bring friends along. The intangible benefits are high and must be considered in all customer relations.

Managing Capacity and Resources

Does the organization have the capacity and the resources to properly serve the existing customer base? What would be your answer if there was a rapid increase in orders due to a new fad, introduction of a new product line, acquisition of another company, a competitor's demise, and so on?

Good customer relations means not only providing a quality product or service, but also being able to deliver the needed quantity when and where the customers' requirements dictate. Predicting and providing for future demand is tricky, but necessary. Factors that can contribute to building and sustaining the needed capacity are:

- Customer-focused organization culture

- Leadership commitment

- Strategic planning and deployment process

- Continual environmental scanning

- Sound financial management

- Continual risk assessment

- Effective quality system

- Understanding and improving your processes

- Trend and pattern analysis

- Knowing your process capability

- Understanding present and emerging customer needs

- Understanding and working with suppliers

For an example of the impact diverse customer groups may have on product and service development and delivery, consider the following scenario: Marketing efforts are anticipated to result in adding a new customer product line and a new customer segment. The sole manufacturing plant is working at near 100 percent capacity now. What to do before the expected wave of new orders for the new products arrives? Management considers:

- Adopting lean techniques and tools to reduce cycle time and free up space for the needed new equipment and personnel.

- Initiating a study, based on activity-based costing, to determine if any of the existing product lines are unprofitable and can be phased out.

- Renting a local facility and setting up a mini-plant to start producing the new product line. When the new products become a stable source of income, a more permanent facility for making the new products can be found or built, perhaps closer to the customers.

- Outsourcing either the manufacture of the new products or, more likely, some of the existing functions to make room for manufacturing to expand to accommodate the new products.

- Reassessing the product lines currently offered in relation to the new product line to determine whether the business should be restructured and one or more of the existing product lines sold because of lack of fit to the strategy of the reconstituted core business.

- Hiring an organization development consultant to diagnose the existing organizational culture and recommend effective approaches to assimilating the new product lines, new technologies involved, new procedures, and new people.

In meeting the challenges of today's marketplace, many organizations will have to develop the competence and capacity to provide for mass customization. The benefits that will accrue to the organization that does so may include:

- Competitive edge
- Greater attraction to buyers
- Increase in customers' perceived value
- Greater agility in response to changing customer perceptions and demands
- Prestigious reputation for one-to-one selling
- Increased profitability

Customers are your most valued assets; attend to their needs or nothing else matters!

ENDNOTES

1. D. Peppers, M. Rogers, and D. Dorf, "Is Your Company Ready for One-to-One Marketing?" *Harvard Business Review* 77, no. 3 (January–February 1999).
2. R. McKenna, *Relationship Marketing: Successful Strategies for the Age of the Customer* (Reading, MA: Basic Books, 1991).
3. J. M. Juran, *Juran on Planning for Quality* (New York: The Free Press, 1988).
4. GOAL/QPC, *Voice of the Customer*, GOAL/QPC Research Committee Report (Methuen, MA: GOAL/QPC, 1995).
5. R. T. Westcott, "Tapping the Many Voices of the Customer," *The Informed Outlook* (June 2000): 20–23.
6. J. T. Israel, "Feedback to Improve Core Customer Relationships: A Framework to Implement Face-to-Face Surveys," *ASQ 51nd Annual Quality Congress Transactions* (May 6, 1997): 420.
7. U.S. Office of Consumer Affairs/Technical Assistance Research Programs, *Consumer Complaint Handling in America: An Update Study, Part II* (Washington, D.C.: U.S. Office of Consumer Affairs, March 31, 1986), 42–43.
8. Much of the material under this heading has been adapted from articles by D. M. Stowell in *The Quality Management Forum*, a publication of the ASQ Quality Management Division.
9. B. J. Finch, "A New Way to Listen to the Customer," *Quality Progress* (May 1997) 73–76.
10. Israel, "Feedback," 425.
11. B. T. Gale and R. C. Wood, *Managing Customer Value: Creating Quality and Service That Customers Can See* (New York: The Free Press, 1994).
12. T. G. Vavra, *Improving Your Measurement of Customer Satisfaction: A Guide to Creating, Conducting, Analyzing, and Reporting Customer Satisfaction Measurement Programs* (Milwaukee: ASQ Quality Press, 1997), 16–17.

Part V.B.4

13. R. Westcott, "Safeguard Your Customer Base," *The Quality Management Forum* (Summer 1998): 10–13.

14. J. Case, *Open-Book Management: The Coming Business Revolution* (New York: HarperBusiness, 1995).

15. J. Carlzon, *Moments of Truth: New Strategies for Today's Customer-Driven Economy* (New York: HarperBusiness, 1987).

16. K. Albrecht, *At America's Service: How Your Company Can Join the Customer Service Revolution* (New York: Warner Books, 1988).

17. E. Naumann, *Creating Customer Value: The Path to Sustainable Competitive Advantage* (Milwaukee: ASQC Quality Press, 1995).

18. F. F. Reichheld, *The Loyalty Effect: The Hidden Force Behind Growth, Profits, and Lasting Value* (Boston: Harvard Business School Press, 1996).

See Appendix A for additional references for this chapter.

Part V.B.4

Part VI
Supply Chain Management

World-class supply chains organize, plan, and deliver on the basis of what customers value.

—Gene Tyndall, Christopher Gopal,
Wolfgang Partsch, John Kamauff

Chapter 18

Supply Chain Management

A systems view of an organization recognizes that performance is a function of taking in inputs (marketplace requirements, operating funds, raw materials and supplies, and employees) and effectively and efficiently converting them to outputs deemed of value by customers. It is, therefore, in the best interest of organizations that they select and work with suppliers in ways that will ensure high quality of those inputs.

A supplier is any provider whose goods and services may be used at any stage in the design, production, and/or delivery process. *Supply chain management*, defined as the process of effectively integrating and managing the supply chain, is a series of processes including planning, sourcing, making, delivering, and returning. This chapter focuses on the planning, sourcing, and delivering aspects of supply chain management.

Supplier performance is recognized as being about more than just a low purchase price. The costs of transactions, communication, problem resolution, and of switching suppliers all impact overall cost. The reliability of supplier delivery as well as their own internal operational policies, such as inventory levels, all impact overall supply chain performance.

Concern about running out of stock, or a desire to play suppliers against one another for price reductions, used to mean multiple suppliers for the same raw material. This has given way in many industries to working closer with a smaller number of suppliers on longer-term, partnership-oriented arrangements. This also means less variation in vital process inputs.

If suppliers have proven to be effective at controlling the quality of their output, the purchasing organization can reduce the amount of monitoring of the supplier and its input. Compliance to international quality management system standards is often a requirement.

A progressive supplier management process must be supported by top management of all companies involved, and the relationship must also be based on mutual trust. More funds will typically be spent in developing the relationship in order to prevent problems later. This means that total cost of doing business has to be considered. As Deming stated in his 14 points for management, we must "end the practice of awarding business on the basis of price tag alone."[1]

Many of the concepts presented in this chapter are especially focused on the manufacturing industry. This industry has the special situation wherein much of what it purchases is actually incorporated into its own products, as opposed to simply being used as a component of the processes of doing business. Because there is a higher inherent risk, or potential impact, in the manufacturing customer–supplier relationship, organizations such as the Automotive Industry Action Group (AIAG) have developed detailed supplier management guidelines such as CQI-19. Many of these same methods, however, have been adapted in some form by nonmanufacturing organizations for items such as records, data, and software code. This is especially true of partnerships and alliances, which are becoming a widespread way of sharing expertise and resources, and spreading risk, in a complex global environment.

Outsourcing

Outsourcing is contracting out certain processes, or subprocesses, of the organization that often:

- Do not directly contribute to the organization's core business, for example, bookkeeping for a medical consortium.

- Are operations or tasks in which the organization wishes not to engage, for example, laboratory testing of raw materials, breeding animals for medical research, removal of hazardous waste material from a construction site.

- Are operations or tasks for which the organization does not have the expertise, nor wants to develop the expertise, for example, fund-raising for a not-for-profit organization, collection services for an e-commerce organization, or repossession of autos for a finance organization.

(Note: In this chapter the organization dealing with the supplier will be referred to as a *purchaser.*)

A. SUPPLIER SELECTION

> Define, develop, and use criteria for selecting suppliers, including internal rating programs and external certification standards. Assess and manage the impact these programs can have on various internal processes of the organization. (Create)
>
> **Body of Knowledge VI.A**

Supplier Selection

The process for selecting new suppliers should be based on the type of product or service being purchased, uniqueness of the product or service, and total cost. For example, if the item is a standard product (available off the shelf) and does not have a critical impact on the purchaser's performance, then purchase price and availability may be all that needs to be considered. Selection may be as easy as finding companies listed in the yellow pages or an industrial directory and requesting a quote. An example of such a product might be standard office supplies; for a service organization it might be a lawn care service.

This simple view, however, does not suffice for the many purchased products and services that will have a significant performance impact. Aluminum billets for an extruder of automotive brake parts, a new university online research database, or equipment maintenance for an airline—these are examples where the qualification and selection process must be carefully thought through and carried out. In some cases customers may dictate that a particular supplier be used (as is typical for steel used to make automotive components). But in most cases the purchaser must define what criteria will be applied, then make a final decision to determine ways that prospective suppliers will be evaluated against the criteria.

Supplier selection criteria for a particular product or service category should be defined by a cross-functional team. In a manufacturing company, team members would typically be from purchasing, quality, engineering, production, or materials management. Team membership could consist of personnel with technical/applications knowledge of the product or service to be purchased, as well as members of the department that will use the purchased item.

The issues to be used to create the selection criteria will typically include the following:

- Previous experience and past performance with the product/service to be purchased

- Relative level of sophistication of the quality system, including meeting regulatory requirements or customer-mandated quality system registration (for example, ISO 9001, ISO/TS 16049)

- Capability to meet current and potential future capacity requirements and at the desired delivery frequency

- Financial stability of the supplier

- Technical support available and willingness to participate as a partner in developing and optimizing design and a long-term relationship

- Total cost of dealing with the supplier (material cost, communications methods, inventory requirements, incoming verification required)

- Supplier's past track record for business performance improvement

- Supplier's code of conduct and ability to be socially and ethically responsible

Methods for determining how well a potential supplier fits the criteria include:

- Obtaining Dun & Bradstreet or other available financial reports

- Requesting a formal quote, which includes providing the supplier with specifications and other requirements (for example, testing)

- Visits to the supplier by management and/or the selection team

- Confirmation of quality system status either by on-site assessment, a written survey, or request for a certificate of quality system registration

- Discussions with other customers served by the supplier

- Review of databases or industry sources for the product line and supplier

- Evaluation of samples obtained from the supplier (for example, prototyping, lab tests, validation testing)

After information has been gathered, potential suppliers are ranked and a preliminary selection made. Ranking is often done using a standardized scoring system. Final selection might not be completed until the supplier has submitted formal documentation demonstrating that certain quality system and product requirements have been met, and the supplier has demonstrated statistical capability to perform over a preliminary time period.

Suppliers not selected are to be contacted in an appropriate manner. The supplier should be informed as to why their bid was not accepted. This information should include the strengths and weaknesses in the supplier's proposal as well as reasons for not accepting the proposal. Treat all suppliers with objectivity, respect, integrity, and professionalism whether you accept their bid or not. Remember, you might need that supplier in the future.

For many products and services to be purchased, there is often a contract signed stipulating:

- Specifications of the items to be purchased, including quality and testing requirements

- Quantity to be purchased, or purchaser's forecasted demand level

- Price and delivery requirements

- Corrective action process to be followed

- Exclusivity constraints, and nondisclosure agreement

- Terms of the rating system to be used to evaluate supplier's performance

- Time period covered by contract

- Contract cancellation terms

Purchasers strive to reduce the number of suppliers for a given product or service. With fewer suppliers and longer-term relationships, purchasers can invest more time and resources in working with suppliers to improve quality and reduce costs. However, for critical items, it may be wise to identify and qualify backup suppliers.

Assessing Supplier Capabilities

Ratings systems may be used to assess and evaluate suppliers' performance and:

- Trigger suppliers' corrective actions

- Plan actions to improve suppliers' performance

- Comply with end customers' contractual requirements, regulatory requirements, and other external standards

- Determine whether to continue or discontinue business with a supplier

- Provide a basis for recognition of suppliers for work done well

In deciding whether a rating system is needed and, if so, designing the system, there are several considerations, such as:

- Given the nature of the items to be purchased (value, cost, availability, and criticality) and the reputation of the suppliers providing those items, ask whether a rating system is worth the time and effort to design and maintain. Further, will a score be more meaningful to the supplier than reviewing the actual quality, cost, and delivery performance metrics?

- Is quality alone the only criterion to be used as a rating parameter?

- Are charts showing lots accepted as a percentage of lots received, and deliveries received on time as a percentage of deliveries scheduled adequate? These or other quality-related statistics are converted into three or four rating levels, each with ranges of acceptability. Are these ratings sufficient, considering that they tend to relate only to the top layer of costs resulting from poor quality?

- Are more-sophisticated quality and delivery cost indexes appropriate? (For example, for each supplier, the non-value-added costs due to nonconformances, and penalty dollars associated with ranges of those costs, are part of a formula used to compute a cost index for each supplier.) Again, while this added sophistication makes for fairer comparison supplier to supplier, the index still deals with only a fraction of the total cost of poor quality.

- Is a more comprehensive approach appropriate? The method would encompass all aspects of suppliers' performance, such as quality, delivery, price, service, and the effect of nonconformances on the purchaser's as well as the customer's operations. Each factor could be subdivided into contributing factors with assigned weights. This would be the fairest of the considerations, but also the most expensive and cumbersome to maintain.

Caveats

When using a supplier rating system, some points to consider are:

- Both the suppliers and the purchaser must be involved in the design of any rating system to be used, and they must agree on the acceptable level of performance.

- The metrics must be meaningful, fair, objective, and easy to understand, with little chance for error in the methodology used and the interpretation of the metric.

- Costs associated with maintaining the rating system must be significantly lower than the benefits derived from the rating system.

- The number of factors chosen for measurement must be kept to a minimum. Choosing to measure too many factors can result in less effective action.

- The rating system, and its components, must be periodically reviewed for cost-effectiveness, as well as to identify potential for improvement.

See Section C for typical indices used for ongoing tracking of supplier performance.

B. SUPPLIER COMMUNICATIONS

> Develop and implement specific communication methods with suppliers, including regularly scheduled meetings and routine and emergency reporting procedures. Develop explicit expectations and confirm that the supplier is aware of critical product and delivery requirements. (Create)
>
> **Body of Knowledge VI.B**

If suppliers are to meet requirements, they must know and understand them. Requirements may be related to product, process, quality system, purchase transaction handling, logistics, or other related business matters. Following are some examples of requirements that should be clearly spelled out in writing, as well as communicated and/or reinforced by other means:

- *Quote requirements.* Information that is to be included in the quote, and by when and to whom the quote must be submitted.

- *Product technical requirements.* Specifications for product attributes that must be met (for example, physical, chemical, visual, performance, or reliability), and which attributes are more important and why. *Pass through characteristics* (PTC) and special characteristics need to be communicated to suppliers.

- *Process requirements.* Special requirements that must be met related to the process that will produce/deliver the product or service.

- *Product verification and traceability requirements.* Testing that the supplier is obligated to perform, information that is to be provided to the purchaser for verification (for example, statistical data, certificates of analysis), and identification requirements for product batches that allow recall if necessary.

- *Quality management system requirements.* Management processes that the purchaser must have in place in order to help ensure quality, including any specific quality management system standards to which the supplier must be compliant and/or certified.

- *Delivery requirements.* How orders will be placed, how the product is to be protected during shipment, what modes of shipping are to be used, and minimum and/or maximum batch sizes.

- *Order requirements.* The quantity of a particular product that the purchaser currently wants, and the date on which it is due.

- *Corrective actions required.* Process to be followed when problems occur at the purchaser's site for which the supplier is to perform and document a formal investigation and report back to the purchaser what was found and done to resolve the situation.

- *Safety and security safeguards required.* Special requirements needed to protect persons coming in contact with product or service.

- *Environmental protection requirements.* Voluntary and involuntary environmental protection parameters relating to contamination, pollution, destruction, depletion of natural resources, introduction of a harmful organism, and so on.

- *Financial requirements.* Requirements relating to the supplier's financial stability.

- *Management requirements.* Requirements relating to the supplier management's integrity and ethical behavior (for example, adhering to the purchaser's code of conduct).

These requirements may be communicated to the supplier via:

- Formal written specifications or drawings created by the purchaser (communicated either by hard copy or electronic transfer of a CAD file), the supplier, or a third-party organization (for example, ASTM)

- Samples of finished products or components provided to the supplier

- Supplier quality assurance (SQA) requirements manual

- Visits to customer plants by technical, quality, or logistics personnel

- Written contracts spelling out the details of products, volume to be purchased within the contract period, and the purchase price

- Purchase orders and releases (by phone, fax, or mail) or electronic orders placed by electronic data interchange (EDI) or through other electronic communications channels

- Other written communications

- Training provided by the purchaser's organization to supplier personnel

- Purchaser–supplier information exchanges during joint design reviews

- Purchaser furnishing order demand forecasts to suppliers

- Having the supplier visit the purchasing organization on an as-needed basis or a regular basis

- Face-to-face contact by a continuous on-site representative from the purchaser (often the case with government contracts)

The supplier should be aware of not only how normal communications are to be carried out, but also what is to occur in the case of a special or critical event. Appropriate contact points (individual, method of contact) should be clearly defined for each different type of situation.

The explicit expectations and consequences to the supplier for nonconformances should be clearly spelled out in advance of the organization placing an order with the supplier. Suppliers must be made aware of the criticality of quality to the purchaser.

Suppliers must keep the purchaser informed of any change in the status of the order. Process delays in the supplier's organization, late arrival of material from the supplier's supplier, delays caused by the supplier having to rework or replace damaged product, or recalls somewhere in the supply chain are all potential disasters for the purchaser and the purchaser's customer—especially if just-in-time deliveries are expected.

C. SUPPLIER PERFORMANCE

> Define, develop, and monitor supplier performance in terms of quality, cost, delivery, and service levels, and establish associated metrics for defect rates, product reliability, functional performance, timeliness, responsiveness, and availability of technical support. (Create)
>
> **Body of Knowledge VI.C**

In order for suppliers to know how they are performing, they must receive feedback from the purchaser. Since the product or service is usually delivered to a location that is remote from where it is designed and produced, this feedback is the primary mechanism that allows the supplier to maintain performance in line with their purchaser's expectations.

This means that for suppliers providing products or services critical to quality, the purchaser must have a formal process for collecting, analyzing, and reporting supplier performance. Following are some of the more common assessments of supplier performance:

- *Questionnaires/audits.* Suppliers may be requested to fill out a survey containing questions about their organization and how their quality system is designed, and what plans for improvement have been developed. The purchaser may instead conduct an on-site assessment as a means of learning more about the details of the system. The purchaser may also conduct a satisfaction survey within its own organization, asking appropriate employees to rate a particular supplier based on product performance and experiences with supplier communication and problem resolution.

- *Product data.* Suppliers are often requested to provide product quality data with each delivery, which is used in place of formal verification by the purchaser. The purchaser may then analyze the data numerically or statistically, looking at overall rates of compliance to specification as well as process stability and capability. Any verification performed by the purchaser also provides data that can be used for this analysis. Internal performance of the product (for example, number of failures when the product was used by the purchaser) can also be analyzed. A *number of defects analysis* is common for many manufacturing industries. Data from analyses of field failures that indicated the supplier was at fault can also be reported.

- *Delivery performance.* Supplier performance against delivery requirements (for example, total number of days early and total days late) can be tracked based on a comparison of receiving records against order requirements.

- *Corrective actions.* When problems are reported to suppliers with a formal request for corrective action, this triggers a tracking process for ensuring that the supplier responds. These records can be analyzed to determine whether a supplier has been timely in its responses, as well as the effectiveness of the corrective actions.

- *Product price and total cost.* Companies are always trying to reduce the cost of raw materials and services, or at least minimize increases. The ability of suppliers to continually show progress in this area can partially be done through a cost-of-quality analysis (see Chapter 13, Section 5) or a broader financial analysis that looks at the total cost of doing business with the supplier. Supplier-provided data on continual improvement efforts is also desired.

Supplier performance is then analyzed using a standard form (manual or computerized) into which the preceding information is placed. A numeric score is applied to each category along with a total score. The score is usually compared to some minimum level required in order to remain a supplier, and a category label applied based on the score (for example, unacceptable, acceptable, superior). The data should also be reviewed for trends (see Chapter 15, Section 5) that would indicate whether the supplier is improving over the long term.

Reporting of supplier performance is usually done on a regular basis (for example, quarterly), by one of the following:

- The rating information is mailed to the suppliers.

- The rating information is provided as part of a visit to the supplier facility (for example, if there is a significant problem to be addressed).

- The information is entered into an online database so that individual suppliers are able to access their own rating.

- An electronic report is sent to suppliers.

- The report is given during regularly scheduled supplier performance meetings.

Figure 18.1 is an example of a supplier performance report that allows a supplier to quickly see its performance over the past year, as well as compare itself to the purchaser's other suppliers.

Suppliers who receive unacceptable ratings are often given a probationary period in which to resolve their problems, and if they do not take action or are unable to improve, they will usually be replaced. For some products, however, a particular supplier may be the only option, which requires a creative approach in working with them. Suppliers who consistently perform exceptionally well may be given supplier performance awards.

Metrics in common use to measure supplier performance may include:

- Defects (parts per million defective)

- Accuracy (order processing, billing)

- Timeliness (traditional delivery, just-in-time delivery, stock replenishment)

ABC Company
Supplier Performance Report for:

Fourth Quarter 2014

Supplier: XYZ Company, Anywhere U.S.

Category	Possible score	Actual score
Product quality	30	25
Delivery	30	30
Quality system	20	15
Corrective action	20	20
	100	**90**

Performance for past three quarters: 80, 80, 85
Average score of all suppliers: 88
Performance of best supplier: 95

Performance categories:
    Preferred partner 95–100
    Acceptable 80–94
    Probation <80

Figure 18.1   Supplier performance report.

- Completeness (order quantity delivered, required paperwork submitted)

- Responsiveness (to inquiries, to corrective actions, complaint resolution)

- Returns for rework or repair

- Technical support made available (field adjustments, end user training)

- Supplier's process capability (C_{pk})

- Supplier's process performance (P_{pk})

- Cost/price responsiveness

- Compliance

- Warranty performance

Questions to ask when determining the frequency with which suppliers should be measured include:

- What is the purpose of the metric? What is needed by when? How critical is the item(s) to be purchased?

- How much time and money will this measurement require to maintain and use?

- How much of a time interval should there be between taking measurements?

- Can the measurement be used in controlling the overall process? Can an unfavorable trend be corrected, and how quickly?

- What are the risks and consequences of not using the measurement?

- Will the measurement be consistently used over time for trend analysis?

Suppliers can also be provided with benchmarking data that help them understand the levels of performance that can be achieved. Care must, of course, be taken to not violate any confidentiality issues. Letting suppliers know about the best performance being achieved by other suppliers regarding measures such as on-time delivery, parts-per-million (ppm) defect rates, and corrective action effectiveness provides the supplier with an opportunity to know how they compare.

Supplier performance metrics achieve several things. They:

- Reinforce the terms of the contract. (A purchaser's order accepted by the supplier is a contract.)

- Serve to link the supplier organization with the strategic objectives of the purchaser.

- Aid in detecting current or emerging problems.

- Help the purchaser's process owners in understanding the overall process—which factors are important.

- Help in making the decisions needed from the purchaser to keep the supply chain viable.

Each organization typically has its own indices used for tracking supplier performance. Following are some examples:

- *Past performance index* (PPI). This index can be based both on quality and/or delivery and/or best-value measures. It is used for individual materials and can be calculated for each supplier that provides the material. Suppliers can then be compared using the index.

- *Supplier performance index* (SPI). This index can also include both quality and/or delivery measures. It tracks all materials provided by a supplier in order to show overall performance trends.

- *Commodity performance index* (CPI). This index is often used when there is no past performance history.

- *Quality performance index* (QPI). This index can be organized by product or by supplier, and takes into account things such as manufacturing floor failures, scrap, supplier corrective action, and failures at receiving inspection.

- *Delivery performance index* (DPI). This index shows delivery trends and can be organized by product or by supplier. Late, early, and on-time deliveries are considered on the basis of requested delivery dates.

The following formula can be applied to further utilize these indices:[2]

$$\text{Performance index (PI)} = \frac{(\text{Purchased costs} + \text{Nonproductive costs})}{(\text{Purchased costs})}$$

This allows an index to be transformed to a ratio of the total costs of working with a supplier to the purchase price. For example, an index of 1.85 means that every dollar spent with a supplier costs the customer a total of $1.85. The lower the index the better. Of course, systems for capturing nonproductive costs (dealing with late deliveries, quality problems) need to be developed to support this process.

A purchaser's action taken resulting from nonconformances may be one or more of the following:

- Return defectives at the supplier's expense.

- Accept nonconforming products temporarily until the product can be replaced.

- Accept nonconforming product at a discounted price.

- Accept nonconforming product that has been modified, adjusted, or repaired at the supplier's expense.

- Scrap nonconforming product received and deduct price charged from supplier's total invoice.

- Bill supplier for purchaser's internal costs related to the nonconformances.

- Scrap nonconforming product in accordance with purchaser's policy and procedures.

- Make arrangements with the supplier for the purchaser to provide technical assistance or training to improve quality.

D. SUPPLIER IMPROVEMENT

> Define and conduct supplier audits, evaluate corrective and preventive action plans, provide feedback, and monitor process improvements. (Create)
>
> **Body of Knowledge VI.D**

Whether it is to help resolve problems or is simply a part of ongoing continual improvement, ensuring that supplier performance improves is required if an organization is to maintain competitiveness. Improvements may be related to products, processes, systems, value and competitive pricing, or strategies. Feedback to suppliers is an important component for their improvement, helping them to understand strengths and weaknesses from the purchaser's perspective.

When the transaction is business-to-business, evaluate the purchasing process as well as supplier performance. Look at:

- Is the purchasing process measured solely on reducing costs, the head of purchasing measured on "Don't pay too much. Don't run out. And never shut down a line"?

- Is the focus on suppliers absorbing storage costs, causing higher prices?

- Is the total cost of procurement considered (price + poor quality + poor delivery)?

- Are specifications given the suppliers correct and adequately defined?

- Are buyer–supplier relationships more adversarial than collaborative?

Supplier Audits

A focus on the supplier's quality system is one means of supplier improvement and can be done through assessment and scoring of the appropriate processes.

Suppliers that are audited against a quality system standard may be asked to improve particular aspects of the system (for example, better qualification of critical processes or use of statistical process control). Some industries require that registered companies develop their suppliers based on the requirements of the industry quality management standard (for example, ISO/TS 16949 for automotive, AS9100 for aerospace, and TL 9000 for telecommunications).

Audits that are performed against a company's standards or other criteria such as the Baldrige Criteria typically measure strengths and weaknesses. Suppliers are given a score, and some purchaser's require scores to be above a minimum in order to award business.

Assessments done of a supplier's quality system must be done by personnel who are adequately qualified in the assessment process as well as the particular standard being used for the assessment. Perhaps more importantly, they must have the ability to communicate with supplier personnel in a manner that will result in a willingness to listen to the results, rather than their feeling criticized.

Corrective and Preventive Action

A basic aspect of supplier improvement involves the purchaser communicating problems or potential problems. For example, product performance or delivery problems can be documented and communicated to the supplier through a corrective action request. These requests usually require that the supplier respond within a specific period of time, and the response is analyzed to determine whether the actions planned or taken are appropriate to the magnitude of the problem. The purchaser can then monitor future performance to ensure that the action taken by the supplier was effective.

Preventive actions are taken to eliminate the causes of potential noncompliances and nonconformances from occurring. The process involving the interaction between the purchaser and supplier, as well as the supplier's internal processes, are examined for potential for producing defectives. Often, with technical assistance from the purchaser, changes are made to the supplier's process to eliminate or reduce the risk of failure to meet the purchaser's requirements. Coincidental to working to improve the supplier's process, the purchaser would examine the communication content and medium used when placing an order to ensure that all requirements are clearly transmitted and acknowledged.

Corrective actions are taken to correct a problem that has occurred. More than a quick fix, a corrective action seeks out the root cause(s) of the problem, explores solutions, and selects the best solution to implement. Assuming that the selection and implementation work as planned, the same problem should not recur.

Feedback to Suppliers

As a means of maintaining a closer working relationship, some purchasers hold regular meetings with suppliers. These meetings provide the opportunity for detailed discussions to occur that are not as effectively carried out through infrequent phone calls or e-mails between the purchaser and supplier organization. Supplier scorecards, as described previously, are often discussed in these meetings. It is important to provide regular routine feedback to suppliers. Often, suppliers only hear from purchasers when there are problems.

Part VI.D

Monitoring Process Improvements

Purchasers may be interested in monitoring a supplier's process improvements for a number of reasons, including new business, new technology, or corrective action. Process improvements may be periodically reviewed to assure that the desired impact was achieved and that the change was standardized.

Another approach to supplier improvement is to work very closely with those suppliers where greater benefits would be achieved. This might involve providing technical personnel to help the supplier solve product or process problems, or a joint product redesign effort. For a components manufacturer, such joint efforts might include value analysis, lean production, design for manufacturability and assembly, or other improvement techniques that will help improve product and/or reduce costs for both parties. Larger companies that have their own formal educational programs for continual improvement methods often invite or require supplier personnel to attend courses.

E. SUPPLIER CERTIFICATION, PARTNERSHIPS, AND ALLIANCES

> Design and implement supplier certification programs that include process reviews and performance evaluations. Identify strategies for developing customer–supplier partnerships and alliances. (Create)
>
> **Body of Knowledge VI.E**

Supplier Certification

The objective of a supplier certification program is to allow consistent supplier performance to be reflected in operating practices for handling received material and awarding future business. Material from a certified supplier may be verified at a very low level of verification (for example, skip-lot sampling whereby parts will be checked from perhaps only every fifth lot). Suppliers who are certified may also receive higher priority for new business.

The certification process involves the following major steps:

- Development of the certification criteria and process (for example, selection, evaluating, rating, communication, and reaction processes)

- Identification of supplier categories for which certification would be advantageous

- Evaluation of selected suppliers against defined criteria

- Reporting of evaluation results, awarding of certification for those who qualify, and clarification of a future interrelated process (for example, supplier reporting requirements)

- Ongoing monitoring of supplier performance, with actions taken in accordance with the defined certification process

Determining which suppliers for whom certification will be available requires evaluation of the potential impact on both the purchaser and supplier. Certification should be considered if it could significantly reduce costs and enhance the business relationship. Risks or other issues such as regulatory or purchaser-mandated requirements for incoming product verification may rule out the option. Another factor is whether the level of sophistication of the supplier organization and its process technology can support the performance expected from a certified supplier.

Supplier certification programs use the assessment and feedback systems mentioned earlier in this chapter; however, there is usually a tiered rating classification (for example, qualified, preferred, and certified). As a supplier advances from one classification level to the next, the amount of reliance on the supplier for product verification is increased. Performance at a particular level must also be maintained for some minimum amount of time before moving to the next level.

Partnerships and Alliances

By their nature, purchaser–supplier relationships are often less than win/win, and are sometimes even adversarial in nature. A customer typically wants the highest quality, the shortest cycle time, and the lowest possible price, and often views suppliers as interchangeable commodity providers. Conversely, suppliers are motivated to sell goods and services at a price that provides an acceptable profit, but are also motivated to build customer loyalty and create a close-knit relationship to secure future business.

Supplier management has evolved to emphasize the importance of both parties working together to build strategic relationships that are known by many terms: coalition, joint venture, strategic alliance, and partnership. According to Dominick and Lunney, a supplier alliance is a special, formalized relationship with a supplier. An alliance implies that two parties are working together for a common purpose. The notion of partnerships goes even further, implying a shared fate, mutual benefits, and equal relationship. Strategic relationships involve cooperative undertaking between companies and can involve technology, licenses, or supply/marketing agreements.

Some common situations that might lead an organization to develop a purchaser–supplier partnership include:

- The difficulty in obtaining supplies, or the need to maintain stability of product or services in a tight market.

- On the basis of a review of core competencies, a purchaser might recognize that a supplier's capabilities exceed the company's own internal capabilities. In such cases, a better ROA might be attained by outsourcing the production of key components or services to the supplier.

- Cost-cutting pressures resulting from substantial price competition in the market might force a purchaser to search for ways to lower costs, both internally and externally, so that profit margins can be maintained.

- Combining resources can increase capabilities, flexibility, responsiveness, and innovation so that they exceed those realized by purchasers and suppliers engaged in more traditional purchaser–supplier relationships.

Strategic relationships are a viable option when an organization desires to attain technological breakthroughs, enter new markets, and/or develop new products or services.

The importance of creating and maintaining partnering relationships with key suppliers is reflected in the following guidelines for organizations looking for ways to effectively manage partnership relations:

- What key products/services do you purchase from suppliers and/or partners?

- How do you incorporate performance requirements into supplier and/or partner process management? What key performance requirements must your suppliers and/or partners meet to fulfill your overall requirements?

- How do you ensure that your performance requirements are met? How do you provide timely and actionable feedback to suppliers and/or partners? Include the key performance measures and/or indicators and any targets you use for supplier and/or partner assessment.

- How do you minimize overall costs associated with inspections, tests, and process and/or performance audits?

- How do you provide business assistance and/or incentives to suppliers and/or partners to help them improve their overall performance and to improve their abilities to contribute to your current and longer-term performance?

- How do you improve your supplier and/or partnering processes, including your role as supportive customer/partner, to keep current with your business needs and directions? How are improvements shared throughout your organization, as appropriate?

- Do the legal ramifications of the planned partnership prevent setting up the partnering arrangement?

In a survey of its customers, a silicon wafer manufacturer asked them several questions on the nature of purchaser–supplier partnerships. The questions addressed the nature of supplier partnerships, expected benefits from partnerships, and the characteristics exhibited by key suppliers. Following are some of the questions and findings:

Q. *What is a supplier partnership?*

A. Nearly half the customers spoke of shared risks and rewards. Two-fifths described the nature of the relationship as embodying a mutual give-

and-take (analogies ranging from marriage to virtual mergers). One-third spoke of good communications that emphasize honesty and openness. One-fifth talked of the idea of extending the factory to the supplier.

Q. *What benefits do you expect (as the customer) from a supplier partnership relationship?*

A. Nearly half indicated that the expected benefits from a partnership-type relationship would be realized through higher quality (supplier and product), guaranteed supply, and/or attaining desired purchaser–supplier synergies. About one-third expected improved communications and/or improved costs or pricing to be important benefits.

Q. *What are the characteristics of your best suppliers?*

A. The leading characteristics purchasers used to describe their best suppliers included:

- Providing high product quality (52 percent)

- Responsive and flexible service (48 percent)

- Good communications (29 percent)

Nearly one-fifth described their best suppliers as those who "go the extra mile" or have a "can-do" attitude, honor their commitments, and/or provide problem-solving support.[3]

As shown by these answers, especially important characteristics of successful partnerships and alliances include mutual benefit, trust building, open and complete communication, and interdependence of parties.

Not all purchasers or suppliers desire to quickly enter into a partnership or alliance relationship. There is a courtship period in establishing the relationship during which a determination is made as to the viability of entering into a more formal relationship. It is worthwhile to overcome the barriers that exist, as a successful partnership can not only be economically rewarding, but also can endure more mistakes and produce greater rewards than if no such relationship existed.[4]

Even when a firm could perform an activity itself, it often makes business sense to outsource work to suppliers. When it is an essential activity, a partnership or alliance is even more critical. Typical reasons for outsourcing include:

- Improving the customer organization's focus by allowing it to concentrate on essential activities

- Gaining access to world-class capabilities

- Accelerating the benefits of reengineering

- Sharing, and thus reducing, risks

- Freeing noncapital resources or making capital funds available

- Reducing operating costs

- Securing resources not available internally

- Increasing production capacity

- Eliminating a function that is difficult to manage[5]

Steps in developing a partnership or alliance relationship include:

1. Determine materials or services for which a closer relationship would be beneficial.

2. Be aware of any legal implications.

3. Identify suppliers with whom a partnership or alliance will be pursued.

4. Define expectations and potential risks for such a relationship.

5. Communicate and negotiate with suppliers.

6. Implement arrangements that are mutually agreed to.

7. Establish ongoing monitoring and communication to maintain the relationship.

Many of the supplier management processes previously mentioned in this chapter will apply to partnership or alliance arrangements. However, some additional activities that more closely integrate the two organizations in such arrangements include:

- Joint design, marketing, and launch of new products/services

- Sharing of long-term strategies

- Communication of demand and resource planning information beyond a day-to-day or week-to-week horizon

- Lending employees to each other's firm for technology transfer and development opportunities

- Sharing in financial gains achieved by the venture

Partnerships and alliances require an operating philosophy that goes beyond just successfully doing business together. Following are some of the critical aspects necessary to having a successful partnership/alliance:

- *Mutual benefit.* Both parties in a strategic relationship must profit from the relationship. Unless the product is satisfactory and the level of service provided is acceptable, neither party will desire to continue a relationship.[6] Problems should be approached collaboratively; both parties should strive to make money while reducing cycle time. The spirit of a win/win mutual benefit must be pervasive and encourage both parties to seek creative solutions.[7]

- *Trust building.* Both parties should be in the relationship for the long haul so that the relationship is not jeopardized by momentary problems or opportunistic behavior. "Even when the relationship is expected to be a short-term one, trust is still essential to the relationship."[8] Suppliers and customers must feel free to exchange ideas without fearing that proprietary information will be divulged to competitors.

• *Open and complete communication.* All responsibilities and expectations of the relationship must be clearly and frequently communicated. The most indispensable element of a customer–supplier relationship is dialogue and feedback.[9] "Immediate feedback from the client company's market directly to the supplier allows the parties to make quick global estimates and promptly introduce the required changes or improvements. It makes available information and ideas that are very useful to both parties."[10]

• *Interdependence of parties.* Effective partnerships foster mutual assistance, joint planning, and other forms of close collaboration.[11] "As the organization becomes more permeable, insiders flow out and outsiders flow in with ease. Suppliers, strategic partners, customers, and experts . . . become involved in open managerial meetings relating to planning, product design, capital budgeting, personnel systems, and operations. Lead users join product planning and design teams. Customer representatives work directly with in-house personnel . . . the 'organization chart' becomes a series of overlapping circles representing cross-disciplinary projects, alliances, and stakeholder relationships, many of which cut across national borders."[12]

F. SUPPLIER LOGISTICS AND MATERIAL ACCEPTANCE

> Describe the impact that purchased products and services can have on final product assembly or total service package, including ship-to-stock, and just-in-time (JIT). Plan and conduct incoming material inspections. (Understand)
>
> Body of Knowledge VI.F

Logistics

Identification, selection, monitoring, and improvement of suppliers are part of the plan–do–check–act cycle of supplier management. An additional important piece is how the interface between purchaser and supplier is planned and implemented. Materials must be available when needed, but this must be done in a manner that considers the costs of transportation, receipt, and storage. This often requires coordination of schedules across multiple organizations in the supply chain.

Push or pull systems might be used to assure that material is available when needed. Push systems require suppliers to ship according to purchasers' demands. Forecasts and demand must be closely aligned and communicated. Pull systems require purchasers to order product from suppliers as replacements for those items that have been used. Pull systems keep purchasers' inventory lower than the push method.

A *ship-to-stock* program utilizes supplier performance and supplier certification as a means of identifying suppliers whose materials can be received directly into the organization without verification. Material is simply moved directly to storage when received. The advantages of ship-to-stock include reduced inventory levels and elimination of incoming inspection.

Just-in-time programs eliminate raw material storage altogether on some products by having the supplier ship materials in smaller quantities more frequently and directly to the point of use (see Chapter 13, Section 3). In making such decisions, the shipping lot size and frequency must consider the time in transit, cost of shipment, and cost of inventory. For example, nuts and bolts can be maintained in inventory very inexpensively, and infrequent shipments with higher inventory may make more financial sense. An automotive assembly plant, however, would probably not want to maintain a large inventory of car seats covering the full range of different colors and materials. Some organizations allow suppliers to replenish small hardware stock on premises without paperwork. The supplier is paid based on the quantity of hardware used on the final products produced.

Working on a just-in-time basis requires close coordination between purchaser and supplier. When feasible, it is best to level demand rather than have large swings (for example, created by special promotions) that require the supplier to radically adjust output levels. When the type of business makes demand leveling difficult, production plans and schedules must be communicated more frequently. This often involves electronic communications between the purchaser's and supplier's advanced planning and enterprise resource planning systems.

A final method being used to improve and simplify the supply chain is the move toward *modular assembly*. It is the process of transferring additional business back to suppliers, who produce a complete subassembly that was previously assembled by the purchaser. The result is that the purchaser receiving the subassembly as a completed item can more effectively integrate the subassembly into the final assembly.

Material Acceptance

Once product is delivered, purchasers need to determine whether that product meets requirements. This is accomplished by source inspection, certification of suppliers, or receiving inspection. The amount or type of inspection depends on the risk the purchaser assumes (see Chapter 15, Section 2) The risk depends on the type of product purchased as well as the supplier's quality system and history (see Figure 18.2 for types of risks). Purchasers need to have a good understanding of the contract, knowledge of the product, and knowledge about the supplier to determine the appropriate material acceptance system.

Product may be directly sent to stock if a supplier is certified, the product has a *certificate of certification*, or if source inspection has been completed. If a supplier is certified, the assumption is that the product meets requirements and can be sent directly to stock. Product that has a certificate of certification—which is supplier-generated data or independent lab data that demonstrate that the product meets requirements—is also sent to stock after the certification data are reviewed. Product that has been *source inspected*—or inspected by the purchaser

Actual

	Good	Bad
Accept	$1 - \alpha$ Producer's confidence	$1 - \beta$ Type II error Consumer's risk
Reject	α Type I error Producer's risk	$1 - \beta$ Consumer's confidence

Decision

Figure 18.2   Risks in sampling.

at the supplier's facility to confirm that product complies to requirements prior to shipping—can also be directly sent to stock.

Incoming, or *receiving*, inspection is used to verify product once it is received from suppliers. Receiving inspection can be a quick check of packaging, or a complete dimensional, visual, chemical, and/or electrical evaluation. Inspection rates can be 100% for product with mandated requirements or a poor quality history, or much less for other product. If inspection is necessary, the most economical way to accept product is through the use of statistical sampling plans (Chapter 15, Section 2). If the product is rejected per the sampling plan, the supplier is to provide corrective action before any additional shipments can be made.

Management of the Supply Chain

When an organization behaves as an integral part of a supply chain, more than just logistics is involved, assuming a working definition of a *supply chain* is "organizations that are interconnected so as to function as if they are one organization in providing goods and services to customers." The role of *supply chain management* (SCM) is to ensure that the right product or service, in the right quantity, of the right quality, gets to the end customer at the right time.

Sometimes, it may appear that achieving effective management of the supply chain would be akin to successfully herding cats. All the linked organizations are constantly changing, as is the marketplace. It may be inevitable that there will be conflicts, incompatible objectives, and breakdowns in communication.

Integrating the entire supply chain, while it is promoted to improve operating costs and increase customer satisfaction, is a daunting task, a task requiring very careful planning and implementation, highly effective support systems in all participating organizations, extreme patience, effective collaboration, and negotiation. This is especially important when the supply chain reaches across the globe, with the added issues of culture, politics, language, education level, and so on.

Compatible information technology is desirable, as is a centralized locale for all pertinent information. Electronic communication systems are needed to complete the linkage.

Establishing strategic partners is vital to the exchange of information and resources. Additionally, partnerships allow for shared risks as well as benefits. How customer demand will be disseminated among the organizations in the chain and how the pace of production will be planned, monitored, and synchronized is critical.

Deciding early on which organization and what person is in charge of SCM is critical. Someone has to facilitate the big decisions or the chain can collapse. Advice on virtually every topic that has been discussed in this book, and some that haven't, is needed to effectively attain and sustain a fully functional supply chain.

ENDNOTES

1. W. E. Deming, *Out of the Crisis* (Cambridge, MA: MIT Center for Advanced Educational Study, 1986).
2. C. Long, *Advanced Supplier Certification* (Seal Beach, CA: World Class Consulting Group, 1995), 4–14.
3. J. T. Israel, "Feedback to Improve Core Customer Relationships: A Framework to Implement Face-to-Face Surveys," *ASQ 52nd Annual Quality Congress Transactions* (May 6, 1997): 423–24.
4. C. R. Bell, *Customers As Partners: Building Relationships That Last* (San Francisco: Berrett-Koehler, 1994), 7.
5. R. Whitely and D. Hessan, *Customer Centered Growth: Five Proven Strategies for Building Competitive Advantage* (Reading, MA: Addison-Wesley, 1996), 34.
6. D. Peppers, M. Rogers, and B. Dorf, "Is Your Company Ready for One-to-One Marketing?" *Harvard Business Review* 77, no. 16 (January–February 1999).
7. N. Imparato and O. Harari, *Jumping the Curve: Innovation and Strategic Choice in an Age of Transition* (San Francisco: Jossey-Bass, 1994), 227.
8. Bell, *Customers As Partners*, 5.
9. Peppers et al., "Is Your Company Ready," 16.
10. G. Merli, *Co-Makership: The New Supply Strategy for Manufacturers* (Cambridge, MA: Productivity Press, 1991), 63.
11. E. J. Broecker, "Build a Better Supplier–Customer Relationship," *Quality Progress* (September 1999): 67.
12. Imparato and Harari, *Jumping the Curve*, 190–91.

See Appendix A for additional references for this chapter.

Part VII

Training and Development

Part VII

An investment in knowledge always pays the best interest.

—Benjamin Franklin

Training increases skill and competence and teaches employees the "how" of a job. Education increases their insights and understanding and teaches the "why."

—Michael Hammer and James Champy

Training—constant, intensive, lavish, and universal—is another hallmark of companies that produce great customer service.

—William Davidow and Bro Uttal

Training, if done correctly and for the right reasons, is not an expense— it's an investment.

—Russ Westcott

Chapter 19

Training and Development

Technical training has been a part of human activity since the earliest times when survival depended on learning how to find food and use tools for agriculture and hunting. During the Middle Ages, the Roman Catholic Church rose to prominence by educating clerics and aristocrats. Likewise, merchant guilds provided education and apprenticeships to children of guild members, who in turn became guild members and worked in the profession. The industrial revolution of the eighteenth and nineteenth centuries changed education and technical training approaches. Colleges and universities were formed to provide public education, and industries began to provide apprenticeships independent of the guilds.

Later, Frederick W. Taylor's scientific management techniques matched individuals to particular jobs and identified the optimal way in which a job could be performed, therefore increasing production output and efficiency. Henry Ford used these methods to create an assembly line. Using this approach, a person could be trained for a particular, defined job, precluding the need for a broader education. This was a departure from the previous master craftsman model, in which a worker was expected to understand all aspects of the job.

Today, increasingly complex technology, more-comprehensive management systems, accelerated change, and global competition require that employees have formal education in addition to technical training. Also, inasmuch as change is occurring at an ever-increasing rate, the need for continual individual development is crucial. It has been said that the average college graduate may look forward to upward of seven career changes (careers, not just jobs) in his or her working lifetime.

Distinguishing Between Training and Education

The terms *education* and *training* are often used interchangeably. Education, however, is the process of acquiring knowledge and information, usually in a formal manner. Education equips learners to acquire new knowledge by teaching them how to think. Examples are the study and understanding of human behavior, team dynamics, and the principles of statistics. On the other hand, *training* is the process of acquiring proficiency in some skill or skill set. Examples are team leadership and facilitation, and the application of the seven quality control tools. Figure 19.1 compares two workers with relatively equal basic skills and abilities. What differences will emerge if, over a period of time, education is provided to one and

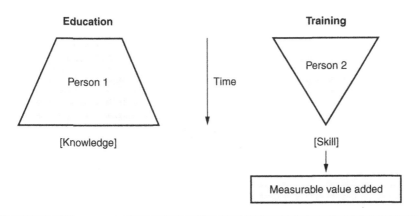

Figure 19.1   Training versus education.

training to the other? If the education process is successful, the worker receiving education will have broadened his or her knowledge base, therefore expanding his or her thinking processes. The worker being trained will have received specific instruction in how to perform tasks for his or her job.

The outcome of education is typically measured by testing comprehension and knowledge retention. Training is usually measured by the learner's ability to demonstrate the learned skill by producing desired outputs (for example, by correctly drawing a blood sample from a patient).

An education course may not involve much training. A training program usually involves some education in the theory or principles underlying the development and need for the skill. Taking a refresher course in preparation for the Certified Manager of Quality/Organizational Excellence examination involves learning some skills in test taking, but is primarily the assimilation, or reawakening, of knowledge in a broad range of subjects, hence mostly education. Unfortunately, the two terms are frequently used interchangeably, for example, "A Sarbanes-Oxley Training Course." Understanding which parts of the course or program are education and which parts are training is important in the design, delivery, and evaluation of the offering.

Quality management is how a business is managed. It's the horizontal, across-the-organization view, including performance measures and integration with strategic planning. To be a Big Q quality manager or director suggests a need to continually reeducate oneself and to continually acquire new skills and sharpen proven skill sets. Also, due to the rapid increase in and importance of knowledge work, there is a need for continual education and training. Often, the competency (the sum of knowledge, experience, skills, aptitude, and attitude) of the workforce can be a factor that differentiates world-class learning organizations from their competitors.

Empowering workers to be responsible for the quality of their work has become routine in many industries. Inspection can often be eliminated when controlling the process and/or preventing defects is emphasized. This requires broader worker capabilities and effective training so that workers will know when and how to react to changing conditions.

A. TRAINING PLANS

> Develop and implement training plans that are aligned with the organization's strategic plan and general business needs, including leadership training and alignment of personal development plans. (Create)
>
> **Body of Knowledge VII.A**

Alignment with Strategic Planning and Business Needs

For most organizations, training is a significant budget item. During downturns in business it is often the first place where cost reduction is ordered. Therefore, it is imperative to view training as a strategic, cost-justified investment. It is the cost of not training that needs to be addressed when considering investing in training. Training is most beneficial to the organization when the training program's role in achieving the goals and objectives of the organization's strategic plan is supported by top management (for example, strategic plans include plans and budget for training).

Juran and Gryna suggest consideration of the following six issues when planning for training:

1. The quality problems and challenges faced by the organization

2. The knowledge and skills needed to solve these problems and meet these challenges

3. The knowledge and skills actually possessed by the jobholders

4. The training facilities and processes already in existence

5. The prevailing climate for training in the organization, based on the record of past programs

6. What needs to be done differently to achieve the desired quality[1]

Top management's support and personal commitment to training efforts should result in:

- The integration of training into business planning as a quality-inducing process.

- Management being role models for reinforcing the daily use of quality principles throughout the organization.

- Trainees grasping the connection between what they are to learn and the strategic objectives of the organization (for example, continual improvement, customer focus, product and service quality, productivity, profit, and employee training and development).

- Preparing workers to deal with changing expectations through training.

- Establishing the acquiring of training skills as a requisite skill set for all management and team leaders.

- Effective training design and delivery.

- Consistent and frequent on-the-job recognition for work done well.

- Coaching to reinforce the worker's use of post-training skills.

- Treatment of training as an investment in the future.

- Application of benefits-to-cost analysis to justify training and to measure results of training. If there is no expected return on training investment (ROTI), training should not be done.

- Training practitioners striving to adequately study, assess, and address the needs of the organization's mainline operations.

- Measuring the training's effectiveness in terms of the improved outcomes of the organization affected by the training (for example, by collaboration/partnering between the training professionals and operations work units to achieve a mutually measurable outcome).

- Treating training as important in building and sustaining a superbly trained workforce. (A significant marketing strategy that may be used to differentiate an organization from its competitors.)

- Realizing the value of training and placing it high on the list of priorities for resource allocation.

At the daily operational level, education might be advantageous to introduce new concepts or principles (for example, the concept of cycle time reduction and its impact on quality, or the principles of process management). Training might be warranted to build new skills, to refresh fading skills, or to qualify individuals to a prescribed standard. Such education and training at the operating level must still be traceable to the organization's strategic plans and objectives.

A proposed training program should be evaluated through a benefit–cost analysis (see Chapter 10, Section 2). The resulting budget should be supported by top management as it identifies the trade-offs between the cost of and the benefits that are realized by doing the training. Depending on the detail desired, the training costs can include trainee salaries, production time lost during training, facilities, training materials and equipment, and trainer or consultant costs. With a focus on the results expected from the training, benefits can include improved customer satisfaction, better product or service quality, reduced scrap, less rework, fewer returns, improved productivity, increased employee retention and improved employee morale, and a more flexible workforce.

Education and training are processes for supporting an organization's strategic objectives. Examples include building a new or updated core competency to address a threatening competitive situation, introducing a state-of-the-art technological change, or increasing customer satisfaction by reducing order response time. Organizations that use a systemic approach for translating the strategic plans and associated training objectives to the lowest levels of the organization, such as those using hoshin planning (discussed in Chapter 5), will have the best chances for success. This process is valuable because it helps everyone in the organization better understand how training supports goals and objectives.

What Training Can and Can Not Do

An organization should be aware that training will not solve all its problems. At times, organizations attempt to use training to solve a problem when lack of skill is not the issue. Training can not remedy a situation caused by poor performance or other root causes that are not skill related. Mager and Pipe offer a diagnostic process for analyzing and correcting performance problems.[2] Table 19.1 offers questions to help direct the actions to take.

The first consideration, before committing any resources, is to clearly differentiate whether the operating problem or situation is a performance deficiency or a knowledge/skill deficiency. It is often stated in the training field that whenever a manager says that a training problem exists, much of the time the problem is found to be something in the system, not the people performing the job. Correcting deficiencies in job execution is often best achieved by changing resources, by providing more objective feedback, or by adding or removing behavioral consequences. For example, if an individual is not performing the job but could do so if his or her life depended on it, retraining is not the answer.

Planning for training should closely resemble the planning done for projects (see Chapter 10). For example:

- A need is identified.

- An objective and outputs and outcomes are stated.

- Stakeholders (trainees) are identified.

- Development work to be done is laid out (work breakdown structure).

- A timetable for development, delivery, and evaluation is set (Gantt chart).

- Resource requirements are specified (trainers, facilities, equipment, materials).

- Applicable metrics are established.

- A budget is developed.

- The plans are approved.

- The training program development is monitored and measured.

- Training is delivered.

- Outputs are evaluated (ability to perform task).

- Outcomes are evaluated (training objective achieved).

- Lessons learned are reviewed.

Table 19.1   Deficiency analysis.

Question	Answer	Action
1. Why does performer fail to do job as trained?	Doesn't understand what is expected.	Ask another question.
2. Why does performer not understand what is expected?	Doesn't recall what was covered in training.	Ask another question.
3. Why doesn't performer recall content of training?	Doesn't have any notes or receive other references as to what was covered.	Ask another question.
4. Why does performer not have reference material from training?	Wasn't given any, or told where to get any.	Ask another question.
5. Were training materials given to the performer?	No. Instructor says none were available and trainees were told to "take notes."	Ask another question.
6. Why didn't performer take notes?	Performer has only sixth grade education and was not familiar with note taking.	Ask another question.
7. Why didn't instructor use handouts?	There was no formal course design and none were provided.	Ask another question.
8. Why was there no course design and no print material available for training use?	Selecting an "experienced old hand" to give the course was considered sufficient.	Ask another question.
9. In the absence of print material, why didn't performer's supervisor detect apparent reason for the performance deficiency?	The supervisor assumed the performer was ignoring or refusing to perform in accordance with the training.	Ask another question.
10. Does the performer need to be disciplined or be retrained?	Retrain, but with an improved training design, support materials, and supervisory reinforcement. Discipline is inappropriate (it was the "fault" of the system, and management's responsibility).	Redesign training. Retrain performer. Tutor supervisor on how to reinforce training.

Source: Reprinted with permission of R. T. Westcott & Associates.

- Documentation of the development and delivery process, outputs, and outcomes is added to the organization's knowledge database.

Training Is a Process

Whether training is conducted one-to-one, on-the-job, through remote electronic interface, or in a classroom, there is a process cycle, as depicted in the training system model, Figure 19.2. Steps in the process are:

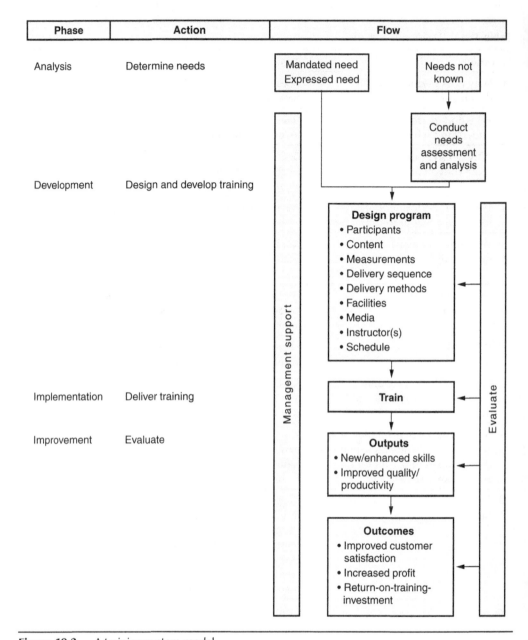

Figure 19.2   A training system model.

1. Determine training needs:

   • Mandated or expressed need—verify and clarify.

   • Needs unknown—conduct needs assessment.

   • Propose training program—obtain approval and funding for design.

2. Design the training program:

- Identify participants.

- Determine objectives, content, and sequence of instruction (if to be designed internally).

- Determine applicable metrics, measurement criteria and process.

- Select/design the training delivery method(s) (if to be delivered by an internal trainer) or assess/select an appropriate external provider.

- Select/design the facilities.

- Select/design the media to be used.

- Select instructor(s)—train instructors as needed.

- Set training schedule.

- Test, evaluate, and modify the training as needed.

3. Deliver the training.

4. Evaluate the effectiveness of the training:

- Instructional objectives met? Desired outputs produced?

5. Post-training:

- Desired outcomes met?

- Maintain the improvement—ROI?

- Sustain the gains (responsibility of the management of the work unit[s] from which trainees came).

B. TRAINING NEEDS ANALYSIS

> Use various tools and techniques such as surveys, performance reviews, regulatory requirements, and gap analysis to identify training needs. (Create)
>
> **Body of Knowledge VII.B**

When training and/or education are determined to be the best solution to the problem or situation, the next step is to determine the needs. Considerations when establishing these needs are:

- Is the need mandated by a regulatory body (for example, safety, hazardous materials, food quality, toxic material use)? Is the need clearly defined?

- Is the need mandated by management in support of a specific strategic objective (for example, customer contact skills or an ISO 9001–based quality system)? Is the need clearly defined?

- If not mandated, is the need directed toward correcting a knowledge/skill deficiency? If so, who are the affected individuals? How many individuals are affected? Where are they located? What do they need to learn to do? What do they presently know about how to do what they are expected to do? What is the expected outcome of the training? Within what time frame must the individuals be trained? Need all individuals affected be trained at one time, together, or individually, or just in time?

- What delivery method is most appropriate for the needed training (instructor-led classroom training, self-directed, on-the-job training, or other)?

- What facilities, methods/programs, trainers, materials, equipment and so on, are available?

- What presently unavailable resources are needed to achieve the training or education objective?

- If primarily a training need, does a benefits–cost analysis justify the training? How will the training be funded (budget, appropriation, grant or subsidy, or other)?

- How should the training effectiveness be measured and evaluated (for example, demonstration of skills learned, on-the-job performance improvement, or return on training investment)?

- What top management commitment and personal involvement are necessary to successfully execute the training and education plans?

A design can be determined once needs have been established, the number of individuals to be affected has been identified, the availability of personnel and facilities has been confirmed, and so on. The needs, timing, resources available, funding, and operating constraints will affect the method of delivery selected. Here are a few examples:

- Two newly hired workers, who need basic safety, housekeeping, and ISO 9001–quality system orientation, when reporting for work might be asked to watch three DVDs and successfully complete a quiz to demonstrate assimilation and understanding of the learning points. (Education)

- All machine operators need to learn how to use a new onboard statistical process control computer terminal to be installed at their machines. Training is needed just before the new system goes online. Appropriate just-in-time training might consist of instructor-led classroom training with each individual demonstrating the requisite skills to perform the task. (Training)

- One-to-one on-the-job training by a skilled operator is one solution for an experienced machine operator transferred to a new work cell where unfamiliar machinery is in use. Another solution could be to send the operator to a course offered by the machinery manufacturer. (Training)

As these examples imply, the variety of designs and the media possible for training and/or education is extensive. For a large percentage of skill-related needs, the use of on-the-job training by a skilled trainer/supervisor and the introduction of job aids (for example, checklists, work instructions, and diagrams) is often an effective solution.

Fade-out is a significant issue. It is the decline of a learned skill as time elapses between training delivery and on-the-job use of the learned skill. For this reason, it is best to schedule training just prior to participants' need for the skill, on the job. Likewise, when a skill is infrequently used, the skill fades out and refresher training may be needed.

Purposes of a Needs Assessment and Analysis

Training may be indicated for one or more of the following reasons:

- To comply with new or changed regulatory and/or customer requirements

- To address new or changed systems, processes, procedures, methods, equipment, or tools

- To add or modify skills

- To refresh previous training to ensure maintenance of a specific skill

- To qualify and/or certify an individual to a specific workmanship standard

- To correct a skill deficiency noted in an individual's performance appraisal

In addition, there are often needs to satisfy that are not strictly training. These education needs could be to:

- Provide company orientation for new or transferred employees.

- Provide knowledge of theories and concepts pertinent to the organization's products or services and practices, such as theory pertaining to electrical currents and transmission.

- Provide knowledge of required and/or acceptable work behaviors.

- Mentor an individual in personal development planning and/or career advancement.

Part VII.B

Assessing Training Needs

An assessment of training needs can range from a companywide periodic assessment in which the analysis provides data for an annual training plan and budget, to a simple observation that a given employee does not know how to perform an assigned task. Many companies address their training needs by matching people to jobs on the basis of formal education acquired, then training them in the specific requirements of the job. For this to be successful, the needs assessment should begin with top management and the organization's strategic plan. The following issues may be appropriate to address:

- Strategic plans, goals, business objectives, and action plans
- Major changes anticipated for the short and long term
- Primary customers served
- Plans for entering a new market (requiring workforce retraining)
- Products or services produced and technologies used presently
- Organizational structure
- Decision makers
- Impact of political realities (internal and external)
- Micro cultures and policies of each business unit
- Budget approval process
- Present core competencies of employees
- Future core competencies employees will need
- History and significance of technical training in the organization
- Competitor's approach to training and education
- Industry standards and regulations affecting technical training

A proper assessment of needs helps prioritize resources to ensure that they are available to address the most critical training needs. Finally, the needs assessment process must be deployed to each business unit, which in turn cascades it downward until the training needs of individual employees are addressed.

There are many techniques and tools for determining training needs and for separating out non-training needs. Data obtained from these needs assessment and analysis tools provide information for designing program content, and a baseline for evaluating training, and aid in selecting participants, instructors, facilities, equipment, and media.

Needs Assessment Techniques and Tools

- Review of existing records determines the magnitude of a training and/or education deficiency. Types of records include performance reports, job descriptions, performance appraisals, meeting minutes, process audit reports, and training programs completed. Output is a matrix showing the records accessed, the needs uncovered, and the magnitude of the need.

- Interviews of exemplary performers may be conducted to ascertain the level of competence that is attainable by performers who exhibit the most effective KESAA factors in the work units from which participants will be selected.[3] Output is a summary of the key KESAA factors for the jobs or work units targeted. See Figure 3.2 for a KESAA requisites analysis sample.

- Focus groups may be used to collect stated needs from a cross-section of key employees, conducted with small groups of eight to 10 employees, using structured discussion questions, with a facilitator. Output is a summarization of the needs surfaced and the tasks, processes, and/or work unit wherefrom the needs emanate.

- Organizational diagnosis for an entire organization examines relationships and communication—vertically, horizontally, and diagonally. The output is a summary of findings and conclusions and recommended actions.

- Job analysis consists of breaking a job down to levels of increasing specificity. Outputs are a sequenced task listing by level, and job inventories.

- Task analysis involves the specification of all overt and covert behaviors pertinent to the performance of a job. Outputs can be stimulus–response tables, flowcharts, time and motion studies, and behavior observation check sheets.

- Front-end analysis can be accomplished through many techniques, for example, a performance audit, root cause analysis, or a competency analysis. The outputs provide data in a variety of formats, usually a matrix.

- Instruments for collecting data for analysis can include tests, questionnaires, surveys, checklists, simulations, games, self-completed assessments, and recorded performance reviews.

- Techniques involving personal interaction can include observations of work being performed, individual or group interviews, brainstorming, focus groups, and *needs analysis by walking around* (NABWA). Outputs would be a categorization of the needs detected, where the needs are prevalent, and the perceived magnitude of the needs.

- Qualitative data analysis techniques can be used to analyze nonquantitative data, such as data expressed in words, phrases, and paragraphs.

- Critical incident analysis is the recording and analysis of personal accounts (examples of situations) of incidents pertinent to needs for training. Similar to collecting personal stories, but briefer.

- Surveys, questionnaires, and checklists are used to collect data about a group's interests in and desires for training. Because the focus is on the employees' interests and desires and not the organizational needs, this method is usually not considered an effective way to surface skills training needs. It may, however, have some value in indicating educational needs.

For a simple approach to determine needs at the individual level:

- Talk with the performers.

- Talk with the performers' bosses.

- Talk with subordinates, peers, and customers with whom the performers have contact.

- Observe a performer and/or give the performer a test.

- Obtain needs from performance appraisals.

When the Need Is to Improve Job Performance

When conducting a needs assessment, the problem that surfaces is frequently a performance problem. Conducting a training program is not a viable solution when job behavior (and attitude), poor supervision, or an inadequacy of job design, material, tools, or equipment are the cause of deficient performance. To determine whether the deficiency is a performance problem rather than lack of knowledge and skill, apply the test questions listed in Table 19.2.

From answers to the questions in the table:

- Select a *job* solution (J) if the problem is the way the task is organized or if the tools, and so on, are inadequate. Note: The skill might not be needed at all if the job/task can be eliminated or redesigned.

- If the performer lacks the requisite knowledge/skills, select a *training* solution (T).

- If the problem is that the performer does not know what is expected of her or him, select a solution that improves performance *feedback* (F).

- If the performer is capable of doing the work, but fails to do it, take action to change the *consequences* (C) of doing the job. Note: An incentive may also be considered, for example, self-assessment of performance, empowerment, or profit sharing.

- Frequently, performers know how to get the job done, but receive more negative than positive consequences for doing so, and really do not know what is expected of them. A solution is to train supervisors in how to provide performance feedback and positive consequences for work done well (a T, F, and C for supervisors).

Of course, a situation might be detected in which both a knowledge/skill deficiency and a performance problem exist. The performance problem should be resolved first so that training efforts are not wasted.

Table 19.2   Distinguishing between performance and skill/knowledge issues.

Relative to target population (TP)	J	T	F	C
Does TP have time to do job well?	X	X		
Does TP have proper facilities in which to work?	X			
Does TP have the proper tools to do the work?	X			
Does TP have proper procedures, instructions, job aids?	X			
Does TP know what they are supposed to do?		X	X	
Has TP ever done the job correctly?		X	X	
Could TP do the job properly if their lives depended on it?		X		X
If TP could do the job in an exemplary way, would they?				X
Are there more negative than positive consequences in doing the job?				X
Does TP know when they are not performing as supervisor expects?			X	
Do supervisors of TP have requisite knowledge/skills?		X	X	X

Source: Reprinted with permission of R. T. Westcott & Associates.

Caveats

Ineffective or poor assessment of needs can negatively impact a training program. Following are examples of corrective actions focused on preventing these problems:

- Training plan changed to address specific organizational goals and objectives.

- Training is necessary to address a specific process or task need.

- Identified job skills are deficient and training is needed immediately.

- The work problem has been clearly identified, and training is the right solution, regardless of the organizational levels of those persons to be trained.

- It is planned that the right participants will be trained in the right skills, by the right trainers, for the right reasons, and at the right time.

- Any purchased or outsourced training is keyed to appropriate business needs and constraints.

- Training is effectively designed, delivered, evaluated, and reinforced to meet the organization's needs. That is, training appropriately addresses the identified gaps.

If the value to be gained by training does not exceed the cost, a less expensive training method should be used, or the training should not take place. People should not be trained until there is an immediate way for them to use the skill. Most of the skills-acquisition process should focus on learning by doing, but sequencing learning activities in the order they are performed on the job is not always best. Building from simpler to more complex sub-tasks may be a better way to build toward achieving mastery of complex tasks.

Circulating a list of available or potential courses for employees to indicate their preference *is not* a needs assessment. Employees often do not know what they need. This may be true if:

- Little or no effective performance feedback is provided, so the employee does not have a clear view of what is expected of her or him nor of her or his performance related to that expectation.

- Employee is unaware of organizational objectives and conditions that could affect his or her job (for example, new product introduction, new process/equipment, new regulations).

- Receiving the list is perceived to mean the employee must check off something.

- The perception is that something additional will be expected if a course is attended.

- The courses listed appear to have no relation to the employee's work.

- Attending a course may be just a way of getting out of doing work.

The skill level of the intended training participants should be assessed so that training can be structured to build on present skill levels. People should not be trained in a skill they already can demonstrate. Finally, if there is a performance problem and lack of skill is not an issue, some other solution is indicated.

C. TRAINING MATERIALS, DEVELOPMENT, AND DELIVERY

Use various tools, resources, and methodologies to develop training materials and curriculum that address adult learning principles and the learning needs of an increasingly diverse workforce. Describe various methods of training delivery: classroom, workbooks, simulations, computer-delivered, on-the-job, and self-directed. Use mentoring and coaching to support training outcomes. (Apply)

Body of Knowledge VII.C

Training and Education—Differences by Organizational Level

Often, the term *training* is not used with top management. Executive education may take the form of multi-day retreats, combining learning and leisure activities, or it could consist of intensive learning events at a prestigious academic institution. For shorter-term education, executive briefings are the norm. *Forums* and *symposia* are other terms used.

Management training is the term typically used when providing education and training courses, workshops, or seminars for supervisors/managers or in preparing individuals to assume a supervisory/managerial role. Many successful companies cascade knowledge down throughout the organization by having management learn first, then having managers instruct their direct reports. It is an excellent way for management to demonstrate support, become personally involved, and better comprehend the subject matter. As the Body of Knowledge for the ASQ CMQ/OE examination suggests, managing requires an eclectic repertoire of skills (for example, technical skills for the functions managed, planning and organizing skills, staffing and people management skills, project management skills, and training, coaching, and mentoring skills). In addition, managers need to develop skills in managing conflict and negotiations, as well as build a solid understanding of variation and the use of measurements.

In most organizations the quality manager is the in-house expert on quality issues and, as such, is expected to be involved in helping identify the quality subject training needs for other managers. The quality manager should ensure that the quality-related technical content of a training program meets the training needs.

It is not enough simply for training to be conducted; it is extremely important that follow-up activities require the manager to use the knowledge or skill gained in the training session. If a manager is not required to employ the new skill immediately, only a small portion of the training is likely to be retained. Additionally, a manager must be given the opportunity to apply the new skill in the environment in which it is expected to be used. The training should be reinforced and evaluated periodically to ensure that the concepts are understood and the skills are practiced.

Training for managers differs from that for other employees because managers often are not expected to actually do the things that are the subject of the training, but rather are expected to be able to oversee proper application of the training. A simple example involves training in statistical process control (SPC).

An operator would be expected to actually use the skills learned in training to record the data and control the process. To do this, the operator would need to understand control chart rules and what action to take when out-of-control conditions are shown on the chart. A manager, however, needs to not only oversee the worker's proper use of SPC, but also needs to interpret the data at a higher level. For example, a manager must determine whether the average or range chart control limits are so broad that action is required at the machine to improve capability even when the process is in control. The manager may also create systems so SPC charts can be properly employed within the organization.

Part VII.C

The ISO 9000 series quality system standards, and other standards, have heightened awareness of the need for training and qualifying personnel who conduct activities pertaining to quality, as defined in the organization's quality plan, procedures, and practices. Typical basic training topics for all employees include quality principles and practices, problem-solving methods, the basic quality tools, working as a team member, team protocols, and interpersonal skills. Training is also needed in the technical aspects of a job.

Skills required in day-to-day activities can be acquired through formal training or through *on-the-job training* (OJT). When practical, employee training may be more effective when formal training is combined with OJT. Both formal training and OJT need a defined structure, clear objectives, and a method for demonstrating competency. Regardless of the training system used, the trainer must be qualified to teach the topic/skill to be trained (including underlying concepts and the reason for training), must know how to properly use requisite tools and references (including any equipment used to deliver training), and should be aware of how to best train adults. Knowles has delineated theories of learning and teaching for adults.[4]

Nonmanagerial employees tend to receive more-specific OJT than do managers. On-the-job-training can be highly effective because the training is typically conducted in the actual work environment—on the same equipment and using the same processes used in day-to-day activities.[5] Historically, OJT normally has been conducted by a manager or other employee familiar with job requirements. Especially in organizations that face rapid rates of change and thus have difficulties keeping current with technology, however, outsourcing training to external training providers has become a trend.

When a supervisor/manager conducts the training, training could be ineffective, abbreviated, and superficial if:

- The time that a manager can devote to the training effort is limited.
- The supervisor/manager lacks the competency to conduct training.
- Training is unplanned.
- Time for training is not a high priority.
- Managers/supervisors who do not do the job routinely lack firsthand knowledge of all the things that must be done to do the job successfully.

There are a few precepts for performer-level training:

- Trainers need to understand that the learner is always in control of what is learned. For a training program or an OTJ learning experience to be fully effective, the learners need to see clearly how what is being taught will benefit them and fulfill a felt need in them.[6] This is true of both managers and other employees, but because managers have the authority to set directions, a failure to recognize this fact can effectively nullify the training efforts.

- A training program should address benefits in terms of the trainee's needs. The information presented must be reinforced with actual hands-on application of the skills. Although hands-on activities can be simulated in a classroom setting, it is better, when feasible, to actually do these activities in the work environment, as described in this example.

A program for teaching internal quality auditing to employees consists of several steps. First, the program establishes the purposes and benefits of internal auditing to the participants and to the organization. Second, the program examines the elements of auditing and explains how to establish an audit schedule, prepare a checklist, conduct an opening meeting, perform the audit, hold the closing meeting, report audit results, and follow up on any problems detected. Classroom training is supplemented with exercises and role-playing to demonstrate and reinforce the skills presented. The procedures the organization follows in preparing for an actual audit, for example, preparing a checklist, are to be followed exactly. Training continues with employees demonstrating competence in all the skills learned by performing an actual audit in a unit of the organization. The trainer(s) should supervise and coach participants throughout the entire auditing process, including the audit team's issuance of the audit report and audit follow-up activities.

Designing the Training Program

ASQ's self-directed learning series *Certified Manager of Quality/Organizational Excellence Program* presents in Module 7 a five-phase instructional design model called *ADDIE*, representing:

1. A. The *analysis* phase provides the opportunity to get the target training audience, including prospective participants and their managers, directly involved in determining what training should take place, how it should be delivered, and who should participate.

2. D. The *design* phase is where decisions regarding course content, delivery methods, measurement and evaluation, and implementation strategies are made.

3. D. In the *development* phase, training materials are created, purchased, and/or modified to meet the training need.

4. I. During *implementation*, the training is delivered to the target audience.

5. E. *Evaluation* consists of determining what final results occurred because of attendance and participation in the training encounter.

Following a needs assessment/analysis, the next step is to design (or purchase) a cost-effective training program. The intent of the program is to produce the desired outputs and outcomes with the least expenditure of resources.

A training program can be as simple as planning for one-to-one OTJ training for an individual, or as involved as training large groups of employees in a new process or the use of new equipment. Regardless, there should be a defined training plan and documented evidence that the training was successfully completed.

The major factors to consider in designing a training program are:

- Who needs the training (participants)? How many are there, and where are they located?

- Why do they need the training? What are they doing now? At what skill level are they now?

- What do they need to learn? How much of what they need is knowledge, and how much is pure skill attainment?

- What measurement(s) will best indicate that participants can do the tasks to which they are assigned (apply the skills acquired)?

- What basis will be used to evaluate the success of the training program?

- What method is best for delivering the training within the organization's resource constraints (for example, classroom, on-the-job, outside training provider, or other method)?

- Where can the training best be delivered (which facility, what room, at or away from the workplace)?

- What media are best to use in delivering the training (for example, audio, visuals, video, print, intranet, or the internet)?

- Who should deliver the training? What trainer qualifications are needed? If not a qualified trainer or facilitator, will training of a trainer be needed? How many trainers are needed?

- When would training best be done? What is the best schedule, considering workplace demands?

- What is the projected return on training investment (ROTI)? Is the planned training worth the investment?

Adult Learning Principles. Before an organization can select the appropriate methods and tools to use in quality training, it must first understand how adults learn. In general, adults exert more control over their lives than do younger people, and this desire for control extends to the learning process as well. Knowles identifies six factors that influence adult learning:

1. Adults have a need to know why they should learn something.

2. Adults have a deep need to be self-directing.

3. Adults have a deeper, broader, greater, different quality of experience than youths.

4. Adults become ready to learn when they experience in their life situation a need to know or to be able to perform more effectively and satisfactorily.

5. Adults enter into a learning experience with a task-centered (or problem-centered or life-centered) orientation to learning.

6. Adults are motivated to learn by both extrinsic and intrinsic motivators.[7]

The andragogical model requires that learners be actively involved in the process of evaluating their learning outcomes. Knowles and Hartl propose the following six questions:

1. What procedures would I use with this particular group to encourage conditions of mutual respect, cooperation rather than competition, support rather than judgment, mutual trust, and having fun while learning?

2. What procedures will I use to involve the learners continuously in planning?

3. What procedures will I use to help the participants diagnose their own learning needs?

4. What procedures can I use to help participants translate learning needs into learning objectives?

5. What procedures can I use to involve the learners with me in designing and managing a pattern of learning experiences?

6. What procedures can I use to involve the learners responsibly in evaluating the accomplishment of their learning objectives?[8]

Learning Objectives. Learning objectives are sometimes called *terminal objectives* because they address what will be learned by the end of the training module or program. These objectives contain a statement of the resulting observable actions planned, the measurable criterion for each action, and the conditions under which performance will be measured.

Bloom's Taxonomy of Educational Objectives categorizes objectives in three domains: cognitive (or mental skills), affective (growth in feelings, emotional areas), and psychomotor (manual, physical skills). The cognitive domain is subdivided into six behaviors:

- Remember (knowledge level)

- Understand (comprehension level)

- Apply (application level)

- Analyze (analysis level)

- Evaluate (evaluation level)

- Create (synthesis level)

The reader will recognize the cognitive domain behaviors from their use in categorizing the complexity level of the Body of Knowledge and test questions for the CMQ/OE exam. (See the Body of Knowledge in Chapter 20.) The affective domain is subdivided into five behaviors: receiving, responding, valuing, organization, and characterization.

Lesson Plans. Lesson plans specify what material will be presented during a particular training session. Johnson lists the following guidelines for the successful development of lesson plans:

1. Lesson plans are crucial for [guiding the trainer to achieving] training success.

2. Every subject must be adequately researched.

3. Develop twice as much material as you think you will need.

4. Ensure that trainees know what's in it for them early on so they are motivated to learn.

5. Practice, practice, practice prior to presentation.

6. Use examples that pertain to the operation where possible.

7. Stimulate questions.

8. Use training aids.

9. Adapt the training to the group's level.

10. Never make excuses. For example, "I've never taught this material before."

11. Remain positive.

12. Follow your lesson plan.[9]

Johnson identifies four types of lesson plans: topical outline, manuscript, sentence, and key word.[10] The type of lesson plan developed depends on the instructor's experience and familiarity with the material, whether he or she has presented it previously, and the degree of formality desired in the presentation of the material. Note: Purchased training programs often include one or more suggested lesson plans.

Competency-based training methods may also be referred to as *individualized instruction, mastery learning,* or *programmed instruction.* There are fundamental differences between what students learn, how they learn, when they learn, and if they learn each task. Competency-based training focuses on these key features:

- *Outputs.* Learners know exactly what they will be able to do upon completion.

- *Learner-centered.* Training is organized to accommodate individuals' needs, for example, speed of learning, need for feedback, sequence of learning (simple to complex).

- *Job breakdown.* Jobs are subdivided into tasks with terminal performance objectives for each task.

- *Mastery.* One task is mastered by the learner before moving to the next (often moving from the simple to the more complex steps before rearranging the steps into the logical work sequence).

- *Performance.* Learners must meet a high job proficiency level, in a job-type environment, to obtain acknowledgment of completion.

- *Competency.* Competency is achieved when the learner has acquired the requisite knowledge, experience, and skill to perform a worthwhile job in a prescribed way.

Methods of Training Delivery

Traditionally, instructional modes have included live instructors, printed handouts, and media aids (for example, whiteboards, chalkboards, flip charts, and overhead projection of slides, or computerized projection). Lectures, discussions, role-plays, simple paper-based games, case studies, workbooks, DVDs, CDs, and self-directed learning with printed materials are often used. Lectures and role playing date back to classical Greece, more than 2000 years ago. Lectures were the primary method of instruction, but creative instructors now use many other tools to enhance learning.

Learner-Controlled Instruction. Increasingly, newer technologies for delivering learner-controlled instruction (LCI), also called *self-directed learning* (SDL), are becoming available. Working without an instructor and at their own pace, adult learners build toward ultimate mastery of the needed knowledge/skill. Learner-controlled instruction works well when there is only one person to train at any given time, when the learners are geographically distant, when training needs to occur at multiple sites simultaneously, when consistency of skill execution is a necessity, or when refresher training is needed.

The trend toward LCI/SDL reinforces the trend toward the use of technology-based training, as new technologies both stimulate and enable direct interaction between the individual and the material to be learned. Internet-based programs with learner–instructor interaction are currently popular for delivery of certain types of standardized training (for example, computer application training). ASQ provides many media choices and topics for self-directed training.

Lectures and Presentations. A *lecture* is a one-dimensional, oral transmission of information to students by an instructor, either in-person or via electronic media. It is still frequently used to convey concepts and content to students, and often is used in combination with other tools. Lectures are one type of presentation, but presentations can also include other oral, visual, and multimedia formats.

Discussion Format. The discussion format allows participants freedom to present views, opinions, and ideas in an unrestrained environment. Round tables and panel discussions are variations. These methods normally work best with a knowledgeable and experienced discussion leader. The *Socratic method* of repeated questioning has been successfully used to elicit and share the accumulated knowledge and experience of course members.

Experiential Training. The focus of this form of training is on experiencing the effects typically encountered in a real-life situation. The experiential approach employs many types of structured experiences (for example, games, simulations, role-plays) to facilitate learning. Typically, participants assume roles within a stated scenario designed to surface one or more learning points. They then play out the scenario to a conclusion under the eye of a skilled facilitator. A well-designed scenario will tend to produce a predictable range of responses highlighting the training content. Experiential training is used more for training in the softer, interpersonal skills areas, such as managing people.

Coaching. Used on a one-to-one basis, or for a small group or team, and conducted at the workplace, coaching is a teaching, learning, and counseling relationship designed to develop job-related knowledge and skills and improve performance. It requires a continuous flow of instructions, comments, explanations, and suggestions from coach to trainee—with the coach demonstrating, listening, questioning, acknowledging learners' experiences, assisting, motivating, encouraging, and rewarding performance. The coaching option is used primarily to teach complex skills and operations, when the number of trainees is small and the training is needed infrequently, and as a follow-on to other forms of employee training. It has the advantage of being flexible and adaptable. Its disadvantage is that its success depends on the competence of the coach.

Coaching can be applied to work groups or teams, in which it closely resembles the sports team coaching model. Finnerty outlines the following steps for effective coaching:

- Define performance goals.
- Identify the resources necessary for success.
- Observe and analyze current performance.
- Set expectations for performance improvement.
- Plan a coaching schedule.
- Meet with the individual or team to get commitment to goals, demonstrate the desired behavior, and establish boundaries.
- Give feedback on practice and performance.
- Follow up to maintain goals.[11]

Case Studies. Many different kinds of learning exercises fall under the category of case studies. Such exercises illustrate the application of study content and show how different approaches can be used to solve problems. Case studies can serve to stimulate intense discussions and idea sharing.

Case studies can be developed in-house or purchased from a variety of sources. A form of mini case study, the *critical incident,* may often be of greater value than a larger, more inclusive case study. The critical incident is usually derived from real situations within the organization for which the training is designed. A critical incident might consist of just a few sentences describing a specific type of event or condition without reference to names or locations. Critical incidents are usually inserted throughout the training to illustrate specific learning points. The advantages of critical incidents are:

- They are easier to prepare than a fully developed case study.

- Participants can usually identify with the situation (it is their organization).

- Discussion is more targeted, with less confusion generated than with the multifaceted case study.

- They take less discussion time and get to the learning points quickly.

Concerns relating to critical incidents are:

- Data used to compile critical incidents must be collected prior to course design, necessitating a plan and time to do so.

- A critical incident is a carefully crafted, succinct representation (usually written) designed to engender learning about how to respond to a specific event/situation/condition. A critical incident should not be confused with anecdotal material ("war stories") that is used extemporaneously to illustrate a point and/or to inject humor.

- Care must be taken to not target, purposely or accidentally, any person or work unit in the company. Data must appear anonymous.

Workbooks. Workbooks contain a collection of discussion topics, exercises, extra readings, and other reference material. They may be used to supplement other materials provided during classroom presentations. Workbooks can serve several purposes:

- As a learning tool actively used during the presentation to encourage note taking (filling in the blanks); as self-tests, as a supplement to material presented in class; as a more job-specific interpretation of material presented in a generic textbook; and as a reference to be used during class testing.

- To demonstrate mastery of each stage of the training: specific notes, research data, or checklists compiled by participants and signed off by the instructor.

- As a guide to be used by the trained person back on the job; the guide might contain workmanship standards and other reference material.

Workbooks can combine some or all of the features in the previous list. They can range from a binder for filing class handouts and making notes to a more formal reference manual.

Instructional Games, Simulations, and Role Playing. Experience has shown that adult learners prefer to practice rather than just listen to lectures, and that they prefer to interact with other learners when in a group learning environment.

Instructional games are activities designed to augment other training methods in order to focus the participants' learning toward specific training results. For example, *in-box exercises* usually present each participant with a variety of papers (reports, charts, tables) that resemble what a manager might find in an in-box. The participant analyzes the documents and takes what he or she considers appropriate action for each item. Responses are either discussed in class or

Part VII.C

evaluated off-line by the instructor, with instructional notes affixed to the documents. (This method could be used to instruct future internal quality system auditors in the document analysis phase of internal auditing.)

Simulations resemble instructional games but also include correspondence between some aspect of the game and reality. *Role playing* consists of spontaneously performing in an assigned scenario.

Remote Learning. This includes educational institutions that offer low-residency or completely online learning programs. Remote learning is especially popular with nontraditional students who would not be able to attend classes in person. This type of learning requires a sustained trainee commitment and self-discipline to successfully complete.

Distance Learning. One popular form of distance learning is where students in more than one location are scheduled and linked together electronically (for example, via cable TV or satellite TV) to enable one instructor to simultaneously teach students in multiple locations. The video provides face-to-face contact between the students and the instructor. Audio interaction between student and instructor and between the students may be included.

Computer-Based Instructional Techniques. Although much training continues to be conducted using the traditional techniques of lecture, discussion, and on-the-job training, technology-based approaches are rapidly moving to the forefront. Computers, electronic communications, and the internet have created dramatic new opportunities to provide learning. New products and techniques are appearing nearly every day.

Examples of existing computer-related technology used include:

- Instructional modules embedded within computer software (help screens, wizards, pop-ups)

- Learning from mistake-proofing software (spelling and grammar checkers, templates)

- Websites (offering technical knowledge, testing, articles, links to other sites)

- Internet access:

  - Online equipment use and repair instructional manuals

  - Webinars (interactive education and training modules)

  - Articles, research papers, books

  - Forums, chat rooms, and blogs

- Intranets (in-house internet-like networks providing training and education)

A quality manager's activities in the area of training technology may include being familiar with the techniques available, understanding technical jargon so as to make wise selections, and serving on multifunctional teams that develop technology-based training packages.

Job Aids. Job aids are virtually any type of media that can support or substitute for formal training and/or provide reinforcement or reference after training. Often, providing a job aid can be the simplest and most cost-effective way to assist performers in doing their jobs. A few types of job aids are:

1. Procedure manual

2. Laminated checklist hung at a workstation

3. Message on a computer screen, a buzzer, or other physical/aural interruption warning of a missing step or incorrectly performed function

4. Nested (drop-down) computer help screens taking the learner to increasingly greater detail

5. Instructions printed on the back of a form giving detailed instructions for completing the form

6. Pertinent information included for each critical step described on a shop work order or traveler

7. Tool mounting board that has a clearly marked place for each type of tool

8. Diagnostic decision tree for solving a problem

9. Audio device accessed by a learner wearing earphones that guides the learner through each task step in the sequence and at the pace expected upon achieving mastery

Rossett and Gautier-Downes cite eight situations in which job aids are appropriate:

1. The individual can not be expected to remember how to do a task because he or she is rarely required to do it.

2. To offer support for individuals who confront lengthy, difficult, and information-intensive challenges.

3. Without the aid, the consequences of error are high.

4. Performance relies on a large body of information.

5. Performance is dependent on knowledge, procedures, or approaches that change frequently.

6. Employee turnover is high and the task is simple.

7. Employees are expected to act in an empowered way, with emphasized or new standards in mind.

8. There is little time or few resources for training.[12]

On-the-Job Training. Much skills training occurs through on-the-job training (OJT). The learner is usually an employee who has been newly hired, transferred, or promoted into a position and lacks the knowledge and skill to perform some specific job component(s). A more experienced employee (peer or supervisor) is usually assigned to work with the trainee. Specific tasks are demonstrated and

Part VII.C

performed in the actual work environment to help the trainee gain the knowledge or skills previously lacking.

Johnson presents six principles of OJT:

1. It's usually used for skills training.

2. It's useful for individuals or small groups.

3. Without a consistent OJT program, there is a strong possibility that people are learning incorrect techniques through trial and error or from their teammates.

4. TQM requires OJT in the workplace, whether it be shop floor, computer, or a sales call.

5. OJT must have a plan, even though it may not be as formal as those used in the lecture method.

6. The OJT teaching process is tell them, show them, have them show you, and repeat the process until performance is satisfactory.[13]

Like all training programs, OJT programs require a needs analysis, training objectives, clear statement of responsibilities, the procedures and work instructions for the specific job/task, and the basis for measuring job/task mastery.

Inconsistencies can result in the way employees perform their duties when it is common for an employee who is familiar with the job to train another employee, without objectives or a planned system. In addition, the lack of structure can cause bad habits to be included in the training. Another problem occurs when a relatively inexperienced employee is responsible for training others. The employee might know how to do the job, but, as anyone who has done training knows, it is much more difficult to teach someone to do a job than to do it yourself.

It has been estimated that up to 75 percent of all training is OJT. OJT provides instant feedback on the learner's achievements, and OJT relates directly to the job/task where training is needed. The trainer should positively reinforce improvement through as many iterations as necessary for the trainee to achieve mastery.

Hands-on training can be supplemented with photos of properly completed tasks at each stage of production and/or videos of workers properly performing the tasks to enhance the learning experience. All training, even OJT, should be planned to ensure completeness, consistency, and correctness of instruction. Performance improvement is virtually assured when planned, structured OJT is combined with formal training and positive reinforcement.

Other Training Delivery Techniques

Other options for providing training include:

- Using external experts to deliver a packaged program or to custom design and deliver an organization-specific program.

- Training and qualifying in-house trainers to deliver an externally developed program.

- Augmenting training presented by in-house trainers with known subject matter experts from outside the organization.

- Utilizing webinars (training prepared for delivery via the web).

- Establishing book reading discussion groups or forums focusing on material to be learned.

- Taking guided and focused tours of other organizations.

- Participating in a benchmarking team, or on an internal audit team.

- Inviting more-experienced people from other organizations to come in and talk.

- Sending individuals to a manufacturer's technical training course.

- Partnering with a local college or university to bring programs to the organization.

- Periodically reexamining the job(s) for ways to improve the processes and perhaps eliminate the need for training in a particular area, or simplify the training needed.

- Establishing a buddy system until the trainee has mastered the job.

- Periodically rotating jobs and cross-training workers to provide additional operation effectiveness and keep performers motivated.

- Partnering with local organizations with common interests to share training costs and introduce a variety of experiences for all the partners' employees.

Keys to Making Training More Effective

Design the training with consideration for learning styles and preferences:

- *Seeing.* Participant needs to be able to actually see, or if not, to be able to visualize what is being taught. Demonstrate, show examples, or paint a word picture to illustrate.

- *Hearing.* Participant needs to hear and understand what is being taught. Paraphrase a second time. Check with participant to determine if instruction is getting through and is understood as intended.

- *Feeling.* Participant needs to touch and feel. As appropriate, allow participant to feel surfaces and shapes. Allow for participants to feel the effect of hot/cold, wind/water, and other forces of nature. Allow for experiencing inner feelings: sadness, joy, anger, disappointment, enthusiasm, and other emotions.

- *Doing.* Provide hands-on opportunity for the participant to try to replicate what is instructed.

When delivering training, the trainer should remember to KISS (keep it simple, Sam or Sylvia). When participants are so enthralled with the gadgets and gizmos used in the training that they forget the training message, the trainer has gone too far. A theme-park type of production is seldom needed, practical, or economical for presenting training. Additionally, when training delivery is totally dependent on the technology, and the technology is difficult to use, it can detract from learning or disrupt the training, especially when an equipment malfunction occurs.

Training delivered by straight lecture, although a prevalent method, is often boring and fades rapidly (if it sticks at all). Trainees might understand little of the message if they are absorbed in taking notes. For this reason, the use of job aids and workbooks should be considered both to augment initial training and to provide reinforcement on the job.

Whenever possible, avoid training an individual in a skill or topic for which the learner already has competence. Doing so may mean the learner becomes disengaged or distracted from the learning process. The learner could also be disruptive when bored. If part of the training is redundant for a learner, the instructor has a few choices:

- Appoint the pre-informed learner as a co-instructor for the segment where the learner could become bored. (This suggests an in-depth needs analysis, with participant interviews where their competencies and strengths are assessed and potential co-instructors are invited to prepare to share in the instruction of a training module.)

- Divide the participants and design the training for basic and advanced levels.

- Allow the pre-informed participant to choose between remaining in the class (and participating constructively) or temporarily leaving until called back.

In skills training, the charisma of the trainer is less important than the ability of the trainer to transfer knowledge and skills to the participant. Training is not intended to be pure entertainment, but does not preclude the judicious use of humor and having fun while learning.

D. TRAINING EFFECTIVENESS AND EVALUATION

Assess training effectiveness and make improvements based on feedback from training sessions, end-of-course test results, on-the-job behavior or performance changes, and departmental or area performance improvements. (Create)

Body of Knowledge VII.D

Training Effectiveness

As indicated in the training model in Figure 19.2, all phases of the training process should be evaluated. Evaluation is essential in determining whether the training program meets the objectives of the training plan. Evaluation includes:

1. Verification of the design (for example, subject content and delivery methods)

2. Applicability of facilities, equipment and tools, and media to be used

3. Qualifications of the trainer

4. Selection of the participants

5. Measures to be used to assess training effectiveness (validation)

6. Measures to be used to assess outcomes resulting from training (validation)

Technical training effectiveness can be greatly enhanced by four key considerations:

1. Appropriate preparation of the training facilities

2. Appropriate timing of the training relative to when performance is required

3. Appropriate sequence of training relative to skills mastery

4. Appropriate feedback indicating performance difficulties and progress

Figure 19.3 describes five levels for evaluating training. Kirkpatrick is credited with defining the first four levels (reaction, learning, behavior, and results) for evaluating training.[14] Robinson and Robinson expanded level three to distinguish between Type A (Are participants applying the skills and behavior as taught?) and Type B (Are participants applying non-observable skills, for example, mental skills, learning to the job?) learning.[15] Level 5 in Figure 19.3 is a perspective addressed by Westcott and Phillips.[16]

Level 1. The *reaction* level provides the lowest-value information and results and is frequently and easily used.

Level 2. The *learning* level is used to obtain a more in-depth assessment of whether specific training objectives were met.

Level 3. The *behavior* (job applications) level assesses whether or not the training is applied back on the job, usually after some time has passed.

Level 4. The *results* level measures the quantitative difference between the outcomes of the work units affected prior to their people receiving training (the baseline) and the outcomes some time after the training ended. The objectives for training measured could be a decrease in scrap rate, an increase in number of savings accounts opened, increased classroom attendance, elimination of medication errors in a hospital, and so on.

Part VII.D

No.	Level	Questions	Comments
1	Reaction	Were the participants pleased with the training?	The typical "smile" sheets collected at the end of a program, session, or module.
2	Learning	Did the participants learn what was intended for them to learn?	Were the training objectives met? Typically determined from some kind of test.
3	Behavior	Did participants change their behavior on the basis of what was taught?	Typically determined from an assessment of how learned behaviors are applied on the job.
4	Results	Was there a positive affect on the organization resulting from participants' changed behavior?	Typically measured from pretraining versus post-training analysis of the organization's outcomes. Usually a "quantity" type measure (increased production, lower rejects, number of time periods without a customer complaint, and so on).
5	ROTI	Was there a measurable net dollar payback for the organization resulting from participants' application of learned behavior?	Return on training investment (ROTI) is based on the dollar valued added by the investment in the training.

Figure 19.3   Levels of training evaluation.

Level 5. The ROTI level offers the highest-value information and results, but is not used as frequently and is more difficult to assess. Level 5 is based on placing dollar values on the baseline, the results, and the improvement, then determining the value received for the dollars spent. When expressed as a ratio, a $3 return for every $1 spent is a useful minimum ROTI. Quality training programs that score best at all levels are likely to be very successful.

Two formulas may be used to evaluate at level 5: the *benefits-to-cost ratio* (BCR) and the *return on training investment* (ROTI).

$$BCR = \frac{\text{Program benefits}}{\text{Program costs}}$$

$$ROTI = \frac{\text{Net program benefits (total benefits} - \text{costs)}}{\text{Program costs}}$$

A rule of thumb is that if ROTI is less than $3.00 (or a ratio of 3:1), meaning $3 of benefits obtained from every $1 spent, then training should not be considered (unless mandated).

Training program development costs are usually included in the first year (when training may extend over one year) unless the costs substantially exceed the first-year benefits. In this case, costs may be prorated over the period in which the training is delivered.

What Causes Ineffectiveness or Failure?

The ineffectiveness or failure of a quality training program is likely to be linked to one or more of the following causes:

- Cultural resistance by line managers
- Doubt as to the usefulness of the training, which occurs when:
  - No linkage exists with the strategic plans of the organization.
  - No apparent connection is evident between the behaviors to be learned and their application on the job.
  - No projected objectives are established for post-training improvement.
  - The question of "What's in it for me?" is inadequately addressed for participants and their supervisors.
- Lack of participation (involvement) by line managers
- Technique versus problem orientation
- Inadequacies of leaders
- Mixing of levels of participants
- Lack of application during the course
- Language too complex
- Lack of participation by the training function
- Operational and logistical deficiencies[17]

Additional issues include:

- There is no or weak partnering among managers/supervisors, trainers, and participants mutually involved in achieving the training objectives.
- The training program is poorly planned and delivered. Problems could include:
  - Inadequate needs assessment and analysis
  - Training content (objectives, subjects, media, and demonstrations) does not match needs
  - Lack of appropriate metrics and measures for evaluation
  - Overemphasis on theory and technique versus skill application
  - Lack of practice during the course
  - Inadequacies of trainers
  - Ineffective selection of participants

Part VII.D

- There is a lack of or inadequate reinforcement of participants' success in learning and applying learning on the job.

Rationale for Ongoing Training Evaluation

If the training is new or is a major revision to previous training, the following need to be determined:

- From the design verification phase, are there projections indicating that the training program will be worth the resources to be expended, and that the outcomes will support the organization's strategic plans?
- Does it make sense to go further if the appropriate resources can not be made available?
- Would it be more cost-effective to continue with in-house design or to consider a training provider's product?
- If going forward with the design and delivery of the program appears feasible, which of the possible alternatives available have the greatest positive impact on the organization? Which have the greatest positive impact in the short term? In the long term?

During the delivery of training, the following should be frequently evaluated:

- Is the training achieving stated objectives?
- Are the right people attending the training?
- What parts of the training are yielding the most benefit to the participants? What parts are yielding the least? Why?
- What modifications must be made in-flight to correct a problem or deficiency?
- If this or similar training is to be done again, what should be done differently? Why? How?
- Are there facility problems that need to be corrected immediately?
- Is the trainer succeeding in producing trained participants? If not, why?

After the training, the following questions should be asked:

- Are the participants satisfied? If not, why?
- Are the participants' organizations satisfied? If not, why?
- Have all the training plan requirements been met?
- How can the training design and delivery be improved?
- Did the training produce the desired outcomes?

Note: Some organizations mistakenly measure training progress by the number of training programs conducted or people that flow through a classroom rather than by how effectively the training is used to achieve the organization's strategic objectives.

Reinforcing Quality Training

Numerous ways exist to reinforce quality training. Cash awards are of dubious value and are not recommended in connection with training in relatively affluent societies. Positive reinforcement is used during the training to shape the participants' behavior and is vital when the trained person properly applies the skills learned back on the job.

In most situations, a key to reinforcement is to provide more positive than negative consequences for appropriate behavior/performance. Another key point is to provide positive performance feedback to the participant immediately following an observation of work done well. The types and frequencies of consequences can be collected through an analysis of the job/task environment during the needs assessment phase. An analysis will often show that participants have, prior to training, received a negative balance of consequences.

For example, a lathe operator might get raw material late or receive material of an inferior quality, causing excessive tool replacement. This in turn makes the operator's job more difficult and the output late, resulting in pressure (or criticism) from supervisors. The solution of this type of problem is up to management, and it should be resolved before any training is conducted. Training will not solve such a problem, and failure to solve it ahead of time will likely detract from the intent and waste training funds.

As an example, first-line supervisors receive training in interpreting and taking action based on control chart data. On returning to the workplace from training, the next level of management fails to acknowledge the new skill and berates the supervisors for not pushing product out the door fast enough. More positively, supervisors could take special care to acknowledge their trained people with positive performance feedback when the learned skills are applied and the work is done properly. When properly given, performance feedback for work not up to expectation is a helpful rather than a punitive action.

Negative consequences for poor performance in a work environment can take many forms, ranging from verbal abuse from supervisors or coworkers when a mistake is made to pay deductions for rejected product. Contributors to poor performance include inadequate training or instructions; poor working conditions; lack of proper tools, adequate equipment, and facility maintenance; lack of positive feedback when work is done well; and inadequate communication from management. Removal of conditions like these, along with positive reinforcement for doing the job right, are among the outcomes of acceptable performance.

Training should occur just in time, that is, immediately prior to the context in which it is to be used. The longer the time that elapses between the training and the opportunity to put the knowledge/skill gained into practice, the more likely the knowledge/skill gained will fade out. In such cases, learning can be reinforced through a refresher course. A refresher course recaps previous learning in a shorter time period, at a faster pace, and in a more intense manner. Face-to-face instruction might not be required. The use of technological methods may be sufficient.

Most employees find value in training that helps them do a better job easier and supports their growth and development. Therefore, employees who are motivated to increase their proficiency are simultaneously working to improve their organization's competitive advantage and themselves. Note: *Never* use training as a punishment or position it so it is perceived as such.

Training and Education As Tools in the Management of Quality

An integrated training program driven by strategic organizational goals and objectives, for personnel at every organizational level, is a powerful process for continual improvement. Given the rapidity and constancy of change:

- Organizations are transitioning into learning organizations with an emphasis on acquisition of knowledge.

- Individuals are committing to lifelong learning as a personal goal.

- The viable organization's delivery of a quality service or product relies on the competence of its people. Knowledge and skills are integral to competency development and enhancement.

- The organization that has adopted a mind-set that training and education of its people is an *investment*, not an *expense*, is moving toward the right goal.

Distinguishing Between Training, Education, and Individual Development

Training and education have been discussed extensively in previous sections. The remaining issue is how those two topics differ from *individual development* (often called *professional development* or *career development*)? First, *training* is targeted to build or enhance skills. Second, *education* is aimed at broadening one's knowledge base. *Development* infers a formal or informal program leading to or adding to an individual's repertoire of skills, knowledge, wisdom, and experience. This is accomplished through a variety of actions, often over the working lifetime of the individual. Such actions may include:

- Building experience and responsibility through a variety of occupational assignments and venues

- Gaining knowledge through formal and informal education

- Acquiring and enhancing skills

- Accumulating insights through exposure to those more expert, and through networking

- Developing wisdom (from analyzing data collected, to synthesizing information, to building knowledge, to gaining wisdom)

For the majority of people, individual development occurs though serendipity, chance encounters with growth-enhancing experiences. For a more goal-oriented individual, development occurs through following a grand plan.

Throughout much of the 1960s, '70s, and '80s, development of individuals was considered to be a responsibility of employers. During those times, managers learned how to guide their employees in their career development plans. Organizations published career ladders and steps individuals should take to broaden their knowledge and skills for the employees' growth and development. This effort was not universally successful. It became apparent that the real responsibility for development rested with the individuals, not their boss. More recently, and especially with a more mobile, transient workforce, individual development is the individual's responsibility, sometimes with some support and resources from their employer. The text in Chapter 8 and Figure 8.5 describe a model of the mutual investment made by the organization and the individual leading to the individual's growth and personal development.

ENDNOTES

1. J. M. Juran and F. M. Gryna, eds., *Juran's Quality Control Handbook*, 4th ed. (New York: McGraw-Hill, 1988), 11.4–11.5.
2. R. F. Mager and P. Pipe, *Analyzing Performance Problems or You Really Oughta Wanna: How to Figure Out Why People Aren't Doing What They Should Be, and What to Do About It*, 2nd ed. (Belmont, CA: David S. Lake, 1997).
3. R. T. Westcott, *Stepping Up to ISO 9004:2000* (Chico, CA: Paton Press, 2003), 32–39.
4. M. Knowles, *The Adult Learner: A Neglected Species* (Houston: Gulf, 1973).
5. R. S. Johnson, *Quality Training Practices* (Milwaukee: ASQC Quality Press, 1993), 79.
6. L. Kelly, ed., *The ASTD Technical and Skills Training Handbook* (New York: McGraw-Hill, 1995), 214.
7. M. Knowles, "Adult Learning," in *The ASTD Training and Development Handbook: A Guide to Human Resources Development*, 3rd ed., ed. R. L. Craig (New York: McGraw-Hill, 1996), 171–72.
8. M. S. Knowles and D. E. Hartl, "The Adult Learner in the Technical Environment," in *The ASTD Technical and Skills Training Handbook*, ed. L. Kelly (New York: McGraw-Hill, 1995), 12.
9. R. S. Johnson, *TQM: The Mechanics of Quality Processes* (Milwaukee: ASQC Quality Press, 1993), 147–48.
10. Ibid., 147.
11. M. F. Finnerty, "Coaching for Growth and Development," in *The ASTD Training and Development Handbook: A Guide to Human Resources Development*, ed. R. L. Craig (New York: McGraw-Hill, 1996), 423.
12. A. Rossett and J. H. Gautier-Downes, *A Handbook of Job Aids* (San Diego: Pfeiffer & Company, 1991).
13. Johnson, *TQM*.
14. D. L. Kirkpatrick, "Techniques for Evaluating Training Programs," a four-part series beginning in the November 1959 issue of the *Training Director's Journal*.
15. D. G. Robinson and J. C. Robinson, *Training for Impact: How to Link Training to Business Needs and Measure the Results* (San Francisco: Jossey-Bass, 1990).

16. R. T. Westcott, "A Quality System Needs Assessment," in *In Action: Conducting Needs Assessment (17 Case Studies)*, ed. J. J. Phillips and E. F. Holton III (Alexandria, VA: American Society for Training and Development, 1995), 235; "Applied Behavior Management Training," in *In Action: Measuring Return on Investment*, vol. 1, ed. J. Phillips, (Alexandria, VA: American Society for Training and Development, 1994), 85–104; "Behavior Management Training," in *Human Resources Management and Development Handbook*, 2nd ed. (New York: AMACOM, 1994), 897–911; and "ROQI: Overlooked Quality Tool," *The Total Quality Review* (November/December, 1994): 37–44.

17. Juran and Gryna, *Quality Control Handbook*.

See Appendix A for additional references for this chapter.

Chapter 20

The Certified Manager of Quality/ Organizational Excellence Body of Knowledge

Total quality management addresses the quality of management as well as the management of quality.

—V. Daniel Hunt

CERTIFIED MANAGER OF QUALITY/ORGANIZATIONAL EXCELLENCE (CMQ/OE) COMPLETE BODY OF KNOWLEDGE (BoK)—2013

The topics in this new BoK include descriptive details (subtext) that will be used by the Exam Development Committee as guidelines for writing test questions. This subtext is also designed to help candidates prepare for the exam by identifying specific content within each topic that may be tested. The subtext is not intended to limit the subject matter or be all-inclusive of what might be covered in an exam but is intended to clarify how the topics relate to a Manager's role. The descriptor in parentheses at the end of each entry refers to the maximum cognitive level at which the topic will be tested. A complete description of cognitive levels is provided at the end of this document.

   I. Leadership (25 Questions)

   A. *Organizational Structures.* Define and describe organizational designs (i.e., matrix, flat, and parallel) and the effect that a hierarchical management structure can have on an organization. (Apply)

   B. *Leadership Challenges*

   1. *Roles and responsibilities of leaders.* Describe typical roles, responsibilities, and competencies of people in leadership positions and how those attributes influence an organization's direction and purpose. (Analyze)

   2. *Roles and responsibilities of managers.* Describe typical roles, responsibilities, and competencies of people in management positions and how those attributes contribute to an organization's success. (Analyze)

551

3. *Change management.* Use various change management strategies to overcome organizational roadblocks and achieve desired change levels, and review outcomes for effectiveness. Define and describe factors that contribute to an organization's culture. (Evaluate)

4. *Leadership techniques.* Develop and implement techniques that motivate employees and sustain their enthusiasm. Use negotiation techniques to enable parties with different or opposing outlooks to recognize common goals and work together to achieve them. Determine when and how to use influence to resolve a problem or move a project forward. (Create)

5. *Empowerment.* Apply various techniques to empower individuals and teams. Identify typical obstacles to empowerment and appropriate strategies for overcoming them. Describe and distinguish between job enrichment and job enlargement, job design and job tasks. (Apply)

C. *Teams and Team Processes*

1. *Types of teams.* Identify different types of teams and their purpose, including process improvement, self-managed, temporary or ad hoc (special project), and work groups or workcells. (Understand)

2. *Stages of team development.* Define and describe the classic stages of team development: forming, storming, norming, performing. (Apply)

3. *Team-building techniques.* Apply basic team-building steps such as using ice-breaker activities to enhance team introductions and membership, developing a common vision and agreement on team objectives, identifying and assigning specific roles on the team. (Apply)

4. *Team roles and responsibilities.* Define and describe typical roles related to team support and effectiveness such as facilitator, leader, process owner, champion, project manager, and contributor. Describe member and leader responsibilities with regard to group dynamics, including keeping the team on task, recognizing hidden agendas, handling disruptive behavior, and resolving conflict. (Analyze)

5. *Team performance and evaluation.* Evaluate team performance in relation to established metrics to meet goals and objectives. Determine when and how to reward teams and celebrate their success. (Evaluate)

D. *ASQ Code of Ethics.* Identify and apply behaviors and actions that comply with this code. (Apply)

II. Strategic Plan Development and Deployment (18 Questions)

    A. *Strategic Planning Models.* Define, describe, and use basic elements of strategic planning models, including how mission, vision, and values as guiding principles relate to the plan. (Apply)

    B. *Business Environment Analysis*

        1. *SWOT analysis.* Analyze an organization's strengths, weaknesses, opportunities, and threats, and develop and prioritize actions to take in response to that analysis. Identify and analyze risk factors that can influence strategic plans. (Analyze)

        2. *Market forces.* Define and describe various forces that drive strategic plans, including existing competition, the entry of new competitors, rivalry among competitors, the threat of substitutes, bargaining power of buyers and suppliers, current economic conditions, and how well the organization is positioned for growth and changing customer expectations. (Apply)

        3. *Stakeholder analysis.* Identify and differentiate various internal and external stakeholders, as well as their perspectives, needs, and objectives to ensure that the organization's strategic objectives are aligned with those of the stakeholders. (Analyze)

        4. *Technology.* Describe how changes in technology can have long- and short-term influences on strategic planning. (Understand)

        5. *Internal capability analysis.* Identify and describe the effects that influence an organization's internal capabilities: human resources, facilities capacity, and operational capabilities. Analyze these factors in relation to strategy formation. (Analyze)

        6. *Legal and regulatory factors.* Define and describe how these factors can influence strategic plans. (Understand)

    C. *Strategic Plan Deployment*

        1. *Tactical plans.* Identify basic characteristics of tactics: specific, measurable, attainable, relevant, time-specific, and linked to strategic objectives. Evaluate proposed plans to determine whether they meet these criteria. (Evaluate)

        2. *Resource allocation and deployment.* Evaluate current resources to ensure they are available and deployed in support of strategic initiatives. Identify and eliminate administrative barriers to new initiatives. Ensure that all internal stakeholders understand the strategic plan and have the competencies and resources to carry out their responsibilities. (Evaluate)

        3. *Organizational performance measurement.* Develop these and ensure that they are aligned with strategic goals, and use the measures to evaluate the organization against the strategic plan. (Evaluate)

4. *Quality in strategic deployment.* Support strategic plan deployment by applying continuous improvement and other quality initiatives to drive performance outcomes throughout the organization. (Create)

III. Management Elements and Methods (30 Questions)

A. *Management Skills and Abilities*

1. *Principles of management.* Define and apply basic management principles such as planning, leading, delegating, controlling, organizing, and re-sourcing, in various situations. (Apply)

2. *Management theories and styles.* Define and describe management theories such as scientific, organizational, behavioral, learning, systems thinking, and situational complexity. Define and describe management styles such as autocratic, participative, transactional, transformational, management by fact, coaching, and contingency approach. Describe how management styles are influenced by an organization's size, industry sector, culture, and competitors. (Apply)

3. *Interdependence of functional areas.* Describe the interdependence of an organization's areas (human resources, engineering, sales, marketing, finance, research and development, purchasing, information technology, logistics, production, and service) and how those dependencies and relationships influence processes and outputs. (Understand)

4. *Human resources (HR) management.* Apply HR elements in support of ongoing professional development: setting goals and objectives, conducting performance evaluations, developing recognition programs, ensuring that succession plans are in place where appropriate. Develop quality-supportive responsibilities to include in job descriptions for positions throughout the organization. (Apply)

5. *Financial management.* Read, interpret, and use various finance tools including income statements, balance sheets, and product/service cost structures. Manage budgets and use the language of cost and profitability to communicate with senior management. Use potential return on investment (ROI), estimated return on assets (ROA), net present value (NPV), internal rate of return (IRR), and portfolio analysis to analyze project risk, feasibility, and priority. (Analyze)

6. *Risk management.* Identify the kinds of risk that can occur throughout the organization, from such diverse processes as scheduling, shipping/receiving, financials, production and operations, employee and user safety, regulatory compliance and changes. Describe and use risk control and mitigation methods: avoidance, reduction, prevention, segregation, and transfer. (Apply)

7. *Knowledge management (KM).* Use KM techniques in identifying core competencies that create a culture and system for collecting and sharing implicit and explicit knowledge among workers, customers, competitors, and suppliers. Capture lessons learned and apply them across the organization to promote best practices. Identify typical knowledge-sharing barriers and how to overcome them. (Apply)

B. *Communication Skills and Abilities*

1. *Communication techniques.* Define and apply various modes of communication used within organizations, such as verbal, non-verbal, written, and visual. Identify factors that can inhibit clear communication and describe ways of overcoming them. (Apply)

2. *Interpersonal skills.* Develop skills in empathy, tact, friendliness, and objectivity. Use open-minded and non-judgmental communication methods. Develop and use a clear writing style, active listening, and questioning and dialog techniques that support effective communication. (Apply)

3. *Communications in a global economy.* Identify key challenges of communicating across different time zones, cultures, languages, terminology, and business practices, and identify ways of overcoming them. (Understand)

4. *Communications and technology.* Identify how technology has affected communications, including improved information availability, its negative influence on interpersonal communications, and the new etiquette for e-communications. Use appropriate communication methods to deliver different kinds of messages in a variety of situations. (Apply)

C. *Project Management*

1. *Project management basics.* Use project management methodology and ensure that each project is aligned with strategic objectives. Define the different phases of a project: initiation, planning, execution, monitoring and controlling, and closure. Recognize the importance of keeping the project on-time, and within budget. (Apply)

2. *Project planning and estimation tools.* Use tools such as risk assessment, benefit–cost analysis, critical path method (CPM), Gantt chart, PERT, and work breakdown structure (WBS) to plan projects and estimate related costs. (Apply)

3. *Measure and monitor project activity.* Use tools such as cost variance analysis, milestones, and actual vs. planned budgets to monitor project activity against project plan. (Evaluate)

4. *Project documentation.* Use written procedures and project summaries to document projects. (Apply)

D. *Quality System*

1. *Quality mission and policy.* Develop and monitor the quality mission and policy and ensure that it is aligned with the organization's broader mission. (Create)

2. *Quality planning, deployment, and documentation.* Develop and deploy the quality plan and ensure that it is documented and accessible throughout the organization. (Create)

3. *Quality system effectiveness.* Evaluate the effectiveness of the quality system using various tools: balanced scorecard, internal audits, feedback from internal and external stakeholders, skip-level meetings, warranty data analytics, product traceability and recall reports, and management reviews. (Evaluate)

E. *Quality Models and Theories*

1. *Organizational and Performance Excellence.* Define and describe common elements and criteria of performance excellence models such as the Malcolm Baldrige National Quality Award (MBNQA), Excellence Canada, and European Excellence Award (EFQM). Describe how their criteria are used as management models to improve processes at an organization level. (Understand)

2. *ISO quality management standards.* Define and describe how the ISO 9001 standards can be used to support quality management systems. (Understand)

3. *Other quality methodologies.* Describe and differentiate methods such as total quality management (TQM), continuous improvement, and benchmarking. (Apply)

4. *Quality philosophies.* Describe and apply basic methodologies and theories proposed by quality leaders such as Shewhart, Deming, Juran, Crosby, Feigenbaum, and Ishikawa. (Apply)

IV. Quality Management Tools (30 Questions)

A. *Problem-Solving Tools*

1. *The seven classic quality tools.* Select, interpret, and evaluate output from these tools: Pareto charts, cause and effect diagrams, flowcharts, control charts, check sheets, scatter diagrams, and histograms. (Evaluate)

2. *Basic management and planning tools.* Select, interpret, and evaluate output from these tools: affinity diagrams, tree diagrams, process decision program charts (PDPCs), matrix diagrams, prioritization matrices, interrelationship digraphs, and activity network diagrams. (Evaluate)

3. *Process improvement tools.* Select, interpret, and apply tools such as root cause analysis, PDCA, six sigma DMAIC (define, measure,

analyze, improve, control), and failure mode and effects analysis (FMEA). (Evaluate)

4. *Innovation and creativity tools.* Use various techniques and exercises for creative decision-making and problem-solving, including brainstorming, mind mapping, lateral thinking, critical thinking, the 5 whys, and design for six sigma (DFSS). (Apply)

5. *Cost of quality (COQ).* Define and distinguish between prevention, appraisal, internal, and external failure cost categories and evaluate the impact that changes in one category will have on the others. (Evaluate)

B. *Process Management*

1. *Process goals.* Describe how process goals are established, monitored, and measured and evaluate their impact on product or service quality. (Evaluate)

2. *Process analysis.* Use various tools to analyze a process and evaluate its effectiveness on the basis of procedures, work instructions, and other documents. Evaluate the process to identify and relieve bottlenecks, increase capacity, improve throughput, reduce cycle time, and eliminate waste. (Evaluate)

3. *Lean tools.* Identify and use lean tools such as cycle-time reduction, 5S, just-in-time (JIT), kanban, value stream mapping, single-minute exchange of die (SMED), poka-yoke, kaizen, and overall equipment effectiveness (OEE). (Apply)

4. *Theory of constraints (TOC).* Define key concepts of TOC: systems as chains, local vs. system optimization, physical vs. policy constraints, undesirable effects vs. core problems, and solution deterioration. Classify constraints in terms of resources and expectations as defined by measures of throughput, inventory, and operating expense. (Understand)

C. *Measurement: Assessment and Metrics*

1. *Basic statistical use.* Use techniques such as the goal-question-metric (GQM) model and others to identify when, what, and how to measure projects and processes. Describe how metrics and data gathering methods affect resources and vice versa. (Apply)

2. *Sampling.* Define and describe basic sampling techniques such as random and stratified. Identify when and why sampling is an appropriate technique to use. (Understand)

3. *Statistical analysis.* Calculate basic statistics: measures of central tendency (mean, median, mode), and measures of dispersion (range, standard deviation, and variance). Identify basic distribution types (normal, bimodal, skewed) and evaluate run charts, statistical process control (SPC) reports, and other control charts to make data-based decisions. (Evaluate)

4. *Measurement systems analysis.* Define basic measurement terms: accuracy, precision, bias, and linearity. Understand the difference between repeatability and reproducibility in gauge R&R studies. (Understand)

5. *Trend and pattern analysis.* Interpret graphs and charts to identify cyclical, seasonal, and environmental data trends. Evaluate control chart patterns to determine shifts and other trend indicators in a process. (Evaluate)

6. *Process variation.* Analyze data to distinguish between common and special cause variation. (Analyze)

7. *Process capability.* Recognize process capability (C_p and C_{pk}) and performance indices (P_p and P_{pk}). (Understand)

8. *Reliability terminology.* Define and describe basic reliability measures: mean time between failures (MTBF) and mean time to repair (MTTR). Understand the value of reliability for estimating the probability of being able to meet requirements or specifications, typically for a specific period of time. (Understand)

9. *Qualitative assessment.* Identify subjective measures such as verbatim comments from customers, observation records, and focus group output. Describe how they differ from objective measures, and determine when measurements should be captured in categories rather than numeric values. (Analyze)

V. Customer-Focused Organizations (17 Questions)

A. *Customer Identification and Segmentation*

1. *Internal customers.* Define and describe the impact an organization's treatment of internal customers will have on external customers. Develop methods for energizing internal customers to improve products, processes, and services and evaluate the results. (Evaluate)

2. *External customers.* Define external customers and describe their impact on products and services. Develop strategies for working with them and integrating their requirements and needs to improve products, services, and processes. (Evaluate)

3. *Customer segmentation.* Define and describe the process of customer segmentation and its impact on aligning service and delivery to meet customer needs. (Evaluate)

B. *Customer Relationship Management*

1. *Customer needs.* Use quality function deployment (QFD) to analyze customer needs in relation to products and services offered. Use the results of the analysis to prioritize future development in anticipation of changing customer needs. (Analyze)

2. *Customer satisfaction and loyalty.* Develop systems to capture positive and negative customer perceptions and experiences, using tools such as voice of the customer, listening posts, focus groups,

complaints and warranty data, surveys, and interviews. Use customer value analysis to calculate the financial impact of existing customers and the potential results of losing those customers. Develop corrective actions and proactive methods to improve customer satisfaction, loyalty, and retention levels. (Create)

3. *Customer service principles.* Develop and deploy strategies that support customer service principles: courtesy, politeness, smiles, cheerfulness, attention to detail, active listening, empathy, rapid response, and easy access for information and service. (Apply)

4. *Multiple and diverse customer management.* Establish and monitor priorities to avoid or resolve conflicting customer requirements and demands. Develop methods and systems for managing capacity and resources to meet the needs of multiple customers. Describe the impact that diverse customer groups can have on all aspects of product and service development and delivery. (Evaluate)

VI. Supply Chain Management (15 Questions)

A. *Supplier Selection.* Define, develop, and use criteria for selecting suppliers, including internal rating programs and external certification standards. Assess and manage the impact these programs can have on various internal processes of the organization. (Create)

B. *Supplier Communications.* Develop and implement specific communication methods with suppliers, including regularly scheduled meetings and routine and emergency reporting procedures. Develop explicit expectations and confirm that the supplier is aware of critical product and delivery requirements. (Create)

C. *Supplier Performance.* Define, develop, and monitor supplier performance in terms of quality, cost, delivery, and service levels, and establish associated metrics for defect rates, product reliability, functional performance, timeliness, responsiveness, and availability of technical support. (Create)

D. *Supplier Improvement.* Define and conduct supplier audits, evaluate corrective and preventive action plans, provide feedback, and monitor process improvements. (Create)

E. *Supplier Certification, Partnerships, and Alliances.* Define and implement supplier certification programs that include process reviews and performance evaluations. Identify strategies for developing customer–supplier partnerships and alliances. (Create)

F. *Supplier Logistics and Material Acceptance.* Describe the impact that purchased products and services can have on final product assembly or total service package, including ship-to-stock, and just-in-time (JIT). Plan and conduct incoming material inspections. (Understand)

VII. Training and Development (15 Questions)

A. *Training Plans.* Develop and implement training plans that are aligned with the organization's strategic plan and general business needs, including leadership training and alignment of personal development plans. (Create)

B. *Training Needs Analysis.* Use various tools and techniques such as surveys, performance reviews, regulatory requirements, and gap analysis to identify training needs. (Create)

C. *Training Materials/Curriculum Development and Delivery.* Use various tools, resources, and methodologies to develop training materials and curriculum that address adult learning principles and the learning needs of an increasingly diverse workforce. Describe various methods of training delivery: classroom, workbooks, simulations, computer-delivered, on-the-job, and self-directed. Use mentoring and coaching to support training outcomes. (Apply)

D. *Training Effectiveness and Evaluation.* Assess training effectiveness and make improvements based on feedback from training sessions, end-of-course test results, on-the-job behavior or performance changes, and departmental or area performance improvements. (Create)

Topics for the Constructed-Response (Essay) Portion of the Certified Manager of Quality/Organizational Excellence Exam

Candidates will be presented with three open-ended questions from which they can select the two that they prefer to answer. Candidates will have 45 minutes in which to write responses to the two chosen situations. Prior to the start of the constructed-response portion of the exam, candidates will be given 5 minutes to review and select their situations. Candidates may split their time spent on the problems as they like. Their responses will be graded on their knowledge of quality management as it relates to the content areas listed below and in the following skills and abilities: communication, critical thinking, personnel management, general management.

CR-1. Leadership. Demonstrate knowledge of the quality manager's role in organizational leadership and as quality champion and customer advocate. Deploy change agent strategies in support of organization-wide continuous improvement efforts. Develop teams and participate on them in various roles.

CR-2. Strategy Development and Deployment. Develop and maintain organizational focus on the importance of quality and performance excellence. Create quality policies and procedures in support of the strategic plan, and integrate those policies and processes into the tactics developed to support the strategic plan.

CR-3. Management. Demonstrate management abilities in human resources, financial, risk, and knowledge management applications. Use effective communication methods in various situations to support continuous improvement efforts.

Select and use appropriate tools and methodologies to plan, implement, and evaluate projects. Develop, deploy, and evaluate quality plans that can be used throughout the organization. Evaluate and recommend appropriate quality models or systems to implement in various situations.

CR-4. Customer Focus. Identify and segment customers using a variety of criteria and tools. Identify and prioritize product or service design and development on the basis of customer requirements and feedback. Solicit customer input proactively and combine with market analysis and other research to achieve organizational goals. Use customer expectations and feedback to manage continuous improvement projects.

CR-5. Supplier Management. Develop and deploy supplier management systems from selection process through partnership agreements, including mutually beneficial continuous improvement programs. Identify methods for assessing supplier performance at various levels of customer-supplier relationships.

CR-6. Training and Development. Demonstrate knowledge and ability in developing, implementing, and evaluating needs assessment, training delivery methods, and outcomes of training efforts.

Levels of Cognition
(Based on Bloom's Taxonomy—Revised (2001)

In addition to content specifics, the subtext for each topic in this BoK also indicates the intended complexity level of the test questions for that topic. These levels are based on "Levels of Cognition" (from Bloom's Taxonomy—Revised, 2001) and are presented below in rank order, from least complex to most complex.

Remember (Knowledge Level). Recall or recognize terms, definitions, facts, ideas, materials, patterns, sequences, methods, principles, etc.

Understand (Comprehension Level). Read and understand descriptions, communications, reports, tables, diagrams, directions, regulations, etc.

Apply (Application Level). Know when and how to use ideas, procedures, methods, formulas, principles, theories, etc.

Analyze (Analysis Level). Break down information into its constituent parts and recognize their relationship to one another and how they are organized; identify sublevel factors or salient data from a complex scenario.

Evaluate (Evaluation Level). Make judgments about the value of proposed ideas, solutions, etc., by comparing the proposal to specific criteria or standards.

Create (Synthesis Level). Put parts or elements together in such a way as to reveal a pattern or structure not clearly there before; identify which data or information from a complex set is appropriate to examine further or from which supported conclusions can be drawn.

B. INTEGRATING THE BoK AS A SYSTEM

Up to this point the BoK has been presented as seven separate parts. In reality, the quality manager or director seldom deals with only one part at a time in performing her or his job—in planning, organizing, staffing, directing, and controlling. Typically, problem solving, decision making, and overseeing a function will call for thinking and acting using combinations of all or several of the BoK parts as a system for reaching a resolution.

In the CMQ/OE examination, the multiple-choice questions will not be presented as clusters addressing one part of the BoK at a time, but will be randomly interspersed. Even at that, it is only the constructed response (CR) questions that more realistically test the participant on the value of treating the BoK as a system. As a guideline, it is recommended that when answering a CR question, the exam taker should run a self-check against the memorized parts of the BoK, asking, Which parts of the BoK should be integrated in preparing the CR answer?

In the CMQ/OE refresher courses given by ASQ it is recommended that participants commit to memory as much of the BoK structure as possible in order to facilitate the integration mentioned above. Also, class participants are involved with a case study with the instruction (1) scan the case to get an overview of its content, (2) list the accomplishments made, and the issues and concerns not adequately addressed, (3) note on the list the parts of the BoK that could be combined to either strengthen the gains or address the weaknesses. The exercise is often done as a total group effort, either with a volunteer leader, or leaderless. The case study is used to help the participants pull it all together in discussing the decisions, actions, and events of a simulated organization over a span of time. The case study is provided in Section C.

(Note: the examination does not include a case study.)

C. APPLYING THE BoK—CASE STUDY*

Glo, Inc. (GLO) produces and distributes products based on a proprietary process for depositing reflective metallic material on plastic substrates. Their products are highway and construction site warning signs, educational institution signage, and containers for personal grooming products.

GLO employs a total of 440 workers and management. The breakdown is shown in Table 20.1.

Originally called Yonkers Signboard Co., the company was founded by the Batterson brothers in 1937. It was inherited by Alfred Batterson, son of one of the brothers, after an auto accident in 1973 killed the owners. The cosmetic container line was introduced in 1974 when Al became the CEO and reorganized the company as Glo, Inc. Al was instrumental in capturing a significant share of the cosmetic container market, partly because of the patent on their deposition process.

Al, supported by his top team, lead GLO in a series of quality initiatives from 1994 through 1998:

• Introduction of strategic planning

---

* Reprinted with permission of R. T. Westcott & Associates

Table 20.1   Employee breakdown at Glo, Inc.

Functions	Location	Employee total	Management	Nonmanagement
Administrative:	Yonkers, NY			
Officers/staff		10	4	6
Marketing		17	5	12
Engineering		7	5	2
Finance		13	4	9
Human resources		9	3	6
Purchasing		4	2	2
Sales offices:	Yonkers, NY	(included above)		
	Chicago, IL	12	2	10
	Miami, FL	5	1	4
	Denver, CO	4	1	3
	San Francisco	10	3	7
Plants:				
Outdoor signs	Troy, NY	95	7	88
Containers	Cicero, IL	116	11	105
Indoor signs	Mobile, AL	27	3	24
Containers	Downey, CA	69	6	63
Warehouses:	Yonkers, NY	7	1	6
	Cicero, IL	14	2	12
	Pomona, CA	21	2	19

- Introduction of SPC in the plants
- Introduction of a companywide enterprise resource planning computer system
- Implementation of an ISO 9001:1994–based quality management system (QMS) at all plants and warehouses, and certification of all locations
- Entry into the Empire State Quality Award (obtained site visit level)

Some of the deficiencies noted by the Empire State Quality Award site visit team included:

- There is no evidence that senior leadership solicits and reviews key performance information from all locations.
- There is inadequate evidence of how the company addresses its public responsibilities.

- There is insufficient evidence that corporate strategy (including goals and objectives) has been adequately deployed to all locations, and that there are facility action plans to support such goals and objectives.

- There is no coherent process evident for discerning the satisfaction of customers, nor is there evidence of actions taken to specifically improve customer satisfaction and retention.

- There is no evidence that GLO makes an effort to distinguish its customer base beyond just three categories: external signage, internal signage, and containers.

- It is unclear how the human resource policies and practices promulgated by headquarters are applied at the various locations.

- There is insufficient evidence that employee training and development is universally utilized at all locations.

- There is no evidence that production management participate in new product design or changes to design to ensure manufacturability.

- There is no evidence of existing or pending partnering with key suppliers.

- The only information reported is financial and operational results. There are no results shown for customer focus, market penetration, employee well-being and satisfaction, or supplier partnering.

GLO has shown relatively steady progress in recent years, throughout the ups and downs of the economy. GLO appears poised for a major upturn in growth and profitability, partially due to new military contracts for both external and internal signage, and also an upsurge in sales of women's cosmetics (lipstick especially).

In the strategic planning for years 2002–2007, the top team identified three goals: (1) improve customer satisfaction and retention, (2) introduce "lean thinking" as a means to improve product production and delivery, and reduce costs, and (3) prepare an application for the Malcolm Baldrige National Quality Award, to be submitted for the 2006 award program.

Glancing Forward Two Years

Looking at the following information through the CMQ/OE BoK lens, how would you evaluate the work GLO has done in the last two years (for example, what was done well, and what wasn't?) Be ready to present your rationale based on QM theories/principles.

1. GLO has neither added nor dropped any of its locations, or modified its employee count and mix. GLO has recently hired a director of corporate quality to head a top-level Award Task Force to guide the changes and preparation for applying for the Baldrige award. It is expected that a management person from each of the plants and each headquarters function will serve on this task force. The stated objective is to win the

Baldrige Award. (It is assumed by the rank and file that this means "at any cost.")

2. The director has hired Baldrige Award coordinators for each of the plants, reporting to the director but with a "dotted-line" relationship with the plant managers.

3. Responding to the deficiencies cited by the Empire State site visit team, teams have been established at some of the plants to address the deficiencies at the plant level. The coordinators send a status report to the quality director quarterly.

4. Human Resources devised a temporary reward system to recognize team achievements with a pay bonus. There is inconsistent information at the locations as to the criteria to be used and how the bonus is to be computed. No team has received a bonus yet. The director of quality opposed the bonus plan but was overruled by the majority of the task force. One of the teams from Cicero has applied for the bonus and been rejected by the vice president of human resources. These team members feel they have been wronged and have appealed to the director of quality to intervene on their behalf.

5. The task force wants to have Human Resources conduct an employee survey, the company's first, to provide data that can be analyzed to aid in improving employee satisfaction. Human Resources is resisting the request on several grounds: (a) with so much going on in the company, the timing is not good, (b) HR has reservations about the practicality of surveying employees, expressing fear that it can do more harm than good, (c) concern exists that HR does not have the expertise to design, implement, and analyze a survey, and (d) HR really doesn't have the expertise to evaluate outside resources that could help.

6. The coordinators at the two product container plants have been collaborating and have developed good support from their plant managers in setting up improvement teams to address the Baldrige criteria. They frequently share ideas, techniques, and tools via e-mail and other media, although they have never met face to face.

7. Sales and production maintain a traditional adversarial relationship, as does purchasing with suppliers.

8. There are no integrated plans and programs for employee training and development. What training is done is on-the-job training for persons having an impact on quality—skills training to qualify employees for their assigned tasks—an ISO 9001 requirement. Requests to attend outside training and educational events are seldom approved. Those employees who pursue a formal education do so on their own.

9. The director receives status reports, via e-mail, from each of the plant coordinators on a quarterly basis. These are summarized and presented at the quarterly management meeting.

10. Two of the coordinators have been pressing the director to hold a joint meeting of the coordinators with the task force members, at least quarterly, suggesting teleconferencing as a means for doing so.

11. The quality director has not yet personally visited any sites outside of New York state. It is unclear whether the director has initiated any action at sites and with other internal functions than just the plants.

12. The top team's attention has very recently been focused on the development of a new market with a new product line—rear-view mirrors for vehicles. This new focus resulted from a "brilliant idea" that the process used to develop the mirror-like finish on lipstick containers could be used for rear-view mirrors, especially for military vehicles. The resulting product could, ultimately, replace all metal and glass-type vehicle mirrors at a significant savings to vehicle manufacturers. (It is noted that the strategic planning process did not surface any future indication that a shift in product and marketplace was imminent.)

13. The goals from the strategic plan have taken somewhat of a "back seat," except that the quality director is now viewed as the "owner" of the Baldrige Award initiative.

14. GLO employees do participate as volunteers and elected officials within their communities. These efforts are not company sponsored, not recognized by the company, and are undocumented.

15. Recent financials place GLO as an attractive target for a hostile takeover by a huge conglomerate.

16. A Malaysian company has perfected a deposition process that is competitive with GLO's. GLO alleges their process was stolen.

Appendix A

References

A list that the preparers of the CMQ/OE examination may use to create questions is available for download from http://prdweb.asq.org/certification/control/manager-of-quality/references).

QUALITY MANAGEMENT—GENERAL

(These references address multiple sections and topics from the Body of Knowledge.)

Bauer, J. E., G. L. Duffy, and R. T. Westcott, eds. *The Quality Improvement Handbook.* 2nd ed. Milwaukee: ASQ Quality Press, 2006.

Beecroft, G. D., G. L. Duffy, and J. W. Moran, eds. *The Executive Guide to Improvement and Change.* Milwaukee: ASQ Quality Press, 2003.

Cartin, Thomas J., *Principles and Practices of Organizational Performance Excellence.* Milwaukee: ASQ Quality Press, 1999.

Christensen, E. H., K. M. Coombes-Betz, and M. S. Stein. *The Certified Quality Process Analyst Handbook.* Milwaukee: ASQ Quality Press, 2007.

Dorf, R. C., ed. *The Technology Management Handbook.* Boca Raton, FL: CRC Press, 1999.

Duffy, Grace L., ed. *The ASQ Quality Improvement Pocket Guide.* Milwaukee, WI: ASQ Quality Press, 2013.

Evans, J. R., and W. M. Lindsay. *The Management and Control of Quality.* 6th ed. Cincinnati: South Western, 2004.

Feigenbaum, A. V. *Total Quality Control.* 3rd rev. ed. New York: McGraw-Hill, 1991.

GOAL/QPC. *The Memory Jogger II: Tools for Continuous Improvement and Effective Planning.* 2nd ed. 2010; *The Six Sigma Memory Jogger II.* 2002; *The Process Management Memory Jogger: Building Cross-Functional Excellence.* 2008; *Value Methodology: To Reduce Cost and Improve Value Through Function Analysis.* 2008. Salem, NH.

Juran, J. M., ed. *A History of Managing for Quality: The Evolution, Trends, and Future Directions of Managing for Quality.* Milwaukee: ASQC Quality Press, 1995.

Juran, J. M., and A. B. Godfrey, eds. *Juran's Quality Handbook.* 5th ed. New York: McGraw-Hill, 1999.

Liebesman, S. *Competitive Advantage: Linked Management Systems.* Chico, CA: Paton Professional, 2011.

Pyzdek, T. and P. Keller, *The Handbook for Quality Management: A Complete Guide to Operational Excellence,* 2nd ed. New York: McGraw-Hill, 2013.

———. *The Six Sigma Handbook: A Complete Guide for Green Belts, Black Belts, and Managers at All Levels.* 3rd ed. Milwaukee: ASQ Quality Press, 2009.

ReVelle, J. B. *Quality Essentials: A Reference Guide from A to Z.* Milwaukee: ASQ Quality Press, 2004.

ReVelle, J. B., ed. *Manufacturing Handbook of Best Practices: An Innovation, Productivity, and Quality Focus.* Boca Raton, FL: St. Lucie Press, 2002.

Siebels, D. L. *The Quality Improvement Glossary.* Milwaukee: ASQ Quality Press, 2004.

Sirkin, M. *The Secret Life of Corporations: Understanding the True Nature of Business.* White Plains, NY: New Chrysalis Press, 2004.

Summers, D. C. S. *Quality.* 2nd ed. Upper Saddle River, NJ: Prentice Hall, 2000.

Tague, N. R. *The Quality Toolbox.* 2nd ed. Milwaukee: ASQ Quality Press, 2005.

Townsend, P. L., and J. E. Gebhardt. *The Excutive Guide to Understanding and Implementing Employee Engagement Programs: Expand Production Capacity, Increase Revenue, and Save Jobs.* Milwaukee: ASQ Quality Press, 2007.

West, J. E., and C. A. Cianfrani. *Unlocking the Power of Your QMS: Keys to Business Process Improvement.* Milwaukee: ASQ Quality Press, 2004.

PART I LEADERSHIP

A. Chapter 1 Organizational Structures

Ashkenas, R., D. Ulrich, T. Jich, and S. Herr. *The Boundaryless Organization: Breaking the Chains of Organizational Structure.* San Francisco: Jossey-Bass, 1995.

Harrington, H. J., and F. Voehl. *The Organizational Alignment Handbook: A Catalyst for Performance Acceleration.* Boca Raton, FL: CRC Press, 2012.

Hesselbein, F., and P. M. Cohen, eds. *Leader to Leader: Enduring Insights on Leadership from the Drucker Foundation's Award-Winning Journal.* San Francisco: Jossey-Bass, 1999.

B. Chapter 2 Leadership Challenges

Attong, M., and T. Metz. *Change or Die: The Business Process Improvement Manual.* Milwaukee: ASQ Quality Press, 2013.

Bellman, G. M. *Getting Things Done When You Are Not in Charge: How to Succeed from a Support Position.* San Francisco: Berrett-Koehler, 2001.

Benowitz, E. A. *Cliffs Quick Review Principles of Management.* Hoboken, NJ: Wiley Publishing, 2001.

Blank, W. *The 108 Skills of Natural Born Leaders.* New York: AMACOM, 2001.

Camarota, A. G. *Finding the Leader in You: A Practical Guide to Expanding Your Leadership Skills.* Milwaukee: ASQ Quality Press, 2005.

Covey, S. R. *Principle-Centered Leadership.* New York: Summit Books, 1991.

Cramer, A., and Z. Karabell. *Sustainable Excellence: The Future of Business in a Fast-Changing World.* New York: Macmillan-Rodale, 2010.

Duck, J. D. *The Change Monster: The Human Forces That Fuel or Foil Corporate Transformation and Change.* New York: Random House (Crown Business), 2001.

Ducoff, N. *No-Compromise Leadership: A Higher Standrad of Leadership Thinking and Behavior.* Sanford, FL: DC Press, 2009.

Everly, G., Strause, D., and Everly III, G. *The Secrets of Resilient Leadership.* Milwaukee: ASQ Quality Press, 2009.

Gawande, Atul, *The Checklist Manifesto: How to Get Things Right.* New York: Metropolitan Books-Henry Holt and Company, 2009.

Goleman, D. *Working with Emotional Intelligence.* New York: Bantam Books, 1998.

Gostick, A., and C. Elton. *The Carrot Principle: How the Best Managers Use Recognition to Engage Their People, Retain Talent, and Accelerate Performance.* New York: Free Press, 2007.

Hacker, S., and T. Roberts. *Transformational Leadership: Creating Organizations of Meaning.* Milwaukee: ASQ Quality Press, 2004.

Heath, C., and D. Heath, *Switch: How to Change Things When Change Is Hard.* New York: Crown Business, 2010.

Hersey, P., *The Situational Leader.* Escondido, CA: Center for Leadership Studies, 2004.

Hersey, P., K. Blanchard, and D. E. Johnson. *Management of Organizational Behavior: Leading Human Resources.* Upper Saddle River, NJ: Prentice-Hall, 2001.

Hesselbein, F., and P. M. Cohen, eds. *Leader to Leader: Enduring Insights on Leadership from the Drucker Foundation's Award-Winning Journal.* San Francisco: Jossey-Bass, 1999.

Hirzel, R. C. "Leadership Is Personal." Paper published by the ASQ Human Development and Leadership Division. Milwaukee, 2003.

Hopen, D. "Guiding Corporate Behavior: A Leadership Obligation, Not a Choice," *The Journal for Quality and Participation* 25 (Winter 2002):15–19

Hutton, D. *The Change Agent's Handbook.* Milwaukee: ASQ Quality Press, 1994.

Jossey-Bass. *Business Leadership: A Jossey-Bass Reader.* San Francisco: Jossey-Bass, 2003.

Kotter, J. P. *Leading Change.* Boston: Harvard Business School Press, 2012.

Kouzes, J., and B. Posner. *The Leadership Challenge.* 4th ed. San Francisco: Jossey-Bass, 2008.

Labovitz, G., and V. Rosansky. *Rapid Improvement.* Milwaukee: ASQ Quality Press, 2013.

Lee, J. *Rising Above All.* Milwaukee: ASQ Quality Press, 2013.

Miller, K. *The Change Agent's Guide to Radical Improvement.* Milwaukee: ASQ Quality Press, 2002.

Mundy, Lee. *A Journey to Quality Leadership,* Milwaukee: ASQ Quality Press, 2011.

Palmer, B. *Making Change Work: Practical Tools for Overcoming Human Resistance to Change.* Milwaukee: ASQ Quality Press, 2004.

Pauley, J. A., and J. Pauley, *Communication: The Key to Effective Leadership.* Milwaukee: ASQ Quality Press, 2009.

Perseus Publishing. *Best Practice: Ideas and Insights From the World's Foremost Business Thinkers.* Cambridge, MA: Perseus, 2003.

Pietenpol, D. *Leadership, Quality, and Learning.* Milwaukee: ASQ Quality Press, 2008.

Senge, P. *The Fifth Discipline.* New York: Random House, 2005.

Shearer, C. *Everyday Excellence: Creating a Better Workplace Through Attitude, Action, and Appreciation.* Milwaukee: ASQ Quality Press, 2006.

Smart, B. D. *Topgrading: How Leading Companies Win by Hiring, Coaching, and Keeping the Best People.* New York: Portfolio-Penguin Group, 2005.

Weiner, E., and A. Brown. *Future Think: How to Think Clearly in a Time of Change.* Upper Saddle River, NJ: Pearson-Prentice Hall, 2006.

Weiss, A. *"Good Enough" Isn't Enough: Nine Challenges for Companies That Choose to Be Great.* New York: AMACOM, 2000.

C. Chapter 3 Teams and Team Processes

Dreo, H., P. Kunkel, and T. Mitchell. *The Virtual Teams Guidebook for Managers.* Milwaukee: ASQ Quality Press, 2003.

McDermott, L. C., N. Brawley, and W. W. Waite. *World Class Teams: Working across Borders.* New York: John Wiley & Sons, 1998.

Scholtes, P. R., B. L. Joiner, and B. J. Streibel. *The Team Handbook.* 3rd ed. Madison, WI: Joiner Associates, 2003.

Wilson, S. "Forming Virtual Teams." *Quality Progress* (June 2003): 36–41.

D. Chapter 4 ASQ Code of Ethics

Anderson, B. *Bringing Business Ethics to Life: Achieving Corporate Social Responsibility.* Milwaukee: ASQ Quality Press, 2004.

AuBuchon, D. "Integrity in Management." *The Quality Management Forum* (Fall 2004).

Geissler, P. *Managing with Conscience for Competitive Advantage.* Milwaukee: ASQ Quality Press, 2004.

Sarbanes-Oxley Act of 2002. Public Law 107-204, July 30, 2002. (Addresses concerns, among other issues, about corporate responsibility for financial reports. A top corporate officer must review and sign financial reports signifying that "the report does not contain any untrue statement of a material fact or omit to state a material fact necessary in order to make the statements made, in light of the circumstances under which such statements were made, not misleading.")

Stimson, W. A. "A Deming Inspired Management Code of Ethics." *Quality Progress* (February 2005): 67–75.

PART II STRATEGIC PLAN DEVELOPMENT AND DEPLOYMENT

A. Chapter 5 Strategic Planning Models

Cobb, C. G. *From Quality to Business Excellence: A Systems Approach to Management.* Milwaukee: ASQ Quality Press, 2003.

Colletti, J. *Hoshin Kanri Memory Jogger.* Salem, NH: GOAL/QPC, 2013.

Haines, S. G. *Strategic and Business Planning: The Systems Thinking Approach.* Amherst, MA: HRD Press, 1999.

National Institute of Standards and Technology. *Baldrige Performance Excellence Program: Criteria for Performance Excellence.* Gaithersburg, MD: NIST, 2012. (Individual copies of the criteria booklets may be obtained free of charge from: Baldrige Performance Excellence Program, NIST, Administration Building, Room A600, 100 Bureau Drive, Stop 1020, Gaithersburg, MD 20899-1020, telephone (301) 975-2036, fax (301) 948-3716, e-mail nqp@nist.gov or download from www.baldrige.nist.gov/Criteria.htm). Note: There are separate criteria for healthcare and for education.

B. Chapter 6 Business Environment Analysis

Babcock, C. *Management Strategies for the Cloud Revolution: How Cloud Computing Is Transforming Business and Why You Can't Afford to Be Left Behind.* New York: McGraw-Hill, 2010.

C. Chapter 7 Strategic Plan Deployment

DeFeo, J. A. "Strategic Deployment," Section 13 in *Juran's Quality Handbook.* 5th ed. J. M. Juran and A. B. Godfrey, eds. New York: McGraw-Hill, 1999.

Haines, S. G. *Strategic and Business Planning: The Systems Thinking Approach.* Amherst, MA: HRD Press, 1999.

PART III MANAGEMENT ELEMENTS AND METHODS

A. Chapter 8 Management Skills and Abilities

Principles of Management, Management Theories, and Tools

Hersey, P., K. Blanchard, and D. E. Johnson. *Management of Organizational Behavior: Leading Human Resources*. Upper Saddle River, NJ: Prentice-Hall, 2001.

Hofstede, G., G. J. Hofstede, and M. Mikov. *Cultures and Organizations*. 4th ed. New York: McGraw-Hill, 2010.

Liker, J. *The Toyota Way: 14 Management Principles from the World's Greatest Manufacturer*. New York: McGraw-Hill, 2004.

Schein, E. H. *The Corporate Culture Survival Guide: Sense and Nonsense About Culture Change*. San Francisco: Jossey-Bass, 1999.

Schermerhorn Jr., J. R., J. G. Hunt, and R. N. Osborn. *Organizational Behavior*. 9th ed. New York: John Wiley & Sons, 2005.

Senge, P. M. *The Fifth Discipline: The Art & Practice of the Learning Organization*. New York: Doubleday, 1990.

Senge, P. M., A. Kleiner, C. Roberts, R. B. Ross, and B. J. Smith. *The Fifth Discipline Fieldbook: Strategies and Tools for Building a Learning Organization*. New York: Doubleday, 1994.

Woodson, W., P. Tillman, and B. Tillman. *Human Factors Design Handbook*. 2nd ed. New York: McGraw-Hill, 1992.

Interdependence of Functional Areas

Cobb, C. G. *From Quality to Business Excellence: A Systems Approach to Management*. Milwaukee: ASQ Quality Press, 2003.

Sirkin, M. *The Secret Life of Corporations: Understanding the True Nature of Business*. White Plains, NY: New Chrysalis Press, 2004.

Human Resources Management

Holbeche, L. *Aligning Human Resources and Business Strategy*. New York: Butterworth Heinemann, 2001.

Mathis, R. L., and J. H. Jackson. *Human Resource Management*. 11th ed. Mason, OH: Thomson South-Western, 2000.

Financial Management

Chang, R. Y., and M. W. Morgan. *Performance Scorecards: Measuring the Right Things in the Real World*. San Francisco: Jossey-Bass, 2000.

Drickhamer, D. "House of Cards." *Industry Week* (January 2005): 49–51.

Finkler, S. A. *Finance and Accounting for Nonfinancial Managers*. 3rd ed. New York: Aspen Publishers, 2003.

Garrison, R. H., and E. W. Noreen. *Managerial Accounting*. Boston: McGraw-Hill/Irwin, 2003.

George, S. "How to Speak the Language of Senior Management." *Quality Progress* (May 2003): 30–36.

Hoisington, S. H., and E. C. Menzer. "Learn to Talk Money." *Quality Progress* (May 2004): 44–49.

Kaplan, R. S., and D. P. Norton. *The Balanced Scorecard: Translating Strategy into Action*. Boston: Harvard Business School Press, 1996.

Livingston, J. L., and T. Grossman. *The Portable MBA in Finance and Accounting*. 3rd ed. New York: John Wiley & Sons, 2001.

Ryan, J. *Making the Economic Case for Quality.* An ASQ White Paper. Milwaukee: American Society for Quality, 2004.

Tracy, J. A. *Accounting for Dummies: A Reference for the Rest of Us.* 2nd ed. New York: Hungry Minds, 2001.

Risk Management

Drickhamer, D. "House of Cards." *Industry Week* (January 2005): 49–51.

Getto, G. "Risk Management Supporting Quality Management of Software Acquisition Projects," in *Software Quality Professional (ASQ)* 2, no. 2 (2000): 42–53.

Goodden, R. L. *Product Liability Prevention: A Strategic Guide.* Milwaukee: ASQ Quality Press, 2000.

Hutchins, G., and D. Gould. "The Growth of Risk Management." *Quality Progress* (September 2004): 73–75.

Kolka, J. W. "ISO 9001 and 9004: A Framework for Disaster Preparedness." *Quality Progress* (February 2002): 57–62.

Snow, A. "Integrating Risk Management into the Design and Development Process." *Medical Device & Diagnostic Industry* (March 2001): 99–113.

Vinas, T., and J. Jusko. "5 Threats That Could Sink Your Company." *Industry Week* (September 2004): 53–62.

Westcott, R. T. *Stepping Up to ISO 9004:2000.* Chico, CA: Paton Press, 2005, Chapter 4.

Knowledge Management

Bajaria, H. J. "Knowledge Creation and Management: Integrated Issues." *ASQ's 54th Annual Quality Conference Proceedings.* Milwaukee: ASQ, 2002.

Davenport, T. H., and L. Prusak. *Working Knowledge: How Organizations Manage What They Know.* Boston: Harvard Business School Press, 1998.

Shockley III, W. "Planning for Knowledge Management." *Quality Progress* (March 2000).

Von Krogh, G., K. Ichijo, and I. Nonaka. *Enabling Knowledge Creation: How to Unlock the Mystery of Tacit Knowledge and Release the Power of Innovation.* New York: Oxford University Press, 2000.

Wilson, L. T., and D. Asay. "Putting Quality in Knowledge Management." *Quality Progress* (January 1999): 25–31.

Product Development

Cooper, R. G. *Winning at New Products: Accelerating the Process from Idea to Launch.* 3rd ed. Cambridge, MA: Perseus, 2001.

Monczka, R. M., R. B. Handfield, T. V. Scannell, G. L. Ragatz, and D. J. Frayer. *New Product Development: Strategies for Supplier Integration.* Milwaukee: ASQ Quality Press, 2000.

Reilly, N. B. *The Team Based Product Development Guidebook.* Milwaukee: ASQ Quality Press, 1999.

B. Chapter 9 Communication Skills and Abilities

Brounstein, M. *Communicating Effectively for Dummies: A Reference for the Rest of Us.* New York: John Wiley & Sons, 2001.

Harrington, H. J., and F. Voehl. "Managing Global Quality: Directing a Worldwide Organization Demands Keen Strategy and Innovative Planning." *Quality Digest* (November 2004): 33–37.

Morrison, T., W. A. Conaway, and G. A. Borden. *Kiss, Bow, or Shake Hands: How to Do Business in Sixty Countries.* Holbrook, MA: Adams Media Corporation, 1994.

C. Chapter 10 Project Management

Baker, S., and K. Baker. *The Complete Idiot's Guide to Project Management*. Indianapolis, IN: Alpha Books, 2000.

Barkley, B. T., and J. H. Saylor. *Customer-Driven Project Management: Building Quality into Project Processes*. 2nd ed. New York: McGraw-Hill, 2001.

Chapman, C., and S. Ward. *Project Risk Management*. New York: John Wiley & Sons, 2003.

Chatfield, C. S., and T. D. Johnson. *Microsoft Project 2000 Step by Step*. Redmond, WA: Microsoft Press, 2002.

Conklin, J. D. "Smart Project Selection." *Quality Progress* (March 2003): 81–83.

Cooper, R. G. *Winning at New Products: Accelerating the Process from Idea to Launch*. 3rd ed. Cambridge, MA: Perseus, 2001.

Dobson, M. *Project Management for the Technical Professional*. Upper Darby, PA: Project Management Institute, 2001.

Fleming, Q. W., and J. M. Koppelman. *Earned Value: Project Management*. Newtown Square, PA: Project Management Institute, 2000.

Frame, J. D. *Managing Risk in Organizations: A Guide for Managers*. New York: John Wiley & Sons, 2003.

————. *The New Project Management*. 2nd ed. San Francisco: Jossey-Bass, 2002.

Graham, R. J., and R. L. Englund. *Creating an Environment for Successful Projects*. 2nd ed. Milwaukee: ASQ Quality Press, 2003.

Kerzner, H. *Project Management: A Systems Approach to Planning, Scheduling, and Controlling*. 8th ed. New York: Van Nostrand Reinhold, 2003.

LaBrosse, M. A. *Accelerated Project Management*. New York: HNB, 2002.

Lewis, J. P. *Project Planning, Scheduling & Control: A Hands-On Guide to Bringing Projects in on Time and on Budget*. 3rd ed. Chicago: Probus, 2001.

Lowenthal, J. N. *Six Sigma Project Management: A Pocket Guide*. Milwaukee: ASQ Quality Press, 2002.

Milosevic, D. Z. *Project Management Toolbox: Tools and Techniques for the Practicing Project Manager*. New York: John Wiley & Sons, 2003.

Phillips, J. J., T. W. Bothell, and G. L. Snead. *The Project Management Scorecard: Measuring the Success of Project Management Solutions*. New York: Butterworth Heinemann, 2002.

PMI Standards Committee. *A Guide to the Project Management Body of Knowledge*. Upper Darby, PA: Project Management Institute, 2000.

Pyzdek, T. "Selecting Winning Projects." *Quality Digest* (August 2000): 26.

Rad, P. F., and G. Levin. *Achieving Project Management Success Using Virtual Teams*. Boca Raton, FL: J. Ross, 2003.

Stevenson, N. *Microsoft Project for Dummies*. Foster City, CA: IDG, 2000.

Uyttewaal, E. *Dynamic Scheduling with Microsoft Project 2002*. Boca Raton, FL: J. Ross, 2003.

————. *The Portable MBA in Project Management*. New York: John Wiley & Sons, 2003.

Westcott, R. T. *Simplified Project Management for the Quality Professional*. Milwaukee: ASQ Quality Press, 2004.

Wysocki, R. K., and J. P. Lewis. *The World Class Project Manager: A Professional Development Guide*. Cambridge, MA: Perseus, 2001.

D. Chapter 11 Quality System

Arter, D. R. *Quality Audits for Improved Performance*. 3rd ed. Milwaukee: ASQ Quality Press, 2003.

Arter, D. R., C. A. Cianfrani, and J. E. West. *How to Audit the Process-Based QMS*. Milwaukee: ASQ Quality Press, 2003.

Palmes, P. C. *Process Driven Comprehensive Auditing.* Milwaukee: ASQ Quality Press, 2005.

———. *The Internal Auditing Pocket Guide.* Milwaukee: ASQ Quality Press, 2003.

———. *Continual Improvement Assessment Guide: Promoting and Sustaining Business Results.* Milwaukee: ASQ Quality Press, 2004.

West, J., and C. A. Cianfrani. *Unlocking the Power of Your QMS: Keys to Business Performance Improvement.* Milwaukee: ASQ Quality Press, 2005.

E. Chapter 12 Quality Models and Theories

Bernhart, M. S., and F. J. Maher. *ISO 26000 in Practice.* Milwaukee: ASQ Quality Press, 2011.

Blazey, M. L. *Insights to Performance Excellence 2013–2014: Understanding the Integrated Management System and the Baldrige Criteria: An Inside Look at the 2005 Baldrige Award Criteria.* Milwaukee: ASQ Quality Press, 2013.

Brown, M. G. *Baldrige Award Winning Quality: How to Interpret the Baldrige Criteria for Performance Excellence.* 14th ed. New York: Productivity Press, 2005.

Byrnes, M. A., and J. C. Baxter. *There Is Another Way! Launch a Baldrige-Based Quality Classroom.* Milwaukee: ASQ Quality Press, 2005.

Cianfrani, C. A., and J. E. West. *ISO 9001:2008 Explained Expanded: Optimizing Your QMS for Success.* Milwaukee: ASQ Quality Press, 2013.

Collins Jr., J. W., and D. S. Steiger. *The Memory Jogger 9001:2008: Implementing a Process Approach Compliant to ISO 9001:2008 Quality Management Systems.* Salem, NH: GOAL/QPC, 2011.

Crosby, P. B. *Quality Is Free.* New York: Mentor Books, 1979.

Deming, W. E. *The New Economics.* 2nd ed. Cambridge, MA: MIT Center for Advanced Educational Studies, 1994.

———. *Out of the Crisis.* Cambridge, MA: MIT Center for Advanced Engineering Study, 1986.

Imai, M. *Kaizen: The Key to Japan's Competitive Success.* New York: Random House Business Division, 1986.

Ishikawa, L. *Guide to Quality Control.* Tokyo: Asian Productivity Organization, 1982.

Leonard, D., and M. McGuire. *Executive Guide to Understanding and Implementing the Baldrige Criteria: Improve Revenue and Create Organizational Excellence.* Milwaukee: ASQ Quality Press, 2007.

Myhrberg, E. V. *A Practical Field Guide for ISO 9001:2008.* Milwaukee: ASQ Quality Press, 2009.

Russell, J.P. *Continual Improvement Assessment Guide.* Milwaukee: ASQ Quality Press, 2004.

———. *The Internal Auditing Pocket Guide.* Milwaukee: ASQ Quality Press, 2003.

West, J. E., and C. A. Cianfrani. *Unlocking the Power of Your QMS: Keys to Business Performance Improvement.* Milwaukee: ASQ Quality Press, 2005.

Westcott, R. T. *Stepping Up to ISO 9004:2000: A Practical Guide for Creating a World-Class Organization.* Chico, CA: Paton Press, 2003.

PART IV QUALITY MANAGEMENT TOOLS

A. Chapter 13 Problem-Solving Tools

Seven Classic Quality Tools and Basic Management and Planning Tools

Andersen, B., T. Fagerhaug, B. Henriksen, and L. F. Onsøyen. *Mapping Work Processes.* Milwaukee: ASQ Quality Press, 2008

Brassard, M., and D. Ritter. *The Memory Jogger 2*. 2nd ed. Salem, NH: GOAL/QPC, 2010.

Process Improvement Tools

ABS Consulting—L. N. Vanden Heuvel, D. K. Lorenzo, R. L. Montgomery, W.E. Hanson, and J. R. Rooney. *Root Cause Analysis Handbook*. 3rd ed. Milwaukee: ASQ Quality Press, 2008.

Andersen, B., and T. Fagerhaug. *Root Cause Analysis: Simplified Tools and Techniques*. 2nd ed. Milwaukee: ASQ Quality Press, 2006.

Barry, R., and A. C. Smith. *The Manager's Guide to Six Sigma in Healthcare: Practical Tips and Tools for Improvement*. Milwaukee: ASQ Quality Press, 2005.

Brassard, M., L. Finn, D. Ginn, and D. Ritter. *The Six Sigma Memory Jogger II: A Pocket Guide of Tools for Six Sigma Improvement Teams*. Salem, NH: GOAL/QPC, 2002.

GOAL/QPC. *The Problem Solving Memory Jogger: Seven Steps to Improved Processes*. Lawrence, MA: GOAL/QPC, 2000.

Munro, R. A. *Six Sigma for the Shop Floor*. Milwaukee: ASQ Quality Press, 2002.

Okes, D., *Root Cause Analysis: The Core of Problem Solving and Corrective Action*. Milwaukee: ASQ Quality Press, 2009.

Pande, P. S., and L. Holpp. *What Is Six Sigma?* New York: McGraw-Hill, 2001.

Pande, P. S., R. R. Cavanagh, and R. P. Neuman. *The Six Sigma Way: How GE, Motorola, and Other Top Companies Are Honing Their Performance*. New York: McGraw-Hill, 2000.

Plenert, G. *Strategic Continuous Process Improvement: Which Quality Tools to Use, and When to Use Them*. New York: McGraw-Hill, 2012.

Pries, K. H. *Six Sigma for the Next Millennium*. 2nd ed. Milwaukee: ASQ Quality Press, 2009.

Six Sigma Academy. *The Black Belt Memory Jogger: A Pocket Guide for Six Sigma Success*. Salem, NH: GOAL/QPC, 2002.

Stamatis, D. H. *Failure Mode Effect Analysis: FMEA from Theory to Execution*. 2nd ed. Milwaukee: ASQ Quality Press, 2003.

Tague, N. R. *The Quality Toolbox*. 2nd ed. Milwaukee: ASQ Quality Press, 2005.

Watson, G. *Six Sigma for Business Leaders: A Guide to Implementation*. Salem, NH: GOAL/QPC, 2004.

Innovation and Creativity Tools

Cook, H. E. *Design for Six Sigma As Strategic Experimentation: Planning, Designing, and Building World-Class Products and Services*. Milwaukee: ASQ Quality Press, 2005.

GOAL/QPC. *The Design for Six Sigma Memory Jogger*. Salem, NH: GOAL/QPC, 2004.

Hidahl, J. W. "DFMA/DFSS." In *Manufacturing Handbook of Best Practices*, edited by J. B. ReVelle. Boca Raton, FL: St. Lucie Press, 2002.

Mader, D. P. "Design for Six Sigma: You Need More Than Standard Six Sigma Approaches to Optimize Your Product or Service Development." *Quality Progress* (July 2002): 82–86.

Tague, N. R. *The Quality Toolbox*. 2nd ed. Milwaukee: ASQ Quality Press, 2005.

Ungvari, S. F. "TRIZ." Chapter 19 in *Manufacturing Handbook of Best Practices: An Innovation, Productivity, and Quality Focus*, edited by J. B. ReVelle. Boca Raton, FL: St. Lucie Press, 2002, 399–425.

Watson, G. H. *Design for Six Sigma: Innovation for Enhanced Competitiveness*. Salem, NH: GOAL/QPC, 2005.

Cost of Quality

Beecroft, G. D. "Cost of Quality and Quality Planning Affect the Bottom Line." *The Quality Management Forum* (Winter 2001).

DeFeo, J. A. "The Tip of the Iceberg: When Accounting for Quality, Don't Forget the Often Hidden Costs of Poor Quality." *Quality Progress* (May 2001): 29–37.

Freiesleben, J. "Quality Problems and Their Real Costs." *Quality Progress* (December 2004): 49–55.

Gryna, F. M. "Section 8: Quality and Costs." In *Juran's Quality Handbook*. 5th ed. Edited by J. M. Juran and A. B. Godfrey New York: McGraw-Hill, 1999.

Wood, D. C., ed. *Principles of Quality Costs: Financial Measures for Strategic Implementation of Quality Management*. 4th ed. Milwaukee: ASQ Quality Press, 2012.

B. Chapter 14 Process Management

Process Goals and Analysis

Alukal, G., and A. Manos. *Lean Kaizen: A Simplified Approach to Process Improvement*. Milwaukee: ASQ Quality Press, 2006.

Christensen, E. H., K. M. Coombes-Betz, M. S. Stein, *The Certified Quality Process Analyst Handbook*. Milwaukee: ASQ Quality Press, 2007.

Imai, M. *Gemba Kaizen: A Commonsense Approach to a Continous Improvement Strategy*. 2nd ed. Milwaukee: ASQ Quality Press, 2012.

Lareau, W. *Office Kaizen 2: Harnessing Leadership, Organizations, People, and Tools for Office Excellence*. Milwaukee: ASQ Quality Press, 2011.

Windsor, S. *An Introduction to Green Process Management*. Milwaukee: ASQ Quality Press, 2011.

Lean Tools

Hinckley, C. M. *Make No Mistake!: An Outcome-Based Approach to Mistake-Proofing*. Portland, OR: Productivity Press, 2001.

Lareau, W. *Office Kaizen: Transforming Office Operations into a Strategic Competitive Advantage*. Milwaukee: ASQ Quality Press, 2003.

Macinnes, R. L. *The Lean Enterprise Memory Jogger: Create Value and Eliminate Waste throughout Your Company*. Salem, NH: GOAL/QPC, 2002.

MCS Media. *The New Lean Pocket Guide XL: Tools for the Elimination of Waste!* Chelsea, MI: MCS Media, 2006.

Ohno, T. *Toyota Production System: Beyond Large-Scale Production*. Portland, OR: Productivity Press, 1988.

ReVelle, J. B. *Manufacturing Handbook of Best Practices: An Innovation, Productivity, and Quality Focus*. Boca Raton, FL: St. Lucie Press, 2002.

Rooney, S. A., and J. K. Rooney. "Lean Glossary." *Quality Progress* (June 2005): 41–47.

Schonberger, R. J. "Make Work Cells Work for You." *Quality Progress* (April 2004): 58–63.

Tapping, D., T. Luyster, and T. Shuker. *Value Stream Management: Eight Steps to Planning, Mapping, and Sustaining Lean Improvements*. New York: Productivity Press, 2002.

Trischler, W. R. *Understanding and Applying Value-Added Assessment: Eliminating Business Process Waste*. Milwaukee: ASQC Quality Press, 1996.

Voelkel, J. G., and C. Chapman. "Value Stream Mapping." *Quality Progress* (May 2003): 65–69.

Theory of Constraints

Dettmer, W. W. *Breaking the Constraints to World-Class Performance*. Milwaukee: ASQ Quality Press, 1998.

———. *Goldratt's Theory of Constraints: A Systems Approach to Continuous Improvement*. Milwaukee: ASQ Quality Press, 1997.

Nave, D., "How to Compare Six Sigma, Lean, and the Theory of Constraints." *Quality Progress* (March 2002): 73–78.

C. Chapter 15 Measurement: Assessment and Metrics

Andersen, B. *Business Process Improvement Toolbox.* Milwaukee: ASQ Quality Press, 1999.

Anderson, M. J., and S. L. Kraber. "Eight Keys to Successful DOE." *Quality Digest* (July 1999): 39–43.

ASQ Statistics Division. *Improving Performance Through Statistical Thinking.* Milwaukee: ASQ Quality Press, 2000.

Barrentine, L. B. *Concepts for R&R Studies.* 2nd ed. Milwaukee: ASQ Quality Press, 2003.

Blank, R. *Basics of Reliability.* New York: Productivity Press, 2004.

Borror, C. M., ed. *The Certified Quality Engineer Handbook.* 3rd ed. Milwaukee: ASQ Quality Press, 2009.

Brassard, M., L. Finn, D. Ginn, and D. Ritter. *Six Sigma Memory Jogger II: A Pocket Guide for Six Sigma Improvement Teams.* Salem, NH: GOAL/QPC, 2002.

Brassard, M., and D. Ritter. *The Creativity Tools Memory Jogger.* Salem, NH: GOAL/QPC, 1998.

Carey, R. G., and R. C. Lloyd. *Measuring Quality Improvement in Healthcare: A Guide to Statistical Process Control Applications.* Milwaukee: ASQ Quality Press, 2001.

Crossley, M. L. *The Desk Reference of Statistical Quality Methods.* Milwaukee: ASQ Quality Press, 2000.

Hahn, G. J., W. Q. Meeker, and N. Doganaksoy. "Speedier Reliability Analysis." *Quality Progress* (June 2003): 58–64.

Hunter, J. S. "Improving an Unstable Process." *Quality Progress* (February 2004): 68–71.

———. "Making a Decision Under Uncertain Circumstances." *Quality Progress* (April 2003): 83–85.

Kimothi, S. K. *The Uncertainty of Measurements: Physical and Chemical Metrology Impact and Analysis.* Milwaukee: ASQ Quality Press, 2002.

Okes, D. *Performance Metrics: The Levers for Process Management.* Milwaukee: ASQ Quality Press, 2013.

Payne, G. C. "Calibration: What Is It?" *Quality Progress* (May 2005): 72–76.

Schilling, E. G. "Acceptance Sampling." In *Juran's Quality Handbook.* 5th ed. Edited by J. M. Juran and A.B. Godfrey. New York: McGraw-Hill, 1999, Section 46.1–46.87.

Stephens, K. S. *The Handbook of Applied Acceptance Sampling: Plans, Procedures, and Principles.* Milwaukee: ASQ Quality Press, 2001.

West, J. E., and C. A. Cianfrani. *Unlocking the Power of Your QMS: Keys to Business Performance Improvement.* Milwaukee: ASQ Quality Press, 2005.

Wheeler, D. J. *Understanding Variation: The Key to Managing Chaos.* Knoxville, TN: SPC Press, 1993.

Wood, D., ed. *Principles of Quality Costs: Financial Measures for Strategic Implementation of Quality Management.* 4th ed. Milwaukee: ASQ Quality Press, 2013.

PART V CUSTOMER-FOCUSED ORGANIZATIONS

A. Chapter 16 Customer Identification and Segmentation

Westcott, R. T. "Quality-Level Agreements for Clarity of Expectations." *The Informed Outlook* (December 1999): 13–15.

B. Chapter 17 Customer Relationship Management

Albrecht, K., and R. Zemke. *Service America in the New Economy.* New York: McGraw-Hill, 2002.

Barlow, J., and C. Møller. *A Complaint Is a Gift: Using Customer Feedback As a Strategic Tool.* San Francisco: Berrett-Koehler, 1996.

Becker, K. "Are You Hearing Voices?" *Quality Progress* (February 2005): 28–35.

Camarota, A. G. *Finding the Leader in You.* Milwaukee: ASQ Quality Press, 2004.

Cochran, C. "Leveraging Customer Complaints into Customer Loyalty." *Quality Digest* (December 2004): 26–28.

Allen, D. R., and T. R. Rao. *Analysis of Customer Satisfaction Data.* Milwaukee: ASQ Quality Press, 2000.

Fisher, C. M., and J. T. Schutta. *Developing New Services: Incorporating the Voice of the Customer into Strategic Service Development.* Milwaukee: ASQ Quality Press, 2003.

Fornell, C. *The Satisfied Customer: Winners and Losers in the Battle for Buyer Preference.* New York: Palgrave-Macmillan, 2007.

Harris, E. K. *Customer Service: A Practical Approach.* Upper Saddle River, NJ: Prentice Hall, 2000.

Hayes, B. E. *Measuring Customer Satisfaction and Loyalty: Survey Design, Use, and Statistical Analysis Methods.* 3rd ed. Milwaukee: ASQ Quality Press, 2008.

Jeffries, R. D., and P. R. Sells. "Customer Satisfaction Measurement Instruments: In Healthcare, Does One Size Fit None?" *Quality Progress* (February 2000): 118–23.

Kessler, S. *Customer Satisfaction Toolkit for ISO 9001:2000.* Milwaukee: ASQ Quality Press, 2003.

LeBoeuf, M. *How to Win Customers and Keep Them for Life.* Rev. ed. New York: Berkeley Books, 2000.

McKenzie, R. *The Relationship-Based Enterprise: Powering Business Success Through Customer Relationship Management.* New York: McGraw-Hill, 2001.

Mody, A. "New Imperative: To Keep Customers, Deliver an Exceptional Experience." *The Quality Management Forum* (Fall): 5–7.

Naumann, E., and S. H. Hoisington. *Customer Centered Six Sigma: Linking Customers, Process Improvement, and Financial Results.* Milwaukee: ASQ Quality Press, 2001.

Newell, F. *Loyalty.com: Customer Relationship Management in the New Era of Internet Marketing.* New York: McGraw-Hill, 2000.

Nykamp, M. *The Customer Differential: The Complete Guide to Implementing Customer Relationship Management.* New York: AMACOM, 2001.

Plsek, P. E. "Creative Thinking for Surprising Quality: The Ability to Innovate Is a Must in Today's Competitive Marketplace." *Quality Progress* (May 2000): 67–73.

Rosenbluth, H. F., and D. M. Peters. *The Customer Comes Second: Put Your People First and Watch 'Em Kick Butt.* New York: HarperCollins, 2002.

Schultz, G. *The Customer Care & Contact Center Handbook.* Milwaukee: ASQ Quality Press, 2003.

Sewell, C., and P. B. Brown. *Customers for Life: How to Turn That One-Time Buyer into a Lifetime Customer.* New York: Doubleday, 2002.

Timm, P. R. *Seven Power Strategies for Building Customer Loyalty.* New York: AMACOM, 2001.

Ulwick, A. W. *What Customers Want: Using Outcome-Driven Innovation to Create Breakthrough Products and Services.* New York: McGraw-Hill, 2005.

Vavra, T. G. *Customer Satisfaction Measurement Simplified: A Step-by-Step Guide for ISO 9001:2000 Certification.* Milwaukee: ASQ Quality Press, 2002.

Warner, C. M. In *Real World Customer Service Strategies That Work.* Sevierville, TN: Insight, 2004.

Westcott, R. T. "Stepping Up to ISO 9004:2000: Focusing on the Customer." *The Informed Outlook* (July 2001): 3–8 and (August 2001): 19–24.

———. "Tapping the Many Voices of the Customer." *The Informed Outlook* (June 2000): 20–23.

———. "Safeguard Your Customer Base." *The Quality Management Forum* (Summer 1998): 10–13.

———. "Unconditional Guarantee: Implications for Your Business." *The Quality Management Forum* (Spring 1994): 3–6.

Wilburn, M. W. *Managing the Customer Experience: A Measurement-Based Approach.* Milwaukee: ASQ Quality Press, 2007.

Xie, M., K. C. Tan, T. N. Goh. *Advanced QFD Applications.* Milwaukee: ASQ Quality Press, 2003.

Zeithaml, V. A., A. Parasuraman, and L. L. Berry. *Delivering Quality Service: Balancing Customer Perceptions and Expectations.* Milwaukee: ASQ Quality Press, 2002.

PART VI SUPPLY CHAIN MANAGEMENT

Chapter 18 Supply Chain

Andrews, D. L. "How to Manage Cross-Cultural Change." *Chief Supply Chain Officer* (May 2005): 34–39.

Ayers, J. B. *Supply Chain Project Management: A Structured Collaborative and Measurable Approach.* 2nd ed. Boca Raton, FL: CRC Press, 2010.

Balasubramanian, R., and S. Baumgardner. "Good Supplier Management Aids New Product Launch." *Quality Progress* (June 2004): 49–57.

Barney, D. "Get Ripped!: 20 Steps to a Lean, Mean Supply Chain Machine." *Chief Supply Chain Officer* (May 2005): 18–25.

———. "10 Rules of Supply Chain Excellence." *Chief Supply Chain Officer* (February 2005): 22–29.

Bolstorff, P., and R. Rosenbaum. *Supply Chain Excellence: A Handbook for Dramatic Improvement Using the SCOR Model.* 2nd ed. New York: AMACOM, 2003.

Boone, T., and R. Ganeshan. *New Directions in Supply-Chain Management: Technology, Strategy, and Implementation.* New York: AMACOM, 2002.

Bossert, J. L., ed. *The Supplier Management Handbook.* 6th ed. Milwaukee: ASQ Quality Press, 2004.

CQI-19 AIAG Sub-tier Supplier Management Process Guideline, Version I, Issued August 2012.

Dittmann, P. J. *Supply Chain Transformation: Building and Executing an Integrated Supply Chain.* Milwaukee: ASQ Quality Press, 2013.

Dominick, C., and S. Lunney. *The Procurement Game Plan: Winning Strategies and Techniques for Supply Management Professionals.* Fort Lauderdale, FL: J. Ross, 2012.

Fawcett, S. E., and G. M. Magnan. *Achieving World-Class Supply Chain Alignment: Benefits, Barriers, and Bridges.* Center for Advanced Purchasing Studies, 2001. http://www.capsresearch.org.

Gilmore, D. "Integrated Supply Chains Require Effective Sales and Operations Planning." *Chief Supply Chain Officer* (May 2005): 48–47.

Gordon, S. "Seven Steps to Measure Supplier Performance." *Quality Progress* (August 2005): 20–25.

Handfield, R. B., and E. L. Nichols Jr. *Supply Chain Redesign: Transforming Supply Chains into Integrated Value Systems.* Upper Saddle River, NJ: Prentice Hall, 2002.

"How to Give a Quality Score to Your Supplier." Metric Stream. Accessed August 1, 2013. http://www.metricstream.com/insights/qualityScore.htm.

Navas, D. "The Global Supply Chain: 3PLs Lead the Way." *SCS* (May 2005): 10–17.

Norausky, P. H. *The Customer and Supplier Innovation Team Guidebook.* Milwaukee: ASQ Quality Press, 2000.

ReVelle, J. B., ed. *Manufacturing Handbook of Best Practices: An Innovation, Productivity, and Quality Focus.* Boca Raton, FL: St.Lucie Press, 2002, Chapters 16 and 17.

Stauffer, D. "Risk: The Weak Link in Your Supply Chain." *Harvard Business Review* (March 1, 2003): 3–5.

Supply and Demand Executive: Solutions-Based Intelligence for Supply Chain ROI . Magazine published five times per year, Northbrook, IL, omeda.com.

Supply Chain Metric.com. Accessed August 1, 2013. http://www.supplychainmetric. com/.

Terry, L. "Supply Chain Execution Expands Its Footprint: The Distinction between Supply Chain Planning and Supply Chain Execution Software Is Beginning to Blur, As Businesses Build Cross-Functional, Integrated Demand-Driven Networks." *SCS* (May 2005): 18–25.

Watkins, D. K. "Quality Management's Role in Global Sourcing." *Quality Progress* (April 2005): 24–31.

Chapter 19 Training and Development

Allen, M. W. *Michael Allen's Guide to E-Learning: Building Interactive, Fun, and Effective Learning Programs for Any Company.* Hoboken, NJ: John Wiley & Sons, 2003.

Kruse, K., and J. Keil. *Technology-Based Training: The Art and Science of Design, Development, and Delivery.* San Francisco: Jossey-Bass, 2000.

Phillips, J. J., *Handbook of Training Evaluation and Measurement Methods,* 3rd ed. Woburn, MA: Butterworth-Heinemann, 1997.

——. *Return on Investment in Training and Performance Improvement Programs.* Houston, TX: Gulf, 1997.

Rosenberg, M. J. *e-Learning: Strategies for Delivering Knowledge in the Digital Age.* New York: McGraw-Hill, 2001.

Rossett, A. *The ASTD E-Learning Handbook: Best Practices, Strategies, and Case Studies for an Emerging Field.* New York: McGraw-Hill, 2002.

——. *First Things Fast: A Handbook for Performance Analysis.* San Francisco: Pfeiffer, 1999.

——. *Training Needs Assessment.* Techniques in Training and Performance Development Series. Englewood Cliffs, NJ: Educational Technology Publications, 1987.

Rothwell, W. J., and H. C. Kazanas. *Mastering the Instructional Design Process: A Systematic Approach.* 3rd ed. San Francisco: Pfeiffer, 2003.

Stetar, B. "Training: It's Not Always the Answer." *Quality Progress* (March 2005): 44–49.

Westcott, R. T. "Mini-Scule: If You Have No Time or Money to Provide Training, Try a Mini-Scule." *Quality Progress* (June 2005): 104.

Appendix B

Glossary and Acronyms

A

A-B-C analysis—A systematic collection and analysis of the behavior observed of an individual or a work group for the purpose of determining the cause of specific behaviors.

acceptable quality limit (AQL)—The quality level that is the worst tolerable process average when a continuing series of lots is submitted for acceptance sampling.

acceptance sampling—Inspection of a sample from a lot to decide whether to accept or not accept that lot. There are two types: attributes sampling and variables sampling. In *attributes* sampling, the presence or absence of a characteristic is noted in each of the units inspected. In *variables* sampling, the numerical magnitude of a characteristic is measured and recorded for each inspected unit; this involves reference to a continuous scale of some kind.

acceptance sampling plan—Specific plan that indicates the sampling sizes and the associated acceptance or nonacceptance criteria to be used. In attributes sampling, for example, there are single, double, multiple, sequential, chain, and skip-lot sampling plans. In variables sampling, there are single, double, and sequential sampling plans. For detailed descriptions of these plans, see ANSI/ISO/ASQ A35342.

accreditation—Certification, by a duly recognized body, of the facilities, capability, objectivity, competence, and integrity of an agency, service, or operational group or individual to provide the specific service or operation needed. For example, the Registrar Accreditation Board (U.S.) accredits those organizations that register companies to the ISO 9000 series standards.

accuracy—A characteristic of measurement that addresses how close an observed value is to the true value. It answers the question, "Is it right?"

ACSI—The American Customer Satisfaction Index is an economic indicator, a cross-industry measure of the satisfaction of U.S. customers with the quality of the goods and services available to them—both those goods and services produced within the United States and those provided as imports from foreign firms that have substantial market shares or dollar sales.

action plan—The detailed plan to implement the actions needed to achieve strategic goals and objectives (similar to, but not as detailed as a *project plan*).

active listening—Listening closely to what others are saying (for example, rather than what you think of what they're saying or what you want to say back to them).

activity-based management—Managing with an accounting system (activity-based costing) that allocates costs to products based on resources employed to produce the product.

ad hoc team—See *temporary team.*

ADDIE—An instructional design model (*analysis, design, development, implementation,* and *evaluation*).

adult learning principles—Key principles of how adults learn that impact how education and training of adults should be designed.

affinity diagram—A management and planning tool used to organize ideas into natural groupings in a way that stimulates new, creative ideas. Also known as the *KJ method.*

agile approach—Means to change rapidly to meet changing customer and business direction. Also see *lean approach.*

AIAG—Automotive Industry Action Group.

alignment—Action taken to ensure that a process or activity allows traceability from an action level upward to support the organization's strategic goals and objectives.

alliance—An alliance can be the first step toward a partnership. See *partnership/ alliance.*

alpha risk—Type 1 error; rejecting a process or lot when it is acceptable. Also see *producer's risk.*

analogies—A technique used to generate new ideas by translating concepts from one application to another.

analysis of variance (ANOVA)—A basic statistical technique for analyzing experimental data. It subdivides the total variation of a data set into meaningful component parts associated with specific sources of variation in order to test a hypothesis on the parameters of the model or to estimate variance components. There are three models: fixed, random, and mixed.

analytical thinking—Breaking down a problem or situation into discrete parts to understand how each part contributes to the whole.

AND—activity network diagram. A management and planning tool used to diagram the sequential relationships of events or processes or deliverables. The critical path method (CPM) and the program evaluation review technique (PERT) are derived from the arrow diagram.

andon board—A visual device (usually lights) displaying status alerts that can easily be seen by those who should respond.

AOQ—Average outgoing quality.

AOQL—Average outgoing quality limit.

APICS—American Production and Inventory Control Society.

appraisal cost—Costs incurred to determine the degree of conformance to quality requirements.

AQL—See *acceptable quality limit*.

AS9100—An international quality management standard for the aeronautics industry embracing the ISO 9001 standard.

ASME—American Society of Mechanical Engineers.

ASQ—American Society for Quality, a society of individual and organizational members dedicated to the ongoing development, advancement, and promotion of quality concepts, principles, and technologies.

assessment—An estimate or determination of the significance, importance, or value of something.

assignable cause—See *common cause* or *special cause*.

ASTD—American Society for Training and Development.

ASTM—American Society for Testing and Materials.

attribute data—Does/does not exist data. The control charts based on attribute data include fraction defective chart, number of affected units chart, count chart, count-per-unit chart, quality score chart, and demerit chart.

audit—A planned, independent, and documented assessment to determine whether agreed-on requirements are being met. Common types of audits are of the quality management system, processes, products, and services. When an audit is to check on conformance to a standard, specifications, contract terms, or regulations, it may be called a *compliance audit*.

audit program—The organized structure, commitment, schedules, and documented methods used to plan and perform audits.

audit scope—The depth or extent and boundaries within which the audit will be conducted.

audit team—The group of trained individuals conducting an audit under the direction of a team leader, relevant to a particular system, product, process, service, contract, project, or standard.

audit types—"Internal" or "first party" (organization being audited by itself), "external" or "second party" (an organization conducting an audit of a supplier, customer, or other company), and "external" or "third party" (audit conducted by a registrar or another party).

auditee—The individual or organization being audited.

auditor—An individual or organization carrying out an audit.

autocratic management—Autocratic managers are concerned with developing an efficient workplace and often have little concern for people (theory X assumptions about people). They typically make decisions without input from subordinates. These managers rely on their positional power.

autonomation—Use of specially equipped automated machines capable of detecting a defect in a single part, stopping the process, and signaling for assistance. See *jidoka*.

availability—The ability of a process or equipment to be in a state to perform its designated function under stated conditions at a given time. Availability can be expressed by the ratio:

$$\frac{\text{Uptime}}{\text{Downtime}}$$

average—The sum of all the pertinent data divided by the number of observations collected. Also see *mean*.

average chart—A control chart in which the subgroup average, X-bar, is used to evaluate the stability of the process level.

average outgoing quality (AOQ)—The expected average quality level of outgoing product for a given value of incoming product quality.

average outgoing quality limit (AOQL)—The maximum average outgoing quality over all possible levels of incoming quality for a given acceptance sampling plan and disposal specification.

B

balance sheet—A financial statement showing the assets, liabilities, and owner's equity of a business entity.

balanced scorecard—Translates an organization's mission and strategy into a comprehensive set of performance measures to provide a basis for strategic measurement and management, typically using four balanced views: financial, customers, internal business processes, and learning and growth.

Baldrige Performance Excellence Program (BPEP)—The Baldrige National Quality Award was established by Congress in 1987 to raise awareness of quality management and to recognize U.S. companies that have implemented successful quality management systems. A *Criteria for Performance Excellence* is published each year. Three awards may be given annually in each of five categories: manufacturing businesses, service businesses, small businesses, education institutions, and healthcare organizations. The award is named after the late Secretary of Commerce Malcolm Baldrige, a proponent of quality management. The U.S. Commerce Department's National Institute of Standards and Technology manages the award, and ASQ administers it. The major emphasis in determining success is achieving results.

batch processing—Running large batches of a single product through the process at one time, resulting in queues awaiting next steps in the process.

BATF—Bureau of Alcohol, Tobacco, and Firearms.

bathtub curve—Also called *life-history curve* or *Weibull curve*. A graphic demonstration of the relationship of failures over the life of a product versus the probable failure rate. Includes three phases: early or infant failure (break-in), a stable rate during normal use, and wear-out.

behavior management—The management methodology and practices adapted from B. F. Skinner's theories: a practice used in managing people.

behavioral theories—Motivational theories, notably those of Abraham Maslow, Frederick Herzberg, Douglas McGregor, and others.

benchmarking—An improvement process in which a company measures its performance against that of best-in-class organizations (or others that are good performers), determines how those organizations achieved their performance levels, and uses the information to improve its own performance. Areas often benchmarked include strategies, operations, processes, and procedures.

benefit–cost analysis—Collection of the dollar value of benefits derived from an initiative and the associated costs incurred and computing the ratio of benefits to cost.

beta risk—Type 2 error; the possibility that a bad product will be accepted by a consumer. See *consumer's risk*.

bias—A characteristic of measurement that refers to a systematic difference.

Big Q, little q—A term used to contrast the difference between managing for quality in all processes and products (Big Q) and managing for quality in a limited capacity (little q).

binomial distribution—Defines the probability of successes from a given number of trials.

Black Belt—Full-time leader responsible for implementing Six Sigma process improvement projects using pertinent methodologies, such as DMAIC, DOE, and others. Usually, the Black Belt trains the Green Belts, and often serves for a two-year assignment overseeing eight to ten Six Sigma projects.

blemish—An imperfection that is severe enough to be noticed, but should not cause any real impairment with respect to intended normal or reasonably foreseeable use. (See also *defect, imperfection*, and *nonconformity*.)

block diagram—A diagram that shows the operation, interrelationships, and interdependencies of components in a system. Boxes, or blocks (hence the name), represent the components; connecting lines between the blocks represent interfaces. There are two types of block diagrams: a *functional* block diagram, which shows a system's subsystems and lower-level products, their interrelationships, and interfaces with other systems; and a *reliability* block diagram, which is similar to the functional block diagram except that it is modified to emphasize those aspects influencing reliability.

Bloom's Taxonomy (levels of cognition)—See Chapter 20, page 561.

body language—The expression of thoughts and emotions through movement or positioning of the body.

bottom line—An essential point or primary consideration. The line at the bottom of a financial statement that states the net profit or loss incurred.

boundaryless organization—An organization without the internal or external boundaries limiting traditional structures. (Also known as a *network organization*, a *modular corporation*, or a *virtual corporation*.)

BPR—Business process reengineering. See *process reengineering*.

brainstorming—A problem-solving tool that teams use to generate as many ideas as possible related to a particular subject. Team members begin by offering all their ideas; the ideas are not discussed or reviewed until after the brainstorming session.

breakthrough—A method of solving chronic problems that results from the effective execution of a strategy designed to reach the next level of quality. Such change often requires a paradigm shift within the organization.

brown fields—Abandoned, idle, or underused commercial or industrial facilities or site, often where use is complicated by real or potential environmental contamination.

BSI—British Standards Institute.

business partnering—The creation of cooperative business alliances between constituencies within an organization or between an organization and its customers or suppliers. Partnering occurs through a pooling of resources in a trusting atmosphere focused on continuous, mutual improvement. See also *customer–supplier partnership*.

business processes—Processes that focus on what the organization does as a business and how it goes about doing it; the functional processes (generating output within a single department) and cross-functional processes (generating output across several functions or departments).

C

calibration—The comparison of a measurement instrument or system of unverified accuracy to a measurement instrument or system of a known accuracy to detect any variation from the true value.

capability maturity model (CMM)—Description of key elements of an effective software process, covering planning practices, engineering, managing software development and maintenance.

capability ratio (C_p)— The specification tolerance width divided by the process capability.

capital expenditure—Money for improvements that will have a useful life of more than a year.

cascading training—Training implemented in an organization from the top down, where each level acts as trainers to those below.

case study—A prepared scenario (story) that, when studied and discussed, serves to illuminate the learning points of a course of study.

cash flow statement—A financial statement showing the flow of cash in and out of an enterprise within a given time period.

catchball—A term used to describe the interactive process of reaching consensus in developing and deploying policies and plans with hoshin planning.

cause-and-effect diagram—A tool for analyzing process variables. It is also referred to as the *Ishikawa diagram* because Kaoru Ishikawa developed it, and the *fishbone diagram* because the complete diagram resembles a fish skeleton. The diagram illustrates the main causes and sub-causes leading to an effect (symptom). The cause-and-effect diagram is one of the seven tools of quality.

CBT—Computer-based training. Training delivered via computer software.

c-chart—Count control chart. See also *attribute data*.

CDC—Centers for Disease Control and Prevention.

CE mark—A mark placed on a product signifying that the product complies with the essential/safety requirements of the relevant European regulations; from the French, Conformité Européenne.

cell—A layout of workstations and/or various machines for different operations (usually in a U shape) in which multitasking operators proceed with a part from machine to machine to perform a series of sequential steps to produce a whole product or major subassembly.

cellular team—The cross-trained individuals who work within a cell.

central tendency—The propensity of data collected on a process to concentrate around a value situated somewhere midway between the lowest and highest values.

centralization—Relates to the locus of the decision-making authority within an organization.

certification—The receipt of a document from an authorized source stating that a device, process, or operator has been certified to a known standard.

certification to a standard—A process in which an accredited, independent third-party organization conducts an on-site audit of a company's operations against the requirements of the standard to which the company wants certification. Upon successful completion of the audit, the company receives a certificate indicating that it has met the standard requirements. The third party (registrar) lists the organization receiving certification (registration). For example, an ISO 9001–based quality management system (QMS) is implemented, audited, passes, and is certified as compliant with the standard. The registrar lists the organization as having received a certificate. The organization is registered.

CFR—Code of Federal Regulations.

cGMP—current good manufacturing practices.

chain reaction—A series of interacting events described by W. Edwards Deming: improve quality > decrease costs > improve productivity > increase market share with better quality and lower price > stay in business, provide jobs, and provide more jobs.

chaku–chaku—(Japanese) Means *load–load* in a cell layout where a part is taken from one machine and loaded into the next.

champion—An individual who has accountability and responsibility for many processes or who is involved in making strategic-level decisions for the organization. The champion ensures ongoing dedication of project resources and monitors strategic alignment (also referred to as a *sponsor*).

chance cause—Same as *common cause*, a random and uncontrollable cause of variation.

change agent—The person who takes the lead in transforming an organization into a quality-focused organization by providing guidance during the planning phase, facilitating implementation, and supporting those who pioneer the changes.

change management—The strategies, processes, and practices involved in creating and managing change.

changeover—Changing a machine or process from one type of product or operation to another.

characteristic—A property that helps to identify or to differentiate between entities and that can be described or measured to determine conformance or nonconformance to requirements.

charter—A documented statement officially initiating the formation of a committee, team, project, or other effort in which a clearly stated purpose and approval is conferred.

check sheet—A simple data-recording device. The check sheet is custom designed for the particular use, allowing ease in interpreting the results. The check sheet is one of the seven tools of quality. Check sheets should not be confused with data sheets and checklists. Sometimes called *tally sheet*.

checklist—A tool for organizing and ensuring that all important steps or actions in an operation have been taken. Checklists contain items that are important or relevant to an issue or situation. Checklists should not be confused with check sheets and data sheets.

chi-square—A measurement of how well a set of data fits a proposed distribution, such as a normal distribution.

chronic problem—A long-standing adverse situation that can be remedied by changing the status quo. For example, actions such as revising an unrealistic manufacturing process or addressing customer defections can change the status quo and remedy the situation.

clean room—Workplace or process location within which the air is filtered to a specified level and/or additional environmental controls are present to prevent failures due to contamination or to ensure the personal safety of the workers.

cloud computing—A model for enabling convenient, on-demand network access to a shared pool of configurable computing resources, for example, networks, servers, storage, applications, and services, that can be rapidly provisioned and released with minimal management effort or service provider interaction. The cloud model promotes availability and is composed of five essential characteristics, three service models, and four deployment models. (National Institute of Standards and Technology, Information Technology Laboratory.)

CMI—Certified mechanical inspector (ASQ).

coaching—A continual improvement technique by which people receive one-to-one learning through demonstration and practice and that is characterized by immediate feedback and correction.

code of conduct—The expected behavior that has been mutually developed and agreed on by a team, and communicated to the workforce.

comment cards—Printed cards or slips of paper used to solicit and collect comments from users of a service or product.

common causes of variation—Causes that are inherent in any process all the time. A process that has only common causes of variation is said to be stable or predictable or in control. Also called *chance causes*.

companywide quality control (CWQC)—(Japanese origin) Similar to total quality management.

competence—Refers to a person's ability to learn and perform a particular activity. Competence consists of *knowledge, experience, skills, aptitude,* and *attitude* components (KESAA factors).

competency-based training—A training methodology that focuses on building mastery of a predetermined segment or module before moving on to the next.

competitive analysis—The gathering of intelligence relative to competitors in order to identify opportunities or potential threats to current and future strategy.

complaint handling—The process and practices involved in receiving and resolving complaints from customers.

complexity—In an organizational context, the number of different entities (job title, reporting levels, functional departments, and physical work locations) that comprise the organization.

complexity theory—The theory concerned with the interaction among the parts of a system, as well as the interaction between the system and its environment.

compliance—An affirmative indication or judgment that the supplier of a product or service has met the requirements of the relevant specifications, contract, or regulation; also the state of meeting the requirements.

computer-based training—Any instruction delivered via a computing device.

concurrent engineering—A process in which an organization designs a product or service using input and evaluations from business units and functions early in the process, anticipating problems, and balancing the needs of all parties. The emphasis is on upstream prevention versus downstream correction. Sometimes called *simultaneous engineering*.

conflict resolution—A process for resolving disagreements in a manner acceptable to all parties.

conformance—An affirmative indication or judgment that a product or service has met the requirements of a relevant specification, contract, or regulation.

consensus—Finding a proposal acceptable enough that all team members can support the decision, and no member opposes it.

constancy of purpose—Occurs when goals and objectives are properly aligned to the organizational vision and mission. (First of Deming's 14 steps.)

constraint—A constraint may range from the intangible (for example, beliefs, culture) to the tangible (for example, posted rule prohibiting smoking, buildup of work-in-process awaiting the availability of a machine or operator).

constraint management—Identifying a constraint and working to remove or diminish the constraint, while dealing with resistance to change.

construct—A formally proposed concept representing relationships between empirically verifiable events and based on observed facts.

consultative—A decision-making approach in which a person talks to others and considers their input before making a decision.

consumer's risk—For a sampling plan, refers to the probability of acceptance of a lot the quality of which has a designated numerical value representing a level that is seldom desirable. Usually, the designated value will be the lot tolerance percent defective (LTPD). Also called *beta risk* or *type 2 error*.

content analysis—A qualitative analytical technique for categorizing and analyzing the contents of documents.

continual process improvement (CPI)—The actions taken throughout an organization to increase the effectiveness and efficiency of activities and processes in order to provide added benefits to the customer and organization. It is considered a subset of total quality management and operates according to the premise that organizations can always make improvements. Continual improvement can also be equated with reducing process variation.

continuous probability distribution—A graph or formula representing the probability of a particular numeric value of continuous (variable) data, based on a particular type of process that produces the data.

continous quality improvement (CQI)—A philosophy and actions for repeatedly improving an organization's cabilities and processes with the objective of customer satisfaction.

contract review—Systematic activities carried out by an organization before agreeing to a contract to ensure that requirements for quality are adequately defined, free from ambiguity, documented, and can be realized by the supplier.

control chart—A basic tool that consists of a chart with upper and lower control limits on which values of some statistical measure for a series of samples or subgroups are plotted. It frequently shows a central line to help detect a trend of plotted values toward either control limit. It is used to monitor and analyze variation in a process to see whether the process is in statistical control.

control limits—(1) Calculated boundaries of a process within specified confidence levels, expressed as upper control limit (UCL) and lower control limit (LCL). (2) The limits on a control chart used as criteria for signaling the need for action or for judging whether a set of data does or does not indicate a "state of statistical control."

control plan—A document, or documents, that may include the characteristics for quality of a product or service, measurements, and methods of control.

core competency—Pertains to the unique features and characteristics of an organization's overall capability.

corporate culture—See *organization culture*.

correction—When a problem occurs (1) find out how bad it is, (2) decide what to do to keep it from having a larger impact, and (3) determine what to do with what has already been impacted. Doing 1 and 2 is containment action, and 3 is remedial action. This is correcting the problem, but not the causes.

corrective action—Once a problem has been corrected, decide whether or not it was of enough significant importance (based on frequency, impact, risk, and so on) to warrant investigating the causes, and take action to eliminate the root cause(s) and symptom(s) of an existing deviation or nonconformity to prevent recurrence.

correlation—Refers to the measure of the strength of the relationship between two sets of numbers or variables. (A *scatter chart* may be used in the analysis.)

correlation coefficient—Describes the magnitude and direction of the relationship between two variables.

cost–benefit analysis—Compares the potential or actual benefits with the estimated or real cost associated with a problem solution or process improvement, as a ratio or in dollars.

cost of poor quality—The costs associated with providing poor-quality products or services.

cost of quality (COQ)—The total costs incurred relating to the quality of a product or service. There are four categories of quality costs: *internal failure costs*

(costs associated with defects found before delivery of the product or service), *external failure costs* (costs associated with defects found during or after product or service delivery), *appraisal costs* (costs incurred to determine the degree of conformance to quality requirements), and *prevention costs* (costs incurred to keep failure and appraisal costs to a minimum).

count chart—A control chart for evaluating the stability of a process in terms of the count of events of a given classification occurring in a sample.

count-per-unit chart—A control chart for evaluating the stability of a process in terms of the average count of events of a given classification per unit occurring in a sample.

C_p—A widely used process capability index. It is expressed as

$$\frac{\text{Upper spec limit} - \text{Lower spec limit}}{6\sigma}$$

C_{pk}—A widely used process capability index. It is expressed as

$$\frac{(\text{Ratio with smallest answer}) \text{ Upper specification limit} - X\text{-bar}}{3\sigma}$$

or

$$\frac{X\text{-bar} - \text{Lower specification limit}}{3\sigma}$$

Crawford slip method—A method of anonymously gathering and presenting data from a group.

creativity, stages of—One model gives the following stages: generate, percolate, illuminate, and verify. May also be defined as visualization, exploration, combination, and modification.

criteria—Stated objectives, guidelines, principles, procedures, and/or standards used for measuring a project, process, product, or performance.

criterion—A standard, rule, or test on which a judgment or decision can be based.

critical incident—An event that has greater than normal significance, often used as a learning or feedback opportunity.

critical path—Refers to the sequence of tasks that takes the longest time and determines a project's completion date.

critical path method (CPM)—An activity-oriented project management tool that uses arrow-diagramming techniques to demonstrate both the time and cost required to complete a project. It provides one time estimate—normal time—and allows for computing the critical path.

critical success factors (CSF)—Factors identified by the organization as critical to the organization's success in achieving its strategic goals and objectives.

critical thinking—The careful analysis, evaluation, reasoning (both deductive and inductive), clear thinking, and systems thinking leading to effective decisions.

critical-to-quality (CTQ)—Characteristics that, from a customer's perception of quality, are critical to the achievement of quality goals, objectives, standards, and/or specifications.

cross-functional team—A group consisting of members from more than one department, work unit, or technical discipline that is organized to accomplish a project.

CSR—Customer service representative.

culture—See *organization culture.*

culture change—Major proposed or actual change in organizational operating principles, behavior, and attitude.

cumulative sum control chart (CUSUM)—A control chart on which the plotted value is the cumulative sum of deviations of successive samples from a target value. The ordinate of each plotted point represents the algebraic sum of the previous ordinate and the most recent deviations from the target.

current reality tree—A technique used in applying Goldratt's theory of constraints to identify undesirable effects (similar to root cause analysis).

customer—Recipient of a product or service provided by a supplier. See also *external customer* and *internal customer.*

customer council—A group usually composed of representatives from an organization's largest customers who meet to discuss common issues.

customer delight—The result achieved when customer requirements are exceeded in unexpected ways the customer finds valuable.

customer loyalty/retention—The result of an organization's plans, processes, practices, and efforts designed to deliver their services or products in ways that create retained and committed customers.

customer oriented organization—An organization whose mission, purpose, and actions are dedicated to serving and satisfying its customers.

customer relationship management (CRM)—Refers to an organization's knowledge of its customers' unique requirements and expectations, and using that knowledge to develop a closer and more profitable link to business processes and strategies.

customer satisfaction—The result of delivering a product or service that meets customer requirements, needs, and expectations.

customer segmentation—Refers to the process of differentiating customers based on one or more characteristics for the purpose of developing a marketing strategy to address specific segments. The intent is to better address customers' needs, and improve customer satisfaction and organizational effectiveness.

customer service—Activities dealing with customer questions; also may be the designation of the department that takes customer orders or provides post-delivery services.

customer–supplier partnership—A long-term relationship between a buyer and supplier characterized by teamwork and mutual confidence. The supplier is considered an extension of the buyer's organization. The partnership is based on several commitments. The buyer provides long-term contracts and uses fewer suppliers. The supplier implements quality assurance processes so that incoming inspection can be minimized. The supplier also helps the buyer reduce costs and improve product and process designs.

customer value—There are five factors of influence on customer value: price, product/service quality, innovation, and organization image relative to competition. When customers are satisfied with their perception of the balance of the product/service meeting their need or want, the quality is satisfactory, and the price is right for them—customer value has been achieved.

cycle time—Refers to the elapsed time that it takes to complete a process from the start of the process to completion.

cycle time reduction—To reduce the time that it takes, from start to finish, to complete a particular process.

D

data—Quantitative or qualitative facts presented in descriptive, numeric, or graphic form. Two types of numerical data are *measured*, or *variable* data, and *counted*, or *attribute* data.

data mining—The process of searching a large computer database (for example, a customer database) for previously undetected patterns and relationships, with the intent to transform the data into information for making decisions about strategy.

decision matrix—A matrix used by teams to evaluate problems or possible solutions. For example, after a matrix is drawn to evaluate possible solutions, the team lists them in the far left vertical column. Next, the team selects criteria to rate the possible solutions, writing them across the top row. Then, each possible solution is rated on a scale of 1 to 5 for each criterion and the rating recorded in the corresponding grid. Finally, the ratings of all the criteria for each possible solution are added to determine its total score. The total score is then used to help decide which solution deserves the most attention.

defect—A product's or service's nonfulfillment of an intended requirement or reasonable expectation for use, including safety considerations. They are often classified, such as:

- Class 1, *critical*, leads directly to severe injury or catastrophic economic loss.

- Class 2, *serious*, leads directly to significant injury or significant economic loss.

- Class 3, *major*, is related to major problems with respect to intended normal or reasonably foreseeable use.

- Class 4, *minor*, is related to minor problems with respect to intended normal or reasonably foreseeable use. See also *blemish*, *imperfection*, and *nonconformity*.

defective—A product that contains one or more defects relative to the quality characteristics being measured.

delighter—Feature of a delivered product or service that unexpectedly pleases a customer.

demerit chart—A control chart for evaluating a process in terms of a demerit (or quality score), such as a weighted sum of counts of various classified nonconformities.

Deming cycle—See *plan–do–check–act cycle*.

Deming Prize—Award given annually to organizations that, according to the award guidelines, have successfully applied companywide quality control based on statistical quality control and will keep up with it in the future. Although the award is named in honor of W. Edwards Deming, its criteria are not specifically related to Deming's teachings. There are three separate divisions for the award: the Deming Application Prize, the Deming Prize for Individuals, and the Deming Prize for Overseas Companies. The award process is overseen by the Deming Prize Committee of the Union of Japanese Scientists and Engineers in Tokyo.

demographics—Variables among buyers in the consumer market, which include geographic location, age, sex, marital status, family size, social class, education, nationality, occupation, and income.

dependability—The degree to which a product is operable and capable of performing its required function at any randomly chosen time during its specified operating life, provided that the product is available at the start of that period. (Nonoperation-related influences are not included.) Dependability can be expressed by the ratio

$$\frac{\text{Time available}}{\text{Time available} + \text{Time required}}$$

deployment—Used in strategic planning to describe the process of cascading *goals*, *objectives*, and *action plans* throughout an organization.

design failure mode and effects analysis (DFMEA)—See *FMEA*.

design for manufacturing (DFM)—The design of a product for ease in manufacturing. Also called *design for assembly* (DFA).

Design for Six Sigma (DFSS)—The aim is for a robust design that is consistent with applicable manufacturing processes and assures a fully capable process that will produce quality products.

design of experiments (DOE)—A branch of applied statistics dealing with planning, conducting, analyzing, and interpreting controlled tests to evaluate the factors that control the value of a parameter or group of parameters.

design review—Documented, comprehensive, and systematic examination of a design to evaluate its capability to fulfill the requirements for quality.

designing-in quality versus inspecting-in quality—See *prevention versus detection.*

desired quality—Refers to the additional features and benefits a customer discovers when using a product or service that lead to increased customer satisfaction. If missing, a customer may become dissatisfied.

deviation—A nonconformance or departure of a characteristic from specified product, process, or system requirements.

diagnostic journey and remedial journey—A two-phase investigation used by teams to solve chronic quality problems. In the first phase, the diagnostic journey, the team moves from the symptom of a problem to its cause. In the second phase, the remedial journey, the team moves from the cause to a remedy.

dimensions of quality—Different ways in which quality may be viewed, for example, meaning of quality, characteristics of quality, or drivers of quality.

DiSC—A profiling instrument that measures characteristic ways in which a person behaves in a particular environment. Four dimensions measured are dominance, influence, steadiness, and conscientiousness.

discrete probability distribution—The measured process variable takes on a finite or limited number of values; no other possible values exist. A discrete variable could be the number of people in a room.

disposition of nonconformity—Action taken to deal with an existing nonconformity; action may include correct (repair), rework, regrade, scrap, obtain a concession, or amend a requirement.

dissatisfiers—Those features or functions that the customer or employee has come to expect, which, if they are no longer present, would result in dissatisfaction.

distance learning—Learning where student(s) and instructor(s) are not colocated; interaction through electronic means.

distribution—Describes the amount of potential variation in outputs of a process; it is usually described in terms of its shape, average, and standard deviation.

DMAIC—A methodology used in a Six Sigma initiative: *define, measure, analyze, improve, control.*

Dodge–Romig sampling plans—Plans for acceptance sampling developed by Harold F. Dodge and Harry G. Romig. Four sets of tables were published in 1940: single-sampling lot tolerance tables, double-sampling lot tolerance tables, single-sampling average outgoing quality limit tables, and double-sampling average outgoing quality limit tables.

downsizing—The planned reduction in workforce due to economics, competition, merger, sale, restructuring, or reengineering.

drivers of quality—Crucial factors that when controlled, the product or service will be controlled. These factors might include processes, customers, products, services, employee satisfaction, total organizational focus on providing quality products/services, and so on.

E

earned value analysis (EVA)—A methodology used to measure project performance by comparing planned work with actual work accomplished to determine if performance is adhering to plan.

education—Refers to the individual learner's process to acquire new or refreshed knowledge. See also *training*.

efficiency—Ratio of output to the total input in a process, with an objective to use less resources, such as time, cost.

eighty–twenty (80–20) rule—A term referring to the Pareto principle, which suggests that most effects come from relatively few causes; that is, 80 percent of the effects come from 20 percent of the possible causes.

employee involvement—A practice within an organization whereby employees regularly participate in making decisions on how their work areas operate, including making suggestions for improvement, planning, objectives setting, and performance monitoring.

empowerment—A condition whereby employees are given the authority to make decisions and take action in their work areas, within stated bounds, without prior approval. For example, an operator can stop a production process upon detecting a problem, or a customer service representative can send out a replacement product if a customer calls with a problem.

end users—External customers who purchase products/services for their own use—*consumers*.

engineering change order (ECO)—An order to make a change in a process, product, or service after the initial release of the product or service design. See *concurrent engineering* for a process for reducing ECOs.

entropy—Tendency of a system or process to run down and collapse.

environmental analysis/scanning—Identifying and monitoring factors from both inside and outside the organization that may impact the long-term viability of the organization.

environmental management system (EMS)—A management system for addressing the environmental policies, objectives, principles, procedures, authority, responsibility, accountability, and implementation of an organization's practices for managing its impact on the environment in which it operates.

EPA—Environmental Protection Agency.

equity theory—A theory that states that job motivation depends on how equitable the individual believes the rewards or punishment to be.

error-proofing—See *poka-yoke.*

ethics—An individual or an organization's adherence to a belief or documented code of conduct that is based on moral principles and tries to balance what is fair for individuals and the organization with what is right for society.

EU—European Union.

event—The starting or ending point for a task or group of tasks. An occurrence of some attribute.

executive education—Usually refers to the education (and training) provided to top management.

expectancy theory—A motivational theory inferring that what people do is based on what they expect to gain from the activity.

expected quality—Also known as *basic quality,* the minimum benefit or value a customer expects to receive from a product or service.

experimental design—A formal plan that details the specifics for conducting an experiment, such as which responses, factors, levels, blocks, treatments, and tools are to be used.

explicit knowledge—Represented by the captured and recorded tools of the day, for example, procedures, processes, standards, and other like documents. See also *tacit knowledge.*

exponential distribution—A continuous distribution where data are more likely to occur below the average than above it. Typically used to describe the break-in portion of the bathtub curve.

external audit—Audit performed by anyone or any organization outside the organization being audited. See *second-party audit* or *third-party audit.*

external customer—A person or organization who receives a product, a service, or information, but is not part of the organization supplying it. See also *internal customer.*

external failure costs—Costs associated with defects found during or after delivery of the product or service.

F

facilitator—A trained individual who is responsible for creating favorable conditions that will enable a team to reach its purpose or achieve its goals by bringing together the necessary tools, information, and resources to get the job done. A facilitator addresses the processes a team uses to achieve its purpose.

factor analysis—A statistical technique that examines the relationships between a single dependent variable and multiple independent variables. For example, it is used to determine which questions on a questionnaire are related to a specific question such as "Would you buy this product again?"

failure mode analysis (FMA)—A procedure for determining which malfunction symptoms appear immediately before or after a failure of a critical parameter in a system. After all the possible causes are listed for each symptom, the product is designed to eliminate the problems.

failure mode and effects analysis (FMEA)—A procedure in which each potential failure mode of every sub-item of an item is analyzed to determine its effect on other sub-items and on the required function of the item. Typically, two types of FMEAs are used: DFMEA (design) and PFMEA (process).

failure mode effects and criticality analysis (FMECA)—A procedure that is performed after a failure mode and effects analysis to classify each potential failure effect according to its severity and probability of occurrence.

false customer—An individual or group within a process that performs activities that do not add value to the product or service.

fault tree analysis (FTA)—Technique for evaluating the possible causes that might lead to the failure of a product or service.

FDA— Food and Drug Administration.

feasibility study—Examination of technical and cost data to determine the economic potential and practicality of a project or application of equipment. NPV may be used in this analysis.

feedback—The interpersonal communication response to information received (written or oral); it may be based on fact or feeling and helps the party who is receiving the information judge how well he/she is being understood by the other party. More generally, feedback is information about a process or performance and is used to make decisions that are directed toward improving or adjusting the process or performance as necessary.

feedback loops—Pertains to open-loop and closed-loop feedback. Open-loop feedback focuses on how to detect or measure problems in the inputs and how to plan for contingencies. Closed-loop feedback focuses on how to measure the outputs and how to determine the control points where adjustment can be made.

filters—Relative to human-to-human communication, those perceptions (based on culture, language, demographics, experience, and so on) that affect how a message is transmitted by the sender and how a message is interpreted by the receiver.

finding—A conclusion of importance based on observation(s) and/or research, for example, an audit finding.

first-party audit—Audit of a process or product/service by auditing personnel employed by the organization in which the audit is performed. Also called *internal audit.*

fishbone diagram—See *cause-and-effect diagram.*

fitness for use—A term used to indicate that a product or service fits the customer's defined purpose for that product or service.

five S (5S)—(Japanese) Five practices for maintaining a clean and efficient workplace. Briefly the term embraces: *seiri* (sort/separate), *seiton* (arrange and identify), *seiso* (clean up), *seiketsu* (standardize), *shitsuke* (develop habit of always following first four S's).

five whys—A repetitive questioning technique to probe deeper to surface the root cause of a problem by asking *why* five times (more or fewer, as needed).

flowchart—A graphical representation of the steps in a process. Flowcharts are drawn to better understand processes. The flowchart is one of the seven basic tools of quality.

focus group—A discussion group consisting of eight to 10 participants, usually invited from a segment of the customer base to discuss an existing or planned product or service, led by a facilitator working from predetermined questions (focus groups may also be used to gather information in a context other than customers). Information from a focus group is often used as a basis for forming survey questions.

force field analysis—A technique for analyzing the forces that aid or hinder an organization in reaching an objective.

formal communication—The officially sanctioned information within an organization, which includes publications, memoranda, training materials/events, public relations information, and company meetings.

fourteen (14) points—W. Edwards Deming's 14 management practices to help organizations increase their quality and productivity. They are:

1. Create constancy of purpose for improving products and services.

2. Adopt a new philosophy.

3. Cease dependence on inspection to achieve quality.

4. End the practice of awarding business on price alone; instead, minimize total cost by working with a single supplier.

5. Improve constantly and forever every process for planning, production, and service.

6. Institute training on the job.

7. Adopt and institute leadership.

8. Drive out fear.

9. Break down barriers between staff areas.

10. Eliminate slogans, exhortations, and targets for the workforce.

11. Eliminate numerical quotas for the workforce and numerical goals for management.

12. Remove barriers that rob people of pride of workmanship, and eliminate the annual rating or merit system.

13. Institute a vigorous program of education and self-improvement for everyone.

14. Put everybody in the company to work to accomplish the transformation.

fraction defective chart (*p*-chart)—An attribute control chart used to track the proportion of defective units.

frequency distribution—Set of all the various values from individual observations, and the frequency of their occurrence in the sample population. Statistically, a display of a large volume of data so that the central tendency (average or mean) and distribution are clear.

functional organization—An organization organized by discrete functions, for example, marketing/sales, engineering, production, finance, and human resources.

funnel experiment—An experiment that demonstrates the effects of tampering. Marbles are dropped through a funnel in an attempt to hit a flat-surfaced target below. The experiment shows that adjusting a stable process to compensate for an undesirable result, or an extraordinarily good result, will produce output that is worse than if the process had been left alone.

future reality tree—A technique used in the application of Goldratt's theory of constraints to show what to change and how to identify any new unfavorable aspects to be addressed prior to the change.

G

gage blocks—Standards of precise dimensions, used in combination to form usable length combinations. The blocks are traceable to national standards in the country of use (NIST in the United States).

gage repeatability and reproducibility (GR&R)—The evaluation of a gauging instrument's accuracy by determining whether the measurements taken with the gage are repeatable (that is, there is close agreement among a number of consecutive measurements of the output for the same value of the input under the same operating conditions) and reproducible (that is, there is close agreement among repeated measurements of the output for the same value of input made under the same operating conditions over a period of time). *Repeatability* is the variation in results on a single gage when the same part is measured repeatedly by the same person. *Reproducibility* is the variation from person to person using the same gage.

gainsharing—A type of program that rewards individuals financially on the basis of organizational performance.

Gantt chart—A type of bar chart used in process/project planning and control to display planned work and finished work in relation to time. Also called a *milestone chart* when interim checkpoints are added. May be used in the planning stage as well as in tracking progress.

gap analysis—A range of techniques that compares a company's existing state to its desired state (as expressed by its long-term plans) to help determine what needs to be done to remove or minimize the gap between them.

gatekeeper—The role of an individual (often a facilitator) in a group meeting in helping ensure effective interpersonal interactions (for example, someone's ideas are not ignored due to the team moving on to the next topic too quickly).

geographic information system (GIS)—A computer-based method of collecting and displaying data in relation to a specific point or location on earth to which each datum is related—the computer program maps the data.

geographic organization—An organization structured by geography, territory, region, or the like.

geometric dimensioning and tolerancing (GDT)—A method used to minimize production costs by considering the functions or relationships of part features in order to define dimensions and tolerances.

goal—A statement of general intent, aim, or desire; it is the point toward which management directs its mission, efforts, and resources; goals are usually nonquantitative. A goal is measured by the objectives supporting the goal.

goal–question–metric (GQM)—A method used to define measurement of a project, process, or product on three levels (conceptual, operational, quantitative).

go/no-go—State of a unit or product. Two parameters are possible: *go* conforms to specifications, and *no-go* does not conform to specifications.

grade—A planned or recognized difference in requirements for quality.

grapevine—The informal communication channels over which information flows within an organization, usually without a known origin, and without any confirmation of its accuracy or completeness (sometimes referred to as the *rumor mill*).

Green Belt—An individual trained on the improvement methodology of Six Sigma who will lead a process or quality improvement team.

group dynamics—The interaction (behavior) of individuals within a team.

groupthink—Most or all team members coalesce in supporting an idea or decision that hasn't been fully explored, or some members secretly disagree but go along with the other members in apparent support.

H

Hawthorne effect—Concept that every change in workplace environment results (initially, at least) in increased productivity. This demonstrates the importance of human factors in motivating the workforce. (Based on studies by Elton Mayo at the Hawthorne Plant of Western Electric Company in Chicago in 1924.)

heijunka—Act of leveling the variety or volume of items produced in a process over time. Used to avoid excessive batching of product types, volume fluctuations, and excess inventory.

hierarchy structure—Describes an organization that is organized around functional departments/product lines or around customers/customer segments and is characterized by top-down management (also referred to as a *bureaucratic model* or *pyramid structure*).

histogram—A graphic summary of variation in a set of data. The pictorial nature of the histogram lets people see patterns that are difficult to see in a simple table of numbers. The histogram is one of the seven tools of quality.

hold point—A point, defined in an appropriate document, beyond which an activity must not proceed without the approval of a designated organization or authority.

horizontal structure—Describes an organization that is organized along a process flow or value-added chain, eliminating hierarchy and functional boundaries (also referred to as a *systems structure*).

hoshin kanri, hoshin planning—Japanese-based strategic planning/policy deployment process that involves consensus at all levels as plans are cascaded throughout the organization, resulting in improved actionable plans and continual monitoring and measurement.

house of quality—A diagram (named for its house-shaped appearance) that clarifies the relationships between customer needs and product features. It helps correlate market or customer requirements and analysis of competitive products with higher-level technical and product characteristics, and makes it possible to bring several factors into a single figure. Also known as *quality function deployment* (QFD).

human relations theory—A theory focusing on the importance of human factors in motivating employees.

hygiene factors—A term used by Frederick Herzberg to label dissatisfiers. See *dissatisfiers*.

I

IEEE—Institute of Electrical and Electronics Engineers.

imagineering—Creative process used to develop, in the mind's eye, a process without waste.

imperfection—A quality characteristic's departure from its intended level or state without any association to conformance to specification requirements or to the usability of a product or service. See also *blemish*, *defect*, and *nonconformity*.

implied warranty—Implicit promise, not necessarily documented, that states that a product must reasonably operate or comply with the ordinary purposes for which it is intended or used.

in-control process—A process in which the statistical measure being evaluated is in a state of statistical control; that is, the variations among the observed sampling results can be attributed to a constant system of chance/common causes. The process may also be described as *stable*. See also *out-of-control process*.

incremental improvement—Improvements implemented on a continual basis. See *kaizen*.

indicators—Predetermined measures used to determine how well an organization is meeting its customers' needs and its operational and financial performance objectives. Such indicators can be either *leading* or *lagging* indicators. *Indicators* may also refer to devices used to measure lengths or flow.

indirect customers—Customers who do not receive process output directly, but are affected if the process output is incorrect or late.

individual development—A process that may include education and training, but also includes many additional interventions and experiences to enable an individual to grow and mature intellectually and emotionally, as well as professionally.

informal communication—The unofficial communication that takes place in an organization as people talk freely and easily; examples include impromptu meetings and personal conversations (verbal or e-mail).

information—Data transformed into an ordered format that makes it usable and allows one to draw conclusions.

information system—Technology-based systems used to support operations, aid day-to-day decision making, and support strategic analysis. Other names often seen include *management information system, decision system, information technology* (IT), *data processing*.

input—Material, product, or service that is obtained from an upstream internal provider or an external supplier and is used by the receiver to produce an output.

inspection—Measuring, examining, testing, and gauging one or more characteristics of a product or service and comparing the results with specified requirements to determine whether conformity is achieved for each characteristic.

intellectual property—The concepts, ideas, thought, processes, and programs that are definable, measurable, and proprietary in nature (includes copyrights, patents, trademarks, computer software).

interactive multimedia—A term encompassing technology that allows the presentation of facts and images with physical interaction by the viewers; for example, taking a simulated certification exam on a computer, or receiving training embedded in transaction processing software.

interdependence—Shared dependence between two or more items.

interfaces—Interaction between individuals, departments, work units, outside organizations, and so on, that allows the meaningful exchange of information.

intermediate customers—Distributors, dealers, or brokers who make products and services available to the end user by repairing, repackaging, reselling, or creating finished goods from components or subassemblies.

internal audit—An audit conducted within an organization by members of the organization to measure its strengths or weaknesses against its own procedures and/or external standards—a first-party audit.

internal capability analysis—A detailed view of the internal workings of the organization; for example, determining how well the capabilities of the organization match to strategic needs.

internal customer—The recipient (person or department) of another person's or department's output (product, service, or information) within an organization. See also *external customer.*

internal failure costs—Costs associated with defects found before the product or service is delivered.

internal rate of return (IRR)—An organization's acceptable rate of return from investments. Also, the discount rate that causes net present value to equal zero.

International Organization for Standardization (ISO)—Based in Geneva, Switzerland, it is the worldwide controller of ISO standards.

interrelationship digraph—A management and planning tool that displays the relationship between factors in a complex situation. It identifies meaningful categories from a mass of ideas and is useful when relationships are difficult to determine.

intervention—An action taken by a leader or a facilitator to support the effective functioning of a team or work group.

inventory—A term encompassing all forms of physical accumulation of materials, supplies, work in process, and finished goods held in temporary storage or warehoused. The term is also used by Goldratt to mean "all the money the system invests in things it intends to sell" (see *theory of constraints*).

Ishikawa diagram—See *cause-and-effect diagram.*

is/is not matrix—A tool that helps to differentiate what is distinctive about a problem.

ISO—A prefix for a series of standards published by the International Organization for Standardization. *Iso* also means *equal* in Greek.

ISO 9000 series standards—A set of individual but related international standards and guidelines on quality management and quality assurance developed to help companies effectively document the quality system elements to be implemented to maintain an efficient quality system. The standards, initially published in 1987, and revised in 1994, 2000, and 2008–2009, are not specific to any particular industry, product, or service. The standards were developed by the International Organization for Standardization, a specialized international agency for standardization composed of the national standards bodies of countries worldwide.

ISO 14000 series—A set of standards and guidelines relevant to developing and sustaining an environmental management system.

J

jidoka—Japanese method of autonomous control involving the adding of intelligent features to machines to start or stop operations as control parameters are reached, and to signal operators when necessary.

job aid—Any device, document, or other media that can be provided to a worker to aid in correctly performing tasks (for example, a laminated setup instruction card hanging on a machine, photos of product at different stages of assembly, or a metric conversion table).

job description—A narrative explanation of the work, responsibilities, and basic requirements of a job.

job enlargement—Expanding the variety of tasks performed by an employee.

job enrichment—Increasing the worker's responsibilities and authority in work to be done.

job specification—A list of the important functional and quality attributes (knowledge, skills, aptitudes, and personal characteristics) needed to succeed in the job.

joint planning meeting—A meeting involving representatives of a key customer and the sales and service team for that account to determine how better to meet the customer's requirements and expectations.

Juran's trilogy—See *quality trilogy.*

JUSE—Union of Japanese Scientists and Engineers.

just-in-time (JIT) manufacturing—An optimal material requirement planning system for a manufacturing process in which there is little or no manufacturing material inventory on hand at the manufacturing site and little or no incoming inspection.

just-in-time training—Providing job training coincidental with, or immediately prior to, an employee's assignment to a new or expanded task.

K

kaikaku—A Japanese term that means a breakthrough improvement in eliminating waste.

kaizen—A Japanese term that means incremental and unending improvement by doing little things better and setting and achieving increasingly higher standards. The term was made famous by Masaaki Imai in his book *Kaizen: The Key to Japan's Competitive Success.*

kaizen blitz/event—An intense, short time frame (typically three to five consecutive days), team approach to employ the concepts and techniques of continual improvement (for example, to reduce cycle time or increase throughput).

kanban—A system inspired by Taiichi Ohno's (Toyota) visit to a U.S. supermarket. The system signals the need to replenish stock or materials or to produce more of an item (also called a *pull* approach).

Kano model—A representation of the three levels of customer satisfaction defined as dissatisfaction, neutrality, and delight. Named after Noriaki Kano.

kansei engineering—A Japanese term referring to the translation of consumers' psychological feelings about a product into perceptual design elements (sensory engineering, emotional usability).

KESAA factors—See *competence.*

KJ method—See *affinity diagram.*

knowledge management—Involves transforming data into information and the acquisition or creation of knowledge, as well as the processes and technology employed in identifying, categorizing, storing, retrieving, disseminating, and using information and knowledge for the purposes of improving decisions and plans.

KRA (key result area)—Critical customer requirements that are important for the organization's success. Also known as *key success factor* (KSF).

L

lateral thinking—A process that includes recognizing patterns, becoming unencumbered with old ideas, and creating new ones.

LCALI—A process for operating a listening post system for capturing and using formerly unavailable customer data. LCALI stands for *listen, capture, analyze, learn,* and *improve.*

leader—An individual recognized by others as the person to lead an effort. Normally one can not be a leader without one or more followers. The term is often used interchangeably with *manager.* A leader may or may not hold an officially designated management-type position. See *manager.*

leadership—An essential factor in a quality improvement effort. Organization leaders must establish a vision, communicate that vision to those in the organization, and provide the tools, knowledge, and motivation necessary to accomplish the vision.

lean approach/lean thinking—A focus on reducing cycle time and waste using a number of different techniques and tools, for example, value stream mapping, and identifying and eliminating monuments and non-value-added steps.

lean manufacturing—Applying the lean approach to improving manufacturing operations.

learner-controlled instruction (LCI)—When a learner works without an instructor, at an individual pace, building mastery of a task. Computer-based training is a form of LCI. Also called *self-directed learning.*

learning curve—The time it takes to achieve mastery of a task, a body of knowledge, or a skill.

learning organization—An organization that has a policy to continue to learn and improve its products, services, processes, and outcomes—"an organization that is continually expanding its capacity to create its future" (Senge).

lesson plan—A detailed plan created to guide an instructor in delivering training and/or education.

life cycle—A product life cycle is the total time frame from product concept to the end of its intended use; a project life cycle is typically divided into six stages: concept, planning, design, implementation, evaluation, and closeout.

life history curve—See *bathtub curve.*

linear regression—The mathematical application of the concept of a scatter diagram where the correlation is actually a cause-and-effect relationship.

linear responsibility matrix—A matrix providing a three-dimensional view of project tasks, responsible person, and level of relationship.

line balancing—A method of proportionately distributing workloads within the value stream to meet *takt* time.

listening post data—Customer data and information gathered from designated organizational listening posts.

little q, Big Q—The difference between managing for quality in a limited capacity (q) to managing for quality across all business processes and products (Q). Attributed to J. M. Juran.

long-term goals—Goals that an organization hopes to achieve in the future, usually in three to five years. They are commonly referred to as *strategic goals.*

lost customer analysis—Analysis to determine why a customer or segment of customers was lost or defected to a competitor.

lot—A defined quantity of product accumulated under conditions that are considered uniform for sampling purposes.

lot tolerance percent defective (LTPD)—See *consumer's risk.*

lower control limit (LCL)—Control limit for points below the central line in a control chart.

M

macro processes—Broad, far-ranging processes that often cross functional boundaries.

maintainability—The probability that a given maintenance action for an item under given usage conditions can be performed within a stated time interval when the maintenance is performed under stated conditions using stated procedures and resources. Maintainability has two categories: *serviceability,* the ease of conducting scheduled inspections and servicing, and *repairability,* the ease of restoring service after a failure.

Malcolm Baldrige National Quality Award (MBNQA)—Earned by the organization qualifying under the criteria of the Baldrige Performance Excellence Program of NIST.

management by fact—A business philosophy that decisions should be based on data.

management by policy—The organizational infrastructure that ensures that the right things are done at the right time.

management by walking around (MBWA)—A manager's planned, but usually unannounced, walk-through of the organization to gather information from employees and make observations; may be viewed in a positive light by virtue of giving employees opportunity to interact with top management; has the potential of being viewed negatively if punitive action is taken as a result of information gathered.

management levels—A typical hierarchy of management levels is top management (executive level, upper management, top team), middle management (directors, general managers, plant managers, department managers), and first-level supervision (persons directly supervising workers).

management representative—A person appointed to act on management's behalf to manage the quality/environment system. Also, this person usually handles the interface with a registration body.

management responsibility categories—Planning, organizing, staffing, directing, and controlling (POSDC).

management review—Scheduled formal review and evaluation by management of the status and adequacy of the quality/environmental management system(s) in relation to the organization's strategic objectives and policies.

management styles—The predominant personal styles used by managers; styles may be based on prevalent management theories and assumptions about people. Style categories include authoritarian, autocratic, combative, conciliatory, consensual, consultative, democratic, disruptive, ethical, facilitating, intimidating, judicial, laissez-faire, participative, promotional, secretive, shared, or shareholder management.

management training—Usually refers to training and/or education provided to any management or professional-level person from frontline supervision up to, but usually not including, executives.

manager—An individual who manages and is responsible for resources (people, facilities, equipment, material, money, time). A person officially designated with a management-type position title. A manager is granted authority from above, whereas a leader's role is derived by virtue of having followers. The terms *manager* and *leader* are often and unfortunately used interchangeably.

market-perceived quality—The customer's opinion of your products or services as compared to those of your competitors.

Master Black Belt (MBB)—Six Sigma quality expert responsible for strategic implementation within the organization. The MBB is qualified to instruct other Six Sigma Black Belts and Green Belts on the methodologies, tools, and applications in all functions and levels of the organization, and acts as a resource on process management.

material review board (MRB)—A quality control committee or team, usually employed in manufacturing or other materials-processing installations, that has the responsibility and authority to deal with items or materials that do not conform to fitness-for-use specifications. An equivalent, the *error review board*, is sometimes used in software development.

matrix chart/diagram—A management and planning tool that shows the relationships among various groups of data; it yields information about the relationships and the importance of task/method elements of the subjects. Typically, a matrix displays the relationship between two topics—with, perhaps, the impact of a third element—such as a personnel requirements matrix. There are many varieties of matrices, for example, see *quality function deployment*.

matrix structure—Describes an organization that is organized into functional and product/project departments; it brings together teams of people to work on projects and is driven by product or project scope. Basically, functional departments obtain, train, maintain, and sustain the appropriate people, who are deployed, as needed, to product/project departments or work units. A given person may be based in a functional department (say, software developers) and deployed to one or more product/project work teams (say, a new product development team and also a team working on improving the QMS).

mean—A measure of central tendency, the arithmetic average of all measurements in a data set.

mean time between failures (MTBF)—The average time interval between failures for repairable product for a defined unit of measure (for example, operating hours, cycles, or miles).

means (in hoshin planning usage)—The step of identifying the ways by which multiyear objectives will be met, leading to the development of action plans.

measurement—Refers to the reference standard or sample used for the comparison of properties.

median—The middle number or center value of a set of data when all the data are arranged in sequence.

mentor—A person who voluntarily assumes a role of trusted advisor and teacher to another person. The mentor may or may not be the mentored person's organizational superior or even in the same organization. Usually, the only reward the mentor receives is self-gratification in having helped someone else.

metric—A standard of measurement or evaluation.

metrology—Science and practice of measurements.

micro processes—Narrow processes made up of detailed steps and activities that could be accomplished by a single person.

micromanaging—Managing every little detail (for example, executive approving requisition for paper clips).

milestone—A specific time when a critical event is to occur; a symbol placed on a milestone chart to locate the point when a critical event is to occur. (An upward-pointing triangle signifies the scheduled time of an event, a downward-pointing triangle signifies completion of an event.)

milestone chart—A Gantt chart on which event starting and ending times are indicated.

mind mapping—A technique for creating a visual representation of a multitude of issues or concerns by forming a map of the interrelated ideas.

mission statement—An explanation of the core purpose or reasons for existing as an organization; it provides the focus for the organization and defines its scope of business. The mission may define customers or markets served, distinctive competence, or technologies used.

mistake-proofing—See *poka-yoke*.

mitigation—Risk response strategy that decreases risk by lowering the probability of a risk event's occurrence or reduces the effect of the event should it occur.

mode—The value that occurs most frequently in a data set.

moment of truth (MOT)—An MOT is described by Jan Carlzon, former CEO of Scandinavian Air Services in the 1980s, as, "Any episode where a customer comes into contact with any aspect of your company, no matter how distant, and by this contact, has an opportunity to form an opinion about your company."

monitoring—Systematic and periodic or continuous surveillance or testing of a product or process to determine the level of compliance with industry, engineering, or regulatory requirements. No action is implied.

monument—The point in a process that necessitates a product waiting in a queue before processing further; a barrier to continuous flow.

motivation—Two types of motivation are *extrinsic* and *intrinsic*. Motivating a person means providing a work environment in which the person feels motivated; that is, one person can not directly motivate another person.

muda—(Japanese) An activity that consumes resources but creates no value; the seven categories of muda (waste) are correction, processing, inventory, waiting, overproduction, internal transport, and wasted motion.

multi-attribute evaluation—Simpler than QFD, this process rank-orders and weights customer requirements relative to the competition. In addition, it estimates the cost of each requirement in order to prioritize improvement actions.

multivariate control chart—A control chart for evaluating the stability of a process in terms of the levels of two or more variables or characteristics.

multivoting—A decision-making tool that enables a group to sort through a long list of ideas to identify priorities.

murmurs—A technique to gather information on consumer behavior by watching customers use the product or service.

Myers-Briggs Type Indicator (MBTI)—A method and instrument for identifying a person's personality type based on Carl Jung's theory of personality preferences.

mystery shopper—A person who pretends to be a regular shopper in order to get an unrestrained view of how a company's service process works.

N

n—Sample size (the number of units in a sample).

NAICS—North American Industry Classification System; a system replacing the Standard Industrial Classification (SIC), used to classify organizations according to the products or services produced.

natural team—A work group having responsibility for a particular process.

***n*-chart**—Number defective chart for attribute data, used where each unit is inspected from a given lot.

negotiation—A process in which individuals or groups work together to achieve common goals.

next operation as customer (NOAC)—Concept that the organization comprises service/product providers and service/product receivers, or internal customers.

NIST—National Institute of Standards and Technology (U.S.).

nominal group technique—A technique similar to brainstorming, used by teams to generate ideas on a particular subject. Team members are asked to silently come up with as many ideas as possible and write them down. Each member is then asked to share one idea, which is recorded. After all the ideas are recorded, they are discussed and prioritized by the group.

nonconformity—The result of nonfulfillment of a specified requirement. See also *blemish, defect,* and *imperfection.*

nondestructive testing (NDT) and evaluation—Testing and evaluation methods that do not damage or destroy the product being tested.

non-value-added—Tasks or activities that can be eliminated with no deterioration in product or service functionality, performance, or quality in the eyes of the customer.

norm (behavioral)—Expectation of how a person or group will behave in a given situation based on established protocols, rules of conduct, or accepted social practices.

normal distribution—A bell-shaped distribution for continuous data where most of the data are concentrated around the average, and it is equally likely that an observation will occur above or below the average.

np-**chart**—A control chart for attribute data showing the number of defective units in a subgroup. Requires a constant subgroup size.

NPV (net present value)—A discounted cash flow technique for finding the present value of each future year's cash flow.

O

objective—A quantitative statement of future expectations and an indication of when the expectations should be achieved; it supports goals, clarifying and measuring what people must accomplish.

objective evidence—Verifiable qualitative or quantitative observations, information, records, or statements of fact pertaining to the quality of an item or service or to the existence and implementation of a quality system element.

objective setting—See *S.M.A.R.T. W.A.Y.*

observation—An item or incidence of objective evidence found during an audit.

OC (operating characteristic) curve—For a sampling plan, the OC curve indicates the probability of accepting a lot based on the sample size to be taken and the fraction defective in the batch.

one-to-one marketing—The concept of knowing customers' unique requirements and expectations and marketing to these. See also *customer relationship management.*

on-the-job training (OJT)—Training conducted at the workstation, typically done one-on-one.

open book management—An approach to managing that exposes employees to the organization's financial information, provides instruction in business literacy, and enables employees to better understand their role and contribution and its impact on the organization.

operating characteristic curve—See *OC curve*.

operating expense—All the money the system spends turning inventory into throughput (Goldratt's theory of constraints).

optimization—Achieving planned process results that meet the needs of the customer and supplier alike and minimize their combined costs.

organization culture—The collective beliefs, values, attitudes, manners, customs, behaviors, and artifacts unique to an organization.

organization development (OD)—An organization-wide (usually) planned effort, managed from the top, to increase organization effectiveness and health through interventions in the organization's processes using behavioral science knowledge and methodologies.

original equipment manufacturer (OEM)—An organization that uses product components from one or more other outside organizations to build a product it sells under its own name and brand. For example, an organization that furnishes the completed seats that are installed in the automobile that is sold under the auto assembler's brand is an OEM. Sometimes the term is misused to refer to the outside organization that supplies only components.

OSHA—Occupational Safety and Health Administration (U.S.).

out of spec—A term used to indicate that a unit does not meet a given specification.

outcome—The measurable result of a project, a quality initiative, or an improvement. Usually, some time passes between the completion of the action and the realization of the outcome, for example, improved productivity, quality, customer satisfaction, profits, and so on.

out-of-control process—A process in which the statistical measure being evaluated is not in a state of statistical control (that is, the variations among the observed sampling results can not all be attributed to a constant system of chance causes; special or assignable causes exist.) See also *in-control process*.

output—The deliverables resulting from a process, project, quality initiative, improvement, and so on. Outputs include data, information, documents, decisions, and tangible products. Outputs are generated both from the planning and management of the activity and the delivered product, service, or program. *Output* is also the item, document, or material delivered by an internal provider (supplier) to an internal receiver (customer).

outsourcing—A strategy and an action to relieve an organization of processes and tasks in order to reduce costs, improve quality, reduce cycle time (for example, by parallel processing), reduce the need for specialized skills, and increase efficiency. Often, the primary intent is to save money through cheaper labor costs.

P

panels—Groups of customers recruited by an organization to provide ad hoc feedback on performance or product development ideas.

paradigm—The standards, rules, attitudes, culture, and so on, that influence the way an organization lives and behaves.

paradigm shift—Advent and acceptance of a totally new model that is theory- or custom-shattering and displaces and/or discredits older theories and models, for example, a major organizational culture change such as adopting the BPEP criteria as the new business model.

parallel structure—Describes an organizational model in which groups, such as quality circles or a quality council, exist in the organization in addition to and simultaneously with the line organization. Also referred to as *collateral structure*.

parameter design (Taguchi)—The use of design of experiments in identifying the major contributors to variation.

Pareto chart—A basic tool used to graphically rank causes from most significant (or frequent) to least significant (or frequent). It utilizes a vertical bar graph in which the bar height reflects the frequency or impact of causes.

Parkinson's law—States that work expands to fit the organization developed to perform it, and there is a tendency for each work unit within the organization to try to build up its importance by expanding the number of jobs and personnel it controls. Sometimes expressed as "work expands to fit the available time."

participative management—A style of managing whereby the manager tends to work from theory *Y* assumptions about people, involving the workers in decisions made. See *theory Y*.

partnership/alliance—A strategy and a formal relationship between a supplier and a customer to engender cooperation for their mutual benefit, such as reducing costs of ownership, maintenance of minimum stocks, just-in-time deliveries, joint participation in design, exchange of information on materials and technologies, new production methods, quality improvement strategies, and the exploitation of market synergy.

payback period—The number of years it will take the results of a project or capital investment to recover the investment from net cash flows.

p-**chart**—Fraction defective chart (also called a *proportion chart* or *percent chart*).

PDSA cycle—Plan–do–study–act cycle (a variation of PDCA) See *plan–do–check–act cycle (PDCA)*.

performance appraisal/evaluation—A formal method of measuring employees' progress against performance standards and providing feedback to them.

performance management system—A system that supports and contributes to the creation of high-performance work and work systems by translating behavioral principles into procedures.

performance plan—A performance management tool that describes desired performance and provides a way to assess the performance objectively.

PERT (program/project evaluation and reporting technique) chart—An enhanced AND that graphically demonstrates the relationship among project elements. Unlike the critical path method (CPM), PERT uses three time estimates rather than one.

pilot test—Small-scale implementation of a process or an operation to test its capability, design, and performance to requirements.

plan–do–check–act (PDCA) cycle—A four-step process for quality improvement. In the first step (plan), a plan to effect improvement is developed. In the second step (do), the plan is carried out, preferably on a small scale. In the third step (check), the effects of the plan are observed. As part of the last step (act), the results are studied to determine what was learned and what can be predicted. The plan–do–check–act cycle is sometimes referred to as the Shewhart cycle because Walter A. Shewhart discussed the concept in his book *Statistical Method from the Viewpoint of Quality Control*, and as the Deming cycle because W. Edwards Deming introduced the concept in Japan. The Japanese subsequently called it the Deming cycle. Sometimes referred to as *plan–do–study–act* (PDSA).

Poisson distribution—A distribution used for discrete data, applicable when there are many opportunities for occurrence of an event but a low probability (less than 0.10) on each trial.

poka-yoke—(Japanese) A term that means to mistake-proof a process by building safeguards into the system that avoid or immediately find errors. It comes from *poka*, which means *error*, and *yokeru*, which means *to avoid*.

PONC—Price of nonconformance: the cost of not doing things right the first time.

population—A group of people, objects, observations, or measurements about which one wishes to draw conclusions.

portfolio analysis—A process of comparing the value of proposed projects or acquisitions relative to the financial impacts on current projects as well as the potential for impact on resources of the proposed projects or acquisitions.

P_{pk}—Potential process capability statistic used in the validation stage of a new product launch (uses the same formula as C_{pk}, but a higher value is expected due to the smaller time span and fewer data from the sample).

ppm—Parts per million.

precision—A characteristic of measurement that addresses the consistency or repeatability of a measurement system when the identical item is measured a number of times.

pre-control—A control process, with simple rules, based on tolerances. It is effective for any process where a worker can measure a quality characteristic (dimension, color, strength) and can adjust the process to change that characteristic, and where there is either continuous output or discrete output totaling three or more pieces.

prerequisite tree—A technique used to identify obstacles in the application of Goldratt's theory of constraints.

prevention costs—Costs incurred to keep internal and external failure costs and appraisal costs to a minimum.

prevention versus detection—A term used to contrast two types of quality activities. *Prevention* refers to those activities designed to prevent nonconformances in products and services. *Detection* refers to those activities designed to detect nonconformances already in products and services. Another phrase used to describe this distinction is *designing-in quality versus inspecting-in quality.*

preventive action—Reviewing procedures, processes, and products/services to evaluate risks, and take action to eliminate the potential causes of a nonconformity, defect, or other undesirable situation in order to prevent occurrence.

primary customer—The individual or group who directly receives the output of a process.

principled negotiation—Based on a win–win orientation, includes:

* Separate the people from the problem.
* Focus on interest, not position.
* Understand what both sides want to achieve.
* Invent options for mutual gain.
* Insist on objective criteria.

priorities matrix—A tool used to choose between several options that have many useful benefits, but where not all of them are of equal value.

probability—Likelihood of occurrence.

probability distribution—A mathematical formula that relates the values of characteristics to their probability of occurrence in a population.

problem solving—A rational process for identifying, describing, analyzing, and resolving situations in which something has gone wrong without explanation.

procedure—A document that answers the questions What has to be done? Where is it to be done? When is it to be done? Who is to do it? Why do it? (Contrasted with a work instruction, which answers, How is it to be done? With what materials and tools is it to be done?) In the absence of a work instruction, the instructions may be embedded in the procedure.

process—An activity or group of activities that takes an input, adds value to it, and provides an output to an internal or external customer; a planned and repetitive sequence of steps by which a defined product or service is delivered.

process analysis—Defining and quantifying the process capability from data derived from mapping and measurement of the work performed by the process.

process capability—A statistical measure of the inherent process variability for a given characteristic. See C_p, C_{pk}, and P_{pk}.

process capability index—The value of the tolerance specified for the characteristic divided by the process capability. There are several types of process capability indexes, including the widely used C_p and C_{pk}.

process control—Methodology for keeping a process within prescribed boundaries and minimizing the inherent variation in the process.

process decision program chart (PDPC)—A management and contingency planning tool that identifies all events that can go wrong and the appropriate countermeasures for these events. It graphically represents all sequences that can lead to an undesirable effect.

process improvement—The act of changing a process to reduce variability and cycle time and make the process more effective, efficient, and productive.

process improvement team (PIT)—A natural work group or cross-functional team whose responsibility is to achieve needed improvements in existing processes. The life-span of the team is based on the completion of the team's purpose and specific objectives.

process management—The collection of practices used to implement and improve process effectiveness; it focuses on holding the gains achieved through process improvement and assuring process integrity.

process mapping—The flowcharting of a work process in detail, including key control measurements.

process organization—A form of departmentalization where each department specializes in one phase of the process.

process owner—The manager or leader who is responsible for ensuring that a total process is effective and efficient.

process quality audit—An analysis of elements of a process and appraisal of completeness, correctness of conditions, and probable effectiveness.

process reengineering—See *reengineering*.

process village—Refers to an area where machines are grouped by type of operation performed by the machines (contrast with a cell layout).

producer's risk—For a sampling plan, the probability of not accepting a lot the quality of which has a designated numerical value representing a level that is generally desirable. Usually, the designated value will be the acceptable quality level. Also called *alpha risk* and *type 1 error*.

product life cycle management (PLM)—Concern for a product's viability, reliability, use, and disposition from its design through manufacturing, delivery, customer use, and ultimate discard.

product organization—A departmentalization where each department focuses on a specific product type or family.

product orientation—A tendency to see customers' needs in terms of a product they want to buy, not in terms of the services, value, or benefits the product will produce.

product quality audit—A quantitative assessment of conformance to required product characteristics.

product warranty—The organization's stated policy that it will replace, repair, or reimburse a customer for a defective product, providing the product defect occurs under certain conditions and within a stated period of time.

product/service liability—The obligation of a company to make restitution for loss related to personal injury, property damage, or other harm caused by its product or service.

professional development plan—An individual development tool for an employee. Working together, the employee and management create a plan that coordinates the individual's career needs and aspirations with organizational demands.

profit and loss statement—A financial statement showing the income and expenses resulting in a profit or loss for an organization within a specified period of time.

profound knowledge, system of—As defined by W. Edwards Deming, states that learning can not be based on experience only; it requires comparisons of results to a prediction, plan, or an expression of theory. Predicting why something happens is essential to understand results and to continually improve. The four components of the system of profound knowledge are appreciation for a system, knowledge of variation, theory of knowledge, and understanding of psychology.

program evaluation and review technique (PERT)—An event-oriented project management planning and measurement technique that utilizes an arrow diagram to identify all major project events and demonstrates the amount of time (critical path) needed to complete a project. It provides three time estimates: optimistic, most likely, and pessimistic.

project life cycle—Six sequential phases of project management: concept, planning, design, implementation, evaluation, and closeout.

project management—The management of activities and events involved throughout a project's life cycle.

project plan—All the documents that comprise the details of why the project is to be initiated, what the project is to accomplish, when and where it is to be implemented, who will have responsibility, how the implementation will be carried out, how much it will cost, what resources are required, and how the project's progress and results will be measured.

project team—A designated group of people working together to produce a planned project's outputs and ultimate outcome.

psychographic customer characteristics—Variables among buyers in the consumer market that address lifestyle issues and include consumer interests, activities, and opinions.

pull system—See *kanban.*

Q

quality—A subjective term for which each person has his or her own definition. In technical usage, quality can have two primary meanings: (1) the characteristics of a product or service that bear on its ability to satisfy stated or implied needs, and (2) a product or service free of deficiencies.

quality assessment—The process of identifying business practices, attitudes, and activities that are enhancing or inhibiting the continual achievement of quality improvement in an organization.

quality assurance/quality control (QA/QC)—Two terms that have many interpretations because of the multiple definitions for the words *assurance* and *control.* For example, *assurance* can mean the act of giving confidence, the state of being certain, or the act of making certain; *control* can mean an evaluation to indicate needed corrective responses, the act of guiding, or the state of a process in which the variability is attributable to a constant system of chance causes. One definition of *quality assurance* is all the planned and systematic activities implemented within the quality system that can be demonstrated to provide confidence that a product or service will fulfill requirements for quality. One definition for *quality control* is the operational techniques and activities used to fulfill requirements for quality. Often, however, *quality assurance* and *quality control* are used interchangeably, referring to the actions performed to ensure the quality of a product, service, or process.

quality audit/assessment—A systematic, independent examination and review to determine whether quality activities and related results comply with planned arrangements, and whether these arrangements are implemented effectively and are suitable to achieve the objectives.

quality auditor—A person trained in the auditing/assessing of the appropriate application of quality principles, policies, protocols, and practices supporting the producing of high-quality products or services that meet customer needs and expectations and comply with applicable standards.

quality characteristics—The unique characteristics of products and services by which customers evaluate their perception of quality.

quality circles—Quality improvement or self-improvement study groups composed of a small number of employees—10 or fewer—and their supervisor, who meet regularly with an aim to improve a process.

quality control—See *quality assurance.*

quality cost reports—A system of collecting quality costs that uses a spreadsheet to list the elements of quality costs against a spread of the departments, areas, or projects in which the costs occur, and summarizes the data to enable trend analysis and decision making. The reports help organizations review prevention costs, appraisal costs, and internal and external failure costs.

quality costs—See *cost of quality.*

quality council—The group driving the quality improvement effort and usually having oversight responsibility for the implementation and maintenance of the quality management system; operates in parallel with the normal operation of the business. Sometimes called *quality steering committee.*

quality engineering—The analysis of a manufacturing system at all stages to maximize the quality of the process itself and the products it produces.

quality function—The entire spectrum of activities through which an organization achieves its quality goals and objectives, no matter where these activities are performed.

quality function deployment (QFD)—A multifaceted matrix in which customer requirements are translated into appropriate technical requirements for each stage of product development and production. The QFD process is often referred to as "listening to the voice of the customer." See also *house of quality.*

quality function mission—Derived from and an input into the organization's mission, the quality function mission statement includes a customer focus, a supplier focus, and an employee focus. The statement represents the basic direction the organization intends to follow regarding quality.

quality improvement—Actions taken in any or all parts of the organization to increase the effectiveness and efficiency of activities and processes in order to provide added benefits to both the organization and its customers.

quality inspection—A number of possible activities used with an intent to ascertain or verify compliance to stated standards, prescribed measurements, or acceptable practices.

quality level agreement (QLA)—Internal service/product providers assist their internal customers in clearly delineating the level of service/product required in quantitatively measurable terms. A QLA may contain specifications for accuracy, completeness, timeliness, usability, service availability, or responsiveness to needs. The QLA provides, in writing, what a service/product receiver expects from an upstream provider, furnishes data to measure whether the quality acceptance level has been met, and is the basis for trending progress toward improvement, and ultimate recognition for quality achievement.

quality loss function—A parabolic approximation of the quality loss that occurs when a quality characteristic deviates from its target value. The quality loss function is expressed in monetary units—the cost of deviating from the target increases as a quadratic function the farther the quality characteristic moves from the target. The formula used to compute the quality loss function depends on the type of quality characteristic being used. The quality loss function was first introduced in this form by Genichi Taguchi.

quality management—All activities of the overall management function that determine the quality principles, policy, mission, objectives, responsibilities, and practices that when implemented through quality planning, quality assurance, quality control, and continual quality improvement within the quality system provide quality products and services leading to customer satisfaction and organizational benefits.

quality management system (QMS)—The organizational structure, processes, procedures, and resources designed and implemented to maintain and continually improve quality management, products, and services.

quality manual—Document stating the organization's quality policy and describing the quality system of an organization.

quality metrics—Quantitative measurements that give an organization the ability to set objectives and evaluate actual performance versus plan.

quality plan—The document, or documents, stating the specific quality practices, resources, specifications, and sequence of activities relevant to a particular product, project, or contract. The types of documents differ widely depending on the industry, type and size of organization, type of product or service produced, and other factors.

quality planning—The activity of establishing quality objectives and quality requirements.

quality policy—An organization's formally stated beliefs about quality, and the acceptable behavior that will lead to the expected result.

quality principles—Rules, guidelines, or concepts that an organization believes in, collectively. The principles are formulated by senior management with input from others and are communicated and understood at every level of the organization.

quality score chart (Q chart)—A control chart for evaluating the stability of a process in terms of a quality score. The quality score is the weighted sum of the count of events of various classifications in which each classification is assigned a weight.

quality steering committee—See *quality council.*

quality trilogy—A three-point approach to managing for quality. The three points are *quality planning* (developing the products and processes required to meet customer needs), *quality control* (meeting product and process objectives), and *quality improvement* (achieving unprecedented levels of performance). Attributed to Joseph M. Juran.

questionnaires—See *surveys.*

queue processing—Processing in batches (contrast with continuous flow processing).

queue time—Wait time of product awaiting the next step in a process.

quincunx—A teaching tool that creates frequency distributions. Beads tumble over numerous horizontal rows of pins, which force the beads to the right or left. After a random journey, the beads are dropped into vertical slots. After many beads are dropped, a frequency distribution results. In the classroom, quincunxes are often used to simulate a manufacturing process. The quincunx was invented by English scientist Francis Galton in the 1890s.

R

radar chart—A visual method to show in graphic form the size of gaps between a number of both current organization performance indicators and ideal performance indicators. The resulting chart resembles a radar screen or a spider's web.

random cause—Cause of variation due to chance and not assignable to any factor. See *common cause*.

random number generator—Used to select a stated quantity of random numbers from a table of random numbers. The resulting selection is then used to pull specific items or records corresponding to the selected numbers to comprise a random sample.

random sampling—A sampling method in which every element in the population has an equal chance of being included.

range—A measure of dispersion, the highest value minus the lowest value.

range chart (R chart)—A control chart in which the subgroup range, R, is used to evaluate the stability of the variability within a process.

ratio analysis—The process of relating isolated business numbers, such as sales, margins, expenses, debt, and profits, to make them meaningful.

rational subgroup—A subgroup that is expected to be as free as possible from assignable causes (usually consecutive items).

recognition and reward system—Management's recognition of work done well by individuals or groups, and any monetary or nonmonetary reward that is provided to those persons recognized.

record—Document or electronic medium that furnishes objective evidence of activities performed or results achieved, for example, a filled-in form.

red bead experiment—An experiment developed by W. Edwards Deming to illustrate that it is impossible to put employees in rank order of performance for the coming year based on their performance during the past year because performance differences must be attributed to the system, not to employees. Four thousand red and white beads, 20 percent red, in a bin, and six people are needed for the experiment. The participants' goal is to produce white beads because the customer will not accept red beads. One person begins by stirring the beads and then, blindfolded, selects a sample of 50 beads. That person passes the bin to the next person, who repeats the process, and so on.

When everyone has his or her sample, the number of red beads for each is counted. The limits of variation between employees that can be attributed to the system are calculated. Everyone will fall within the calculated limits of variation that could arise from the system. The calculations will show that there is no evidence one person will be a better performer than another in the future. The experiment shows that it would be a waste of management's time to try to find out why, say, John produced four red beads and Jane produced 15; instead, management should improve the system, making it possible for everyone to produce more white beads.

reengineering—Completely redesigning or restructuring a whole organization, an organizational component, or a complete process. It's a "start all over again from the beginning" approach, sometimes called a *breakthrough*. In terms of improvement approaches, reengineering is contrasted with incremental improvement (kaizen).

Registrar Accreditation Board (RAB)—An organization that evaluates the competency and reliability of registrar organizations that audit and register client organizations to an appropriate standard, such as ISO 9001 or ISO 14001.

registration—See *certification to a standard.*

regression analysis—A statistical technique for estimating the parameters of an equation relating a particular variable to one or more variables.

reinforcement of behavior—The process of providing positive consequences when an individual is applying the correct knowledge and skills to the job. It has been described as *catching people doing things right and recognizing their behavior.* Caution: Less than desirable behavior can also be reinforced unintentionally.

reliability—In measurement systems analysis, the ability of an instrument to produce the same results over repeated administration—consistency. In reliability engineering it is the probability of a product performing its intended function under stated conditions for a given period of time. See also *mean time between failures.*

reliability engineering—Science of including those factors in the basic design that will ensure the required degree of reliability, availability, and maintainability.

remedial journey—See *diagnostic journey.*

remedy—Something that eliminates or counteracts a problem cause: a solution.

repair—Action taken on a nonconforming product so that it will fulfill the intended usage requirements, although it may not conform to the originally specified requirements. See *rework.*

repeatability and reproducibility (R & R)—A measurement validation process to determine how much variation exists in the measurement system (including the variation in product, the gage used to measure, and the individuals using the gage).

reproducibility—Variation in the average of the measurements made by different appraisers using the same measuring instrument when measuring the identical characteristics on the same part.

resistance to change—A person or group's unwillingness to change beliefs, habits, and ways of doing things.

resource requirements matrix—A tool used to relate the resources required to the project tasks requiring them (used to indicate types of individuals needed, material needed, subcontractors, and so on).

response surface—A graphical representation of the relationship between important independent variables, controlled factors, and a dependent variable.

RETAD—Rapid exchange of tooling and dies, the same concept as *SMED*.

return on assets (ROA)—A measure of the return generated by the earning power of the organization's investment in assets, such as facilities, large equipment, and so on.

return on equity (ROE)—The net profit after taxes, divided by the previous year's tangible stockholders' equity, and then multiplied by 100 to provide a percentage (also referred to as *return on net worth*).

return on investment (ROI)—An umbrella term for a variety of ratios measuring an organization's business performance and calculated by dividing some measure of return by a measure of investment and then multiplying by 100 to provide a percentage. In its most basic form, ROI indicates what remains from all money taken in after all expenses are paid.

return on net assets (RONA)—Measure of an organization's earning power from investments in assets calculated by dividing net profit after taxes by the previous year's tangible total assets, multiplied by 100 to provide a percentage.

return on training investment (ROTI)—A measure of the return generated by the benefits obtained by the organization's investment in training.

reverse engineering—Developing new design specifications by inspection and analysis of the process steps (from last to first) used to produce an existing product.

rework—Action taken on a nonconforming product so that it will fulfill the specified requirements (may also pertain to a service).

right the first time—The concept that it is beneficial and more cost-effective to take the necessary steps up front to ensure that a product or service meets its requirements than to provide a product or service that will need rework or not meet customers' needs. In other words, an organization should engage in defect prevention more than defect detection.

risk assessment/management—The process of determining what present or potential risks are possible in a situation (for example, project plan) and what actions might be taken to eliminate or mitigate them.

risk priority number (RPN)—The priority of risks assessed expressed as a number.

robustness—The condition of a product or process design that remains relatively stable with a minimum of variation even though factors that influence operations or usage, such as environment and wear, are constantly changing.

role playing—A training technique whereby selected participants, designated to assume a particular role, spontaneously interact in an assigned scenario.

root cause analysis (RCA)—A set of quality techniques that can be used to distinguish the cause of defects or problems. It is a structured approach that focuses on finding the decisive or original source of a problem or condition.

run—Consecutive points on one side of the centerline on an SPC chart.

run chart—A line graph showing data collected during a run or an uninterrupted sequence of events. A trend is indicated when the series of collected data points up or down.

S

sales leveling—A strategy of establishing a long-term relationship with customers to lead to contracts for fixed amounts and scheduled deliveries in order to smooth the flow and eliminate surges.

sample—A finite number of items of a similar type taken from a population for the purpose of examination to determine whether all members of the population would conform to quality requirements or specifications.

sample plan—Documented plan showing the scheduled number of samples to be taken from a lot for the purpose of acceptance or rejection of the lot. There are several pre-designed sampling plans available.

sample size—The number of units in a sample chosen from a population.

sampling—The process of drawing conclusions about a population based on a part of the population.

satisfier—Term used to describe the quality level received by a customer when a product or service meets requirements.

SCAMPER—A list of seven questions used by a team to stimulate creativity.

scatter diagram—A graphical technique used to analyze the relationship between two variables. Two sets of data are plotted on a graph, with the *y*-axis being used for the variable to be predicted and the *x*-axis for the variable being used to make the prediction. The graph will show possible relationships (although two variables might appear to be related, they might not be; those who know most about the variables must make that evaluation). The scatter diagram is one of the seven tools of quality.

scenario planning—A strategic planning process that generates multiple stories/ scenarios about possible future conditions, allowing an organization to look at the potential impact on them, and different ways they could respond.

scientific management—Finding the one best way to perform a task so as to increase effectiveness, quality, productivity, and efficiency.

scope—The total number of products, services, processes, people, operations, that will be affected by an initiative, project, or other action.

scope creep—In a project, job, or other work situation, the gradual expansion of responsibilities and work load, often invisible in early stages until the additional time and cost appear as a variation from estimates.

scorecard—Any evaluation device that formally specifies criteria and a means for rating performance.

secondary customer—Individuals or groups from outside the process boundaries who receive process output but who are not the reason for the process's existence.

second-party audit/assessment—An action carried out by a customer on their suppliers.

segmentation—See *customer segmentation.*

SEI capability maturity model—A model used to determine current process capabilities and identify critical software issues for improvement.

selective listening—One hears what they are predisposed to hear.

self-control—Three elements comprise workers' self-control: knowing what they are supposed to do, knowing what they are actually doing and how well, and being able to control the process.

self-directed learning—See *learner-controlled instruction.*

self-inspection—The process by which employees inspect their own work according to specified rules.

self-managed team—A team that requires little supervision and manages itself and the day-to-day work it does; self-directed teams are responsible for whole work processes, with each individual performing multiple tasks.

sensor—In an inspection or monitoring system, a device that detects a condition out of the normal and provides a notification signal of the changed condition.

service level agreement (SLA)—See *quality level agreement.*

setup time—The time taken to change over a process to run a different product or service.

seven basic tools of quality—Tools that help organizations understand their processes in order to improve them. The tools are the cause-and-effect diagram, check sheet, control chart, flowchart, histogram, Pareto chart, and scatter diagram. See individual entries.

seven management tools of quality—The tools used primarily for planning and managing are the activity network diagram (AND), or arrow diagram, affinity diagram (KJ method), interrelationship digraph, matrix diagram, priorities matrix, process decision program chart (PDPC), and tree diagram.

shape—(1) Pattern or outline formed by the relative position of a large number of individual values obtained from a process. (2) Removal of material from an item using a shaper or shaver tool.

shared leadership—Management approach in which the manager believes that the many functions of management can be effectively spread among various teams or individuals.

Shewhart cycle—See *plan–do–check–act cycle*.

shift—Abrupt change in an important variable in a process. Examples include broken tools, dropped gages, parts slipping, oil stops flowing, missed ingredient in a mix.

ship-to-stock program—An arrangement with a qualified supplier whereby the supplier ships material directly to the buyer without the buyer's incoming inspection; often a result of evaluating and approving the supplier for certification.

SIC (standard industrial classification)—Replaced by *NAICS*.

sigma—Greek letter (σ) that stands for the standard deviation of a process.

silo—(as in functional silo). An organization where cross-functional collaboration and cooperation is minimal and where the functional silos tend to work toward their own objectives, sometimes to the detriment of the organization as a whole. The allusion to "silo" is the mental picture of a vertical farm structure dedicated to serving one purpose without due regard to its relation to the farm as a whole entity.

single-minute exchange of die (SMED)—A goal to be achieved in reducing the setup time required for a changeover to a new process; the methodologies employed in devising and implementing ways to reduce setup.

single-piece flow—A method whereby the product proceeds through the process one piece at a time rather than in large batches, eliminating queues and costly waste.

SIPOC analysis—A macro-level analysis of the suppliers, inputs, processes, outputs, and customers.

situational leadership—Leadership theory that maintains that leadership style should change based on the person and the situation involved, with the leader displaying varying degrees of directive and supportive behavior.

Six Sigma approach—A quality philosophy; a collection of techniques and tools for use in reducing variation; a program of improvement.

six sigma quality—Term generally used to indicate that a process is well controlled, that is, within process limits $\pm 3\sigma$ from the centerline in a control chart, and requirements/tolerance limits $\pm 6\sigma$ from the centerline. The term was originated by Motorola.

skewness—Measure of a distribution's symmetry, a skewed distribution has a longer tail on the right or left side, with its hump (probability) pushed to the opposite side.

skip-level meeting—Evaluation technique that occurs when a member of senior management meets with persons two or more organizational levels below, without the intervening management present, to allow open expression about the effectiveness of the organization.

skip-lot sampling—An acceptance sampling plan in which some set number of lots in a series is accepted without inspection. When the set number of lots is received without inspection, the next lot is inspected unless problems surface that merit all lots being inspected until the problem is eliminated and confidence is restored.

slack time—The time an activity can be delayed without delaying the entire project; it is determined by calculating the difference between the latest allowable date and the earliest expected date. Also called *float*.

S.M.A.R.T. W.A.Y.—A template for setting objectives—*specific, measurable, achievable, realistic, time, worth, assign, yield*.

Society of Automotive Engineers (SAE)—International society for the exchange of ideas advancing the engineering of powered transportation systems.

spaghetti chart—A before-improvement chart of existing steps in a process, with lines showing the many back and forth interrelationships (the resulting chart resembles cooked spaghetti). It is used to identify the redundancies and other wasted movements of people and material.

span of control—How many subordinates a manager can effectively and efficiently manage.

special causes—Causes of variation that arise because of special circumstances. They are not an inherent part of a process. Special causes are also referred to as *assignable causes*, as contrasted with *common causes*.

special characteristics—Any characteristics that may affect safety and/or regulatory requirements, degradation, customer satisfaction, annoyance, and/or other criteria.

specification—The engineering requirement used for judging the acceptability of a particular product/service based on product characteristics such as appearance, performance, and size. In statistical analysis, specification refers to the document that prescribes the requirements to which the product or service has to conform.

sponsor—The person who supports a team's plans, activities, and outcomes—the team's "backer." The sponsor provides for resources and helps define the mission and scope to set limits. The sponsor may be the same individual as the "champion."

stable process—Process that is in control, with only common causes of variation present.

stakeholder—People, departments, and outside organizations that have an investment or interest in the success of—or may be impacted by actions taken by—the organization.

stakeholder analysis—The identification of stakeholders and delineation of their needs.

stakeholder requirements matrix—A matrix for capturing and categorizing the needs of identified stakeholders.

standard—A statement, specification, or quantity of material against which measured outputs from a process may be judged as acceptable or unacceptable.

standard deviation—A calculated measure of variability that shows how much the data are spread around the mean.

standardized work—Documented and agreed-on work instructions and practices that embody the present best known methods and work sequence to be followed by all performers of each manufacturing or assembly step in a process.

statement of work (SOW)—A description of the actual work to be accomplished. It is derived from the work breakdown structure and, when combined with the project specifications, becomes the basis for the contractual agreement on the project. See also *scope*.

statistical confidence—The level of accuracy expected of an analysis of data. Most frequently it is expressed as either a "95% level of significance" or "5% confidence level." Also called *statistical significance*.

statistical process control (SPC)—The application of statistical techniques to control a process.

statistical quality control (SQC)—The application of statistical techniques to control quality. Often, the term *statistical process control* is used interchangeably with *statistical quality control*, although statistical quality control includes acceptance sampling as well as statistical process control.

statistical thinking—A philosophy of learning and action based on fundamental principles:

- All work occurs in a system of interconnected processes.

- Variation exists in all processes.

- Understanding and reducing variation are vital to improvement.

steering committee—A special group established to guide and track initiatives or projects.

storyboarding—A technique that visually displays thoughts and ideas and groups them into sequenced categories (scenes), making all aspects of a process visible at once. Often used to communicate to others the activities performed by a team as they improve a process.

strategic fit review—A process by which senior managers assess the future of each project or initiative proposed for a particular organization in terms of its ability to advance the mission, strategies, goals, and objectives of the organization.

strategic planning—A process for identifying and setting an organization's long-range vision, mission, goals, and objectives, and identifying the actions needed to ultimately achieve the goals.

stratified random sampling—A technique for segmenting (stratifying) a population prior to drawing a random sample from each strata, the purpose being to increase precision when members of different strata would, if not stratified, cause an unrealistic distortion.

structural variation—Variation caused by regular, systematic changes in output, such as seasonal patterns and unaccustomed "blips" in long-term trends.

suboptimization—The result occurring when an individual business function fails to focus on the overall organizational objectives for producing higher efficiency and effectiveness of the entire system, and instead focuses on the individual function's improvement.

supplier—Source of materials, services, or information input provided to a process. Internal suppliers provide materials or services to internal customers.

supplier audits—Reviews that are planned and carried out to verify the effectiveness of a supplier's quality program, drive improvement, and increase value.

supplier certification—Process of evaluating the performance of a supplier with the intent of authorizing the supplier to self-certify shipments if such authorization is granted.

supplier performance—The monitoring and measurement of supplier conformance to standards, good manufacturing practices, industry norms, and the customer's purchase contract, often with the use of specialized performance metrics and/or supplier audits.

supplier quality assurance—Confidence that a supplier's product or service will fulfill its customers' needs. This confidence is achieved by creating a relationship between the customer and supplier that ensures that the product will be fit for use with minimal corrective action and inspection. According to J. M. Juran, there are nine primary activities needed: (1) define product and program quality requirements, (2) evaluate alternative suppliers, (3) select suppliers, (4) conduct joint quality planning, (5) cooperate with the supplier during the execution of the contract, (6) obtain proof of conformance to requirements, (7) certify qualified suppliers, (8) conduct quality improvement programs as required, and (9) create and use supplier quality ratings.

supplier selection strategy and criteria—Selection of new suppliers is based on the type and uniqueness of the product or service to be purchased, and the total cost. Suppliers of commodity-type items and basic supplies may be selected from directories and catalogs. For more-sophisticated products and services, stringent evaluation criteria may be established.

supply chain—The series of processes and/or organizations that are involved in producing and delivering a product to the final user.

supply chain management (SCM)—The process of effectively integrating and managing components of the supply chain.

support systems—Starting with top management commitment and visible involvement, support systems are a cascading series of interrelated practices or actions aimed at building and sustaining support for continual quality improvement.

surveillance—Continual monitoring of a process.

surveillance audit—The regular audits conducted by registrars to confirm that a company registered to the ISO 9001 standard still complies; usually conducted on a six-month or one-year cycle.

survey—Act of examining a process or of questioning a selected sample of individuals to obtain data about a process, product, or service. A survey is generally conducted on a selected sample of a population to collect information about predetermined questions. A customer satisfaction survey is one example. Surveys may be conducted orally by a survey-taker, by paper and pencil, by computer online, and so on. Responses are tabulated and analyzed to surface significant areas for change.

SWOT analysis—An assessment of an organization's key *strengths, weaknesses, opportunities,* and *threats*. It considers factors such as the organization's industry, competitive position, functional areas, and management.

symptom—An indication of a problem or opportunity.

system—A network of interdependent actions, processes, or events that work together to accomplish a common mission and goal.

system of profound knowledge (SoPK)—See *profound knowledge*.

systems approach to management—A management theory that views the organization as a unified, purposeful combination of interrelated parts; managers must look at the organization as a whole and understand that activity in one part of the organization affects all parts of the organization (also known as *systems thinking*).

T

tacit knowledge—Unarticulated heuristics and assumptions used by any individual or organization. The knowledge that comes from experience over time.

tactical plans—Short-term plans, usually of one- to two-year duration, that describe actions the organization will take to meet its strategic business plan.

tactics—The techniques and processes that help an organization meet its objectives.

Taguchi loss function—Pertains to where product characteristics deviate from the target intended and losses increase according to a parabolic function. Merely attempting to produce a product within specifications doesn't prevent loss (loss that is inflicted on society after shipment of a product). Any points beyond the center of the process, in either direction, even though within specifications, Taguchi considers a loss.

Taguchi methods—The American Supplier Institute's trademarked term for the quality engineering methodology developed by Genichi Taguchi. In this engineering approach to quality control, Taguchi calls for off-line quality control, online quality control, and a system of experimental design to improve quality and reduce costs.

takt time—The available production time divided by the rate of customer demand. Operating to takt time sets the production pace to customer demand.

tally sheet—Another name for check sheet.

tampering—Action taken to compensate for variation within the control limits of a stable system. Tampering increases rather than decreases variation, as evidenced in the funnel experiment.

TARP—U.S. Office of Consumer Affairs/Technical Assistance Research Programs.

task—A specific, definable activity to perform an assigned function, usually within a specified time frame.

taxonomy—Classification of terms or objects.

team—A group of two or more people who are organized to work together and held accountable for the accomplishment of a task and specific performance objective.

team building/development—The process of transforming a group of people into a coordinated team and developing the team to achieve its purpose.

team dynamics—Interactions that occur among team members under different conditions.

team facilitation—Process of dealing with both the role of the facilitator on the team and the techniques and tools for facilitating the team. See *facilitator.*

team growth, stages of—Refers to the four development stages through which groups typically progress: *forming, storming, norming,* and *performing.* Knowledge of the stages helps team members accept the normal problems that occur on the path from forming a group to becoming a team. It is suggested that *adjourning* be added to the list to deal with closing down a team's work.

team leader—A person designated to be responsible for the ongoing work and success of the team, and keeping the team focused on the task assigned.

team performance evaluation, recognition and rewards—Special metrics are needed to evaluate the work of a team (to avoid focus on any individual on the team) and as a basis for the recognition and reward for team effort and achievements.

team-based organization/structure—A function or entire entity that consists primarily of multiple teams.

telecommuting—Working individually, or as part of a group, performing at least some work away from the organization's primary location, and accomplishing tasks with the aid of electronic technologies.

temporary/ad hoc team—A team, usually small, formed to address a short-term objective or emergency situation.

theory of constraints (TOC)—Eliyahu Goldratt's theory deals with techniques and tools for identifying and eliminating the constraints (bottlenecks) in a process, to achieve greater flow of money.

theory of knowledge (TOK)—A belief that management is about prediction, and people learn not only from experience, but also from theory. When people study a process and develop a theory, they can compare their predictions with their observations; profound learning results.

theory X and theory Y—A theory developed by Douglas McGregor that maintains that there are two contrasting assumptions about people, each of which is based on the manager's view of human nature. Theory X managers take a negative view and assume that most employees do not like work and try to avoid it. Theory Y managers take a positive view and believe that employees want to work, will seek and accept responsibility, and can offer creative solutions to organizational problems.

third-party audit—External audits conducted by personnel who are neither employees of the organization, nor a supplier, but are usually employees of certification bodies or of registrars.

three-sixty-degree (360°) feedback process—A people performance evaluation method that provides feedback from the perspectives of self, peers, direct reports, superiors, customers, and suppliers.

throughput—The rate at which the entire system generates money through sales of product or service (Goldratt's theory of constraints).

throughput time—The total time required (processing + queue) from concept to launch, or from order received to delivery, or raw materials received to delivery to customer.

TickIT—A certification of quality management systems that conform to the requirements of the ISO 9001 standard, specifically pertaining to software development.

tier—Level, rank, sequence.

TJC—The Joint Commission, formerly the Joint Commission on Accreditation of Healthcare Organizations (JCAHO).

TL 9000—Quality management standard series for the telecommunications industry.

tolerance—The variability of a parameter permitted and tolerated above or below a nominal value.

tolerance design (Taguchi)—Provides a rational grade limit for components of a system; determines which parts and processes need to be modified and to what degree it is necessary to increase their control capacity; a method for rationally determining tolerances.

tolerance limit—The maximum and minimum limit values a product may have and still meet engineering or customer requirements.

tool—Any implement or technique used for making a desirable change to materials, process, product, or approach that contributes to a quality product or service. (A narrow definition—a device used by hand, or a fixture in a machine, that cuts, strikes, shapes, marks/tags, positions, polishes, or heat-treats material in a process.)

tool life—Minimum amount of useful production that can be expected from a tool.

top management commitment—Participation and visible involvement of the organization's highest-level officials in their organization's quality improvement efforts.

total productive maintenance (TPM)—Methodologies for reducing and eventually eliminating equipment failure, setup and adjustment, minor stops, reduced speed, product rework, and scrap; preventive maintenance.

total quality management (TQM)—A term initially coined by the Naval Air Systems Command (U.S.) to describe its management approach to quality improvement. Total quality management (TQM) has taken on many meanings. Simply put, TQM is a management approach to long-term success through customer satisfaction. TQM is based on the participation of all members of an organization in improving processes, products, services, and the culture in which they work. TQM benefits all organization members and society. Various methods for implementing TQM are found within the teachings of such quality leaders as Philip B. Crosby, W. Edwards Deming, Armand V. Feigenbaum, Kaoru Ishikawa, J. M. Juran, and others. The Baldrige Performance Excellence Program (U.S.) and other criteria-based programs embody the principles of TQM.

traceability—The ability to track the history, application, or location of an item or activity, and like items or activities, by means of recorded identification.

training—The skills that employees need to learn in order to perform or improve the performance of their current job or tasks, and the process of providing those skills.

training evaluation—The techniques and tools used and the process of evaluating the effectiveness of training.

training needs assessment—The techniques and tools used and the process of determining an organization's training needs.

transactional leadership—A style of leading whereby the leader sees the work as being done through clear definition of tasks and responsibilities and the provision of resources as needed.

transformational leadership—A style of leading whereby the leader articulates the vision and values necessary for the organization to succeed.

transition tree—A technique used in applying Goldratt's theory of constraints.

tree diagram—A management and planning tool that shows the hierarchy of subtasks required to achieve an objective.

trend—Consecutive points plotted against a time period that show a pattern, and help to identify any unexpected occurrences. Trend plotting of sequential data points show the direction and rate of change of an organization, work unit, or process over time.

trend analysis—The charting of data over time to identify a tendency or direction.

trilogy—See *quality trilogy.*

TRIZ—(Russian) A theory of problem solving that aids in the solution of inventive problems. A set of analytical and knowledge-based tools that are typically hidden subconsciously in the minds of creative inventors.

***t*-test**—A method for testing hypotheses about the population mean; the *t*-statistic measures the deviation between the sample and population means, in terms of the number of standard errors.

type I error—An incorrect decision to reject something (such as a statistical hypothesis or a lot of products) when it is acceptable. Also known as *producer's risk* and *alpha risk.*

type II error—An incorrect decision to accept something when it is unacceptable. Also known as *consumer's risk* and *beta risk.*

U

***u*-chart**—Count per unit chart. Attribute control chart used to show the average number of defects in a sample; uses variable sample size. A *c*-chart uses a fixed sample size.

unconditional guarantee—An organizational policy of providing customers unquestioned remedy for any product or service deficiency.

unity of command—The concept that a subordinate should be responsible to only one superior. Note: A matrix-type organization negates this concept.

upper control limit (UCL)—Control limit for points above the central line in a control chart.

upper specification limit (USL)—Maximum limit for dimensions as specified for a product to be acceptable.

USDA—U.S. Department of Agriculture.

V

validation—Confirmation by examination of objective evidence that specific requirements and/or a specified intended use are met.

validity—Refers to the ability of a feedback instrument, and validation action taken, to measure what it was intended to measure. Validity may be measured three ways: (1) criterion related, (2) construct related, and (3) content related.

value added—Parts of the process that add worth from the external customers' perspective.

value chain—See *supply chain*.

value stream—The primary actions required to bring a product from concept to placing the product in the hands of the end user.

value stream mapping—The technique for mapping the value stream, typically done for the present perception and then the future perspective.

values—Statements that clarify the behaviors that the organization expects in order to move toward its vision and mission. Values reflect an organization's personality and culture.

variable control chart—Data resulting from the measurement of a parameter or a variable. Control charts based on variable data include average (*X-bar*) chart, individuals (*X*) chart, range (*R*) chart, sample standard deviation (*s*) chart, and CUSUM chart.

variable cost—Cost that varies with production quantity, such as material and direct labor.

variable sampling plan—A plan in which a sample is taken and a measurement of a specified quality characteristic is made on each unit. The measurements are summarized into a simple statistic, and the observed value is compared with an allowable value defined in the plan.

variables—Quantities that are subject to change.

variance—The difference between a planned amount (usually money or time) and the actual amount. In math, the measure of dispersion of observations based on the mean of the squared deviations from the arithmetic mean. The square of the standard deviation, given by formula.

variation—A change in data, a characteristic, or a function that is caused by one of four factors: *special causes, common causes, tampering,* or *structural variation*. See individual entries.

verification—The act of reviewing, inspecting, testing, checking, auditing, or otherwise establishing and documenting whether items, processes, services, or documents conform to specified requirements.

vertically integrate—To bring together more of the steps involved in producing a product in order to form a continuous chain owned by the same firm; typically involves taking on activities that were previously in the external portion of the supply chain.

virtual team—A boundaryless team functioning without a commonly shared physical structure or physical contact, using electronic technology to link the team members.

vision—A statement that explains what the company wants to become and what it hopes to achieve.

visual control—A technique of positioning all tools, parts, production activities, and performance indicators so that the status of a process can be understood at a glance by everyone; providing visual cues to aid the performer in correctly processing a step or series of steps, to reduce cycle time, to cut costs, to smooth flow of work, and to improve quality.

vital few, useful many—A term used by J. M. Juran to describe his use of the Pareto principle, which he first defined in 1950. (The principle was used much earlier in economics and inventory control methodologies.) The principle suggests that most effects come from relatively few causes; that is, 80 percent of the effects come from 20 percent of the possible causes. The 20 percent of the possible causes are referred to as the *vital few*; the remaining causes are referred to as the *useful many*. When Juran first defined this principle, he referred to the remaining causes as the *trivial many*, but realizing that no problems are trivial in quality assurance, he changed it to *useful many*.

voice of the customer—The perceived understanding of the customers' needs and expectations (*voice*) interpreted and passed downward throughout the organization to ensure, at all levels, that the organization is responding to the customers' voice.

W

walk the talk—Not only talking about what one believes in, but also being observed acting out those beliefs. Employees' buy-in to the TQM concept is more likely when management is seen involved in the process, every day.

walkabout—A visual, group technique used during strategic planning for resolving resource planning conflicts among organizational components.

warranty—A manufacturers' published statement that defective or deficient product or service experienced by the customer, within a prescribed time period, will be remedied by the manufacturer.

waste—Activities that consume resources but add no value; visible waste (for example, scrap, rework, downtime) and invisible waste (for example, inefficient setups, wait times of people and machines, inventory).

Weibull distribution—A distribution of continuous data that can take on many different shapes and is used to describe a variety of patterns; in relation to the bathtub curve, used to define when the "infant mortality" rate has ended and a steady state has been reached (decreasing failure rate).

WIIFM—"What's in it for me?" Ask and answer WIIFM before suggesting that a change/improvement will be acceptable to affected persons.

win–win—Outcome of a negotiation that results in both parties being better off.

wisdom—The culmination of the continuum from data to information to knowledge to wisdom.

work analysis—The analysis, classification, and study of the way work is done. Work may be categorized as value-added (necessary work), or non-value-added (rework, unnecessary work, idle). Collected data may be summarized on a Pareto chart showing how people within the studied population work. The need for and value of all work is then questioned, and opportunities for improvement identified. A time use analysis may also be included in the study.

work breakdown structure (WBS)—A project management technique by which a project is divided into tasks, subtasks, and units of work to be performed, displayed on a chart.

work group—A team type composed of people from one functional area who work together on a daily basis and whose goal is to improve the processes of their function.

work instruction—A document that answers the question "How is the work to be done?" See *procedure*.

workbook—A collection of exercises, questions, or problems to be solved during training; a participant's repository for documents used in training (for example, handouts).

world-class quality—A term used to indicate a standard of excellence; the best of the best.

X

x-axis—Horizontal axis on a control chart, run chart, or other chart.

X-bar chart—Average chart.

Y

y-axis—Vertical axis on a control chart, run chart, or other chart.

yield—Ratio between salable goods produced and the quantity of raw materials and/or components input at the beginning of the process.

Z

zero defects—A performance standard popularized by Philip B. Crosby to address a dual attitude in the workplace: people are willing to accept imperfection in some areas, while in other areas they expect the number of defects to be zero. This dual attitude has developed because of the conditioning that people are human and humans make mistakes. The zero-defects methodology states, however, that if people commit themselves to watching details and avoiding errors, they can move closer to the goal of perfection.

zero investment improvement—Another name for a *kaizen blitz*.

Index

A

A-B-C behavior analysis, 139–40, 144
absolutes of quality management (Crosby), 307
acceptable quality limit (AQL), 400
acceptance sampling, 399–400
accrual basis bookkeeping, 170
accuracy, 425
    versus precision, 411
achieved availability, 424
acid test ratio, 175
action plans, 88, 117, 256
    deployment, 122
    preparing, 93
active listening, 206–7, 210–11
activity network diagram (AND), 243, 323–24
activity-based costing (ABC), 178, 352
activity-based management (ABM), 178
ad hoc teams, 56
ADDIE instructional design model, 531
adult learning principles, 532–33
affinity diagram, 318, 324
Aguayo, Rafael, 431
alignment, of business processes and performance measures, 221–22
alliances, supplier, 505–9
alpha (α) risk (type I error), 400
American Productivity (and Quality) Center (APQC), 280, 354
Americans with Disabilities Act (ADA), 150
analogies, in problem solving, 341
analysis of variance (ANOVA), 405
analytical thinking, versus creative, 338–39
ANSI/ASQ Z1.4 standard, 400
Ansoff, H. Igor, 86
appraisal costs, 349
arithmetic mean, 402
ASQ Certified Manager of Quality/ Organizational Excellence examination, preparing for, xxiii–xxvi, xxvii–xxviii
ASQ Code of Ethics, 81–83
ASQ Futures of Quality study, xv
Athos, Anthony, 21

attributes control charts, 408
audit
    four types (Ishikawa), 310
    metrics, 277
    post-project, 254
    quality, 270–73
    supplier, 498, 502–3
    tools, 277
auditing, xxi
authority
    forms of, 3
    lack of as roadblock to change, 30
autocratic management, 144
availability
    in OEE, 380
    in reliability, 424–25
average, 420
average outgoing quality limit (AOQL), 400

B

Baker, Edward M., 131
balance sheet, 170–72
    ratios derived from, 175
balanced scorecard (BSC), 179, 268–70
Baldrige Performance Excellence Program (BPEP), 279, 280, 291
    category descriptions, 280–81
    core values and concepts, 135–36
    using criteria as management model, 281–83
bathtub curve, 403–5, 423
behavior management, 139–41
behavioral theories, 137
Bell Laboratories, 303
benchmarking, 296–303
    in business environment analysis, 105–7
    code of conduct, 300
    in project risk assessment, 228
    steps in, 297–98
    what it isn't, 302
benefit–cost analysis, in projects, 228
Bennis, Warren, 1
best judgment sampling, 399

W

Z

e Knowledge Center
ww.asq.org/knowledge-center

Learn about quality. Apply it. Share it.

Q's online Knowledge Center is the place to:

- Stay on top of the latest in quality with Editor's Picks and Hot Topics.

  Search ASQ's collection of articles, books, tools, training, and more.

  Connect with ASQ staff for personalized help hunting down the knowledge you need, the networking opportunities that will keep your career and organization moving forward, and the publishing opportunities that are the best fit for you.

e Knowledge Center Search to quickly sort through hundreds of books, articles, :her software-related publications.

.asq.org/knowledge-center

Ask a Librarian

Did you know?

- The ASQ Quality Information Center contains a wealth of knowledge and information available to ASQ members and non-members

- A librarian is available to answer research requests using ASQ's ever-expanding library of relevant, credible quality resources, including journals, conference proceedings, case studies and Quality Press publications

- ASQ members receive free internal information searches and reduced rates for article purchases

- You can also contact the Quality Information Center to request permission to reuse or reprint ASQ copyrighted material, including journal articles and book excerpts

- For more information or to submit a question, visit **http://asq.org/knowledge-center/ ask-a-librarian-index**

Visit www.asq.org/qic for more information.

TRAINING   CERTIFICATION   CONFERENCES   MEMBERSHIP   **PUBLICATIONS**   The Global Voice of Qu